COSMOS&
CULTURE

Cultural Evolution in a Cosmic Context

Edited by
Steven J. Dick
and Mark L. Lupisella

NASA SP-2009-4802

Library of Congress Cataloging-in-Publication Data

Cosmos and Culture : Cultural Evolution in a Cosmic Context / Steven J. Dick and Mark Lupisella, editors.
    p. cm. -- (NASA SP ; 4802)
  Includes bibliographical references and index.
  1. Cosmology--History. 2. Astronomy--History. 3. Culture--Origin. 4. Social evolution. 5. Human evolution. I. Dick, Steven J. II. Lupisella, Mark.
  QB981.C8263 2009
  523.109--dc22
                            2009004348

ISBN 978-0-16-083119-5

9 780160 831195   90000

For sale by the Superintendent of Documents, U.S. Government Printing Office
Internet: bookstore.gpo.gov Phone: toll free (866) 512-1800; DC area (202) 512-1800
Fax: (202) 512-2104 Mail: Stop IDCC, Washington, DC 20402-0001

ISBN 978-0-16-083119-5

Table of Contents

Part 1: The Cosmic Context

Part 2: Cultural Evolution

Part 3: Cosmos and Culture

Introduction

Cosmic evolution, the idea that the universe and its constituent parts are constantly evolving, has become widely accepted only in the last 50 years. It is no coincidence that this acceptance parallels the span of the Space Age. Although cosmic evolution was first recognized in the physical universe early in the 20th century, with hints even earlier, the relationships among planets, stars, and galaxies, and the evolution of the universe itself, became much better known through the discoveries by planetary probes and space telescopes in the latter half of the century. It was also during the last 50 years—a century after Darwin proposed that evolution by natural selection applies to life on our own planet—that researchers from a variety of disciplines began to seriously study the possibilities of extraterrestrial life and "the biological universe."[1] Considering biology from this broader cosmological perspective has expanded biological thinking beyond its sample-of-one straightjacket, incorporating biology into cosmic evolution. Astrobiology is now a robust discipline even though it has yet to find any life beyond Earth.[2]

But there is a third component to cosmic evolution beyond the physical and the biological. Even if we only know of culture on one planet so far, cultural evolution has been an important part of cosmic evolution on Earth, and perhaps on many other planets. Moreover, it also dominates the other two forms of evolution in terms of its rapidity. Humans were not much different biologically 10,000 years ago, but one need only look around to see how much we have changed culturally. Yet, unlike the study of biological evolution, which has made great progress since Darwin's *Origin of Species*, the scientific study of cultural evolution languished after Darwin's death for the better part of a century. Only within the past few decades has significant progress been made, and concerned with advancing their fledgling science, cultural evolutionists have yet to expand their thinking beyond their current planetary sample-of-one concerns.[3] But if life and intelligence do exist beyond Earth, it is likely that culture will arise and evolve. In this volume authors with diverse backgrounds in science, history, and anthropology consider culture in the context of the cosmos, including the implications of the cosmos for our own culture.

Expanding the horizons of the science of cultural evolution to include a cosmic context has many potential benefits. As biology has benefited from broader cosmological considerations, the science of cultural evolution could also benefit from thinking in more general, theoretical terms about the origin and evolution of cultures. As cultural evolutionists broaden their minds to include cosmic perspectives, their insights could help guide the already substantial and continuing search for intelligent life elsewhere in the cosmos. Not least, a cultural evolutionary science that includes a cosmic context should allow for a better understanding of the relationships among physical, biological, and cultural evolution—steps perhaps toward a cosmic evolutionary synthesis. All of these benefits could inform the future of humanity and life in the universe. Conversely, greater attention to these problems should help us understand how our expanding knowledge of the cosmos impacts culture and cultural evolution.

We are acutely aware that "culture" is an amorphous and ambiguous term, with an uneasy relationship to its cousin "society."[4] Like many complex concepts, dwelling on perfect definitions of culture, and in particular, *cultural evolution*, can be tricky and perhaps even distracting, because there are often blurry boundaries and intractable counter-examples. But despite the importance of clear distinctions and definitions, imperfect definitions should not prevent exploratory analysis. Often, in pursuing analyses that tolerate imperfect definitions, we find contexts and usages that help clarify, however unsatisfying those definitions may still ultimately remain. Indeed, in this book, we do not focus explicitly on defining cultural evolution, or, for that matter, life, intelligence, and culture. These matters are touched on in various ways in some chapters, but it was not an explicit intention of this effort—indeed, the authors invoke varying uses of "culture." Nevertheless, perhaps increased clarity will come from considering the broader and theoretical explorations of the authors' contributions.

This volume is divided into three parts, beginning with the nature and history of cosmic evolution, then focusing on cultural evolution, and finally tackling more explicit themes of the relationships between cosmos and culture. In Part 1, Eric Chaisson, an astronomer who—more than anyone—has explored the significance and possibilities of cosmic evolution over the last three decades, provides an overarching and coherent perspective of the subject from a scientific point of view.[5] Steven Dick, an astronomer and historian of science who has written widely on extraterrestrial life and astrobiology, offers an overview of the history of the idea of cosmic evolution, how it has affected culture so far, and its implications for humanity's future.

Part 2 focuses on cultural evolution itself, and as such is dominated by authors in the social sciences and humanities. Kathryn Denning, an anthropologist at York University in Canada who has become deeply involved with the SETI community, provides an overview of the field of cultural evolution, or "social evolution" as she terms it. She makes it clear why the field is a difficult one fraught with dangers, even in the terrestrial context. One of the central problems in the field has been the lack of a robust theory, but toward that goal the philosopher Daniel Dennett, the author of *Darwin's Dangerous Idea*, supports the notion of memes (the cultural equivalent to genes) as a cultural evolution model, and finds that cultural possibility is far less constrained than genetic possibility. Indeed, psychologist Susan Blackmore, well known for her book *The Meme Machine*, warns in this section that the blind replication of memes can be extremely destructive—and possibly cause extinction. She provides an intriguing "alternative Drake Equation" for survivability of intelligent civilizations based on memes and kinds of replication. Howard Bloom provokes us with a very broad notion of culture and a multiplanet mandate deeply rooted in evolution. Systems theorist John Smart draws from a number of unique disciplines, applying an informational, evolutionary, and developmental systems model to understand the universe and the role of culture within it.

NASA engineer and scientist Mark Lupisella opens Part 3 by exploring a framework for the relationships between the cosmos and culture, and offers a "cosmocultural" perspective whereby the coevolution of cosmos and culture gives rise to cosmic value. But why worry about cosmos and culture? Physicist Paul Davies argues that life, mind, and culture are of fundamental significance to the grand story of the cosmos because life is based on a universal Darwinian mechanism that has allowed the cosmos to generate its own self-understanding through science, rational reasoning, and mathematics that may ultimately lead to cultural evolution on a large enough scale to allow the universe to both create and steer itself toward its destiny. This suggests a potential abundance of life in the cosmos, and astronomer Seth Shostak argues that human beings, like other intelligent species, may pass through a short self-destruction bottleneck and survive for very long time periods after dispersal in space, giving rise to many long-lived technologically advanced civilizations throughout the galaxy. If so, one of the great questions is whether humans can communicate with extraterrestrials, and Doug Vakoch, a psychologist at the SETI Institute who has written broadly on interstellar communication, explores the potential utility of using our understanding of cosmic evolution to communicate with extraterrestrial intelligence.

Historian David Christian argues for using cosmic evolution in an expanded view of history he terms "big history." But the place of humans in the scheme of cosmic evolution remains problematic in part because we lack definitive evidence of extraterrestrials, and in part because we cannot fathom our human future. Complexity theorist James Gardner suggests that our transhuman future might be memetically engineered using an "intelligent universe" worldview, which would contribute to a benign future for humans who will not likely be a dominant force in the future. Finally, the volume concludes with paired articles by Steven Dick, who plays out one specific scenario—a postbiological universe—that results from taking culture in the cosmos seriously, and by JoAnn Palmeri, a historian of science who examines a specific case of how one far-seeing astronomer, Harlow Shapley, took the cosmos seriously as an element integral to our terrestrial culture.

In the end, at least four general themes emerge from the volume: 1) Long-term cosmic perspectives can be theoretically and practically illuminating for reflecting on culture; 2) cosmology deeply affects and informs culture; 3) culture may have surprising significance in overall cosmic evolution; and 4) expansion into the wider universe is an important, perhaps critical, endeavor. It is our firm belief that these are themes that can and should be more deeply investigated as our terrestrial culture learns more about the cosmos around us.

While we have certainly fallen well short of exhausting the subject, we have nevertheless attempted an initial exploration of perspectives from a variety of thinkers and practitioners. The material is biased toward natural and scientific perspectives, and arguably toward mechanistic and perhaps reductionist views (e.g., memes as a mechanism of cultural evolution). Eastern perspectives are not properly represented, but perhaps will be in the future.

This book is one of several on the societal impact of spaceflight in the NASA History Series, and is directly relevant to NASA's mandate to "provide for long-range studies of the potential benefits to be gained from, the opportunities for, and the problems involved in the utilization of aeronautical and space activities for peaceful and scientific purposes." Much of NASA's work may be seen as filling in the gaps in our knowledge of cosmic evolution. Perhaps the largest gap is the still very much open question of whether humans are alone in the universe, and what this means for humanity. We hope this book will stimulate a more serious field of inquiry into how culture and cosmos relate based not only on how we understand our own cultural evolution, but on broader theoretical grounds as well. It is only a first tentative step toward the scientific study of the relationship between cosmic and cultural evolution, of placing the rapidly growing science of cultural evolution within a cosmic context, and urging a greater appreciation of the role that the cosmos should play in our culture.

Steven J. Dick, former NASA Chief Historian
Mark L. Lupisella, NASA Goddard Space Flight Center
May 2009

Endnotes

1. Steven J. Dick, *The Biological Universe: The Twentieth Century Extraterrestrial Life Debate and the Limits of Science* (Cambridge: Cambridge University Press: 1996). There is nevertheless a deep and fascinating background to the idea of extraterrestrial life extending at least to the ancient Greeks. See Steven J. Dick, *Plurality of Worlds: The Origins of the Extraterrestrial Life Debate from Democritus to Kant* (Cambridge: Cambridge University Press, 1982); Michael J. Crowe, *The Extraterrestrial Life Debate,* 1750-1900 (Cambridge: Cambridge University Press, 1986); and Karl S. Guthke, *The Last Frontier* (Ithaca, NY: Cornell University Press, 1990).

2. Steven J. Dick and James E. Strick, *The Living Universe: NASA and the Development of Astrobiology* (New Brunswick, NJ: Rutgers University Press, 2004). This volume shows how astrobiology developed in the mid-1990s out of NASA's exobiology program, which dates back almost to the origins of NASA in 1958.

3. For an entrée into the literature of cultural evolution see Kevin Lalande and G. R. Brown, *Sense & Nonsense: Evolutionary Perspectives on Human Behaviour* (Oxford: Oxford University Press, 2002) and the chapters in Part 2 of this volume.

4. For debated differences between the concepts of culture and society a good starting point is Nigel Rapport and Joanna Overing, *Social and Cultural Anthropology: The Key Concepts* (London and New York: Routledge, 2000), entries on "culture" and "society."

5. E. Chaisson, *Cosmic Dawn: The Origins of Matter and Life* (Boston: Little, Brown and Company, 1981); *Cosmic Evolution: The Rise of Complexity in Nature* (Cambridge: Harvard University Press, 2001); and *Epic of Evolution: Seven Ages of the Cosmos* (New York: Columbia University Press, 2006).

Part 1

The Cosmic Context

Chapter 1

Cosmic Evolution
State of the Science

Eric J. Chaisson

Evolution, broadly considered, has become a powerful unifying concept in all of science, providing a comprehensive worldview for the new millennium. Among all of nature's diverse systems, energy—acquired, stored, and expressed—is a principal driver of the rising complexity of galaxies, stars, planets and life-forms in the expanding universe. Our cultural curiosity is both a result of, and a key to understanding, myriad cosmic-evolutionary events that have shaped our material origins.

Introduction

Emerging now from modern science is a unified scenario of the cosmos, including ourselves as sentient beings, based on the time-honored concept of change. Change does seem to be universal and ubiquitous in nature, much as the ancient Greek philosopher Heraclitus claimed long ago that "everything flows and nothing stays." Nowadays we have evidence for change virtually everywhere, some of it obvious, other subtle. From galaxies to snowflakes, from stars and planets to life itself, scientists are weaving an intricate pattern penetrating the fabric of all the natural sciences—a sweepingly inclusive worldview of the order and structure of every known class of object in our richly endowed universe.

Cosmic evolution is the study of the many varied developmental and generational changes in the assembly and composition of radiation, matter, and life throughout all space and across all time. These are the changes that have produced our galaxy, our Sun, our Earth, and ourselves. The result is a grand evolutionary synthesis bridging a wide variety of scientific specialties—physics, astronomy, geology, chemistry, biology, and anthropology, among others—a genuine narrative of epic proportions extending from the very beginning of time to the present, from the Big Bang to humankind.

While entering this new age of synthesis, today's researchers are truly embracing interdisciplinarity; we are thinking bigger, broader, and more holistically. We are deciphering how all known objects—from atoms to galaxies, from cells to brains, from people to society—are interrelated. For the more we examine nature, the more everything seems related to everything else. Our appreciation for evolution now extends well beyond the subject of biology; indeed, the concept of evolution, generally considered, has become a potent unifying factor in all of science. Yet questions remain: how valid are the apparent continuities among nature's historical epochs and how realistic is the quest for unification? Can we reconcile the observed constructiveness of cosmic evolution with the inherent destructiveness of thermodynamics? Specifically how have the magnificent examples of order all around us arisen from chaos?

We especially want to know about the origins of the diverse structures spanning our universe, notably those often characterized by the intuitive term "complexity"—a state of intricacy, complication, variety, or involvement, as in the interconnected parts of a system. Particularly intriguing is the rise of complexity over the course of time, indeed dramatically so within the past half-billion years since the start of the Cambrian Era on Earth. Resembling a kind of Neoplatonism, perhaps some underlying principle, a unifying law, or an ongoing process creates, organizes, and maintains all structures in the universe, enabling us to study everything on uniform, common ground—"on the same mental page," so to speak.

Recent research, guided by notions of mathematical elegance and bolstered by vast new observational databases, suggests affirmative answers to some of those queries: islands of ordered complexity—namely, open systems that are galaxies, stars, planets, and life-forms—are more than balanced by great seas of increasing disorder elsewhere in the environments beyond those systems. All is in quantitative agreement with valued precepts of thermodynamics, especially nonequilibrium thermodynamics. Indeed, the underlying, ubiquitous phenomenon mentioned above may simply be energy itself. Energy flows engendered largely by the expanding cosmos do seem to be as universal a currency in the origin of structured systems as anything yet found in nature. Furthermore, the optimization of such energy flows might well act as the motor of evolution broadly conceived, thereby affecting all of physical, biological, and cultural evolution, the sum total of which constitutes cosmic evolution—much as presented in Figure 1.

Cosmic evolution writ large

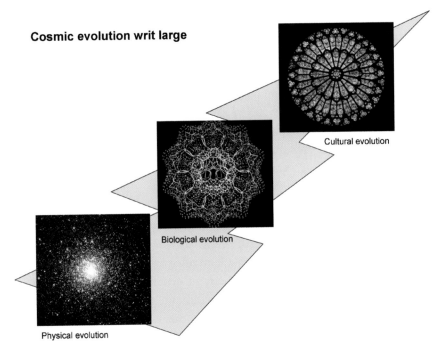

Cultural evolution

Biological evolution

Physical evolution

Figure 1. **Cosmic evolution writ large**: Changes in the physical, biological, and cultural domains are governed by underlying scientific principles that guide the emergence of increasingly complex structures in the universe. Resembling the beautiful stained-glass window in the south transept of the great Gothic cathedral in Paris (shown at top right), the pattern at center actually represents a pseudo-colored array of atoms viewed along the axis of a double-helical DNA molecule some two nanometers across. (Red denotes oxygen atoms; blue, nitrogen; green, carbon; yellow, phosphorus; hydrogen is not shown.) Likewise, images of colorful globular star clusters (as at bottom left, where thousands of aged red giants dominate youthful blue stars) exemplify change-filled events in the earlier universe; shown here is the M80 star cluster nearly 120 light-years across and about 28,000 light-years distant.

Taken together, stars, genes, and art represent manifest expressions of complexity rising over the course of cosmic time. Increasing energy densities typify the construction of physical and biological structures, such as fusing stars and functioning molecules; even more energy density is needed to fashion cultural entities, such as organized societies and today's global civilization. The flow of energy, as dictated by nonequilibrium thermodynamics in an expanding universe, does seem to provide a powerful means to explain the growth of order, form, and complexity on all scales, from quarks to quasars, from microbes to minds. (Images courtesy of Cathedrale Notre-Dame de Paris; University of California, San Francisco; STScI/NASA)

Heraclitus, with his unifying mantra of "all flows (παντα ρει)," would likely be proud of modern cosmic-evolutionary ideas, but he would also be surprised by our huge array of empirical findings supporting those ideas. Others have been down this path before, most originally perhaps the 19th century encyclopedist Robert Chambers (1844), who anonymously penned a pre-Darwinian tract of wide insight, and the mid-20th century astronomer

Harlow Shapley (1930), whose "cosmography" went well beyond biology by classifying all known structures according to dimensional size and scale. Among others, philosopher Herbert Spencer (1896) championed the notion of increasing complexity in biological and cultural evolution, the mathematician Alfred North Whitehead (1925) sought to undergird broad scientific thinking with his "organic philosophy," and the biologist E. O. Wilson (1998) appealed to "consilience" for unification in the sciences.

Arrow of Time

Figure 2 (a) shows the archetypal illustration of cosmic evolution—the arrow of time. Regardless of its shape or orientation, such an arrow represents a symbolic guide to the sequence of events that have changed systems from simplicity to complexity, from inorganic to organic, from chaos to order. That sequence, as determined by a large body of post-Renaissance data, accords well with the idea that a thread of change links the evolution of primal energy into elementary particles, the evolution of those particles into atoms, in turn of those atoms into galaxies and stars, and of stars into heavy elements, the evolution of those elements into the molecular building blocks of life, of those molecules into life itself, and of intelligent life into the cultured and technological society that we now share. Despite the compartmentalization of today's academic science, evolution knows no disciplinary boundaries.

As such, the most familiar kind of evolution—biological evolution, or neo-Darwinism—is just one, albeit important, subset of a broader evolutionary scheme encompassing much more than mere life on Earth. In short, what Darwinian change does for plants and animals, cosmic evolution aspires to do for all things. And if Darwinism created a revolution of understanding by helping to free us from the notion that humans differ from other life-forms on our planet, then cosmic evolution extends that intellectual revolution by treating matter on Earth and in our bodies no differently from that in the stars and galaxies beyond.

Anthropocentrism is neither intended nor implied by the arrow of time—which is why some researchers prefer to draw it opening up in variety and diversity as in Figure 2 (a), instead of pointing anywhere in particular, other than toward the future generally. Anthropic principles notwithstanding, there is no logic to support the idea that the universe was conceived to produce specifically us. We humans are surely not the culmination of the cosmic-evolutionary scenario, nor are we likely to be the only technologically competent beings that have emerged in the organically rich universe. The arrow merely provides a convenient symbol, artistically depicting a mixture of chance and

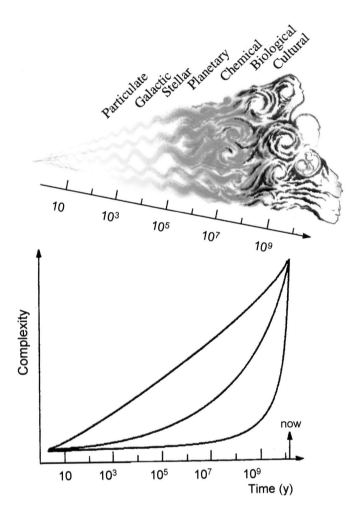

Figure 2. (a) **Arrow of Time**: This stylized arrow of time highlights salient features of cosmic history, from its fiery origins some 14 billion years ago (at left) to the here and now of the present (at right). Sketched diagonally across the top are the major evolutionary phases that have produced, in turn, increasing amounts of order and complexity among all material things: particulate, galactic, stellar, planetary, chemical, biological, and cultural evolution. Cosmic evolution encompasses all of these phases, each of which represents a coarse temporal duration when the emergence of key systems flourished in nature. Time is assumed to flow linearly and irreversibly, unfolding at a steady pace, much as other central tenets are presumed, such as the fixed character of physical law or the notion that 2 + 2 = 4 everywhere. (Drawing by Lola Judith Chaisson)

(b) **Rising complexity, intuitively judged**: Graphed here qualitatively is the rise of order, form, and complexity of localized material structures throughout the history of the universe. This family of curves represents more an innate feeling than a quantitative proof, in accord with the subjective impression that complex ordered structures have generally increased (with some exceptions) over the course of time. Whether this rise of complexity has been linear, exponential, or hyperbolic (as sketched here), current research aims to specify this curve and to characterize it empirically. (For an objective view, see Figure 5) necessity that operate together while building increasingly complex structures from spiral galaxies to rocky planets to thinking beings.

Nor does time's arrow mean to imply that "lower," primitive life-forms biologically change directly into "higher," advanced organisms, any more than galaxies physically change into stars, or stars into planets. Rather, with time— much time—the environmental conditions suitable for spawning primitive life eventually changed into those favoring the emergence of more complex species; likewise, in the earlier universe, environments were ripe for galactic formation, but now those conditions are more conducive to stellar and planetary formation. Change in the surrounding environment often precedes change in ordered systems, and the resulting system changes have *generally* been toward greater amounts of diverse complexity.

Figure 2 (b) graphs the widespread impression that material assemblages have become more organized and complex, especially in relatively recent times. This family of curves refers to "islands" of complexity that are systems per se—whether swollen stars or buzzing bees—not to the vastly, indeed increasingly disorganized sea of chaos surrounding them. Modern science aims to explain this rise of complexity and to do so with known scientific principles that avoid mysticism, vitalism, creationism, and the like.

Nonequilibrium Thermodynamics

Cosmic evolution, as understood today, is governed largely by the known laws of physics, particularly those of thermodynamics. Note the adverb "largely," for this is not an exercise in traditional reductionism. Of all the known principles of nature, thermodynamics perhaps most pertains to the concept of change—yet change as driven, again for emphasis, by a combination of randomness and determinism, of chance and necessity. Literally, thermodynamics means "movement of heat"; a more insightful translation (in keeping with the wider connotation in Greek antiquity of motion as change) would be "change of energy."

To be sure, the cosmic-evolutionary narrative is much too complicated to be explained merely by equilibrium thermodynamics—the kind most often used to describe closed systems isolated from their environments and having maximum entropy states. All structures, whether galaxies, stars, planets, or life-forms, are demonstrably open, nonequilibrium systems with flows of energy in and out being a central feature. And it is this energy, often called available, or "free," energy—literally the ability to do work—that helps to build structures.

At face value, the second law of thermodynamics—arguably the most cherished principle in all of physics—practically prohibits systems from changing spontaneously toward more ordered states. Structures left alone naturally tend to break down and increase entropy. When unattended, for example, domestic households grow more disorderly: lawns become unkempt, stoves greasy, roofs leaky. Even human beings who fail to eat gradually become less ordered and die; and when we die we decay to ultimate disorder, thereby returning our elemental resources to Earth and the universe that gave us life. All things will eventually degenerate into chaotic, randomized, less ordered states.

By utilizing energy, however, order can be achieved temporarily, or at least the environmental conditions made conducive for the potential rise of order within open systems ripe for growth. To extend our example, some human sweat and hard work—an energy flow—can put a disarrayed house back in order, yet this reordering comes at the expense of those cleaning the house; we get tired and increasingly disordered ourselves. In turn, humans can become reinvigorated (i.e., personally reenergized or reordered) by eating again—which is also an energy flow—but this renewed order arises, further in turn, at the expense of the agricultural environment that was ravaged to produce the food consumed.

In short, energy flow does play an important role in creating, ordering, and maintaining complex systems—all quantitatively in accord with the second law of thermodynamics. None of nature's ordered structures, not even life itself, is a violation (nor even a circumvention) of the second law. Considering both any system of order as well as its surrounding environment, we find good agreement with modern, nonequilibrium thermodynamics. In this way, both order and entropy can increase together—the former locally and the latter globally. (For quantitative details, see Chaisson 2001.)

Championed decades ago by the German-Canadian systematist Ludwig von Bertalanffy (1932) and later espoused by the German quantum mechanic Erwin Schroedinger (1944), the need for energy is now recognized as an essential feature, not only of biological systems such as plants and animals, but also of physical systems such as stars and galaxies; indeed acknowledged for social systems, too, such as a city's inward flow of food and resources amidst its outward flow of products and wastes. The analysis is much the same for any open system, provided we think in broad, interdisciplinary terms.

Figure 3 is a schematic diagram, adapted from the work of Belgian physical chemist Ilya Prigogine (1972) and American immunologist Jonas Salk (1982), illustrating the emergence of structure in the presence of energy flow. By crossing certain energy thresholds that depend on a system's status, bifurcations can occur, fostering the emergence of whole new hierarchies of novel structures that display surprising amounts of coherent behavior. Such

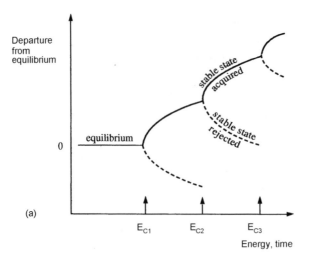

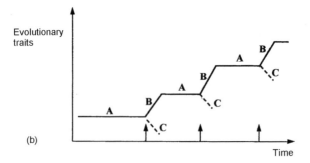

Figure 3. (a) **A physicist's visualization of rising complexity**: Sketched here is an arbitrary equilibrium coordinate for an open system as a function of both time and energy, either of which quantity serves to illustrate the extent of departure of that system from equilibrium. The time axis makes clear that this is a historical, evolutionary process, whereas the parallel energy axis denotes the free energy flowing through the open system as a vital part of that process. At certain critical energies, labeled here E_c, a system can spontaneously change, or bifurcate, into new, nonequilibrium, dynamic steady states. Statistical fluctuations—that is chance—affect which fork the system selects—that is necessity—upon bifurcation (vertical arrows), namely which spatial structure is achieved. Not all new systems survive (solid curve); some are rejected (dashed curve). The process, as always, is an interplay of randomness and determinism, therefore the end result is inherently unpredictable, as with all of evolution.

(b) **A biologist's visualization of rising complexity**: Events in evolutionary biology mimic those of the diagram in (a), although the results are richer in structural detail, system function, and energy flow. In phases marked A, the main task of a species is to survive and thus persist until such time that the environment changes (vertical arrows), after which further evolution occurs—along phase B toward renewed survival and perhaps speciation or along phase C toward extinction.

Neither upward rising graph implies progress or inevitability, but they do suggest a *general trend* toward increased complexity with time—a trend undeniable among organized systems observed throughout nature.

dissipative structures can export some of their entropy (or dissipate some of their energy) into their external environments. Accordingly, order is often created and sustained by routine consumption of substances rich in energy, accompanied by a discharge of substances low in energy.

How does such structuring actually occur? How can ordering emerge from a condition where originally there was no such thing? We know well that fluctuations—random deviations from some average, equilibrium value of, for example, density, temperature, or pressure—are common phenomena in nature. Fluctuations inevitably yet stochastically appear in any system having many degrees of freedom. Normally, as in equilibrium thermodynamics, such instabilities regress in time and disappear; they just come and go by chance, the statistical fluctuations diffusing as quickly as they initially arose. Even in an isolated system, such internal fluctuations can generate local, microscopic reductions in entropy, but the second law ensures that they will always balance themselves out. Microscopic temperature fluctuations, for instance, are said to be thermally relaxed. Nor can an open system *near* equilibrium change spontaneously to new and interesting structures. But should those fluctuations become too great for an open system to damp, that system will then depart far from equilibrium and be forced to regroup. Such reorganization generates a "dynamic steady state," provided the amplified fluctuations are continuously driven and stabilized by a flow of energy from the surroundings— namely, provided the energy flow rate exceeds the thermal relaxation rate. Systematic, coherent cycling is often the result, since under these conditions the spontaneous creation of macroscopic structures dissipates energy more rapidly than the ensuing, and damaging, heat can smooth out those structures. Furthermore, since each successive reordering often causes more complexity than the preceding one, such systems become even more susceptible to fluctuations. Complexity itself consequently creates the conditions for greater instability, which in turn provides an opportunity for greater reordering. The resulting phenomenon—termed "order through fluctuations"—is a distinctly evolutionary one, complete with feedback loops that help drive the system further from equilibrium. And as the energy consumption and resulting complexity accelerate, so does the evolutionary process. This is the realm of true thermo*dynamics*, the older, established subject of that name more properly labeled "thermostatics."

Numerous examples abound throughout nature, and not just among physical systems, but for biological and social ones as well. Naturally occurring phenomena such as convection cells in a pot of warm water, river eddies behind rocks in flowing streams, and atmospheric storms that grow into hurricanes all display enhanced order when energies flow above some threshold. Yet biological systems also obey the rules of nonequilibrium thermodynamics, for we and our living relatives are demonstrable examples of dynamic steady states that have emerged via energetically enhanced neo-Darwinism. Even artificially made devices such as kitchen refrigerators and coherent lasers, among a whole host of similar examples of culturally produced systems, promote or maintain order when amply fed with sufficient energy.

Three Eras in Natural History

The origin of nature's many varied structures depends on the flow of free energy. And this, like the arrow of time itself, is a direct consequence of the expansion of the universe. Independently pioneered by astrophysicists Thomas Gold (1962) and David Layzer (1976), among others, time marches on and free energies surge because the cosmos dynamically evolves. Indeed, it is cosmic expansion, and nothing more, that has caused the entire universe to depart from its initial state of thermodynamic equilibrium. The stark contrast between myriad hot stars and the vast, cold interstellar space surrounding them now guarantees a state of nonequilibrium.

The run of density and temperature in the standard, Big Bang model of the universe, shown in Figure 4 (a), encapsulates the essence of change on the largest observable scale (Chaisson 1998). Knowing only the density and temperature of something, we can derive a great deal about its physical properties. Here our interest centers on the big picture— the whole universe—so the curves of this figure pertain to nothing in particular, just everything in general. They show the main trends, minus the devilish details, of big-bang cosmology: the cooling and thinning of radiation and matter based largely on measures of the microwave background radiation and of the distant receding galaxies (Figure 4 [b]).

Radiation completely ruled the early universe. Life was nonexistent and matter only a submicroscopic precipitate suspended in a glowing fireball of blinding light, x rays, and gamma rays. Structure of any sort had yet to emerge; the energy density of radiation was too great. If single protons managed to capture single electrons to make hydrogen atoms, the radiation was so fierce as to destroy them immediately. The first few hundreds of millennia after the beginning of time were uniform, symmetrical, informationless, and boring. We call it the Radiation Era.

Eventually, and inevitably so, the primacy of radiation gave way to matter. As the universe naturally cooled and thinned owing solely to its expansion,

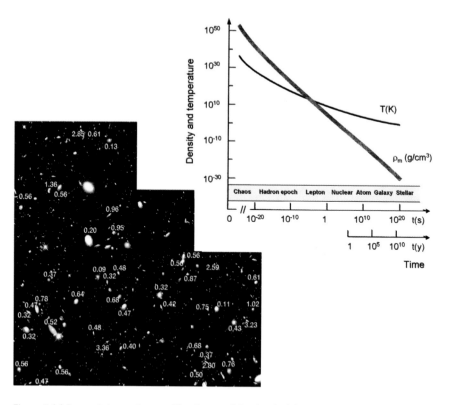

Figure 4. (a) **An evolving universe**: The change of the density (ρ) of matter and the temperature (T) of radiation, from near the origin of the universe to the present. The thick width of the density curve displays the range of uncertainty in total mass density, whose true value depends on the amount of "dark matter." By contrast, the cold cosmic background temperature is very accurately measured today (2.7 K), and its thin curve equally accurately extrapolated back into the hot, early universe. The recent finding that universal expansion is accelerating should not much affect these curves.

(b) **Hubble deep field**: This fabulously rich collection of thousands of galaxies, with their measured red shifts (proportional to galaxy recessional velocity) superposed, bolsters the standard Big Bang model of the universe, as characterized by the curves of density and temperature above. However complex astronomical structures may seem, including huge galaxy clusters and peculiar filaments and voids on even larger scales than that shown here, all physical systems are simpler than any biological systems—grand spiral galaxies much less complex than the most primitive microbes. (Image courtesy STScI/NASA; redshift data courtesy Keck Observatory/CARA)

the charged particles became bound into neutral atoms, which are among the simplest of all structures. This represents a change of first magnitude, for it was as though an earlier, blinding fog had lifted—its uniformity punctured, its symmetry broken. The universe slowly became transparent, meaning that photons no longer scattered about aimlessly and destructively. The Radiation Era gradually transformed into the Matter Era, an event claimed by some researchers to be the greatest change of all time; it occurred about a half-million years after the Big Bang.

With the onset of the Matter Era, matter literally began dominating radiation. Natural history became more interesting. The results, over billions of years and minus the details, were galaxies, stars, planets, and life, one by-product of which is intelligence—at least on one planet called Earth. And this, in turn, has anthropogenically changed nearly everything on our planet.

Some 14 billion years after the beginning of space and time, the Life Era has now begun, at least locally. Here, the emergence of technologically intelligent life, on Earth and perhaps elsewhere, heralds a whole new era—one where life, in its turn, has gradually come to dominate matter. This second of two great transformations was not triggered by the origin of life; rather, it is technologically advanced life (perhaps as early as the onset of agriculture yet at least by later industrialization) that differs dramatically from primitive life and from other types of inanimate matter scattered throughout the universe.

These are not anthropocentric statements. Technology, despite all it pitfalls, enables life to manipulate matter, even to control it, much as matter evolved to overwhelm radiation billions of years ago. Accordingly, matter is now beginning to lose its dominance, at least at those isolated locales of hi-tech civilization, such as on planet Earth. To use a popular cliché, life is now taking matter into its own hands, for nonsentient nature could not have built books, machines, museums, and the like. Humankind constructs such artificial things; they are products of cultural evolution. Our narrative has transitioned across all known time from plain and simple protogalaxies to stratified societies of extraordinary order. We have reached the here and now.

Key questions flood the mind: what caused the plethora of changes throughout the ages and how has complexity actually increased with time? Have humans truly become the agents of change on Earth, able to tinker with both matter and energy, including genes and environments, more than these ingredients now affect us? How did the neural network within human brains acquire the sophistication needed to fashion nations, weapons, cathedrals, philosophies, and scenarios of cosmic evolution? In short, what caused us to become conscious enough to contemplate our complex selves?

Empirically Measuring Complexity

To appreciate the crux of the historical appearance of structured matter and life, we return to the greater cosmic environment and to some of the thermodynamic issues raised earlier. In brief, when the universe broke its symmetry a few thousand centuries after the Big Bang, equilibrium was also destroyed.

Temperature gradients became established owing naturally to the expansion of the cosmos. And that meant free energy began flowing, in fact increasingly so as the temperatures of matter and radiation diverged with time. These are the environmental conditions that are favorable for the potential growth of order, form, and structure—indeed, of complexity.

But how shall we characterize complexity, a slippery term for many researchers? In biology alone, much as their inability to reach consensus on a definition of life, biologists cannot agree on a complexity metric. Evolutionist John Maynard Smith (1995) uses nonjunk genome size, biologist John Tyler Bonner (1988) employs being morphology and behavioral flexibility, theorist Stuart Kauffman (1993) charts the number of cell types in organisms, and bioengineer Thomas McMahon (1983) appeals to cellular specialization. All these attributes of life have qualitative worth, yet all are hard to quantify in practical terms. We must push the envelope beyond mere words, beyond biology.

Putting aside as unhelpful the traditional quantitative ideas of information content (of the Shannon-Weiner type, which is admittedly useful in some contexts, but controversial in others) and of negative entropy (or "negentropy," which Schroedinger first adopted but then quickly abandoned), we return to the quantity with greatest appeal to physical intuition—energy. More than any other term, energy seemingly has a central role to play in any attempt to unify physical, biological, and cultural evolution. Energy is an underlying, universal driver like no other in all of modern science.

Not that energy has been overlooked in many previous discussions of systems' origin and assembly. Biometrician Alfred Lotka (1922), physicists Philip Morrison (1964) and Freeman Dyson (1979), biologist Harold Morowitz (1968), ecologist Harold Odum (1988), and geographer Vaclav Smil (1999), just to name a few, have championed the cause of energy's organizational abilities. Even so, the quantity of choice cannot be energy alone, for a star clearly has more energy than an amoeba, a galaxy much more than a single cell. Yet any biological system is surely more complex than any inanimate entity. Thus, absolute energies are not as telling as relative values, which depend on a system's size, composition, and efficiency. Nor are maximum energy principles or minimum entropy states likely to be operative, as nature is neither black nor white, but more like shades of grey throughout. Rather, organization is seemingly governed by the *optimum* use of energy—not too little as to starve a system, yet not too much as to destroy it.

To characterize complexity objectively—that is, to normalize all such structured systems on that same level page—a kind of energy density is useful, much as it was competing energy densities of radiation and matter that dictated events in the earlier universe. Moreover, it is the *rate* at which free energy transits complex systems of given mass that seems most constructive. Hence, "energy rate density" becomes an operational term whose meaning and measurement are clear and easily understood. In this way, neither new science nor appeals to nonscience are needed to justify the impressive hierarchy of the cosmic-evolutionary story, from stars to plants to society.

The modeled flow of energy through a wide variety of open systems, be they animate or inanimate, does closely resemble the intuitive rise in complexity implied by Figure 2 (b). Complexity has indeed increased over the course of history, and at a rate that is at least exponential in recent times. Figure 5 plots a sampling of findings, where energy rate densities, in units of erg/second/gram, are graphed as horizontal histograms proportional to various systems' historical longevities. As expected, yet here only briefly stated: red giant stars are more complex than main-sequence stars, eukaryotes more complex than prokaryotes, animals more complex than plants, industrial society more complex than hunter-gatherers, and so on up the system hierarchy. To be sure, energy flow diagnostics have also been used recently by some unfettered historians, including David Christian (2004) and Fred Spier (2005), to bolster their pioneering studies of "big history," which parallels the subject of cosmic evolution.

This is not to say, by any means, that galaxies per se evolved into stars, or stars into planets, or planets into life. Rather, this analysis suggests that galaxies gave rise to environments suited to the birth of stars, that some stars spawned environments conducive to the formation of planets, and that countless planets likely fostered environments ripe for the origin of life. Cosmic evolution, to repeat, incorporates both developmental and generational change.

Nor do these evolutionary phases, or historical durations, have well-determined start and stop times—or stop times necessarily at all. The horizontal histograms of Figure 5 serve to reinforce that each of these phases once begun did not end; stars and galaxies, for example, first emerged in the earlier universe, as also implied by the diagonal phases atop Figure 2's arrow of time, yet both such systems continue presently developing and evolving, as do plants and animals that emerged much later. In fact, as depicted by those histograms, and unlike customary geological periods that do have set time intervals, currently all evolutionary phases noted in Figures 2 and 5 are engaged simultaneously and indefinitely.

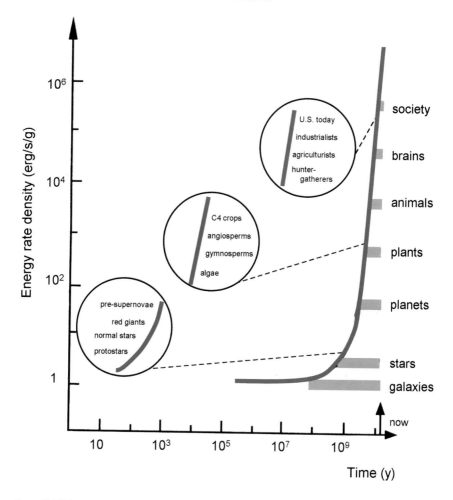

Figure 5. **Rising complexity, empirically based**: The increase in energy rate density, plotted as histograms starting at those times when various open structures dominantly emerged in nature, has been especially rapid in the last billion years, much as expected from human intuition and Figure 2 (b). The solid blue curve approximates the increase in normalized energy flow that best characterizes order, form, and structure throughout the history of the universe. The three insets (circled) show greater detail of further calculations of energy rate densities passing through stars, plants, and societies, which are classic examples of physical, biological, and cultural evolution, respectively, all of which are now operative in our increasingly complexified universe. (Adapted from Chaisson 1998, 2001, 2003)

Evolution, Broadly Considered

The word *evolution* need not be the sole province of biology, its utility of value only to life scientists. Charles Darwin never used it as a noun, in fact only once as a verb in the very last sentence of his 1859 classic, *On the Origin of Species.* Nor need the principle of natural selection be the only mechanism of evolutionary change, past and present. Darwin surely embraced it as we do today to describe much of biological change, but there too he cautioned us: "I am convinced that Natural Selection has been the main but not exclusive means of modification."

Actually, the term selection is itself a misnomer, for there is no known agent in nature that deliberately selects. Selection is not an active force or promoter of evolution as much as a passive pruning device to weed out the unfit. As such, selected objects are simply those that remain after all the poorly adapted or less fortunate ones have been removed from a population of such objects. A better term might be "nonrandom elimination," a phrase long championed by one of the 20th century's leading evolutionists, Ernst Mayr (1997). What we really seek to characterize is the aggregate of adverse circumstances responsible for the deletion of some members of a group. Accordingly, selection can be generally taken to mean preferential interaction of any object with its environment—a more liberal interpretation that also helps widen our view of evolution.

Selection works alongside the flow of resources into and out of all open systems, not just life-forms. Ordered systems are selected partly for their ability to command energy; and this energy is the "force," if there is any at all, in evolution. Briefly and broadly, selection occurs in the inanimate world as well as among animate objects, often providing a formative step in the production of order. It is energy flow and selection that together, working in tandem, underlie the self-assembly noted in Figure 3—the former driving an initial system beyond equilibrium, the latter aiding the emergence of higher order in that system. Even more strongly stated, it may well be that energy flow rate itself is the trait most often selected by successful systems of the same kind. A handful of cases will suffice, among many others so documented (Chaisson 2001, 2003, 2004), to illustrate the action of this energy-selection duo among a spectrum of increasingly ordered systems in successive phases of cosmic evolution.

First, consider stars as an example of physical evolution. Growing complexity can serve as an indicator of stellar aging—a developmental process—allowing stars to be tracked as their interiors undergo cycles of nuclear fusion causing them to change in size, color, brightness, and elemental composition, all the while passing from "birth" to maturity and thence to "death"; red giant stars, for instance, are clearly more complex than normal, main-sequence stars such as our current Sun, which is in turn more complex than protostars perched on the verge of stardom, as noted in Figure 5. At least as regards energy flow, material resources, and structural integrity while experiencing change, stars have much in common with life. None of which claims that stars are alive, a common misinterpretation of such an eclectic stance. Stars do not evolve in the strict and limited biological sense; yet close parallels are apparent, including populations, variation, modification, selection, adaptation, and perhaps even a kind of reproduction among the stars—a generational process—reminiscent of the following Malthusian inspired scenario:

Galactic clouds spawn clusters of stars, only a few of which (the more massive ones unlike the Sun) enable other, subsequent groups of stars to emerge in turn, with each generation's offspring showing slight variations, especially among the heavy elements contained within. Waves of "sequential star formation" propagate through many such clouds like slow-motion chain reactions over eons of time—shock waves from the death of old stars triggering the birth of new ones—neither one kind of star displaying a dramatic increase in number nor the process of regeneration ever being perfect. Those massive stars modified by gravity and selected by nature to endure the fires needed to produce heavy elements are in fact the very same stars that often produce shocks to create new populations of stars, thereby both episodically and gradually enriching the interstellar medium with greater elemental complexity on timescales measured in millions of millennia. As always, the necessary though perhaps not sufficient conditions for the growth of complexity depend on the environmental circumstances and on the availability of energy flows in such (here, galactic) environments. On and on, the cycle churns; build up, break down, change—a stellar "evolution" minus any genes, inheritance, or overt function, for these are the value-added qualities of biological evolution that go well beyond the evolution of physical systems.

Next, consider plants as an example of biological evolution. Here, we trace the rise in complexity with evolution among plant life, much as we could for myriad and wondrous life-forms both more and less advanced. And here natural selection—that is genuine neo-Darwinism—is clearly at work, making use of energy rate densities well in excess of those of galaxies, stars, and planets. As shown in Figure 5, energy-flow diagnostics display a clear increase in complexity among various plants that best locally and temporarily the normal entropy process: photosynthesis operates more efficiently in flowering angiosperms than in gymnosperms or algae and, in turn, more efficiently still for more organized, cultivated (C4) crops such as corn and sugarcane. Similar trends are apparent for animals, yet with even higher and rising energy rate densities along a broad evolutionary sequence spanning protocells, prokaryotes, ectotherms, and endotherms. To be sure, system functionality and genetic inheritance are two factors, above and beyond mere system structure, tending to enhance order among animate systems that are clearly living compared to inanimate systems that are clearly not. Unsurprisingly, then, life-forms require the acquisition of more energy per unit mass for their well-being.

Onward across the bush of life (or the arrow of time)—cells, tissues, organs, organisms—we find much the same story unfolding. Starting with life's precursor molecules (the realm of chemical evolution) and all the way up to human brains exemplifying the most complex clump of animate matter known, we encounter the same *general* trend found earlier for stars: the greater the perceived complexity of the system, the greater the flow of energy density through that system—either to build it, or to maintain it, or both.

Finally, consider society as an example of cultural evolution. Here, the cosmic-evolutionary narrative continues, yet with greater normalized energy flows to account for the rise of our obviously complex civilization. As plotted in Figure 5, once more we can trace social progress, again in energy consumption, for a variety of human-related advances among our hominid ancestors. Quantitatively, hunter-gatherers of a million years ago utilized considerably less energy rate density than did agriculturists of several thousand years ago; and these, in turn, much less than pioneering industrialists and now contemporary western society. The path to today's civilization is undoubtedly paved with increased energy use.

Machines, too—and not just computer chips, but also ordinary motors and engines that typified the fast-paced economy of the 20th century—can be cast in evolutionary terms, though here the mechanism is less Darwinian than Lamarckian with its emphasis on accumulation of acquired traits. Either way, energy remains the driver and with rapidly ramping pace. Aircraft engines, for example, display clear evolutionary trends as engineering improvement and customer selection over generations of products have made engines more intricate, complex, and efficient—all the while utilizing enriched flows of energy density—from the Wright engine of the early 1900s to the F-117 Nighthawk of the 1990s. Automobiles, from the pioneering Model Ts to today's gadget-rich SUVs, can be likewise analyzed, as can the vaunted silicon chips that so clearly now accelerate our 21st century economy.

Humankind is now moving toward a time, possibly as soon as within a few generations, when we will no longer be able to expect nature to adjust rapidly enough to ensure our own survival. Rather, civilization on Earth will either have to adapt to the natural environment with ever-accelerating speed, or generate artificial environmental conditions needed for our ecological existence. From two magnificent yet local systems—society and machines—will likely emerge a symbiotically functioning technoculture, the epitome (as far as we know) of complexity writ large in nature—a new technology-based system that will likely require yet greater values of energy rate density, as the curve in Figure 5 continues racing upward. This is truly the onset of the Life Era, wherein sentient, manipulative cyborgs potentially become the agents of change—or it will be a passing event in spacetime whereby human life on Earth and its great cultural experiment end.

Conclusion

This article has taken the liberty of using the word "evolution" in an intentionally provocative way, to capture ontological, ecological, and phylogenetic change on all spatial and temporal scales by means surely including, but not restricted to, natural selection. Within the grand scenario of cosmic evolution, general trends have been identified among nature's myriad changes affecting galaxies, stars, planets and life-forms throughout an extremely long duration of natural history, from the Big Bang to humankind. The result is a unifying worldview of considerable scope and insight, a scientific posture that not only embeds all cultures on Earth in a cosmic setting yet also itself creates a transcendent culture that people of all persuasions can know, welcome, and embrace. We have been especially alert to any universal process—developmental or generational, gradual or punctual—that might have allowed for, indeed driven, evolution from time immemorial. More than any other single factor, energy flow would seem to be the principal means whereby all of nature's diverse systems have naturally spawned complexity in an expanding universe, in fact some of them evolving impressive degrees of order characteristic of life, mind, and civilization. Energy, specifically humanity's use of it optimally and wisely, will also likely guide our fate along the future arrow of time. For we, too, partake in the cosmic-evolutionary narrative, an epic-class story of rich natural history for the new millennium.

References

Bonner, J. T., 1988, *The Evolution of Complexity*. Princeton: Princeton University Press.

Chaisson, E. J., 1998, "The cosmic environment for growth of complexity," *BioSystems* 46:13.

———, 2001, *Cosmic Evolution: The Rise of Complexity in Nature*. Cambridge: Harvard University Press. (For a popular rendition of this work, consult *Epic of Evolution*. New York: Columbia University Press, 2006.)

———, 2003, "A unifying concept for astrobiology," *Int. Journal Astrobiology* 2:91.

———, 2004, "Complexity: An energetics agenda," *Complexity: Journal of Santa Fe Institute* 9:14.

Chambers, R., 1844, *Vestiges of the Natural History of Creation*. London: Churchill.

Christian, D., 2004, *Maps of Time*. Berkeley: University of California Press.

Darwin, C., 1859, *On the Origin of Species*. London: J. Murray.

Dyson, F., 1979, "Time without end: physics and biology in an open universe," *Reviews of Modern Physics* 51:447.

Gold, T., 1962, "The arrow of time," *American Journal of Physics* 30:403.

Kauffman, S., 1993, *The Origins of Order*. Oxford: Oxford University Press.

Layzer, D., 1976, "The arrow of time," *Astrophysical Journal* 206:559.

Lotka, A., 1922, "Contribution to the energetics of evolution," *Proceedings of National Academy of Sciences* 8:147.

Maynard Smith, J., 1995, "Non-junk DNA," *Nature* 374:227.

Mayr, E., 1997, *This is Biology*. Cambridge: Harvard University Press.

McMahon, T. and Bonner, J. T., 1983, *On Size and Life*. San Francisco: W. H. Freeman.

Morowitz, H. J., 1968, *Energy Flow in Biology*. New York: Academic Press.

Morrison, P., 1964, "A thermodynamic characterization of self-reproduction," *Reviews of Modern Physics* 36:517.

Odum, H., 1988, "Self-organization, transformity, and information," *Science* 242:1132.

Prigogine, I., Nicolis, G., and Babloyantz, A., 1972, "Thermodynamics of evolution," *Physics Today* 11:23 and 12:38.

Salk, J., 1982, "An evolutionary approach to world problems," Paris: UNESCO.

Schroedinger, E., 1944, *What is Life?* Cambridge: Cambridge University Press.

Shapley, H., 1930, *Flights from Chaos*. New York: McGraw Hill.

Smil, V., 1999, *Energies*. Cambridge: MIT Press.

Spencer, H., 1896, *A System of Synthetic Philosophy*. London: Williams and Norgate.

Spier, F., 2005, "How big history works," *Social Evolution & History* 4:25.

von Bertalanffy, L., 1932, *Theoretische Biologie*. Berlin: Borntraeger.

Whitehead, A. N., 1925, *Science and the Modern World*. New York: Macmillan.

Wilson, E. O., 1998, *Consilience: The Unity of Knowledge*. New York: Knopf.

Links

Links to Internet resources for "cosmic evolution" are available at: *http://www.tufts.edu/as/wright_center/cosmic_evolution*.

Chapter 2*

Cosmic Evolution
History, Culture, and Human Destiny

Steven J. Dick

During the course of the 20th century, a powerful new idea gradually entered human consciousness and culture: that we are part of a cosmos billions of years old and billions of light years in extent; that all parts of this cosmos are interconnected and evolving; and that the stories of our galaxy, our solar system, our planet, and ourselves are part and parcel of the ultimate master narrative of the universe, a story we now collectively term "cosmic evolution." Even as in some quarters of popular culture, heated debate continues over Darwinian evolution 150 years after the idea was published, over the last 50 years the much more encompassing idea that Carl Sagan embodied in the phrase "the cosmic connection" has become more and more a part of our daily lives, and will even more in the future as our cosmic consciousness increases.[1]

Cosmic evolution provides the proper universal context for biological evolution, revealing that the latter is only a small part of the bigger picture, in which everything is evolving, including life and culture. The more we know about science, the more we know culture and cosmos are connected, to such an extent that we can now see that the cosmos is inextricably intertwined with human destiny, both in the short term and the long-term, impinging on (and arguably essential to) questions normally reserved for religion and philosophy. It is the purpose of this chapter to uncover the historical evolution

---

* Parts of the first section of this chapter are updated from chapter 1 of Steven J. Dick and James E. Strick, *The Living Universe: NASA and the Development of Astrobiology* (New Brunswick: Rutgers University Press, 2004).

of this new understanding of the cosmos, describe the effects on culture so far, and outline the potentially far-reaching impact on the future of humanity.

Cosmic Evolution and History

The idea of cosmic evolution implies a continuous evolution of the constituent parts of the cosmos from its origins to the present. Planetary evolution, stellar evolution, and the evolution of galaxies could in theory be seen as distinct subjects in which one component evolves but not the other, and in which the parts have no mutual relationships. Indeed, in the first half of the 20th century scientists treated the evolution of planets, stars, and galaxies for the most part as distinct subjects, and historians of science still tend to do so.[2] But the amazing and stunning idea that overarches these separate histories is that the entire universe is evolving, that all of its parts are connected and interact, and that this evolution applies not only to inert matter, but also to life, intelligence, and culture. Physical, biological, and cultural evolution is the essence of the universe.[3] This overarching idea is what is called cosmic evolution, and the idea has itself evolved to the extent that some modern scientists even talk of a cosmic ecology the "life of the cosmos" and the "natural selection" of universes.[4]

Although the question of extraterrestrial life is very old, the concept of a full-blown cosmic evolution—the connected evolution of planets, stars, galaxies, *and* life on Earth and beyond—is much younger. As historian Michael Crowe has shown in his study of the plurality of worlds debate, in the 19th century a combination of ideas—the French mathematician Pierre Simon Laplace's "nebular hypothesis" for the origin of the solar system; the British naturalist Robert Chamber's application of evolution to other worlds; and Darwinian evolution on this world—gave rise to the first tentative expressions of parts of this world view. The philosophy of Herbert Spencer extended it to the evolution of society, although not to extraterrestrial life or society. But some Spencerians, notably Harvard philosopher John Fiske in his *Outlines of a Cosmic Philosophy Based on the Doctrine of Evolution* (1875), did extend evolutionary principles to life on other planets.[5]

Neither astronomers nor biologists tended to embrace such a broad philosophical, and empirically unsupported, concept as full-blown cosmic evolution. Influenced by Darwin, 19th century astronomers and popularizers did occasionally propound the rudiments of the idea. In England, Richard A. Proctor proposed an evolutionary view in which all planets would attain life in due time. In France, Camille Flammarion argued that life began by spontaneous generation, evolved via natural selection by adaptation to its environment, and was ruled by survival of the fittest wherever it was found in the universe. In this scheme of cosmic evolution, anthropocentrism was banished; Earth was not unique, and humans were in no sense the highest form of life. Thus were the general outlines of the idea of cosmic evolution spread to the populace, not only by these forerunners of Carl Sagan, but (as historian Bernard Lightman has shown) by a variety of Victorian popularizers of science.[6]

But such a set of general ideas is a long way from a research program. In the first half century of the post-Darwinian world, cosmic evolution did *not* find fertile ground among astronomers who were hard-pressed to find evidence for it. Spectroscopy, which displayed the distinct "fingerprints" of each of the chemical elements, did reveal to astronomers that those same elements were found in the terrestrial and celestial realms. This confirmed the widely assumed idea of "uniformity of nature," that both nature's laws and its materials were everywhere the same. Astronomers recognized and advocated parts of cosmic evolution, as in William Herschel's ruminations on the classification of nebulae, the British astrophysicist Norman Lockyer's work on the evolution of the elements, or the American astronomer George Ellery Hale's *Study of Stellar Evolution* (1908). In their published writings, however, Hale and his colleagues stuck very much to the techniques for studying the evolution of the physical universe. Even Percival Lowell's *Evolution of Worlds* (1909) spoke of the evolution of the physical universe, not a "biological universe" full of life, his arguments for Martian canals built by an alien intelligence notwithstanding. Although Lowell was a Spencerian, had been influenced by Fiske at Harvard, and had addressed his graduating class on "the nebular hypothesis" two years after Fiske's *Cosmic Philosophy* (1874), he did not apply the idea of advanced civilizations to the universe at large.[7]

Even in the first half of the 20th century, astronomers had to be content with the uniformity of nature argument confirmed by spectroscopy. In an article in *Science* in 1920, the American astronomer W. W. Campbell (a great opponent of Lowell's canalled Mars) enunciated exactly this general idea of widespread life via the uniformity of nature argument, "If there is a unity of materials, unity of laws governing those materials throughout the universe, why may we not speculate somewhat confidently upon life universal?" he asked. He even spoke of "other stellar systems . . . with degrees of intelligence and civilization from which we could learn much, and with which we could sympathize."[8]

That was about all the astronomers of the time could say. As Helge Kragh concluded in his history of the Big Bang cosmology, "during the nineteenth century the static clockwork universe of Newtonian mechanics was replaced with an evolutionary worldview. It now became accepted that the world has not always been the same, but is the result of a natural evolution from some previous state probably very different from the present one. Because of the evolution of the world, the future is different from the past – the universe acquired a history." But the 19th century went only so far: "The Victorian conception of the universe was, in a sense, evolutionary, but the evolution was restricted to the constituents of the universe and did not, as in the world models of the 20th century, cover the universe in its entirety."[9]

For the most part, biologists were also reluctant cosmic evolutionists even at the beginning of the 20th century. The British naturalist Alfred Russel Wallace, cofounder with Darwin of the theory of natural selection, wrote in 1903 that "[o]ur position in the material universe is special and probably unique, and . . . it is such as to lend support to the view, held by many great thinkers and writers today, that the supreme end and purpose of this vast universe was the production and development of the living soul in the perishable body of man." While he believed in a modicum of physical evolution in his small solar system-centric universe, he concluded that intelligence beyond Earth was highly improbable, calculating the physical, cosmic, and evolutionary improbabilities against the evolution of an equivalent moral or intellectual being to man, on any other planet, as a hundred million million to one. Clearly, for this pioneer in evolution by natural selection there was no cosmic evolution in its fullest sense, no biological universe.[10]

Similarly, Lawrence J. Henderson, a professor of biological chemistry at Harvard, wrote 10 years after Wallace, "[t]here is . . . one scientific conclusion which I wish to put forward as a positive statement and, I trust, fruitful outcome of the present investigation. The properties of matter and the course of cosmic evolution are now seen to be intimately related to the structure of the living being and to its activities; they become, therefore, far more important in biology than has been previously suspected. For the whole evolutionary process, both cosmic and organic, is one, and the biologist may now rightly regard the universe in its very essence as biocentric." Clearly, Henderson grasped essential elements of cosmic evolution, used its terminology, and believed his research into the fitness of the environment pointed in that direction. Yet, although he had a productive career at Harvard until his death in 1942, Henderson never enunciated a full-blown concept of cosmic evolution, nor did any of his astronomical colleagues.[11]

Henderson's idea of a biologically robust cosmic evolution in 1913 was largely stillborn; perhaps it was in part because just a few years later the British astronomer James Jeans's theory of the formation of planetary systems by close stellar encounters convinced the public, and most scientists, that planetary systems were extremely rare. This idea remained entrenched until the mid-1940s. Without planetary systems, cosmic evolution was stymied at the level of the innumerable stars, well short of the biological universe. In the absence of evidence, cosmic evolution was left to science fiction writers like Olaf Stapledon, whose *Last and First Men* and *Star Maker* novels in the 1930s embraced it in colorful terms. But Henderson had caught the essence of a great idea—that life and the material universe were closely linked, a fundamental tenet of cosmic evolution that would lay dormant for almost a half century.

The humble and sporadic origins of the idea of cosmic evolution demonstrate that it did not have to become what is now the leading overarching principle of 20th century astronomy. But it did, helped along by the Big Bang cosmology featuring a universe with a beginning slowly unfolding over time. The history of the Big Bang cosmology therefore parallels to some extent the history of cosmic evolution in its grandest sense, and Edwin Hubble's empirical observations of galaxies consistent with the concept of an expanding universe added a further dimension to the new world view.[12] Almost all astronomers today view cosmic evolution as a continuous story from the Big Bang to the evolution of intelligence, accepting as proven the evolution of the physical universe, while leaving open the still unproven question of the biological universe, whose sole known exemplar remains the planet Earth. The central question remains how far cosmic evolution commonly proceeds. Does it end with the evolution of matter, the evolution of life, the evolution of intelligence, or the evolution of culture? Today, by contrast with 1950, cosmic evolution is the guiding conceptual scheme for a substantial research program.

When and how did astronomers and biologists come to believe in cosmic evolution as a guiding principle for their work, and how did it become a serious research program? In her pioneering book, *Unifying Biology: The Evolutionary Synthesis and Evolutionary Biology*, historian Betty Smocovitis has emphasized that with the rise of the modern synthesis in biology, by midcentury evolution had become a unifying theme for biology, with Julian Huxley and others also extolling its place in cosmic evolution. By the 1940s, Smocovitis wrote, "cosmic, galactic, stellar, planetary, chemical, organic evolution and cultural evolution emerged as a continuum in a 'unified' evolutionary cosmology."[13] But it was only in the 1950s and 1960s that the cognitive elements—planetary science, planetary systems science, origin of life studies, and the Search for Extraterrestrial Intelligence (SETI)—combined to form a robust theory of cosmic evolution, as well as to provide an increasing amount of evidence for it. Only then, and increasingly thereafter, were serious claims made for disciplinary status for fields known as exobiology, astrobiology, and bioastronomy—the biological universe component of cosmic evolution. And only then did government funding become available, as the search for life became one of the prime goals of space science, and cosmic evolution became public policy.

We have already hinted at why this coalescence had not happened earlier, Spencerian philosophy and the ideas of Flammarion, Proctor, and Henderson notwithstanding. Although the idea of the physical evolution of planets and biological evolution of life on those planets in our solar system had been around for a while—and even some evidence in the form of seasonal changes and spectroscopic evidence of vegetation on Mars—not until the space program did the technology become available, resulting in large amounts of government funding poured into planetary science so that these tentative conclusions could be further explored. Moreover, if evolution was truly to be conceived as a cosmic phenomenon, planetary systems outside our solar system were essential. Only in the 1940s, when the nebular hypothesis came back into vogue, could an abundance of planetary systems once again be postulated. During a 15-year period from 1943 to 1958, the commonly accepted frequency of planetary systems in the galaxy went from 100 to one billion, a difference of seven orders of magnitude. The turnaround involved many arguments, from the observations of a few possible planetary companions in 1943, to binary star statistics, the nebular hypothesis, and stellar rotation rates. Helping matters along was the dean of American astronomers, Henry Norris Russell, whose 1943 *Scientific American* article "Anthropocentrism's Demise" enthusiastically embraced numerous planetary systems based on just a few observations by Kaj Strand and others. By 1963, the American astronomer Peter van de Kamp announced his discovery of a planet around Barnard's star, and the planet chase was on, to be truly successful only at the end of the century.[14]

Thus was one more step in cosmic evolution made plausible by midcentury, even though it was a premature and optimistic idea, since only in 1995 were the first planets found around Sun-like stars, and those were gas giants like Jupiter. But what about life? That further step awaited developments in biochemistry, in particular the Oparin-Haldane theory of chemical evolution for the origin of life. The first paper on the origins of life by the Russian biochemist Aleksandr Ivanovich Oparin was written in 1924, elaborated in the 1936 book, *Origin of Life*, and reached the English world in a 1938 translation. By that time the British geneticist and biochemist J. B. S. Haldane had provided a brief independent account of the origin of life similar to Oparin's chemical theory. By 1940, when the British Astronomer Royal, Sir Harold

Spencer Jones, wrote *Life on Other Worlds*, he remarked that "It seems reasonable to suppose that whenever in the Universe the proper conditions arise, life must inevitably come in to existence."[15]

The contingency or necessity of life would be one of the great scientific and philosophical questions of cosmic evolution, but in any case the Oparin-Haldane chemical theory of origin of life provided a basis for experimentation, beginning with the famous experiment of Stanley Miller and Harold Urey in 1953, in which amino acids—the building blocks of proteins and life—were synthesized under possible primitive Earth conditions. By the mid-1950s, another step of cosmic evolution was coming into focus—the possibility of primitive life. Again, the optimism was premature, but the point is that it set off numerous experiments around the world to verify another step in cosmic evolution. Already in 1954, Harvard biochemist George Wald proclaimed the Oparin-Haldane process a natural and inevitable event, not just on our planet, but on any planet similar to ours in size and temperature. By 1956, Oparin had teamed with Russian astronomer V. Fesenkov to write *Life in the Universe*, which expressed the same view of the inevitability of life as had Wald.[16]

What remained was the possible evolution of intelligence in the universe. Although hampered by a lack of understanding of how this had happened on Earth, discussion of the evolution of intelligence in the universe was spurred on by the famous paper by the American physicists Giuseppe Cocconi and Philip Morrison in *Nature* in 1959. "Searching for Interstellar Communications," showed how the detection of radio transmissions was feasible with radio telescope technology already in hand. In the following year astronomer Frank Drake, a recent Harvard graduate, undertook just such a project (Ozma) at the National Radio Astronomy Observatory (NRAO), ushering in a series of attempts around the world to detect such transmissions. And in 1961, Drake, supported by NRAO director Otto Struve, convened the first conference on interstellar communication at Green Bank, West Virginia. Although a small conference attended by only 11 people including Struve, representatives were present from astronomy, biology, and physics, already hinting at the interdisciplinary nature of the task.[17] Thus by 1961, the elements of the full-blown cosmic evolution debate were in place.

It was at the Green Bank meeting that the now-famous Drake Equation was first formulated. The equation $N = R_* \times f_p \times n_e \times f_l \times f_i \times f_c \times L$—purporting to estimate the number (N) of technological civilizations in the galaxy—eventually became the icon of cosmic evolution, showing in one compact equation not only the astronomical and biological aspects of cosmic evolution, but also its cultural aspects. The first three terms represented the number of stars in the galaxy that had formed planets with environments suitable for life; the second two terms narrow the number to those on which life and intelligence actually develop; and the final two represent radio communicative civilizations. "L," representing the lifetime of a technological civilization, embodied the success or failure of cultural evolution. Unfortunately, depending on who assigned values to the parameters of the equation, it yielded numbers ranging from one (Earth) to many millions of technological civilizations in the galaxy. Drake and most others in the field recognized then, and recognize even now almost 50 years later, that this equation is a way of organizing our ignorance. At the same time, progress has been made on at least one of its parameters; the fraction of stars with planets (f_p) is now known to be between 5 and 10 percent for gas giant planets around solar type stars.

The adoption of cosmic evolution was by no means solely a Western phenomenon. On the occasion of the fifth anniversary of Sputnik, Soviet radio astronomer Joseph Shklovskii wrote *Universe, Life, Mind* (1962). When elaborated and published in 1966 as *Intelligent Life in the Universe* by Carl Sagan, it became the bible for cosmic evolutionists interested in the search for life. Nor was Shklovskii's book an isolated instance of Russian interest. As early as 1964, the Russians convened their own meetings on extraterrestrial civilizations, funded their own observing programs, and published extensively on the subject.[18]

Thus, cosmic biological evolution first had the potential to become a research program in the early 1960s when its cognitive elements had developed enough to become experimental and observational sciences, and when the researchers in these disciplines first realized they held the key to a larger problem that could not be resolved by any one part, but only by all of them working together. At first this was a very small number of researchers, but it has expanded greatly over the last 40 years, especially under NASA patronage. The idea was effectively spread beyond the scientific community by a variety of astronomers. As early as 1958 cosmic evolution was being popularized by Harvard astronomer Harlow Shapley in *Of Stars and Men*; and Shapley used it thereafter in many of his astronomical writings emphasizing its impact on culture.[19] The idea was spread much more by Sagan's *Cosmos* (1980), Eric Chaisson's works beginning with *Cosmic Dawn: The Origins of Matter and Life* (1981), and in France by Hubert Reeves *Patience dans l'azur: L'evolution cosmique* (1981), among others.[20] By the end of the century cosmic evolution was viewed as playing out on an incomparably larger stage than conceived by A. R. Wallace a century ago.

The catalyst for the unified research program of cosmic evolution—and for the birth of a new scientific discipline—was the Space Age. No one would claim that a field of extraterrestrial life studies, or cosmic evolution, existed in the first half of the 20th century. Even by 1955, when Otto Struve pondered the use of the word "astrobiology" to describe the broad study of life beyond Earth, he explicitly decided against a new discipline: "[t]he time is probably not yet ripe to recognize such a completely new discipline within the framework of astronomy. The basic facts of the origin of life on Earth are still vague and uncertain; and our knowledge of the physical conditions on Venus and Mars is insufficient to give us a reliable background for answering the question" of life on other worlds. But the imminent birth of "exobiology" was palpable in 1960 when Joshua Lederberg coined the term and set forth an ambitious but practical agenda based on space exploration in his article in *Science* "Exobiology: Experimental Approaches to Life Beyond the Earth." Over the next 20 years numerous such proclamations of a new discipline were made. By 1979, NASA's SETI chief John Billingham wrote that "over the past twenty years, there has emerged a new direction in science, that of the study of life outside the Earth, or exobiology. Stimulated by the advent of space programs, this fledgling science has now evolved to a stage of reasonable maturity and respectability."[21]

The extent to which NASA had served as the chief patron of cosmic biological evolution is evident in its sponsorship of many of the major conferences on extraterrestrial life, although the Academies of Science of the United States and the USSR were also prominent supporters. It was NASA that adopted exobiology as one of the prime goals of space science, and it was from NASA that funding would come, despite an early but abortive interest at the National Science Foundation.[22] Pushed by prominent biologists such as Joshua Lederberg, beginning already in the late 1950s soon after its origin, NASA poured a small but steady stream of money into exobiology and the life sciences in general. By 1976, $100 million had been spent on the Viking biology experiments designed to search for life on Mars from two spacecraft landers. Even as exobiology saw a slump in the 1980s in the aftermath of the Viking failure to detect life on Mars unambiguously, NASA kept exobiology alive with a grant program at the level of $10 million per year, the largest exobiology laboratory in the world at its Ames Research Center, and evocative images of cosmic evolution (Figure 1). Cosmic evolution's potential by the early 1960s to become a research program was converted to reality by NASA funding.

This is true not only of NASA's exobiology laboratory and grants program, but also of its SETI program. Born at Ames in the late 1960s, quite

Figure 1. Cosmic evolution is depicted in this image from the exobiology program at NASA Ames Research Center (ARC), 1986. Upper left: the formation of stars, the production of heavy elements, and the formation of planetary systems, including our own. At left prebiotic molecules, RNA, and DNA are formed within the first billion years on primitive Earth. At center: the origin and evolution of life leads to increasing complexity, culminating with intelligence, technology, and astronomers. Upper right: contemplating the universe. The image was created by David DesMarais, Thomas Scattergood, and Linda Jahnke at ARC in 1986 and reissued in 1997.

separate from the exobiology program, NASA SETI expended some $55 million prior to its termination by Congress in 1993. It was the NASA SETI program that was the flag bearer of cosmic evolution. As it attempted to determine how many planets might have evolved intelligent life, all of the parameters of cosmic evolution, as encapsulated in the Drake Equation, came into play.

With the demise of a publicly funded NASA SETI program in 1993, the research program of cosmic evolution did not end. The remnants of the NASA SETI program were continued with private funding, and similar, if smaller, SETI endeavors are still carried out around the world. Within NASA, a program of cosmic evolution research continued, with its images subtly changed. In 1995, NASA announced its Origins program, which two years later it described in its Origins Roadmap as "following the 15 billion year long chain of events from the birth of the universe at the Big Bang, through the formation of chemical elements, galaxies, stars, and planets, through the mixing of chemicals and energy that cradles life on Earth, to the earliest self-replicating organisms—and the profusion of life." Any depiction of "intelligence" is conspicuously absent from the new imagery (Figure 2), for due to congressional action, programmatically it could no longer be supported with public funding. With this proclamation of a new Origins program, cosmic

Figure 2. Cosmic evolution, as it appeared in the Roadmap for NASA's Office of Space Science Origins Theme, 1997 and 2000.

evolution became the organizing principle for most of NASA's space science effort. In a broad sense, most of NASA's space science program can be seen as filling in the gaps in the story of cosmic evolution.

In 1996 the "Astrobiology" program was added to NASA's lexicon. The NASA Astrobiology Institute, centered at NASA's Ames Research Center, funds numerous centers nationwide for research in astrobiology at the level of several tens of millions of dollars. Its paradigm is also cosmic evolution, even if it also tends to avoid mention of extraterrestrial intelligence due to congressional disapproval stemming from cancellation of the NASA SETI program in 1993. No such restriction is evident at the SETI Institute in Mountain View, California, headed by Frank Drake. The Institute has under its purview tens of millions of dollars in grants, all geared to answering various parameters of the Drake Equation, the embodiment of cosmic evolution, including the search for intelligence.

As we enter the 21st century, there is no doubt about the existence of a robust cosmic evolution research program. NASA is its primary patron and even many scientists without government funding now see their work in the context of this research program. Other agencies, including the European Space Agency, are also funding research essentially in line with the Origins and Astrobiology programs, not to mention their spacecraft, which help to fill in the gaps in the grand narrative of cosmic evolution. Within the last 40 years, all the elements of a new discipline gradually came into place: the cognitive elements, the funding resources, and the community and communications structures common to new disciplines. As we enter the 21st century, cosmic evolution is a thriving enterprise, providing the framework for an expansive research program and drawing in young talent sure to perpetuate a new field of science that a half century ago was nonexistent.

Cosmic Evolution and Culture

Since Darwin propounded his theory of evolution by natural selection, evolution has been much more than a science. It has been a worldview that has affected culture in numerous ways, and different cultures in diverse ways.[23] As we have noted, in her history of the modern evolutionary synthesis in biology, historian Betty Smocovitis found that by the late 1950s and early 1960s the wider culture was "permeated with evolutionary science" and "resonated with evolutionary themes."[24] The leaders of that evolutionary synthesis, including Julian Huxley, Theodosius Dobzhansky, Ernst Mayr, and George Gaylord Simpson, espoused an "evolutionary humanism," a secular progressive vision of the world that, for Huxley at least, was "the central feature of his worldview and of his scientific endeavors." In books and articles, each of these scientists addressed the future of mankind in evolutionary terms. Huxley (grandson of Darwin's chief defender T. H. Huxley) "offered an inquiry . . . into an ethical system, an ethos, grounded in evolution, now a legitimate science, with its fundamental principle of natural selection, verifiable and testable through observation and experiment." Cosmic evolution was part of this worldview, even if Mayr and Simpson would later express serious doubts about the chances for success of exobiology and SETI programs.[25]

As Palmeri also points out in Chapter 15 of this volume, in the 1950s and 1960s Harlow Shapley was a prime example of a cosmic evolution evangelist from the astronomical side, being among the first to popularize the cosmic evolutionary perspective with "missionary zeal." In Shapley's view, this perspective inspired a religious attitude, should be incorporated into current religious traditions, and went beyond those traditions in questioning the need for the supernatural. He even spoke of a "stellar theology," a view that had broader implication for ethics. Cosmic evolution has also been used to bolster the idea of biological evolution, though apparently with little impact to this day among skeptical Americans. Shapley's books *Of Stars and Men: The Human Response to an Expanding Universe* (1958), *The View from a Distant Star* (1963), and *Beyond the Observatory* (1967) spread these ideas worldwide.

During the second half of the 20th century, then, the evolutionary view of the universe was not only fully in place both from the point of view of at least some astronomers and biologists, but was also spreading to the broader culture. Instead of the small and relatively static universe accepted at the turn of the 20th century, humanity was now asked to absorb the idea of an expanding (now known to be accelerating) universe 13.7 billion light-years in extent, full of billions of evolving galaxies floating in an Einsteinian space time with no center. The Big Bang theory, though still in competition in the 1950s with Fred Hoyle's Steady State theory that denied an overarching linear cosmic evolution, would receive increasing confirmation through the detection of the cosmic microwave background in 1965, and its study at ever-finer resolution through the COBE and WMAP satellites. The Hubble Space Telescope and other spacecraft brought the impact of this worldview directly to the people, through spectacular imagery of objects in the evolutionary narrative, and through more global images such as the Hubble Deep Field. The biological universe full of life was conjectured, but not proven, though SETI and astrobiology programs received much popular attention, particularly in the case of the supposed fossil life found in the Mars rock (evidence hotly contested, in part because of the high stakes for broader worldviews).[26]

In seeking the impact of the new universe on culture in the modern era, we need to remember that "culture" is not monolithic and that "impact" is a notoriously vague term. Thus it is no surprise that the new universe and its master narrative of cosmic evolution evoked different meanings for different groups. Cosmic consciousness in the form of a biological universe was expressed in many forms in popular culture, some of them unpalatable to most scientists: belief in UFOs and extraterrestrial abduction, space-oriented religious cults, and ever more elaborate alien scenarios in science fiction. Indeed, all three of these developments may be seen as ways that popular culture attempts to work out the worldview implied by the new universe. The UFO debate and alien science fiction both had their predecessors in the late 19th century, but only in the second half of the 20th century did they come into their own as major elements of popular culture. During this time, evolutionary themes became common in science fiction, notably in Arthur C. Clarke's work such as *Childhood's End*. Some of the most popular films of all times featured aliens, among them *Star Wars, Close Encounters of the Third Kind, ET: The Extraterrestrial, War of the Worlds*, and *Men in Black*. Obviously, and understandably, popular culture became preoccupied with whether the biological universe is hostile or friendly.[27]

Although human reactions to the new universe and cosmic evolution have not been monolithic, certain underlying themes are pervasive. The increased awareness of the new universe and the possibility of a biological universe largely dashed any remaining hopes for an anthropocentric universe with all that implies for religion and philosophy.[28] Even though the idea that the universe was made for humans survives in the form of the elegantly misnamed "anthropic principle," in fact that principle is (to use L. J. Henderson's term from 1913 mentioned earlier), a "biocentric" principle of the fine-tuning of universal laws that points to the possible abundance of life in the universe in many forms, rather in human form only.[29] And if life is common throughout the universe, then our religions, philosophies, and other human endeavors are too parochial and will need to be significantly altered, expanded, or discarded. As physicist Paul Davies has said, "if it turns out to be the case that the universe is biofriendly . . . then . . . the scientific, theological and philosophical implications will be extremely significant."

The religious and philosophical implications of astronomical discoveries have been discussed especially since the time of the Copernican revolution, which made Earth a planet and the planets potential Earths.[30] A few farsighted thinkers reflected these implications in the early 20th century. Much to the chagrin of the Catholic Church, the French Jesuit priest, philosopher, and paleontologist, Pierre Teilhard de Chardin, famously made the evolution of the cosmos the central theme of his posthumous book *The Phenomenon of Man* (1955). Here he embraced cosmic evolution, and argued for a teleological evolution in which man would end in a collective consciousness called the "noosphere," which would ultimately lead to the Omega Point, the maximum level of consciousness, which he also identified with God.[31] Though the idea was not accepted within the Catholic church, a few have followed in Teilhard's footsteps, including the Catholic priest Thomas Berry and physicist Brian Swimme, whose book *The Universe Story*, emphasizes the religious significance of cosmic evolution.[32]

The new universe of the late 20th century has spawned renewed analysis of the relation of humans to the cosmos, both inside and outside established religions. Biologist Ursula Goodenough argues in *The Sacred Depths of Nature* that cosmic evolution is a shared worldview capable of evoking an abiding religious response. "Any global tradition," she writes, "needs to begin with a shared worldview—a culture-independent, globally accepted consensus as to how things are." She finds this consensus in "our scientific account of Nature, an account that can be called The Epic of Evolution. The Big Bang, the formation of stars and planets, the origin and evolution of life on this planet, the advent of human consciousness and the resultant evolution of cultures—this is the story, the one story, that has the potential to unite us, because it happens to be true."[33] She calls her elaboration of the religious implications "religious naturalism."

Similarly, but with the Christian tradition, the British biochemist and Anglican priest, Sir Arthur Peacocke, has called cosmic evolution "Genesis for the third millennium." He believes that "any theology—any attempt to relate God to all-that-is—will be moribund and doomed if it does not incorporate this perspective [of cosmic evolution] into its very bloodstream."[34] Michael Dowd and Connie Barlow, who consider themselves, "evangelists of cosmic evolution," have proposed "evolutionary Christianity"—very different from Huxley's evolutionary humanism, but both with evolution as a central concept. Evolutionary Christianity embraces cosmic evolution, variously termed "the Great Story" and the "epic of evolution," much more than did Huxley's original evolutionary humanism, undoubtedly because cosmic evolution has been so much more developed over the last 50 years, complete with evocative images from the Hubble Space Telescope.[35]

While Freeman Dyson among others have argued that the age-old mystery of God will be little changed by human attempts to read his mind, others argue that the new universe not only could, but should, lead to a new "cosmotheology" or a new "cosmophilosophy." Among the elements such a cosmotheology must take into account are 1) that humanity is in no way physically central to the universe, but located on a small planet circling a star on the outskirts of the Milky Way galaxy; 2) that humanity is probably not central biologically, even if our morphology may be unique; 3) that humanity is likely somewhere near the bottom, or at best midway, in the great chain of being—a likelihood that follows from the age of the universe and the youth of our species; 4) that we must be open to radically new conceptions of God grounded in cosmic evolution, including the idea of a "natural" rather than a "supernatural" God; and 5) that it must have a moral dimension, a reverence and respect for life that includes all species in the universe.[36]

Each of these elements of cosmotheology provides vast scope for elaboration. Perhaps the most radical consequences stem from the fourth principle that states that we must be open to new conceptions of God, stemming from our advancing knowledge of cosmic evolution and the universe in general. As the God of the ancient Near East stemmed from ideas of supernaturalism, our concept of a modern God could stem from modern ideas divorced from supernaturalism. The billions of people attached to current theologies may consider this no theology at all, for a transcendent God above and beyond nature is the very definition of their theology. The supernatural God "meme," which we should remember is an historical idea the same as any other, has been very efficient in spreading over the last few thousand years, picking up new memes such as those accepted by Christianity and other religions. Nonetheless, the idea of a "natural" God in the sense of a superior intelligence is appealing to some. A natural God need not intervene in human history, nor be the cause for religious wars such as witnessed through human history. It remains an open question whether a natural God fulfills the apparent need that many have for "the Other"; such a "God" is different enough from tradition concepts that some may wish to call it a cosmophilosophy rather than a cosmotheology.[37] In any case some will see it as an important part of religious naturalism.

Over the next centuries or millennia, religions will likely adjust to these cosmotheological principles. The adjustment will be most wrenching for those monotheistic religions that see man in the image of God (Judaism, Christianity, and Islam), a one-to-one relationship with a single godhead. It will be less wrenching for Oriental religions that teach salvation through individual enlightenment (Buddhism and Hinduism) rather than through a Savior, or that are this-worldly (Confucianism) rather than other-worldly. The adjustment will be not be to the physical world, as in Copernicanism, nor to the biological world, as in Darwinism, where man descended from the apes but still remained at the top of the terrestrial world. Rather the adjustment will be to the biological, or even postbiological, universe, in which intelligences are likely to be superior to us.

Even the possibility of life beyond Earth raises such theological questions, but particularly intriguing are impact scenarios in the event of the actual discovery of such life. The impact would undoubtedly very much depend on how the discovery was made and the nature of the discovery. Finding microbial life and even complex but nonsentient life might be of more interest to science than to philosophy or theology as scientists probed the nature of the newfound life and determined whether it was based on the same DNA structure and biochemistry as life on Earth. The discovery of intelligent life, on the other hand, would be of immediate interest not only to science, but to such age-old philosophical problems as the nature of objective knowledge (would we perceive the universe in the same way as extraterrestrials?) and theology, typically meaning the relationship between humans and God, but now recast as the relationship between all intelligent beings in the universe and God. In general, the urgency of the societal implications of extraterrestrial intelligence would depend on whether physical contact was made (considered unlikely to the extent that evidence for UFOs is weak), or if contact was made via a remote radio signal through a SETI program. If the latter, a great deal would depend on the message received, if indeed it were decipherable.

While all of these scenarios are interesting to contemplate, most compelling, and most discussed, is the problem of how the discovery of clear evidence of a signal from extraterrestrial intelligence would affect theology on Earth, even if no message were deciphered. This is still a complex question because there are many terrestrial theologies and they would undoubtedly be affected in different ways. And there would be much discussion, and perhaps no consensus, even within a particular theology. We know this will be the case because the discussion has already been underway for over 500 years. As Michael J. Crowe—one of the premier historians of the extraterrestrial life debate—has emphasized, extraterrestrials have already influenced life on Earth and the history of ideas in many areas in the sense that the possibility of their existence and the implications of their discovery have been the subject of discussion for centuries.[38]

Real SETI programs in the 20th century, however, made the problem more real even if the same concerns were raised again and again.[39] Ernan McMullin (a priest and philosopher at the University of Notre Dame) and George Coyne (the Jesuit director of the Vatican Observatory) are among those who have recently provided reflections from within the Catholic tradition. McMullin related the problem to that faced by 16th century Europeans discovering the peoples of Mesoamerica. Fully aware of Thomas Paine's objections to Christianity in the late 18th century, McMullin noted that "the proven reality of ETI [Extraterrestrial Intelligence] might even more effectively encourage a broadening among the theologians and religious believers generally of the realization that the Creator of a galactic universe may well choose to relate to creatures made in the Creator's own image in ways and on grounds as diverse as those creatures themselves." The problems of such a broadening of Christian doctrine related for McMullin to three issues: original sin, soul and body, and incarnation. He speculated that an omnipotent creator might want "to try more than once the fateful experiment of allowing freedom to a creature," such as the Eve/apple event in the Garden of Eden. He pointed to the possibility that aliens might or might not have souls; if they did "God also might elect to become incarnate in their nature or to interact in some other way with them" depending on their response to an Eden-like challenge. Regarding incarnation, which he calls "the defining doctrine of the Christian tradition," McMullin suggests that conflicting theological interpretations of that doctrine would influence anyone faced with the ETI situation. Thus the discovery of ETI would result in a range of answers from Christian theologians with regard to whether Christ would become incarnate on another world ranging from "certainly yes" to "certainly no." McMullin's own answer is "maybe."[40]

George Coyne, at the time Director of the Vatican Observatory, posed similar reservations about a definitive answer. He concluded that with the discovery of ETI "theologians must accept a serious responsibility to rethink some fundamental realities within the context of religious belief."[41] Among those realities are the nature of a human being, and whether Jesus Christ could exist on more than one planet a one time. While theologians are limited in their ability to answer such questions, varying interpretations of Christian doctrines suggests that were a discovery of ETI actually made, a way would be found for Christian doctrine to absorb it, though perhaps not easily. The alternative would be extinction, and Christianity has shown its ability to adapt to scientific discovery, if very slowly at times.

The extraterrestrial life debate has also stimulated Jewish thought about the implications of ETI. Rabbi Norman Lamm, for example, noted, "this challenge must be met forthrightly and honestly" and called those who shrink from pursuing it "parochial and provincial." Citing astronomers who emphasize our peripheral place in the new universe, Rabbi Lamm noted that "[n]ever before have so many been so enthusiastic about being so trivial." Cautioning that extraterrestrial life is far from proven, Lamm explored "a Jewish exotheology," and concluded that "[a] God who can exercise providence over one billion earthmen can do so for then billion times that number of creatures throughout the universe."[42]

The case where an extraterrestrial message is decoded is even more startling. Astronomer Jill Tarter, a pioneer in the field of SETI, believes an extraterrestrial message, unambiguously decoded, might be "a missionary campaign without precedent in terrestrial history," leading to the replacement of our diverse collection of terrestrial religions by a "universal religion." Alternatively, a message that indicates long-lived extraterrestrials with no need for God or religion might undermine our religious worldview completely.[43]

If there was any consensus, it was that terrestrial religions would adjust to extraterrestrials—an opinion echoed in late 20th century studies of religious attitudes toward the problem.[44] As McMullin and others have pointed out, various extraterrestrial theological scenarios have also been worked out in detail in science fiction, including C. S. Lewis's *Perelandra* and Walter Miller's *A Canticle for Leibowitz*. More recently, Maria Dorrit Russell has taken up these questions in her novels, *The Sparrow* and *Children of God*. These fictional scenarios nevertheless represent deep thought about a problem that has now been with us for 500 years in hypothetical form, and that will be given greater urgency as soon as a discovery is made.

The impact of the new cosmos and its master narrative of cosmic evolution need not be couched solely in terms of theology. Mark Lupisella and John Logsdon have proposed a "cosmocentric ethic," which they characterize as one which "(1) places the universe at the center, or establishes the universe as the priority in a value system, (2) appeals to something characteristic of the universe (physical and/or metaphysical) which might then (3) provide a justification of value, presumably intrinsic value, and (4) allow for reasonably objective measurement of value."[45] A cosmocentric ethic would have some of the same concerns as cosmotheology, devoid of the theological implications. For example, a cosmocentric ethic would dictate how we treat extraterrestrial life-forms, whether primitive or intelligent, taking into account not only our own homocentric interests, but also the interests of the other life-forms. The prospects of terraforming entire planets also raise the question of whether questions of terrestrial environmental ethics should be extended to the cosmic stage. In the context of spaceflight, human interaction in general—whether among ourselves or with other intelligence—would seem to demand a reorientation toward a cosmic rather than a geocentric perspective.

Quite aside from theological and philosophical implications, cosmic evolution provides humanity a cosmic context in time, allowing us to place humanity in the 13.7 billion-year history of the universe. Although it is difficult to grasp that span of time, attempts have been made for several decades using the "cosmic calendar," which conflates the history of the universe into a single year, showing humans arising in the last 1.5 hours of the last day of cosmic history, with the European Age of Discovery taking place one second ago.[46] More substantively, a small but increasing discipline known as "big history" seeks to incorporate human history into cosmic history in a more systematic way.[47] As seen in Chapter 13 of this volume, big history links our understanding of human history with our understanding of other historical sciences, such as cosmology, geology, and biology. It allows us to appreciate the emergent properties of culture in the same way as the emergent properties along the earlier path of cosmic evolution. And it highlights our unique collective learning ability and capacity for symbolic thought that results in our need to find meaning. In short, it reintegrates humans with the long history of the cosmos whence they sprang.

Finally, cosmic evolution integrates humans into the cosmos quite literally by teaching us that we are all "star stuff." Once again, Harlow Shapley was an early proponent of this perspective. "Mankind is made of star stuff," he wrote already in 1963, "ruled by universal laws. The thread of cosmic evolution runs through this history, as through all phases of the universe—the microcosmos of atomic structures, molecular forms, and microscopic organisms, and the macrocosmos of higher organisms, planets, stars, and galaxies. Evolution is still proceeding in galaxies and man—to what end, we can only vaguely surmise."[48] The colorful terminology of star stuff and "starfolk" was picked up by Carl Sagan among others; its integration of humans into the cosmos encourages us to be "at home in the universe" in the felicitous phrase used by several distinguished scientists in the late 20th century.[49] We now know that the atoms in our bodies were forged in nuclear reactions in stellar furnaces, spewed into the universe in supernovae explosions, and incorporated into our bodies through the long process of the evolution of life over the last 3.8 billion years on Earth. We recognize that after death, our bodily atoms will be dispersed once again through the universe, recycled to once again become star stuff in a cycle of events that will end only with the death of the universe itself. We are part and parcel of the universe, and at the hour of our death when we return to the universe, the old phrase from the *Book of Common Prayer* based on Genesis and often used in burial ceremonies—"earth to earth, ashes to ashes, dust to dust"—need only be slightly altered to "earth to earth, ashes to ashes, stardust to stardust" to be literally true. Cosmic evolution provides us with a master narrative in which our own birth, life, and death are integral parts of the universe, without recourse to the supernatural. In the end, that may be the ultimate message of the new universe and cosmic evolution.[50]

While only a small portion of humanity yet realizes the implications of the new universe and cosmic evolution, the incorporation of these ideas into educational curricula and the general reawakening to our place in the universe ensure these ideas are an increasingly important role in culture. Such educational curricula have emerged from the astrobiology and SETI programs, and are reaching an increasing number of students. The SETI Institute's *Life in the Universe* curriculum "Voyages Through Time" provides standards-based materials for a one-year high school integrated science course using cosmic evolution as its unifying theme. Its six modules include Cosmic Evolution, Planetary Evolution, Origin of Life, Evolution of Life, Hominid Evolution, and Evolution of Technology. The Wright Center for Science Education at Tufts University is also a valuable educational resource directly centered on "Cosmic Evolution: From Big Bang to Humankind," not surprising since the Center's director is Eric Chaisson.[51]

Following in the tradition of Shapley's *Of Stars and Men* (1958), a variety of popular books are also bringing cosmic evolution to a broader audience including Neil DeGrasse Tyson's *Origins: Fourteen Billion Years of Cosmic Evolution* (also a Nova special on PBS); *The Universe Story: From the Primordial Flaring Forth to the Ecozoic Era—A Celebration of the Unfolding of the Cosmos* by physicist Brian Swimme and theologian Thomas Berry; *Children of the Stars: Our Origin, Evolution and Destiny* by astronomer Daniel Altschuler; and *Atoms of Science: An Exploration of Cosmic Evolution* by astrophysicist Hubert Reeves. In short, an increasing number of people around the world are seeing their place for the first time within this naturalistic worldview. This recognition represents for humanity a return to the cosmos, a more sophisticated integration of culture and cosmos that humans possessed when cultures began, ranging from Stonehenge and the ancient civilizations such as Sumer and Egypt to Native Americans and the Australian aborigines.[52]

Cosmic Evolution and Human Destiny: Three Scenarios

In addition to the impact of the new universe on culture, cosmic evolution also provides a window on long-term human destiny. Although historians are understandably loathe to use the word "destiny," associating it with the misguided "Manifest Destiny" doctrine in which American colonists viewed it as their inherent right to expand westward and seize territory from the Native Americans, the word can and must be dissociated from that historical event. In fact, the concept of "destiny" has often been used in the context of theological discussion. A little over a month after the outbreak of World War II in 1939, theologian Reinhold Niebuhr began his Gifford Lectures on "Human Destiny," published in 1941 under the title *The Nature and Destiny of Man*, in which he concluded that human destiny must lie outside of history, outside of nature, in the supernatural realm espoused by Christianity. In 1947, just after the War's end, the French biophysicist and philosopher Pierre Lecomte du Noüy published his volume *Human Destiny*, which espoused confidence in the broad scope of evolution in the universe, but ultimately found human destiny in God. And as we have seen, human destiny was explicit in Teilhard de Chardin's works, written in the first half of the 20th century.

In the realm of the natural world, in the broadest sense we have only a limited number of destinies whether we like it or not. Cosmic evolution provides at least three vastly different scenarios of what the long-term human future may be. The ultimate product of cosmic evolution may be only planets, stars, and galaxies—a "physical universe" in which life is extremely rare. This has, in fact, been our chief worldview for the last several millennia, the plurality of world tradition notwithstanding. Almost all of the history of astronomy, from Stonehenge through much of the 20th century, encompasses the people, the concepts, and the techniques that gave rise to our knowledge of the physical universe. Babylonian and Greek models of planetary motion; medieval commentaries on Aristotle and Plato; the astonishing advances of Galileo, Kepler, Newton, and their comrades in the Scientific Revolution; the details of planetary, stellar and galactic evolution—all these and more address the physical universe. The physical universe is truly amazing in its own right, boasting a whole bestiary of remarkable objects.

For millennia, our perceptions of the destiny of human life on Earth were tied to the physical universe as represented by the geocentric system associated with Aristotle, with Earth at the center and the heavens above. This cosmological worldview provided the very reference frame for daily life, religious and intellectual. Writers from Claudius Ptolemy to Dante Alighieri touted it as the true system of the world in which humans sought meaning. The heliocentric system of Copernicus changed all that, making Earth a planet and the planets potential Earths. Societal uproar followed this daring new cosmological worldview. Since then the history of modern astronomy has been one of the increasing decentralization of humanity. In the 1920s, Harlow Shapley showed our solar system at the periphery of our Milky Way galaxy rather than its center, and since then billions of galaxies have been discovered beyond our own.[53]

In the physical universe scenario, all is not lost with respect to the status of humanity. In a universe in which life on Earth is unique or rarely duplicated, humans may still have an important role. Indeed, in such a universe, stewardship of our pale blue dot takes on special significance for life in the universe depends on our actions over long periods of time bounded only by physical reality. In two billion years the Sun will have increased in brightness enough to induce a runaway greenhouse effect on our home planet. Long before that we will likely have escaped to another star, offering our species longevity. The process will repeat until star formation in galaxies halts in 100 trillion years.[54] Assuming we don't remain Earthbound, the destiny of life in the physical universe is for humans—sooner or later—to populate the universe. Many options exist for humans in a universe devoid of life and many scenarios in science fiction address this possibility. Isaac Asimov has played out one scenario in his Foundation series, and the philosopher John Leslie has addressed some of the philosophical implications.[55]

The second possible outcome of cosmic evolution reveals a quite different destiny. The biological universe—the universe in which cosmic evolution commonly ends in life, mind, and intelligence—means that we will almost certainly interact with extraterrestrials. Ideas about a possible biological universe date back to ancient Greece in a history that is now well known.[56] It is the universe that astrobiology and SETI program are attempting to prove. There is again no lack of ideas about human-extraterrestrial interaction in such a universe. Science fiction is filled with possibilities, from the horrors of a war of the worlds to warm and fuzzy ETs. Arthur C. Clarke—author of *Childhood's End, Rendezvous with Rama*, and *2001: A Space Odyssey* and its sequels, among much other "alien literature"—is the prophet of this worldview replete with extraterrestrials. In such a universe, humanity may join what has been called a "galactic club" whose goal is to enhance knowledge.[57]

Taking a long-term view not often discussed, cosmic evolution may have already resulted in a third scenario. Cultural evolution in a biological universe may have already produced, or replaced, biologicals with artificial intelligence, constituting what I have called a "postbiological universe."[58] This idea requires us to take cultural evolution just as seriously as astronomical and biological evolution. It requires us to contemplate cultural evolution on cosmic "Stapledonian" time scales as did Olaf Stapledon in his novels *Last and First Men* (1930) and *Star Maker* (1937). While astronomers are accustomed to thinking in these terms for physical processes, they are not accustomed to thinking on cosmic time scales for biology and culture. But cultural evolution now completely dominates biological evolution on Earth. Given the age of the universe, and if intelligence is common, it may have evolved far beyond us. If intelligence is highly valued for its evolutionary advantage, extraterrestrials would long ago have sought the best way to improve their intelligence, and it is likely to have involved artificial intelligence, yielding the postbiological universe. Nor does L, the lifetime of a technological civilization, need to be millions of years for such a scenario. It is possible that such a universe would exist if L exceeds a few hundred or a few thousand years where L is defined as the lifetime of a technological civilization that has entered the electronic computer age (which on Earth approximately coincides with the usual definition of L as a radio communicative civilization.) Indeed, some predict Earth will be postbiological in a few generations.[59]

Such a postbiological universe would have sweeping implications for SETI strategies, for our worldview, and for the destiny of life on Earth if it has already happened throughout the universe. We may see our own future in the evolution of extraterrestrial civilizations, perhaps another motivation for searching. How such postbiologicals—whether terrestrial or extraterrestrial—would use their knowledge and intelligence is a valuable question that, at present, is unanswerable. Whether one relishes or opposes the idea of a universe dominated by machines, the transition to such a universe presents many moral dilemmas and raises with renewed urgency the ancient philosophical question of destiny and free will.

In short, both in our relationship with extraterrestrials and with God—however conceived—human destiny would be quite different in a universe full of biologicals or postbiologicals than if we were alone. If extraterrestrial intelligence is abundant, it will be our destiny to interact with that intelligence—whether for good or ill—for life identifies with life. It is here that the fifth Cosmotheological Principle, or the cosmocentric ethic, comes into play. The moral dimension—a reverence and respect for extraterrestrial intelligence that may be morphologically very different from terrestrial life-forms—will surely challenge a species that has come to blows over superficial racial and national differences. If we are wise, humanity will realize that our species is one—a necessary realization before we have any hope of dealing with extraterrestrial beings in a morally responsible way.

Although the physical, biological, and postbiological universe may be facts that the universe imposes on us, humans will still have great scope for choice and free will within these broad scenarios. The founders of the modern evolutionary synthesis emphasized this point already at the middle of the 20th century. George Gaylord Simpson for one, echoing Huxley's evolutionary humanism, wrote, "it is another unique quality of man that he, for the first time in the history of life, has increasing power to choose his course and to influence his own future evolution. It would be rash, indeed, to attempt to predict his choice. The possibility of choice can be shown to exist. This makes rational the hope that choice may sometime lead to what is good and right for man. Responsibility for defining and for seeking that end belongs to all of us."[60]

Whether intelligence is rare or abundant, whether extraterrestrial life is of a lower order or a higher order than *Homo sapiens*, human destiny is intimately connected with cosmic evolution. Driven by the astronomical, biological, and cultural components of cosmic evolution, the universe may have generated any of the three outcomes described here: the physical universe, the biological universe, or the postbiological universe. Which of the three the universe has produced in reality we do not yet know—this is one of the many challenges of astrobiology with its goal of analyzing the future of life as well as its past and present. Ours may be a cosmos in which humanity is not central, yet where humans can be at home in the universe in which they play a role. Whatever its long-term destiny, it is surely the destiny of humanity in the near future to follow the trail of scientific evidence wherever it may lead even if it means abandoning old scientific, philosophical, and theological ideas. Humans have always known intuitively that culture and cosmos are intertwined. We are just now beginning to realize what this coevolution may mean.

Endnotes

1. Carl Sagan, *The Cosmic Connection: An Extraterrestrial Perspective* (Garden City, NY: Doubleday, 1973). After Sagan's death the book was reissued as *Carl Sagan's Cosmic Connection: An Extraterrestrial Perspective* (Cambridge and New York: Cambridge University Press, 2000), with new contributions by Freeman Dyson, Ann Druyan, and David Morrison.

2. Percival Lowell confined himself to planets in *The Evolution of Worlds* (New York: Macmillan Company, 1909) and George Ellery Hale dealt only with stars in *The Study of Stellar Evolution* (Chicago: University of Chicago Press, 1908). Among historians, stellar evolution has been treated in David DeVorkin's work on the development of the Hertzsprung-Russell diagram, but no history of ideas of cosmic evolution exists.

3. In making the distinctions between physical, biological, and cultural evolution, I do not mean to deny their physical basis, but rather to imply that the three possible endpoints of cosmic evolution are physical, biological, and cultural, a point elaborated in the last section of this paper. Biological and cultural evolution cannot occur without their physical basis. This vast sweep of evolution was enunciated already in 1957 by evolutionary biologist Julian Huxley, among others, notably in his *New Bottles for New Wine* (New York: Harper and Brothers, 1957).

4. On the natural selection of universes, see Lee Smolin, *The Life of the Cosmos* (New York and Oxford: Oxford University Press, 1997). Freeman Dyson, *Infinite in All Directions* (New York: Harper and Row, 1988), p. 51, proposes "cosmic ecology." It is important to note that "evolution" has general and specific meanings. When scientists speak about "cosmic evolution" they usually have a general idea of "development" in mind. When Smolin speaks of the "natural selection" of universes that may compose the multiverse, he is applying the more specific idea of Darwinian evolution to astronomy. On the general idea of evolution see Peter J. Bowler, *Evolution: The History of an Idea* (Berkeley and Los Angeles: University of California Press, 1983; revised edition, 1989).

5. Michael J. Crowe, *The Extraterrestrial Life Debate, 1750–1900* (Cambridge: Cambridge University Press, 1986), pp. 224–225, 274–277, 464–465. Simon Schaffer has shown the place of the nebular hypothesis in a general "science of progress" in early Victorian Britain, "The Nebular Hypothesis and the Science of Progress," in *History, Humanity and Evolution: Essays for John C. Greene*, J. R. Moore, ed. (Cambridge: Cambridge University Press, 1989), pp. 131–164. On the role of Spencer and Fiske in 19th century origin of life debates, see James Strick, *Sparks of Life: Darwinism and the Victorian Debates over Spontaneous Generation* (Cambridge, MA: Harvard University Press, 2000), pp. 94–95 and passim.

6. See Proctor's *Other Worlds than Ours* (London, 1870), *Our Place among Infinities* and *Science Byways*—the latter published in 1875, and the 1872 edition of Flammarion's *La pluralite des mondes*. Flammarion's *La pluralite* reached 33 editions by 1880 and was reprinted until 1921, while Proctor's *Other Worlds than Ours* reached 29 printings by 1909, making him the most widely read astronomy writer in the English language. On Proctor and Flammarion see Crowe, *The Extraterrestrial Life Debate*, pp.

367–386. In his book *Victorian Popularizers of Science: Designing Nature for New Audiences* (Chicago: University of Chicago Press: 2007), historian Bernard Lightman makes the case that these and lesser known popularizers used the concept of cosmic evolution to narrate an evolutionary epic long before it was accepted by scientists or incorporated into any research program. An early case of 19th century astronomical evolution is the astronomer/popularizer Robert S. Ball, "The Relation of Darwinism to other Branches of Science," *Longman's Review* 2 (November 1883): 76–92.

7. On Lowell as Spencerian, and as influenced by Spencer's American disciple John Fiske, see David Strauss, *Percival Lowell: The Culture and Science of a Boston Brahmin* (Cambridge, MA: Harvard University Press, 2001), pp. 97–165.

8. W. W. Campbell, "The Daily Influences of Astronomy," *Science* 52 (10 December 1920): 543–552, 540. David DeVorkin had found archival evidence that Hale's interest in cosmic evolution extended beyond the physical universe to the biology and culture; "Evolutionary Thinking in American Astronomy from Lane to Russell," presented at a session on "Evolution and 20th Century Astronomy," History of Science Society Meeting, Denver, Colorado, 8 November 2001.

9. Helge Kragh, *Cosmology and Controversy: The Historical Development of Two Theories of the Universe* (Princeton, NJ: Princeton University Press, 1996), p. 4. See also Stephen Toulmin and June Goodfield, *The Discovery of Time* (Chicago: University of Chicago Press, 1982).

10. The quotation is from A. R. Wallace, "Man's Place in the Universe," *The Independent* (New York) 55: 473–483: 474. This was expanded into a book *Man's Place in the Universe* (London and New York: McClure, Phillips & Co., 1903), and Wallace's thoughts on the improbabilities of humans on any other planet are found in the Appendix to its London, 1904 edition, pp. 326–336. On Wallace's astronomy see Steven J. Dick, "The Universe and Alfred Russel Wallace," in Charles H. Smith and George Beccaloni, eds., *Natural Selection and Beyond: The Intellectual Legacy of Alfred Russel Wallace* (Oxford: Oxford University Press, 2008), pp. 320–340; also Dick, *The Biological Universe* (reference 14 below), chapter 1. On Wallace himself see Michael Shermer, *In Darwin's Shadow: The Life and Science*

of Alfred Russel Wallace (Oxford: Oxford University Press, 2002); for
Wallace's "heresy" in breaking with Darwin on the matter of the evolution of the human brain, see pp. 157–162.

11. L. J. Henderson, *The Fitness of the Environment* (New York: MacMillan
Company, 1913), reprinted with an Introduction by Harvard biologist
George Wald (Gloucester, MA: Peter Smith, 1970), p. 312. The com-
plexity of Henderson's ideas on the fitness of the environment and their
connection to modern ideas on the subject are analyzed in detail in Iris
Fry, "On the Biological Significance of the Properties of Matter: L. J.
Henderson's Theory of the Fitness of the Environment," *J. History of
Biology* 29 (1996): 155–196.

12. Helge Kragh, *Cosmology and Controversy* (1996), reference 9.

13. Vassiliki Betty Smocovitis, *Unifying Biology: The Evolutionary Synthesis
and Evolutionary Biology* (Princeton, NJ: Princeton University Press,
1996), p. 165.

14. Dick, *The Biological Universe: The Twentieth Century Extraterrestrial Life
Debate and the Limits of Science* (Cambridge: Cambridge University Press,
1996), chapter 4.

15. Spencer Jones, *Life on Other Worlds* (New York: MacMillan, 1940), p.
57. On Oparin see Iris Fry, *The Emergence of Life on Earth: A Historical
and Scientific Overview* (New Brunswick, NJ: Rutgers University Press,
2000), chapter 6, and Dick, *The Biological Universe*, chapter 7.

16. A. I. Oparin and V. G. Fesenkov, *Life in the Universe* (New York, 1961);
George Wald, "The Origin of Life," *Scientific American* (August, 1954): 44.

17. For details of SETI history see Dick, *The Biological Universe*, chapter 8.

18. Joseph Shklovskii and Carl Sagan, *Intelligent Life in the Universe* (San
Francisco: Holden-Day, 1966). In May 1964, the Armenian Academy of
Sciences sponsored a meeting on extraterrestrial intelligence at Byurakan
Astrophysical Observatory. The Proceedings are G. M. Tovmasyan, ed.,
Extraterrestrial Civilizations (1965; English translation, 1967). For a list
of further Soviet meetings see Dick, *The Biological Universe*, pp. 484–485.

19. On Shapley's uses of cosmic evolution see JoAnn Palmeri, chapter 15 in this volume, and her dissertation, "An Astronomer Beyond the Observatory: Harlow Shapley as Prophet of Science," (University of Oklahoma, 2000).

20. While Sagan's views have reached a vast worldwide audience through the TV series *Cosmos*, Chaisson has been most persistent and explicit about cosmic evolution as a leading idea and about its impact on culture. In addition to *Cosmic Dawn*, see *The Life Era: Cosmic Selection and Conscious Evolution* (New York: W.W. Norton, 1987); *Cosmic Evolution: The Rise of Complexity in Nature* (Cambridge, MA: Harvard University Press, 2001); and *Epic of Evolution: Seven Ages of the Cosmos* (New York: Columbia University Press, 2006). In addition see his Web site at *http://www.tufts.edu/as/wright_center/cosmic_evolution/docs/splash.html*.

21. Otto Struve, "Life on Other Worlds," *Sky and Telescope* 14 (February 1955): 137–146; Joshua Lederberg, "Exobiology: Experimental Approaches to Life Beyond the Earth," in Lloyd V. Berkner and Hugh Odishaw, *Science in Space* (New York: McGraw Hill, 1961), pp. 407–425; John Billingham, *Life in the Universe* (Cambridge, MA: MIT Press, 1981), p. ix.

22. In 1960 the NSF's John Wilson looked forward to funding space biology. But NASA took an early dominant lead, which it has continued to hold. By 1963 NASA's life sciences expenditures (including exobiology) had already reached $17.5 million. Toby Appel, *Shaping Biology: The National Science Foundation and American Biological Research, 1952-1975* (Baltimore: Johns Hopkins University Press, 2000), p. 132.

23. John C. Greene, Science, *Ideology and World View: Essays in the History of Evolutionary Ideas* (Berkeley: University of California Press, 1981) and Peter J. Bowler, *Evolution: The History of an Idea* (Berkeley: University of California Press, revised edition, 1989).

24. Smocovitis, *Unifying Biology*, pp. 142–153: 148. Connie Barlow's book of readings, *Evolution Extended: Biological Debates on the Meaning of Life* (Cambridge, MA: MIT Press, 1995), clearly shows these wider evolutionary themes.

25. Smocovitis, *Unifying Biology*, pp. 139, 146–148. See Julian Huxley, *Evolutionary Humanism* (Buffalo, NY: Prometheus books, 1992; first edition 1964); Theodosius Dobzhansky, *Mankind Evolving: The Evolution of the Human Species* (New Haven and London: Yale University Press, 1969; first edition, 1962), especially chapter 12; George Gaylord Simpson, *The Meaning of Evolution: A Study of the History of Life and of its Significance for Man* (New Haven, CT: Yale University Press, 1949). On the connections of evolution and extraterrestrial life see Dick, *The Biological Universe*, pp. 389–398.

26. Kathy Sawyer, *The Rock from Mars: A Detective Story on Two Planets* (New York: Random House, 2006).

27. See Dick, *The Biological Universe*, chapter 5.

28. On the increasing decentralization of humans through history see Richard Berenzden, "Geocentric to Heliocentric to Galactocentric to Acentric: The Continuing Assault on the Egocentric," in Arthur Beer and K. Aa. Strand, eds., *Copernicus: Yesterday and Today* (Oxford: Pergamon Press, 1975), pp. 65–83; also Peter van de Kamp, "The Galactocentric Revolution: A Reminiscent Narrative," *Publications of the Astronomical Society of the Pacific* 77 (October 1965): 325–335. For an important history that expresses a contrary view on the place of the Earth and humans in the universe see Dennis Danielson, "The Great Copernican Cliché," *American Journal of Physics* 69, no. 10 (October 2001): 1029–1035 and Danielson, "The Bones of Copernicus," *American Scientist* 97, no. 1 (January–February 2009): 50–57.

29. On the anthropic principle and its philosophical implications see John Barrow and Frank Tipler, *The Anthropic Cosmological Principle* (New York: Oxford University Press, 1986), *Universe or Multiverse?* Bernard Carr, ed. (Cambridge: Cambridge University Press, 2007) and Steven J. Dick, "Cosmology and Biology," *Proceedings of the 2008 Conference of the Society of Amateur Radio Astronomers* (American Radio Relay League; National Radio Astronomy Observatory, Green Bank, WV, 2008), pp. 1–16.

30. The intellectual transformation wrought by the Copernican theory has been discussed in Hans Blumenthal, *The Genesis of the Copernican World* (Cambridge, MA: MIT Press, 1987); Thomas Kuhn, *The Copernican*

Revolution: Planetary Astronomy in the Development of Western Thought (Cambridge, MA: Harvard University Press, 1992), and Steven J. Dick, *Plurality of Worlds*, chapter 4.

31. Teilhard de Chardin, *The Phenomenon of Man* (New York: Harper Collins, 2002), was first published in French in 1955, in English in 1959. The Harper edition also has an Introduction by Sir Julian Huxley. See also Teilhard's *The Future of Man* (New York: Doubleday, 2004), and on Teilhard himself Ursula King, *The Life and Vision of Teilhard de Chardin* (New York: Orbis Books, 1996).

32. Thomas Berry and Brian Swimme, *The Universe Story; From the Primordial Flaring Forth to the Ecozoic Era—A Celebration of the Unfolding of the Cosmos* (New York: Harper, 1994).

33. Ursula Goodenough, *The Sacred Depths of Nature* (Oxford: Oxford University Press, 1998).

34. Arthur Peacocke, "The Challenge and Stimulus of the Epic of Evolution to Theology," in Steven J. Dick, ed., *Many Worlds: The New Universe, Extraterrestrial Life and the Theological Implications* (Philadelphia: Templeton Foundation Press, 2000); Paul Davies, "Biological Determinism, Information Theory, and the Origin of Life," ibid., pp. 15–28.

35. Rev. Michael Dowd, *Thank God for Evolution: How the Marriage of Science and Religion Will Transform Your Life and Our World* (New York: Viking, 2008), and "Evolutionary Christianity," DVD, described as "seeing the entire history of the Universe and emergent complexity of matter, life, consciousness, culture and technology is a God-glorifying, Christ-edifying way"; also Amy Hassinger, "Welcome to the Ecozoic Era," *UU[Unitarian Universalist] World* (Spring, 2006): 26–32. A major theme of Connie Barlow's edited volume *Evolution Extended: Biological Debates on the Meaning of Life* (Cambridge, MA: MIT Press, 1995) is the relationship between theology and evolution. See also their Web sites at *http://www.thegreatstory.org/CB-writings.html* and *http://www.thegreatstory.org/*.

36. Steven J. Dick, "Cosmotheology: Theological Implications of the New Universe," in Dick, *Many Worlds*, pp. 191–210; Steven J. Dick, "Kosmotheologie—Neu Betrachtet," in *Leben im All: Positionen aus*

Naturwissenschaft, Philosophie und Theologie, Tobias Daniel Wabbel, ed. (Dusseldorf, Germany: Patmos, 2005), pp. 156–172. The latter collection of essays shows interest in the subject is not limited to the English-speaking world.

37. The idea of a nontranscendent natural God has a long history, and has been raised most recently among scientists in Fred Hoyle, *The Intelligent Universe: A New View of Creation and Evolution* (New York: Holt, Rinehart and Winston, 1983); E. W. Harrison, "The Natural Selection of Universes Containing Intelligent Life," *Quarterly Journal of the Royal Astronomical Society* 36, no. 3 (1995): 193; and James Gardner, *The Intelligent Universe: AI, ET and the Emerging Mind of the Cosmos* (Franklin Lakes, NJ: New Page Books, 2007), p. 159 and Gardner, *Biocosm: The New Scientific Theory of Evolution: Intelligent Life is the Architect of the Universe* (Makawao, Maui, HI: Inner Ocean Publishing, 2003).

38. For the historical discussion on theological implications of extraterrestrial life see Michael J. Crowe, "A History of the Extraterrestrial Life Debate," *Zygon* 32 (June 1997): 147–162; Dick, *The Biological Universe* and R. O. Randolph, Margaret S. Race, and Chris P. McKay, "Reconsidering the Theological and Ethical Implications of Extraterrestrial Life," *CTNS [Center for Theology and the Natural Sciences] Bulletin* 17, no. 3 (1997): 1–8.

39. Thomas F. O'Meara gives the best in-depth discussion of current thinking about extraterrestrials and Christianity in "Christian Theology and Extraterrestrial Intelligent Life" *Theological Studies* 60 (1999): 3–30. Another discussion is Ted Peters, "Exotheology: Speculations on Extraterrestrial Life," chapter 6 in his *Science, Theology and Ethics* (Burlington, VT: Ashgate, 2003). The role of extraterrestrials in the Mormon church is detailed in Erich Robert Paul, *Science, Religion and Mormon Cosmology* (Urbana and Chicago: University of Illinois Press, 1992).

40. Ernan McMullin, "Life and Intelligence Far from Earth: Formulating Theological Issues," in Steven J. Dick, ed., *Many Worlds*, pp. 151–176: 162, 169, 171.

41. George V. Coyne, "The Evolution of Intelligent Life on Earth and Possibly Elsewhere: Reflections from a Religious Tradition," in Dick, *Many Worlds*, pp. 177–190.

42. Norman Lamm, "The Religious Implications of Extraterrestrial Life," in *Challenge: Torah Views on Science and its Problems*, Aryeh Carmell and Cyril Domb, eds., (Jerusalem and New York: Feldheim, 1978), pp. 354–398.

43. Jill Tarter, "SETI and the Religions of the Universe," in Dick, *Many Worlds*, pp. 143–150.

44. See, for example, Michael Ashkenazi, "Not the Sons of Adam: Religious Response to ETI," *Space Policy* 8 (1992): 341–350. In interviews with 21 religious authorities from a variety of religions, the author found that none believed extraterrestrial intelligence created theological or religious problems, not even the 17 who believed such extraterrestrials existed. For the broader debate see Dick, *The Biological Universe*, pp. 514–526.

45. Mark Lupisella and John Logsdon, "Do We need a Cosmocentric Ethic?" (International Astronautical Congress paper IAA-97-IAA.9.2.09, 6-10 October 1997), p. 1.

46. Carl Sagan was among the first to use the Cosmic Calendar in his Pulitzer Prize-winning book, *The Dragons of Eden* (New York: Random House, 1977), chapter 1, and again in his Cosmos television series, first aired on PBS in 1980. It has been used as a teaching tool ever since; see, for example, *http://visav.phys.uvic.ca/~babul/AstroCourses/P303/BB-slide.htm*. Each month represents a little more than a billion years.

47. David Christian, *'Maps of Time': An Introduction to 'Big History'* (Berkeley, CA: University of California Press, 2004) and Fred Spier, *The Structure of Big History: From the Big Bang Until Today* (Amsterdam: Amsterdam University Press, 1996).

48. Shapley, *The View from a Distant Star: Man's Future in the Universe* (New York: Basic Books, 1963), p. 5. See also Palmeri, chapter 15, this volume.

49. Stuart Kauffman, *At Home in the Universe: The Search for the Laws of Self-Organization and Complexity* (Oxford: Oxford University Press, 1995); John Wheeler, *At Home in the Universe* (New York: Springer-Verlag, 1996).

50. The details of where the atoms of our bodies originate and how they are recycled are detailed in John Gribbin, *Stardust: Supernovae and Life—The Cosmic Connection* (New Haven: Yale University Press, 2000). The sentiment is found several times in the Bible: Ecclesiastes 3:20, "All go to one place; all are from the dust, and all turn to dust again"; Job 10:9, "Remember that you fashioned me like clay; and will you turn me to dust again?"; Job 34:15, "All flesh would perish together, and all mortals return to dust"; Genesis 3:19, "By the sweat of your face you shall eat bread until you return to the ground, for out of it you were taken; you are dust, and to dust you shall return."

51. The curriculum, developed by the SETI Institute, the California Academy of Sciences, NASA Ames Research Center, and San Francisco State University, is available on CD-ROM. This and other educational curricula are described, and available, at *http://www.seti.org/epo*. The Wright Center program on cosmic evolution may be accessed at *http://www.tufts.edu/as/wright_center/cosmic_evolution/docs/splash.html*.

52. On this astronomical heritage, see E. C. Krupp, *Echoes of the Ancient Skies: The Astronomy of Lost Civilizations* (Cambridge, MA: Harper & Row, 1983).

53. See reference 28, including Danielson's contrary view of the decentralization of humanity.

54. For an exciting explication of the physical evolution of the cosmos over the long term, see Fred Adams and Greg Laughlin, *The Five Ages of the Universe: Inside the Physics of Eternity* (New York: The Free Press, 1999). Adams and Laughlin distinguish five eras: primordial, stelliferous, degenerate, black hole, and the dark era.

55. John Leslie, *The End of the World: the Science and Ethics of Human Extinction* (London and New York: Routledge, 1996).

56. The history of the extraterrestrial life debate is treated in Steven J. Dick, *Plurality of Worlds: The Origins of the Extraterrestrial Life Debate From Democritus to Kant* (Cambridge: Cambridge University Press, 1982); Steven J. Dick, *The Biological Universe: The Twentieth Century Extraterrestrial Life Debate and the Limits of Science* (Cambridge: Cambridge University Press, 1996) and its abridgement and update, *Life on Other Worlds* (Cambridge: Cambridge University Press, 1998); and Michael J. Crowe, *The Extraterrestrial Life Debate, 1750–1900: The Idea of a Plurality of Worlds from Kant to Lowell* (Cambridge: Cambridge University Press, 1986).

57. The history of ideas about a biological universe is in Dick, *The Biological Universe*. For an illustrated guide to the long-term possibilities of life see Peter Ward, *Future Evolution: An Illuminated History of Life to Come* (New York: Henry Holt and Co., 2001).

58. The arguments for such a universe are laid out in chapter 14 of this volume.

59. Hans Moravec, *Mind Children: The Future of Robot and Human Intelligence* (Cambridge: Harvard University Press, 1988) and *Robot: Mere Machine to Transcendent Mind* (Oxford: Oxford University Press, 1999); Ray Kurzweil, *The Age of Spiritual Machines: When Computers Exceed Human Intelligence* (New York: Penguin Books, 1999) and *The Singularity is Near: When Humans Transcend Biology* (New York: Penguin Books, 2006).

60. Closing paragraph in George Gaylord Simpson, *The Meaning of Evolution* (New Haven: Yale University Press, 1949).

Part 2

Cultural Evolution

Chapter 3

Social Evolution
State of the Field

Kathryn Denning

Social Evolution In Cosmic Context

Placing Earth into the largest possible context is easier in some ways than others. High school students can identify the place of our Sun in the typology of stars. We know our solar system's mailing address within our galaxy, and how to find our galaxy within the local group neighborhood. We can study our home world's geology and atmosphere objectively, and classify Earth appropriately in the ever-growing list of extrasolar planets. Our knowledge of other stars, galaxies, and planets changes, but we have observed external realities in relation to which we can locate ourselves.

It becomes more difficult when we discuss life, because, at the time of writing, none of any kind has been discovered elsewhere. We are, for the moment, still positioning Earth's life in relation to ideas—rumored phantoms which have yet to materialize in our view, no matter how logically likely they might be. So, when we discuss intelligent life-forms with technological societies in the absolute absence of extraterrestrial cases, we are philosophically and scientifically adrift. We can mark Earth's physical coordinates on the galactic map, and we can find our star and planet in tables and typologies, but we cannot, in any way, position human civilization in relation to any other technological civilization.

And yet, while we wait for data about extraterrestrial intelligence with which to anchor ourselves, we muse about our place in the cosmos. We boldly sketch our hypothetical neighbors, debate how we might find them, guess what they might be thinking and doing, and wonder what we should say to them. These speculations are driven simultaneously by our knowledge of *their* potential neighborhoods (planetary systems and habitable zones), and our knowledge of *ourselves* (our own planet, its biota, and societies). With respect to imagining life and civilizations elsewhere, we are, therefore, caught between logics that tug in different directions and do not easily mesh.

This poses significant challenges. For example, the processes of working downwards from generalities about the universe, and working upwards from the particularities of Earth, promote competing perspectives about our place in the cosmos. Few thinkers can effectively balance both. The balancing act requires scholars from the humanities and social sciences to expand their horizons and wonder whether we can simultaneously be intelligent agents determining our own futures, dwelling in historical time with all its contingencies, *and* part of much larger patterns with knowable rules and predictable outcomes. It also requires scholars primarily trained in the physical sciences to take a closer look at Earth's societies to develop the most nuanced understanding possible of the data and theory we have at our disposal and to consider how, exactly, knowledge of our own case might relate to other cases.

In this chapter, I attempt to facilitate the latter task by providing an overview of some of the most difficult, contentious, and promising areas in social evolution research, as pertinent to culture in the cosmos. The modern literature about social evolution runs many disciplines wide and several centuries deep; so this is necessarily a selective review, shaped by my own perspective that is rooted in anthropology, biological anthropology, archaeology, and the history and philosophy of science. Much of the chapter addresses background issues relevant to the general problem of integrating social evolution on Earth into syntheses about cosmic evolution and to the particular problem of SETI (the Search for Extraterrestrial Intelligence). I begin with some essential preliminaries about social evolution and SETI—the data, competing epistemologies, why social evolution matters, motivations for studying social change, and disciplinary differences. The challenges of researching social evolution are best illustrated in context, so I then provide an extended case study which examines approaches to the perennially fascinating subject of collapse. In the remaining sections, I briefly review the current status of selected relevant debates in the method and theory of social evolutionary studies including the relationship of biology and culture, a new Modern Synthesis/Holistic Darwinism, complexity theory, hologeistic studies, interactions between civilizations, the roles of contingency and convergence, and the lifetimes of civilizations. I conclude that there are many promising routes forward. The blossoming of new theoretical perspectives which accommodate complex systems, the development of improved tools for studying the history of societies on Earth, and our increased awareness of our own subjectivities in these studies will enable ever-better investigations of how civilizations develop, interact, and expire or endure.

Before proceeding, a note on terminology is warranted. In this chapter, I use the term 'social evolution' in a way that is interchangeable with 'cultural evolution' and 'sociocultural evolution.' This may, to some readers, be debatable. For example, 'social evolution' is arguably broader as it can include research with social species other than humans. However, in the strictly human realm which is the focus of this chapter, usage is inconsistent. The terminology itself has evolved over the last two centuries—i.e., 'social evolution' does not mean the same thing today as it did in 1890. Further, scholars from disciplines ranging from anthropology to evolutionary biology use the terms differently, and researchers from different continents tend toward different conventions. Broad-ranging discussions with historical terrestrial and hypothetical extraterrestrial dimensions can rapidly become patience-trying and nonsensical if they try to distinguish precisely between these terms, and so I have elected to gloss over this, use 'social evolution' as a catch-all, and refer to specific sociocultural phenomena where appropriate.

All that said, the first order of business is to comment specifically upon social evolution within the field of SETI.

Social Evolution in SETI

Ideas about social evolution are integral to SETI. However, contemporary mainstream social scientific ideas about evolution are not; in fact, the treatment of social evolution within SETI discourse is quite distinctive and idiosyncratic. SETI's different approach clearly doesn't stem from the data about extraterrestrials, since we have none, so it seems safe to assume that it partly derives from different disciplinary orientations, as described later in this chapter. But it also stems from SETI's starting points.

SETI assumes, obviously, that extraterrestrial intelligence (ETI) with detectable technology may well exist. What makes this assumption scientifically plausible is a trio of premises: 1) that evolution on Earth tends to produce complexity; 2) that biological, social, and technological evolution will work the same way elsewhere in the galaxy as they have here; and 3) that these processes will therefore eventually produce approximately equivalent (not identical) results wherever suitable conditions exist. The latter two premises are consistent with two astronomical principles, i.e., the Copernican

Principle of Mediocrity (which says that Earth is not special), and the uniformity of the laws of nature throughout the universe. These principles may be generally accepted in physics, but their biological/social/technological instantiations are vigorously disputed by evolution researchers along with the premise about evolution's drive towards complexity (Carroll 2001). Nonetheless, I will not address that directly here. Instead, I will focus briefly on specific ideas about social evolution in SETI that build upon those contested premises.

The premises above have led to the practice of generating predictions about civilizations elsewhere based upon social evolution on Earth. Assumptions about the development of Earth's societies have thus shaped conjectures about alien societies on topics including their possible characteristics, appropriate search strategies, and the wisdom of seeking contact. More specifically, as I have discussed elsewhere at some length (see Denning 2006, 2007b, 2007c, in press, and citations therein), SETI thinkers have used information about human civilizations in these ways:

- to provide numerical values to be used in predictive models concerning civilizations' longevity and development (e.g., in discussions of the Drake factor "L")
- to illustrate different potential outcomes of contact between civilizations with a view to human-extraterrestrial (ET) contact
- to characterize the general evolution of ET civilizations up to and beyond a level of technology that is SETI-detectable and/or spacefaring (e.g., energy consumption, use of radio waves, development of weaponry, risk of self-annihilation, level of technological development in relation to ours, and/or potential patterns of colonization)
- to speculate about the characteristics of ET civilizations, particularly their peacefulness or aggression
- to speculate about visible technological signatures they might produce (e.g., deliberate transmissions or beacons, electromagnetic [EM] spectrum leakage, astroengineering projects like Dyson spheres, and/or probes)
- to speculate about the likely form and content of any signal they might send us, and what kind of transmission from Earth (form and content) is appropriate for us to send

In other words, thought about extraterrestrial Others is deeply infused with thought about social evolution on Earth. But it is very notable that SETI thinkers work with this information differently from scholars in social sciences and the humanities, sometimes to the chagrin of the latter. When scientists writing on SETI draw on social evolution, they tend to:

- develop syntheses that pull all human experience together into a single narrative, instead of keeping the threads separate (which reinforces unilinear evolutionary thinking, instead of the multilinear perspective that is the social scientific norm)
- use isolated cultural analogies, rather than doing systematic cross-cultural comparisons
- extrapolate more, and make bolder hypotheses about the future
- assume not just that the laws of nature are universal, but that intelligent perceptions, understandings, and expressions of them could be universal, too
- lean towards the quantitative rather than the qualitative, for example using the Earth record to estimate values for "L"
- assume fundamental similarities between physical, chemical, biological, social, and technological realms

These are substantial differences of approach compared to most social scientists (Denning 2006, 2007b, 2007c, in press) which can result in diametrically opposed opinions about cultural matters. But rather than pitting the approaches against each other, or dismissing one in favor of the other—as, for example, the historian George Basalla recently did in his critique of SETI (2006)—we do have the option of exploring their potential complementarity (Denning 2006). We also have the option of pinpointing testable propositions and checking them against the available Earth data instead of continuing to debate at the level of abstraction.

Given the frequency with which social evolution on Earth is invoked in SETI discussions, it seems clear that developing the best possible understanding of it would be useful. There is a barrier here, however: many scholars in the humanities and social sciences emphasize the contingencies and particularities in human history, which tend to suggest that (Copernicus notwithstanding) we *are* unique—that technological, social intelligence would not arise on other worlds, and thus SETI is futile. Personally, I consider this argument a nonstarter because we cannot accurately predict the odds of other intelligences arising and developing civilization and interstellar communication; and even if the odds are vanishingly small and there is only one other in the vastness of space, it is worth it to look. Using data from history on Earth to argue that SETI cannot possibly succeed thus seems illogical to me.

I would argue that data and theory about social evolution are applicable to SETI, for three reasons. First, even if a detection never comes, it benefits us to think about humanity and our own future in the broadest possible way (Langhoff et al. 2007). Second, the case study of humanity is already constantly and unavoidably employed within SETI thinking, and so we may as well do our best to fine-tune its use. Third, if a detection is ever made, we will immediately begin making inferences about the entities that produced the signal (Denning 2007c), and it would be extremely useful to know what we can and cannot sensibly assume about them. Despite all the speculation mentioned above, this area is still under-theorized. So, a careful and comprehensive investigation of social evolution on Earth seems warranted within the SETI field. Of course, such an investigation might indicate that we still understand social evolution's workings so poorly, or with such uneven reliability, that we should not use Earth data *at all* in speculations about intelligent life on other worlds—i.e., we should assume we know *nothing*, and attempt to *refrain* from extrapolating or using Earth analogies. Even so, that might be more useful than the current state of affairs, which underestimates our collective ignorance about humanity's history.

The next order of business, then, is a review of some essential background to the study of social evolution.

Vital Preliminaries

The Presence of Pachyderms

When there's an elephant in the room, it's wise to introduce it. In the hall of social evolution, there is a herd of them which many of us assiduously ignore, even when they trumpet at each other and poke us with their trunks. Here, I name just a few.

Any survey of current approaches to social evolution is dogged by disunity. There is no one field upon which one can report; there is no single accepted outline of social evolution's course(s); there is little consensus about social evolutionary processes; there are longstanding, even vituperative, debates about appropriate analytical methods for studying culture change; and there are widely divergent purposes animating studies and theories of social evolution. This unruliness and complexity means that a neatly bounded, linear summary is out of the question. Rather, in discussing the 'state of the field,' we have to work with and through this disunity.

The disunity stems from a host of factors including disciplinary traditions, the complex nature of the data, limitations inherent in our methods, and the larger socio-political significance of the ideas. It requires some explanation for several reasons. First, the current diversity of approaches to social evolution is incomprehensible without some idea of how the situation came to be this way. Second, each approach has embedded assumptions, strengths and weaknesses, and some appreciation of those can be helpful. Third, programmatic statements about how we now 'should' study social evolution—and there are plenty—get us nowhere when their issuers fail to recognize that there are very good reasons for the current diversity of approaches and indeed, for these approaches' incommensurabilities. Any reasonable way forward has to accommodate this diversity rather than regarding it as a shortcoming born of a lack of scientific rigor, or an untidy mess which should be reduced to a singular approach. Accordingly, the following short comments sketch a few of the elephants that we need to watch as we consider the different ways of studying social evolution.

Onward, then, to what we know, what we don't, and why.

The Nature of the Data

Those who routinely work with historical and archaeological data know their pitfalls all too well. The archaeologist Robert Hall once observed, on the subject of one of North America's largest and youngest pre-Columbian sites, that

> [C]onsidering the size of the Cahokia site, approaching six square miles, and considering the length of the Mississippian occupation, at least six centuries, let's say 25 generations, and considering the small area explored archaeologically, less than a quarter of one percent of the site, just the ambition to make a definitive statement at this time about Cahokia presumes the confidence a scholar might assume who seeks to understand the operations and inner workings of the United States Congress by monitoring the archaeologically visible activity of one legislative wastebasket (Hall, 1975).

Our knowledge about past societies is not comprehensive. For example, even though the last decade has seen a vast increase in archaeological work on New World states, this has yet to be fully integrated into comparative syntheses (Smith and Schrieber 2006). We also have not successfully deciphered or translated all the ancient texts available to us; e.g., two millennia of ancient Mayan scripts have only been effectively engaged by scholars for several decades, and much is not yet understood.

The problem is not merely one of degree. Hall neatly encapsulated the tremendous archaeological problem of fractional data at large and complex sites, but left room for hope that *someday*, if Cahokia is fully excavated, we might *then* fully understand. One of Hall's contemporaries neatly dispensed with that hope by remarking of archaeology that it "is the discipline with the theory and practice for the recovery of unobservable hominid behaviour patterns from indirect traces in bad samples" (Clarke 1973, 17). And Clarke wasn't even trying to get at what the hominids were *thinking* about, which is, arguably, a major purpose of studying past people.

In other words, the only partial recovery of data is only part of the problem. At its core, the archaeological enterprise is altogether more difficult and altogether more doomed than Hall's quip about Cahokia suggests. That the epic journey of *Homo sapiens* has taken us from the savannah to space is indisputable, but we do not have one simple, comprehensive account of this multigenerational sojourn—and we never will, no matter how much we excavate. Rather, we have grainy snapshots, faded sketches, souvenirs of mysterious purpose, maps of unspecified scales drawn long after the fact, and stories which change with each storyteller and occasion.

Archaeologists work with jumbled puzzle pieces: some thoughts lead to behaviors, some behaviors leave material traces, some of those material traces preserve, some of those traces that preserve are discovered, some of those discovered traces can be reassembled, and some of those reassembled can be meaningfully interpreted. Those working with texts instead of material culture have a similar problem: of the sum of everything ever written, a fraction is recovered, a fraction of that can be deciphered and translated, a fraction of that can be understood, a fraction of that is true, and only a fraction of that is relevant to anything we might actually want to know.

Compounding this are differences of opinion about analytical units in the study of the past, which, logically enough, produce immense differences in our models of how those units interact. There is, for example, no agreement upon what a "city-state" is or was (Smith and Schrieber 2006, 7), which certainly complicates analyses of their characteristics, their behavior over time, and what networks of city-states do. Things don't come out of the ground labeled, ordered, and packaged. We impose labels upon them, and those labels differ from archaeologist to archaeologist, and may or may not have any bearing upon the human reality as it was lived. One cannot discover a civilization; instead, we discover buildings, potsherds, and ancient garbage, study their attributes, and proceed to decide whether they belong together or apart. A civilization is a matter of definition rather than a real bounded entity in the world. Should we consider industrial Europe to be essentially a different civilization from its precursor? (Arnason 2006). Was predynastic

Egypt under Narmer the same as the civilization ruled by Cleopatra VII three thousand years later (Zerubavel 2003)? Should we lump Sumeria and Babylonia together? What about Sparta and Athens? Judea, Palestine, and Israel? The states comprising the former Yugoslavia? Australia and England? Is India one civilization? Is China? Is California its own civilization now (Chytry 2006)?

Archaeologists and historians create history's pageant and we start simply by grouping our data. We create the actors by naming ancient peoples and drawing distinctions between them in ways that they themselves would never have recognized. We decide on the size of the stage by placing edges on the areas we study. And we determine the length of the acts by dividing up time. We do all these things according to our best guesses early in our study of an ancient culture and then find ourselves struggling within and against those very structures. We strive, for example, to bridge the gaps between the Mesolithic and the Neolithic, or precontact and postcontact eras, but the gaps are of our own, modern manufacture.

These aspects of the data and our engagements with them contribute to differences in how archaeologists and historians approach knowledge compared to physical scientists.

On Knowing

Because the topic of social evolution spans multiple disciplines in disparate realms of the humanities, social sciences, and sciences, running the gamut from history to biology, philosophy to physics, it's essential to acknowledge differences in ideas about how we know things, what we can know, and how confident we can be in our knowledge. Reality, truth, and knowledge are matters about which there is less consensus than one might hope. This is a massive discussion in itself, but here, I will only touch upon some key epistemological issues concerning multiple explanations for past phenomena.

Culture influences our understanding of the world. Our biological perception equipment is influenced by our mental constructions; we do not simply 'see the world as it is,' either in the literal sense of vision or in the metaphorical sense of overall apprehension. Our explanations for the patterns we observe are produced in part by what we are taught about the rules of causation, i.e., 'how the world works.' Documenting variation in cultural logics is part of the work of anthropology, and is fascinating in itself. What is crucial here, however, is this anthropological point: that contemporary science is as cultural as shamanism, opera, Catholicism, or the Boy Scouts. It does not stand outside of culture in a space of perfect objectivity. Scientists are people, and they are subject to the influences of their times. Theories explaining the world change diachronically or vary synchronically not only because of variation in the available *data*, but because of change and variation in the *people* producing the theories. Objectivity itself is culturally constituted (Daston and Galison 2007). This is an essential point in relation to any history of social evolutionary thought; from the outset, it is important to acknowledge that just as humanity as a whole is not simply progressing down a linear historical path, neither are scholars simply progressing down a linear path towards an evermore precise understanding of how cultures change. Different, incommensurable explanations for the same cultural phenomena exist simultaneously.

Moreover, these different explanations can be equally valid, particularly when we are discussing events and processes from long ago, as we often must with social evolution. This is not extreme postmodernism, but a consequence of the fact that we can *discover* the world, but we *decide* upon the truth. Philosopher Richard Rorty (1989, 4–5) famously explained that "We need to make a distinction between the claim that the world is out there and the claim that truth is out there . . . [because] where there are no sentences there is no truth . . . The world is out there, but descriptions of the world are not. Only descriptions of the world can be true or false." Drawing from Rorty, Keith Jenkins (1991, 5) explains that just as the world and truth are different things, so are the past and history. Although the past really happened—in the same way that the world is indeed out there—history is something we make. Furthermore, he says

> [T]he past and history are not stitched into each other such that only one historical reading of the past is absolutely necessary. The past and history float free of each other, they are ages and miles apart. For the same object of enquiry can be read differently by different discursive practices (a landscape can be read/interpreted differently by geographers, sociologists, historians, artists, economists, etc.) whilst internal to each, there are different interpretive readings over time and space. (Jenkins 1991, 5)

The sticking point is that, as Jenkins puts it, history is "epistemologically fragile": "there is no real account, no proper history, that, deep down, allows us to check all other accounts against it: there is no fundamentally correct 'text' of which other interpretations are just variations; variations are all there are" (1991, 11). This does not mean that *all* interpretations are equally valid, because the data will always constrain the options. It does mean, however, that there will never be just one real and true history.

Furthermore, we cannot always decide which of two historical interpretations is more real and more true because we do not have the luxury of dealing with simple systems with controllable tests. Reasoning about the past is thus complex in the extreme (Wylie 2002). Particular problems include: the challenge of disentangling correlation from causation, especially when chronologies are imprecise; the difficulty of tacking back and forth between the past and present through analogical reasoning; and the fundamental disjunction between material traces of human behavior and those humans' conceptual worlds. These problems can be wiggled around at times, but they simply cannot be eliminated methodologically. They are part of the deal of studying human history. Even when dealing with recent, written history instead of the cryptic world of ancient fragmentary objects, the skill of thinking historically—navigating between familiarity and unfamiliarity—takes a long time to learn, and does not provide us with certainty (Wineburg 2001, 5).

The point here is two-fold: in principle, the realities of working with the past can run counter to traditional scientific thinking; and in practice, different disciplines may not share ideas about appropriate methods and worthwhile results. Many scientists operate according to the assumption that there is one truth, and their task is to find it, and that they have achieved success when they have a simple explanation with a singular answer—even though this model of inquiry stands on shaky logical ground (Allen et al. 2001). Many scientists also believe that a good explanation for an observed phenomenon must have predictive value, i.e., speak to the future instead of merely accurately describing the past. If something can be cast in a formula instead of a narrative, they find the former to be more satisfying. However, much scientific explanation is actually of narrative form (more on this below), and the utility of simple formulas is questionable when we are dealing with complex systems with intelligent agents. As Allen et al. put it, "[m]any questions posed by the human condition in today's world are not susceptible to a single answer" (2001, 476).

Obviously, philosophy has a great deal more to say on the subject, but the salient point here is that different disciplines bring different models of truth, knowledge, and methods to the study of social evolution and this is partly responsible for some of the debates. (See Denning 2006 for specific comments in relation to SETI.) Another contributor is the differences in our purposes: to what end are we studying social evolution, anyway?

Why Even Ask?
The Purposes of Inquiry into Social Evolution

Reasons for studying social evolution have been varied, but they all have one thing in common: they connect to much bigger agendas.

Most cultures have an origin story that explains who humans are, what their relationships are to other humans, gods, animals, and the natural world, and how they came to exist. This is the broader context within which the study of social evolution is situated. (And, of course, the context for the modern battle between creationism and evolutionism.) Empirical inquiries that went beyond traditional narratives are known from many ancient cultures; the profession of historian is among the oldest. My comments here will be restricted to modern western traditions of scholarship, but they are not the only ones of relevance.

It is noteworthy that the study of social evolution substantially predated modern biological evolutionary theory. It was obvious that human societies changed, but before fossils and their patterning were understood—starting in the early 19th century with Smith's geological work (Winchester 2001)—it was not widely recognized that biological macroevolution had occurred, so no theory was required to explain it. In addition, the biological world was seen within Christianity to be simply the work of God's creation whereas the social world could clearly be shaped by men.

In the recent European context, debates about social evolution developed in step with the humanities, social sciences, and natural history, for the polymaths of the 17th and 18th centuries frequently wondered about humanity's natural state and the development of civil society. (This became increasingly possible as agnosticism and atheism emerged as viable alternatives.) As usual, these were not disinterested musings; modern science was born at a time of bloody revolutions in Europe, with decades of civil war and killing, and so it was that scholars like Thomas Hobbes sought to deduce, logically and scientifically, the best way for human beings to live. Social evolution has always been political.

This is even more the case today; as the young Marx famously wrote in 1845, as he was beginning to develop his own theory of social evolution, the point is not just to interpret the world, but to change it (Marx 1998 [1845]). Indeed, the French Revolution of 1789 had crystallized a radical assumption— dear to revolutionaries ever since—"that they could renovate society completely, by reference to abstract principles, not to precedent," and this in turn sparked an academic interest in "identifying the underlying forces of historical development . . . which could be turned into allies if they were understood" (Close

1985, 7, 9). Today, many take it for granted that we can, collectively, engineer a truly different society—that we can act either violently or peacefully upon ideas about human nature and society to convert governments from monarchies to republics, install or remove democracies, and institute or abolish socialist practices. Or that we can work internationally on projects of global scope, like peace-keeping, the eradication of smallpox, the elimination of child labor, or the control of carbon emissions. Accordingly, a great deal of work in the social sciences is applied in nature, i.e., it specifically aims to understand processes of social change in order to better effect change. This principle also guides future-oriented work in social evolution, as demonstrated by the *Journal of Conscious Evolution*, and *World Futures: The Journal of General Evolution*, produced by General Evolution Research Group/Club of Budapest.

Just as social evolutionary thought has served the purposes of revolutionaries, it has also served to explain and legitimate various status quos. The development of theories of unilineal evolution—i.e., stages through which all human societies eventually progress, like 'savagery, barbarism, and civilization'—was rather convenient in 18th and 19th century England and America, since it explained the positions of different human societies relative to one another, and justified the domination of some 'primitive' cultures by those who were more evolved, i.e., more 'civilized.' This also connected with biological essentialism, particularly the contemporary polygenic theories of race, which in turn connected to Social Darwinism and eugenics, which have been used to support everything from slavery to genocide, though to the chagrin of Darwin himself (Glick 2008). For reasons like this, it is often uncomfortable for modern anthropologists to claim social evolutionists like Lewis Henry Morgan and Edward Burnett Tylor among the founders of their discipline, for their theories were predicated upon the ethnocentric classification and ranking of human societies in ways that served colonialist agendas.

In sum, western theories of social evolution which imbue so much of our thinking today are not timeless. They emerged from a very specific political moment, and inevitably, carry within them European biases of the 17th through 19th centuries. The legacies of all these ideas mentioned above survive in modern social evolutionary thought, and so the politics of their origin remain with us. Naturally enough, some scholars have continued to study social evolution with the aim of refuting the ideas sketched above—e.g., replacing the unilinear model with a multilinear one, thereby privileging the idea of local adaptations over universal progress (Steward 1955)—and thus, another major reason for studying social evolution has been to respond to previous ideas about social evolution.

Finally, of course, as illustrated by this volume, some scholars seek to understand social evolution because they wish to place it with chemistry, biology, and astronomy within the framework of cosmic evolution. Some might argue that this reach for a comprehensive theory of everything is a modern secular substitute for religion, but others regard it as simply a scientific worldview.

So, there have been, and are, a host of different reasons for studying social evolution. The theories produced wander far from their contexts of origination, but they bring their baggage with them. And this matters, because what we say about social evolution has real effects in the world.

Why It Matters what We Say About Social Evolution

What scientists believe and say about the subjects of their inquiry has real effects on those subjects. For example, Descartes' argument that animals are without minds, are essentially unconscious, and unable to feel pain or to suffer, was used by early modern vivisectionists to justify their activities (Nash 1989, 17). Of course, the zoological knowledge of Descartes and his contemporaries was incomplete; they knew nothing of great apes or dolphins, and nothing of human evolution, and this made it easy for them to divide the world into animal automata and men with minds and souls (Coetzee 1999, 61). But regardless of the reason for Descartes' error, his theories had practical consequences for living, sensate beings.

How, then, should we theorize when the subjects are human? Social scientists often feel that we have a special duty of care to our subjects. Not least because of our awareness of the skeletons in our disciplinary closets—for examples, see Gould's classic *The Mismeasure of Man*, 1996 (1981)—many contemporary social scientists tend to extreme caution when theorizing about socially volatile topics, because our statements can have immediate, serious, practical consequences. Indeed, it is arguable that we have to be more cautious than some other scientists. If, for example, a palaeontologist makes a bold conjecture about therapsid phylogeny or a cosmologist proposes a new model of dark matter, it is unlikely to affect the distribution of aid to regions where children starve to death. However, some social scientists work on subjects where this is precisely what is at stake. A new therapsid phylogeny or dark matter model is also unlikely to contribute directly to a person being enslaved. But this is precisely the kind of injustice to which previous theorists' guesses about human beings have contributed. We cannot forget that scholarly models of human biological or cultural evolution have, at times, justified or encouraged social inequality and crimes against humanity.

Social evolutionary theory is among the more easily abused products of social science for several reasons. It positions different cultures in relation to each other, and does so in ways that can lead easily to characterizations of people as superior or inferior. It explicitly suggests the best ways to engineer societies, and in such projects, there will always be winners and losers. An additional complication is that it is difficult to separate out long-term human cultural and biological evolution from each other.

To elaborate: prior to the massive waves of exploration of recent centuries, the peoples of the Americas developed their own cultures, while those of Africa developed others, and those of Europe developed others, etc. The western intellectual tradition has unfortunately tended to characterize some cultures as superior and others as inferior, which has in turn prompted searches for the ultimate causes of these differences. It is popularly assumed that these cultural differences have their roots in human biological variation, and in turn that the global distribution of power we observe today is a result of the inherent biological superiority of some groups of people over others. Diamond (1997/2005), amongst others, has provided a book-length refutation of this notion, explaining the importance of environmental variables in world history (more about this below), but the idea is still prevalent. Similarly, a wealth of research indicates that biological differences between human populations are superficial, and that 'race' is biologically meaningless because there is more variation within populations than between them—and yet, there are still scholars who claim significant differences in IQ between different human 'races,' and who link these to patterns in human cultural evolution. For example, the psychologist Rushton has recently argued that Africa's current economic underdevelopment is a continuation of a long pattern of cultural stagnation born of its peoples' inferior IQ—an argument which has been dismantled at length by the archaeologist/anthropologist MacEachern (2006). The problem here, then, is that social evolutionary constructs which have elevated some cultures and debased others—usually due to information about culture as inadequate as Descartes' information about biology was—have contributed to biological arguments about human beings which are deeply racist, and have real effects in the world.

What we say about social evolution matters in yet more complicated ways. Even our theories about the mechanisms of evolutionary change matter in society, because they affect the way people consider the social status quo. If one ascribes to a reductionist version of natural selection, i.e., the 'survival of the fittest,' then, famously, the fittest are those who survive and thrive—and those who fail, do so because they are inherently inferior, rather than because of unlucky initial situations, chance events in their lives, or consistent inequalities of treatment in their environments. If one assumes that sexual selection plays a dominant role in producing the status quo, then it follows that males and females are continually at odds, each engineering or outwitting the other to suit their own best interests. Obviously, all this has implications for our thinking about class structure and relationships between the sexes. Conversely, if one thinks in terms of some less popularly known evolutionary processes—such as drift, through which adaptively neutral traits can become widespread; or selection for groups of characteristics which are transmitted together, including adaptive, neutral, and maladaptive traits; or environmental change, through which the previously well-adapted can be slowly or quickly obliterated; or group selection, through which cooperation between individuals or even between species can be favored over competition—then there are quite different implications for our understanding of the world in which we live, and our social behavior may vary accordingly.

Finally, what we say about social evolution matters even with respect to specific cultural traits. Many have assumed, for example, that the status quo is produced primarily by selection, from which it follows that any widespread trait has a survival advantage. In turn, it follows that a given cultural characteristic (say, farming) became widespread because it is a superior lifestyle and highly adaptive for everyone. That is quite different from the proposition that agriculture had, and has, *some* advantages for *some* members of society, *some* of the time, or from the recognition that actually, farming barely works well enough to keep most people in the world alive (Wright 2004). (Indeed, many archaeologists now consider that the advent of farming was a collapse of sorts, an inefficient fall-back option after the exhaustion of easily available resources.) Further, the formerly common assumption that farming was only invented once, and diffused to other societies, produced a very different model of world history from one which assumes that farming emerged multiple times in multiple places, as we now know to be fact. The diffusionist model was used to portray one society as vital and generative and others as mere copycats, but the independent invention model respects the innovative capacities of all societies and peoples.

It can be seen, then, that there are social implications to what we say about the large-scale patterns of social evolution, the mechanisms of evolution, and the evolution of specific cultural traits. It might be argued that this is behind us now, since our theories of social evolution have developed beyond the Victorian era, and since we now have a better understanding of human biological variation. However, theories of social evolution and world history still have very real effects today. One recent, vivid example is provided by Jared Diamond, who writes in his 2005 postscript to his 1997 world-historical synthesis *Guns, Germs and Steel*, that shortly after the book's publication it was favorably reviewed by Bill Gates. This in turn spawned the distribution of the book within business consulting firms, and a mass of correspondence from economists and business leaders asking "what is the best way to organize human groups, organizations, and businesses so as to maximize productivity, creativity, innovation, and wealth?" (Diamond 1997/2005, 433). We have, then, a recent example of an essentially historical book focused upon topics like the origins and development of agriculture, *directly* generating new discourse and practices within global capitalism.

In short, the subject of social evolution is not a harmless intellectual playground, a place for exuberant 'maybes.' Without exaggeration, it can be deadly serious.

Antipathies, Anxieties, Identities

The loadedness of theories about social evolution has meant that many in the social sciences and humanities consider it a pernicious subject, one to be avoided. It has also meant that when it *is* addressed, skeptical treatments of social evolutionary theory can be badges of disciplinary identity. This theme will reemerge in context later in this chapter, but it is sufficiently significant to warrant an introduction here.

First, there is the issue of who, exactly, is talking. The academy itself has evolved considerably in recent decades, and this has relevant effects. It is often observed by philosophers and historians of science that it matters who is doing the science (e.g., Harding 2003, Haraway 1988). It would be, for example, logical for scholars from groups which were once systematically excluded from the academy or the body politic on the basis of their biology—women, and racialized minorities—to be sensitive to evolutionary arguments that evoke biological determinism. (Evolutionary theory can be a powerful weapon against racism, for the evidence clearly indicates that human beings everywhere are much more alike than they are different. And yet it is also easily co-opted into racist and sexist discourse.) Likewise, it would make sense for academics from subaltern backgrounds to be more vigilant for theories which evoke colonialism or deny the importance of diversity.

Related to this is the problem of reductionism in evolutionary theory. There are multiple forms of reductionism in science and philosophy, but broadly speaking, what concerns us here is the idea that complex phenomena are best explained by reducing them to their smallest components, most basic laws, and fundamental arrows of causation. This has ostensibly been a guiding principle for much modern science. This particularly makes sense for physical scientists who are invested in a universe with knowable unchanging rules and predictability. Social scientists, on the other hand, work in the world of humans where very little is logical, comparatively little is systematic, and not much is unchanging. We also have to contend with the fact that our subjects are sentient, with free will and agency, which makes it difficult to write equations precisely predicting their behavior. As a result of this, we are often more in the business of uncovering and describing human behavior than we are of distilling it down into axioms and prognostications.

Moreover, to many scholars in the social sciences and humanities, reductionism is ideologically problematic for several reasons. For example, for many anthropologists the details of a culture should not be reduced down to straightforward patterns or sequences because the details—the intricacies of human lives—*are the point*. Often we seek to understand people in their own right, and on their own terms rather than from an external perspective. Furthermore, as Eric Wolf argued in his classic work, *Europe and the People Without History*, "the world of humankind constitutes a manifold, a totality of interconnected processes, and inquiries that disassemble this totality into bits and then fail to reassemble it falsify reality" (1982, 3).

When historical patterns are distilled into their simplest forms, uncertainty is omitted. The 'maybes' and the imprecisions which are inherent to historical scholarship are dropped. This matters. Not least, this matters because the resulting theories are inevitably biased, and those who lose out are, disproportionately, those without the power to talk back. Stories can be told about their pasts that the powerful would not tolerate being told about their own. But the distortion resulting from oversimplification is only part of the problem. Another problem is silencing—or the comparative invisibility of some people who are left in history's shadows. We have to ask: when historical patterns are distilled into simple forms, *whose* details are most often elided? Typically, it is the people whom anthropologists have traditionally studied: those who were not part of the industrialized European system; those who are today marginalized, oppressed, or engulfed by nation-states. This includes those who have lived by hunting and foraging, or in small-scale villages, those whose traditions do not include written records, or whose civilizations have been subsumed within others.

Historically, when these peoples have been included in grand narratives of humanity's journey (instead of simply left out), they have often been treated as anachronisms, representatives of lifeways from the distant past, rather than as contemporary human beings. Many anthropologists feel a particular allegiance to these groups because of the intrinsic interest of their cultures, but also because their very survival—cultural, linguistic, and physical—is threatened. Some are falling to the juggernaut of globalization, while others are still deliberately targeted by governments—persecuted, displaced, denied rights, forcibly assimilated, etc.—as a continuation of colonizations begun centuries or decades ago. And so it is that some anthropologists, and other scholars, too, spend their careers attempting to be witnesses for those who have ended up on the wrong side of power, and to ensure that their stories are told. And so it is that some anthropologists and social scientists today tend to see all grand historical syntheses, including social evolutionary schemes, as part of a colonial strategy of domination.

Anthropology itself began as a colonial project, and we are still dealing with that legacy. As part of the process of decolonizing the discipline, many anthropologists consider it part of their job description to defend against the misuse of anthropological and archaeological data, and to argue against oversimplifications which, intentionally or not, privilege some human beings over others or rationalize systemic social injustice.

All this is germane to this chapter because it identifies some of the academic tensions surrounding the subject of social evolution, and explains what for some observers can be a puzzle—i.e., why much contemporary social scientific scholarship concerning human culture is not easily recruited into the project of building social evolutionary theory.

Now, having introduced some of the elephants in the room, I will proceed to illustrate their behavior through an extended case study on a topic central to social evolutionary thought: collapse.

Case Study: The Unsteady State of 'Collapse'

The study of social collapse has received a great deal of attention, both scholarly and popular, in recent years (e.g., Diamond 2005, Wright 2004). This is of particular interest here for multiple, intertwined reasons. First, dominant, recurring themes in culture/cosmos discussions include the possibility that our own civilization will collapse, thereby halting our technological progress, and the related question of the longevity of hypothesized extraterrestrial civilizations—the crucial "L" of the Drake Equation (e.g., NASA report by Langhoff et al. 2007). Second, collapse is an obviously important macroevolutionary process, but researchers' approaches to collapse vary substantially, highlighting different disciplinary and analytical orientations to social evolutionary phenomena. Further, popular discourse about collapse clearly demonstrates the current political, economic, and environmental significance of social evolutionary thought. Finally, a close look at collapse enables us to pinpoint some persistent questions about the general relationship of the past to the present and future.

Guns, Germs, Steel, and Collapse

It is useful to begin with a recent, popular overview of the topic. Jared Diamond's hefty *Collapse: How Societies Choose to Fail or Succeed* (2005) has, like his previous, Pulitzer Prize-winning *Guns, Germs, and Steel: The Fates of Human Societies* (1997), become an international bestseller. As an academic trained first in physiology and then in evolutionary biology, and later a professor of geography and environmental history, Diamond aimed to create 'big-picture' syntheses that address common assumptions and questions about humanity's history and future. In *Guns, Germs, and Steel*, Diamond sought to explain the historical pattern of European colonization of other continents through reference to deep environmental history. Attacking the commonly held racist assumption that European societies achieved domination because of inherently superior characteristics of Europeans themselves, Diamond contends that instead, European societies were lucky—they just happened to develop in a biogeographical context that led easily to the colonization and conquest of other lands. In *Collapse*, Diamond addressed what lies ahead for our society; by comparing the collapses and successes of multiple societies, he summarized the eight environmental causes for collapse as being "deforestation and habitat destruction, soil problems (erosion, salinization, and soil fertility losses), water management problems, overhunting, overfishing, effects of introduced species on native species, human population growth, and increased per-capita impact of people" (Diamond 2005, 6). However, none of these challenges is in itself enough to induce collapse. Diamond specifies his five-point framework for understanding possible environmental collapses: "Four of those sets of factors—environmental damage, climate change, hostile neighbours, and friendly trade partners—may or may not prove significant for a particular society. The fifth set of factors—the society's responses to its environmental problems—always proves significant" (Diamond 2005, 11). The model is multifactorial, but a unifying theme running through it is the concept of 'overshoot,' or a population unwisely exceeding carrying capacity (Tainter 2006), and a correlated argument in favor of sustainable development today.

Though his work has received much acclaim—indeed, Diamond holds a National Medal of Science—it has also provoked significant critiques from within the academic community, particularly from those who specialize in disciplines such as anthropology, archaeology, and history, that generated the data and primary works from which Diamond weaves his stories. Some believe that Diamond simplifies to the point of being wrong, while others object that his emphases are badly placed (Johnson 2007, Powell 2008). Indeed, Diamond acknowledges in a 2005 postscript to *Guns, Germs, and Steel* that not everyone is convinced by his arguments. For example, on the question of why, in the 19th century, Europe rather than China held the balance of global power, Diamond favors explanations in deep ecological history, whereas "a large majority of social scientists still favours proximate explanations" (1997/2005, 431)—explanations based in recent historical contingencies and culture.

Environment or Culture? Structure or Contingency? Culprits or Victims?

The critiques extend further, and have political and moral undertones. Some scholars, for example, believe that Diamond tends not only towards environmental determinism, but also towards Eurocentrism. Others object that Diamond's accounts of world history distribute blame in convenient ways. In the case of global inequality, they say, he argues that the winners are just lucky, not to blame for making decisions that led to the condition of the world's have-nots. In the case of collapse, they say, Diamond argues that the losers made bad decisions, and are to blame for their own sorry ends (Johnson 2007).

Of course, *both* deep environment and recent cultural contingencies and choices play a role in generating historical patterns. This has been appreciated since the Annales school of historical analysis suggested that the history of any given place can be best understood by looking at time on multiple scales, i.e., long-term environmental history, mid-term sociopolitical structures, and short-term events (Braudel 1980). The trick, then, is figuring out the balance, and choosing whether to emphasize environmental constraints or human agency, structure, or contingency (Bintliff 1999). But this is not merely a scholarly nicety to be debated in conference rooms. The choice has consequences, and not just for our understanding of those long dead.

For example, do we regard the tragedy of the Rwandan genocide as essentially a Malthusian collapse (Diamond 2005), or as essentially political?

Or how do we explain the current war in Darfur, which has claimed hundreds of thousands of lives and displaced millions? As an ethnic/religious war or a consequence of climate-driven ecological crisis? It is, of course, both, and the global community needs to take both into account in deciding courses of action in Darfur and places like it, according to the Secretary General of the United Nations (Moon 2007). The problem comes when the situation is oversimplified, some scholars say, because an overemphasis on resource shortages as the conflict's cause "whitewashes the Sudan government," elides their war crimes, and also tends to suggest that climate change leads inexorably to genocide (IRIN 2007). Likewise, characterizations of the conflict as being between Arabs and Africans, or between pastoralists and agriculturalists, do hold elements of truth, but oversimplify matters into convenient binaries that distort the real picture and hamper constructive interventions (IRIN 2007). Overall, Africa's shocking record of civil war from 1970 onwards is not well understood because the precise relationships between ethnic diversity and political disorder, between natural resources and state failure, between poverty and strife, between political reform/democratization and instability, are complex; too often, the causes and symptoms of state failure in Africa have been confused, and the real patterns are obscured (Bates 2008). It matters because the explanations proffered determine the international community's responses in emergency situations like these, and their overall approach towards investment in, and relations with, Africa.

Of Diamond and Dinosaurs: the Perils of Synthesis

Obviously Diamond's arguments are significant, but so is his general mode of inquiry. In the epilogue of *Guns, Germs, and Steel* (1997/2005, 424), he explicitly argues that world history should employ the methods of historical sciences like astronomy, evolutionary biology, and climatology, which tackle developmental trajectories by comparing different systems to deduce cause-effect relationships. This method of cross-cultural comparison, juxtaposing societies from different patches of space and time to uncover larger patterns, is relatively uncontroversial and often-enough attempted though methodologically challenging (more below). However, the framing raises concerns for some: Diamond states that he is "optimistic that historical studies of human societies can be pursued as scientifically as studies of dinosaurs" (1997/2005, 425). Although this may sound like a good idea, it has generated much friction. Many social scientists don't particularly *want* to treat human beings and their societies as we treat erstwhile reptilians, for the host of reasons addressed above. Diamond's reply to such critiques is that we need both comparative syntheses *and* detailed case studies: "In both chemistry and physics, the need for both approaches has been recognized for a long time. . . . One no longer finds specialists on molybdenum decrying the periodic table's sweeping superficiality, nor advocates of the periodic table scorning mere descriptive studies of individual elements" (quoted in Johnson 2007). In *Collapse*, he emphasizes the need for both "good individual studies and good comparisons" (Diamond 2005, 19).

Some scholars would argue that this reply still misses the point of the critique about comparative syntheses concerning humanity's history, for the objection is not to multiple methods, or to superficiality in itself; rather, it is an abiding concern about compacting world history into tidy, easily summarized, powerful master narratives (Fulford 1999). The alarm escalates when an author tells a story as compelling as Diamond's, and especially when one author's version of history gains as much popularity as Diamond's has, because it can quickly come to dominate the arena. This is risky because when a complex situation is reduced to a sketch, biases inevitably come into play, and whether an author intends it or not, simplified history is a perennial tool of the powerful.

The Magic Wand of History: Now You See Them, Now You Don't

The distortion of history by political interests is a sore point in the historical disciplines because it is absolutely commonplace; it is the norm, not the exception, and requires our constant vigilance. Nation-states particularly need founding myths, and that has frequently encouraged them to erase or diminish the histories of their predecessors, or those whom they currently subjugate, or those whose land they intend to occupy. Most notoriously, the Nazis had a special archaeology division (Arnold 1992). *Raiders of the Lost Ark* didn't invent that, but neither did the Nazis. For example, from their earliest days, the white settler states of Africa claimed, in the face of abundant evidence to the contrary, that impressive ancient sites like Great Zimbabwe had been built by Phoenicians, Arabs, or the Queen of Sheba, rather than by black African civilizations. Or, even more boldly and astoundingly, they claimed that there had been no significant settlement in the territory at all prior to the earliest European arrivals (Hall 1984). And in the United States of America, the impressive mound sites of the Mississippi River Valley—including Cahokia's Monks Mound, covering 15 acres—were, in the 19th century, often attributed to mysterious 'Moundbuilders,' lost Israelites, roaming Vikings, ambitious Phoenicians, King Arthur, and wandering Welshmen, now disappeared. The mounds were attributed to just about anyone except the people who actually built them, Native Americans (Feder 2006), who were, not coincidentally, being forcibly relocated at that time. This myth survives even today. In each case—and there are many more like them—claims about the accomplishments, existence, and/or survival of a people who produced prominent archaeological sites were explicitly used by invading powers to justify their expansionist agendas. The connection to theories about collapse is this: if a society is labeled as 'collapsed,' then the people are labeled as 'extinct,' and thus their descendants are neatly excised from the body politic. When they speak, their voices are heard as mysterious echoes on the wind, if they're heard at all.

There are very few simple truths in archaeology, but here is one: ancient sites were all built by people who are now dead. Though in reality none of them survive, in the modern imagination, some are construed as being more alive than others. Some are represented as having cultural descendants who carry on their traditions: for example, Europeans and Americans often claim cultural continuity with the democracy and science of the ancient Greeks. Select others whose societies are labeled as failed, fallen, or 'collapsed,' are popularly supposed to have left few or no descendants, and are thus relegated exclusively to the past—people whose time has come and gone. They are celebrated as 'mysteriously disappeared,' and popular books are written about their 'lost wisdom' (Denning 1999). And since they are officially gone, their descendants are thus either ignored or written out of the present as anachronistic exceptions, the last strag—gling survivors of a doomed and degenerated culture who will surely finish disappearing any minute now. So it is that in popular discourse about 'the Maya collapse,' the Maya people themselves are represented as extinct, as vanished, despite the fact that millions of Maya are alive today amongst the other indigenous peoples of Central America. In fact, the 'collapse' in question refers only to the end of the Classic Maya period around 800–1100 AD, specifically to the abandonment of *some* lowland centres. Other Maya centres, like Chichen Itza and Lamanai, continued to thrive, and new 'Postclassic' Maya polities arose and endured in the millennium after the 'collapse'—with sufficient numbers and strength that it took the Spanish conquistadors the better part of two centuries to subdue them even with smallpox on their side. The Maya are still here and the wars are not over; in Chiapas and Guatemala, in particular, the Maya and other indigenous peoples have long been fighting for basic rights and freedoms—indeed, for recognition of their existence. Partly as a result of those struggles, indigenous cultures, languages, and political groups are now on the upswing once more in Guatemala and Mexico.

This is the kind of 'detail' that gets lost in redaction, when history is simplified too much and only the most general patterns are drawn out. (Other 'details' include the survival of the Arawak, who are widely supposed to have been obliterated in the Columbian invasion, and the Tasmanians, also supposed to be long gone. Both groups left descendants whose voices are finally being heard again in the international community.) This is not merely a matter of political correctness, good global citizenship, or guilty liberal outrage on behalf of the forgotten or silenced subaltern. It is a matter of accuracy in terms of social evolutionary events. What really happens in collapses? If people don't simply die out, then what do they really do? And what really drives these processes labelled as 'collapse'?

The reader will not, by now, be surprised to learn that there is little consensus. When we return to the primary literature on collapse synthesized by Diamond and others, it's evident that much remains unclear.

What Archaeologists Really Know About the Causes of Past Collapses

Joseph Tainter, anthropologist, historian, and author of multiple significant works on collapse (e.g., 1988, 1995, 1996, 2000, 2006), carefully reviewed the archaeological literature in relation to the popular notion of 'overshoot.' He notes that "The literature on sustainability and the human future emphasizes the belief that population and/or mass consumption caused resource degradation and collapse in earlier societies," and describes the way that archaeological cases are recruited as evidence that humanity has exceeded resource limits (2006, 59–60). The concepts of overshoot and case studies like Easter Island's collapse are now "in the wild," Tainter argues—that is, they are ideas loosed from their academic origins, proliferating and mutating in the public imagination. But are they based on secure foundations? Reviewing the archaeological cases cited by Diamond and others, Tainter concludes that overshoot hypotheses are not borne out very well by the archaeological evidence; even some iconic examples, such as Easter Island, are equivocal. Indeed, there are several different ways to tell the Easter Island story, with very different implications (Powell 2008, Denning and Jones 2005). In sum, Tainter argues, "There does not presently appear to be a confirmed archaeological case of overshoot, resource degradation, and collapse brought on by overpopulation and/or mass consumption" (2006, 71).

Such confirmation may come in time, but it is simply not here now. Neither do we have crystal clear pictures about climate change and collapse. For example, in recent years, palaeoclimate research has documented widespread droughts in western Asia and the eastern Mediterranean region around 8,200, 5,200, and 4,200 years before present—time periods which coincide with significant changes or collapses of archaeologically known cultures. Particularly prominent is the temporal association between the 4.2 ka drought and dramatic changes in several Bronze Age societies based upon cereal farming. However, the nature of the correlation is still much disputed and discussed by specialists: "uncertainty about the causal linkage between abrupt climate change and social collapse derives from chronological imprecision and the uncertain ability of societies to adapt to the abruptness, magnitude and duration of environmental change" (Staubwasser and Weiss 2006, 373; see also Weiss and Bradley 2001).

A similar situation prevails in studies of ancient New World states, where, Smith and Schrieber note in their summary of recent research, "a dramatic explosion of scientific data on Holocene climate and environmental changes" is shifting archaeologists' understanding of culture change (2006, 26). However, there is a polarization between "environmentalists and culturalists," i.e., those who find an approximate correlation of a significant environmental event and a collapse to be adequate explanation for the collapse, and those who argue that human agency and resilience must also be taken into consideration (Smith and Schrieber 2006). In many cases, it can be legitimately argued both ways, and good methodologies that integrate the perspectives are still uncommon. Smith and Schrieber hope that in time, "we will be in a far better position to evaluate models of the collapse of the lowland Classic Maya" and other polities (2006, 27). In a review of Demarest et al.'s recent volume about the terminal classic, Mayanist Elizabeth Graham says that "the fact that we still have so much to debate, exemplified by the many views expressed in this volume, suggests that we have not got all that much closer to understanding exactly what happened during these centuries of transition from the Maya Classic to Postclassic, about 800 to 1100," and emphasizes that we still need more empirical work to understand the great variability between regions, and that catastrophism is the easy way out (2005, 210–214). So, popular convictions about the Maya collapse notwithstanding, expert meta-analysis says that we still don't know for sure what happened. (More on this below.)

Bad timing and communication gaps are partially the culprits here, as for so many human dilemmas. Radiocarbon dates for events thousands of years ago quite frequently include error ranges of several centuries. Add to this the standard difficulties of inferring social processes from archaeological and ancient textual evidence, and exact chains of causality become difficult to establish. We can certainly *infer* that dramatic climate change generated the observed social changes—e.g., reduced agricultural production, reduced population, religious and political collapses and foreign invasion, transitions from urban to nonurban lifeways, regional abandonment and relocation to track moving habitats—but precise models concerning the nature and sequence of changes, particularly models which hold in detail for multiple cases and accommodate their variability, which account for one region's success and another's failure, are not easy to produce. As archaeological and palaeoclimate data are obtained, as analyses accumulate, and as dating is refined, the details of the picture will be filled in, but there will always be limits. And the more one knows, the less straightforward things become.

Connecting the Dots: Evolving Stories About Collapse

Here is what we do know for sure about collapse: perspective matters when we connect the dots. Perspectives change over time. It isn't just deliberate manipulation that changes historical stories—it is also the evolution of disciplines, and the embeddedness of their authors in societies and in scientific traditions.

Explanations for the Mayan collapse, for example, are notorious for having shifted over the last century, as Mayan specialists Rice et al. (2004) explain. Initial 19th century explorations of the Maya lowlands fostered a romantic image of a lost civilization, its mysterious ruins swallowed by the jungle. Clearly, at some point, the Maya had ceased building their phenomenal pyramids and temples, and the 'mystery' set western imaginations racing through the bestselling works of Catherwood and Stephens. In an era of European expansion, it was unthinkable for westerners that a people might choose to stop creating monumental stone structures and do things differently—e.g., build with perishable materials that are hard to see today—so it was assumed that there must have been a catastrophe. And since there had obviously been a catastrophe, no-one bothered much to look at what came afterwards, i.e., the still rather impressive phase of Mayan civilization now known as the Postclassic, for which there is abundant evidence. (The terminology itself is instructive: had the continuous Mayan civilization been divided into different analytical categories—perhaps Maya A, Maya B, Maya C—and the dividing lines drawn at different times, the entire structure of the discussion would be different.) In the mid-20th century, when historical thinking focused upon the rise and fall of empires, the Mayan scenario was still assumed to be one of dramatic decline. So, of course, the cause needed to be found. Subsequent speculations, based on still-patchy evidence, pinned the blame on influences such as "earthquake activity, climatic change (drought), epidemic diseases such as malaria and yellow fever, foreign conquest, 'cultural decadence,' agricultural (soil) exhaustion, and revolt of the lower classes" (Rice et al. 2004). It has also been observed that in the latter half of the 1900s, the explanations cycled through energy crises, war, and environmental stress according to what was foremost in the minds of the Mayanists at the time.

At any rate, by the late 1970s, as archaeological research in the region increased, it was already becoming evident that the 9th and 10th centuries were a time of transition and renewal, and that the picture was quite complex. Certainly, building traditions changed and certain political institutions passed, some dynasties ended, religious practices were transformed, and overall population declined in the southern Maya region. However, this took centuries and varied incredibly from region to region. *Some* Mayan states clearly fragmented, but the civilization did not end (Rice et al. 2004). For example, at Lamanai, with its *continuous* occupation from at least 1000 BC to the present, the evidence of the Classic-Postclassic transition shows changes in the elites who were in power, but the lives of nonelites seem to have changed rather little, except for economic shifts like a renewed focus on long-distance trade (Graham 2004, 2006)—not unlike the sorts of shifts seen in historic Europe when political regimes changed. Big, highly visible things, like cathedrals, palaces, and parliament buildings, can change dramatically, even when most people's lives just go on as usual. In short, we might ask whether the general 'Mayan collapse' is a meaningful concept at all, or whether it was, essentially, invented by previous generations of archaeologists, and then wildly reinterpreted and misinterpreted by others.

Only part of the variability in explanation is attributable to the development of the data set. True, as there are more dots to connect, the number of different ways to connect them grows, but there is more at work here than that. Allen et al. explain this beautifully through the Dust Bowl ecological disaster of the 1930s, describing three different versions of it (2001, 478–479, citing Cronon's work). All three versions agree on the facts, but weave those points together differently. One historian tells a "tragedy of ecological degradation," while another historian tells a heroic American tale of recovery through technological change; and Plenty-Coups, a chief of the Crow people, tells of the loss of the buffalo and a lifeway. Plenty-Coups's story ends with "After that, nothing happened." His story was over, and later events belonged to someone else's story. Allen et al. ask, "[h]ow can there be agreement on the facts, as some science would have it, but diametrically opposed narratives . . . or no narrative . . . ?" The point is, they say, that "scientists always use narrative, and thus benefit from being self-conscious narrators. Science cannot make an indefinite number of observations, and so selects, just like a narrator." Indeed, persuasive science depends on narratives (Harré, Brockmeier, and Mühlhäusler 1999, 69; see also Landau 1991). Furthermore, our stories tend to follow certain patterns. For collapses, there's nothing as satisfying as a good catastrophe (Rose 1999). As Gould (1999, xi) noted, we "especially like stories about growth and progress (or the obverse tragedies of death and destruction)," and predictable endings. Our preference for certain sorts of stories may mean that in attempts to really understand the past, we will always be fighting a losing battle; as Howard Gardner explains, not only do human beings like narratives, but we prefer simple, unsophisticated narratives, particularly binary stories of good and evil (1996, 49). Even in the face of rational analysis, those emotionally appealing stories are the ones that stick. At any rate, no story and no scientific account can connect *all* the dots, and so scientists and authors emphasize some points and ignore others, decide when to start and when to stop, and deliver messages in keeping with their worldviews. As we obtain more dots, the data set may enlarge *or* constrain the number of plausible interpretations. It rarely permits just one.

In any case of collapse, where we begin and end the story is important. As discussed above, this has implications for our positioning of people alive today, but it also determines where and when we focus our historical research. Tainter (1995) notes that in many ancient societies, it was assumed that human societies had life spans and would someday die only to be replaced by others. Empires were assumed to be unsustainable, and history was therefore assumed to be cyclical. We, on the other hand, have tended to believe that complex societies should endure. Therefore, historical collapses are compelling violations of our expectations; they attract our attention, demand explanation, provoke anxiety, and invite the telling of cautionary tales. We may even invent them sometimes, because we need their dark ink to draw our own mortal fears. But what if we shifted focus? Recently, some archaeologists have begun to examine what happens *after* 'collapse'; in looking at the frequent reemergence of complex societies and rise of second-generation states, they emphasize processes of transformation and regeneration, not simple disappearance (Schwartz and Nichols 2006). This, of course, feels more hopeful, but what does it all really mean for *us*, anyway?

Of Parables and Predictions:
What Can the Past Really Tell Us About Our Future?

There has long been a debate between those who believe that human beings are sufficiently inventive to be able to maneuver beyond constraints, and those who believe that resources have firm limits and we approach those limits at our peril (e.g., Boserup 1965 vs. Malthus 2004 [1798]). It is unsurprising that in our time—when the world's population is nearing seven billion, we can measure our collective effect upon Earth's climate, and our information networks permit the collation of worldwide data about famine—there is grave concern about sustainable resource use, ecological footprints, deforestation, and carbon emissions.

It is also unsurprising that history has been drawn into the discussion to bolster the case for change. After all, 'revelations' from the archaeological past play a guiding role in our increasingly secular society; like religious prophecies, they orient us and tell us how we should live (Denning 1999). But do we really need to invoke the Maya, or the Easter Islanders, or the Mesopotamians, or anyone else, to argue for sustainability? Does it really help on any level beyond the rhetorical? Are these tales of collapse mere parables, or science, or both?

Archaeologists have, in recent years, been grappling with some realities about the relationship of the past and the present. On one hand, we know that the ancient past is a player upon our modern stage—it is, "at best, a Rorschach test for contemporary concerns, and at worst, a text constructed in a metanarrative with a conscious or subconscious agenda of legitimating the conquering Western capitalist tradition" (Rice et al. 2004). And many archaeologists realize that we are implicated in those processes, because we provide the raw material and stories which contemporary minds reflect upon and rearrange at will. On the other hand, we also believe that material traces of ancient lives are real, and careful empirical work with that evidence can teach us something worth knowing about the past, and about ourselves.

But *what*? What *exactly* can these inquiries teach us about the past, or ourselves?

Of course it tells us where we came from, and that is useful to know. But does it really go beyond that? Some scientists, like Diamond (2005, 8), continue to optimistically argue that knowledge of the past really can help us make better decisions about the future, perhaps even averting catastrophe. For example, an interdisciplinary collective of scientists called IHOPE (Integrated History and future Of People on Earth) seeks to

i) map the integrated record of biophysical and human system change on the Earth over the last several thousand millennia, with higher temporal and spatial resolution in the last 1000 and the last 100 years.

ii) Understand the socioecological dynamics of human history by testing human-environment system models against the integrated history

iii) Based on these historical insights, develop credible options for the future of humanity. (Costanza et al. 2007, 523)

But they themselves don't answer their own fundamental question: "how does the history of human-environment systems generate useful insights about the future?" (2007, 525) They propose various sophisticated strategies for improved synthesis and modeling, etc., but seem to accept, as affirmatively answered, precisely that which needs to be addressed: *Does* the history of human-environment systems really generate useful insights about the future? and if so, what form do those insights take?

To reiterate: We know the past is used as a shopping mall of sorts, a source of anecdotes, bold accessories to festoon rhetoric about the present and future. We know that theories about the nature of history affect people's beliefs about today's world and how we should act in it. We know the past provides great fodder for popular movies like *Troy*, *300*, and *Apocalypto*, which recycle and regenerate prevalent ideas about war and international relations. We also know that, studied well, the past can provide us with a more sophisticated understanding of complex systems and how they generally function. And, of course, when analyzing any particular modern situation, it helps to know about the historical trajectory that produced it. So far, so clear. But there is still a crucial, live question concerning insights for the future: what sort of relationship do the past and present really have—i.e., in what sense are they really each other's analogs? (Holtorf 2000–2007). And following on from that, can our explanations of disconnected events long-past truly be expected to provide useful predictions about our own global system?

The subject of scientific prediction is a matter of enduring tension. As Stephen Jay Gould (1999) described it, in the historical sciences, explanation and prediction must be teased apart; these disciplines are not like experimental science, wherein a good explanation of a past process results in a prediction which can then be tested in a rerun of the same process. This does not diminish their scientific standing, but does limit their prognosticative value: "Narrative explanations may be as detailed, as decisive, and as satisfying as anything learned by the experimental method, but they do not permit prediction from a known starting point" (1999, xi). There are those who would certainly disagree, arguing that if we can model past systems with sufficient detail and precision, we will see regularities that *will* enable prediction. This is very much a live debate, and one that resists easy resolution. In fact, it is the axis around which swirls at least 50 years of archaeological theory, and the jury is still out.

Perhaps the understanding of past systems will help us in a different, indirect way with our own. Tainter argues persuasively that while we need to look to past collapses for information about our own future, they will not give us simple answers about what we should do next. He suggests, rather, that past cases can help us to understand the general nature of our present systems. He describes a pattern common to scientific research and any other kind of "societal problem-solving": "problem-solving evolves along a path of increasing complexity, higher costs, and declining marginal returns" (1995, 402). In every society, increasing complexity involves escalation in complex problems, which requires increasing investment in problem-solving, which coincides with diminishing returns on those investments, until a point is reached where it is clear that "the cost of overcoming our problems is too high relative to the benefits conferred, and that *not* solving our challenges is the economical option" (1995, 404). *This*, then, is collapse in Tainter's (1988) understanding—not a catastrophe, but a rational adaptation, by which some members of society actually benefit. And accordingly, one of our tasks in sustainability research is to know where we are in terms of our own complex system's trajectory—to know where we are in history, and understand the current state of our own problem-solving capacities (Tainter 1996). This is something that the experiences of past societies can hint at, but not tell us outright. To know, we must look in the mirror, not the microscope.

Generalizing: From Collapse to Other Social Evolutionary Processes

The challenge for those interested in collapse is four-fold: keep working on the recovery and primary interpretation of data; continue developing sophisticated models to integrate those interpretations, appreciating that the more we know, the harder the integration will get; keep questioning the stories told about the past, because they can legitimately, and will inevitably, be told in different ways and the choices have consequences; and keep asking exactly how, and to what extent, models of the past relate or apply to our present and future.

This set of challenges has been delineated with respect to collapse, but I would argue that the same set applies to other social evolutionary phenomena.

For example, the phenomena of contact, or intercivilizational encounters, pose exactly the same kinds of analytical difficulties.

These challenges, then, are relevant in multiple ways to the larger subject of this volume: culture in the cosmos. If we want to use humanity's past to make assessments about our own future—with or without the perturbation of contact from an extraterrestrial intelligence—or about possible trajectories of social evolution on other worlds, then these are the issues with which we must continue to grapple.

Theory And Method In Social Evolutionary Studies: The State of Key Debates

The foregoing sections have introduced the conspirators, including data, theory, and theorists, which make social evolution an intricate and often intractable research area, and have illustrated their actions in the context of a case study. These should be kept in mind as I now turn briefly to some key areas in the current literature concerning social evolution. This survey is far from comprehensive; it merely highlights a few debates, theories, and methodological approaches of specific relevance to social evolution in cosmic perspective. (A plethora of social scientific literature on social evolution exists, so those who seek more general overviews of this area may wish to consult Sanderson [1990, 2007] and Rousseau [2006], for example, as starting points.)

How Are Biological Evolution and Social Evolution Related?

It has been remarked that "[t]he analogy of society as an organism is old, attractive, and disreputable"—indeed, it dates back at least as far as Roman rhetoric (Back 1971, 660). The debate about whether this is an appropriate analogy, or indeed, whether biology and culture are related as analogs or as part of a continuous whole, is likewise old, attractive, and disreputable. Unfortunately, the debate about the real relationship of biological and cultural evolution has often revolved more around abstractions than reality, and has tended to be unresolvable because of its framing, not to mention touchy because of its implications for social justice.

An astounding amount of ink has been used on this discussion, much of it turning on semantics (e.g., what exactly should "evolution" be defined as including? What about "evolutionary theory"?), much of it fussing with arcane detail, and much of it along the lines of "if only my esteemed opponent was familiar with X body of work, it would be obvious that . . ." or other venerable academic versions of "yes it is/no it isn't." For example, scholars have argued at length over whether it is technically accurate to refer to cultural evolution as Lamarckian, on the grounds that genetic material is not actually changed by the acquisition of new cultural traits (Hodgson and Knudsen 2006). As with any other longstanding debate of this form, this hints at something interesting about the construction of knowledge, but tells us rather little about the world.

And yet it *is* important to know whether Darwinism's applicability to cultural traits (e.g., in archaeology) is strictly in the realm of metaphor, or not metaphorical at all (O'Brien et al. 2003). The history of social evolutionary theory and Darwinian biological evolutionary theory can be of help here, because these discourses do have a familial relationship, though not in the way usually assumed. It is often supposed that ideas about social evolution derive from the theory of biological evolution, but in fact, many of the concepts in Darwinian evolutionary theory actually developed from social theory. As anthropologist Christopher Hallpike noted,

> The idea that societies have developed according to some regular principles was current long before it was supposed that biological species could ever change. Aristotle, Lucretius, Ibn-Khaldun, Vico, Hume, Hegel, Comte, and Marx all developed theories of social evolution independently of any contribution of biology, many of whose evolutionary concepts have in fact been derived from social prototypes— 'competition,' 'adaptation,' 'selection,' 'fitness,' 'progress,' and so on. (1988, 29)

Indeed, when Darwin first published, this migration of concepts was wryly remarked upon by one of his contemporaries:

> Darwin, whom I have looked up again, amuses me when he says he is applying the 'Malthusian' theory also to plants and animals, as if with Mr. Malthus the whole point were not that he does not apply the theory to plants and animals but only to human beings—and with geometrical progression—

as opposed to plants and animals. It is remarkable how Darwin recognizes among beasts and plants his English society with its division of labour, competition, opening-up of new markets, 'inventions,' and the Malthusian 'struggle for existence.' It is Hobbes's *bellum omnium contra omnes*, and one is reminded of Hegel's *Phenomenology*, where civil society is described as a 'spiritual animal kingdom,' while in Darwin the animal kingdom figures as civil society. . . .

(Karl Marx, in a letter to Engels,
18 June 1962 in McLellan 2000, 565)

No wonder, then, that the broad contours of biological evolutionary theory can be easily applied to social evolution, since Darwinism itself is deeply imbued with18th and 19th century social theory refracted through the natural kingdom. But the question remains, to what extent is modern-day biological evolutionary theory, with all its post-Darwin refinements and extensions, applicable to social evolution?

It seems an odd question to some scholars, given the plethora of disanalogies between biological and social evolution, which include: the genotype/phenotype distinction in biology (no solid cultural equivalent), the horizontal as well as bidi-rectional vertical transmission of cultural traits, the fact that cultural change can be truly intentional or teleological, and the disparate and interdependent nature of cultural traits (ideas/behaviors/words/things). For some, it is hard to imagine that the theory and methodology for studying the biological evolution of spe-cies, or their traits, could be appropriate for studying cultural change within a society, or the evolution of societies in general. For others, however, it is seen as the only way forward. For example, in their recent article "Towards a unified sci-ence of cultural evolution," evolutionary psychologists Mesoudi et al. argue that there is essentially a one-to-one correspondence, i.e., the analytical approaches of Darwinian evolutionary biology are basically all that we need to understand cul-ture change, that "the structure of a science of cultural evolution should broadly resemble the structure of evolutionary biology," and that we should be working towards "the cultural equivalent of molecular genetics" (2006, 329). They con-demn anthropology harshly for being "much less demonstratively productive" than evolutionary biology, "particularly in terms of establishing a secure body of data and theory that earns and deserves the attention of researchers working in sister disciplines," and wonder why anthropology is, compared to biology, such a failure (Mesoudi et al. 2006, 328). The answer, they contend, is anthropolo-gists' comparative unwillingness to use "simplifying assumptions" and "crude but workable methods" to render complex systems tractable, and thus "contribute to the steady accumulation of reliable knowledge that will ultimately form the basis of a sophisticated understanding of the phenomena in question" (2006, 330).

Some anthropologists' replies are predictably testy. Commentary upon the article shows considerable skepticism about Mesoudi and colleagues' convictions about the best way forward (see individual respondents' remarks at the end of Mesoudi et al. 2006). We also might wonder whether Mesoudi et al. were aware of sophisticated work being done at centers like the AHRC Centre for the Evolution of Cultural Diversity in the U.K., and the School of Evolution and Social Change at Arizona State University. But ultimately, their critique bangs up against a problem described earlier in this chapter, i.e., that anthropologists have good reasons for their attitude. The social consequences of a crudely reductionist approach to, say, fruit fly genetics are probably trivial compared to the demonstrated results of reducing human beings or their societies into conveniently tractable analytical units, suitable for a provisional, rough analysis. As noted previously, governments have an unpleasant habit of acting on as-yet-incomplete and maybe-not-quite-precisely-accurate analyses concerning the relationships of nature and nurture, genes and behavior, and some cultures to others. They disenfranchise, colonize, sterilize, enslave, segregate, displace, 'reeducate,' incarcerate, and murder people on the basis of such analyses. Therefore, many anthropologists would argue that we cannot afford to simplify our subjects because of the potential cost in human suffering.

At any rate, the general debate about biological evolution and social evolution continues (e.g., Cordes 2006, Nunn et al. 2006, Nelson 2006) and seems unlikely to conclude anytime soon. Nelson (2006) argues persuasively that the narrow form of what he calls "Universal Darwinism" should be rejected by social scientists—not because of the philosophical and moral issues of reductionism noted above, but simply because cramming the details of social phenomena into a biological framework does not work. However, he suggests that the broader form of Universal Darwinism may be roomy enough for us. He writes:

> The most prominent variety of Universal Darwinism argues for close counterparts between the variables and mechanisms of cultural evolution and biological evolution, for example proposing the concept of "memes" as units of culture. Other Universal Darwinists propose, more flexibly, that human culture and biological species both change over

time through a process that involves variation and selection, but that the details of the processes may be very different. . . . [T]he narrower form of Universal Darwinism should not be acceptable to social scientists. The differences in the details of cultural evolution and biological evolution are considerable. On the other hand, if Universal Darwinism provides a roomy intellectual tent welcoming scholars studying a variety of topics, with the unifying element being a dynamic theory involving variation and selection, but with the key variables and mechanisms being recognized as perhaps differing greatly between biology and human culture, we can be happy in that camp. (Nelson 2006, 491).

That said, it may be most productive for all concerned to focus less on theoretical positioning, and more on questions that can actually be empirically evaluated. For example, there has been some intriguing work about the use of specific methods originating in evolutionary biology to study culture.

Recently, Nunn et al. (2006) used a computer simulation to evaluate the sensitivity of two comparative methods to different levels of horizontal transmission of cultural traits. Rather than just assuming or disputing the suitability of methods borrowed from evolutionary biology, the team specifically tested the use of phylogenetic comparative methods in cross-cultural comparisons. These methods rely on principles including the use of phylogenetic trees to represent relationships between human societies, and the vertical transmission of cultural traits along this tree, from ancestors to descendants, resulting in cultural evolution by descent with modification. Given that some scholars have indeed been using such phylogenetic methods to study culture change, Nunn et al. elected to test their sensitivity to a number of variables using computer simulations. Ultimately, they found that these methods are appropriate only in quite specific conditions, and that they are considerably confounded by horizontal transmission, which is a common cultural phenomenon. They suggest that more empirical data concerning rates of horizontal transmission would help enormously in creating new statistical approaches to questions of culture change.

Other researchers have been working to create precise mathematical models of key processes in cultural evolution. For example, 'demographic transition'—a group of effects including reductions in mortality and fertility, and an increase in socioeconomic development—shows puzzling variability in its onset in different societies (Borenstein et al. 2006). Mathematical models drawing by analogy from evolutionary biology's concept of 'niche construction,' whereby an organism modifies its own environment, can explain this to a certain extent. Borenstein and colleagues note that one cultural trait, such as degree of education, is transmitted vertically from generation to generation, changing the cultural environment and affecting the horizontal transmission of other cultural traits such as fertility control (2006, 93). What is notable in this particular case, however, is the modesty of the authors in understanding that such models may have explanatory power and lead to useful understandings about cultural change, and yet at the same time be severely limited in their capacity to accurately and fully represent the real world.

These kinds of studies are helpful in moving the discussion forward. Another way forward lies in the renovation of evolutionary biology itself.

A New Modern Synthesis and Holistic Darwinism

Theories of social evolution have often been substantially entangled with theories of biological evolution in two ways: first, through analogy, and second, through 'grand theories' that combine the realms of the biological and the social into a single explanatory framework. Therefore, recent shifts in biological models herald changes in theories of social evolution.

There is a growing sense among some evolutionary biologists that the 'Modern Synthesis' of the 1940s requires a significant update; the accumulation of new understandings in biology has triggered a theoretical crisis (Pennisi 2008). The 'Modern Synthesis' combined Darwin's ideas about natural selection with genetics, and included the now-familiar processes of natural selection, sexual selection, and genetic drift, etc., which work upon variations produced through genetic mechanisms like mutation and recombination. Now, advances in genome mapping, proteomics, knowledge of gene regulation and epigenetic modifications, amongst other areas, calls for a fuller integration of molecular biology into evolutionary theory, and indeed, these subjects are now being fused at the undergraduate level.

Similarly, Peter Corning notes that present-day evolutionary theory has absorbed many critiques of neo-Darwinism, and incorporates a variety of new emphases: evolution as a multilevel process, group selection theory, symbiosis, symbiogenesis, advanced game theory, phenotypic plasticity/organism-environment interactions, social learning/cultural transmission, the nuances of the genome, hierarchy theory, systems biology, autocatalysis, self-organization, and network dynamics (Corning 2005, 1–2). He suggests, therefore, that a new paradigm is emerging: "Holistic Darwinism," according to Corning, is a convergence of research which challenges the individualistic, selfish-gene theory, and endeavors to better explain the evolution of complex biological systems by incorporating theories of cooperation and synergy. Instead of just the selfish gene, we also have the "selfish genome." In this paradigm, the relationship between genes, phenotypes, and higher levels of organization is bidirectional: the latter are not mere epiphenomena, but "distinct evolutionary units" which influence the fate of their components (Corning 2005, 2). The emphasis within this body of ideas upon synergy, teleonomy, emergence, cybernetics processes, and superorganisms, lends itself beautifully to the study of human cultures and political systems (Corning 2005, 4).

Corning argues that this body of work holds significant unifying potential. Most researchers in the social sciences have assumed that human societies are largely governed not by biology but by cultural systems, and as noted—given the 20th century's history of racism and genocide justified in scientific language—have been exceptionally wary of doctrines evoking biological determinism. Accordingly, for example, many rejected the implications of E. O. Wilson's *Sociobiology: The New Synthesis* (1975) as ominous anathema. But what if evolutionary biology itself continues to become better balanced, less reductionist, more able to describe complex, higher-order systems? What if, for example, the substantial evidence for cooperation and synergy in nature took its place alongside the evidence for competition (Corning 2005, 24)? Perhaps then, Corning suggests, a fusion of biological reasoning and social science might be palatable to more social scientists.

One example of contemporary substantial cross-over between the biological sciences and the social sciences is to be found in complexity theory.

Coping with Complexity: Emergence

The study of complex systems is an interdisciplinary endeavor which is changing many fields of inquiry concerning natural, artificial, and human systems. In systems with interacting agents, nonlinear, unpredictable properties and effects can emerge; computational models are increasingly shedding light upon how this works. This may well revolutionize the study of social evolution, because it opens up new ways of understanding social change both today and long ago.

Much existential angst has been experienced by those working with the past when it comes to establishing causality. A great deal of archaeological theory of recent decades has focused upon the question of how we know what we know, and the limits of that knowledge; when there are multiple potential explanations for any observed pattern in the archaeological record, and few opportunities for straightforward hypothetico-deductive reasoning, what is one to do? In other words, we may be able to describe more or less *what* happened, but establishing *why* is altogether more fraught—particularly if one is thinking in linear terms.

Bentley and Maschner (2007) point out that decades ago, archaeologists were inclined to conceive of social systems as tending towards equilibrium, and to think about cultural evolution as being societies transitioning from one steady state to another through either positive or negative feedback. This was obviously problematic in multiple ways, both theoretical and practical, and so complexity theory is useful in considering social systems with many interacting agents. Most important, complexity theory's collection of approaches helps us in thinking about emergence, or the unpredictable appearance of new, complex properties in social systems as they increase in size, or as our scales of analysis change.

Through work at the Santa Fe Institute and Britain's Centre for the Evolutionary Analysis of Cultural Behaviour, amongst other centers, complexity theory's suite of approaches is gaining popularity among archaeologists. The time is right because the necessary computing power is now readily available, and the general orientation of complexity theory is well suited to the particular dilemmas of understanding past societies. On the whole, their aim is to understand the emergent properties of complex systems—e.g., the effect of modifying different variables, which is arguably more fruitful than trying to precisely predict the system's trajectory (Bentley and Maschner 2007). They also emphasize the interactions between agents (i.e., people!), in contrast to environmental determinist approaches, which privilege environmental variables and suppose that human beings always act rationally in relation to resources, which in reality, they manifestly do not. And, furthermore, complexity theory reorients our thinking about social evolution away from simplistic reductionist Darwinian approaches that emphasize the vertical transmission of cultural traits, and helps us explore the horizontal spread of ideas and things.

More specifically, Bentley and Maschner (2007) note that complexity theory is finding application in:

- the observation of power-law distributions, e.g., for accumulation of material wealth and prestige
- new theories about the behavior of networks, e.g., in the exchange of goods and ideas
- the description of neutral or random copying of ideas from one individual to another, eventually producing scale effects, without any particular advantage or attachment to the idea (which is a useful counter to the notion that if a trait is dominant, it must be selectively advantageous in some way)

- accounting for episodes of abrupt change or punctuated equilibrium
- understanding, via chaos theory, how tiny variations in system input can have huge effects
- exploration of self-organized critical states which hover on the edge between stasis and chaos (drawing from Stuart Kauffman's 'NK landscapes')
- mapping information cascades, including the fractal behavior of information spread
- agent-based modeling, including simulations of colonization events and the spread of agriculture, which can demonstrate the effects of various inputs into the system (e.g., varying mortality and fertility rates)

This is clearly a fruitful direction for research into social evolution. However, it, too, will have limits and liabilities in its application, as illustrated by the case of the rank-size analysis of cities. Cities in a nation have an intriguing tendency to follow a log-normal distribution, whereby the second-largest city's population is half the size of the largest city's population, and the third-largest city's population is one-third the size, etc. This has had interesting effects among archaeological researchers: first, some have focused their efforts upon explaining deviations from this pattern; and second, some have attempted to use rank-size analysis to make sense of patterns among tiny, nonurban communities, to which the model was never intended to apply (Smith and Schrieber 2006, 16) The success of the mathematical model in explaining *some* patterns thus exerts a sort of methodological tyranny. Nonetheless, it contributes to our arsenal of tools with which to understand the past.

Another area of social evolution research that has been greatly facilitated by improvements in computing—in this case, databases—is the area of cross-cultural comparison, or hologeistic studies.

Throwing the Database at the Questions

There are two basic ways to examine long-term cultural change: first, by using synchronic ethnographic data and attempting to track backwards by comparing different coexisting cultures; and second, by using diachronic archaeological/historic data and comparing successive cultures along a particular shared trajectory. This is the subject of an old division in anthropology, going back to 1896, when Franz Boas denounced the unilineal evolutionism of his contemporaries Spencer, Morgan, and Tylor. When comparing different societies, they tended to assume that similar patterns must be the result of similar processes—that correlations imply the same causation—while Boas argued that the same cultural pattern can arise in multiple societies from different, indeed unique, historical trajectories. Boas argued that appropriate anthropological methods should trace each society's development independently, an orientation that has remained at odds with cross-cultural comparisons (Chrisomalis 2006, 379). To this day, most cross-cultural comparisons use ethnographic rather than historical data; they compare societies as though they are frozen in time. Further, Chrisomalis (2006) notes, in hologeistic studies, archaeological data tend to be treated as ethnographic data, which drastically underuses their potential.

Chrisomalis pleads for a methodological shift towards a greater use of archaeological data of key events for the study of cross-cultural processes of change—that is, he argues that we should use the *event* rather than the entire *culture* as the unit of analysis. He demonstrates through a very interesting study in historical ethnomathematics, examining the advent of numerical notation systems in different societies, e.g., Roman, Greek, Inka, Babylonian, Hindu-Arabic, and Chinese. His results show multilinear evolution at work: multiple *different* processes of transformation and replacement produced the same overall trend away from cumulative/additive systems, such as Roman numerals, and towards ciphered/positional systems, such as Hindu-Arabic numerals (Chrisomalis 2006, 393).

This kind of approach holds a great deal of promise. In the past, there have been many empirical analyses testing specific points of various social evolutionary theories against particular case studies, and there have also been many attempts at general theoretical syntheses. However, there have been fewer attempts to bring the full force of all our comparative ethnographic and archaeological data to bear upon social evolutionary questions. As electronic databases improve in comprehensiveness and accessibility, it is becoming increasingly possible. Substantial efforts in archaeological data management (e.g., the Archaeological Data Service in the U.K., the Digital Archaeological Record project at Arizona State University, and the Archaeoinformatics initiative) have been initiated in the last two decades, partly for the safe preservation and sharing of archaeological data—a perennial issue in a discipline with artifacts, maps, notes, field logs, photographs, and sketches, as well as more quantitative data—but also as a means of tackling questions that require extensive comparison between sites and cultures.

These enhanced databases can be used to pioneer new approaches, like Chrisomalis's, or to reuse old ones. For example, using the electronic Human Relations Area Files Collection of Archaeology, Peregrine et al. (2004)

recently resurrected an analytical approach pioneered some 50 years ago and explored in anthropology during the 1960s: Guttman scaling. This method identifies a clear hierarchy among a group of traits. In a Guttman scale, at the top are traits that imply the presence of the traits listed below them. Peregrine et al. argue that if traits form a Guttman scale, there are clear evolutionary implications. That is, following Carneiro, "the order in which the traits are arranged, from bottom to top, is the order in which the societies have evolved them" (Carneiro 1970, cited in Peregrine et al. 2004, 145).

Using a random sample of 20 archaeological cases from the eHRAF, Peregrine et al. found a clear Guttman scale of traits, as follows:

- Writing
- Towns exceeding 1,000 in population
- Political state of 10,000 in population
- Full-time craft specialists
- Full-time government specialists
- Social stratification or slavery
- Subsistence economy based on food production
- Intersocietal trade

That is, if there is an economy based on food production (i.e., farming, rather than hunting/foraging), then there must be intersocietal trade, and so on up the hierarchy with the presence of writing indicating the presence of all the other traits. Peregrine et al. infer, on the basis of this scale's validity in their sample of 20 cases, "that there are general sequences in cultural evolution that hold for both historic and prehistoric cases. While not all cases must evolve in precisely this way, a valid Guttman scale cannot occur unless most cases behave in the manner described in the scale" (2004, 147).

While the general association of these traits would not be a surprise to anyone who teaches Intro to Ancient Civilizations, this assertion of a general sequence in cultural evolution *would* be surprising to many, because as the authors note, among anthropologists, "while it is widely accepted that cultures have generally become more complex over time, it is not widely accepted that societies generally develop traits in ordered evolutionary sequences" (Peregrine et al. 2004, 145). And indeed, analyses like these may still not necessarily compel such a conclusion. Long-established critiques question the evolutionary significance of Guttman scales. For example, Farrell (1969) noted that to subscribe to the argument that a Guttman scale demonstrates an evolutionary sequence is to assume precisely that which needs to be proven—and that the argument is subject to empirical testing with cases that are better documented than the average prehistoric society. His test with a modern ethnographic case showed that the existence of a Guttman scale does *not* accurately predict an evolutionary sequence. And so, he argued, "evolutionary inferences from Guttman scale patterns must be made with considerable caution" (1969, 280). Moreover, he wondered whether the use of the evolutionary metaphor can cause a distortion in thinking about patterns of development; perhaps we should be focusing on the variations instead of the commonalities.

Chrisomalis (2006) notes, too, that Guttman scales don't work with some common patterns in history, such as the replacement of one trait by another (instead of the retention of the oldest trait and accumulation of additional ones), or the simple loss of traits instead of their addition. Further, Guttman scalograms fail to capture multilinearity and do not actually establish direct evolutionary connections between traits, or tell us anything about the processes of cultural change; the mere fact that fire-agriculture-writing-steam engines would produce a perfect Guttman scale for any number of cultures doesn't tell us much about the real relationship of those variables (Chrisomalis 2006, 384).

Peregrine et al. did attempt a test of the hypothesis that the cultural traits on their Guttman scale evolved in a sequence. Tracing the actual chronological development of societies in eight world regions, ranging from the Nile River Valley to the Yellow River valley to Highland Peru, they found that the sequence generally held, but that traits often emerge simultaneously in the archaeological record in bursts that they refer to as "punctuated equilibrium." So, for example, "once social stratification evolves both government and craft specialists also evolve . . . once the population of polities grows above 10,000, both cities and writing tend to appear . . . once sedentarism evolves so does social inequality and a reliance on domesticates" (2004, 148). Again, these clusters of traits would come as no surprise to anthropologists, who have tended to classify cultures typologically according to their degree of complexity; although the classic classification of 'band–tribe–chiefdom–state' is deeply contested, such labels are still a useful, common shorthand for the sorts of characteristics a society displays. The sequence is not particularly surprising, either, given the causal connections between some of these traits.

What *is* surprising is the conclusion of Peregrine and colleagues: that these clusters can be seen as "evolutionary 'stages,' similar to those proposed by a number of anthropologists in the middle of the last century that are now considered highly suspect. . . . We conclude that there are universal patterns in cultural evolution" (2004, 149). This statement is startling because of its boldness in the face of most current anthropological thinking—wherein

multilinear rather than unilinear evolution is heavily emphasized, simplifi-
cations are discouraged, and claims about universals are eschewed—but also
because it appears to move from an interesting pattern in a specific dataset
to an incredibly general conclusion. Claims to universal patterns in cultural
evolution have to contend with a host of questions. For example: Are there
universal patterns for hunting/foraging societies and industrial civilizations
as well as ancient civilizations? Is the strength of the pattern spurious because
the analysis is based upon selected early civilizations that arrived at similar
end points? What about those which arrived at different end points? What
about the societies that had or have, for example, food production but no
slavery? Those that had towns exceeding 1,000 in population but no writing?
Those that had or have intersocietal trade and no food production? Were they
merely halted on their inexorable evolutionary journey by historical events?
Did they not have enough time? Or was some crucial variable lacking to
propel them into the next 'stage'? What if we choose other criteria for studying social complexity, criteria other than these traditional anthropological
variables of writing, craft specialization, etc.? Is there still a 'universal pattern'?
And finally, of course: *Why?* If there is indeed a universal pattern, is it because
of a single organizing principle or mechanism, or because of a series of interconnected processes? As Chrisomalis (2006, 385) puts it, "[f]or any theory of
cultural evolution to be validated, moreover, the how and why questions must
be answered satisfactorily, not simply 'in what order.'"

The hows and whys *can* be tackled. For example, a key step along the
way to civilization was the consolidation of larger communities; this ran
counter to an established trend of villages fissioning, and set the stage for
the emergence of institutionalized social inequality. Given the importance of
the phenomenon, some anthropologists and archaeologists have attempted
to formally model the fissioning process through concepts such as an "irrita-
tion coefficient"—which notes that causes of conflict escalate geometrically
in relation to population size—or "scalar stress," which emphasizes the possibility of new institutions emerging to handle the new social and informational demands of a society in conflict due to expanding population size and
intensifying population density (Bandy 2004, 323). Cost-benefit analysis can
be used to analyze the probability of a village fissioning, considering factors
such as resource depletion, internal conflict, self-defence against neighbor-
ing communities, and availability of land. A formal evolutionary approach
thus produces hypotheses—e.g., "a regional system of villages with a steadily
increasing population can be expected to demonstrate an initially high rate
of fissioning followed by a cessation of fissioning and the appearance of the

materialized manifestations of higher-level integrative practices" (Bandy 2004, 324)—which are at least somewhat amenable to testing with ethnographic and archaeological data. However, even though some case studies lend support to this particular hypothesis, it does not suggest the model is *universally* applicable, not least because in human societies, ideology (e.g., egalitarianism) can and does override other forces (Bandy 2004, 332).

In sum, vast quantities of ethnographic and archaeological data are increasingly available to us, with which to try new ways of searching for patterns and interrogating our assumptions about social evolution. In conjunction with new ways of understanding complex systems, this bodes well for future studies. But even so, substantial dilemmas may remain. One of the most important is the question of the relative roles of contingency and convergence in evolution.

Contingency vs. Convergence

This is a perennial question in both biological and social evolution, and a key problem currently being tackled in astrobiology (Chyba 2005). It is crucial to the matter of life on other worlds (Dick 1999)—intelligent or otherwise—because if the influence of contingency on evolution substantially outweighs that of convergence, we probably have rather worse odds of discovering any life elsewhere, much less conversing with it. It is also, independently and in its own way, crucial to the social sciences. Indeed, the archaeologist and historian Bruce Trigger noted towards the end of his long career, that "[t]he most important issue confronting the social sciences is the extent to which human behaviour is shaped by factors that operate cross-culturally as opposed to factors that are unique to particular cultures . . . At the centre of this debate is a fundamental question: given the biological similarities and the cultural diversity of human beings, how much the same or how differently are they likely to behave under analogous circumstances?" (Trigger 2003, 3).

There is no consensus, but because the question is so crucial to understanding humanity, many are currently using hologeistic studies to address it. Trigger's own assessment, after comparing seven early civilizations, is that the truth lies somewhere in the middle; there are enough significant consistencies and variations that we can say neither that social evolution is driven by convergence nor that it is driven by contingency (2003, 684–688).

For now, then, this remains a big question of history, which advancing theory and method and ever-improving data, may help us to better understand. There are many more questions like it, but I will briefly address only two more, of particular pertinence to 'culture in the cosmos': what happens when civilizations encounter others, and how long do civilizations last?

Interactions Between Civilizations

What happens when different civilizations meet? 'Contact' and its sequelae are, of course, important matters within the subject of culture in the cosmos. Hypothetical future encounters between *Homo sapiens* and intelligent beings from another world have long been a popular topic for speculation. Thus, "intercivilizational encounters" on Earth, to borrow a term from Arnason (2006), might be considered a prime area to search for information on what happens when disparate cultures meet—as anthropologists have frequently noted when commenting upon SETI (Dick 2006).

However, this is also a surprisingly difficult subject. In actuality, contact is much more complicated than it is usually made out to be. Further, notions about what civilizations are and how they interact, are so deeply entrenched that it is a challenge to recognize our cultural assumptions and biases. And, as with the case of collapse, contact between cultures occupies the realm of myths and legends about humanity's past, and is frequently the subject of cautionary tales and just-so stories.

Any nation's history is shaped by encounters with others, and this influences the way that we see history itself. For example, the Cold War was integral to American ideas about the unfolding of history, so much so that when communism fell in Europe and the Berlin Wall came down, the neoconservative political philosopher and American government policy advisor Francis Fukuyama suggested that we had reached "the end of history," i.e., the final stage of the global ideological and political evolution of humanity (Fukuyama 1992). This implies that two superpowers—two civilizations—can have a standoff, but that eventually, one system will triumph and subsume the other. This is interesting in itself, but of more significance here is the reply of Samuel Huntington, i.e., his model of the 'clash of civilizations,' based on the idea that although various modern innovations originating in the West (industrialization, etc.) have diffused worldwide, shared modernity is merely a shallow overlay on top of a much older and deeper structure of different civilizations with major disparities in worldviews and modes of thought. The perils of such a global condition are often belabored in political discussion. Crucially, this is not merely an academic matter, for the "clash of civilizations" concept underpins the contemporary American "war on terror," through the formulation of "the-West-against-the-rest" (Robertson 2006, 426). Indeed, Chen (2006, 427) wonders whether Huntington's 1993 "The Clash of Civilizations?" was "the most influential academic essay on Earth," and considers its "civilizationalism" to be "one of the most powerfully dangerous articulations emerging in the historical scene"—essentially an amplified right wing nationalism clothed in the guise of history.

The idea of "the clash of civilizations" has become particularly entrenched in American thought since September 2001, but it is only one way of representing intercivilizational encounters, which do, after all, run the gamut from conflict and conquest to coexisting interconnection to fusion (Arnason 2006). The case of India, Arnason notes, provides multiple useful examples: the outward spread of Buddhism from India to East Asia, Alexander's invasion, the long coexistence of Islam and Hinduism, and the period of British rule all demonstrate different patterns of intercivilizational encounter. Commonalities among these patterns include asymmetry, and violence and destruction, but also productivity, i.e., the generation of new cultural patterns. At the same time, some encounters leave comparatively little enduring change in traditions or ways of thinking.

Observing that there has not yet been a systematic attempt to create a typology of intercivilizational encounters, Arnason proposes a return to the theories of Benjamin Nelson, who regarded such encounters as being "contacts and confrontations between different macro- or meta-structures of consciousness [which] can, in principle, take a wide variety of forms: some encounters lead to unilateral assimilation, [while] others are conducive to innovations which may affect the most central structures of consciousness" (Arnason 2006, 45–46). Ultimately, Arnason suggests, the "clash of civilizations" is not real, but an artifact of a way of thinking about what a civilization is; it is more fruitful to think of a "mobile labyrinth of civilizations, all of them caught up in the modern transmutation, but each of them possessing specific legacies and resources that can be activated in inventive ways" (2006, 52). Similarly, Robertson argues that even the concept of a "civilization" is loaded with "considerable ideological and perspectival baggage" (2006, 422).

There is an incredible wealth of historical and anthropological data at our disposal concerning 'contact,' but to use it well requires preparation. If we can think in the broadest possible terms about what a civilization is, appreciate the full range of their possible interactions, and suspend our belief in the mythologies of our continents and nations—whether about the 'discovery' of the New World by the Old, the defeat of communism by capitalism, or the war on terror—then we will be better situated to understand the information we have about past contacts on Earth.

This is important both for an academic understanding of contact processes, and for another reason. The history of exploration on Earth has shown that often, people find largely what they expect to find. For example, the earliest illustrations of the New World drawn by people from the Old World, included portraits of dog-headed cannibals—a species that many medieval Europeans assumed existed in faraway lands (but to this day never encountered by modern science). It is little wonder, then, that European monarchs and religious leaders found it easy to treat the peoples of the New World as less than fully human. We all have a remarkable capacity to slot our observations into preconceived frameworks, and act accordingly. In other words, our intellectual models of contact *generate* history as surely as they recount it.

The Future: Of Bombs and Bottlenecks

What lies ahead for humanity? How can we know? And how long might extraterrestrial societies endure?

Crystal balls aside, there are two primary modes of reckoning our future: extrapolation from our present circumstances, and projection based on our knowledge of the paths of civilizations which came before us. Central to both are our deepest hopes and fears about human nature, and our beliefs about the tools we create and the societies we make.

Within the context of 'culture in the cosmos,' the Drake factor "L," or the lifetime of transmitting civilizations, is frequently discussed since SETI's chances of success may depend upon it (Shostak this volume, Sagan 1980, Denning in press and citations therein). Of course, there is a distinction to be drawn between the civilization's actual lifetime, and the period during which the civilization is "on the air," there being a host of reasons other than extinction which might cause a civilization to 'go dark' in different portions of the EM spectrum (Drake 2008). Both lines of inquiry tend to revolve around our beliefs about the evolution of technology whether for communications or for weaponry. These in turn tend to rest on a unilineal, progressivist model of technological evolution—i.e., that if radio technology develops on another world, so, probably, will weapons of mass destruction—despite abundant evidence from the history of science and technology that our 'stuff' evolves in less predictable and necessary ways (Denning 2007c).

Both discussions—about our own future and about the hypothetical life course of extraterrestrial civilizations—illustrate our deep ambivalence about technology. Some of of humanity's oldest myths concern the double edge of the technological sword. With increasing knowledge and godlike power, as the stories go, comes great peril. The tales of Adam and Eve, Prometheus, and Pandora, and the Mayan story of the Rebellion of the Tools, all speak of the risks of knowing too much, having too much power, or wielding technology inappropriately. And today, humanity does have powers previously known only to the gods of legend, and gathers more each day. Guesses about where this will lead are frequently based on ideas about human nature, themselves often rooted in ideas about biological and social evolution. They play off our tendencies towards aggression, competition, and revenge against our predilections for altruisim, cooperation, and reciprocity, and make much of the fact that we have "stone age minds and the might of the gods" (Small and Jollands 2006, 347) or, as Ronald Wright put it, that "we are running twenty-first century software on hardware last upgraded 50,000 years ago" (2004, 35).

Some are cautiously optimistic, suggesting that there is a period of intense danger, or a bottleneck, that comes with the advent of weapons of mass destruction, but that civilizations could develop the ethical frameworks necessary to live with such technologies indefinitely, or that spacefaring technology would tend to evolve at about the same time, offering protection against extinction (Sagan 1980, Shostak this volume). Others argue that in the human case, the accidental and incidental impacts of modern technology, combined with the potential malevolent uses of it, leave us at great risk. One noteworthy analysis by Small and Jollands draws upon biological and cultural evolutionary thinking to predict both the diffusion of lethal technologies—consider the increasing number of individuals and groups with access to nuclear weapons—and a corresponding escalation in the destructive potential of aggressive elements of society, i.e., the "hawks" among us. The authors note that "the very people who are the most evolutionarily unsuited to living in a technologically advanced world are most likely to predominate in the corridors of power," which is a concern not only because of their potential for deliberate malevolent use of technology, but also because "hawks" are more likely to "ignore incidental causes of harm to nature or society and to deny the risk of unforeseeable or accidental causes. They are also likely to claim that the future can take care of itself and to advocate technological optimism, unrestrained growth and consumerism as appropriate economic and political philosophies" (Small and Jollands 2006, 352).

All this is important, not only for our own future—which could use more rigorous attention (Lupisella et al. 2003)—and not only for estimates of "L," but also for our characterizations of hypothetical extraterrestrial civilizations. Will those who have survived long enough to be detected by us be peaceful or hostile? Opinions about this question shape debates about present-day policy here on Earth concerning our own transmissions to space (Michaud 2007). Thus, despite the already abundant literature forecasting our own future and hypothesizing about extraterrestrial civilizations' possible pasts, it may yet benefit from further hologeistic investigations concerning the evolution of technology on Earth, and simulations using some of the new analytical methods sketched earlier.

Summary

In sum, diverse approaches to the study of social evolution are currently in play. Some old debates concerning the precise relationship of biological evolution and social evolution continue, and seem unlikely to disappear, but the overall discourse is increasingly being shaped by developments in the study of complex systems, the advent of better computing power, and advances in electronic archiving of archaeological and anthropological data. Some key methodological issues can never be fully resolved—e.g., the nature of the data and the bias/standpoint of the observer—but the research community is clearly getting better at dealing with complex systems and is starting to ask better questions. Disciplinary differences are also unlikely to disappear, but even these are starting to blur in some new, potentially productive ways. For those interested in questions of culture in the cosmos, some particularly exciting routes forward include: potential new approaches to old questions (intercivilizational contact, the longevity of civilizations, the evolution of technology, and the roles of contingency and convergence in evolution); a heightened awareness of different modes of explanation, and careful attention to their strengths, weaknesses, and implications; a steadily improving understanding of biological change, which does feed into models of cultural change; a developing attention to how biology and culture are and are not similar; and, finally, an increasing appreciation for the significance of the stories we tell ourselves about our social worlds.

Conclusions

People have long studied social evolution to know who we are, how we got here, where we are going, and who Others are in relation to us. Now, we also wish to use social evolution to help us understand how the entire universe fits together, and to build theories of other intelligent beings in the cosmos. These are tall orders given that we might legitimately wonder how much we really grasp about the pasts of our own societies. And yet if we wish our inquiries to be grounded in the world instead of untethered abstractions, we must find ways to use the evidence we have. And although the study of culture in the cosmos is necessarily just beginning, it is now, truly, a work in progress.

Each line of investigation mentioned in this chapter has its challenges, weaknesses, and strengths, and these should be kept in mind when working across disciplinary lines, as we must do. To best use Earth cases in relation to cosmic questions, we need to understand the limits of the data, the methods used to study them, the reasons for which they have been studied, and the narratives and ideological positions they support. Without this kind of awareness, we run the risk of importing biased, oversimplified factoids and theories into the study of culture in the cosmos, and missing out on real discoveries. It is better yet to design our own cosmos-oriented empirical studies about cultural evolutionary processes and technological evolution, rather than borrowing the results of research designed for other purposes. There may be tremendous strength in fusing the bold hypotheses of the hard sciences with the cautions and caveats of the social sciences. As humanity's investigation of space proceeds and the frame within which we see ourselves becomes ever-larger, support for this kind of research may grow.

These are exciting times: after centuries of trying, we may yet develop rigorous, inclusive approaches that can do justice to all humanity's experiences, and can explain history's patterns without oversimplifying them or disrespecting its agents. This would itself be a hugely meaningful accomplishment, and a cosmic perspective can only help us achieve it. And then if, someday, we discover another, distant dataset, we may better know how to see it.

Acknowledgments

My thanks go to many members of the SETI community for fascinating discussions about the possible characteristics of extraterrestrial societies and how we think about them. My colleagues and students in anthropology at York University keep me immersed in a rich anthropological environment, and Derek Douglas provided valuable library assistance while he was a research student there. Part of this work was written while I stayed at the Green Bank Observatory in West Virginia; I greatly appreciate the hospitality of that community of scientists. This paper was completed while I was on sabbatical from York, for which I am grateful to my department and to Robert Drummond, Dean of the Faculty of Arts. Billions of human beings, alive and dead, furnished mindboggling data. I am also indebted to the editors, Steve Dick and Mark Lupisella, for their invitation, inspiration, and epic patience.

References

Aberle, David. 1989. Review of *The Eighth Day: Social Evolution and the Self-Organization of Energy*, by Richard Newbold Adams. *American Anthropologist* 91, no 3 (September 1989): 776–777.

Allen, T. F. H., Joseph A. Tainter, J. Chris Pires, and Thomas W. Hoekstra. 2001. "Dragnet Ecology—'Just the Facts, Ma'am'—The Privilege of Science in a Postmodern World," *Bioscience* 51(6): 475.

Arnason, Johann. 2006. "Understanding Intercivilizational Encounters," *Thesis Eleven* 86:39–53.

Arnold, Bettina. 1992. "The past as propaganda: How Hitler's archaeologists distorted European prehistory to justify racist and territorial goals," *Archaeology* (July/August)1992: 30–37.

Back, Kurt. 1971. "Biological Models of Social Change," *American Sociological Review* 36:660–667.

Bandy, Matthew S. 2004. "Fissioning, Scalar Stress, and Social Evolution in Early Village Societies," *American Anthropologist* 106(2): 322–333.

Basalla, George. 2006. *Civilized Life in the Universe: Scientists on Intelligent Extraterrestrials* (Oxford: Oxford University Press).

Bates, Robert H. 2008. *When Things Fell Apart: State Failure in Late-Century Africa* (Cambridge: Cambridge University Press).

Bentley, R. A. and H. D. G. Maschner. 2007. "Complexity Theory" in *Handbook of Archaeological Theories*. R. A. Bentley, H. D. G. Maschner, C. Chippendale, eds. (Lanham, MD: AltaMira Press), pp. 245–270.

Bintliff, John, ed. 1999. *Structure and Contingency: Evolutionary Processes in Life and Human Society* (London: Leicester University Press).

Borenstein, Elhanan, Jeremy Kendal, and Marcus Feldman. 2006. "Cultural niche construction in a metapopulation," *Theoretical Population Biology* 70: 92–104.

Boserup, Ester. 1965. *The Conditions of Agricultural Growth: The Economics of Agrarian Change under Population Pressure* (Chicago: Aldine).

Braudel, Fernand. 1980. *On History* (Chicago: Chicago University Press).

Carroll, Sean B. 2001. "Chance and necessity: the evolution of morphological complexity and diversity," *Nature* 409 (6823): 1102–1109.

Chen, Kuan-Hsing. 2006. "Civilizationalism," *Theory, Culture and Society* 23(2-3): 427.

Chrisomalis, Stephen. 2006. "Comparing Cultures and Comparing Processes: Diachronic Methods in Cross-Cultural Anthropology," *Cross-Cultural Research* 40: 377–404.

Chyba, Christopher. 2005. "Contingency and the Cosmic Perspective" in *The New Astronomy: Opening the Electromagnetic Window and Expanding Our View of Planet Earth*, Wayne Orchiston, ed. (Springer: Netherlands), pp. 27–39.

Chytry, Joseph. 2006. "California Civilization: Beyond the United States of America?" *Thesis Eleven* 85 (May): 8–36.

Clarke, David. 1973. "Archaeology: The Loss of Innocence," *Antiquity* 47(185): 6–18.

Close, David. 1985. "The Meaning of Revolution" in *Revolution: A History of the Idea*, edited by D. Close and C. Bridge. (London & Sydney: Croom Helm), pp. 1–14.

Coetzee, J. M. 1999. *The Lives of Animals* (Princeton, NJ: Princeton University Press).

Cordes, Christian. 2006. "Darwinism in economics: from analogy to continuity," *Journal of Evolutionary Economics* 16:529–541.

Corning, Peter. 2005. *Holistic Darwinism: Synergy, Cybernetics, and the Bioeconomics of Evolution* (Chicago: University of Chicago Press).

Costanza, Robert, Lisa Graumlich, Will Steffen, Carole Crumley, John Dearing, Kathy Hibberd, Rik Leemans, Charles Redman, and David Schimel. 2007. "Sustainability or Collapse: What Can We Learn from Integrating the History of Humans and the Rest of Nature?" *Ambio* 36 (7): 522–526. Available online: *www.igbp.kva.se/documents/Costanza_2007_Ambio.pdf*.

Daston, Lorraine and Peter Galison. 2007. *Objectivity* (New York: Zone Books).

Denning, Kathryn. In press. "'L' on Earth." In *Culture in the Cosmos: Extraterrestrial Life and Society,* (eds. Douglas Vakoch and Albert Harrison. Berghahn Press).

Denning, Kathryn. 2007a. "Cultural Evolution: An Introduction for Visionary Scientists and Scientific Visionaries." For NASA Ames conference, "The Future of Intelligence in the Cosmos." 30 June–1 July 2007, NASA Ames Research Center, Moffett Field, California. Organizers: Drs. Stephanie Langhoff, Carl Pilcher, Gregory Laughlin, Seth Shostak, Jill Tarter. (SETI Institute and NASA Ames Research Center.)

Denning, Kathryn. 2007b. "Cultural Evolution At Home . . . and Away?" Bioastronomy 2007 conference, San Juan, Puerto Rico, July 2007. Abstract in: *Astrobiology* 7(3): 480.

Denning, Kathryn. 2007c. "Being Technological," International Astronautical Federation—58th International Astronautical Congress 2007, vol. 2, pp. 1316–1329.

Denning, Kathryn. 2006. "Ten Thousand Revolutions: Conjectures about Civilizations." 57th International Astronautical Congress, IAC 2006, vol. 3, pp. 1682–1692.

Denning, Kathryn. 1999. "Apocalypse past/future: Archaeology and folklore, writ large." *Archaeology and Folklore* A. Gazin-Schwartz and C. Holtorf, eds. (London: Routledge), pp. 90–105.

Denning, Kathryn and Christopher Jones. 2005. "Historical consciousness and sustainable futures." Paper presented by Jones at World Futures

Studies Federation conference, Futures Generations for/by Future Generations. Corvinus University, Budapest, Hungary, 23 August 2005.

Demarest, Arthur A., Prudence M. Rice, and Don S. Rice, eds. 2004. *The Terminal Classic in the Maya lowlands: collapse, transition, and transformation* (Boulder, CO: Colorado University Press).

Diamond, Jared. 2005. *Collapse: How Societies Choose to Fail or Succeed* (New York: Penguin).

Diamond, Jared. 1997/2005. *Guns, Germs, and Steel: The Fates of Human Societies* (New York: W. W. Norton).

Dick, Steven J. 2006. "Anthropology and the Search for Extraterrestrial Intelligence: An historical view," *Anthropology Today* 22(2): 3–7.

Dick, Steven J. 1999. *The Biological Universe: The Twentieth Century Extraterrestrial Life Debate and the Limits of Science* (Cambridge: Cambridge University Press).

Diener, Paul. 1980. "On Distinguishing Functional Ecology and Evolution in Cultural Theory," *Central Issues in Anthropology* 2(2): 1–22.

Drake, Frank. 2008. "SETI: From Pioneering Research to Recent Achievements." Talk presented at *Searching for Life Signatures* conference, International Academy of Astronautics, 22 September 2008, UNESCO, Paris.

Farrell, Joseph. 1969. "Guttman Scales and Evolutionary Theory: An Empirical Examination Regarding Differentiation in Educational Systems," *Sociology of Education* 42(3): 271–283.

Feder, Kenneth. 2006. *Frauds, Myths, and Mysteries: Science and Pseudoscience in Archaeology*, 5th ed. (New York: McGraw Hill).

Fukuyama, Francis. 1992. *The End of History and the Last Man* (Free Press).

Fulford, Robert. 1999. *The Triumph of Narrative: Storytelling in the Age of Mass Culture* (Toronto: House of Anansi Press).

Gardner, Howard with Emma Laskin. 1996. *Leading Minds: An Anatomy of Leadership* (New York: Basic Books).

Glick, Thomas F. 2008. "The Anthropology of Race Across the Darwinian Revolution" in *A New History of Anthropology*, Henrika Kuklick, ed. (Oxford: Blackwell), pp. 225–241.

Gould, Stephen Jay. 1999. "Introduction: The scales of contingency and punctuation in history" in Bintliff, ed. *Structure and Contingency: Evolutionary Processes in Life and Human Society* (London: Leicester University Press).

Gould, Stephen Jay. 1996(1981). *The Mismeasure of Man* (New York: W.W. Norton & Co.).

Graham, Elizabeth. 2006. "An Ethnicity to Know." *Maya Ethnicity: The Construction of Ethnic Identity from Preclassic to Modern Times*, edited by Frauke Sachse. *Acta Mesoamerica*, vol. 19. (Markt Schwaben: Verlag Anton Saurwein), pp. 109–124.

Graham, Elizabeth. 2005. "Maya Political History," *Antiquity* 79(303): 210–214.

Graham, Elizabeth, 2004. "Lamanai Reloaded: Alive and Well in the Early Postclassic," *Research Reports in Belizean Archaeology* 1. Institute of Archaeology, NICH, Belize, Pp. 223–241.

Hall, Martin. 1984. "The Burden of Tribalism: The Social Context of Southern African Iron Age Studies," *American Antiquity* 49(3): 455–467.

Hallpike, Christopher R. 1988. *The Principles of Social Evolution* (Oxford: Clarendon Press).

Haraway, Donna. 1988. "Situated Knowledges: The Science Question in Feminism and the Privilege of Partial Perspectives," *Feminist Studies* 14(3): 575–599.

Harding, Sandra, ed. 2003. *The Feminist Standpoint Theory Reader* (London: Routledge).

Harré, Rom, Jens Brockmeier, and Peter Mühlhäusler. 1999. *Greenspeak: A Study of Environmental Discourse* (London: Sage Publications).

Hodgson, Geoffrey and Thorbjørn Knudsen. 2006. "Dismantling Lamarckism: why descriptions of socio-economic evolution as Lamarckian are misleading," *Journal of Evolutionary Economics* 16:343–366.

Holtorf, Cornelius. 2000–2007. "Beyond Analogies" *Monumental Past: The Life-histories of Megalithic Monuments in Mecklenburg-Vorpommern (Germany).* Electronic monograph. University of Toronto: Centre for Instructional Technology Development. *https://tspace.library.utoronto.ca/citd/holtorf/6.7.html.*

Huntington, Samuel P. 1993. "The Clash of Civilizations?" *Foreign Affairs,* 72(3): 22–49.

IRIN 2007. "SUDAN: Climate change—only one cause among many for Darfur conflict." 28 June 2007. IRIN NEWS (Integrated Regional Information Networks), *UN Office for the Coordination of Humanitarian Affairs.* Online: *www.irinnews.org/Report.aspx?ReportId=72985.*

Jenkins, Keith. 1991. *Re-thinking History* (London: Routledge).

Johnson, George. 2007. "A Question of Blame When Societies Fall," *New York Times,* Science section, 25 December 2007. Online: *www.nytimes.com/2007/12/25/science/25diam.html.*

Landau, Misia. 1991. *Narratives of Human Evolution* (New Haven, CT: Yale University Press).

Langhoff, Stephanie, Carl Pilcher, Greg Laughlin, Jill Tarter, and Seth Shostak, eds. 2007. "Workshop Report on the Future of Intelligence in the Cosmos." Report of a workshop jointly sponsored by NASA Ames Research Center, the SETI Institute, and the University of California at Santa Cruz, held at Ames, 30 June–1 July 2007. NASA Ames, Moffett Field, California.

Lupisella, Mark, Jerome Glenn, Christopher Jones, Jim Dator, James Dewar, David Fromkin, Jakub Ryzenko, Allen Tough, William Marshall, and Gill

Stuart. 2003. "The horizons project: Global mechanisms for long-term survival and development." 54th International Astronautical Congress of the International Astronautical Federation, the International Academy of Astronautics and the International Institute of Space Law, vol. 1, pp. 2641–2644.

MacEachern, Scott. 2006. "Africanist archaeology and ancient IQ: racial science and cultural evolution in the twenty-first century," *World Archaeology*, 38(1): 72–92.

Malthus, Thomas. 2004(1798). *An Essay on the Principle of Population* (Whitefish, MT: Kessinger Publishing reprints).

Marx, Karl. 1998(1845). *The German Ideology Including Theses on Feuerbach and Introduction to the Critique of Political Economy*. R. M. Baird and S. E. Rosenbaum, eds. (Amherst, NY: Prometheus Books).

McLellan, David, ed. 2000. *Karl Marx: Selected Writings* (Oxford: Oxford University Press).

Michaud, Michael. 2007. *Contact with Alien Civilizations* (New York: Copernicus Books).

Mesoudi, Alex, Andrew Whiten, and Kevin Laland. 2006. "Towards a unified science of cultural evolution," *Behavioural and Brain Sciences* 29:329–383.

Moon, Ban Ki. 2007. "A Climate Culprit in Darfur," *Washington Post* 16 June 2007:A15.

Nash, Roderick Frazier. 1989. *The Rights of Nature: A History of Environmental Ethics* (Madison, WI: University of Wisconsin Press).

Nelson, Richard. 2006. "Evolutionary social science and universal Darwinism," *Journal of Evolutionary Economics* 16:491–510.

Nunn, Charles L., Monique Borgerhoff Mulder, and Sasha Langley. 2006. "Comparative Methods for Studying Cultural Trait Evolution: A Simulation Study," *Cross-Cultural Research* 40:177–209.

O'Brien, Michael, R. Lee Lyman, and Robert D. Leonard. 2003. "What is Evolution? A Response to Bamforth," *American Antiquity* 68(3): 573–580.

Pennisi, Elizabeth. 2008. "Modernizing the Modern Synthesis," *Science* 321(5886): 196–197.

Peregrine, Peter, Carol Ember, and Melvin Ember. 2004. "Universal Patterns in Cultural Evolution: An Empirical Analysis Using Guttman Scaling," *American Anthropologist* 106(1): 145–149.

Powell, Eric A. 2008. "Do Civilizations Really Collapse?" *Archaeology* 61 vol. 2 (March/April 2008).

Rice, Prudence M., Arthur A. Demarest, and Don S. Rice. 2004. "The Terminal Classic and the 'Classic Maya Collapse' in Perspective," in Demarest, Arthur A., Prudence M. Rice, and Don S. Rice, eds. *The Terminal Classic in the Maya lowlands: collapse, transition, and transformation* (Boulder, CO: Colorado University Press). Available online: *www.famsi.org/reports/00085/section01.htm*.

Robertson, Roland. 2006. "Civilization," *Theory, Culture and Society* 23(2–3): 421–436.

Rousseau, Jerome. 2006. *Rethinking Social Evolution* (Montreal/Kingston: McGill-Queen's University Press).

Rorty, Richard. 1989. *Contingency, Irony, and Solidarity* (Cambridge: Cambridge University Press).

Rose, Mark. 1999. "Godzilla's Attacking Babylon!" *Archaeology* (22 September 1999). Available online (with worthwhile illustrations): *www.archaeology.org/online/features/godzilla*.

Sagan, Carl. 1980. *Cosmos*. (New York: Random House).

Sanderson, Stephen K. 2007. *Evolutionism and Its Critics: Deconstructing and Reconstructing an Evolutionary Interpretation of Human Society* (Boulder, CO: Paradigm Publishers).

Sanderson, Stephen K. 1990. *Social Evolutionism: A Critical History* (Oxford: Blackwell).

Schwartz, G. M. and John J. Nichols, eds. 2006. *After Collapse: The Regeneration of Complex Societies.* (Tucson, AZ: University of Arizona Press).

Small, Bruce and Nigel Jollands. 2006. "Technology and ecological economics: Promethean technology, Pandorian potential," *Ecological Economics* 56(3): 343–358.

Smith, Michael E. and Katharina J. Schrieber. 2006. "New World States and Empires: Politics, Religion, and Urbanism," *Journal of Archaeological Research* 14 (1): 1–52.

Steward, Julian. 1955. *Theory of Culture Change: The Methodology of Multilinear Evolution* (Champaign, IL: University of Illinois Press).

Staubwasser, Michael and Harvey Weiss. 2006. "Holocene climate and cultural evolution in late prehistoric—early historic West Asia," *Quaternary Research* 66:372–387.

Tainter, Joseph. 1988. *The Collapse of Complex Societies* (Cambridge: Cambridge University Press).

Tainter, Joseph. 1995. "Sustainability of Complex Societies," *Futures* 27(4): 397–407.

Tainter, Joseph. 1996. "Complexity, Problem Solving, and Sustainable Societies" in Robert Constanza, Olman Segura, Juan Martinez-Alier, eds. *Getting Down to Earth: Practical Applications of Ecological Economics* (Washington, DC: Island Press).

Tainter, Joseph. 2000. "Global Change, History, and Sustainability" in Roderick McIntosh, Joseph Tainter, and Susan McIntosh, eds. *The Way the Wind Blows: Climate, History, and Human Action* (New York: Columbia University Press), pp. 331–356.

Tainter, Joseph. 2006. "Archaeology of Overshoot and Collapse," *Annual Review of Anthropology* 35:59–74.

Trigger, Bruce. 2003. *Understanding Early Civilizations: A Comparative Study* (Cambridge: Cambridge University Press).

Weiss, Harvey and Raymond Bradley. 2001. "What Drives Societal Collapse?" *Science* 291:609–610.

Wilson, E. O. 1975. *Sociobiology: The New Synthesis* (Cambridge, MA: Belknap Press).

Winchester, Simon. 2001. *The Map That Changed the World: William Smith and the Birth of Modern Geology* (New York: Harper Collins).

Wineburg, Sam. 2001. *Historical Thinking and Other Unnatural Acts* (Philadelphia, PA: Temple University Press).

Wolf, Eric. 1982. *Europe and the People Without History* (Berkeley/LA: University of California Press).

Wright, Ronald. 2004. *A Short History of Progress* (Toronto: Anansi Press).

Wylie, Alison. 2002. *Thinking From Things: Essays in the Philosophy of Archaeology* (Berkeley, CA: University of California Press).

Zerubavel, Eviatar. 2003. *Time Maps: Collective Memory and the Social Shape of the Past* (Chicago: University of Chicago Press).

Chapter 4*

The Evolution of Culture

Daniel C. Dennett

Cultures evolve. In one sense, this is a truism; in other senses, it asserts one or another controversial, speculative, unconfirmed theory of culture. Consider a cultural inventory of some culture at some time—say 1900 AD. It should include all the languages, practices, ceremonies, edifices, methods, tools, myths, music, art, and so forth that compose that culture. Over time, that inventory changes. Today, 100 years later, some items will have disappeared, some multiplied, some merged, some changed, and many new elements will appear for the first time. A verbatim record of this changing inventory through history would not be science; it would be a database. This is the truism: cultures evolve over time. Everybody agrees about that. Now let's turn to the controversial question: how are we to explain the patterns to be found in that database? Are there any good theories or models of cultural evolution?

1. Science or Narrative?

One possibility is that the only patterns to be found in cultural evolution defy scientific explanation. They are, some might want to say, *narrative* patterns, not scientific patterns. There is clearly something to this, but it won't do as it stands for many scientific patterns are also historical patterns, and hence are revealed and explained in narratives—of sorts. Cosmology, geology, and biology are all historical sciences. The great biologist D'Arcy Thompson once said: "Everything is the way it is because it got that way."

If he is right—if *everything* is the way it is because it got that way—then every science must be, in part, a historical science. But not all history—the

---

* The first Annual Charles Simonyi Lecture, Oxford University, 17 February 1999, posted at *http:// www.edge.org/3rd_culture/dennett/dennett_p1.html* and reprinted here by permission.

recounting of events in temporal sequence—is *narrative,* some might want to say. Human history is unique in that the patterns it exhibits require a different *form* of understanding: *hermeneutical* understanding or *Verstehen,* or—you can count on the Germans to have lots of words for claims like this—*Geisteswissenschaft* (approximately: spiritual science). I think this, too is partly right; there *is* a particular sort of understanding that is used to make sense of narratives about human agents. It is also true that the mark of a *good* story is that its episodes unfold *not* as the predicted consequences of general laws and initial conditions, but in delightfully surprising ways. These important facts do not show, however, that cultural evolution escapes the clutches of science and must be addressed in some other realm of inquiry. Quite the contrary; the humanistic comprehension of narratives and the scientific explanation of life processes, for all their differences of style and emphasis, have the same logical backbone. We can see this by examining the special form of understanding we use when following—and creating—good narratives.

Mediocre narratives are either a pointless series of episodes in temporal order—just "one damn thing after another"—or else so utterly predictable as to be boring. Between randomness and routine lie the good stories, whose surprising moments make sense in retrospect, in the framework provided by the unsurprising moments. The perspective from which we can understand these narratives is what I have called *the intentional stance:* the strategy of analyzing the flux of events into *agents* and their (rational) *actions* and *reactions.* Such agents—people, in this case—*do things for reasons,* and can be predicted, up to a point, by cataloguing their reasons, their beliefs and desires, and calculating what, given those reasons, the most rational course of action for each agent would be. Sometimes the most rational course is flat obvious, so while the narrative is predictive (or true), it is uninteresting and unenlightening. To take a usefully simple case, a particular game of chess is interesting to the extent that we are surprised by either the brilliant moves that outstrip our own calculations of what it would be rational to do, or the blunders, which we thought too suboptimal to predict.

In the wider world of human activity, the same holds true. We don't find the tale of Jane going to the supermarket on her way home from work interesting precisely because it all unfolds so predictably from the intentional stance; today she never encountered any interesting options, given her circumstances. Other times, however, the most rational thing for an agent to do is far from obvious, and may be practically incalculable. When we encounter these narratives, we are surprised (sometimes delighted and sometimes appalled) by the actual outcome. It makes sense in retrospect, but who'd have guessed that she'd decide to do *that*? The vast mass of routinely rational human behavior doesn't make good novels, but it is just such humdrum rational narrative that provides the background pattern that permits us to make sense, retrospectively, of the intriguing vagaries we encounter, and to anticipate the complications that will arise when the trains of events they put in motion collide.

The traditional model used by historians and anthropologists to try to explain cultural evolution uses the intentional stance as its explanatory framework. These theorists treat culture as composed of goods—possessions of the people, who husband them in various ways, wisely or foolishly. People carefully preserve their traditions of fire-lighting, house-building, speaking, counting, justice, etc. They trade cultural items as they trade other goods. And of course some cultural items (wagons, pasta, recipes for chocolate cake, etc.) are definitely goods, and so we can plot their trajectories using the tools of economics. It is clear from this perspective that highly prized cultural entities will be protected at the expense of less favored cultural entities, and there will be a competitive market where agents both "buy" and "sell" cultural wares. If a new method of house-building or farming or a new style of music sweeps through the culture, it will be because people perceive advantages to these novelties.

The people on this model are seen as having an autonomous rationality; deprive a person of his goods, and he stands there naked but rational and full of informed desires. When he clothes himself and arms himself and equips himself with goods, he increases his powers, complicates his desires. If Coca Cola bottles proliferate around the world, it is because more and more people prefer to buy a Coke. Advertising may fool them. But then we look to the advertisers or to those who have hired them, to find the relevant agents whose desires fix the values for our cost-benefit calculations. *Cui bono?* Who benefits? The purveyors of the goods, and those they hire to help them, etc. On this way of thinking, then, the relative "replicative" power of various cultural goods—whether Coke bottles, building styles or religious creeds—is measured in the marketplace of cost-benefit calculations performed by the people.

Biologists, too, can often make sense of the evolution (in the neutral sense) of features of the natural world by treating them as goods belonging to various members of various species—one's food, one's nest, one's burrow, one's territory, one's mate[s], one's time and energy. Cost-benefit analyses shed light on the husbandry engaged in by the members of the different species inhabiting some shared environment.[1] Not every "possession" is considered a good, however. The dirt and grime that accumulates on one's body, to say nothing of the accompanying flies and fleas, are of no value or of negative value, for instance. These hitchhikers are not normally considered as goods by biologists except when the benefits derived from them (by *whom?*) are manifest.

This traditional perspective can obviously explain many features of cultural and biological evolution, but it is not uniformly illuminating, nor is it obligatory. I want to show how theorists of culture—historians, anthropologists, economists, psychologists, and others—can benefit from adopting a different vantage point on these phenomena. It is a different application of the intentional stance, one which still quite properly gives pride of place to the *cui bono* question, but which can provide alternative answers that are often overlooked. The perspective I am talking about is Richard Dawkins's *meme's-eye point of view*, which recognizes—and takes seriously—the possibility that cultural entities may evolve according to selectional regimes that make sense only when the answer to the *cui bono* question is that it is the cultural items *themselves* that benefit from the adaptations they exhibit.[2]

2. Memes as Cultural Viruses

Whenever costs and benefits are the issue we need to ask *cui bono?* A benefit by itself is not explanatory; a benefit in a vacuum is indeed a sort of mystery; until it can be shown how the benefit actually redounds to enhance the replicative power of a replicator, it just sits there, alluring, perhaps, but incapable of explaining anything.

We see an ant laboriously climbing up a stalk of grass. Why is it doing that? Why is that adaptive? What good accrues to the ant by doing that? That is the wrong question to ask. No good at all accrues to the ant. Is it just a fluke, then? In fact, that's exactly what it is: a fluke! Its brain has been invaded by a fluke (*Dicrocoelium dendriticum*)—one of a gang of tiny parasites that need to get themselves into the intestines of a sheep in order to reproduce.[3] (Salmon swim up stream; these parasitic worms drive ants up grass stalks to improve their chances of being ingested by a passing sheep.) The benefit is not to the reproductive prospects of the ant but the reproductive prospects of the fluke.[4] Dawkins points out that we can think of the cultural items, memes, as parasites, too. Actually, they are more like a simple virus than a worm. Memes are supposed to be analogous to genes, the replicating entities of the cultural media, but they also have vehicles, or phenotypes; they are like not-so-naked genes. They are like viruses.[5] Basically, a virus is just a string of nucleic acid with an attitude—and a protein overcoat. A viroid is an even more naked gene. And similarly, a meme is an information packet with an attitude—with some phenotypic clothing that has differential effects in the world that thereby influence its chances of getting replicated. (What is a meme *made of*? It is made of information, which can be carried in *any* physical medium. More on this later.)

And in the domain of memes, the ultimate beneficiary, the beneficiary in terms of which of the final cost-benefit calculations must apply is the meme itself, not its carriers. This is not to be heard as a bold empirical claim, ruling out (for instance) the role of individual human agents in devising, appreciating, and securing the spread and prolongation of cultural items. As I have already noted, the traditional perspective on cultural evolution handsomely explains many of the patterns to be observed. My proposal is rather that we adopt a perspective or point of view from which a wide variety of different empirical claims can be compared, *including the traditional claims*, and the evidence for them considered in a neutral setting, a setting that does not prejudge these hot-button questions.

In the analogy with the fluke, we are invited to consider a meme to be like a parasite which commandeers an organism for its own replicative benefit, but we should remember that such hitchhikers or *symbionts* can be classified into three fundamental categories: *parasites*, whose presence lowers the fitness of their host; *commensals*, whose presence is neutral (though, as the etymology reminds us, they "share the same table"); and *mutualists*, whose presence enhances the fitness of both host and guest. Since these varieties are arrayed along a continuum, the boundaries between them need not be too finely drawn; just where benefit drops to zero or turns to harm is not something to be directly measured by any practical test, though we can explore the consequences of these turning points in models.

We should expect memes to come in all three varieties, too. This means, for instance, that it is a mistake to assume that the "cultural selection" of a cultural trait is always "for cause"—always because of some perceived (or even misperceived) benefit it provides to the host. We can always ask if the hosts, the human agents that are the *vectors*, perceive some benefit and (for that reason, good or bad) assist in the preservation and replication of the cultural item in question, but we must also be prepared to entertain the answer that they do not. In other words, we must consider as a real possibility the hypothesis that the human hosts are, individually or as a group, either oblivious to, or agnostic about, or even positively dead set against, some cultural item, which nevertheless is able to exploit its hosts as vectors.

The most familiar cases of cultural transmission and evolution—the cases that tend to be in the spotlight—are innovations that are obviously of some direct or indirect benefit to the genetic fitness of the host. A better fishhook catches more fish, feeds more bellies, makes for more surviving grandchildren, etc. The only difference between stronger arms and a better fishhook in the (imagined) calculation of impact on fitness is that the stronger arms might be passed on quite directly through the germ line, while the fishhook definitely must be culturally transmitted. (The stronger arms *could* be culturally transmitted as well. A tradition of body building, for instance, could explain why there was very low [genetic] heritability for strong adult arms, and yet a very high rate of strong adult arms in a population.) But however it might be that strong arms or fishhooks are transmitted, they are typically supposed to be a good bargain from the perspective of genetic fitness. The bargain might, however, be myopic—only good in the short run. After all, even agriculture, in the long run, may be a dubious bargain if what you are taking as your *summum bonum* is Darwinian fitness.[6] What alternatives are there?

First, we need to note that in the short run (evolutionarily speaking—that is, from the perspective of a few centuries or even millennia) something might flourish in a culture independently of whether it was of actual benefit to genetic fitness, but strongly linked to whether it was of *apparent* benefit to genetic fitness. Even if you think that Darwinian fitness enhancement is the principle driving engine of cultural evolution, you have to posit some swifter, more immediate mechanism of retention and transmission. It's not hard to find one. We are genetically endowed with a biased quality space: some things feel good and some things don't. We tend to live by the rule: *if it feels good, keep it.* This rough and ready rule can be tricked, of course. The sweet tooth is a standard example. The explosion of cultural items—artifacts, practices, recipes, patterns of agriculture, trade routes—that depend quite directly on the exploitation of the sweet tooth has probably had a considerable net *negative* effect on human genetic fitness. Notice that explaining the emergence of these cultural items by citing their "apparent" benefit to genetic fitness does not in any way commit us to the claim that people think that they are enhancing their genetic fitness by acquiring and consuming sugar. The rationale is not theirs, but Mother Nature's. They just go with what they like.

Still, given what people innately like, they go on to figure out, ingeniously and often with impressive foresight, how to obtain what they like. This is still the traditional model of cultural evolution, with people husbanding their goods in order to maximize what they prefer—and getting their preferences quite directly from their genetic heritage. But this very process of rational calculation can lead to more interesting possibilities. As such an agent complicates her life, she will almost certainly acquire new preferences that are themselves culturally transmitted symbionts of one sort or another. Her sweet tooth may lead her to buy a cookbook, which inspires her to enroll in a culinary arts program, which turns out to be so poorly organized that she starts a student protest movement, in which she is so successful that she is invited to head an educational reform movement, for which a law degree would be a useful credential, and so on. Each new goal will have to bootstrap itself into the memosphere by exploiting some preestablished preference, but this recursive process, which can proceed at breakneck speed relative to the glacial pace of genetic evolution, can transform human agents indefinitely far away from their genetic beginnings. In an oft-quoted passage, E. O. Wilson claimed otherwise: "The genes hold culture on a leash. The leash is very long, but inevitably values will be constrained in accordance with their effects on the human gene pool."[7]

But Wilson's leash is indefinitely long and elastic. Consider the huge space of *imaginable* cultural entities, practices, values. Is there any point in that vast space that is utterly unreachable? Not that I can see. The constraints Wilson speaks of can be so co-opted, exploited, and blunted in a recursive cascade of cultural products and meta-products that there may well be traversable paths to every point in that space of imaginable possibilities. I am suggesting, that is, that cultural possibility is less constrained than genetic possibility. We can articulate persuasive biological arguments to the effect that certain imaginable species are unlikely in the extreme—flying horses, unicorns, talking trees, carnivorous cows, spiders the size of whales—but neither Wilson nor anybody else to my knowledge has yet offered parallel grounds for believing that there are similar obstacles to trajectories in imaginable cultural design space. Many of these imaginable points in design space would no doubt be genetic cul-de-sacs, in the sense that any lineage of *Homo sapiens* that ever occupied them would eventually go extinct as a result, but this dire prospect is no barrier to the evolution and adoption of such memes in the swift time of cultural history.[8] To combat Wilson's metaphor with one of my own: the genes provide not a leash but a launching pad, from which you can get almost anywhere, by one devious route or another. It is precisely in order to explain the patterns in cultural evolution that are *not* strongly constrained by genetic forces that we need the memetic approach.

The memes that proliferate will be the memes that replicate one way or another—by hook or by crook. Think of them as entering the brains of culture members, making phenotypic alterations thereupon, and then submitting themselves to the great selection tournament—not the Darwinian genetic fitness tournament (life is too short for that) but the Dawkinsian meme-fitness tournament. It is their fitness as memes that is on the line, not their host's genetic fitness. And the environments that embody the selective pressures that determine their fitness are composed in large measure of other memes. Why do their hosts put up with this? Why should the overhead costs of establishing a whole new system of differential reproduction be borne by members of *Homo sapiens*? Note that the question to be asked and answered here is parallel to the question we ask about any symbiont-host relationship: why do the hosts put up with it? And the short answer is that it is too costly to eradicate, but this just means that the benefits accruing to the machinery that is being exploited by the parasites are so great that keeping the machinery and tolerating the parasites (to the extent that they are tolerated) has so far been the best deal available. And whether or not in the long run (millions of years) this infestation will be viewed as mutualism or commensalism or parasitism, in the short run (the last few millennia) the results have been spectacular—the creation of a new biological type of entity: a person.

I like to compare this development to the revolution that happened among the bacteria roughly a billion years ago. Relatively simple *prokaryotes* got invaded by some of their neighbors, and the resulting *endosymbiotic* teams were more fit than their uninfected cousins, and prospered. These *eukaryotes*, living alongside their prokaryotic cousins, but enormously more complex, versatile and competent thanks to their hitchhikers, opened up the design space of multicellular organisms. Similarly, the emergence of culture-infected hominids has opened up yet another region of hitherto unoccupied and untraversable design space. We live alongside our animal cousins, but we are enormously more complex, versatile, and competent. Our brains are bigger, to be sure, but it is mainly due to their infestation by memes that they gain their powers. Joining forces with our own memes, we create new candidates for the locus of benefit, new answers to *cui bono*?

3. Darwin's Path to Memetic Engineering

The meme's-eye view doesn't just open up new vistas for the understanding of patterns in culture; it also provides the foundation for answering a question left dangling by the traditional model of cultural evolution. The traditional view presupposes rational self-interested agents, intent on buying and selling, and improving their lot. *Where did they come from?* The standard background assumption is that they are just animals whose *cui bono?* question is to be dealt with in terms of the impact on genetic fitness, as we have seen. But when people acquire other interests, including interests directly opposed to their genetic interests, they enter a new space of possibilities—something no salmon or fruit fly or bear can do. How could this great river of novelty get started?

Here I think we can get help from Darwin's opening exposition of the theory of natural selection. In the first chapter of *Origin of Species,* Darwin introduces his great idea of natural selection by an ingenious expository device, an instance of the very gradualism that he was about to discuss. He begins not with natural selection—his destination—but what he calls *methodical selection*: the deliberate, foresighted, intended "improvement of the breed" by animal and plant breeders. He begins, in short, with familiar and uncontroversial ground that he can expect his readers to share with him:

"We cannot suppose that all the breeds were suddenly produced as perfect and as useful as we now see them; indeed, in several cases, we know that this has not been their history. The key is man's power of accumulative selection: nature gives successive variations; man adds them up in certain directions useful to him."[9] But, he goes on to note, in addition to such methodical selection, there is another process, which lacks the foresight and intention, which he calls *unconscious selection*:

> At the present time, eminent breeders try by methodical selection, with a distinct object in view, to make a new strain or sub-breed, superior to anything existing in the country. But, for our purpose, a kind of Selection, which may be called Unconscious, and which results from every one trying to possess and breed from the best individual animals, is more important. Thus, a man who intends keeping pointers naturally tries to get as good dogs as he can, and afterwards breeds from his own best dogs, but he has no wish or expectation of permanently altering the breed.[10]

Long before there was deliberate breeding, unconscious selection was the process that created and refined all our domesticated species, and even at the present time, unconscious selection continues. Darwin gives a famous example: "There is reason to believe that King Charles's spaniel has been unconsciously modified to a large extent since the time of that monarch."[11] There is no doubt that unconscious selection has been a major force in the evolution of domesticated species.[12] In our own time, unconscious selection goes on apace, and one ignores it at our peril. Unconscious selection in bacteria and viruses for resistance to antibiotics is only the most notorious and important example. Consider the "genes for longevity" that have recently been bred into laboratory animals such as mice and rats. It is probably true, however, that much if not all of the effect that has been obtained in these laboratory breeding experiments has simply undone the unconscious selection for short-livedness at the hands of the suppliers of those laboratory animals. The stock the experimenters started with had shorter life expectancy than their wild cousins simply because they had been bred for many generations for early reproductive maturity, and robustness, and short lives came along as an unintended (unconscious) side consequence.[13]

Darwin pointed out that the line between unconscious and methodical selection was itself a fuzzy, gradual boundary: "The man who first selected a pigeon with a slightly larger tail, never dreamed what the descendants of that pigeon would become through long-continued, partly unconscious, and partly methodical selection."[14] And both unconscious and methodical selection, he notes finally, are but special cases of an even more inclusive process, natural selection, in which the role of human intelligence and choice stands at zero. From the perspective of natural selection, changes in lineages due to unconscious or methodical selection are merely changes in which one of the most prominent selective pressures in the environment is human activity. It is not restricted, as we have seen, to domesticated species. White-tailed deer in New England now seldom exhibit the "white flag" of a bobbing tail during headlong flight that was famously observed by early hunters; the arrival of human beings today is much more likely to provoke them to hide silently in underbrush than to flee. Those white flags were too easy a target for hunters with guns, it seems.

This nesting of different processes of natural selection now has a new member: genetic engineering. How does it differ from the methodical selection of Darwin's day? It is just less dependent on the preexisting variation in the gene pool, and proceeds more directly to new candidate genomes with less overt and time-consuming trial and error. Darwin had noted that in his day "Man can hardly select, or only with much difficulty, any deviation of structure excepting such as is externally visible; and indeed he rarely cares for what is internal."[15] But today's genetic engineers have carried their insight into the molecular innards of the organisms they are trying to create. There is evermore accurate foresight, but even here, if we look closely at the practices in the laboratory, we will find a large measure of exploratory trial and error in their search of the best combinations of genes.

We can use Darwin's three levels of genetic selection, plus our own fourth level, genetic engineering, as a model for four parallel levels of *memetic* selection in human culture. In a speculative spirit, I am going to sketch how it might go using an example that has particularly challenged some Darwinians, and hence been held up as a worthy stumbling block—a cultural treasure untouchable by evolutionists: music. Music is unique to our species, but found in every human culture. It is manifestly complex, intricately designed, an expensive consumer of time, energy and materials. How did music start? What was or is the answer to its *cui bono* question? Steven Pinker is one Darwinian who has recently declared himself baffled about the possible evolutionary origins and survival of music, but that is because he has been looking at music in the old-fashioned way, looking for music to have some contribution to make to the genetic fitness of those who make and participate in the proliferation of music.[16] There may well be some such effect that is important, but I want to make the case that there might also be a purely *memetic* explanation of the origin of music. Here, then, is my Just-so Story, working gradually up Darwin's hierarchy of kinds of selection.

Natural Selection of Musical Memes.

One day one of our distant hominid ancestors sitting on a fallen log happened to start banging on it with a stick—*boom boom boom. For no good reason at all.* This was just idle diddling, a by-product, perhaps, of a slightly out of balance endocrine system. This was, you might say, mere nervous fidgeting, but the repetitive sounds striking his ears just happened to feel to him like a slight improvement on silence. A feedback loop was closed, and the *repetition*—*boom boom boom*—was "rewarding." If we leave this individual all by himself, drumming away on his log, then we would say that he had simply developed a habit, *possibly* therapeutic in that it "relieved anxiety," but just as possibly a *bad* habit—a habit that did him and his genes no good at all, but just exploited a wrinkle that happened to exist in his nervous system, creating a feedback loop that tended to lead to individual replications of drumming by him under various circumstances. No musical appreciation, no insight, no goal or ideal or project need be imputed to our solitary drummer.

Now introduce some other ancestors who happen to see and hear this drummer. They might pay no attention, or be irritated enough to make him stop or drive him away, or they might, again *for no reason*, find their imitator-circuits tickled into action; they might feel an urge to drum along with musical Adam. What are these imitator circuits I've postulated? Just whatever it takes to make it somewhat more likely than not that some activities by conspecifics are imitated, a mere reflex if you like—of which we may see a fossil trace when spectators at a football match cannot help making shadow kicking motions more or less in unison with the players on the field. One can postulate reasons why having some such imitative talents built-in would be a valuable adaptation—one that enhances one's genetic fitness—but while this is both plausible and widely accepted, it is, strictly speaking, unnecessary for my Just-so Story. The imitative urge might just as well be a function-less by-product of some other adaptive feature of the human nervous system. Suppose, then, that for no good reason at all, the drumming habit is *infectious*. When one hominid starts drumming, soon others start drumming along in imitation. This could happen. A perfectly pointless practice, of no utility or fitness-enhancing benefit at all, could become established in a community. It might be positively detrimental: the drumming scares away the food, or uses up lots of precious energy. It would then be just like a disease, spreading simply because it *could* spread, and lasting as long as it could find hosts to infect. If it was detrimental in this way, variant habits that were less detrimental—less virulent—would tend to evolve to replace it, other things being equal, for they would tend to find more available healthy hosts to migrate to. And of course such a habit *might* even provide a positive benefit to its hosts (enhancing their reproductive chances—a familiar dream of musicians everywhere, and it might be true, or have been true in the past). But providing a genetic benefit of this sort is only one of the paths such a habit might pursue in its mindless quest for immortality. Habits—good, bad, and indifferent—could persist and replicate, unappreciated and unrecognized, for an indefinite period of time, provided only that the replicative and dispersal machinery is provided for them. The drumming virus is born.

Let me pause to ask the question: what is such a habit made of? What gets passed from individual to individual when a habit is copied? Not stuff, not packets of material, but pure information, the information that generates the pattern of behavior that replicates. A cultural virus, unlike a biological virus, is not tethered to any particular physical medium of transmission.[17]

Unconscious Selection of Memes.

On with our Just-so Story. Some of the drummers begin to hum, and of all the different hums, a few are more infectious than the rest, and those hominids who happen to start the humming in these ways become the focus of attention, as sources of humming. A competition between different humming patterns emerges. Here we can begin to see the gradual transition to unconscious selection. Suppose that being such a focus of humming happens to feel good—whether or not it enhances one's genetic fitness slightly (it might, of course; perhaps the females tend to be more receptive to those who start the winning hums). The same transition to unconscious selection can be seen among viruses and other pathogens, by the way. If scratching an itch feels good, and also has the side effect of keeping a ready supply of viral emigrés on one's fingertips, the part of the body most likely to come in contact with another host, one is unconsciously selecting for just such a mode of transmission by one's myopic and uncomprehending preference for scratching when one itches—and this does not depend on scratching having any fitness-enhancing benefits *for you*: it may be, like the ant's hankering for the top of the grass stem, a desire that benefits the parasite, not the host. Similarly, if varying tempo and pitch of one's hums feels good, and also happens to create a ready supply of more attention-holding noises for spreading to conspecifics, one's primitive aesthetic preference can begin to shape, unconsciously, the lineages of humming habit that spread through one's community.

Brains in the community begin to be infected by a variety of these memes. Competition for time and space in these brains becomes more severe. The infected brains begin to take on a structure as the memes that enter "learn" to cooperate on the task of turning a brain into a proper meme-nest with lots of opportunities for entrance and exit (and hence replication).[18] Meanwhile, any memes out there "looking for" hosts will have to compete for available space therein. Just like germs.

Methodical Selection of Memes.

As the structure grows, it begins to take on a more active role in selecting. That is to say, the brains of the hosts, like the brains of the owners of domesticated animals, become evermore potent and discerning selective agencies—still largely unwitting, but nevertheless having a powerful influence. Some people, it turns out, are better at this than others. As Darwin says of animal breeders, "Not one man in a thousand has accuracy of eye and judgment sufficient to become an eminent breeder."[19]

We honor Bach, the artistic genius, but he was no "natural" doodler—an intuitive genius just "playing by ear." He was the master musical technologist of his day, the inheritor of musical instruments that had had their designs honed over several millennia, as well as some relatively recent additions to the music maker's toolbox—a fine system of musical notation and keyboard instruments that permitted the musician to play many notes at once and an explicit, codified, rationalized *theory* of counterpoint. These mind-tools were revolutionary in the way they opened up musical design space for Bach and his successors.

And Bach, like the one man in a thousand who has the discernment to be an eminent animal breeder, knew how to breed new strains of music from old. Consider, for instance, his hugely successful chorale cantatas. Bach shrewdly chose, for his breeding stock, *chorales*—hymn melodies that had already proven themselves to be robust inhabitors of their human hosts, *already domesticated* tunes his audiences had been humming for generations, building up associations and memories, memes that had already sunk their hooks deeply into the emotional habits and triggers of the brains where they had been replicating for years. Then he used his technology to create variations on these memes, seeking to strengthen their strengths and damp their weaknesses, putting them in new environments, inducing new hybrids.

Memetic Engineering.

What about memetic engineering? Was Bach, in virtue of his highly sophisticated approach to the design of replicable musical memes, not just a *meme breeder* but a *memetic engineer*? In the light of Darwin's admiring comment on the rare skill—the genius—of the good breeder, it is interesting to note how sharply our prevailing attitudes distinguish between our honoring the "art" of selective breeding and our deep suspicion and disapproval of the "technology" of gene-splicing. Let's hear it for *art*, but not for *technology*, we say, forgetting that the words share a common ancestor, *techné*, the Greek word for art, skill, or craft in any work. We retreat in horror from genetically engineered tomatoes, and turn up our noses at "artificial" fibers in our clothing, while extolling such "organic" and "natural" products as whole grain flour or cotton and wool, forgetting that grains and cotton plants and sheep are themselves products of human technology, of skillful hybridization and rearing techniques. He who would clothe himself in fibers unimproved by technology and live on food from nondomesticated sources is going to be cold and hungry indeed.

Besides, just as genetic engineers, for all their foresight and insight into the innards of things, are still at the mercy of natural selection when it comes to the fate of their creations (that is why, after all, we are so cautious about letting them release their brainchildren on the outside world), so, too, the memetic engineer, no matter how sophisticated, still has to contend with the daunting task of winning the replication tournaments in the memosphere. One of the most sophisticated musical memetic engineers of the age, Leonard Bernstein, wryly noted this in a wonderful piece he published in 1955 entitled "Why don't you run upstairs and write a nice Gershwin tune?"[20] Bernstein had credentials and academic honors aplenty in 1955, but no songs on the Hit Parade. "A few weeks ago a serious composer-friend and I . . . got boiling mad about it. Why shouldn't we be able to come up with a hit, we said, if the standard is as low as it seems to be? We decided that all we had to do was to put ourselves into the mental state of an idiot and write a ridiculous hillbilly tune." They failed—and not for lack of trying. As Bernstein wistfully remarked, "It's just that it would be nice to hear someone accidentally whistle something of mine, somewhere, just once."[21] His wish came true, of course, a few years later in 1961, when *West Side Story* burst into the memosphere.

4. Conclusions

There is surely much, much more to be said—to be discovered—about the evolution of music. I chose it as my topic because it so nicely illustrates the way the traditional perspective on culture and the evolutionary perspective can join forces, instead of being seen to be in irresolvable conflict. If you believe that music is *sui generis*, a wonderful, idiosyncratic feature of our species that we prize in spite of the fact that it has *not* been created to enhance our chances of having more offspring, you may well be right—*and if so, there is an evolutionary explanation of how this can be true.* You cannot evade the obligation to explain how such an expensive, time-consuming activity came to flourish in this cruel world, and a Darwinian theory of culture is an ally, not an opponent, in this investigation.

While it is true that Darwin wished to contrast the utter lack of foresight or intention in natural selection with the deliberate goal-seeking of the artificial or methodical selectors in order to show how the natural process could in principle proceed without any mentality at all, he did not thereby establish (as many seem to have supposed) that deliberate, goal-directed, intentional selection is not a subvariety of natural selection! There is no conflict between the claim that artifacts (including abstract artifacts—memes) are the products of natural selection, and the claim that they are (often) the foreseen, designed products of intentional human activity.

Some memes are like domesticated animals; they are prized for their benefits, and their replication is closely fostered and relatively well understood by their human owners. Some memes are more like rats; they thrive in the human environment in spite of being positively selected against—ineffectually—by their unwilling hosts. And some are more like bacteria or viruses, commandeering aspects of human behavior (provoking sneezing, for instance) in their "efforts" to propagate from host to host. There is artificial selection of "good" memes—like the memes of arithmetic and writing, the theory of counterpoint, and Bach's cantatas, which are carefully taught to each new generation. And there is unconscious selection of memes of all sorts—like the subtle mutations in pronunciation that spread through linguistic groups, presumably with some efficiency advantage, but perhaps just hitchhiking on some quirk of human preference. And there is unconscious selection of memes that are positively a menace, but which prey on flaws in the human decision-making apparatus, as provided for in the genome and enhanced and adjusted by other cultural innovations—such as the "abducted-by-aliens" meme, which makes perfect sense when its own fitness as a cultural replicator is considered. Only the meme's-eye perspective unites all these possibilities under one view.

Finally, one of the most persistent sources of discomfort about memes is the dreaded suspicion that an account of human minds in terms of brains being parasitized by memes will undermine the precious traditions of human creativity. On the contrary, I think it is clear that *only* an account of creativity in terms of memes has much of a chance of giving us any way to *identify with* the products of our own minds. We human beings extrude other products, on a daily basis, but after childhood, we don't tend to view our feces with the pride of an author or artist. These are mere biological by-products, and although they have their own modest individuality and idiosyncrasy, it is not anything we cherish. How could we justify viewing the secretions of our poor infected brains with any more pride? Because we *identify with* some subset of the memes we harbor. Why? Because among the memes we harbor are those that put a premium on identifying with just such a subset of memes! Lacking that meme-borne attitude, we would be mere *loci* of interaction, but we have such memes—that is who we are.

Endnotes

1   Such organisms need not be deemed to be making conscious decisions, of course, but the rationality, such as it is, of the "decisions" they make is typically anchored to the expected benefit to the individual organism. See Elliot Sober and David Sloan Wilson, *Unto Others: The Evolution and Psychology of Unselfish Behavior* (Cambridge: Harvard University Press, 1998), for important discussions of gene, individual, and group benefits of such decision-making.

2. Sober and Wilson (1998) note that there is a gap in their model of cultural evolution: "We can say that functionless [relative to human individual and group fitness] behavior should be more common in humans than other species, but we cannot explain why a particular functionless behavior has evolved in a particular culture. That kind of understanding probably requires detailed historical knowledge of the culture, and it may turn out that some behaviors evolved mainly by chance," p. 171. Dawkins's theory of memes, as briefly sketched in a single chapter of *The Selfish Gene* (Oxford: Oxford University Press, 1976), but see also Dawkins, "Viruses of the Mind," in Bo Dahlbom, ed., *Dennett and his Critics* (Oxford: Blackwell, 1993), is hardly a theory at all, especially

compared to the models of cultural evolution developed by other biologists, such as Cavalli-Sforza and Feldman, *Cultural Transmission and Evolution: A Quantitative Approach* (Princeton, NJ: Princeton University Press, 1981); Lumsden and Wilson, *Genes Mind and Culture: The Coevolutionary Process* (Cambridge: Harvard University Press, 1981), and Boyd and Richerson, *Culture and the Evolutionary Process* (Chicago: The University of Chicago Press, 1985). Unlike these others, Dawkins offers no formal development, no mathematical models, no quantitative predictions, and no systematic survey of relevant empirical findings. But Dawkins does present an idea that is overlooked by all the others, including Sober and Wilson in this passage, and it is, I think, a most important idea. It is the key to understanding how we can be not just guardians and transmitters of culture, but cultural entities ourselves— all the way in.

3. Mark Ridley, *Animal Behaviour, 2nd ed.* (Boston: Blackwell Science, 1995), p. 258.

4. Strictly speaking, to the reproductive prospects of the fluke's genes (or the fluke's group's genes), for as Sober and Wilson (1998) point out (p. 18) in their use of *D. dendriticum* as an example of altruistic behavior, the fluke that actually does the driving in the brain is a sort of kamikaze pilot who dies without any chance of passing on its own genes, benefiting its [asexually reproduced] near-clones in other parts of the ant.

5. Dawkins, 1993.

6. See Jared Diamond, *Guns, Germs, and Steel: The Fates of Human Societies* (New York: W. W. Norton & Company, 1997) for fascinating reflections on the uncertain benefits of abandoning the hunter-gatherer lifestyle.

7. E. O. Wilson, *On Human Nature* (Cambridge: Harvard University Press, 1978), p. 167.

8. Boyd and Richerson, "Punishment Allows the Evolution of Cooperation (or Anything Else) in Sizable Groups," *Ethology and Sociobiology* 13 (1992): 171–195) show that "Virtually any behavior can become stable within a social group if it is sufficiently buttressed by social norms." (quoted from Sober and Wilson, 1998, p. 152). Our biology strongly

biases us to value health, nutritious food, the avoidance of bodily injury, and of course having lots of offspring, so a sheltered theorist might suppose that it is highly unlikely that any human group could ever support a fashion for, say, bodily fragility or bulimia, or the piercing of bodily parts, or suicide, or celibacy. If even these practices can so readily overturn our innate biases, where can Wilson's leash do any serious constraining?

9. Charles Darwin, 1859, *On the Origin of Species,* Harvard Facsimile Edition, (Cambridge: Harvard University Press, 1964), p. 30.

10. Ibid., p. 34.

11. Ibid., p. 35.

12. On unconscious selection of both domesticated plants and animals, see Jared Diamond, *Guns, Germs and Steel.*

13. Daniel Promislow, personal correspondence.

14. Darwin, p. 39.

15. Ibid., p. 38.

16. Steven Pinker, *How the Mind Works* (New York: W. W. Norton & Company, 1997), writes: "What benefit could there be to diverting time and energy to the making of plinking noises, or to feeling sad when no one has died? . . . As far as biological cause and effect are concerned, music is useless," p. 528. On p. 538, he contrasts music with the other topics of his book: "I chose them as topics because they show the clearest signs of being adaptations. I chose music because it shows the clearest signs of not being one."

17. This is not the decisive difference some critics of memes have declared. We can readily enough imagine virus-like symbionts that have alternate transmission media—that are (roughly) indifferent to whether they arrive at new hosts by direct transportation (as with regular bacteria, viruses, viroids, fungi...) or by something akin to the messenger-RNA transcription process: they stay in their original hosts, but imprint their information on some messenger element (rather like a prion, we may imagine)

that then is broadcast, only to get transcribed in the host into a copy of the "sender." And if there could be two such communication channels, there could be twelve or a hundred, just as there are for transmission of cultural habits.

18. Sober and Wilson (1998) describe circumstances in which individuals of unrelated lineages thrown into group situations can be selected for cooperativity. Just how—if at all—this model can be adapted for memic coalescence is a topic for further research.

19. Darwin, p. 32.

20. *New York Times*, April 1955. Reprinted in *The Joy of Music* (New York: Simon and Schuster, 1959), pp. 52–62.

21. Ibid., p. 54.

Chapter 5

The Big Burp and the Multiplanetary Mandate

Howard Bloom

Evolution is shouting a message at us. Yes, evolution herself. That imperative? Get your ass off this planet. Get your asses, your burros, your donkeys, and as many of your fellow species as you can—from bacteria and plants to fish, reptiles, and mammals—off this dangerous scrap of stone and find new niches for life. Take the Grand Experiment of Cells and DNA, the 3.85-billion-year Project of Biomass, to other planets, moons, orbiting habitats, and galaxies. Give life an opportunity to thrive, to reinvent itself, to turn every old disaster, every pinwheeling galaxy, into new opportunity. Do this as the only species nature has generated that's capable of deliberate travel beyond the atmosphere of Earth. Do it as the only species able to take on the mission of making life multiplanetary. Accept that mission—the Greening of the Universe—or you may well eliminate yourself and all the species that depend on you—from the microorganisms making folic acid and vitamin K in your gut to wheat, corn, cucumbers, chickens, cows, the yeast you cultivate to make beer, and even the bacteria you use to make cheese. What's worse, if you fail to take life beyond the skies, the whole experiment of life—including rainforests, whales, and endangered species—may die in some perfectly normal cosmic catastrophe.

Where does this imperative to pierce the sky and to fly beyond the well of Earth's gravity come from? What does it have to do with the role of culture in the cosmos? And, most important, how does the relationship between culture and the cosmos tell us that space is a key to our future, a key to our evolutionary obligations, and a key to our ecological destiny?

Let's start with a basic question whose answer may come as a surprise. What is culture and when did it begin? Culture is the multigenerational hard-drive of memory, change, and innovation. Culture transforms a record of the past into a prediction of the future; it transforms memory into tradition—into rules of how to proceed. And culture is profoundly social. It exists not just in one mind, but binds together mobs of minds in a common enterprise.

When did culture first appear in this 13.73-billion-year-old universe? The answer is surprising. Most evolutionary experts say that human culture kicked off 35,000 to 45,000 years ago. Paleontologists studying prehistoric Europe call this period The Cultural Explosion.[1] Thirty-five thousand to forty-five thousand years ago,[2] men and women began to perforate, grind, polish, and drill bone, ivory, antler, shell, and stone into harpoons, fishhooks, buttons, ornaments, sewing needles, and awls.[3] Frosting the cake, humans also invented musical instruments,[4] calendars marked on pieces of antler,[5] and paintings on the walls of caves.[6]

Then there's the **un**-standard answer about culture's beginnings, a rebel timeline of human culture that a relatively new paleoanthropological school is fighting for. This new scientific movement has made its digs in Africa, not Europe,[7] and has come up with radically different dates. Culture, says this upstart school, started approximately 280,000 years ago[8] when humans invented the makeup industry,[9] then followed that with the invention of jewelry, beads, and trade.[10]

But both of these paleoanthropological schools are wrong about the first birth of culture. Dramatically wrong. In 1997, a cohort of colleagues and I started a new discipline. Its name is paleopsychology. Paleopsychology's mandate is to "trace the evolution of sociality, mentation, cognition, and emotion from the first 10^{-32} second of the Big Bang to today."[11] Paleopsychology is cross-disciplinary. It embraces every science that its participants can bring to the table. Activists in the field have included physicists, mathematicians, microbiologists, animal behaviorists, evolutionary biologists, evolutionary psychologists, entomologists, mycologists, anthropologists, cognitive scientists, and neurobiologists. And paleopsychology gives a far different answer to the question of culture's starting date.

Culture didn't begin 45,000 or 280,000 years ago. Culture began roughly 3.85 billion years ago.[12] Yes, I said billion! It began when the cosmos was less than 10 billion years old. It began when this planet was still so new that planetesimals—hunks of rock the size of small moons—were raining down on this globe's face, deforming this planet as savagely as a swift kick distorts a soccer ball.[13]

How could this be? There weren't even primitive brain cells 3.85 billion years ago, much less intelligent societies. Or were there? The story of how culture emerged way, way back when begins with the Big Bang. Culture is a social thing. And this has never been a cosmos of loners. From the git-go 13.73 billion years ago this has been a social universe, a cosmos of tight, intimate bunches, a cosmos of massive mobs and of huge communities. The Big Bang was profoundly social. In its first flick 13.73 billion years ago the Big Blast[14] set the first mob in motion. It precipitated roughly 10^{88} quarks.[15] Those quarks rushed into a social process—ganging up in groups of three, trios we call protons and neutrons. The social process of trio-making involved rules of etiquette, the laws of attraction and repulsion that dictate what sort of quarks you, if you were a quark, should hook up with and what sort of quarks you should avoid. Then came another act of sociality, the shotgun marriage of protons and neutrons in families of between 2 and 10.[16] These proton and neutron families were born of social urgency. Any neutron that didn't elbow its way into a particle cluster, any neutron that didn't join a particle gang, disintegrated after less than 10.6 minutes.[17] It underwent beta decay.[18] This was natural selection working on an instant scale. When it came to quarks and neutrons, only the social survived. And sociality—the behavior of couples, trios, teams, crowds, and swarms—is at culture's core.

When did another ingredient of culture, social memory—a memory that gives a foundation of knowledge, perception, and direction to an entire society—first arise? A firm answer is more elusive than you might think. Why? For the first 300,000[19] years ABB (After the Big Bang), the cosmos was host to a massive social dance. Particle gangs moved at superspeed, colliding with each other like bullets smashing head to head then bouncing away with ferocious velocity.[20] Astonishingly, the particles involved—particularly the protons—came out of each crash with all their mass and form intact. Was this act of identity-retention a primitive form of memory? Was it tradition arisen before its time?

Then another basic of culture emerged: mass behavior. Particle families ricocheted from one smash-up to another so quickly that the speed of serial collisions defied belief. We call this form of superspeed bump-em-car behavior a plasma. But despite all the mayhem and non-stop crashes, the plasma showed a shocking form of coordinated social behavior. Elbow room between particle gangs was hard to find. Yet particle clusters in synchronized swaths that went from one end of the cosmos to the other bunched together tightly then parted again. They collaborated in a cosmos-spanning Busby Berkeley style of choreography. When they crowded together, these super-synchronized chorus lines formed the peak of a wave. When the cosmos-spanning chorus lines of particle gangs gave each other just a hint of elbow room, they formed that wave's trough. These pressure waves[21] washed across the cosmos like tsunamis in the sea. The physicists who discovered these early surges and swells used another metaphor to describe them—the metaphor of music.[22] Thanks to mega-mass behavior and thanks to social behavior on the grandest scale, astrophysicists say this early cosmos and its plasma rang like a massive gong.[23] Or, to put it in the words of *Science Magazine*, "the big bang had set the entire cosmos ringing like a bell."[24]

Thanks to mega-mass behavior and social behavior, the particles of this cosmos rocked and rolled to their own self-generated beat.

So a mere 300,000 years into the universe's existence, three primitive precursors of culture's components had emerged: sociality, a primordial form of memory and coordinated mass behavior. Had we arrived at culture yet? Not by a long shot. But the first hints of its rudiments arose an astonishingly long time ago. Remember, culture's most crucial substrate is sociality. And sociality still had a few more surprises up its sleeve before it would cough out culture.

Three hundred thousand years After the Big Bang (ABB) came another mass astonishment, another radical act of sociality—the Big Break. The particles in the plasma slowed down (we call that deceleration "cooling"), separated, and gave each other more space.[25] But more space did not mean solitude. It did not mean time off from social gatherings. In fact, it meant the very opposite. Puny particles called electrons discovered for the first time in their 300,000-year existence that they were not satisfied on their own. They had an electromagnetic hunger, an electromagnetic craving for a sort of sociality this universe had never known before. And there was another surprise in the offing. The protons at the heart of particle families discovered that they, too, felt they were missing something. They discovered that they, too, had an electromagnetic longing at their core.

The upshot of these longings in the hearts of particles was shocking. If you picture a proton as the size of the Empire State Building, an electron is so small you could hold it in your hand like a baseball. Or, to put it differently, a proton is more than 1,842 times as massive as an electron.[26] So if you and I had been around to bet on the outcome of protons' and neutrons' new electromagnetic lusts, the last thing we'd have guessed is that these social drives would bring electrons and protons together in tight synergies. And, even if one proton **did** manage to hook up with an electron somewhere in this cosmos, we'd have considered it a freak event, a fluke, something that could not and would not ever happen again. But we'd have been dead wrong. Three hundred thousand years ABB, electrons discovered that their needs fit the longings of protons perfectly. No matter where the electron was and no matter what its life history, pick any proton in this universe at random, flip it an electron from anywhere you please, and the fit was more precise than anything even the makers of the ultimate high-precision scientific device, CERN's Large Hadron Collider,[27] have ever been able to achieve.

In a paper in the physics magazine *PhysicaPlus*—"The Xerox Effect: On the Importance of Pre-Biotic Evolution"[28]—I called this sort of thing manic mass production and supersynchrony. Supersynchrony refers to those landmark events in which the same thing happens at the same time all across the face of the cosmos. Supersynchrony was at work 13.73 billion years ago when roughly 10^{88} nearly identical quarks precipitated at precisely the same time from the space time manifold, from a spreading sheet of speed. Supersynchrony was at work when that vast mob of quarks appeared in every nook, cranny, and wrinkle of this huge unfolding universe.

On the other hand, the amazing number of precipitations of quarks from mere speed is manic mass production. Yes, there was variety among the first quarks. There were between 8 and 18 species.[29] But only 8 to 18 in a cosmos that is supposedly random? And roughly 10^{87} identical copies of each quark type? This is manic mass production on a scale that defies belief. It is impossible. At least it is impossible in the eyes of our current assumptions about randomness.

What are our current notions of the role of randomness in the evolution of the universe? The leading expert on cosmic evolution in the astronomical community, Tufts University's Eric Chaisson, writes in his book *Cosmic Evolution: The Rise of Complexity in Nature*, "Contingency—randomness, chance, stochasticity—pervades all of dynamic change on every spatial and temporal scale, an issue to which this book [*Cosmic Evolution*] returns repeatedly."[30] In other words, randomness prevails during every epoch of cosmic evolution from the Big Bang to today. And randomness prevails at every size from the multigalactically gigantic to the impossibly small. What does Chaisson mean by "randomness"? Says he, randomness is "disorder."[31] It's the form of unpredictable chaos known as "entropy."[32]

What's entropy? Physicists invented the idea of entropy in the 19th century to cope mathematically with the power loss in steam engines. It's based on the disordered state of water molecules that escape from a steam engine's cylinders, molecules that are no longer neatly imprisoned for work in the engine's chambers. Instead these molecular escapees—the participants in a leak of steam—bounce around at "random." The metaphor that conveys randomness more colorfully to both scientists and to the general public is the image of six monkeys at six typewriters. The monkeys peck away at the keyboard in a thoroughly haphazard manner. But give them enough time, says the six-monkeys-model-of-randomness, and the illiterate beasts will eventually type out the works of Shakespeare. Give them a bit more time, and they'll randomly peck out the evolution of the cosmos.[33] From utter disorder, order can emerge through a series of arbitrary accidents.

But it may be time to toss the current concept of the "random" away. It may be time to rid ourselves of the "stochasticity" of the six monkeys with six typewriters and to realize that this universe runs like a railroad train. It has a lot of freedom, yet it is rigidly constrained. A locomotive has many routes it can take to get from New York to L.A., but it cannot leave the rails. It cannot plow through pastures of corn, through houses, under oceans, through wormholes, or fly the Jet Stream. A train—and our universe—has a limited number of paths it can take.

Have other instances of supersynchrony and manic mass production appeared in the evolution of the cosmos? Yes. It's happened at every turn, as we're about to see. What do supersynchrony, manic mass production, and railroad trains have to do with culture and the cosmos? What do they have to do with an evolutionary imperative to take ecosystems off this fragile planet and to seed them in space? And what do they have to do with entropy? Far more than you might think.

In the Big Break approximately 300,000 years ABB, the new proton, neutron, and electron teams—atoms of helium, hydrogen, and lithium—discovered yet another social gatherer, a force of mass attraction that had never manifested itself in quite this way before. We call it gravity. And over the next 200 million years or so,[34] this subtle, terribly weak force created entirely new forms of sociality. Gravity swept loose atoms into new herds and flocks, into wisps of gas.[35] Those gas wisps kicked off the era of the Great Gravity Crusades. Wisp battled wisp to see which could use its gravity to dragoon the most new atoms. When one wisp battled another, the bigger always won, cannibalizing its competitor.[36] In the end the call of gravity that tugged atoms together led to the formation of two vast and astonishing new things—galaxies and stars.[37] This was not a sign of a universe tending toward disorder. And it wasn't a sign of randomness, a sign of stochasticity.

Once again, supersynchrony and manic mass production were king. Galaxies and stars assembled by the billions and all were pretty much the same.[38] Yes, there was far more variation than there had been among quarks, protons, and atoms. And the simultaneous timing was not so exquisitely precise. But when you leave Penn Station in Manhattan, there are only two directions you can take—west to tunnels under the Hudson River or east to tunnels under the East River.[39] As you get farther from Manhattan there are more switchpoints you can follow and your options open up, they multiply. The farther this cosmos got from its first simple laws—the law of speed, the law that converts speed to matter, and the laws of attraction and repulsion— the looser the mesh of limitations that held this cosmos in its weave. The farther this unfolding universe got from the first flick of the Big Bang, the more freedom it achieved. Yet this expanding cosmos was still limited by its equivalent of railroad tracks. It was still a captive to the basic pattern of galaxies and stars. The universe was still rigidly constrained.

Roughly 20 million to 30 million years after the Big Break the biggest of the stars, the grandest mega-mobs of atomic nuclei spawned by gravity from one end of the universe to the other, once again underwent something new. And these mega-mobs and high-mass stars did their gruesome new trick pretty much at the same time.[40] They went nova! They collapsed upon themselves, dying with screams of photons, streams of light, and with groans of outpoured energy. It was a cosmic massacre. But it was also supersynchrony.

Everything tends to disorder, says the rule of entropy. Nothing good should come from death. But in this cosmos, something of value usually does. The gift of the death of the first massive stars was a new form of supersynchronous social assembly, a gift of the social pressures in the crumpling stars' crunched and tortured hearts.[41] Until now there had only been three forms of atoms—hydrogen, helium, and lithium. But as the stars imploded, the resisting nuclei of hydrogen, helium, and lithium atoms were shoved violently together with a force that overrode the powers with which these nuclei normally maintained their identity. The results were four new forms of proton-neutron teams, four new elements, iron, carbon, nitrogen, and oxygen.[42] This was the very opposite of disorder. It was the very opposite of entropy. Even in the midst of death, the cosmos built new things.

In a random universe we would have expected a million new forms of atoms or more. But this is a cosmos with railroad constraints, a cosmos where supersynchrony and manic mass production reign. Hence the number of new forms of atom-cores was pathetically tiny by the standard of six-monkey-at-six-typewriter randomness. And thanks to manic mass production, the number of precise duplicates of these four new atomic nuclei was vast.

Once again we had the primitive precursors of culture. Carbon, which was crunched together in the heart of the first generation of dying stars,[43] is a collective, a team, a tight-knit social gathering of 18 to 20 protons, neutrons, and electrons.[44] And it has a primal form of tradition and memory; you can run a carbon particle-team through a host of natural catastrophes, and the atom will go through only three minor changes. Those changes are called isotopes. But the carbon atom's basic identity, its coherence as a society with its own distinct characteristics, will stubbornly remain the same. Carbon will insist on remaining carbon. This is so close to culture and tradition that it's scary.

This raises the big question once again. When did culture begin? When did evolution go from supersynchrony to the rise of collective tradition, collective innovation, collective differentiation, and the collective process that carries a group treasury of habits, attitudes, technology, and instructional stories from one generation to another down the line of time? Protons and carbon had a strange semblance of memory. So did stars and galaxies. Stars worked in pretty much the same way generation after generation. New galaxies assembled in forms that aped their elders. And there was something akin to tradition in the way that the first seven forms of atoms—hydrogen, helium, lithium, iron, carbon, nitrogen, and oxygen— continued to appear in era after era of cosmic change. There was even collective innovation and collective creativity. The second generation of stars, stars like ours, had new forms of atomic nuclei to chew on. And using those nuclei, they attained new powers. Inventive first-[45] and second-generation star-deaths mashed together roughly 85 new forms of atomic nuclei, 85 new elements from scandium and titanium to potassium and platinum.[46] So why isn't this culture?

This isn't culture because the maintenance of old ways was only a semblance of tradition and memory. It was a precursor, but not the real thing. The maintenance of identity and of old ways of doing things—things like the particle-munch in the heart of a star and the evolution of spiral arms of galaxies—was a product of the cosmos's forces, formulas, processes, and shapes. It was the persistence of the natural equivalent of railway tracks—the laws of the universe—the cosmos's rigid constraints. Supersynchrony and manic mass production weren't culture. They weren't really memory. Then what's the difference between the persistence of the laws of nature and memory? And why does nature have laws anyway?

A railroad train follows the same precise path thousands of other trains have taken. Why? Because the rails restrict its movement. The memory is not in the train, it's in the tracks. But the form of memory that would generate culture is a guidance system inside the train itself. It's an accumulation of lessons learned from experiences that have worked and experiences that haven't. And culture is something more. It's a story, a vision, a worldview that dictates a future path, a future path that may be utterly new, utterly old, utterly right, or utterly wrong. A culture is a memory that imagines futures and makes them real. It's an internal record of the past that steers us into the unknown of the next minute, the next decade, and the next century.

The story of the cosmos's next big move toward culture calls for a new field of study, one that lies in the gap between cosmology, theoretical physics, astronomy, and astrochemistry. Astrophysics has a specialization—a very small one—called nucleocosmochronology. Nucleocosmochronology is dedicated to fixing the dates for the rise of the 92 natural atomic nuclei and to pinning down key dates in the evolution of the cosmos.[47] It helps folks like me—multidisciplinary theorists, paleopsychologists, makers of cosmic time lines, and tellers of the cosmos's stories. It promises to help us understand when the nuclei of critical atoms like chlorine, calcium, sodium, potassium, and phosphorus first appeared.

There is need for another specialization to complement nucleocosmochronology. It is moleculocosmochronology, a study that establishes the dates at which the first molecules appeared.[48] Like the quark trios that make protons and neutrons, and like atoms, galaxies, and stars, a molecule is a social group, a coalition of atoms with its own distinct identity. One of the most common molecules found in space, for example, is hydrogen cyanide.[49] Hydrogen cyanide is an atomic trio, an atomic three musketeers. It is a tightly knit chorus line of one hydrogen atom, one carbon atom, and one nitrogen atom. The carbon atom at hydrogen cyanide's center holds the hydrogen atom to one of its sides and locks the nitrogen atom to its other side as if it had linked elbows with each of its two partners to hold them together as an unstoppable team. But astrochemists and molecular astrophysicists haven't yet pinned down the date of hydrogen cyanide's first appearance in this cosmos.[50]

When the number of atoms in a molecule climbs higher, our ignorance becomes worse. As Jan M. Hollis of the NASA Goddard Space Flight Center in Greenbelt, Maryland, said in 2004, "At present . . . there is no accepted theory addressing how interstellar molecules containing more than 5 atoms are formed."[51]

We do know this: carbon was the great seductress, hostess, and mix-mistress of the new element brigade.[52] And carbon's talent for introducing atoms to each other then hosting them as they gelled in stable families resulted in yet more supersynchrony. The result defied belief. It was the manic mass production of biomolecules. These carbon-based atom-teams arose in hot clouds of interstellar gas,[53] in cold clouds of interstellar gas,[54] in spicules of interstellar ice,[55] in the shrouds of dying stars,[56] in comets,[57] in meteorites,[58] and in just about everything in between.[59] Today, 10 percent of the volume of interstellar ice grains is composed of biomolecules.[60] As of 2000, we had detected 120 forms[61] of molecules in space.[62] One hundred of them were organic.[63] A mere 120 early molecules in a universe of six-monkey-and-six-typewriter randomness does not compute. The number should be in the billions. But one thing we know for sure: manic mass production and a loose supersynchrony once again ruled. The cosmos was still hurtling down the narrow railroad tracks of cosmic destiny. Biomolecules in space included carbon dioxide, carbon monoxide, methanol, ammonia polyols, dihydroxyacetones, glycerols, sugar acids, and sugar alcohols. And these molecules were all over the place.

The dates of molecular evolution may remain obscure, but the emergence and complexification of molecules set the stage for culture. They set the stage for the Big Burp—the emergence of REALLY complicated molecules. And they set the stage for those really big molecules' progeny, living creatures like you and me. The date of the Big Burp was far earlier than you might imagine. It was less than 10 billion years ABB,[64] just a tad more than two-thirds of the way into this cosmos's existence.

Supersynchrony suggests that the Big Burp happened on planets scattered across the length and breadth of the universe.[65] Manic mass production hints at the very same thing. But the only planet where we are sure the Big Burp occurred is ours: Mama Earth.

In the Big Burp, sociality went big time in a whole new way. First, this planet began its own gravitational social gathering process. It kidnapped, captured, recruited, and compacted leftover matter from the shards of a newly ignited sun.[66] Then came the second stage of moleculogenesis.[67] Massive teams of molecules in underground water pockets, above-ground puddles, and seas of this early world wove the walls of lipid balloons, greasy micro-sacks walling off a micro-pool of water, a microscopic inner sea. What clues hint that these envelopes were among the first mega-projects produced by the Big Burp, produced by this second-stage of moleculogenesis?

Take a chunk of the Murchison meteorite. Grind it up. It contains the simple biochemicals found all over the cosmos, simple molecules wrapped around the great atomic introducer, seducer, and recruiter: carbon. Slip the powdered bits of the Murchison meteorite into water, and the social gathering of simple biomolecules begins. Your water is rapidly filled with tiny bubbles, water balloons held together by the waterproof envelope of an interwoven[68] molecular mega-community.[69] We call that self-woven oilcloth bag—that microscopic balloon of molecular fabric—a "membrane." And membranes—bio-envelopes—produced protective playpens for more molecular socializing. Far, far more.

A mere 9.9 billion years ABB, the molecular sociality of the Big Burp took advantage of membranes and went whole hog into moleculogenic overdrive, spitting out molecules that were enormous—chain-ganging as many as 62 million atoms into a single molecular strand.[70] Supersynchrony and manic mass production also went into overdrive, apparently producing the same massive atomic communities—the same mega-molecules—all over this planet's face. And those massive atom-teams soon formed their own social alliances, alliances that were driven by something very new—culture. Culture began when these mega-teams of atoms developed internal memory.[71] Culture began when atomic mega-teams braided new strategies into their molecular strands, kept the strategies that worked, reproduced them in multitudes, and discarded or packed away in the cold storage of "junk DNA" the strategies that failed. It sometimes took storing five failed strategies to construct the mega-strategy from which a new breakthrough would be made.[72]

These huge new atom communities were RNA and DNA. RNA and DNA were as social as could be. They used membranes as fortifications, no-go zones, corrals within which RNA, DNA, and their membrane-weaving partners could maintain a specialized mini-sea—a Jell-O or Gatorade rich in vitamins, organic molecules, enzymes,[73] sugars, carbohydrates, fatty acids,[74] and proteins.[75] That gel is better known as cytoplasm.

The Big Burp had produced cells. And each of these cells was a working community of 10^{11} atoms[76]—a hundred trillion atoms combined to pursue a highly complex common purpose. But, more important, a hundred trillion atoms with a heritage passed on from mother to daughter, a past recorded in a literal inner-circle, an interior ring of genes.[77] A hundred trillion atoms with the ability to evade danger and to find food. A hundred trillion atoms with the ability to make future predictions based on an accumulated data base, based on the store of information that gene-strings cadge, corner, and maintain.[78] And a hundred trillion atoms with the ability to rejigger their collective memory's instructions on how to make the next move. A hundred trillion atoms with the ability to reprogram their instruction-set, their genome. In other words, these clusters of a hundred trillion atoms contained the first molecules in the history of the cosmos to have the advantage of memory and the advantage of culture. But how did these culture-driven molecular mobile cities manage to skyhook themselves into new niches, to turn new wastes into food, and to gain new abilities? The answer, once again, is sociality.

No cell is an island. The ancestral cells we're talking about were bacteria. And no bacterium can live alone. Put a single bacterium in solitary confinement. Give it its own petri dish with agar spread across the bottom as food. The bacterium will not become calm and meditative, enjoying its solitude. It will do the opposite. It will split over and over again, giving birth to a huge bacterial family.[79] And each new family member in turn will multiply like crazy to conquer more of the agar.[80] Solitary bacterial cells create communities of unbelievable size around themselves in a very short amount of time. Give them a few weeks and the total bacterial tribe in your petri dish will have a population of 7 trillion[81]—more than all the humans who have ever lived. And that supersized society will not be a disorganized mass of individuals.[82] Far from it. Individual bacteria share their information with a complex chemical language.[83] The result is an information-processing web, a massively parallel-processed computation-and-connection machine, what one leading researcher on this form of social integration among bacteria, Eshel Ben-Jacob of the University of Tel Aviv, calls a "creative web."[84] Your bacterial culture, the bacterial mega-society in your petri dish, will be a research and development machine, a collective intelligence. According to Ben-Jacob it will be capable of spotting problems and working to solve them, often producing solutions this cosmos has never previously seen. And at the heart of that collective expansion-and-innovation web will be, guess what? A collective memory. A collective way of doing things. A culture.

A culture complete with monuments and with pyramids. The bacterial colonies of the first 3.5 billion years of life have left us their architecture, their massive public works projects. They're called stromatolites.[85] Stromatolites are stone structures the size of your mattress poking from the shallow seas around Australia and fossilized in the rocks of Michigan. How are they produced? They're created by bacterial teams contributing to a massive multigenerational enterprise. A colony of bacteria exudes a gooey foundation on which it sits. Each bacterium sucks a key portion of its food—carbon dioxide—from the shallow waters of the sea. This triggers the precipitation of particles of calcium carbonate—grains of limestone—from the water. The falling microbits of stone pile up in the glue-like base of the bacterial colony.[86] The next bacterial colony lives on top of this ultra-thin limestone residue, and in its lifetime leaves a second slick of lime. Millions or trillions of colonies later, those thin slicks of limestone add up. They create a monument nearly as big in comparison to a single bacterium as the Moon is to you and me. Quite an accomplishment for creatures with collective computational powers and creativity, but without brains.

Bacteria were the founders of culture. But they were not the only cultural creatures to appear in the next 3.5 billion years of life's evolution. They were not the only culture-gifted children of the Big Burp. In 1983, John Tyler

Bonner wrote a classic book, *The Evolution of Culture in Animals*.[87] Bonner revealed culture in myxobacteria, slime molds, birds, whales, elephants, social insects, and chimpanzees.

Then came human culture, another multigenerational, multilayered group project that accumulated memories, habits, and methods of turning new niches of barrenness into paradise. We were born one of the most pathetic creatures this Earth has ever seen. Other animals were birthed with biological equipment for thermoregulation[88]—for making it through sizzling heat and biting cold. They were born with fur coats. Not us. We were born as naked as hairless mole rats, like pieces of meat tossed to the crocodile jaws of the elements. Like cheetahs and our cousins, the chimps,[89] we were born with a lust to eat meat. We needed this high-protein diet to fuel our energy-hungry big brains.[90] But we were born without a stitch of hunting equipment. We emerged from the womb without fangs and teeth. We were born without the four legs that give horses, gazelles, and lions their speed.

We were also born without the equipment to be successful vegetarians. Our cousins, mountain apes,[91] had huge bellies capable of breaking down the cellulose fortresses that protect the cells of leaves. We, on the other hand, had relatively tiny tummies[92] that didn't stand a chance against the vegetable roughage, the greenery that surrounded us. Culture was our only means of rescuing ourselves. First we invented artificial fangs and teeth 2.5 million years ago.[93] We invented the Oldowan stone tool kit.[94] Then we tamed fire[95] and invented cooking [96] as a way to predigest our meals so that our compact digestive system (and its bacterial tenants)[97] could extract the fuel from the toughest foods. The small abdomen that cooking made possible gave us a mobility our knuckle-walking cousins had never possessed.[98] According to evolutionary neurobiologist John Skoyles, it also gave us the swiftness of marathon runners.[99] We couldn't outrace a zebra or an antelope, but we could outlast them in a long-distance run.[100] Then we could take advantage of the animal's fatigue to move in for the kill. What's more, we were the first—and so far, the only—species able to hurl a stone at high velocity with perfect aim.[101] We were pitchers par excellence. We could literally knock a bird out of the sky with a stone[102] or kill a fast-moving rat or rabbit with an overhand toss.[103] Which meant that we could hunt small game in ways that claws and fangs had never made possible.

Somewhere along the line we also invented clothing[104] and marched off to the far north,[105] equipped to shield ourselves from winter snow and ice. We also invented architecture during the ice ages, building palaces with frameworks of Mammoth tusks and Mammoth ribs and an outer skin made of Mammoth hides.[106] And we invented ways to feed two needs that obsess us in a manner few animals will ever know—identity and vanity.[107] We invented makeup 280,000 years ago[108] to differentiate your tribe from mine and to let you compete for attention with your tribemates. We invented long-distance trade[109] 140,000 years ago[110] so that folks in the interior of a continent could show off by wearing jewelry made of sea creatures' shells[111] and so that coastal dwellers could make tools out of obsidian mined in the mountains far inland. We invented beads[112] to let each other know who was on top of the tribe's wealth and who was not.[113] Finally, 10,000 years ago, we invented agriculture[114] and cities.[115] Cities gave birth to subcultures,[116] and the competition between human cultures and subcultures went into overdrive.

Without material breakthroughs, human culture would never have achieved its current heights. In fact, without our host of material inventions—the spear, the plow, the fireplace, the coat, the boat, the brick, the book, and the laptop—we would have grubbed along forever as hunter-gatherers. Human culture was a dance between material innovations and innovations of the mind. Human culture layered new concepts, new languages, and new forms of data processing, data storing, worldview making, scenario creating, and future prediction. Human culture worked with the multigenerational stubbornness of the bacteria that built stromatolites. But instead of constructing physical monuments the size of moons, human cultures built new mind tools—words, concepts, metaphors, religions, creation myths, tales of legendary heroes, sagas of triumphs and defeats, and entire worldviews[117]—mind tools that from the very first were celestomanic . . . sky-obsessed. Obsessed with the heavens and the stars. Cultures crafted new mind tools that could decipher the Earth below and the cosmos slowly wheeling above our heads.

One hundred and twenty five thousand generations of this layering have made us conscious, and have misled us into a peculiar arrogance. We think that we have reshaped this planet more than any creatures that have ever come before. We think that we have plundered the pitifully small pool of resources on this Earth and that now we must make sacrifices to appease a nature angered by our transgressions. We are wrong. Very wrong.

Bacteria over two billion years ago[118] utterly polluted this planet's atmosphere by farting out a toxic gas that seemed to threaten all of life. That gas was oxygen.[119] And yet other bacteria invented ways to turn that poison to food and fuel.[120] They invented strategies for recruiting the uncountable molecules of a poison into biomass.

The mud that covers the bottom of the sea is not just a product of inanimate nature.[121] It is a massive desecration of 70 percent of this Earth's pristine rocky surface,[122] a fertile sludge generated by the burrowing and swimming creatures of the sea.[123] It is the recruitment of gazillions of inanimate atoms into the grand project of biomass.

Microbes long ago raped the naked Earth above the seas, piercing its cloak of stone.[124] They produced chemicals that turned a tiny bit of this planet's coat of rock into sludge.[125] Microbes spat out mineral particles from which new rocks would be made. And microbes opened cracks in the planet's native stone. Then plants dug their roots into the microscopic cracks and split the virgin bedrock.[126] If Charles Darwin is right, every fruitful field now covered with soil was the product of a massive landscaping effort left to us by millions of generations of earthworms who "sinned" against nature by doing plastic surgery on our pristine planet's face.[127] The earthworms turned jagged outcrops and crevasses into gentle hills, slopes, and valleys. We use the worms' violation of Mother Nature to grow our plants and we worship the nature-desecrating worms' legacy—rainforests and greenery.

Meanwhile bacteria have continued to outdo us in the research and development business, constantly remaking this rocky orb. They profane the planet by following nature's imperative for the grand experiment of life. That imperative? Take as many inanimate molecules as you can grab and press-gang them into the family of cells and DNA. Be fruitful and multiply. Turn poisons into delicacies and barren wastes into candy. Be consumerist as hell. Be materially rapacious. Make as much of this inanimate globe as you can into biomass. Do what quarks, atoms, galaxies, and stars have done. Defy disorder. Shatter the rules of entropy.

What does this mean for you and me? What does it mean for the culture of human beings? Our culture is one among many this planet has spawned. But we think our culture is unique. And it is. Our culture is built on brains and on the passions of the hypothalamic-pituitary-adrenal-gonadal axis. Our culture is built on emotion, reason, and, literally, balls and guts. As a result, our culture froths with poetry, music, storytelling, technology, high aspirations, self-hating philosophies, and consciousness.

Our culture is also built on something no bacterium or chimp can conceive. It's built on an ancestor worship[128] that keeps our ancient trail of insights alive for hundreds of generations and passes them down the line. We worship ancestors more than we know. In science, we invoke their names to validate our scientific claims. We refer to Plato, Aristotle, Newton, Darwin, and Einstein. We do it in our journal articles. We do it in our lectures and in our conventions. We do it all the time. In political life, we invoke our founding fathers—Jefferson, Washington, Benjamin Franklin, and Alexander

Hamilton. Islam invokes the memory of Mohammed and has produced tens of thousands of pages recording nearly every moment of his life.[129] Buddhism is built on the memory of Siddhartha Gautama, the Buddha.[130] And antiglobalism and anticapitalism keep alive the spirit of the French Revolution, Karl Marx, and Michele Foucault. The result is a layer-upon-layer crepe-cake of thought-tools that accumulates the way that bacterial stromatolites rise from the bottom of the sea and reach for the sky.[131] But this multilayered monument exists in imagination and achievement. It exists as a product of human minds.

What can our culture—with these unique powers—do for the 3.85-billion-year experiment of the bioprocess? What can our culture do for the family of cells and DNA? What can it do for the mega-project of life? What, if any, is our mandate from this cosmos's history?

Our universe has shown a remarkable ability to reinvent itself and to create radically new forms—quarks, protons, galaxies, and stars—without culture and without human beings. Then the universe has used these new creations to create even more. It has created us, complete with our dogmas, our passions, and our fantasies. As incarnations of nature, as the most complex forms of social dance protons have yet conceived, it is our obligation to contribute to this cosmic reinvention, to this invention of enormous change, and to this production of massive surprise.

First off, we are NOT running out of resources. We are running out of ingenuity. We are using less than a quadrillionth of the resources of this planet. Geomorphologists point out that when you look at Earth from space, "few if any natural landforms on Earth bear the unmistakable mark of life."[132] There is 1.097 sextillion cubic meters of rock, magma, and iron beneath our feet. (1,097,509,500,000,000,000,000[133]) That's over a sextillion-cubic-meter stock of raw materials we haven't yet learned to use. We haven't yet learned to turn that sextillion-cubic-meter stockpile into fuel, food, or energy. We haven't yet recruited it into the clan of biomass, into the family of DNA. We haven't yet pulled it into the enterprise of life.

Is there any indication that we could or should transform more of this material into animals and greenery? Yes. The first clue comes from our clever relatives bacteria. Two miles beneath your feet and mine, even as we speak, bacteria are turning granite into food and fuel, into raw material for the grand project of biomass.[134] Anything bacteria can do, we can do better.

The second clue? We are the only species that can take the DNA-and-cell experiment off this planet, off this one fragile terrarium of Earth. We are the only species that can plant ecosystems—biomass—on other planets and moons in this solar system. We are the only species that can carry life to other stars and galaxies. And taking life beyond Earth is an absolute necessity. Why?

The next mass extinction—the next great climate catastrophe—is inevitable, no matter how many Kyoto treaties, carbon sequestration schemes, and heroes of sustainability like Al Gore we have. Let's get to the bitter bottom line. There have been roughly 142 mass extinctions on this globe.[135] That's one species apocalypse every 26 million years.[136] What's more, carbon dioxide levels in our Earth's early atmosphere were 100 to 1,000 times[137] what they are today.[138] And there were no smokestacks or tailpipes anywhere in sight. In our 226-million-year[139] sweep around the center of our galaxy,[140] we accumulate 30 million kilograms of space dust per year. Every 100,000 years we whiffle through a cloud of interplanetary powder that triples that amount.[141] These dust immersions radically change the climate on the surface of our little sphere. And every 143 million years we plow through a spiral arm of our galaxy and hit a patch of cosmic rays that plunges us into an ice age.[142]

But there's more. There have been 60 glaciations, ice ages, in the two million years[143] since *Homo habilis*[144] began the trek that led to the evolution of you and me. What's more, in the last 120,000 years, the era of us physically modern men and women, us *Homo sapiens*,[145] there have been 20 global warmings[146]—20 hothouse punches in which the planet's temperature has shot up between 10 and 18 degrees in a mere two decades or less.[147] And that is just the beginning of the list of Mother Nature's atrocities. The sun itself has set us on the path to a slow boil. Good old Sol is now 43 percent brighter (43 percent hotter) than it was when Earth began.[148] Yet Earth has been in danger of freezing like an iceball over and over again[149] and has spent the last 420,000 years[150] in an ice age that only stopped for a brief pause roughly 12,000 years ago, when we humans were released from the deep freeze and began the steps that would lead to the invention of agriculture and cities, both of which we concocted roughly 10,000 years ago.[151]

Just to show how many natural flukes can resculpt our weather, until 10,000 years ago the Gulf Stream shifted its route every 1,500 years,[152] leaving former warm areas in the cold, and making former frigid zones semitropical. Then there's the Milankovich Effect, an eccentric wobble (a precession) in our planet's rotation around the Sun that resculpts our climatic patterns every 22,000, 41,000, and 100,000 years.[153]

The climatic stability we think is natural is not.[154] It is a 12,000-year-long oddity, a total departure from Mother Nature's norm.[155] Unless we learn far, far more about meteorological engineering than we know today, the relatively stable weather we've bathed in since the departure of the last Ice Age 12,000 years ago will someday change entirely. Carbon sequestration may well be our first attempt at macro-meteorological tinkering. And it may lead to far more sophisticated ways to control our climate. But we have to ditch the fantasy that every climate glitch is our fault and that we must atone by shunning consumption, by sacrificing to the planet, and by making Mother Nature happy. Mother Nature's way is instability and catastrophe. She killed off stars; and she has killed off more species than we can count. Mother Nature, to quote a chapter title from my book *The Lucifer Principle: A Scientific Expedition Into the Forces of History*, is a "bloody bitch."[156]

Evolution has put us in the bull's eye of disaster. We are a hydrophilic species. We are water lovers. Sixty percent of the humans on this globe live in coastal areas.[157] As Plato said, we are dotted like frogs around a pond.[158] And every coastal city we prize, from New York to Shanghai, will someday end up under the sea or on a mountaintop. That will happen with or without our carbon emissions. It's happened to many a water-loving species before us. That's why we find the fossils of sea creatures on mountaintops. The message? Without making some very big moves, all of us coastal frogs will someday either find ourselves far too high and dry or we will drown.

Mother Nature and the evolutionary process have also provided a solution to the certainty of catastrophe. For 3.85 billion years, the imperative of biomass has been to accessorize the standard backbone of life[159]—to customize the molecular backbone of the DNA-and-cell system with as many ways of making a living, of consuming the inedible, of crawling into crevasses and crannies, and of soaring to new heights as it can. With that trick, the family of DNA has ensured that when the next big mass extinction hits, some life-forms will be stripped away, but other of life's experiments, her variations on her Big Burp theme, will survive.

Bacteria are the ultimate survivors, the ultimate evangelists preaching through their actions the imperatives of evolution, the commandments of the cosmos, and the obligations of life. Lesson number one from bacteria is this: without consumption, there would be no ecosystems. There would be no life. A bacterial colony expands by guzzling the fuel of photons, by harnessing inanimate chemistry, and by stitching lifeless atoms of nitrogen, hydrogen, and carbon into the molecules of proteins and sugars, into the weave of cell walls, into the braids of genes, and into the soup of protoplasm in between. A bacterial colony expands by recruiting, seducing, and conquering as many inanimate molecules as it can, bringing them into the family of biomass, the family of life. It expands by inventing new ways to consume.[160]

Bacterial lesson number two: carve out as many new niches as you can; race with all your might and creativity to outwit the next catastrophe—nature's next mass extinction. As we've seen, bacteria have invented ways to flourish in the toxic bath of oxygen that drowned this planet roughly two billion years ago.[161] They've learned to flourish where there is no oxygen at all.[162] They've invented ways to be fruitful and multiply eating the steel of oil pipelines[163] and the metal and PVC plastic[164] in the plumbing of skyscrapers.[165] They've invented ways to munch the most abundant metal in the crust of Earth—aluminum[166]—and to turn it into bio-stuff. They've created techniques for living in plumes of water with a searing 120 degrees of heat and to press-gang inanimate sulfur atoms into the metabolic processes of life.[167] They've pioneered ways to thrive in the radioactive cooling pools of nuclear plants.[168] They've shown that in all probability they will take the carnage left by a nuclear Armageddon, eat it, and turn it into yet more mega-teams of innovators and of micro-inventors—transforming it into yet more bacteria.

But that is the merest hint of bacteria's obsessive imperative to find new niches for life. Between 50 trillion and 500 trillion bacteria are in your throat and gut right now.[169] They've worked out a deal that makes you a niche, a portable home, and a gatherer of their groceries. The bacterial colonies in your throat defend you from hostile microorganisms;[170] and the bacterial colonies in your stomach and intestines digest much of your food for you. All you have to do is give them a nice, warm place to live. They've worked out a similar deal with migrating waterfowl, who fly bacterial colonies thousands of miles, allowing them to spread intercontinentally.[171] Bruce Moffett, a microbiologist at the University of East London, even suspects that bacteria have worked out ways to fly high, thrive in clouds, and to make the weather they like the best.[172] The result? Bacteria have survived every mass extinction with which this planet has threatened to wipe out biomass.

Now the trick is to spread this invention of new niches, this recruitment and radical upgrade of dead atoms, this next step in evolution that we call life, beyond one tiny, fragile nest. The biggest unfilled niche for life exists above our heads.

There's a simple trick nature has taught us via birds. There are more than twice as many bird species as species of mammals[173]—twice as many kinds of feathered sky-soarers as furry, down-to-Earth ground walkers. The lesson?

Those who fly find more environmental pockets of riches than those who remain Earthbound.

We are the only species on the face of this planet who can fly beyond the atmosphere. We are the only beings whose culture has created spaceships. We are the only life-forms who have walked on the Moon. We are the only bio-mechanisms who can take ecosystems to the planets and the stars.

Our mission, should we choose to accept it, is to innovate our way around every climatic catastrophe nature throws our way. It is to spread the products of the Big Burp and to expand life's unique form of manic mass production and supersynchrony. It is to find more protective niches—niches in this solar system and beyond—for the family of cells and DNA. Our evolutionary mandate is to give life a shot at pulling all of this cosmos into the evolutionary process. Our evolutionary mandate is to recruit all of this universe into the process we call nature, the process we call culture, the process we call ecosystems, the process we call life. Our evolutionary mandate is to do what galaxies, stars, and molecules have done—defy disorder and laugh at entropy. Our evolutionary mandate is to bring space to life by bringing life to space! Our evolutionary mandate is to green the universe.

Endnotes

1. Susan L. Hurley and Nick Chater, *Perspectives on Imitation: From Neuroscience to Social Science* (Cambridge, MA: MIT Press, 2005), p. 150.

2. S. McBrearty and A. S. Brooks, "The revolution that wasn't: a new interpretation of the origins of modern human behavior," *Journal of Human Evolution* 39, no. 5 (2000): 453–563. R. G. Klein, *The Human Career* (Chicago, IL: University of Chicago Press, Chicago, ed. 2, 1999).

3. S. McBrearty and A. S. Brooks, "The revolution that wasn't: a new interpretation of the origins of modern human behavior," *Journal of Human Evolution* 39, no. 5 (2000): 453–563. R. G. Klein, *The Human Career* (Chicago, IL: University of Chicago Press, Chicago, ed. 2, 1999).

4. Luis Benítez-Bribiesca, "The Biology of Music," *Science Magazine* 292, no. 5526. (29 June 2001): 2432–2433. Josie Glausiusz, "The Genetic Mystery of Music: Does a mother's lullaby give an infant a better chance for survival?" *Discover Magazine* 22, no. 8 (2001).

5. Alexander Marshack, "Evolution of the Human Capacity: The Symbolic Evidence," *Yearbook of Physical Anthropology* (New York: Wiley-Liss, 1989). Alexander Marshack, "The Tai Plaque and Calendrical Notation in the Upper Palaeolithic," *Cambridge Archaeological Journal* (1991): 25. Alexander Marshack, "On 'Close Reading' and Decoration versus Notation," *Current Anthropology* (February 1997): 81.

6. H. Valladas, J. Clottes, J. M. Geneste, M. A. Garcia, M. Arnold, H. Cachier, and N. Tisnérat-Laborde, Palaeolithic paintings. "Evolution of prehistoric cave art," *Nature* 413, no. 6855 (4 October 2001): 479.

7. Sally McBrearty and Alison S. Brooks, "The revolution that wasn't: a new interpretation of the origins of modern human behavior," *Journal of Human Evolution* 39, no. 5 (2000): 453–563. Carl Zimmer, "Great Mysteries of Human Evolution: New discoveries rewrite the book on who we are and where we came from," *Discover Magazine* 24, no. 09 (2003).

8. Alan L. Deino and Sally McBrearty, "Ar dating of the Kapthurin Formation, Baringo, Kenya," *Journal of Human Evolution* 42, no. ½ (2002): 185–211.

9. Lawrence S . Barham, "Systematic Pigment Use in the Middle Pleistocene of South-Central Africa," *Current Anthropology* 43, no. 1 (2002).

10. James Harrod, "Researching the Origins of Art. Religion, and Mind: Middle Paleolithic Art, Symbols, Mind." Retrieved from the World Wide Web 25 April 2004, *http://www.originsnet.org/mindmp.html*. Larry Barham and Simon Denison, ed., "From art and tools came human origins," *British Archaeology Magazine*. Editor: Simon Denison Issue no 42, March (1999). Council for British Archaeology. Retrieved from the World Wide Web 25 April 2004, *http://www.britarch.ac.uk/ba/ba42/ba42feat.html*. Robert G. Bednarik, "The earliest known palaeoart." First published in Vladimir Vasil'evich Bobrov (ed.), *Pervobytnaya arkheologiya: chelovek i iskusstvo, Kemerovskii gosudarstvennyi universitet, Novosibirsk*: 23–31. Retrieved 11 August 2007, from the World Wide Web *http://mc2.vicnet.net.au/home/aura/shared_files/kemerovo.pdf*.

11. Howard Bloom, "Manifesto for a New Psychological Science," *ASCAP— Across-Species Comparisons and Psychopathology Society* 10, no. 7 (1997): 20–21, 27.

12. Pennsylvania State University geoscientist James F. Kasting feels that the consensus date for the origin of life on Earth is roughly four billion years. (James F. Kasting, "Planetary Atmospheres: Warming Early Earth and Mars," *Science* 23 [May 1997]: 1213–1215.) Evidence tends to pin the date to an undetermined period before 3.85 billion years ago. See: Heinrich D. Holland, "Evidence for Life on Earth More Than 3850 Million Years Ago," *Science* (1997): 38–39. Norman R. Pace, "A Molecular View of Microbial Diversity and the Biosphere." *Science* (1997): 734–740; S. J. Mojzsis, G. Arrhenius, K. D. Mckeegan, T. M. Harrison, A. P. Nutman, and C. R. L. Friend, "Evidence for life on Earth before 3,800 million years ago," *Nature* 7 (November 1996): 55–59. NASA News Releases, "When Life Began On Earth," press release, 5 November 1996. Retrieved 13 November 1996, from the World Wide Web *http://spacelink.msfc.nasa.gov/NASA.News/NASA.News.Releases/Previous. News.Releases/96.News.Releases/96-11.News.Releases/96-11-05.When.Life. Began.On.Earth.* January 1999. John M. Hayes, "The earliest memories of life on Earth," *Nature* (1996): 21–22.

13. Richard A. Kerr, "Early Life Thrived Despite Earthly Travails," *Science* 284 (1999): 2111–2113. M. Gogarten Boekels, E. Hilario, and J. P. Gogarten, "The effects of heavy meteorite bombardment on the early evolution— the emergence of the three domains of life," *Origins of Life and Evolution of the Biosphere* 25, nos. 1–3 (1995): 251–264. Abstract retrieved 10 June 1997 from the World Wide Web *http://www.springerlink.com/content/ hl23380073722636/.* Dana Mackenzie, "Moon-Forming Crash Is Likely in New Model," *Science* (1999): 15–16.

14. Charles Seife, "Breakthrough Of The Year: Illuminating the Dark Universe," *Science* 302, no. 5653 (2003): 2038–2039. doi:10.1126/science.302.5653.2038.

15. J. Allday, *Quarks, Leptons, and the Big Bang* (Bristol, England: IOP [Institute of Physics] Press, 1998). L. Bergstrom and A. Goobar, *Cosmology and Particle Astrophysics* (New York: Wiley, 1999). Jeremy Bernstein, *An Introduction to Cosmology* (Englewood Cliffs, NJ: Prentice Hall, 1995), pp. 12–14. Edward L. Wright, "Brief History of the Universe," Astronomy Department, UCLA. Retrieved 12 August 2007, from the World Wide Web *http://www.astro.ucla. edu/~wright/BBhistory.html.* G. H. Hardy, *Ramanujan: Twelve Lectures on Subjects Suggested by his Life and Work* (New York: Chelsea, 1999).

16. A family of two, a neutron and a proton, is deuterium. A family of ten, three protons and seven neutrons, is Lithium 7. Subir Sarkar, "Big Bang Nucleosynthesis: Reprise," in L. Baudis, *Dark Matter in Astrophysics and Particle Physics 1998: Proceedings of the Second International Conference on Dark Matter and Particle Physics, Heidelberg, 1998* (Boca Raton, FL: CRC Press, 1999), p. 108.

17. Bruno Bertotti, *Modern Cosmology in Retrospect* (Cambridge: Cambridge University Press, 1990), p. 185.

18. Michael Zeilik, *Astronomy: The Evolving Universe* (Cambridge: Cambridge University Press, 2002), p. 361.

19. Ron Cowen, "Sounds of the universe confirm Big Bang," *Science News*159, no. 17 (2001). Retrieved 30 March 2002, from the World Wide Web *http://www.sciencenews.org/20010428/fob3.asp.*

20. Michael D. Lemonick, *Echo of the Big Bang* (Princeton, NJ: Princeton University Press, 2003), p. 205.

21. Charles Seife, "Breakthrough Of The Year: Illuminating the Dark Universe," *Science* 302, no. 5653 (2003): 2038–2039. doi:10.1126/science.302.5653.2038.

22. Christopher J. Miller, Robert C. Nichol, and David J. Batuski, "Acoustic Oscillations in the Early Universe and Today," *Science* 292 (2001): 2302–2303. doi:10.1126/science.1060440]. Ron Cowen, "Sounds of the universe confirm Big Bang," *Science News* 159, no. 17 (2001). Retrieved 30 March 2002, from the World Wide Web *http://www.sciencenews.org/20010428/fob3.asp.*

23. These oscillations, these acoustic waves, apparently continued rolling through the early cosmos for a full 400,000 years. George Musser, "The Peak of Success," *Scientific American* 285, no. 2 (2001): 14–15. Retrieved 10 September 2007, from the World Wide Web *http://ehostvgw6.epnet.com/ehost.asp?key=204.179.122.129_8000_-1525769105&site=ehost&return=n& custid=nypl&IP=yes&profile=web&defaultdb=aph.* Daniel J. Eisenstein, Idit Zehavi, David W. Hogg, Roman Scoccimarro, Michael R. Blanton, Robert C. Nichol, Ryan Scranton, Hee-Jong Seo, Max Tegmark, Zheng Zheng, Scott F. Anderson, Jim Annis, Neta Bahcall, Jon Brinkmann, Scott Burles, Francisco J. Castander, Andrew Connolly, Istvan Csabai, Mamoru Doi,

Masataka Fukugita, Joshua A. Frieman, Karl Glazebrook, James E. Gunn, John S. Hendry, Gregory Hennessy, Zeljko Ivezic, Stephen Kent, Gillian R. Knapp, Huan Lin, Yeong-Shang Loh, Robert H. Lupton, Bruce Margon, Timothy A. McKay, Avery Meiksin, Jeffery A. Munn, Adrian Pope, Michael W. Richmond, David Schlegel, Donald P. Schneider, Kazuhiro Shimasaku, Christopher Stoughton, Michael A. Strauss, Mark SubbaRao, Alexander S. Szalay, Istvan Szapudi, Douglas L. Tucker, Brian Yanny, and Donald G. York, "Detection Of The Baryon Acoustic Peak In The Large-Scale Correlation Function Of SDSS Luminous Red Galaxies," preprint. Submitted to the *Astrophysical Journal* 31 December 2004. Retrieved 10 September 2007, from the World Wide Web, *http://cmb.as.arizona.edu/~eisenste/acousticpeak/lrg_largescale.pdf*. Sloan Digital Sky Survey, "The cosmic yardstick—Sloan Digital Sky Survey astronomers measure role of dark matter, dark energy and gravity in the distribution of galaxies," press release, 11 January 2005. Retrieved 10 September 2007, from the World Wide Web *http://www.sdss.org/news/releases/20050111.yardstick.html*.

24. Charles Seife, "Breakthrough Of The Year: Illuminating the Dark Universe," *Science* 302, no. 5653 (2003): 2038–2039. doi:10.1126/science.302.5653.2038.

25. Bertram Schwarzschild, "COBE Satellite Finds No Hint of Excess In The Cosmic Microwave Spectrum," *Physics Today* (1990): 18. Retrieved 10 September 2007, from the World Wide Web *http://www.physicstoday.com/vol-43/iss-3/pdf/vol43no3p17_20.pdf*.

26. The mass of a proton=1,832 the mass of an electron. Charles Loraine Alley and Kenneth Ward Atwood, *Electronic Engineering* (New York: Wiley, 1966), p. 7. The mass of an electron=9.1093897x10(-31) kg. The mass of a proton=1.6726231 x 10(-27) kg. Electron Mass. Fundamental Physical Constants. Latest (2006) values of the constants. "The NIST Reference on Constants, Units, and Uncertainty," National Institute of Standards and Technology. Retrieved 10 September 2007, from the World Wide Web *http://physics.nist.gov/cuu/Constants/index.html*.

27. CERN (Conseil Européen pour la Recherche Nucléaire), "LHC—The Large Hadron Collider." Retrieved 10 September 2007, from the World Wide Web *http://lhc.web.cern.ch/lhc/*.

28. Howard Bloom, "The Xerox Effect: On the Importance of Pre-Biotic Evolution," in *PhysicaPlus*, the online publication of The Israeli Physical Society. 10 January 2004. Retrieved 10 September 2007, from the World Wide Web *http://physicaplus.org.il/zope/home/en/3/mabat_bloom_en*.

29. Encyclopædia Britannica, "quark," Encyclopædia Britannica Online, 2007. Retrieved 10 September 2007, from the World Wide Web *http://www.britannica.com/eb/article-9062172*.

30. Eric J. Chaisson, *Cosmic Evolution: The Rise of Complexity in Nature* (Cambridge: Harvard University Press, 2001), p. 7.

31. Eric J. Chaisson, *Cosmic Evolution: The Rise of Complexity in Nature* (Cambridge: Harvard University Press, 2001), p. 46.

32. Eric J. Chaisson, *Cosmic Evolution: The Rise of Complexity in Nature* (Cambridge: Harvard University Press, 2001), p. 25.

33. The best-known work spoofing the six-monkeys-at-six-typewriters paradigm was: Elmo, Gum, Heather, Holly, Mistletoe, and Rowan, "Notes Towards the Complete Works of Shakespeare," first published for *Vivaria.net* in 2002. Retrieved 10 September 2007, from the World Wide Web *http://www.vivaria.net/experiments/notes/publication/NOTES_EN.pdf* and *http://www.vivaria.net/experiments/notes/documentation/*.

34. Some astronomers set the date of the first stars at 200 million years ABB. Others pin the date of the first star formation to 400 million years ABB. Ron Cowen, "Beryllium data confirm stars' age," *Science News* (September 2004). Retrieved 30 September 2004, from the World Wide Web *http://www.sciencenews.org/articles/20040918/note11.asp*. Cowen's article gives the date of 200 million years ABB. Dennis Overbye, "Astronomers Find The Earliest Signs Yet Of Violent Baby Universe," *New York Times*, Friday, 17 March 2006: Late Edition—Final, Section A, p. 18. Overbye's article gives the date of 400 million years.

35. Evan Scannapieco, Patrick Petitjean, and Tom Broadhurst, "The Emptiest Places," *Scientific American* 287, no. 4 (October 2002). James Glanz, "Astronomers See Evidence of First Light in Universe," *New York Times*, 7

August 2001. Retrieved 13 August 2007, from the World Wide Web *http:// www.nytimes.com/2001/08/07/science/space/07DARK.html?pagewanted=print.*

36. "The most widely accepted picture of how structure formed involves the idea of gravitational instability. A perfectly smooth self-gravitating fluid with the same density everywhere stays homogeneous for all time. But any slight irregularities (which always exist in reality) tend to get amplified by the action of gravity. A small patch of the universe that is slightly denser than average tends to attract material from around itself; it therefore gets even denser and attracts even more material. This instability will form a highly concentrated lump, held together by gravitational forces." Peter Coles, "The end of the old model Universe," *Nature* 393 (June 1998): 741–744.

37. Berkeley University astronomer Hyron Spinrad refers to the process by which gravity pulls mini particles together as macro forms, galaxies, as "the hierarchical merging of gas-rich systems." Hyron Spinrad, *Galaxy Formation and Evolution* (New York: Springer, 2005), p. 42.

38. Amanda Gefter, "Scale in the universe," *New Scientist* (March 2007). Retrieved 13 August 2007, from the World Wide Web *http://space. newscientist.com/article/mg19325941.600;jsessionid=OCFJLFLEGCNP.*

39. Map of the tunnels exiting Pennsylvania Station, NY. From Kenneth M. Mead, Inspector General. U.S. Department of Transportation, Office of the Secretary of Transportation. Letter to The Honorable Frank Wolf, Chairman, Subcommittee on Transportation and Related Agencies, Committee on Appropriations, United States House of Representatives. Conditions in the Tunnels below Pennsylvania Station. 18 December 2000. Retrieved 10 September 2007, from the World Wide Web *http://www.car-tome.org/penn-tunnel-safety.pdf.* Wikipedia, "Pennsylvania Station (New York City)." Retrieved 10 September 2007, from the World Wide Web *http:// en.wikipedia.org/wiki/Pennsylvania_Station_(New_York_City).* Wikipedia, "Pennsylvania Tunnel and Terminal Railroad." Retrieved 10 September 2007, from the World Wide Web *http://en.wikipedia.org/wiki/Pennsylvania_ Tunnel_and_Terminal_Railroad.* Wikipedia, "East River Tunnels." Retrieved 10 September 2007, from the World Wide Web *http://en.wikipedia.org/wiki/ East_River_Tunnels.*

40. Amy J. Berger, "The Midlife Crisis of the Cosmos," *Scientific American* (January 2005).

41. Robert Irion, "The Quest for Population III," *Science* 295, no. 5552 (January 2002): 66–67. doi:10.1126/science.295.5552.66.

42. Timothy C. Beers, "The First Generations of Stars," *Science* 309, no. 5733 (July 2005): 390–391. doi:10.1126/science.1114671. Iron, carbon, nitrogen and oxygen are the four elements Beers feels evolved from the first star deaths. But Beers cautions that, "Astronomers are uncertain which elements might form in these very massive stars during their explosive death throes, but current calculations indicate that they should eject large amounts of iron and only small amounts of carbon." Michael Shull and Fernando Santoro believe that the first generation of high-mass star deaths also produced silicon. Michael Shull and Fernando Santoro, "Critical Metallicity of the IGM." Presented at First Stars III, Santa Fe, New Mexico, 17 July 2007, p. 4. Retrieved 10 September 2007, from the World Wide Web *http://www.lanl. gov/conferences/firststars3/abstracts_and_talks/m_shull_talk.pdf.*

43. For more detail on how a dying star produces heavy elements like iron and carbon, see: Stephen James O'Meara, *Deep-Sky Companions: The Caldwell Objects* (New York: Cambridge University Press, 2003), p. 130.

44. The Carbon Atom. Math and Science Activity Center—*edinformatics.com.* Retrieved 10 September 2007, from the World Wide Web *http://www.edin-formatics.com/math_science/c_atom.htm.*

45. David Arnett and Grant Bazan, "Nucleosynthesis in Stars: Recent Developments," *Science* 276, no. 5317 (May 1997): 1359–1362.

46. For the standard view of nucleogenesis in second generation stars, see Henri Boffin and Douglas Pierce-Price, "Fusion in the Universe: we are all stardust," *Science in School.* Retrieved 10 September 2007, from the World Wide Web *http://www.scienceinschool.org/2007/issue4/fusion/.* Henri Boffin and Douglas Pierce-Price are with the European Organisation for Astronomical Research in the Southern Hemisphere, Garching, Germany.

47. "Nucleocosmochronology is a good way to determine the time at which stars and galaxies were formed ..." Peter Coles and Francesco Lucchin, *Cosmology:*

The Origin and Evolution of Cosmic Structure (New York: John Wiley and Sons, 2002), p. 84. "In effect, nucleocosmochronology is a way of dating the creation of the heavy elements." Richard M. West, *Highlights of Astronomy, International Astronomical Union General Assembly, International Astronomical Union* (Dordrecht, Holland: D. Reidel Publishing Company, 1983), p. 243. Donald D. Clayton and W. David Arnett and James W. Truran, eds., "Galactic Chemical Evolution and Nucleocosmochronology: A Standard Model," in *Nucleosynthesis: Challenges and New Developments* (Chicago, IL: University of Chicago Press, 1985), p. 65.

48. The best approximation to moleculocosmochronology we have is Astrochemistry and Molecular Astrophysics—two fields that search for molecules in space, theorize about how those molecules formed, but don't pin down when. See: David Curtis, Juhan Sonin, Yi-Jeng Kuan, and Lewis E. Snyder, "What is Astrochemistry? Expo/Science & Industry/ Whispers From the Cosmos. Cyberia," National Center for Supercomputer Applications at the University of Illinois in Urbana-Champaign. 1995. Retrieved 10 September 2007, from the World Wide Web *http://archive. ncsa.uiuc.edu/Cyberia/Bima/astrochem.html*. Also see: Centre for Astronomy, NUI Galway. Star Formation & Astrochemistry Group. National University of Ireland, Galway. Retrieved 10 September 2007, from the World Wide Web *http://astro.nuigalway.ie/research/starformation.html#astrochemistry*. For a good example of Astrochemistry, see: Lucy M. Ziurys, "The chemistry in circumstellar envelopes of evolved stars: Following the origin of the elements to the origin of life," *Proceedings of the National Academy of Sciences* 109, no. 33 (August 2006). Retrieved 10 September 2007, from the World Wide Web *http://www.pnas.org/cgi/reprint/103/33/12274.pdf*.

49. For the possible role hydrogen cyanide may have played in the evolu-tion of life, see the following articles (keep in mind that the chemical term for hydrogen cyanide is HCN): Clifford Matthews, "The HCN World: Establishing Protein-Nucleic Acid Life via Hydrogen Cyanide Polymers," in *Cellular Origin and Life in Extreme Habitats and Astrobiology* 6 (2004), (Origins : Genesis, Evolution and Diversity of Life): 121–135. Retrieved 25 September 2007, from the World Wide Web: *http://books.google.com/ books?id=937NljkEbgYC&pg=PA123&dq=%22The+HCN+World:+Establis hing+Protein-Nucleic+Acid+Life+via+Hydrogen+Cyanide+Polymers%22&si g=uJSGsX3vkmyJIrXH13yJqG3n180*. See also A. Brack, "The Chemistry of Life's Origins," in *Cellular Origin and Life in Extreme Habitats and*

Astrobiology 6, (2004), (Origins: Genesis, Evolution and Diversity of Life): 64. For a sense of how central the study of hydrogen cyanide in space has been to fields from star birth to the evolution of DNA, see: W. M. Keck Observatory, "Precursor to Proteins and DNA Found in Stellar Disk," press release, 20 December 2005. Retrieved 25 September 2007, from the World Wide Web *http://www.spaceref.com/news/viewpr.html?pid=18569*. European Space Agency. New results from ESA's Infrared Space Observatory, ISO, show that toxic compounds exist deep in the interior of star-forming clouds. 12 October 2001. Retrieved 25 September 2007, from the World Wide Web *http://www.space.com/scienceastronomy/astronomy/comet_poison_011012.html*. F. Lahuis and E. F. van Dishoeck, "ISO-SWS spectroscopy of gas-phase C_2H_2 and HCN toward massive young stellar objects," *Astronomy and Astrophysics* 355 (2000): 699–712. A. M. S. Boonman, R. Stark, F. F. S. van der Tak, E. F. van Dishoeck, P. B. van der Wal, F. Schäfer, G. de Lange, and W. M. Laauwen, "Highly Abundant HCN in the Inner Hot Envelope of GL 2591: Probing the Birth of a Hot Core?" *Astrophysical Journal* 553, part 2 (2001): L63–L67. P. F. Goldsmith, W. D. Langer, J. Ellder, E. Kollberg, and W. Irvine, "Determination of the HNC to HCN abundance ratio in giant molecular clouds," *Astrophysical Journal* 249, part 1 (October 1981): 524–531. Abstract retrieved 25 September 2007, from the World Wide Web *http://adsabs.harvard.edu/abs/1981ApJ...249..524G*. Keisaku Ishii, Asami Tajima, Tetsuya Taketsugu, and Koichi Yamashita, "Theoretical Elucidation of the Unusually High [HNC]/[HCN] Abundance Ratio in Interstellar Space: Two-dimensional and Two-State Quantum Wave Packet Dynamics Study on the Branching Ratio of the Dissociative Recombination Reaction HCNH+ + e- rarr HNC/HCN + H," *Astrophysical Journal* 636, part 1 (2006): 927–931. And for a summary in plain English of the importance of many of these peer-reviewed articles, see: Peter N. Spotts. How comets may have "seeded" life on Earth. *USATODAY.com*. 7 September 2005. Retrieved 25 September 2007, from the World Wide Web *http://www.usatoday.com/tech/science/space/2005-09-07-comet-earth-life_x.htm*.

50. Clifford Matthews, "The HCN World: Establishing Protein-Nucleic Acid Life via Hydrogen Cyanide Polymers," in *Cellular Origin and Life in Extreme Habitats and Astrobiology* 6, (2004), (Origins: Genesis, Evolution and Diversity of Life): 121–135. Retrieved 25 September 2007, from the World Wide Web: *http://books.google.com/books?id=937NljkEbgYC&pg=PA123&dq =%22The+HCN+World:+Establishing+Protein-Nucleic+Acid+Life+via+Hydrog en+Cyanide+Polymers%22&sig=uJSGsX3vkmyJIrXH13yJqG3n180*. For a full

copy of Matthews "HCN World," see: *http://www.springerlink.com/content/1550537256x24ln4/fulltext.pdf.*

51. National Radio Astronomy Observatory, Scientists Discover Two New Interstellar Molecules: Point to Probable Pathways for Chemical Evolution in Space. Press release, 21 June 2004. Retrieved 10 September 2007, from the World Wide Web *http://www.nrao.edu/pr/2004/GBTMolecules/.*

52. Norman R. Pace, "The universal nature of biochemistry," *Proceedings of the National Academy of Sciences of the United States of America* 98, no. 3 (January 2001): 805–808. Retrieved 17 August 2007, from the World Wide Web *http://www.pnas.org/cgi/content/full/98/3/805.*

53. Shen-Yuan Liu, "Complex molecules in galactic dust cores: Biologically interesting molecules and dust chemistry." Thesis (Ph.D.). University Of Illinois At Urbana-Champaign, Source DAI-B 60/12, p. 6152, June 2000. Abstract retrieved 11 June 2002, from the World Wide Web *http://adsabs.harvard.edu/abs/2000PhDT........16L.*

54. Alexandra Goho, "Space Invaders: The stuff of life has far-flung origins," *Science News* 165, no. 18 (May 2004). Retrieved from the World Wide Web 6 May 2004, *http://www.sciencenews.org/articles/20040501/bob9.asp.*

55. David F. Blake and Peter Jenniskens, "The Ice Of Life," *Scientific American* 285, no. 2 (August 2001): 44–50.

56. Carbon-copy is an almost literal term. Carbon monoxide—CO—is one of the most abundant molecules produced by nova self-destruction. It appears within a mere 100 days of a nova's explosion. Formic acid (HCOOH) and methyl formate (HCOOH3), two other carbon compounds, also pop up frequently in interstellar clouds of molecules, especially in hot regions where the atom-assemblies are packed together heavily, forming what's called a "hot core." See: "Astronomers Find Carbon Monoxide Gas In Supernova Debris," *Dartmouth News*. Retrieved 10 September 2007, from the World Wide Web *http://www.dartmouth.edu/pages/news/releases/jan99/nova.html.* Shen-Yuan Liu, "Complex molecules in galactic dust cores: Biologically interesting molecules and dust chemistry." Thesis (Ph.D.). University Of Illinois At Urbana-Champaign, Source DAI-B 60/12, p. 6152, June 2000. Abstract retrieved

10 September 2007, from the World Wide Web *http://adsabs.harvard.edu/ abs/2000PhDT........16L.*

57. David F. Blake and Peter Jenniskens, "The Ice of Life," *Scientific American* 285, no. 2, (August 2001). Retrieved from the World Wide Web 27 May 2003, *http://web17.epnet.com/citation.asp?tb=1&_ug=dbs+7+ln+en%2Dus+sid +DD49FA4A%2D927E%2D4700%2DA8E2%2D12188543289C%40Session mgr4+6DA1&_us=bs+the++ice++of++life+ds+the++ice++of++life+dstb+KS+gl+S O++%22Scientific++American%22+hd+0+hs+0+or+Date+ri+KAAACBZB0007 5346+sm+KS+so+b+ss+SO+2921&cf=1&fn=1&rn=1.*

58. Francois Raulin, "Prebiotic chemistry in the solar system," in *ESA, Formation of Stars and Planets, and the Evolution of the Solar System*: pp. 151–157 (SEE N91-18922 10-90). Abstract retrieved 10 September 2007, from the World Wide Web *http://adsabs.harvard.edu/abs/1990ESASP.315..151R.*

59. Max P. Bernstein, Scott A. Sandford, and Louis J. Allamandola, "Life's Far-Flung Raw Materials," *Scientific American* (July 1999).

60. David F. Blake and Peter Jenniskens, "The Ice of Life," *Scientific American* 285, no. 2 (August 2001).

61. Shen-Yuan Liu, "Complex molecules in galactic dust cores: Biologically interesting molecules and dust chemistry." Thesis (Ph.D.). University Of Illinois At Urbana-Champaign, Source DAI-B 60/12, p. 6152, June 2000. Abstract retrieved 11 June 2002, from the World Wide Web *http://adsabs. harvard.edu/abs/2000PhDT........16L.*

62. By 2002, the number of molecules we'd found in space had climbed to 130. Rachel Nowak, "Amino acid found in deep space." *New Scientist* (18 July 2002). Retrieved 25 April 2005, from the World Wide Web *http://www. newscientist.com/channel/space/astrobiology/dn2558.*

63. David F. Blake and Peter Jenniskens, "The Ice of Life." *Scientific American* 285, no. 2, (August 2001).

64. James F. Kasting, "Planetary Atmospheres: Warming Early Earth and Mars," *Science* (23 May 1997): 1213–1215. Heinrich D. Holland, "Evidence for Life on Earth More Than 3850 Million Years Ago," *Science* (3 January 1997):

38–39. Norman R. Pace, "A Molecular View of Microbial Diversity and the Biosphere," *Science* (2 May 1997): 734–740. S. J. Mojzsis, G. Arrhenius, K. D. Mckeegan, T. M. Harrison, A. P. Nutman, and C. R. L. Friend, "Evidence for life on Earth before 3,800 million years ago," *Nature* (7 November 1996): 55–59. NASA News Releases, "96-11-05 When Life Began On Earth," press release. Retrieved 1 December 1996, from the World Wide Web *http:// spacelink.msfc.nasa.gov/NASA.News/NASA.News.Releases/ Previous.News. Releases/96.News.Releases/96-11.News.Releases/ 96-11-05.When.Life.Began. On.Earth*, January 1999. John M. Hayes, "The earliest memories of life on Earth," *Nature* (7 November 1996): 21–22. Minik T. Rosing, "13C-Depleted Carbon Microparticles in >3700-Ma Sea-Floor Sedimentary Rocks from West Greenland," *Science* 283, no. 5402 (29 January 1999): 674–676. doi: 10.1126/science.283.5402.674. Minik Rosing and Robert Frei, "U-rich Archaean sea-floor sediments from Greenland—indications of >3700 Ma oxygenic photosynthesis," *Earth and Planetary Science Letters* 217, nos. 3–4 (15 January 2004): 237–244. Paul Rincon, "Oldest evidence of photosynthesis," BBC News Online, 17 December 2003. Retrieved 10 September 2007, from the World Wide Web *http://news.bbc.co.uk/1/hi/sci/tech/3321819.stm*.

65. Charles H. Lineweaver and Tamara M. Davis, "Does the Rapid Appearance of Life on Earth Suggest that Life Is Common in the Universe?" *Astrobiology* 2, no. 3 (2002): 293–304. doi:0.1089/153110702762027871. Retrieved 10 September 2007, from the World Wide Web *http://www.liebertonline.com/ doi/abs/10.1089/153110702762027871?cookieSet=1&journalCode=ast*.

66. Qingzhu Yin, S. B. Jacobsen, K. Yamashita, J. Blichert-Toft, P. Telouk, and F. Albarede, "A short timescale for terrestrial planet formation from Hf–W chronometry of meteorites," *Nature* 418, no. 29 (August 2002): 949–952. Retrieved 10 September 2007, from the World Wide Web *http://www.gps. caltech.edu/classes/ge133/reading/halfnium_core_nature.pdf*. Claude J. Allègre, Gérard Manhès, and Christa Göpel, "The age of the Earth," *Geochimica et Cosmochimica Acta* 59, no. 8:1445–1456. Abstract retrieved 10 September 2007, from the World Wide Web *http://adsabs.harvard.edu/ abs/1995GeCoA..59.1445A*. Wikipedia. Planetary Formation. Retrieved 10 September 2007, from the World Wide Web *http://en.wikipedia.org/wiki/ Planetary_formation*.

67. L. Bada, "The transition from abiotic to biotic chemistry: When and where?" American Geophysical Union, Fall Meeting 2001, abstract #U51A-11

Publication Date: December 2001. Abstract retrieved 17 August 2007, from the World Wide Web *http://adsabs.harvard.edu/abs/2001AGUFM. U51A..11B.*

68. For information on the peptiglycan weave of cellular membranes, see Franklin M. Harold, *The Way of the Cell: Molecules, Organisms and the Order of Life* (New York: Oxford University Press, 2001), pp. 100–109. Jan Sapp, "Cytoplasmic Heretics," *Perspectives In Biology And Medicine* (Winter 1998): 224–242.

69. NASA's Ames Research Center, "Scientists find clues that the path leading to the origin of life begins in deep space," press release. The Astrochemistry Laboratory in the Astrophysics Branch (SSA) of the Space Sciences Division at NASA's Ames Research Center. Retrieved 10 September 2007, from the World Wide Web *http://www.astrochemistry.org/vesicle.html.* Jason P. Dworkin, David W. Deamer, Scott A. Sandford, and Louis J. Allamandola, "Self-assembling amphiphilic molecules: Synthesis in simulated interstellar/precometary ices," *Proceedings of the National Academy of Sciences of the United States of America* 98, no. 3 (30 January 2001): 815–819. Retrieved 10 September 2007, from the World Wide Web *http://www.pnas.org/cgi/content/full/98/3/815.* R. Cowen, "Life's housing may come from space," *Science News* (3 February 2001). Retrieved from the World Wide Web 30 May 2003 *http://www.findarticles.com/cf_0/m1200/5_159/71352457/print.jhtml.*

70. The figure of 62 million atoms is my extrapolation from information given by Margaret Jo Velardo, P.A., Ph.D. McKnight Brain Institute of the University of Florida. Re: atom teams=genes. Personal communication. 22 February 2003, also posted to International Paleopsychology Project. For an idea of the scale of the first molecules to master the art of reproduction, try these numbers. A simple SV40 virus is a collective of atoms so simple that it CANNOT reproduce. It depends on genomes to do its duplication for it. Yet this extremely primitive society of atoms has 326,400 atoms. A molecule that CAN reproduce—the genome of the bacteria E. Coli—has over 300 million atoms. The first self-reproducing molecules were almost certainly atom teams whose numbers were somewhere in between these two extremes. Sources: James K. Hardy, "DNA and RNA Structure and Function," in *Concepts of Biochemistry* (University of Akron, 1998). Retrieved 10 September 2007 from the World Wide Web *http://ull.chemistry.uakron. edu/biochem/10/.* R. Bennewitz, J. N. Crain, A. Kirakosian, J-L Lin, J. L.

McChesney, D. Y. Petrovykh, and F. J. Himpse, "Atomic scale memory at a silicon surface," *Nanotechnology 13* (2002): 499–502. Institute of Physics Publishing. Retrieved 10 September 2007, from the World Wide Web *http://uw.physics.wisc.edu/~himpsel/383_nano.pdf.*

71. For RNA and DNA as memory-libraries and as information-storing molecules, see: Stephen J. Freeland, Robin D. Knight, and Laura F. Landweber, "Molecular Evolution: Do Proteins Predate DNA?" *Science* 286, no. 5440 (22 October 1999): 690–692. doi:10.1126/science.286.5440.690. Retrieved 19 August 2007, from the World Wide Web *http://www.sciencemag.org/cgi/content/full/286/5440/690.* Says Ronald Breaker of Yale University's Department of Molecular, Cellular, and Developmental Biology, "DNA [is] an ideal molecule for information storage and transfer." Ronald R. Breaker, "Making Catalytic DNAs," *Science* 290, no. 5499 (15 December 2000): 2095–2096. doi:10.1126/science.290.5499.2095. Nobel Prize-winning molecular biology pioneer Walter Gilbert, in his 1980 lecture to the Nobel Foundation, declared flat out that, "DNA is **the** information store," [author's emphasis.] Walter Gilbert, "DNA sequencing and gene structure," *Science* (18 December 1981): 1305–1312. Retrieved 10 September 2007, from the World Wide Web *http://www.sciencemag.org/cgi/reprint/214/4527/1305.pdf.*

72. Re: "It sometimes took storing five failed strategies to construct the mega-strategy from which a breakthrough would be made." This is a hypothesis. I've taken the liberty of extrapolating from the results of experiments like the following: B. G. Hall, "Adaptive evolution that requires multiple spontaneous mutations. I. Mutations involving an insertion sequence," *Genetics* (December 1988): 887–97. L. L. Parker, B. G. Hall, "A fourth Escherichia coli gene system with the potential to evolve beta-glucoside utilization," *Genetics* (July 1988): 485–490.

73. Wikipedia, "Cytoplasm." Retrieved 10 September 2007, from the World Wide Web *http://en.wikipedia.org/wiki/Cytoplasm.*

74. Genevieve Thiers, "What is cytoplasm?" *eSSORTMENT.* Pagewise (2002). Retrieved 10 September 2007, from the World Wide Web *http://www.essortment.com/cytoplasm_rkkg.htm.*

75. The Gatorade inside a bacterial cell is not just rich in proteins. It's rich in protein-makers—ribosomes, small protein assembly plants. Socially, this

Gatorade is a very busy place. *CELLSalive!* "Bacterial Cell Structure." Retrieved 10 September 2007, from the World Wide Web *http://www.cell-salive.com/cells/bactcell.htm.*

76.   Ed Rybicki, Ph.D., Department of Microbiology, University of Cape Town. How many atoms are in a cell? Biosci/Bionet. (BIOSCI promotes communication between professionals in the biological sciences.) Retrieved 11 June 2007, from the World Wide Web. *http://www.bio.net/bionet/mm/mol-evol/1997-September/005971.html.*

77.   James R. Lupski, George M. Weinstock, Frans J. de Bruijn, *Bacterial Genomes: Physical Structure and Analysis* (New York: Springer, 1998), p. 8.

78.   For more on RNA and DNA as memory-libraries see: Stephen J. Freeland, Robin D. Knight, and Laura F. Landweber, "Molecular Evolution: Do Proteins Predate DNA?" *Science* 286, no. 5440 (22 October 1999): 690–692. doi:10.1126/science.286.5440.690. Retrieved 19 August 2007, from the World Wide Web *http://www.sciencemag.org/cgi/content/full/286/5440/690.* Ronald R. Breaker, "Making Catalytic DNAs." *Science* 290, no. 5499 (15 December 2000): 2095–2096. doi:10.1126/science.290.5499.2095. Walter Gilbert, "DNA sequencing and gene structure." *Science* (18 December 1981): 1305–1312. Retrieved 10 September 2007, from the World Wide Web *http://www.sciencemag.org/cgi/reprint/214/4527/1305.pdf.*

79.   James A. Shapiro, Personal Communication. 9 February–24 September 1999.

80.   E. Ben-Jacob, A. Tenenbaum, O. Shochet, I. Cohen, A. Czirók, and T. Vicsek. "Cooperative Strategies in Formation of Complex Bacterial Patterns," *Fractals* 3, no. 4 (1995): 849–868.

81.   Eshel Ben-Jacob, Personal Communication. 15 January 1999.

82.   James A. Shapiro, "Thinking About Bacterial Populations as Multicellular Organisms," *Annual Review of Microbiology.* Palo Alto, CA: Annual Reviews, 1998, pp. 81–104. Eshel Ben-Jacob, Israela Becker, Yoash Shapira, and Herbert Levine, "Bacterial linguistic communication and social intelligence," *Trends in Microbiology* 12, no. 8 (1 August 2004): 366–372.

83. E. Ben-Jacob, A. Tenenbaum, O. Shochet, I. Cohen, A. Czirók, and T. Vicsek, "Communication, Regulation and Control During Complex Patterning of Bacterial Colonies," *Fractals* 2, no. 1 (1994): 14–44.

84. Eshel Ben-Jacob, "Bacterial wisdom, Gödel's theorem and creative genomic webs," *Physica A* 248 (1998): 57–76. Marguerite Holloway, "Talking Bacteria." (Interview with Bonnie L. Bassler). *Scientific American* (February 2004). Retrieved 10 September 2007, from the World Wide Web *http://www.sciam.com/article.cfm?chanID=sa006& colID=30&articleID=0001F2DF-27D8-1FFB-A7D883414B7F0000.* Bonnie Bassler, "Cell-to-Cell Communication in Bacteria." Department of Molecular Biology, Princeton University. Retrieved 10 September 2007, from the World Wide Web *http://www.molbio2.princeton.edu/index.php?option=content&task=view&id=27.*

85. J. W. Schopf, Are the oldest 'fossils,' fossils?" *Origins of Life and Evolution of the Biosphere* (January 1976): 19–36. J. William Schopf and Cornelius Klein, eds, *Proterozoic Biosphere: A Multidisciplinary Study* (New York: Cambridge University Press, 1992). J. William Schopf, "Microfossils of the Early Archean Apex Chert: New Evidence of the Antiquity of Life," *Science* (30 April 1993): 640–646. J. William Schopf, *Cradle of Life: The Discovery of Earth's Earliest Fossils* (Berkeley, CA: University of California Press, 1999).

86. University of California Museum of Paleontology, "Cyanobacteria: Fossil Record." Retrieved 10 September 2007, from the World Wide Web *http://www.ucmp.berkeley.edu/bacteria/cyanofr.html.*

87. John Tyler Bonner, *The Evolution of Culture in Animals* (Princeton, NJ: Princeton University Press, 1983).

88. Matt Richardson, M.Sc.(C), and Stephen Cheung, Ph.D., "The basics of thermoregulation," Agriculture Personnel Management Program. University of California, Berkeley. Retrieved 10 September 2007, from the World Wide Web *http://apmp.berkeley.edu/images/stories/ManagementPractices/thermoprimer.pdf.*

89. Craig B. Stanford, "The Predatory Behavior and Ecology of Wild Chimpanzees." Department of Anthropology, University of Southern California, Los Angeles, CA. Retrieved from the World Wide Web 4 April

2004 *http://www-rcf.usc.edu/~stanford/chimphunt.html*. Jane Goodall, *In The Shadow of Man* (Boston: Houghton Mifflin, 1983 [originally published 1971]).

90. Ann Gibbons, "Solving the Brain's Energy Crisis," *Science* 280, no. 5368 (29 May 1998): 1345–1347. Clodagh O'Brien, "Early humans smart but forgetful," *NewScientist.com*. 13 September 2002. Retrieved 13 September 2002, from the World Wide Web *http://www.newscientist.com/news/print. jsp?id=ns99992793*.

91. Dian Fossey, *Gorillas In the Mist* (Boston: Houghton Mifflin, 1983).

92. Our stomachs are 40 percent smaller than those of other animals our size. The extra blood and energy it takes to operate a big belly is shunted to our brain. L. C. Aiello, "The Expensive Tissue Hypothesis and the Evolution of the Human Adaptive Niche: A Study in Comparative Anatomy," in *Science in Archaeology: An Agenda for the Future*. Edited by J. Bayley (London: English Heritage, 1998), pp. 25–36. L. C. Aiello and P. Wheeler, "The Expensive Tissue Hypothesis: the brain and the digestive system in human and primate evolution," *Current Anthropology* 36 (1995): 199–221.

93. Stanley H. Ambrose, "Paleolithic Technology and Human Evolution," *Science* 291, no. 5509 (2 March 2001): 1748–1753.

94. S. Semaw, P. Renne, J. W. K. Harris, C. S. Feibel, R. L. Bernor, N. Fesseha, K. Mowbray, "2.5 million year old stone tools from Gona, Ethiopia," *Nature* (23 January 1997): 333. Constance Holden, "The First Tool Kit," *Science* (31 January 1997): 623. Ken Swisher, "Rutgers scientists discover oldest stone tools to date," press release. 22 January 1997. (New Brunswick/Piscataway, NJ: Rutgers University.) Downloaded 15 April 1998 from *http://uc.rutgers.edu/ medrel/news/envstud/gona.html*. M. W. Marzke, K. L. Wullstein, S. F. Viegas, "Evolution of the Power ("Squeeze") Grip and Its Morphological Correlates in Hominids," *American Journal of Physical Anthropology* (November 1992). Mary W. Marzke, N. Toth, and K. N. An, "EMG Study of Hand Muscle Recruitment During Hard Hammer Percussion Manufacture of Oldowan Tools," *American Journal of Physical Anthropology* (March 1998).

95. A. Skinner, J. Lloyd, C. Brain, and F. Thackeray, "Electron spin resonance and the first use of fire." Paper presented at the 2004 Paleoanthropology Society

Annual Meeting in Montreal, 30–31 March 2004. Discovering Archaeology September/October 1999. Retrieved May 2000, from the World Wide Web *http://www.discoveringarchaeology.com/0599toc/5feature3-fire.shtml*. R. Rowlett, M. G. Davis, and R. B. Graber, 1999. "Friendly Fire: The First Campfires Helped Hominids Survive the Night," *Discovering Archaeology* 1(5): 82–89. N. Alperson-Afil and N. Goren-Inbar, "Out of Africa and into Eurasia with controlled use of fire: Evidence from Gesher Benot Ya'aqov, Israel," *Archaeology, Ethnology and Anthropology of Eurasia* 28, no. 4 (December 2006): 63–78.

96. Richard Wrangham and Nancy Lou Conklin-Brittain, "Cooking as a biological trait," *Comparative Biochemistry & Physiology Part A: Molecular & Integrative Physiology* 136, no. 1 (September 2003): 35–47. Richard Wrangham, Personal Communication, 28 March 2004. Natalie Angier, "Cooking, and How It Slew the Beast Within," *New York Times*, 28 May 2002. Retrieved 1 June 2002, from the World Wide Web *http://www.nytimes.com/2002/05/28/science/social/28COOK.html?pagewanted=print&position=top*. For a report on Richard Wrangham's hypotheses about how cooking helped us eat inedible tubers and poisonous vegetables, see: Elizabeth Pennisi, "Did Cooked Tubers Spur the Evolution of Big Brains?" *Science* 283, no. 5410 (26 March 1999): 2004–2005.

97. The Comm Tech Lab and the Center for Microbial Ecology at Michigan State University. The Microbe Zoo DLC ME Project, *http://commtechlab.msu.edu/sites/dlc me/zoo/*, downloaded September 1999. William B. Whitman, David C. Coleman, and William J. Wiebe, "Prokaryotes: The unseen majority." *Proceedings of the National Academy of Sciences of the United States of America* 95, no. 12, (9 June 1998): 6578–6583. Richard Gallagher, "Monie a Mickle Maks a Muckle," *Science* (10 July 1998): 186.

98. L. C. Aiello, "Hominine preadaptations for Language and Cognition," in *Modelling the Early Human Mind*, edited by P. Mellars and K. Gibson. (Cambridge, UK: McDonald Institute Monographs, 1996), pp. 89–99. L.C. Aiello, "Terrestriality, bipedalism and the origin of language," in *Evolution of Social Behaviour Patterns in Primates and Man*, edited by J. Maynard-Smith. *Proceedings of the British Academy* 88 (1996): 269–289.

99. John R. Skoyles, "Complete online text of selected papers and two books (Odyssey and Leviathan)." Retrieved 20 August 2000, from the World Wide Web *http://www.users.globalnet.co.uk/~skoyles/*, May 1999.

100. Dennis M. Bramble and Daniel E. Lieberman, "Endurance running and the evolution of Homo," *Nature* 432 (18 November 2004): 345–352. Retrieved 21 August 2007, from the World Wide Web *http://www.nature.com/nature/journal/v432/n7015/full/nature03052.html.*

101. P. J. Darlington, Jr., "Group selection, altruism, reinforcement, and throwing in human evolution." *Proceedings of the National Academy of Sciences* 72, no. 9 (September 1975): 3748–3752. For the changes in our physiology that made pitching and running a uniquely human killer combination, changes that arrived with *Homo erectus* 1.7 million years ago, see Alan Walker, "The Search for 'The Missing Link,'" *Science & The City*, Webzine of the New York Academy of Sciences. 3 August 2007. Podcast. Retrieved 10 September 2007, from the World Wide Web *http://www.nyas.org/snc/podcasts.asp.* William H. Calvin, *The Throwing Madonna: Essays On The Brain* (New York: McGraw Hill, 1983).

102. This is the literal source of the saying, "killing two birds with one stone."

103. Richard W. Young, "Evolution of the human hand: the role of throwing and clubbing," *Journal of Anatomy* 202 (2003): 165–174. Retrieved 10 September 2007, from the World Wide Web *http://web.ebsco-host.com/ehost/pdf?vid=3&hid=8&sid=e49a2147-8b03-43a1-a3f5-0d4939532c2e%40SRCSM2.* Barbara Isaac, "Throwing and human evolution," *African Archaeological Review* 5, no 1 (December 1987): 3–17. Abstract retrieved 10 September 2007, from the World Wide Web *http://www.springerlink.com/content/q1212l4r8m7x6x5m/.* For an Australian folk tale on killing an emu (a large, ostrich-like bird) with a stone toss, see The Weeoonibeens and the Piggiebillah, "The Internet Sacred Text Archive." Retrieved 10 September 2007, from the World Wide Web *http://www.sacred-texts.com/aus/alt/alt09.htm.*

104. Certain forms of body lice only live in human clothing. By tracing the remains of these parasites, William J. Burroughs places the date of wearing apparel at 75,000 years ago. William James Burroughs, *Climate Change in Prehistory: The End of the Reign of Chaos* (New York: Cambridge University Press, 2005), p. 133. The most fascinating expert on early human clothing is archaeologist and former fashion industry insider Olga Soffer. For more on her views, see Kate Wong, "The Caveman's New Clothes." Profile Archaeologist Olga Soffer. *Scientific American* 283, no. 5 (November 2000). Retrieved 10 September

2007, from the World Wide Web *http://www.sciam.com/article.cfm?chanID=s a027&articleID=000F05EF-048B-1C73-9B81809EC588EF21.*

105. Patrick Manning, *Migration In World History* (London: Routledge, 2005). M. F. Hammer, T. Karafet, A. Rasanayagam, et al., "Out of Africa and back again: nested cladistic analysis of human Y chromosome variation," *Molecular Biology and Evolution* 15 (1998): 427–441. A. R. Templeton, "Out of Africa? What do genes tell us?" *Current Opinion in Genetics and Development* 7 (1997): 841–847. Kate Wong, "Is Out of Africa Going Out the Door?" *Scientific American* (August 1999). Retrieved July 1999, from the World Wide Web *http://www.sciam.com/1999/0899issue/0899infocus. html.* Clive Gamble, *Timewalkers: The Prehistory of Global Colonization* (Cambridge, MA: Harvard University Press, 1994).

106. Olga Soffer, *The Upper Paleolithic of the Central Russian Plain* (New York: Academic Press, 1985). C. R. Harington, "Wooly Mammoth," in *Animals of Beringia.* (December 1995.) Yukon Beringia Interpretive Centre. Retrieved November 1999, from the World Wide Web *http://www.berin-gia.com/01student/mainb2.html#top.* For a picture of a reconstructed hut made of mammoth bones and skin, see "Mammoth bones saved Ice Age humans from winter's chill" (Chicago: The Field Museum). *http://www. fmnh.org/exhibits/ttt/TTT4a.htm,* May 1999. For further illustrations of mammoth-bone architecture and jewelry, and for a fascinating run-through of Ukrainian pre and ancient history, see Andrew Gregorovich, "Ancient Inventions of Ukraine." (Etobicoke, Ontario, Canada: InfoUkes.) Retrieved May 1999, from the World Wide Web *http://www.infoukes.com/ history/inventions/.* For the most complete set of illustrations of mammoth-bone structures and other ice age buildings, see Wadyslaw Jan Kowalski, "Stone Age Habitats." Retrieved May 1999, from the World Wide Web *http://www.personal.psu.edu/users/w/x/wxk116/habitat/.* See also David Lambert and the Diagram Group, *The Field Guide to Early Man* (New York: Facts on File Publications, 1987) and Kharlena Maria Ramanan, "Neandertal Architecture," *Neandertals: A Cyber Perspective. http://thunder. indstate.edu/~ramanank/structures.html,* May 1999.

107. There is identity and vanity among animals. Bower birds build enormous architectural arches to woo mates. Other birds preen their elaborate plumage to get the attention of the girls. And some birds show off their plumage by dancing in ways that even Michael Jackson and Fred Astaire would find hard

to outdo. On the identity front, whales sing songs that identify their pods and show who is part of our group and who is not. Fitting into one of these pods—and singing the right melody to prove it—can be a matter of life or death for a young whale. Janet Mann, Richard C. Connor, Peter L. Tyack, and Hal Whitehead. *Cetacean Societies: Field Studies of Dolphins and Whales* (Chicago: University of Chicago Press, 2000).

108. Sally McBrearty and Alison S. Brooks, "The revolution that wasn't: a new interpretation of the origins of modern human behavior," *Journal of Human Evolution* 39, no. 5 (2000): 453–563. Lawrence S. Barham, "Systematic Pigment Use in the Middle Pleistocene of South-Central Africa," *Current Anthropology* 43, no. 1 (February 2002).

109. Sally McBrearty and Alison S. Brooks, "The revolution that wasn't: a new interpretation of the origins of modern human behavior," *Journal of Human Evolution* 39, no. 5 (2000): 453–563. Ben Marwick, "Pleistocene Exchange Networks as Evidence for the Evolution of Language," *Cambridge Archaeological Journal* 13, no. 1 (April 2003): 67. Stanley H. Ambrose, "Paleolithic Technology and Human Evolution," *Science* 291, no. 5509 (2 March 2001): 1748–1753. Yaroslav V. Kuzmin, Michael D. Glascock, and Hiroyuki Sato, "Sources of Archaeological Obsidian on Sakhalin Island (Russian Far East)," *Journal of Archaeological Science* 29, no. 7 (July 2002): 741–750. Carl Zimmer, "New discoveries rewrite the book on who we are and where we came from," *Discover Magazine* 24, no. 09 (September 2003). J. Féblot-Augustins, "Mobility strategies in the late Middle Paleolithic of Central Europe and Western Europe: Elements of stability and variability," in *The Middle Paleolithic Occupation of Europe*, edited by W. Roebroeks and C. Gamble (Leiden: University of Leiden Press, 1999), pp. 193–214. N.a. "When did we become civilised? What drove Stone Age people to abandon a hunter-gatherer lifestyle that had served them well for millennia and take on the trappings of modernity?" *New Scientist Magazine* 18 (September 2004): 32–35. K. Liu, "An Annotated Survey of Bead, Glass, Faience and Ornament," *Archeological Publications* 25, no. 3 (Spring 2002): 22–25.

110. Sally McBrearty and Alison S. Brooks, "The revolution that wasn't: a new interpretation of the origins of modern human behavior," *Journal of Human Evolution* 39, no. 5 (2000): 453–563.

111. Melville J. Herskovits, *Economic Anthropology: The Economic Life of Primitive Peoples* (New York: W. W. Norton, 1965 [originally published in 1940]).

112. Christopher Henshilwood, Francesco d'Errico, Marian Vanhaeren, Karen van Niekerk, and Zenobia Jacobs, "Middle Stone Age Shell Beads from South Africa," *Science* 304, no. 5669 (16 April 2004): 16. Bryn Nelson and Constance Holden, "Oldest Beads Suggest Early Symbolic Behavior," *Science* (16 April 2004): 404. Bryn Nelson, "Is this the oldest known piece of jewelry?" *Newsday.com*, 15 April 2004. Retrieved from the World Wide Web 17 April 2004. *http://www.newsday.com/news/health/ny-hsbead0416,0,665750,print.story?coll=ny-health-big-pix* NY Newsday.com.

113. Ian Tattersall, *Becoming Human: Evolution and Human Uniqueness* (New York: Harcourt, 1998). Chapter One: The Creative Explosion. Retrieved 10 September 2007, from the World Wide Web *http://www.human-nature.com/darwin/books/tattersall.html*.

114. Heather Pringle, "The Slow Birth of Agriculture," *Science* (20 November 1998): 1446. D. B. Grigg, *The Agricultural Systems of the World: An Evolutionary Approach* (Cambridge: Cambridge University Press, 1974). Manfred Heun, Ralf Schafer-Pregl, Dieter Klawan, Renato Castagna, Monica Accerbi, Basilio Borghi, and Francesco Salamini, "Site of Einkorn Wheat Domestication Identified by DNA Fingerprinting," *Science* (14 November 1997): 1312–1322. C. Mlot, "Wheat's DNA points to first farms," *Science News* (15 November 1997): 308.

115. Howard Bloom, *Global Brain: The Evolution of Mass Mind From The Big Bang to the 21st Century* (New York: John Wiley and Sons, 2000). Kathleen M. Kenyon, "Excavations at Jericho, 1957–58," *Palestine Excavation Quarterly* 92 (1960): 88–108; Purushottam Singh, *Neolithic Cultures of Western Asia* (New York: Seminar Press, 1974), pp. 33–47. James Mellaart, *Catal-Huyuk: A Neolithic Town in Anatolia* (New York: McGraw-Hill, 1967). Michael Balter, "Why Settle Down? The Mystery of Communities," *Science* (20 November 1998): 1442–1445. Dora Jane Hamblin with C. C. Lamberg-Karlovsky and the editors of Time-Life Books, *The Emergence of Man: The First Cities* (New York: Time-Life Books, 1979), pp. 29–32, 910. David Ussishkin, "Notes on the Fortifications of the Middle Bronze II Period at Jericho and Shechem," *Bulletin of the American Schools of Oriental Research* (November 1989).

116. Howard Bloom, *Global Brain: The Evolution of Mass Mind From The Big Bang to the 21st Century* (New York: John Wiley and Sons, 2000).

117. Howard Bloom, *The Lucifer Principle: a scientific expedition into the forces of history* (New York: Atlantic Monthly Press, 1995).

118. NASA, "NASA Research Indicates Oxygen on Earth 2.5 Billion Years Ago." NASA News Releases. 27 September 2007. *http://www.nasa.gov/home/hqnews/2007/sep/HQ_07215_Timeline_of_Oxygen_on_Earth.html.* "History of Life on Earth." Department of Biological Sciences, Northern Illinois University. Retrieved 10 September 2007, from the World Wide Web *www.bios.niu.edu/johns/bios103/history_of_life.ppt.*

119. Lynn Margulis and Dorion Sagan, *Microcosmos: Four Billion Years of Microbial Evolution* (New York: Summit Books, 1986).

120. Lynn Margulis, *Symbiosis in Cell Evolution: Microbial Communities in the Archean and Proterozoic Eons*, Second Edition (New York: W. H. Freeman, 1993). Lynn Margulis, Personal Communication. 22 March 1997.

121. National Institute of Water and Atmospheric Research. Conceptual depiction of complex interactions in coastal seafloor sediments. Water & Atmosphere online. NIWA Science. National Institute of Water and Atmospheric Research, Auckland, New Zealand. Retrieved 10 September 2007, from the World Wide Web *http://www.niwa.cri.nz/pubs/wa/12-3/images/sediment2_large.jpg/view.* N.a. *Sedimentology. Organic Influences on Sediments* (Derby, UK: University of Derby). Retrieved 10 September 2007, from the World Wide Web *http://www.virtual-geology.info/sedimentology/organic.html.* Wikipedia, "Sedimentology." Retrieved 10 September 2007, from the World Wide Web *http://en.wikipedia.org/wiki/Sedimentology.*

122. Mark Schrope and John Pickrell, "Mysteries of the Deep Sea," *New Scientist Environment* (4 September 2006.) Retrieved 10 September 2007, from the World Wide Web *http://environment.newscientist.com/channel/Earth/deep-sea/dn9967.*

123. John Gage, "Deep-sea spiral fantasies." *Nature* 434 (17 March 2005): 283–284. doi:0.1038/434283a. Published online 16 March 2005. Retrieved 10 September 2007, from the World Wide Web *http://www.nature.com/nature/*

journal/v434/n7031/full/434283a.html. N.a. "Cold Seep Communities," *Astrobiology Magazine* (16 November 2006.) Retrieved 10 September 2007, from the World Wide Web *http://astrobio.net/news/article2146.html*.

124. Sid Perkins, "Attack of the Rock-Eating Microbes!" *Science News* 164, no. 20 (15 November 2003): 315. Retrieved 23 August 2007, from the World Wide Web *http://www.sciencenews.org/articles/20031115/bob9.asp*. W. Bach and K. J. Edwards, "Iron and sulfide oxidation within the basaltic ocean crust: Implications for chemolithoautotrophic microbial biomass production," *Geochimica et Cosmochimica Acta* 67 (15 October 2003): 3871–3887. Thomas M. Bawden, Marco T. Einaudi, Benjamin C. Bostick, Anders Meibom, Joseph Wooden, John W. Norby, Michael J. T. Orobona, and C. Page Chamberlain, "Extreme 34S depletions in ZnS at the Mike gold deposit, Carlin Trend, Nevada: Evidence for bacteriogenic supergene sphalerite," *Geology* 31 (October 2003): 913–916. Katrina J. Edwards, Thomas M. McCollom, Hiromi Konishi, and Peter R. Buseck, "Seafloor bioalteration of sulfide minerals: Results from in situ incubation studies," *Geochimica et Cosmochimica Acta* 67 (1 August 2003): 2843–2856. Katrina J. Edwards, W. Bach, and D. R. Rogers, "Geomicrobiology of the ocean crust: A role for chemoautotrophic Fe-bacteria," *Biological Bulletin* 204 (April 2003): 180–185. Katrina J. Edwards, D. R. Rogers, C. O. Wirsen, and T. M. McCollom, "Isolation and characterization of novel psychrophilic, neutrophilic, Fe-oxidizing, chemolithoautotrophic alpha- and gamma-proteobacteria from the Deep Sea," *Applied and Environmental Microbiology* 69 (May 2003): 2906–2913. R. S. Oremland and J. F. Stolz, Abstract retrieved 10 September 2007, from the World Wide Web *http://aem.asm.org/cgi/content/abstract/69/5/2906*. Ronald S. Oremland and John F. Stolz, The ecology of arsenic, *Science* 300 (9 May 2003): 939–944. Matthias Labrenz, Gregory K. Druschel, Tamara Thomsen-Ebert, Benjamin Gilbert, Susan A. Welch, Kenneth M. Kemner, Graham A. Logan, Roger E. Summons, Gelsomina De Stasio, Philip L. Bond, Barry Lai, Shelly D. Kelly, and Jillian F. Banfield, "Formation of sphalerite (ZnS) deposits in natural biofilms of sulfate-reducing bacteria," *Science* 290 (1 December 2000): 1744–1747.

125. Sid Perkins, "Signs of Life? Organisms' effects on terrain aren't all that easy to perceive," *Science News* 172, no. 5 (4 August 2007). Retrieved 10 September 2007, from the World Wide Web *http://www.sciencenews.org/articles/20070804/bob10.asp*.

126. Sid Perkins, "Signs of Life? Organisms' effects on terrain aren't all that easy to perceive," *Science News* 172, no. 5 (4 August 2007). Retrieved 10 September 2007, from the World Wide Web *http://www.sciencenews.org/articles/20070804/bob10.asp.*

127. Charles Darwin, *The formation of vegetable mould through the action of worms: With observations of their habits* (London: J. Murray, 1904).

128. Lyle B. Steadman, Craig T. Palmer, and Christopher F. Tilley, "The universality of ancestor worship," *Ethnology* 35 (1996). Retrieved 10 September 2007, from the World Wide Web *http://www.questia.com/googleScholar.qst;jsessioni d=GTMVQT7QKn2b1LKtcnFgsHW5Z2DzvrGr5JK3Vny9TLMyDxTLg L1W!1926754150?docId=5000324827.* Personal communications with Lyle Steadman, 1997.

129. These thousand of pages include the four books of the Hadith—the eyewitness accounts of Mohammed's life—and the early Moslem biographies of Mohammed, one of which, al Tabari's History, is 39 books long. See Sahih Bukhari, Translator: M. Muhsin Khan. MSA-USC Hadith Database. (MSA is the Moslem Student Association, an organization allegedly used by Saudi Arabia as a propaganda machine. Because the MSA is an authentic and devout Moslem source, its online English-language translation of Islam's sacred books should be impeccably faithful to the originals.) USC-MSA Compendium of Muslim Texts. University of Southern California. Retrieved 22 August 2005, from the World Wide Web *http://www.usc.edu/dept/MSA/fundamentals/hadithsunnah/bukhari/.* Sahih Muslim, "The Book of Faith (Kitab Al-Iman)' of Sahih Muslim." Translated by Abdul Hamid Siddiqui. From *SearchTruth.com.* Retrieved 19 February 2006, from the World Wide Web *http://www.searchtruth.com/hadith_books.php. Ibn Ishaq.* Ibn Ishaq, "Sirat Rasul Allah: The earliest biography of Muhammad." An abridged version Edited by Michael Edwardes (sometimes spelled Edwards). Retrieved 5 June 2006, from the World Wide Web *http://www.faithfreedom.org/Articles/sira/index.htm.* al-Tabari and A. Guillaume, *The Life of Muhammad: A Translation of Ibn Ishaq's Sirat Rasul Allah* (New York: Oxford University Press, 1955, 18th printing, 2004). *The History of al Tabari: Complete volume set from 1 to 39: English translation of "at Tareekh al Tabari" various translators* (Albany, NY: State University of New York Press). Al Tabari's history alone in English translation comes to 4,700 pages.

130. Wikipedia, "Buddhist Texts." Retrieved 10 September 2007, from the World Wide Web *http://en.wikipedia.org/wiki/Buddhist_texts#Canonical_texts*.

131. For a detailed description of the evolution of human culture, see Howard Bloom, *Global Brain: The Evolution of Mass Mind From The Big Bang to the 21st Century* (New York: John Wiley and Sons, 2000).

132. Sid Perkins, "Signs of Life? Organisms' effects on terrain aren't all that easy to perceive," *Science News* 172, no. 5 (4 August 2007). Retrieved 10 September 2007, from the World Wide Web, *http://www.sciencenews.org/articles/20070804/bob10.asp*.

133. Tom Young, "What is the volume of Earth?" *Physlink.com*—Physics & Astronomy Online. Retrieved 10 September 2007, from the World Wide Web *http://www.physlink.com/Education/AskExperts/ae419.cfm*.

134. Ellen Trimarco, David Balkwill, Mark Davidson, and T. C. Onstott. "In Situ Enrichment of a Diverse Community of Bacteria from a 4-5 km Deep Fault Zone in South Africa," *Geomicrobiology Journal* 23, no. 6 (September 2006): 463–473. Abstract retrieved 10 September 2007, from the World Wide Web *http://www.informaworld.com/smpp/content~content=a759195485~db =all*. Tullis Onstott, Research Statement. The Department of Geosciences at Princeton. Updated 09/25/06. Retrieved 10 September 2007, from the World Wide Web *http://geoweb.princeton.edu/people/onstott/research.html*. Richard Monastersky, "Deep Dwellers. Microbes thrives [*sic*] far below ground," *Science News* (29 March 1997). Retrieved 2 May 2005, from the World Wide Web *http://www.sciencenews.org/pages/sn_arc97/3_29_97/bob1.htm*. Thomas Gold, *The Deep Hot Biosphere* (New York: Springer, 1999).

135. According to David Raup's and J. John Sepkoski's canonical paper on the statistical parameters of "major extinctions," during the last 250 million years, there have been 12 mass extinctions, "with a mean interval between events of 26 million years." If we extend this average—one mass extinction every 26 million years—back through the 3.85 billion years of life on this planet, we arrive at an estimate of 148 mass extinctions since life began. David M. Raup and J. John Sepkoski, "Periodicity of Extinctions in the Geologic Past," *Proceedings of the National Academy of Sciences* 81, no. 3 (1 February 1984): 801–805.

136. David M. Raup and J. John Sepkoski, "Periodicity of Extinctions in the Geologic Past," *Proceedings of the National Academy of Sciences* 81, no. 3 (1 February 1984): 801–805.

137. Donald R. Lowe and Michael M. Tice, "Geologic evidence for Archean atmospheric and climatic evolution: Fluctuating levels of CO2, CH4, and O2 with an overriding tectonic control," *Geology* 32, no. 6 (June 2004): 493–496. doi:10.1130/G20342.1. Abstract retrieved 10 September 2007, from the World Wide Web *http://geology.geoscienceworld.org/cgi/content/abstract/32/6/493*.

138. James F. Kasting, "Theoretical constraints on oxygen and carbon dioxide concentrations in the Precambrian atmosphere." *Precambrian Research* 1987 (34): 205–229. Abstract retrieved 24 August 2007, from the World Wide Web *http://www.ncbi.nlm.nih.gov/sites/entrez?cmd=Retrieve&db =PubMed&list_uids=11542097&dopt=Citation*. Kasting is with NASA Ames Research Center. But Nathan D. Sheldon of the Royal Holloway University of London believes Kasting's figures for CO2 levels are not high enough. See Nathan D. Sheldon, "Precambrian paleosols and atmospheric CO2 levels," *Precambrian Research* 147, nos. 1-2 (10 June 2006): 148–155. Virginia Tech, "Atmospheric Carbon Dioxide Greater 1.4 Billion Years Ago," press release reprinted in *ScienceDaily*, 19 September 2003. Retrieved from the World Wide Web 21 September 2003 *http://www.sciencedaily.com/releases/2003/09/030918092804.htm*.

139. Paul Recer, "Radio astronomers measure sun's orbit around Milky Way," *Associated Press*, 1 June 1999. For a list of the varied estimates of the Sun's orbit around the core of our galaxy, estimates that are all in the 226-million-year ballpark, see Glenn Elert, editor, "Period of the Sun's Orbit around the Galaxy (Cosmic Year)," in *The Physics Factbook*. Retrieved 10 September 2007, from the World Wide Web *http://hypertextbook.com/facts/2002/StacyLeong.shtml*.

140. For the high correlation between mass extinctions and our 226 million-year-trip around the galactic core, see: G. N. Goncharov and V. V. Orlov, "Global repeating events in the history of the Earth and the motion of the Sun in the Galaxy," *Astronomy Reports* 47, no. 11 (November 2003): 925–933.

141. Stephen J. Kortenkamp and Stanley F. Dermott, "A 100,000-Year Periodicity in the Accretion Rate of Interplanetary Dust," *Science* 280, no. 5365 (8 May 1998): 874–876. doi:10.1126/science.280.5365.874. Retrieved 10 September 2007, from the World Wide Web *http://www.sciencemag.org/cgi/content/full/280/5365/874*. Kristen Vecellio, "Interplanetary Dust May Cause Climate Change, Gradual Extinction." Stardust/JPL/NASA. NASA Jet Propulsion Laboratory, California Institute of Technology, 7 May 1998. Retrieved 10 September 2007, from the World Wide Web *http://stardust.jpl.nasa.gov/news/news19.html*. There's a surge of interstellar dust piling up in our solar system at this very moment, the kind that can produce massive climate shifts. See Ron Cowen, "It's Raining Stardust: Spacecraft measures record amount of stellar debris," *Science News* 164, no. 8 (23 August 2003). Retrieved from the World Wide Web 5 September 2003 *http://www.sciencenews.org/20030823/fob2.asp*.

142. Phil Schewe, James Riordon, and Ben Stein, "Ice Ages and Spiral Arms," *Physics News Update*, American Institute of Physics 599 (24 July 2002). Retrieved 10 September 2007, from the World Wide Web *http://www.aip.org/pnu/2002/599.html*.

143. R. Bruce McMillan, Rickard S. Toomey III, Erich Schroeder, Russell W. Graham, Eric C. Grimm, Pietra G. Mueller, Jeffrey J. Saunders, and Bonnie W. Styles, *Ice Ages: When have Ice Ages occurred?* (Springfield, IL. Illinois State Museum. second edition, 2002). Retrieved 10 September 2007, from the World Wide Web *http://www.museum.state.il.us/exhibits/ice_ages/when_ice_ages.html*.

144. Steven Mithen, *The Prehistory of the Mind: the cognitive origins of art, religion and science* (London: Thames and Hudson, 1996). *Encyclopædia Britannica*. "Homo habilis," Encyclopædia Britannica Online, 2007. Retrieved 10 September 2007, from the World Wide Web *http://www.britannica.com/eb/article-9040897*. See also *Encyclopædia Britannica*. "Homo erectus," In Encyclopædia Britannica Online, 2007. Retrieved 25 August 2007, from Encyclopædia Britannica Online: *http://www.britannica.com/eb/article-249981*. *Encyclopædia Britannica*, 2007. "Australopithecus," Encyclopædia Britannica Online. Retrieved 10 September 2007, from the World Wide Web *http://www.britannica.com/eb/article-9011337*.

145. Steven Mithen. , *The Prehistory of the Mind: the cognitive origins of art, religion and science* (London: Thames and Hudson, 1996), pp. 24–26.

146. Technically these instant global warmings are called Dansgaard–Oeschger events. In the 120,000 years since the end of the Eemian interglacial, these instant global warmings have occurred roughly every 1,500 years. Stefan Rahmstorf, "Ocean circulation and climate during the past 120,000 years," *Nature* 419 (12 September 2002): 207–214. doi:10.1038/nature01090. Retrieved 2 October 2007, from the World Wide Web *http://www.nature. com/nature/journal/v419/n6903/full/nature01090.html*.

147. Fenella Saunders, "Chaotic Warnings From the Last Ice," *Discover* 23, no. 6 (June 2002). Retrieved 25 August 2007, from the World Wide Web *http:// discovermagazine.com/2002/jun/breakice*.

148. D. O. Gough, "Solar interior structure and luminosity variations," *Solar Physics* 74, no. 1 (November 1981): 21–34. Abstract retrieved 10 September 2007, from the World Wide Web *http://www.springerlink.com/content/ w316383474k03835/*. N.a., "How To Mend A Broken Climate," interview with Climatologist Ken Caldeira, head of the Caldeira Lab at the Carnegie Institution of Washington's Department of Global Ecology. *Discover* 24, no. 4 (April 2003). Retrieved 10 September 2007, from the World Wide Web *http://discovermagazine.com/2003/apr/breakdialogue*. Gabrielle Walker, "The Longest Winter," *Natural History* 112, no. 3 (April 2003): 44.

149. Richard A. Kerr, "Early Life Thrived Despite Earthly Travails," *Science* 284 (25 June 1999): 2111–2113.

150. Richard A. Muller and Gordon MacDonald, *Ice Ages and Astronomical Causes* (New York: Springer-Praxis, 2000). Retrieved 10 September 2007, from the World Wide Web *http://muller.lbl.gov/pages/IceAgeBook/history_of_climate. html*.

151. Kathleen M. Kenyon, "Excavations at Jericho, 1957–58," *Palestine Excavation Quarterly* 92 (1960): 88–108. M. Gimbutas, "Wall Paintings of Catal Huyuk," *The Review of Archaeology* (Fall 1990). James Mellaart, *Catal-Huyuk: A Neolithic Town in Anatolia* (New York: McGraw-Hill, 1967). Hans Helback, "First impressions of the Catal Huyuk plant husbandry," *Anatolian Studies* XIV (1964): 121–123. Francesco Salamini Borghi, "Site of Einkorn Wheat

Domestication Identified by DNA Fingerprinting," *Science* (14 November 1997): 1312–1322. Howard Bloom, *Global Brain: The Evolution of Mass Mind From The Big Bang to the 21st Century* (New York: John Wiley and Sons, 2000).

152. Stefan Rahmstorf, "Ocean circulation and climate during the past 120,000 years." *Nature* 419 (12 September 2002): 207–214. doi:10.1038/nature01090. Retrieved 2 October 2007, from the World Wide Web *http://www.nature. com/nature/journal/v419/n6903/full/nature01090.html*. Andrew J. Weaver, Oleg A. Saenko, Peter U. Clark, and Jerry X. Mitrovica, "Meltwater Pulse 1A from Antarctica as a Trigger of the Bølling-Allerød Warm Interval," *Science* 299, no. 5613 (14 March 2003): 1709–1713. doi:10.1126/science.1081002. Retrieved 10 September 2007, from the World Wide Web *http://www.sci-encemag.org/cgi/content/full/299/5613/1709*.

153. J. D. Hays, John Imbrie, and N. J. Shackleton, "Variations of the Earth's orbit: Pacemaker of the ice ages," *Science* 194, no. 4270 (10 December 1976): 1121–1132. doi:10.1126/science.194.4270.1121. Retrieved 10 September 2007, from the World Wide Web *http://www.sciencemag.org/cgi/ reprint/194/4270/1121.pdf*. Stefan Rahmstorf, "Timing of abrupt climate change: a precise clock," *Geophysical Research Letters* 30, no. 10 (March 2003). Retrieve 10 September 2007, from the World Wide Web *http://pik-potsdam. de/~stefan/Publications/Journals/rahmstorf_grl_2003.pdf*. Stefan Rahmstorf, "Ocean circulation and climate during the past 120,000 years," *Nature* 419 (12 September 2002): 207–214. doi:10.1038/nature01090. Retrieved 2 October 2007, from the World Wide Web *http://www.nature.com/nature/ journal/v419/n6903/full/nature01090.html*. For a history and explanation of the Milankovich Effect see *Encyclopædia Britannica*, "climate," Encyclopædia Britannica Online. Retrieved 23 November 2000, from the World Wide Web *http://members.eb.com/bol/topic?eu=109112&sctn=19*. For a dissenting voice on the impact of the Milankovich Effect, see Richard A. Muller and Gordon MacDonald, *Ice Ages and Astronomical Causes* (New York: Springer-Praxis, 2000). Retrieved 10 September 2007, from the World Wide Web *http://muller.lbl.gov/pages/IceAgeBook/history_of_climate.html*.

154. Illinois State Museum's director R. Bruce McMillan and seven of his colleagues write, "Our modern climate represents a very short, warm period between glacial advances." R. Bruce McMillan; Rickard S. Toomey III; Erich Schroeder; Russell W. Graham; Eric C. Grimm; Pietra G. Mueller; Jeffrey

J. Saunders; and Bonnie W. Styles, *Ice Ages: When have Ice Ages occurred?* (Springfield, IL. Illinois State Museum. second edition, 2002). Retrieved 10 September 2007, from the World Wide Web *http://www.museum.state.il.us/ exhibits/ice_ages/when_ice_ages.html*. And according to Richard A. Muller and Gordon MacDonald, "It is clear that most of the last 420 thousand years (420 kyr) was spent in ice age.... The very unusual nature of the last 11,000 years stands out in striking contrast to the 90,000 years of cold that preceded it." Richard A. Muller and Gordon MacDonald, *Ice Ages and Astronomical Causes* (New York: Springer-Praxis, 2000). Retrieved 10 September 2007, from the World Wide Web *http://muller.lbl.gov/pages/IceAgeBook/history_of_climate. html*. Adds Stefan Rahmstorf, Professor of Physics of the Oceans at Potsdam University in Germany and Member of the German Advisory Council on Global Change, "Abrupt climate events appear to be paced by a 1,470-year cycle with a period that is probably stable to within a few percent.... This highly precise clock points to an origin outside the Earth system ..." Stefan Rahmstorf, "Timing of abrupt climate change: a precise clock," *Geophysical Research Letters* 30, no. 10 (March 2003). Retrieved 25 August 2007, from the World Wide Web *http://pik-potsdam.de/~stefan/Publications/Journals/ rahmstorf_grl_2003.pdf*. See also Thomas J. Crowley and Gerald R. North, "Abrupt Climate Change and Extinction Events in Earth History," *Science* 240, no. 4855 (20 May 1988): 996–1002. doi:10.1126/science.240.4855.996.

155. Even the most optimistic experts on climatological history compare our temporary truce with the ice to another highly unusual period that lasted 28,000 years. The wildly out-of-character thaw whose example these scientists hope our epoch will follow is: "the interglacial stage following Termination V." EPICA community members, "Eight glacial cycles from an Antarctic ice core." *Nature* 429 (10 June 2004): 623–628. doi:10.1038/nature02599. Retrieved 10 September 2007, from the World Wide Web *http://www. nature.com/nature/journal/v429/n6992/full/nature02599.html*.

156. Howard Bloom, *The Lucifer Principle: a scientific expedition into the forces of history* (New York: Grove/Atlantic, 1997).

157. UNESCO MAB—Man and Biosphere Programme, "People, Diversity and Ecology." Retrieved 10 September 2007, from the World Wide Web *http://www.unesco.org/mab/ecosyst/islands.shtml*. Columbia University's Socioeconomic data and Applications Center puts the percentage of humans living in coastal areas at 40 percent. SEDAC—Socioeconomic data and

Applications Center, "Percentage of Total Population Living in Coastal Areas." July 2007. Retrieved 10 September 2007, from the World Wide Web *http://sedac.ciesin.org/es/papers/Coastal_Zone_Pop_Method.pdf.*

158. John Boardman, Jasper Griffin, and Oswyn Murray, *The Oxford History of the Classical World: Greece and the Hellenistic World* (New York: Oxford University Press, 1988).

159. These insights on the evolution of the Family of DNA were stimulated by the work of David Smillie. David Smillie, "Human Nature and Evolution: language, culture, and race." Paper given at the Biennial Meeting of the International Society of Human Ethology, Amsterdam, August 1992. David Smillie, "Darwin's Tangled Bank: The Role of Social Environments," *Perspectives in Ethology 10: Behavior and Evolution,* edited by P. P. G. Bateson et al. (New York: Plenum Press, 1993), pp. 119–141. David Smillie, "Darwin's Two Paradigms: An "Opportunistic" Approach to Group Selection Theory," *Journal of Social and Evolutionary Systems* 18, no. 3 (1995): 231–255. David Smillie, "Group processes and human evolution: sex and culture as adaptive strategies." Paper presented at the 19th Annual Meeting of the European Sociobiological Society, Alfred, NY, 25 July 1996.

160. Yes, some bacterial colonies work diligently to snatch inanimate atoms and make them part of the bioprocess, part of the extended family of DNA. Autotrophs kidnap carbon dioxide, chemolithoautotrophs press-gang hydrogen, iron, sulfur, ammonia, and nitrites, chemoorganoheterotrophs enslave miscellaneous chemical compounds, and uncategorized bacteria grab and swallow molecules of methane and carbon monoxide. See NASA, "Life on Other Planets in the Solar System—Looking for Extraterrestrial life." *Viability of Micro-organisms.* TABLE 1.2—Microorganisms with Particular Physiological and Nutritional Characteristics. Retrieved 10 September 2007, from the World Wide Web *http://www.resa.net/nasa/extreme_chart.htm.* For another example, see the ways in which bacteria make use of inanimate sulfur atoms in Agnieszka Sekowska and Antoine Danchin's "Sulfur metabolism in Bacteria, with emphasis on Escherichia coli and Bacillus subtilis," *Genetics of Bacterial Genomes.* Pasteur Institute, France. Retrieved 10 September 2007, from the World Wide Web *http://www.pasteur.fr/recherche/unites/REG/sulfur_review.html.*

161. Lynn Margulis, *Symbiosis in Cell Evolution: Microbial Communities in the Archean and Proterozoic Eons*, Second Edition (New York: W. H. Freeman, 1993). Lynn Margulis and Dorion Sagan, *Microcosmos: Four Billion Years of Microbial Evolution* (New York: Summit Books, 1986).

162. Rudolf K. Thauer, Kurt Jungermann, and Karl Decker, "Energy conservation in chemotrophic anaerobic bacteria," *Microbiology and Molecular Biology Reviews* 41, no. 1 (1 March 1977): 100–180. Edward F. DeLong, "Life on the thermodynamic edge," *Science* (20 July 2007): 327–328.

163. Richard D. Bryant, Wayne Jansen, Joe Boivin, Edward J. Laishley, and J. William Costerton, "Effect of Hydrogenase and Mixed Sulfate-Reducing Bacterial Populations on the Corrosion of Steel," *Applied and Environmental Microbiology* (October 1991): 2804–2809.

164. A team led by R. L. Anderson at the Center for Disease Control in Atlanta, Georgia, reports that pipe-eating microbes manage to survive heavy-duty assaults with disinfectants, including chlorine, phenolic, ethanol, quaternary-ammonium, and idiophor. R. L. Anderson, B. W. Holland, J. K. Carr, W. W. Bond, and M. S. Favero, "Effect of disinfectants on pseudomonads colonized on the interior surface of PVC pipes," *American Journal of Public Health* 80, no. 1 (January 1990): 17–21.

165. Andy Coghlan, "Mapping the Slime Cities," *World Press Review* (December 1996): 32–33.

166. J. M. Gonzales, J. E. Brown, F. T. Robb, et al., "Microbial diversity, metabolism, and interaction." Meeting of the American Society for Microbiology. May 1998, Atlanta, GA. J. Travis, "Novel bacteria have a taste for aluminum," *Science News* 153, no. 22 (30 May 1998): 341. For a dissenting opinion, one that states that aluminum is toxic to **all** bacteria, see Rogelio Garciadueñas Piña and Carlos Cervantes, "Microbial interactions with aluminum," *BioMetals* 9, no. 3 (July 1996): 311–316.

167. V. Epshtein, A. S. Mironov, and E. Nudler, "The riboswitch-mediated control of sulfur metabolism in bacteria," *Proceedings of the National Academy of Sciences* (9 April 2003): 5052–5056. Retrieved 10 September 2007, from the World Wide Web *http://www.pnas.org/cgi/content/full/100/9/5052*.

168. The champion of bacteria that have invented ways to thrive in a radioactive environment is Deinococcus radiodurans. For more on Deinococcus radiodurans survival tricks, see: Y. Hua, I. Narumi, G. Gao, B. Tian, K. Satoh, S. Kitayama, B. Shen, "PprI: a general switch responsible for extreme radioresistance of Deinococcus radiodurans," *Biochemical and Biophysical Research Communications* 306, no. 2 (27 June 2003): 354–360. Retrieved 10 September 2007, from the World Wide Web *http://www.cab.zju.edu.cn/INAS/personal%20web/Hyj/paper/PprI_2003.pdf*. J. R. Battista, "Against all odds: the survival strategies of Deinococcus radiodurans," *Annual Review of Microbiology* 51 (1997): 203–224. Retrieved 10 September 2007, from the World Wide Web *http://web.ebscohost.com/ehost/pdf?vid=3&hid=21&sid=fe833a20-4dd5-439f-92eb-669246604d6f%40sessionmgr2*. John Travis, "Two-handed protein may protect DNA," *Science News* 166, no. 1 (3 July 2004). Retrieved 22 July 2004, from the World Wide Web *http://www.sciencenews.org/articles/20040703/note13.asp*. Patrick Huyghe, "Conan the Bacterium," *The Sciences* (July/August 1998): 16–19.

169. Gerald W. Tannock, *Normal Microflora: An Introduction to Microbes Inhabiting the Human Body* (New York: Springer, 1995).

170. Stuart B. Levy, *The Antibiotic Paradox: How Miracle Drugs are Destroying the Miracle* (New York: Plenum Press, 1992). Stuart B. Levy, M.D., "Multidrug Resistance—A Sign of the Times," *The New England Journal of Medicine*, 7 May 1998. The Center for Adaptation Genetics and Drug Resistance, Retrieved January 1999, from the World Wide Web *http://www.healthsci.tufts.edu/labs/Sblevy/home.html* and Retrieved 10 September 2007, from the World Wide Web *http://www.pubmedcentral.nih.gov/articlerender.fcgi?artid=1113828*. Stuart B. Levy, "The Challenge of Antibiotic Resistance," *Scientific American* (March 1998): 46–53. For animal evidence supporting Levy's contention that we are defended by our internal bacterial homesteaders, see S. P. Borriello and F. E. Barclay, "Protection of hamsters against Clostridium difficile ileocaecitis by prior colonisation with non-pathogenic strains," *Journal of Medical Microbiology* (June 1985): 339–350. F. Le Guyader, M. Pommepuy, and M. Cormier, "Implantation of Escherichia coli in pilot experiments and the influence of competition on the flora," *Canadian Journal of Microbiology* (February 1991): 116–121; D. J. Bibel, R. Aly, C. Bayles, W. G. Strauss, H. R. Shinefield, and H. I. Maibach, "Competitive adherence as a mechanism of bacterial interference," *Canadian Journal of Microbiology* (June 1983): 700–703. A. Onderdonk, B. Marshall, R. Cisneros, and S. B.

Levy, "Competition between congenic Escherichia coli K-12 strains in vivo," *Infection and Immunity* (April 1981): 74–79. N. Rikitomi, M. Akiyama, and K. Matsumoto, "Role of normal microflora in the throat in inhibition of adherence of pathogenic bacteria to host cells: in vitro competitive adherence between Corynebacterium pseudodiphtheriticum and Branhamella catarrhalis," *Kansenshogaku Zasshi* (The Journal of the Japanese Association for Infectious Diseases) (February 1989): 118–124; C. S. Impey, G. C. Mead, S. M. George, "Competitive exclusion of salmonellas from the chick caecum using a defined mixture of bacterial isolates from the caecal microflora of an adult bird," *Journal of Hygiene* (December 1982): 479–490. M. Hinton, G. C. Mead, and C. S. Impey, "Protection of chicks against environmental challenge with Salmonella enteritidis by 'competitive exclusion' and acid-treated feed. Letters in applied microbiology," March 1991. F. W. Edens, C. R. Parkhurst, I. A. Casas, and W. J. Dobrogosz, "Principles of ex ovo competitive exclusion and in ovo administration of Lactobacillus reuteri," *Poultry Science* (January 1997): 179–196. M. E. Hume, J. A. Byrd, L. H. Stanker, and H. L. Ziprin, "Reduction of caecal Listeria monocytogenes in Leghorn chicks following treatment with a competitive exclusion culture (PREEMPT)," *Letters in Applied Microbiology* (June 1998): 432–436. M. Aho, L. Nuotio, E. Nurmi, and T. Kiiskinen, "Competitive exclusion of campylobacters from poultry with K-bacteria and Broilact," *International Journal of Food Microbiology* (March–April 1992): 265–275. Katrin Pütsep, Carl-Ivar Brändén, Hans G. Boman, and Staffan Normark, "Antibacterial peptide from H. pylori." *Nature* (22 April 1999): 671–672.

171. D. M. Fallacara, C. M. Monahan, T. Y. Morishita, and R. F. Wack, "Fecal Shedding and Antimicrobial Susceptibility of Selected Bacterial Pathogens and a Survey of Intestinal Parasites in Free-Living Waterfowl," *Avian Diseases* 45, no. 1 (January–March 2001): 128–135. doi:10.2307/1593019.

172. CNN, "Bugs may control weather," *CNN.com* (27 May 2002). Retrieved 15 March 2003, from the World Wide Web *http://www.cnn.com/2002/WEATHER/05/27/bugs.weather/index.html*. Oliver Morton, "The Living Skies: Cloud Behavior and its Role in Climate Change," *The Hybrid Vigor Journal* (April 2002). Retrieved 10 September 2007, from the World Wide Web *http://www.hybridvigor.net/Earth/pubs/HVclouds.pdf*.

173. "There are over 10000 species of birds in the world," Introduction to Bird Species and Ornithology: Number of Bird Species in the World.

Birding.com. Retrieved 10 September 2007, from the World Wide Web *http://www.birding.com/species.asp*. The total number of mammal species, on the other hand, comes to a mere 4,629. World Resource Institute. Species: Mammal species, number. Retrieved 10 September 2007, from the World Wide Web *http://Earthtrends.wri.org/searchable_db/index. php?action=select_countries&theme=7&variable_ID=119)*.

Chapter 6

Evo Devo Universe?
A Framework for Speculations on Cosmic Culture

John M. Smart

The underlying paradigm for cosmology is theoretical physics. In this paper we explore ways this framework might be extended with insights from information and computation studies and evolutionary developmental (evo-devo) biology. We also briefly consider implications of such a framework for cosmic culture. In organic systems, adaptive evolutionary development guides the production of intelligent, ordered, and complex structures. In such systems we can distinguish *evolutionary processes* that are stochastic, creative, and "divergent," and *developmental processes* that produce statistically predictable, robust, conservative, and "convergent" structures and trajectories.

We will briefly model our universe as an evolutionary, information-processing, and developmental system—as an *"evo compu devo" universe* (abbreviated *"evo devo"* hereafter). Our framework will try to reconcile the *majority* of unpredictable, evolutionary features of universal emergence with a *special subset* of potentially statistically predictable and developmental universal trends, including:

- accelerating *advances* in universal complexity (however we define such advances, e.g., Aunger 2007) seen over the last half of the universe's life history in contrast to *deceleration* during the first half
- increasing spatial and temporal (space time) *locality* of universal complexity development
- apparently hierarchical emergence of increasingly matter and energy *efficient* and matter and energy *dense* substrates (platforms) for adaptation and computation
- apparent accelerating emergence, on Earth, of increasingly *postbiological* (technological) forms of intelligence, and their likely future trajectories.

We use the phrase "evo devo" without the hyphen here to distinguish this speculative philosophy and systems theory from the legitimate science of "evo-devo" biology from which we seek insights.

Introduction: Culture and Technology in Universal Context

What are human culture and technology in relation to the cosmos? How do they change over time? To what extent may intelligence (human culture, science, engineering, technology, and successors) reshape our universe in the future? To what extent are intelligent systems constrained or directed by our universe? What universal role, function, or "purpose" may culture and technology serve?

Such humbling questions are the province of astrosociology, the philosophical study of the likelihood, characteristics, and dynamics of extraterrestrial civilizations by analogy to our still poorly understood and singular example on Earth. Although today it is a field with few journals and conferences, questions in astrosociology are informed by astrobiology, evolutionary biology, paleontology, evolutionary psychology, behavioral ecology, macrohistory, and other life, social, informational, physical, and technological sciences and philosophies. Such questions are also regularly contemplated by SETI practitioners, science fiction writers, futures scholars, and other communities (Wikipedia 2007).

These questions are also central to an even more speculative field we may call astrotechnology, the long-term evolution and development of technology in universal context. Extrapolating accelerating computer developments a few generations hence, some scholars foresee a coming "technological singularity" (Adams 1909; Good 1965; Vinge 1993; Broderick 1997; Dennett 1998; Coren 1998; Kurzweil 1999, 2001, 2005; Smart 1999; Clarke 2003), a time when Earth's leading computing systems may encompass and even surpass human cultural intelligence, performance, and autonomy. Dick has argued (1999, 2000, 2003, 2006) that considering the long-term future of Earth's cultural evolution seems critical to understanding the nature of extraterrestrial intelligence, and that higher intelligence may become postbiological, which would in turn impact extraterrestrial behavior in unknown ways.

To consider the cosmic future of culture and technology this paper will introduce three biologically inspired sets of hypotheses (simple models) of universal change. Like descending Matrioshka dolls, each later model is a subset of the prior in a logical-specification hierarchy (Salthe 2002), and each is also increasingly speculative and poorly grounded (Figure 1). All three models can generate testable implications for astrosociology and astrotechnology, though each may need further mathematical and quantitative representation before that can occur.

- The first model, the *informational computational universe* (ICU) hypothesis, considers the universe as a purposeful information processing system in which biological culture, as it arises throughout the universe, has the potential to play some integral (e.g., anthropic) yet transient universe-guiding role.

Figure 1. Relative scope of three models of universal change.

- The second model, the *evo devo universe* (EDU) hypothesis, considers the universe as engaged in both processes of *evolutionary* creativity and processes of hierarchical *development*, including a specific form of *accelerating* hierarchical development we call "STEM compression" of computation.
- The third model, the *developmental singularity* (DS) hypothesis, proposes our universe's hierarchical and energetically dissipative intelligence systems are developmentally constrained to produce, very soon in cosmologic time, a very specific outcome, a *black hole analogous computing system*. Per other theorists (see Smolin 1997) such a structure is likely to be a core component in the *replicative life cycle* of our evo devo universe within the multiverse, a postulated *environment* of universes.

Our arguments will be guided by theories and analogies of emergence (Holland 1995, 1998). As shown in mathematics (Gödel 1934; Chaitin 1998) and computing (Church 1936; Turing 1936), all theories have areas of utility and areas of incompleteness and undecidability. Likewise all analogies have strengths and shortcomings (Hofstadter 1995). We need not assume our universe is *in essence* "computational," "alive," or even "hierarchically dissipative," only that these computational, organic, and thermodynamic analogies may serve to advance our understanding of processes far more complex than our models.

We must also acknowledge the present empirical and quantitative shortcomings of anthropic universe models on which all three of our hypotheses depend. Anthropic models propose that life and intelligence are developmentally destined to emerge in our particular universe, and range from the mathematical (the apparent fine tuning of fundamental universal parameters, e.g., Rees 1999), to the empirical (special universal chemistry that promotes precursors to biogenesis, e.g., Henderson 1913, 1917; Miller 1953; Lazcano 2004), to the teleological (analogies and arguments for systemic function or purpose to cosmic intelligence, e.g., this paper). Today, as acknowledged by even their most adept practitioners (Barrow and Tipler 1986; Krauss et. al. 2008), anthropic universe models proceed more from ignorance and assumption than from knowledge. Though we will introduce one here, we cannot yet validate a framework for generating a probability distribution for possible universe creation, and from there, critiquing anthropic arguments with any rigor. Our theoretical and experimental capacities are quite poor by comparison to the complexities and apparent degrees of freedom in the universe we are modeling. And if there is a multiverse, a space in which universes like ours live, die, and are reborn, framing difficulties only multiply.

Nevertheless, there is a sizable community of scientists and scholars willing to engage in anthropic systems theory even as such philosophy is not always grounded on testable scientific theory, but rather speculation, induction, analogy, argument, and circumstantial evidence. It is to this audience, and to the hope of near-future emergence of testable anthropic hypothesis and theory, that this paper is addressed.

---

1. The Informational Computational Universe Hypothesis

How fundamental a property of the universe is information? How applicable is the analogy of the universe as an information processing system? What system properties do information processing systems and universes potentially share?

Figure 2. The most fundamental reality and control system of our universe may be information. (Credit: Acceleration Studies Foundation. Artist: Marlon Rojas, *Fizbit.com*)

Perhaps most fundamentally, though we lack rigor in making this claim at present, our universe seems to be both "in the shape of" and "shaped by" *information and its emergents*. The ICU hypothesis proposes a cosmos of *information and information processors* (prebiological, biological and postbiological) that play fundamental roles as both *descriptions of and shapers of universal dynamics*.

We will attempt no definitions of information or computation in this brief paper. Like related terms (complexity, emergence, intelligence) there are many useful models for information and computing (Hofkirchner 1999; Floridi 2003, 2008; von Baeyer 2003; Siefe 2006; Brier 2008), but as yet no commonly accepted general theory or philosophy for either. Nevertheless, since at least the founding of the Pythagorean school circa 530 Before Common Era (BCE), with its conviction that the ultimate laws of the universe may be expressed as mathematical ideals, and more generally the writings of Plato (e.g., *Timaeus* 360 BCE) which proposed that a "perfect realm" of ideal forms and ideas undergirds the physical world and is imperfectly executed in it, philosophers have entertained the notion *that the most basic "reality" and "control system" of our universe may be information and the many apparently emergent manifestations of its processing.* Such manifestations include reduction of uncertainty (Shannon 1948, the founder of modern information theory), evolution (Gershenson 2008), development, complexity, structure, math/symbol, physical law, relation, difference, perception, abstract idea, intelligence, meaning, human consciousness, and any form of postbiological "hyperconsciousness" (Wallace 2006) that may one day come.

In this paper, the more easily observable and quantifiable *physical* features of our universe, such as space, time, energy, and matter/mass, will be referred to as STEM. Such features have been surprisingly well characterized mathematically by general relativity and quantum theory. When such features are described in concert with the more abstract and harder-to-quantify manifestations of *information and computation* described above, we shall call this combination a STEM+IC universe (Smart 2002b).

We cannot yet know whether IC, information and its experiential and computational emergents, including intelligence and consciousness, can be fully described as simply a *special set of arrangements* of universal STEM, or whether informational/computational phenomena are something *as or more* "basic" and "real" than the physical universe they coexist with. Resolving this ancient question (Descartes 1641) seems well beyond our present science. As one potential resolution, some propose that a digital physics may eventually emerge—an understanding of our universe as a quantized computing system (Zuse 1969; Wheeler 1983; Deutsch 1985, 1997; Chaitin 1987; Fredkin 1990, 1992; Wolfram 2002; Lloyd 2006) that is discrete (at the Planck scale) but never complete (in its calculations).

While IC may or may not relate to STEM in such a rigorous and reductive manner, what we can observe today is that "mind" in all physical systems has an ever more pervasive impact on "matter" as a direct function of its complexity (Dyson 1988). Therefore, generalizing from the pervasiveness of information in universal systems (Roederer 2005), and the accelerating influence of mind wherever it emerges, there is a necessity for some provisional hypotheses with respect to STEM+IC relationships. We may now define the ICU hypothesis as *any* set of provisional models of information and computation which seem to have the potential to be fundamental, quantitative, predictive, and constraining perspectives on local or universal physical (STEM) processes.

In these early days of information and computation theory we can suggest many such incomplete sets. My own amateur's perspective considers the following claims and subhypotheses particularly important:

- Church-Turing Thesis on Computational Equivalence and Interdependence (Church 1934; Turing 1936). The Church-Turing thesis holds that any physically computable process can be performed on a Turing machine (a universal generic computer). A cornerstone of computability and complexity theory, it allows us to envision all physical processes as potentially unified by a *future universal theory of computation*.

- Gödel's Thesis on Incompleteness (Gödel 1934; Chaitin 1998). Gödel's thesis holds that all formal logical systems and all physical (finite state) computing systems have *areas of incompleteness and undecidability*, e.g., no computing system can be omniscient. Chaitin argues that even some fundamental mathematical facts that cannot be proven with mathematical logic, are "true for no reason," and *were inherited* in our particular universe, e.g., no mathematical system can even fully understand itself (be "self-omniscient").

- Participatory Anthropic Principle (Wheeler 1983; Lloyd 2006). The PAP proposes our universe may be usefully considered as both *information* and an *information processing system*, engaged in *collective observational interactions* that may be modeled on both quantum mechanical and emergent levels of universal structure. It is arguably the most explicit description of an "informational-computational universe" to date, yet it does not require information or computation to be "ultimate" realities.

- Strong Anthropic Principle (Barrow and Tipler 1986). Our universe must possess properties that "allow life to develop within it at some stage in its history" [e.g., properties that make life *developmentally likely*, in a statistical sense]. The SAP may be drawn from the fine tuning problem in cosmology, in which our universe's apparently fundamental constants and initial conditions seem very narrowly restricted to values which may *statistically determine* the emergence of life and complexity (Barrow 2002, 2007).

- "Final" Anthropic Principle (Barrow and Tipler 1986). "Intelligent information processing must emerge in the universe, and persist [e.g., as a *developmental* process]." In other words, not only life, but intelligent life is statistically likely to emerge and persist, due to the special structure of our universe. The FAP may be inferred from both fine tuning and our universe's accelerating emergence history, e.g., an evolutionary developmental emergence record that has run increasingly rapidly over the last six billion years (Sagan 1977) the more intelligent the local system becomes (Coren 1998).

- Intelligence Principle (Dick 2003). This hypothesis holds that "the maintenance, improvement and perpetuation of knowledge and intelligence is the *central driving force of cultural evolution* [in biological systems in the universe, at least], and to the extent intelligence can be improved, it will be improved." Generalizing from Earth's history, it connects cultural evolution to universal intelligence improvement.

- Melioristic Universe (James 1921). Life has an innate tendency to *improve* (ameliorate, make better or more tolerable) some definable aspects of itself (complexity, intelligence, survivability, and perhaps other measures) over its lifespan. This hypothesis is a generalization of the intelligence principle, and may be proposed by quantifying life's melioristic record of complexity and capacity improvement on Earth.

- Hierarchical Universe of Increasingly Intelligent and Energetically Dissipative Complex Adaptive Systems (Simon 1962; de Vaucouleurs 1970; Pattee 1973; Nicolis and Prigogine 1977; Allen and Starr 1982; Salthe 1985, 1993; Moravec 1988; Paul and Cox 1996; Kurzweil 1999; Chaisson 2001). This hypothesis proposes that our universe generates an *emergence hierarchy* of energetically dissipative "complex adaptive systems" (CAS) (Holland 1995, 1998), and that the leading edge of this computational hierarchy increasingly understands and influences universal processes. Furthermore, the dissipation hierarchy is *integral* to universal purpose, structure, and function in a way yet to be determined. In our hierarchical universe, cultural evolution on Earth, and at least in other Earth-like environments, can be expected to produce an *even more advanced and energetically dissipative intelligence*, some coming form of postbiological "life." As a result, Earth's *human culture has the potential to play an important yet transient role* in the hierarchical lineage of universal intelligence emergence.

- Observer Selection Bias Exists But Does Not Invalidate All Anthropic Insights (Barrow and Tipler 1986). Observer selection bias (Bostrom 2002) must accompany *all* anthropic reasoning (universe hypotheses made from our position as intelligent observers). *But if processes of universal development exist, and if they bias intelligence to be a central observer in the universe system,* as they apparently do with intelligence in all developing biological systems, *then theories of universal development* should prove a more fundamental framework to test and ground anthropic insights. In such case, all observer selection models must be a subset of *universal evolutionary development* models, which we will consider in the EDU hypothesis next.

Note the ICU hypothesis simply collects potentially fundamental informational and computational perspectives on universal dynamics. Some are framed in *proto*-evolutionary or developmental fashion, but without explicitly (except in the last subhypothesis) using the terms "evolution" or "development."

The privileging of information and computation as universal fundamentals feels appropriate for at least three reasons. First, there is the tautological (and unhelpful) reason that we, as conscious observers, are biased to see consciousness and its generative processes as special. Second, information and its emergents have apparently manifested on an unreasonably smooth hierarchy emergence continuum over known universal history, beginning from a featureless and isotropic void and ending with today's highly variegated and at least locally intelligent cosmos—this process at least *looks* like it might be developmental. Third, as we will discuss in the EDU hypothesis, information production and computation are in a small subset of processes that have *continually accelerated* over the last six billennia of universal history.

Figure 3. Christian Aristotelian cosmos. (Credit: Peter Apian's *Cosmographia*, 1524)

To some degree, the above collection of ICU hypotheses represents the current perimeter of respectable scientific and philosophical conjecture on the "meaning" or "purpose" of universal dynamics. Note that the central assumptions and biases of the hypotheses are *"info-morphic,"* not "anthropo-morphic." Nevertheless, the only anthropomorphism we have fully

208

escaped in the ICU is the ancient one placing *Homo sapiens* at the center of the universe in some singular, enduring, or guaranteed fashion (Figure 3).

It is beyond our scope here to carefully evaluate whether ICU assumptions and biases are justified, or are anthropic mistakes (observation selection effects). Bostrom (2002) and others would invoke some form of random-observer self-sampling assumption to critique ICU-related thinking. Yet as our last ICU subhypothesis argues, if random observer-moments exist only in *evolutionary* processes, and are an incorrect evaluative framework for all *developmental* processes in the cosmos, then observer selection theory must be revised to conform with our emerging understanding of universal observer intelligence development. In models of the universe, it is today far from clear what the most fundamental frameworks are from which to launch a critique of observer bias. Let us grant that bias exists and move on.

The ICU hypothesis starts us thinking carefully about the impact of cosmic information and computation, but in this era of still-missing information theory, it is unsatisfyingly vague and only mildly prescriptive. As a result, we propose that the next two models, though each is an increasingly specific and speculative subset of ICU hypothesis space, may prove even more useful, testable, and predictive descriptions of universal dynamics.

---

2. The Evo Devo Universe Hypothesis

How applicable is the analogy of the universe as a quasi-organic information processing system engaged simultaneously in *both evolution* and *development*? Which macroscopic aspects of our universe seem to be engaged in evolution? Which aspects seem to be engaged in development? How closely do universal evolutionary and developmental processes parallel known processes in evo-devo biology?

There would be many potential benefits to constructing and verifying even a primitive and tentative model of an *evo devo universe,* one where evolution and development operate as *distinct and complementary* physical processes at both universal and subsystem scales. Whenever we can discover and validate evolutionary or developmental process and structure in our universe, we can better *describe evolutionary possibilities and predict developmental trends, including possibilities and trends* for universal culture and technology, and even

Table 1. Some Linguistic Dichotomies (Polar Word Pairs) with Homology to Evolution and Development.

Evolution	Development
Unpredictability	Predictability(*statistical*)
Chance	Necessity
Indeterminacy	Determinism
Random	Destined
Divergent	Convergent
Branching	Cyclic
Reversible	Irreversible (*on average*)
Possibilities	Constraints
Variety/Many	Unity/Monism
Variability	Stability
Uniqueness	Sameness
Transformation	Transmission
Accidental	Self-organizing
Bottom-up	Top-down
Local	Global
Immaturity	Maturity
Individual	Collective
Instance	Average
Short-term	Long-term
Reductionism first and Holism secondary	Holism first and Reductionism secondary
Analysis (breaking)	Synthesis (joining)
Amorphous	Hierarchical/Directional
Innovative	Conservative
Creativity (of novelty)	Discovery (of constraint)
Period-doubling/Chaos	Period-halving/Order
Experimental	Optimal
Dispersion	Integration
Dedifferentiation	Differentiation
STEM recombination	STEM compression
Nonergodicity	Ergodicity
Innovation	Sustainability
Mind	Body
Belief (unproven)	Knowledge (verified)

come to understand some of the *functional (evo and devo) roles* of culture and technology in the cosmos.

Consider the following very partial set of polar word pairs (Table 1). Compare these words with your knowledge of evolutionary and developmental processes in biological systems at the molecular, cellular, organismic, population, and ecosystem levels. As we will propose, *if we allow for the possibility of both evolution and development at the universal scale,* a case may be made for commonly, though not exclusively, associating the first column with evolutionary and the second with developmental processes in both living and nonliving complex systems.

Like evolution and development itself, each subordinate word pair suggests, in *some future evo devo information theory*, complementary processes contributing to adaptation in complex systems, as well as conflicting models for analyzing change. In considering these dichotomies, the easy observation is that each process or concept has explanatory value in different contexts. The deeper question is when, where, and how they interrelate.

Unfortunately, when theorists describe change in systems larger or smaller than the individual biological organism today, the term "evolution" has been nearly the sole term of art, and outside of biology, even that term is only inconsistently applied. This is true even as a number of apparently irreversible, statistically predictable, and directional universal processes (entropy, acceleration, locality, hierarchy) have been obvious for more than 150 years, processes which on their surface seem very good candidates for being described as "development." This bias toward evolutionary nomenclature may exist because reductionist analysis has always been easier than holistic synthesis for human-initiated science. Evolutionary biology achieved early theoretical characterization (Darwin 1859), and early quantification via reductionist science (Mendelian genetics), while until recently, both embryology and ecosystem development have remained holistic mysteries, too complex for comparatively quantitative or theoretical investigation. Consequently, hypotheses of macrodevelopment (orthogenesis, complexity ratchets, etc.) have not risen above the realm of philosophical speculation, even with great advances in the explanation of evolutionary mechanisms.

Fortunately, this state of affairs may soon change. Beginning in the mid-1990's a new generation of evo-devo biologists have emerged (Steele 1981, 1998; Jablonka and Lamb 1995, 2005; Raff 1996; Arthur 2000; Wilkins 2001; Hall 2003; Müller and Newman 2003; Verhulst 2003; West-Eberhard 2003; Schlosser and Wagner 2004; Carroll 2005; Callebaut and Rasskin-Gutman 2005), whose inquiries are guided by new conceptual and technical advances in the study of evolution and development. The interdisciplinary field of evo-devo biology explores the relationship between evolutionary and developmental processes at the scale levels of cells, organisms, and ecologies (Carroll 2005). It includes such issues as:

- how developmental processes evolve
- the developmental basis for homology (similarity of form in species with a common ancestor)
- the process of homoplasy (convergent evolution of form in species with unique ancestors)

- the roles of modularity and path dependency in biological evolution and development
- how the environment impacts biological evolution and development.

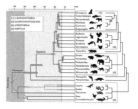

Figure 4. An evo-devo systematics diagram (Milinkovitch and Tzika 2007). (Credit: Michel Milinkovitch, Lab. of Evolutionary Genetics, Free U. of Brussels)

Though this community is just over a decade old, it shows potential to deliver the meta-Darwinian paradigm we have long been seeking in biology, one that reconciles evolution's variety production, and natural selection's contingency and famous *lack* of directionality (e.g., Gould 1977), with the smoothly accelerating and apparently developmental emergence of increasing intelligence and complexity in a special subset of biological systems on Earth over the last four billion years (e.g., Sagan's "Cosmic Calendar" 1977).

A number of scholars in the orbit of the evo-devo community, such as paleontologist Simon Conway Morris (*Life's Solution* 2004) are also contributing greatly to this emerging paradigm. Morris has done persuasive work on "evolutionary convergence" (homoplasy) in the record of life's evolutionary development, documenting the *independent emergence, conservation, and convergence* with respect to a special subset of functional systems and morphologies (eyes, jointed limbs, body plans, emotions, imagination, language, opposable thumbs, tool use, etc.). Many of these homoplasies powerfully advance *individual and cultural information processing and adaptation* over a broad range of evolutionary environments, for all organisms that acquire them.

The streamlined shape of fish fins for example, while invariably first created as an *evolutionary* morphological experiment, *must persist* in the genes of *all* organisms seeking to move rapidly through water on *all* Earth-like planets, as a generic *developmental constraint* imposed by universal physics. In an ICU universe, this makes such advances evolutionary "ratchets" (function that is randomly acquired but statistically irreversible once acquired in a broad range of environments), a type of *developmental optima* (for a given level of environmental complexity) in all universes of our type. As Morris proposes, if the "tape of life" were played twice, on two Earth-like planets, many such "universals" of biological form and function (e.g., the 35 or so generic *body plans* of the Cambrian) should predictably emerge, persist, and converge in both environments. Such convergence must occur even as the *great majority* of details of evolutionary path and species structure in each environment would remain contingently, unpredictably different. Such claims must one day be testable and falsifiable by simulation, and in the nearer term, by long-range experiments in rapid evolutionary systems, such as Richard Lenski's *E. coli* work (Lenski 2004).

Just as in the discovery of biological development, the discovery of universal developmental process, where it exists, would not diminish or negate the *great evolutionary creativity* of our universe. Rather, it would help us understand how universal creativity is also constrained to maintain particular ends, including *hierarchy emergence, universal life cycle, and (future) universe replication*, a superstructure that allows evolution to flourish, but apparently always within circumscribed universal developmental boundaries.

The evo devo universe hypothesis (simple model) will now be presented in brief. It is an aggregation of the following claims and subhypotheses (and others omitted in this sketch):

- The ICU hypothesis (in some variant) as outlined earlier, and:
- The Evo Devo Analogy. Our universe seems analogous to a quasi-organic evolutionary and *developmental* information processing system. As in living systems within it, our universe appears engaged in both unpredictable, creative, and variation-creating evolutionary process and in predictable, conservative, and uniformity-sustaining developmental process. By understanding the intricacies of evolution and development in biology, we may understand them in other substrates, including the universe as a system.

Recalling Teilhard's (1955) evocative phrase, "cosmic embryogenesis," if we consider the Big Bang like a germinating seed, and the expanding universe like an embryo, it must use stochastic, contingent, and localized/reductionist variety creating processes—what we will shortly be calling "evolution"—in its elaboration of form and function just as we see at the molecular scale in any embryo (Figure 5). *At the same time*, all embryos transition through a special subset of statistically predictable, convergent, and global/systemic differentiation milestones, culminating in reproduction, senescence, and the unavoidable termination of somatic (body) life—what is commonly called "development." In other words, if the evo devo analogy has applicability to the universe, there must be both unpredictable new creativity and a predictable set of developmental milestones, reproduction, and ending to our universe.

Consider how genetically identical twins are always *microscopically ("evolutionarily")*

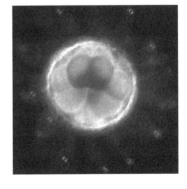

Figure 5. "Cosmic embryogenesis": universe as an evo devo system. (Credit: Ascidian Embryo, SF Exploratorium)

unique (organogenesis, fingerprints [Jain et al., 2002], neural connectivity, etc.) yet also *macroscopically ("developmentally") similar* across a range of convergent emergent aspects (metrics of physical appearance, key psychological attributes, maturation rates, lifespan, etc.). The central mystery of evo-devo biology—and of evo devo universes—is how locally unpredictable selectionist processes nevertheless generate globally predictable, convergent developmental outcomes, in a manner robust to environmental variation (Figure 6).

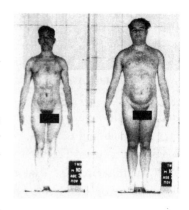

Figure 6. Monozygotic "identical" twins are always highly unique in their "evolutionary" microarchitecture, and occasionally partly so in their convergent developmental macrostructure, as with these twins, one malnourished at birth (Watters 2006). (Credit: J. M. Tanner, Inst. of Child Health, University of London)

• Definition of Evolutionary Processes. Evolutionary processes in biology, and perhaps also in physical, chemical, cultural, technological, and universal systems, are stochastic, creative, divergent (variation creating), nonlinear, and unpredictable. This intrinsic systemic unpredictability, irrespective of context or environment, may be our most useful quantitative definition and discriminator of evolutionary processes at all systems levels. The dynamics of evolutionary change are *random within constraints*, as with genetic drift in neutral theory (Kimura 1983; Leigh 2007). Its fundamental dynamic is *variation and experimentation*.

Biological evolution has been aptly called "tinkering" (Jacob 1977). It *has no foreknowledge* of which strategy will be most successful, so it tries all at hand. It is based on a discrete, quantized set of constraining parameters (such as genes and cellular factors), yet it is continually *shuffling and modifying those parameters in unpredictable ways*. In the universe at large, any process with unpredictability, contingency, generative creativity, and divergence seems at least a candidate for being evolutionary.

• Definition of Developmental Processes. Developmental processes in biology—and we assume also in physical, chemical, cultural, technological, and universal systems—are directional, constraining, convergent, with many previously independent processes *integrating* to form a special subset of outcomes, self-assembling/self-organizing, and statistically predictable *if* you have the right empirical or theoretical aids. This systemic predictability may turn out to be our most useful quantitative definition and discriminator of developmental processes at all systems levels. For example, we can collect empirical evidence of the number and order of stages in the life cycle of any apparently developing system (cell, organism, ecology, solar system, technology platform, etc.) and use this to predict what stage must come next. We are also beginning to access development theoretically, in our models of physical, chemical, and biological development (e.g., see Newman and Bhat 2008 for great work on how genes discovered universal "dynamical patterning modules" in the evolutionary development of *multicellularity*). But high-level predictive quantitative models in developmental biology are today mostly beyond our simulation capacity.

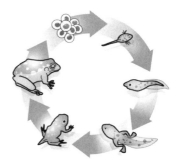

Figure 7. A developmental life cycle (Credit: Acceleration Studies Foundation. Artist: Marlon Rojas, *Fizbit.com*)

Development in biology can also be thought of as cyclical process, a movement from seed, to adapting organism in the environment, to a new seed. For example, the higher (sexual) developmental life cycle includes at least the following irreversible and directional stages:

1. birth (fertilization, cleavage, gastrulation, organ formation)
2. growth
3. maturation
4. courtship/mate selection (when successful)
5. reproduction (when successful)
6. senescence
7. death (recycling)

How many of these stages can we identify in other replicating complex adaptive systems? How many can we find in our universe itself, which by most present accounts appears to be a finite, bounded, and life-limited system? This remains to be seen. In the universe at large, any process with predictability, macrodirectionality, and convergence, or any process with a predictable beginning, ending, and rebeginning (either demonstrated or expected) seems at least a candidate for being developmental.

• Evolutionary and Developmental Interactions and Functions: A Basic Triadic Model. Integrating these processes, evolution comprises the variety of unpredictable and creative pathways by which statistically predictable developmental forms, stages, and destinations (ends, telos) are constructed. Evolution creates novel developmental architecture, but does so *very slowly*, over many successive developmental cycles. Evolution is also *constrained* to act in ways that do not disrupt critical developmental processes

215

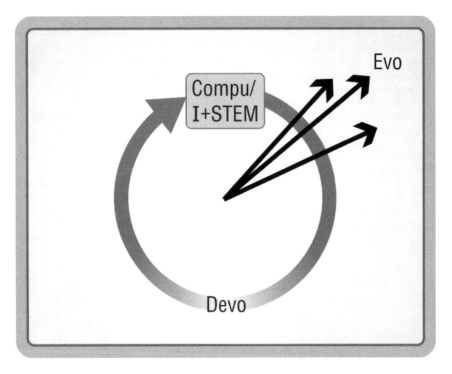

Figure 8. A cartoon of the evo compu devo triad. (Credit: Acceleration Studies Foundation. Artist: Marlon Rojas, *Fizbit.com*)

or terminate the life cycle in each generation. Thus in one sense (variation of form) evolution is the most fundamental, and in another (continuity of form) development is the most fundamental of these two processes. The *two operating together* create information, natural selection, adaptation, plasticity, and universal intelligence.

Our basic evo compu devo (ECD) triad model is a universe of *information processing* (intelligent patterns of physical STEM as adapted structure) *as the central feature*, with the twin processes of *evolution* and *development* as *complementary modes of information processing* in all complex adaptive systems, including the universe as a system (Figure 8). In this model, the primary function of evolution is *basic or neutral information/ intelligence creation and variation, what may be called preadaptive radiation, parameterization, and experimentation, not selection.* By contrast, the primary function of development is *information/intelligence preservation (system sustainability),* which it does *via hierarchical emergence and intelligence transmission* to the progeny. Their interaction, evo devo, is a complex system's way of learning and engaging in natural selection, or "*meaningful" information/intelligence accumulation,* thereby adapting to and shaping its

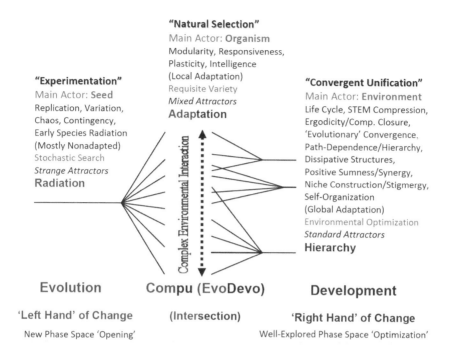

"Natural Selection"
Main Actor: **Organism**
Modularity, Responsiveness,
Plasticity, Intelligence
(Local Adaptation)
Requisite Variety
Mixed Attractors
Adaptation

"Experimentation"
Main Actor: **Seed**
Replication, Variation,
Chaos, Contingency,
Early Species Radiation
(Mostly Nonadapted)
Stochastic Search
Strange Attractors
Radiation

"Convergent Unification"
Main Actor: **Environment**
Life Cycle, STEM Compression,
Ergodicity/Comp. Closure,
'Evolutionary' Convergence,
Path-Dependence/Hierarchy,
Dissipative Structures,
Positive Sumness/Synergy,
Niche Construction/Stigmergy,
Self-Organization
(Global Adaptation)
Environmental Optimization
Standard Attractors
Hierarchy

Complex Environmental Interaction

Evolution   **Compu (EvoDevo)**   **Development**

'Left Hand' of Change   (Intersection)   'Right Hand' of Change

New Phase Space 'Opening'   Well-Explored Phase Space 'Optimization'

Figure 9. A more detailed cartoon of evo compu devo triad dynamics. (Credit: Acceleration Studies Foundation. Artist: Marlon Rojas, *Fizbit.com*)

environment to the greatest extent allowable by that system's internal structure and external environment. Figure 9 is a more detailed cartoon of this ECD dynamic, explored in the longer version of this paper. For our purposes here, note that the triadic ECD model proposes that *evolution, development*, and their *intersection* (evo devo, natural selection, adaptation, computation) are each useful, semi-independent (partially decomposable) analytical perspectives on the dynamics of complex systems.

Note that the ECD model differs subtly from standard evolutionary terminology. In the traditional neo-Darwinian view, evolution is *described* as a quintessentially *adaptive* process, and is *equated* with natural selection on phenotypes in a competitive environment (Gould 2002). In contrast, the evo compu devo model proposes that *divergent variation* (change-creating experimentation) is the essential evolutionary process. We reclassify natural selection (adaptation) as an *evo devo process*, a result of the *interaction* of evolution and development, and *not fully describable* by either process alone. See Reid 2007 for an independent account of this (we believe) fundamentally important conceptual distinction.

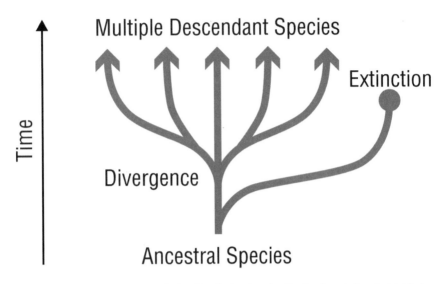

Figure 10. Adaptive radiation in evolution. (Credit: Acceleration Studies Foundation. Artist: Marlon Rojas, *Fizbit.com*)

In summary, the ECD triad model proposes that what biologists typically call "evolution" can be usefully analyzed as *three distinct simultaneous processes*: evolution, natural selection/adaptation/evo devo, and development. Unfortunately, most biologists today, except a few astrobiologists, evo-devo biologists, and theoretical biologists (e.g., Morris 2004), are only willing to consider the *first two* of these three fundamental processes. Even worse, most do not make useful distinctions between even the first two processes (again see Reid 2007 for an excellent exception). The third process (development, hierarchy, orthogenesis) has always been unwelcome in evolutionary theory, perhaps as one should expect it to be. Even the name evolution telegraphs a concern only with accidental, contingent, and selectionist processes in complex systems. Meanwhile, accelerating change, information production, dissipative intelligence hierarchies, and other apparently developmental processes continue apace, waiting patiently for our wits to grow sharp enough to recognize them.

Fortunately, there are interesting early connections emerging between natural selection and information theory. The evo devo process of natural selection, as it "learns" which of many varieties are most fit for a niche, can be said to *create information* in at least the Shannon (1948) definition (reduction of uncertainty) (Devezas and Modelski 2003; Baum 2006; Heylighen 2007a). At the level of the ecosystem, it has also been observed that biological natural selection leads reliably to *increased variety or diversity* of extant forms over time (Gould 1977, 2007; Figure 10). Others (Smith and Szathmary

1995; Kelly 2005) have proposed such additional "evolutionary" (read: evolution plus natural selection) trajectories as increasing ubiquity, increasing specialization, increasing socialization, and increasing complexity of the whole ecosystem, but not necessarily of individuals or even the average organism. Innovative biological theorists (Margulis 1999; Corning 2003) are also building the case that *both competition and cooperation* must be fundamental agents of experimentation, adaptation, and hierarchy creation. As with evolutionary theory, reductionist models of competition have been much easier to describe and defend than systemic-holistic-network models of cooperation and selection for symbiosis and synergy. Fortunately in a world of growing technological connectivity and simulation capacity, this bias is beginning to change.

As we seek evidence for or against the triadic ECD model we would best begin by investigating a number of physical systems in which the *interplay* of experimental, unpredictable (evolutionary) processes and conservative, predictable (developmental) processes appears to have guided the emergence of *adapted* (informational-computational) complexity. At the level of the cosmos, or fundamental physics, good candidates for creative evolutionary process are nonlinear dynamics, chaos, reversible thermodynamics, and quantum mechanics. Examples of apparently developmental physical process are irreversible thermodynamics, classical mechanics, and (real world) relativity. Further examples can be found in the relationship between quantum and classical physics (e.g., Blume-Kohout and Zurek 2005 and "Quantum Darwinism") in stellar nucleosynthesis, in biogenesis (Smith and Morowitz 2006), in multicellularity (Newman and Bhat 2008), in brain development (Edelman 1989 and "Neural Darwinism"), in cognitive selection, in evolutionary psychology, in cultural or "memetic" selection, in evolutionary computation and "artificial life," in technological change—and as we shall explore soon—even in the universe itself, considered as a complex system (Smolin 1992 and "Cosmological Natural Selection"). *In each of these cases* we can identify locally creative and stochastic evolutionary systems that interact to produce *both* selectionist, contingent adaptation *and* predictable developmental hierarchy and trajectory.

Another core concept in evo-devo biology, and in any theory of an evo devo universe, is *modularity*, the study of how discrete adaptive biological modules (gene networks, tissues, organs, organ systems, individuals, etc.) emerge and interact in organic systems. In biology, and perhaps also in other complex systems, modules are defined by evo-devo theorists as adaptive systems which exist at the *interface* of evolution and development. They strike a "critical balance" between variability and stability (Gershenson 2008), dispersion and integration (Heylighen 1999), and other evo vs. devo attributes, and may be self-organized for criticality in several ways (Bak et al. 1987; Adami 1995). See Schlosser and Wagner 2004 for more on biological modularity, and Callebaut and Rasskin-Gutman 2005 more on CAS modularity.

• The Evolutionary Development of Self-Similar Hierarchical Substrates: A Generic Quintet Hierarchy. One of the great lessons of systems research to date is that our universe has great isotropy, self-similarity, and even some scale invariance across all its CAS (von Bertalanffy 1968; Oldershaw 1981, 1989; Nottale et al. 2000). Replicating evolutionary, developmental, and informational-computational processes are pervasive across 30 orders of mass-size magnitude in biology, and may have produced all nonbiological universal complexity as well (Miller 1978; Jantsch 1980; Poundstone 1985; Wolfram 2002). Furthermore, the more evidence we find for evolution, development, and iterative information processing at all *intra*universal systems scales, the more parsimonious it becomes to assume our universe itself has *self-organized its own complexity* (laws, constants, boundary conditions, and emergent evolutionary and developmental structures*) in a manner self-similar to its subsystems.* In other words, a straightforward application of modularity, self-similarity, and quasi-organic analogies to our evo devo universe would argue that its impressive internal complexity would be most likely to have emerged via *a long chain of historical cycling of prior universes in some extrauniversal environment,* some "multiverse" or "metaverse" (Smolin 1997). We will shortly explore this idea and some of its potential cultural and technological implications.

In the modern science story our universe has progressed through a small number of semi-discrete intrauniversal information processing platforms, or STEM+IC "substrates" for computation and adaptation. These major substrates may be placed on a developmental specification hierarchy, as each may emerge from the former at some predictable point in time in universes of our type, each represents a major advance over its progenitor in computational complexity (modeling intelligence), and each relates to the other in a mostly *noncompetitive,* nonevolutionary fashion. Each substrate has also generated (or with astrotechnology, is proposed to soon generate) many semi-independent complex adaptive systems within it. Potential examples of such CAS are listed in parentheses below.

1. AstroPhysics (Universe-as-CAS, constants and laws, matter-energy, space time)
2. AstroChemistry (galaxies, stars, planets, molecules in inorganic and organic chemistry)
3. AstroBiology (cells, organisms, populations, species, ecologies)
4. AstroSociology (culture, economics, law, science, engineering, etc.)

Figure 11. Infrared image of Andromeda Galaxy (M31), 2005. (Credit: Karl Gordon [U. Arizona], JPL-Caltech, NASA, 2005)

5. AstroTechnology (cities, engines, biology-inspired computing, postbiological "life")

A number of insightful systems scholars (Turchin 1977; Miller 1978; Heylighen 1999, 2007b-c) have noted evolutionary processes at all five of these substrate levels. If the EDU hypothesis is correct we must also discover basic developmental processes in these substrates, processes which predictably generate hierarchy and trajectory *independent* of local, chaotic evolutionary variation (see Jantsch 1980; Salthe 1985, 1993; Morris 1998, 2004, 2008 for a range of promising work of this type).

As future astrobiological and information theory research must consider, the above five substrates may represent a generic quintet hierarchy of platforms for cosmic computation, a developmental series that is statistically inevitable in all universes of our type. From *stars onward* in the above list, the replicative, self-organized emergence, and thus potentially evo devo nature of each complex system is apparent from current science (e.g., stars engage in a stelliferous replication cycle, molecules engage in templated replication with variation, and social structure and technology are replicated and varied by human culture). From *galaxies* (Figure 11) *backward* in the above list (the Universe-as-CAS, physical laws, matter-energy, space time, and galaxies) we cannot yet see these as evo devo CAS *unless* we propose a replication and variation cycle for such systems which expresses *outside of our universe*, in the multiverse, as we will do shortly.

For the last three of these five major substrates, consider how *intelligence plays increasingly important evolutionary and developmental roles* in the shaping of system dynamics. One type of intelligence effect can be seen in the variety of increasingly sophisticated (simulation-guided) evolutionary experiments (unique thoughts, behaviors, products) conducted by each individual agent in a (biological, social, technological) population. Another is stigmergy (Abraham et al. 2006; Heylighen 2007a), where *individual evolutionary agents* add signs of their intelligent interactions/learning to the environment, permanently

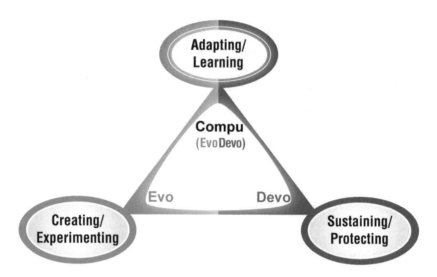

Figure 12. Evo, compu, and devo (creating, adapting, and sustaining) processes seem fundamental to all complex adaptive systems. Consequently, the telos (intrinsic goals/ends/values/drives) of these three processes may be increasingly constraining on CAS as a function of their complexity. (Credit: Acceleration Studies Foundation. Artist: Marlon Rojas, *Fizbit.com*)

altering its selection dynamics in ways that seem *increasingly developmental with time*. A closely related topic is niche construction (Laland et al. 2000; Odling-Smee 2003), which also describes the *increasingly developmental (non-random, predictable, constrained) nature of evolution* in environments that collect signs and structures of artifactual-semiotic intelligence (from foraging trails, to termite mounds, to social rules, to city structure). Stigmergic models explain the "civilizing effect" (Elias 1978) of culture and technology development on individual (evolutionary) behavior, including such understudied long-term trends as the ever-decreasing frequency and severity of human-to-human violence relative to past average behavior (Pinker 2007). As culture and tech develop, humans as evolutionary systems are *increasingly predictably constrained* into special types of ethical social interactions (e.g., laws, codes, positive sum games) irrespective of contingent social history or geography (Johnson 1998; Wright 2000; Gintis 2005). In summary, if we can demonstrate the ECD framework (in some variant) to be useful *across the hierarchy* in coming decades, it can in turn help us predict several aspects of the far future of universal intelligence.

How so? Note that per Figures 9 and 12, we can analyze complex adaptive systems as: 1) computational/ adaptive systems (keeping their evo and devo processes implicit), 2) evo devo systems (making their info processing implicit), or 3) evo, compu, and devo systems (keeping all three perspectives explicit).

Using the latter ECD framework, we can propose that the *three most basic telos* (goals, ends, values, drives) of complex adaptive systems are *creating* (evo), *adapting* (compu), and *sustaining* (devo) system complexity. We may therefore discover that these three telos act as *increasingly powerful constraints on the emergent morality of biological, societal, and technological/postbiological systems.*

In other words, if evo, compu, and devo values increasingly constrain CAS dynamics as intelligence emerges (and eventually discovers itself to be an evo compu devo system), then advanced intelligent life may be expected to be even more *innovation, adaptation, and sustainability oriented* than human culture is today. Elias (1978), Wright (2000), and others would argue the history of human culture has shown such macrodirectionality to date. Anthropology and sociology have documented all three telos in history, with different weightings in different cultures. From the social and cognitive science perspective, these three processes can also be understood as *unverified belief and spirituality* (evo), *verified knowledge and science* (devo), and the *adaptive/ provisional practical knowledge and philosophy* (compu) that bridges them. We will refer to the ECD triad several more times in this paper, to guide our speculations on the future of culture and technology.

• Evo Devo in Creation and Control: The 95/5 Percent Rule of Thumb. This subhypothesis proposes that an average of 95 percent bottom-up/evo and 5 percent top-down/devo creation and control processes operate in complex adaptive systems. In other words, the vast majority (we tentatively propose an average of 95 percent) of the information and computation we use to describe and model both *creation* of a new CAS (or hierarchy) and *control* in a mature CAS (or hierarchy) must involve *bottom-up, local, and evolutionary* processes, with only a very minor, yet critical contribution (again, let us propose an average of 5 percent) coming from *top-down, systemic, developmental* processes. For example, only a small percentage of organismic DNA is expressed in the "developmental toolkit" of any species (e.g., perhaps 2-3 percent of the *Dictyostelium* genome of 13,000 genes, Iranfar et al., 2003). Such developmental genes are also *highly conserved* over macrobiological time. Compare this to the "evolutionary" 97–98 percent of each species genome that recombines and varies far more frequently. For another example, only a very small fraction of cells in a developing metazoan organ (e.g., radial glial cells in the cerebellum) have spatiotemporal destinations that are locationally prespecified (and predictable) in advance, as verified in cell tagging experiments. The *vast majority* (perhaps 95 percent or more) of cells in organogenesis have stochastic destinations (random, contingent "evolutionary" destinations within the scaffolding of the "developmental" cells).

The reasons for the operation of this rule are presently unclear to this author. Perhaps development as a process is far more economical than evolution in its use and generation of information. Perhaps also when (evolutionary) human actors model evo devo systems with our reductionist science, we are biased to see, describe, and quantify far more of the evolutionary than the developmental processes. Whatever the reason(s), in the online version of this paper we cite roughly quantitated examples of this 95/5 percent rule with respect to physical phase transitions,

Figure 13. Iceberg as metaphor for 95 percent bottom-up/evo and 5 percent top-down/devo creation and control in evo devo complex adaptive systems. (Credit: Acceleration Studies Foundation. Artist: Marlon Rojas, *Fizbit.com*)

in DNA libraries and expression, in neural wiring, in ecology, and in power laws in culture and technology dynamics.

If true, the 95/5 percent rule may help explain why the *discovery* of universal developmental processes (predictable patterns of long-range change) has been so difficult not in physics and chemistry, where we have made great strides (e.g., mechanics, relativity, particle physics) but in higher substrates of complexity (biology, society, and technology). These substrates are both more complex and closer to our point of observation. It is particularly here that rare ("5 percent") predictable developmental "signal" would be easily overwhelmed by plentiful ("95 percent") near-random evolutionary "noise." If the 95/5 percent rule is as generic as we suspect, it will increasingly be confirmed in future CAS and modularity research in biological and universal systems.

• Evo Devo, Life Cycle, and Intelligence: Seed, Organism, and Environment (SOE) Intelligence Partitioning. The Disposable Soma theory of aging (Kirkwood 1977, 1999, 2005) highlights the very different choices in energy and information flow that all organisms make with respect to their germline (seed/sperm/egg) versus their somatic (organism/body) tissues. Our "immortal" germline cells are highly repaired/sustained, but engage in little creative/evolutionary activity, except during a *brief period* of reproduction. Cells of the organism (soma) make the exact opposite choice, putting most of their energy and information flow into creative/ evolutionary activities, and as a result being mortal and "disposable" (Figure 14). All complex adaptive systems, both living and nonliving, seem to make this tradeoff through their life cycle, having an "immortal" (read: very slowly changing) set of developmental structures (seed, template) and a "mortal" (rapidly changing but finite) evolutionary body. At the same time, from an information theory perspective, *both* seed and organism extensively use historical regularities in the *environment* to create their evolutionary and sustain their developmental intelligence. In other words, intelligence in complex adaptive systems always partitions into three places over its life cycle: the seed (evo), the organism (compu), and the environment (devo). All three places/spaces contain system complexity.

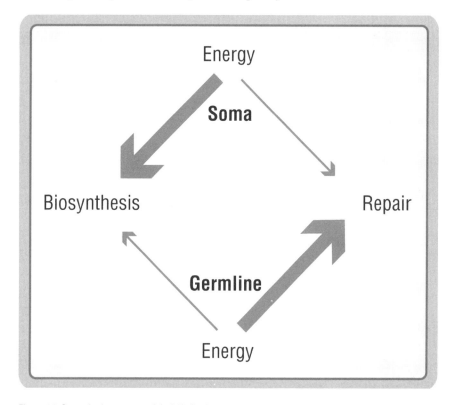

Figure 14. Somatic tissues spend their limited energy budget on biosynthesis, leaving little for repair. Germline tissues make the opposite choice (Kirkwood 1977; Tavernarakis 2007). (Credit: Acceleration Studies Foundation. Artist: Marlon Rojas, *Fizbit.com*)

The strategy of SOE intelligence partitioning can be demonstrated in all five substrates in the quintet hierarchy, and thus may somehow maximize adaptive intelligence. The *mortal organism* phase apparently allows high energy, high competition and cooperation in a naturally selective *environment*, with learning from adaptation flowing to the *immortal seed/germline*. If there is a generic optimization function at work here, it seems reasonable to expect that the postbiological intelligences of tomorrow must *also* gravitate to an SOE partitioned structure, and like us, have *mortal, disposable, constantly changing bodies.*

Furthermore, if our universe is an evo compu devo system, it must also be energetically and informationally partitioned between a germline (seed) of *parameters and special initial conditions* which replicate it, a *finite universal body* (soma) that is initially adaptive then grows increasingly senescent with time, and a *surrounding environment* (the multiverse). An evo devo universe will have *self-organized* much of its present complexity through many prior reproductive cycles in the multiverse. Astrophysicists know our universe has finite matter, energy and time of origin, ever-increasing entropy, and may now be decomposing under accelerating "dark energy" dynamics (Krauss and Scherrer 2008). If it is developmental it must also have some *mechanism of replication.* The leading hypothesis in this area will now be explored.

•   Cosmological Natural Selection (CNS): A Promising Yet Partial Evo Devo Universe Hypothesis. This hypothesis was first proposed, without the CNS name, by philosopher Quentin Smith (1990, 2000) and independently proposed and simulation tested, as CNS, by theoretical physicist Lee Smolin (1992, 1994, 1997, 2006). While speculative, it is perhaps the first viable astrophysical evo devo universe model to date. CNS was born as an attempt to explain the "fine tuning" or "improbable universe" problem. In modern physics and cosmology, there are a number of "fundamental" (empirically/experimentally discovered and apparently not determinable by physical or mathematical theory) *universal parameters.* As far as we can test them with current cosmological models, many of these parameters appear *improbably fine tuned* for the production of physical and chemical conditions necessary for life and complexity (Leslie 1989; Rees 1999; Barrow 2002, 2007).

These include 19 (at present) free parameters in the standard model of particle physics (9 particle masses, 4 matrix parameters for quarks, 4 for neutrinos, and 2 other constants, fine structure and strong coupling) and roughly 15 other constants, ratios, and relations used in our astrophysical models (cosmological constant, gravitational constant, speed of light, reduced Planck's constant, Coulomb force constant, Boltzmann constant, various conservation relations, etc.) Some of these parameters may be eliminated in the future by discovering hidden relationships between them, as occurred to a mild extent in the emergence of quantum theory in the 1930s. At the same time, many more are likely to be *added,* as there are higher-energy levels of unprobed structure and function in our particle physics. High-energy physics, which has delivered *most* of these new parameters, may be analogous to "gene probing" in the biological sciences. There are also numerous cosmic phenomena we still do not understand well (e.g., dark matter and dark energy, black hole physics). Instead of a future "theory of everything," a single equation describing universal relations which might fit on a t-shirt (Weinberg 1993), we can expect a "theory of special things," an economical but still ungainly set of *numerous* fundamental equations and constants that, *working together,* determine our special, complex, and biofelicitous (Davies 2004, 2007) universe.

Like the developmental genes of living organisms, an economical but still ungainly set of fundamental informational parameters which *interact with the environment* to create organismic form in complex and still poorly understood ways, developmental physical parameters may interact with the multiversal environment to dictate many basic features of our universe, such as its lifespan, hierarchical structure, hospitality to internal complexity, and ability to produce black holes. CNS proposes that the special values of our universal parameters are the result of an evolutionary selection process involving universe adaptation in the multiverse, and universe reproduction *via black holes.*

Beginning in the 1980s theorists in quantum gravity began postulating that our universe might "give birth" to new universes via fluctuations in space time over very short distances (Baum 1983; Strominger 1984; Hawking 1987, 1988 1993; Coleman 1988). Some (Hawking 1987; Frolov 1989) proposed that new universe creation might be particularly likely at the central "singularity" inside black holes. The singularity is a region where our equations of relativity fail to hold, depicting energy and space at improbably "infinite" densities. In Smolin's model, what occurs there is a "bounce" that produces a new daughter universe in another region of "hyperspace," one with fundamental parameters that are *stochastically different* from the parent universe. See Susskind 2005 (string theory); Randall 2005 (M-theory); and Smolin 2001 (loop quantum gravity) for some competing proposals that our universe's space time continuum is but a subset of a higher dimensional hyperspace. McCabe (2006) states that research in loop quantum gravity "now appears to support Smolin's hypothesis of a bounce at the center of black holes forming new universes (see also Ashtekar 2006). If true, such a mechanism would mandate an organic type of *reproduction with inheritance for universes,* which would become an extended, branching chain exploring a "phenospace" of potential somatic forms within the multiverse (Figure 15).

Smolin's theory began as an attempt to explore the fine tuning problem via an alternative landscape theory to string theory, one that might prove more readily falsifiable, given its black hole predictions. By the mid-1990s his team had been able to sensitivity test, via simple mathematical simulations, 8 of approximately 20 (by his count) fundamental universal parameters (Smolin 1992, 1994, 1997). In such tests to date, our present universe appears to be fine-tuned both for long-lived universes capable of generating complex life and for the production of hundreds of trillions of black holes, or for "fecundity" of black hole production. If our particular complex universe has self-organized and adapted on top of a broad base of *much more plentiful, much simpler universes*, just as human intelligence could emerge only on a base of vastly more plentiful simpler replicating organic forms (e.g., prokaryotic life), then *fecundity* of black hole production should be validated by theory and observation, in any internally complex evo devo universe.

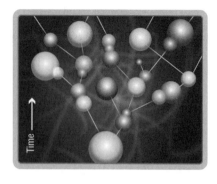

Figure 15. "Baby universes," exploring phenospace on a universal phylogenetic tree (with very low branching and much terminal branching in this cartoon). (Adapted from Linde 1994) (Credit: Acceleration Studies Foundation. Artist: Marlon Rojas, *Fizbit.com*)

Another promising aspect of CNS, also increasingly testable by simulation, is that changes in the parameter values ("genes") of our evo devo universe may provide results analogous to changes geneticists can induce in the genes of evo-devo biological organisms. In biology we can now differentiate between developmental genes (a very small fraction of the typical genome, controlling the development of the organism) and evolutionary genes (a majority of the remaining genes, more involved in regulation in a developed organism and phenotype variation in a population). Developmental genes are *highly conserved* from species to species, and any change in them is almost always either deleterious or catastrophic, particularly in more complex organisms, which have much more "downstream" complexity to protect. We can define evolutionary genes, by contrast, as those that can undergo much more change, as they have few impacts on *internal* processes of development but many impacts on the variety of unique phenotypes, which are in turn subject to *external* natural selection. Evolutionary variants will usually also turn out to be deleterious to adaptation in the environment, but that is a *different process of selection* (external/evo, not internal/devo) with typically milder and far more slowly manifesting effects, on average.

Applying this analogy we find that some fundamental parameters of physics appear *very sensitively tuned* to sustain our universe's internal complexity, with small changes being catastrophic to complexity emergence (this is known in philosophy as the "Fine Tuning Problem"). In the EDU hypothesis, such parameters seem clearly developmental. By contrast, several other parameters (fundamental or derived) produce minor phenotypic variants of the universe when their values are changed by small amounts, making them good candidates for evolutionary process, producing universes that are all developmentally viable but each subtly different, and which may allow some form of external selection on that universe in the multiverse. With respect to developmental parameters, *only very rarely* should changes in them lead to potentially more adaptive features in phenospace such as replication fecundity or internal complexity. Large random changes in such parameters should virtually never have such result (Vaas 1998). With respect to evolutionary parameters, other tests, comparable to those seen in evolutionary variation in biological systems, should be increasingly accessible to simulation.

Looking a few decades or generations ahead, a robust future evo devo simulation science should allow us to construct a *limited phylogenetic tree* (record of likely evolutionary changes in developmental systems), and of *universal systematics* (hierarchical classification of likely universe species, based on recent evolutionary ancestry) for at least the set of possible universes *nearest* to our particular universe in phenospace. We are presently learning to build such models in evo-devo biology (Figure 16), with the great advantage of

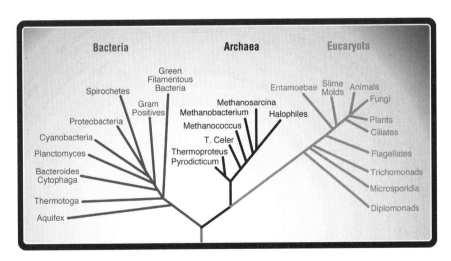

Figure 16. Phylogenetic tree in evo-devo biology. (Credit: Acceleration Studies Foundation. Artist: Marlon Rojas, *Fizbit.com*)

having not one, but many extant biological forms accessible to analysis, with all of apparently common descent.

Unfortunately phylogenetic evo devo universe models are simply not possible in current simulation science. Vaas notes that simulating small variations not only in universal parameters, as in Smolin's present scheme, but also in universal laws, and simulating how such laws emerge from their parameters via symmetry breaking, presumably in both evolutionary and developmental fashion, is presently "beyond any possibility of scientific investigation." Accelerating developments in evo-devo biology, cosmology and computation may one day deliver such possibility, however.

While Smolin's CNS is a promising and clarifying theory, one of its shortcomings is that it provides *no role for systemic intelligence influencing the replication cycle* as occurs at least in all the higher replicators here on Earth. The class of CNS models where emergent intelligence plays some functional role in replication can be called CNS-I (CNS with Intelligence). We will now consider a few CNS-I models that have been proposed to date, and suggest another, evo devo CNS-I, below and in the DS hypothesis to come.

• Evo Devo Cosmological Natural Selection with Intelligence (Evo Devo CNS-I). Strictly speaking, Smolin's CNS and other mildly related work (King 1978, 2001; Nambu 1985) can be considered partial, or gene-centric models of CNS-I, as they allow the self-organization of "genes" (unique fundamental universe-specifying parameters) that can in turn develop increasingly intelligent universes, even those with conscious observers. Where this work stops short is in considering how "postgenetic" intelligence must also grow in strength as the universe body unfolds, and would be expected to nonrandomly influence cosmological natural selection and replication, just as we see postgenetic intelligence (e.g., cultural and technological intelligence) nonrandomly influence CAS replication here on Earth. Models that address this oversight may be called full or high-level CNS-I (Crane 1994; Harrison 1995, 1998; Gardner 2000, 2003, 2005, 2007; Smart 2000, 2002, 2008; Balázs 2002; McCabe 2006; Vidal 2008), and will now be discussed.

In a brave and pioneering paper, the late cosmologist Edward Harrison (1995 and critique: Byl 1996) argued that the "ultimate aim in the evolution of intelligence [e.g., the highest purpose of universal evolution and development] is conceivably the creation of universes that nurture intelligence." As the first peer-reviewed publication on the full CNS-I hypothesis, Harrison originated several evo devo universe ideas. He argued that random variations in Smolin's CNS scheme may have generated the first "low level" universal intelligence in a manner analogous to biogenesis on Earth. He also proposed that just like life's trajectory in Earth's environment, intelligent, computation-rich universes might come to dominate universe ensembles, *if intelligence can be shown to nonrandomly aid in universe reproduction and adaptation.* As tentative evidence for the latter, he noted that speculative theoretical schemes for universe creation already exist in astrophysics (e.g., Farhi and Guth 1987).

In a series of articles and books beginning in 2000, complexity theorist James Gardner has further developed and ventured beyond Harrison's hypothesis. In *Biocosm* (2003), Gardner proposed the selfish biocosm hypothesis, which portrays the universe as a self-organizing self-improving, replication-driven system, in which "highly evolved" internal intelligence plays a key role in future universe reproduction. As the most extensive thesis on CNS-I to date, *Biocosm* is a must read for evo devo scholars. At the same time, we suggest that the EDU and DS hypotheses (Smart 2000 and this paper), as alternative CNS-I proposals, further develop and constrain Gardner's valuable insights. In particular, three important points of difference between the EDU model and Gardner's model should now be mentioned.

First, while Gardner champions Smolin's model of the black hole as a *replicator* in low-level CNS, he does not explore the many attributes that make black hole environments an ideal *attractor* for higher universal intelligence. The latter concept may be central to a mature theory of evo devo CNS-I, as it connects the developmental trajectory of all higher intrauniversal intelligence with Smolin's reproductive mechanism, and makes quantifiable near-term predictions with respect to developmental trends in Earth's intelligence, as we will do in our discussion of STEM compression shortly.

Second, Gardner does not elevate universal development to the same level of importance as universal evolution in his current analysis, which leads to a universe model that is *less constrained and predictable* than one would expect if evo and devo dynamics apply. As one example, Gardner proposes (2003) that a single cycling universe may be as likely as a branching system of universes under the selfish biocosm hypothesis. An evo devo CNS-I model, by contrast, would predict the necessity of a branching tree of self-organizing complexity underlying our universe, and *an abundance of very simple protouniverses coexisting in the multiverse with a comparatively tiny number of complex universes* such as ours, just as abundance of existing replicating bacteria are an evo devo prerequisite to the existence of a comparatively tiny number of replicating humans on Earth. In other words, in an evo devo CNS-I universe, detectable black holes should form an *ecology*, with a distribution of reproductive complexity that has some homology to Earth's ecologies. Our universe must also be tuned to *fecundity* but never a "maximum" of black hole production (Gardner proposes the latter), since the application of energy and information to reproductive vs. somatic activities *always* has a cost-benefit tradeoff in evo-devo biology (Kirkwood 1977; Miller 1978).

Third, and most curiously, Gardner proposes some form of prior intelligent life is likely to have "created," "designed," or "architected" our universe, and that humanity's postbiological descendants may one day become "cosmic engineers" of the next universe(s). Others have made this tellingly anthropomorphic claim as well (Farhi and Guth 1987; Frolov 1989; Harrison 1995). But in any theory of evo devo CNS-I, we should expect such creative influence to be *greatly limited by the inherited constraints of the existing universal developmental cycle*. Reflect on your knowledge of biological systems, and consider how very little "control" (innovation, change) evolutionary intelligence ever has over developmental processes *within any single replication cycle*. It is true humans have significant rational control over technological system design at present, *but technology is not yet its own autonomous substrate.* In every autonomous evo devo CAS inside our universe, from molecules to man, we always see only minor, marginal evolutionary influence on and improvement of the system in each developmental cycle, regardless of complexity of the substrate. This is likely because evolutionary intelligences can never have full knowledge of the implications of any experimental changes they make to evo devo systems in advance, and too much change in developmental architecture always disrupts system survival. As a result, and as evo-devo biology broadly demonstrates, evolution invariably *changes the nature* of developmental systems *very little* in each cycle.

This latter point addresses the critical question of whether end-of-universe intelligences in an evo devo universe could ever become *"gods"* or *"god-like beings,"* omniscient or omnipotent entities able to engage in true creation, design, or engineering of universes, or whether they would merely be *distant natural ancestors* with evo compu devo constraints, mortality, and motivations surprisingly similar to us.

As the ICU hypothesis proposes, such natural intelligences could never be omniscient or omnipotent, but would instead always be *computationally incomplete* (Gödel 1934). Consider the evolution-like phenomenon of free will, our own ability to choose but never fully predict the consequences of our choice, even in what may be an almost entirely deterministic universe at scales relevant to human life. Free will must perennially exist in all CAS, such as they have intelligence, because evo devo intelligence is always built, in large part, out of *stochastic evolutionary systems* of which that intelligence can have only *limited* self-understanding, predictive capacity, and control. So it is also likely to be with any end-of-universe intelligence, as we will discuss in the DS hypothesis to come.

Furthermore, as the EDU hypothesis proposes, physical intelligences apparently partition themselves across three systemic forms as *seed, organism, and environment* (SOE partitioning). Thus the bodies (organisms) of all physical systems, end-of-universe entities included, must always be *mortal* and developmentally fated to become *increasingly senescent* with time (Salthe 1993), just like the universe they reside in. The evo compu devo telos, in turn, would argue that all end-of-universe intelligences must have their own unproven (evolutionary) *beliefs*, adaptive (computational) *practical knowledge and philosophy*, and proven (developmental) *science*. Such intelligences would emerge, just as we did, inside a system whose fundamental structure they *can only mildly influence in any cycle* (evo), *cannot fully understand* (compu), and *did not create* (devo). They would also clearly be simpler and more limited than our own universe-influencing progeny will be. Not gods, but *ancestors*, whose intelligence we can hope to one day equal and eventually exceed, universe willing.

In the EDU framework, the classical religious conception of God, an omnipotent, omniscient, supernatural entity, becomes a hypothesis we "do not need" (Pierre Laplace in De Morgan 1872). In an evo compu devo universe all intelligent beings must have spiritual, philosophical, and scientific (evo, compu, and devo) models, and these models cyclically and incrementally improve themselves via evolutionary and developmental dynamics. But in this framework our theology becomes restricted to unproven (presently poorly evidenced but still subjectively useful) beliefs regarding natural universal process, a hypothesis known as *philosophical* or *scientific naturalism*. It is not pantheism "God is all" but naturalism "nature/universe is all." All this assumes that science has advanced to a point where a self-organizing, evo devo paradigm can well explain most of our internal universal complexity, which today it cannot. Yet to this author, the EDU hypothesis seems the most parsimonious of explanations presently available.

With respect to the expected physical features of an evo devo universe, note that the use of black holes as "genetic" intelligence transmission systems in CNS provides a powerful functional rationale for the emergence of a *relativistic universe*. Note also that quantum cosmology and the quantum mechanism of the black hole bounce each provide functional rationales for the emergence of a *quantum mechanical* universe. But what evo devo rationale might there be for the emergence of a *mathematically simple universe*, exhibiting such "unreasonably effective" and simple approximations as f =ma and

E=mc² (Wigner 1960)? Such underlying simplicities may primarily be due to the assumedly mathematically simple and symmetric physical origins of *any* cycling universe. However there might also be an internal selection mechanism or weak anthropic principle requiring or preserving such simplicities, as they allow intrauniversal intelligence development (universal pattern recognition and STEM manipulation) to be a *strongly nonzero sum game* (Wright 1997,2000). Mathematically elegant universes seem particularly robust to rapid internal intelligence development. Must all evo devo universes start this way and does the lineage grow more or less mathematically elegant with time? Inquiring minds would like to know.

Now recall that seed, organism, and environment (SOE) intelligence partitioning predicts that postbiological intelligence may not, *except through germline (seed) structure and the informational constancies of the multiverse (environment),* transfer its learned information into a new universe. In other words, it seems an inviolable constraint that continually self-aware organismic intelligence cannot enter the next universe, except in its *potential* (seed plus environment) form. If it could, we should expect evidence of ancestor intelligence far and wide throughout our present cosmos, long before our own emergence.

This begs the question of whether any form of *one-way communication* might be possible or desirable between intelligences in successive universes. As we will consider in our discussion of the Fermi Paradox to come, one-way messages are occasionally useful for developmental control, but always constrain evolutionary creativity. In an evo devo universe, it seems the only strategies beneficial to producing further universal complexity would be to attempt small evolutionary improvements in the structure of the seed, and incremental modifications to the multiversal environment. If there were a way to encode and send *any message in the body of the universe itself* (e.g., some obvious message of intelligence, such as a highly nonrandom sequence of numbers buried deep in the transcendental number *Pi*, as occurs in Sagan's novel *Contact* 1997), we may expect several unfortunate consequences. First, the discovery of such an obviously "designed" message by all descendant intelligences would *homogenize their remaining evolutionary searches for universal meaning, while giving the false impression of a designed, and not an evo devo universe,* thus reducing the computational variety of that universe and its successors. Second, the creation of such a message would constrain universal developmental structure to message delivering, not evo devo priorities, again reducing the complexity of successor universes.

Note however that the EDU hypothesis *does* seem to allow ancestor intelligence to leave one-way messages *outside our universe, in the special structure of the multiversal environment,* as a form of *niche construction.* Thus we may very well find evidence of prior cosmic intelligence only when we grow sharp enough to *leave our universe entirely,* a topic we will discuss in the DS hypothesis to come.

Processes of Universal Development

Wherever we find tentative evidence for universal development, we find constraints that may apply to all emergent cultural and technological intelligences. So far, we have considered an evo compu devo telos, hierarchical stage progression, the 95/5 rule, SOE intelligence partitioning, CNS and CNS-I as potentially constraining aspects of an evo devo universe. There are a number of other potentially predictable (with the right empirical and theoretical tools) and irreversible (on average) perspectives on universal developmental process that we may propose. Recall our long list of developmental attributes in Table 1. Let us now explore just three that seem particularly important to understanding the DS hypothesis to come: differentiation, STEM compression, and ergodicity. Others may be found in the online version of this paper.

• Universal Development as Differentiation and Terminal Differentiation (aka, Cosmogonic Philosophy). In biological development, differentiation is often the first process that comes to mind. All organic development begins from a totipotent, stem cell-like zygote, capable of taking *many* adaptive paths, then the replicating cells move through a series of irreversible, branching differentiation steps of steadily decreasing velocity, and the system ends in an array of "terminally differentiated" and functionally highly specialized tissues (Figure 17). This process involves both evolutionary dispersion (at the molecular scale) and developmental integration (at the system scale) of the differentiated tissues into their local environments. Nerve cells are

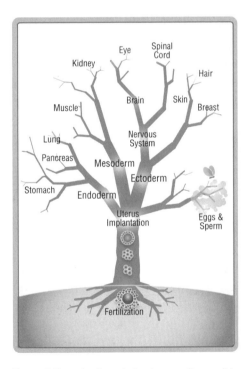

Figure 17. Tree of embryonic development (irreversible steps of developmental differentiation). (Credit: Acceleration Studies Foundation. Artist: Marlon Rojas, *Fizbit.com*)

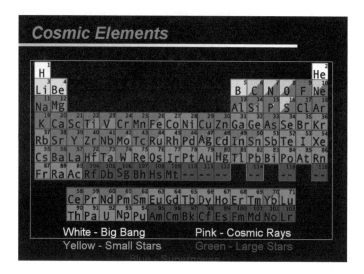

Figure 18. Creation of new elements gets increasingly terminally differentiated over time (NASA/Lochner and Kinnison 2003). (Credit: Your Cosmic Connection to the Elements, James Lochner [USRA] and Suzanne Pleau Kinnison [AESP], NASA/GSFC, 2003)

arguably the most differentiated of metazoan cell types, as they carry high-level environmental information in their synapses, and so lose, on average, even the ability to replace themselves as they age (neural stem cells do not appreciably change this picture). Differentiation as a process is a *stepwise loss of flexibility*, the steep price paid for a short phase of increasing *adaptive complexity* in the mature developed organism. *Only* in the germline cells is totipotency and immortality maintained, but even here flexibility is *frozen* in the process of seed creation, and only returns on the later sprouting of the seed.

When we think of *universal development*, from the Big Bang "seed" to the mature "body," we must expect to find the same sobering process of increasing differentiation and eventually *terminal differentiation* at every computational substrate level whether it be physics, chemistry, biology, culture, or technology. At each level the "tree of evolution" will branch continually, delivering ever-greater diversity of forms with time, but as this is *also* a "tree of differentiation" (development), the *feebleness of branching* must eventually get progressively more noticeable as well. Eventually every evo devo "tree" reaches the *maximum height* allowed for its particular substrate in morphospace or functionspace. Increasingly ergodic recombination (revisiting the same forms) still continues in the lower branches, but as a tool for evolutionary innovation (finding new phase space), the substrate is now exhausted. It has become terminally differentiated. Let us look at a few examples of this process in action.

At the astrophysical/chemical substrate level, we can see this in the production of chemical elements. The production of elements useful for new complexity construction was exhausted by cycling supernovae *many billennia ago* (Figure 18. Elements in dark grey require high energy and exotic conditions to form, are increasingly unstable, and have little utility to the further growth of chemical complexity. Note that the elements necessary for the next leap in the quintet hierarchy, an organic chemistry capable of *biogenesis* on special planets, are made mostly in the first half of elemental phase space (the periodic table) as explored by replicating stellar nucleosynthesis, long before terminal differentiation of elemental innovation occurs. This seems a rather efficient system for universal hierarchy development.

In biology on Earth, we also see terminal differentiation at *every level* of the taxa, from kingdoms to species.

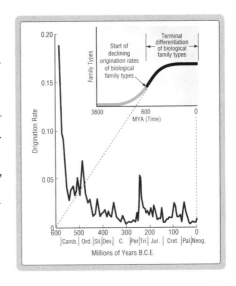

Figure 19. Rate of origination of marine animal families (new families divided by extant families) over time. High rates of origination occur initially and then after major episodes of extinction. The small spikes during the Early Late Cretaceous and Early Cenozoic are associated with the attainment of hitherto unsurpassed levels of global familial diversity. In other words, the evolutionary tree has grown larger than ever, but its marginal branching is now feebler than ever (adapted from Vermiej [1987] and Van Valen and Maiorana [1985]). (Credit: Acceleration Studies Foundation. Artist: Marlon Rojas, *Fizbit.com*)

Diversity continues to go up in the "leading edge" modules of the tree (e.g., species), but the *rate* of diversity innovation is drastically reduced at all levels, and has stopped entirely at all the older, lower levels. There have been no new *kingdoms* for billennia, and the production of *metazoan body plans* stopped entirely in the early Cambrian, 550 million years ago (Müller and Newman 2003).

Figure 19, from Vermiej (1987) shows that even marine animal *families* (a class presently easier to document than *species*) have experienced rapidly declining rates of origination since the Cambrian. We see from this figure that evolution always maintains some creative capacity in reserve, with catastrophe (major extinctions) periodically reinvigorating the system. *Nevertheless,* family innovation as an evo devo process has *progressively exhausted itself over time,* just like our periodic table, only in a more gradual manner, occurring in a more complex adaptive substrate.

We can also observe terminal differentiation in ecosystems, where any long-mature ecology becomes "senescent" (Ulanowicz 1997) brittle and less innovative (unable to host a changing set of species), and thus susceptible to death, disease, fire, succession, or other ecological renewal process.

So while absolute species numbers on Earth are today larger than ever, the branching rates at the end of the evolutionary tree (the average new species generation rates, independent of periodic extinction and origination epochs) and the percentage of novel morphologies and functional specializations introduced into the ecospace by genetic evolution is lower than ever. In other words, the tree of biological developmental differentiation on our planet has nearly reached its maximum height. Since the leading edge of computational change on Earth has been *cultural* evo devo for at least the last two million years, when *Homo habilis* picked up the first stone, increasingly terminal differentiation of biological evo devo systems is perhaps to be expected. Yet the *mechanisms* controlling the timing and location of terminal differentiation in biological morphospace and function space remain mostly obscure to modern science.

Turning next to the genetic dimension of human cultural evolution, we find that even brain-expressed genes in humans clearly follow a terminal differentiation dynamic. Such genes evolve slowly in mammals, but even more slowly in the more complex mammals, like chimps and humans. As Wang et al. (2006) Bakewell et al. (2007) and others report, *evolutionary change in human brain-expressed genes has slowed down both in absolute terms and relative to chimpanzees* since our split from them six million years ago. I have proposed (Smart 2001) that once hominid brains became vessels for external rapidly improving gestural, linguistic, tool-using, and other socially constructed semiotics, algorithms, and grammars, perhaps two million years ago with *H. erectus*, all change in brain genes was increasingly restricted to propagating this exploding new social information base, in an increasingly standardized set of synaptic networks, such as our specialized brain regions for acquiring and using language (Deacon 1997). Human brains thenceforth became functionally specialized to be *carriers and variers* of "memes," culturally transmissible symbols, ideas, behaviors, and algorithms (Dawkins 1976; Blackmore 1999; Aunger 2000) that are no longer recorded mainly in unique gene networks, but rather in unique synaptic connections. *Memetic, not genetic evolution* thus became the leading edge of local computational change. From that point forward major brain changes would be expected to increasingly create *antagonistic plieotropies* (negative effects on legacy systems) and autistic or otherwise socially dysfunctional humans. Our neural phenotype at that point became increasingly *canalized* (stable to small

random changes) around an evolutionary cul-de-sac of initially randomly discovered, meme-propagating architectures. Fortunately the rapidly moving
research in this area should validate or falsify this terminal differentiation
hypothesis in coming years.

Finally, with the advent of digital electronic computers, the leading edge
of evo devo change now seems on the verge of jumping from biological
human culture to our more ethereal and resource-efficient information technology. As computers accelerate all around us, we see global human population saturating (Wattenberg 2005), and the advent of environmental and
resource constraints of our own making (Worldwatch 2008). Some scholars
even see signs of emerging *memetic* terminal differentiation in human culture.
While the size of the tree of cultural innovation will undoubtedly continue to
grow, there may already be a sharply *declining fraction* of truly innovative vs.
derivative and repetitive *human-initiated and understood* cultural knowledge,
products, and behaviors (Stent 1969; Lasch 1991; Barzun 2001; Smart 2005;
Jacoby 2008). At the same time, *technology-initiated and embedded knowledge*
continues to accelerate, and is *increasingly inaccessible to the average biological mind.* Yet the astrotechnological substrate is only at the beginning of its
own "S-curve" of evo devo, having not yet even achieved autonomy from its
biological creators.

Generalizing from a similar set of observations, the great American philosopher Charles S. Pierce (1935) proposed a "cosmogonic philosophy" in
which the long-term evolutionary development of life and intelligence in our
universe must cause it to gradually lose its spontaneous character (reach the
top of its S-curve) in *any* substrate. In Pierce's model, life everywhere seeks to
totally order (as far as it can) and reduce the flexibility of an initially fecund
universal chaos. In EDU terms, the *more evolution* any computational system
has engaged in, on average, the more ways it may become constrained to
follow whatever *final developmental trajectory* exists for that particular system.
Salthe (1981, 1985, 1993) also holds this perspective in his discussion of predictable, progressive and irreversible "universal senescence."

Certainly accelerating development of higher, more intelligent levels of
the universal hierarchy must periodically open up new evolutionary innovation options, yet *acceleration cannot continue forever* in a universe of finite
physical resources and dimensions. As physical substrates, both a coming
technological singularity and a developmental singularity (to be discussed)
would presumably, after *ever-briefer periods* of fantastic new innovation,
each be subject to terminal differentiation and increasing computational
and behavioral constraints, the closer they approach *either* the senescent

structures of a mature universe (body), or the time-frozen germline structures of a mature seed, waiting for its reproduction.

•   Universal Development as STEM Compression of Computation in Dissipative Structures. One of the most curious and apparently developmental processes in our universe is that it seems to be hierarchically constructing special zones of local intelligence (complexity, modeling capacity, meaningful information) which are measurably and predictably more space, time, energy, and matter dense, or *STEM dense* (meaning increasingly *localized* in space, *accelerated* in time, and *dense* in energy and matter flows), and *STEM efficient* (in space, time, energy, and matter resources used per standardized computation or physical transformation), relative to parent structures. Taken together, we may call the twin STEM density and STEM efficiency trends, STEM compression of computation and/or physical transformation in universal development (Smart 1999, 2000, 2002b, and referred to as "MEST compression" in my older literature). To better understand this phenomenon, let us briefly survey both STEM compression trends (density and efficiency) from the partially separable perspectives of space, time, energy, and matter.

Space Compression. Perhaps the most obvious universal developmental trend of these four is space compression or *locality*, the increasingly local (smaller, restricted) spatial zones within which the leading edge of computational change has historically emerged in the hierarchical development of universal complexity. Consider how the leading edge of structural complexity in our universe has apparently transitioned from universally distributed early matter, to galaxies, to replicating stars within galaxies, to solar systems in galactic habitable zones, to life on special planets in those zones, to higher life within the surface biomass, to cities, and soon, to intelligent technology. Each transition to date has involved a *sharply increasing spatial locality* of the system environment (Smart 2000). Even gravity, which has helped organize all of the transitions just listed, is actually not a force in real terms, but as relativity tells us, a process of *space compression* around massive objects. Thus gravity itself seems to be a basic driver (an integral aspect) of universal computational development, as we discuss in the DS hypothesis to come.

At the planetary-cultural level, scholars have noted a type of space compression due to near-instantaneous global digital networks, sensors, effectors, memory, and computation (Broderick 1997; Kurzweil 1999), suggesting an end of geography (O'Brien 1992) or death of distance (Cairncross 1998). Space compression is a real developmental trend, and it impacts future choices for human cultural evolution in ways we are just beginning to appreciate.

Figure 20. Plants, modern human society, and tomorrow's AIs appear to have roughly equivalent scalar "distance" between their intrinsic learning rates (Credit: Acceleration Studies Foundation. Artist: Marlon Rojas, *Fizbit.com*)

Time Compression. We see time compression in the increasingly rapid hierarchical emergence of complexity that has occurred over roughly the last six billion years of the universe's lifespan. Carl Sagan first popularized this acceleration in the metaphor of the Cosmic Calendar (1977). Kurzweil (2005) has compiled 15 separate accounts of emergence frequency for "key events" in Earth and human history, in an attempt to demonstrate that though the event selection process in each case must be subjective, the *acceleration pattern* seen by these at least partially independent observers is apparently not.

How time compressed is the postbiological intelligence substrate likely to be, relative to human culture? Consider the *10 millionfold* difference between the speed of biological thought (roughly 150 km/hr chemical diffusion in and between neurons) and the speed of electronic "thought" (speed-of-light electron flow). The scalar distance between *Phi*-measured learning rates (a topic we will explain shortly) of modern technological society (perhaps 10^7 ergs/s/g) and tomorrow's autonomous computers (perhaps 10^{12} ergs/s/g) is roughly the same as the difference between modern society and *plants* (Figures 20 and 21).

In other words, to self-aware postbiological systems, the dynamics of human thought and culture may be so slow and static by comparison that we will appear *as immobilized in space and time as the plant world appears to the human psyche.* All of our learning, yearning, thinking, feeling, all our desires to merge with our electronic extensions, or to pull their plugs, must move forever *at plantlike pace* relative to postbiological intelligences.

Furthermore, such intelligences are far less computationally restricted, with their near-perfect memories, ability to create variants of themselves,

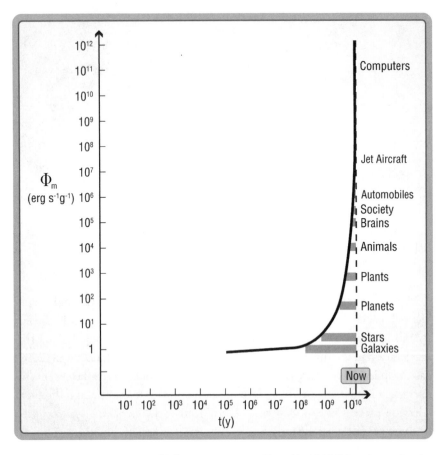

Figure 21. Free energy rate density (*Phi*) values in emergent hierarchical CAS. When the accelerating curve of dissipation rate begins in an expanding early universe is not yet clear. We draw *Phi* beginning at matter condensation (10^5 yrs) to the present. (Adapted from Chaisson 2001). (Credit: Acceleration Studies Foundation. Artist: Marlon Rojas, *Fizbit.com*)

reintegrate at will and think, learn, experiment in virtual space, and share in physical space at the universal speed limit—the speed of light. To be sure, as evo devo systems they must also be bound by developmental cycling and death, but for such systems death comes as archiving or erasure of poorly adapted intelligence architectures and redundant or harmful information, or the death-by-transformation seen in any continually growing system. We can expect that such processes will be far less informationally destructive and subjectively violent than the death we face as biological organisms.

We may be dismayed by such comparisons, yet such leaps in the critical rates of change for new substrates are apparently *built into the developmental physics of our universe.* More than anything else, these leaps define the one-way, accelerating, and developmental nature of the universe's leading evolutionary computational processes over the long term. Discovering such preexistent paths for computational acceleration and efficiency seems the developmental destiny of universal intelligence, though the creative evolutionary paths taken to such destiny are never predictable, and each path adds its own unique value.

Energy Compression. In fascinating and clarifying work, astrophysicist Eric Chaisson (2001) has shown that all complex adaptive systems that use energy flows, so-called dissipative structures, can be placed on an apparently *developmental* universal emergence hierarchy, from galaxies to human societies and beyond, with earlier-emerging systems having far less free energy flow (*Phi*) than recently emerging systems. Free energy is energy available to build structural, adaptive complexity (von Bertalanffy 1932; Schrödinger 1944). *Phi* can be considered a measure not of structural complexity but of *dynamic complexity* (Chaisson 2003), or *marginal learning capacity* of the dissipative structure. It also seems closely related to marginal entropy production (Kleidon and Lorenz 2005).

Note the newest systems, our electronic computers, have roughly *seven orders of magnitude (10 millionfold) greater free energy rate density* than human culture. To me, such a curve is early evidence that postbiological systems represent the next step in a *universal developmental learning hierarchy* for dissipative complex adaptive systems (Figure 21). Below are Chaisson's estimates for *Phi* (free energy rate density, in units of ergs/sec/g) for a set of semi-discrete complex adaptive systems:

It seems unbelievable that our Sun has two orders of magnitude less *Phi* than a houseplant. But remember *Phi* measures not total energy output, but *energy rate density.* Far more energy flows through the same mass or volume of a houseplant, per time, than our Sun, which is *a far simpler object* in terms of both *complexity increase per time,* and *complexity per volume. Phi* seems directly related to the former and indirectly to the latter metric. A system's *level of complexity* is, in Chaisson's view, its *ability to channel matter and energy, per mass or volume, per time,* for info/learning/adaptation (alternatively, evo and devo) activities.

While Chaisson's curve is impressive, what I find nearly as amazing is how studiously we ignore curves of this type—in a general class our organization calls *acceleration studies.* Insightful works on accelerating change, such as Gerard Piel's *The Acceleration of History* (1972), or Richard Coren's *The Evolutionary Trajectory* (1998) are rare, and remain of marginal interest to modern science. When will we wake up?

Note that Chaisson includes both *autonomous and nonautonomous* CAS in this list. Planets are dependent on stellar supernovas for replication within

Table 2. (from Chaisson, 2001)

System	Phi
Pentium II of the 1990s	10^{11}
Intel 8080 of the 1970s	10^{10}
Modern engines	10^5 to 10^8
Society (modern culture)	5×10^5
Brains (human cranium)	1.5×10^5
Animals (human body)	2×10^4
Plants (biosphere)	900
Planets (early Earth)	75
Stars (Sun)	2
Galaxies (Milky Way)	0.5

galaxies, and computers are (presently) dependent on human society for replication on Earth. To the extent that both *evolutionary* variation and *developmental* replication (life cycle) are fundamental to all dissipative CAS, this would imply that the lowest-*Phi* CAS in this figure, galaxies, are likely to replicate as *dependents on their universe* in the multiverse.

Finally, note that Figure 21 appears *effectively asymptotic* today. Something very curious seems to be going on. *When considered on an astronomical scale, universal time has effectively stopped here on Earth, with respect to Phi emergence rates. Some universally important transition appears to lie almost immediately ahead of us.* Wherever postbiological intelligence emerges, dynamic learning becomes effectively instantaneous, from the universe's perspective. We'll speculate more on this in the DS hypothesis to come.

Extrapolating to the future, we can expect fully autonomous computers to have *Phi* values of *at least* 10^{12}, seven orders of magnitude greater than human society (10^5). Even today, our global set of electronic computing systems, while presently far from our level of structural complexity, are learning about the universe, encoding knowledge from their human-aided, quasi-evolutionary searches, as much as 10 millionfold faster than human society, albeit still in narrow ways and only for intermittent periods.

However, if tomorrow's best commercial computers will increasingly improve themselves (self-provision, self-repair, self-evolve), as many designers expect they must, they will be able to exploit their greatly superior learning rate on a *general and continuous basis*, escaping the present need for human manufacturers and consumers in each upgrade cycle. This also assumes that quasi-organic, self-improving computers can be *selected for stability, productivity, and deep symbiosis with humanity*, just as our domestic animals have been intelligently selected for human compatibility over the last 10,000 years (5,000 breeding cycles). Both today's domestic dogs and tomorrow's domestic robots are systems whose detailed brain structures will be a mystery to us, even as we increasingly depend on them. If in turn evolutionary experimentation by computers in ultrafast digital simulation space becomes a useful *proxy* for experimentation in slow physical space (an argument we advance in the longer version of this paper) we can begin to understand how 10 millionfold-accelerated computers might *recapitulate* our 500 million years of metazoan evolutionary developmental learning in as short a period as *50 years.*

Turning briefly to computational *structure*, a universal energy efficiency trend can be observed in the progressively decreasing binding energy levels employed at the leading edge of evo devo computation. As some examples show (adapted from Laszlo 1987), each newly emergent substrate in the quintet hierarchy uses greatly decreased binding energies to create and process information via its physical structure, allowing far greater energy (and space, time, and matter) efficiency of computation:

Finally, energy (and space, time, and matter) density and efficiency may be considered through the framework of Adrian Bejan (2000) and his constructal law, which proposes that for any finite-size system to persist in time (to live), "it must evolve [and develop] in such a way that it provides ever-easier access to the imposed currents that flow through it." Constructal theory, a type of operations research, seeks to describe developmental limits on evolutionary action in nature describing "imperfectly optimal" conditions for animate and inanimate flow systems, and championing both the emergence of and boundaries to all fractal (self-similar) hierarchies in physical systems.

Matter Compression. This may be the hardest of the STEM compression processes to visualize, at first glance. Consider first the astounding growth in matter efficiency and density of computation that produced, in our universe's chemical substrate, *biological cells* on Earth. Early life and pre-life-forms must have been far less genomically and cellularly efficient and dense. DNA folding and unfolding regimes in every eukaryotic (vs. prokaryotic) cell are a marvel of material compression (efficiency and density of genetic computation) that we are only now beginning to unravel. Consider also the density

Table 3.

Hierarchy	Comp. Substrate	Energetic binding system (computational mechanics)
Physics	Matter	Nuclear exchange (strong forces)
Chem	Molecules	Ionic and covalent bonds (electromagnetic (EM) forces)
Bio	Cells	Cell adhesion molecules, peptide bonds (weak EM forces)
Socio	Brains	Synaptic weighting, neural arborization (weaker EM forces)
Tech	Computers	Gated electron flow, single electron transistors (even weaker EM)
Post-Tech?	Black Holes	Gravitons? (Gravity is the weakest of the known binding forces. "Dark energy" is weaker, but repulsive, not binding.)

and efficiency of social computation (increasing human biological *and* material flow efficiency and density) in a *modern city*, vs. nomadic pretechnologic humans. Note the matter compression (increasing efficiency and to a lesser degree growing physical density) in our *digital computing machinery*, in Moore's and a large family of related "laws" in electronic computing, and in emerging nanotechnology, optical, quantum and now single electron transistor devices. Consider next how matter compression creates *nuclear fusion* in a star, the most powerful and plentiful energy source known. Finally, consider the matter compression in the *black hole* forming processes that led to our *initial cosmic singularity*, if the CNS hypothesis is correct, and which lies in our local future if the DS hypothesis (to come) is correct.

If they are to be validated, STEM compression models need to be made much more quantifiable and predictive across the substrate levels. Many fascinating trends or "laws" highlighting some component of STEM efficiency or density have been described for biology or human culture (see Lotka 1922; Zipf 1948; Vermiej 1987; and Winiwarter and Cempel 1992 for a few), but hypotheses of STEM compression as a universal developmental process are much harder to find. Perhaps the first historical example is Buckminster Fuller's (1938, 1979, 1981) concept of *ephemeralization* or "the [universal intelligence efficiency] principle of doing ever more with ever less weight, time, and energy per each given level of functional performance." Fuller also noted *some* spatial and time density trends in human culture, but he did not consider STEM density to be a universal developmental vector for complex systems.

Fortunately the energy density work of Chaisson (2001), Kleidon and Lorenz (2005), and other scholars in nonequilibrium complexity is clearly presented in both universal and developmental terms. We also find a powerful update to Fuller's perspective in the writings of systems theorist Ray Kurzweil, who proposes a "law of accelerating returns," (1999, 2005) where the evolution of universal intelligence must increase both STEM efficiency and time density of computation and productivity. Most recently, Seth Lloyd champions space, time, energy, and matter density increase in his proposal that the "ultimate" universal computer is a black hole (2000a, 2000b), but even Lloyd presently stops short of proposing STEM density as a developmental attractor for all universal intelligence, as we do in the DS hypothesis to come.

• Universal Development as Ergodicity (aka Computational Closure). Random walks vs. ergodic walks in statistical processes may be one of the best *mathematical* ways to discriminate evolutionary from developmental processes, as the former stays perennially unpredictable and the latter converges to an average predictability. In a random walk, such as stock prices under normal conditions, observed events will stay random or stochastic no matter how you sample them (Malkiel 2007). By contrast, an ergodic walk is a sampling process whose average over time converges to the population average. To do this, the population as an entity must adequately sample the entire phase space (behavior, phenomena or state space presently available to the system), within a representative timeframe. Furthermore, the phase space must not be rapidly or unpredictably growing (new behaviors becoming possible) relative to the existing phase space.

In other words, ergodicity requires the emergence of what may be called a computationally closed map (or at least a saturated or very slow-growing map) of the phase space of possible behaviors for a system, and an appropriate sampling technique. In ergodic systems, when you sample an appropriate subset of individuals, over an appropriate length of time, you get a model that allows you to predict up from the sample to the collective and down from the collective ("ensemble") to sample behavior (Tarko 2005).

Ergodicity seems a key precondition to irreversibility, directionality, and hierarchy in information and development theory. It may be only when a system becomes ergodic, which may be the same as saying terminal differentiation is emerging in that particular morphospace and function space, that one can make probabilistically predictive inferences about the system's behavior. In relation to human foresight, this means that *inaccurate generalizations, poor predictions, and flawed models of the future may all be a result of the nonergodicity (the robust evolutionary creativity) of most ensembles, most of the time.* For example, predicting our own cultural evolution seems particularly difficult for individual humans as the phase space of culture historically has grown rapidly and chaotically *relative to us,* and as the sampling is typically done by individual, narrowly intelligent humans. But as global tech intelligence continues to accelerate, and as human culture terminally differentiates, much developmental ergodicity may emerge. We may soon see a "total simulation society" (Brigis 2004) in which collective intelligence, ubiquitous simulation, transparency, and quantification of human behavior will allow emerging technological intelligence to deliver increasingly accurate models of human culture. One example of effective, sample-based trends in cultural prediction is the rise of quantitative marketing and public relations. Another are models that reliably forecast value shifts in countries as a function of their development (e.g., Inglehart and Welzel 2005).

Note that we are arguing here for intelligent technology's ability to increasingly predict the past and future of *human and earlier* systems, both

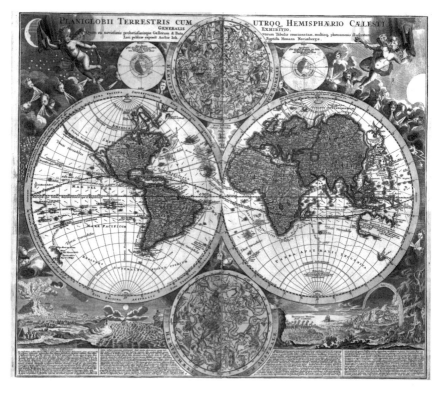

Figure 22. First good maps of Earth. (Credit: Johann Baptiste Homann [German cartographer], 1707)

being simpler and presumably more ergodic (closed) substrates. In an evo devo universe, an AI's ability to predict *its own* evolutionary future (as opposed to its increasingly clearer developmental future) should remain as persistently intractable to the AI as humanity's ability to predict its own social innovation future is to us today. To close our discussion of ergodicity, let us briefly survey ways humans have used *evolutionary* intelligence processes to generate increasingly *closed*, ergodic maps, allowing predictable, directional, and "optimized" *developmental* features to then emerge:

- The salient features of the Earth's surface, a sphere of fixed area, are one obvious eventually ergodic system. Once cartographers had our first good global maps (Figure 22), many aspects of terrestrial exploration "lost their novelty" and predictable, optimized trade routes emerged.
- Human evolutionary psychology, emotions, and morality have many ergodic features as they represent gene-internalized, contextually optimized knowledge accumulated over millions of years in increasingly insulated (niche constructed) environments resulting in predictable group social behaviors (Wright 1997).

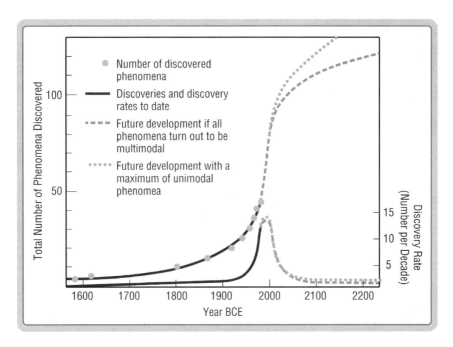

Figure 23. Astronomical discoveries and discovery rate, projected forward (Harwit 1981). (Credit: Acceleration Studies Foundation. Artist: Marlon Rojas, *Fizbit.com*)

- Many aspects of human sociology, culture, and art have become ergodic because human nature changes so slowly, and the number of ways to please and offend human psychology are actually *limited*. Art forms such as classical music, which began to greatly decelerate in rates of evolutionary creativity even in the late 1800s, thus become ergodic as there are limited ways to play the notes of the chromatic scale in a manner aesthetically satisfying to (equally ergodic) human psychology. In such cases only the opening of new phase space (a culture acquiring new creative or psychological capacity, or a genre's recombination with another genre) can reintroduce novelty and unpredictability.

- Many branches of mathematics (e.g., number theory) and science have entered long periods of ergodicity, where new learning ceased to emerge, and have only been reinvigorated (usually only for brief periods) when new computational or investigational methods become available (Horgan 1996).

- Even our maps of astronomical events are rapidly headed toward computational closure, as Martin Harwit (1981) argues (Figure 23). Harwit's estimate predicts the total unique phenomena in a set based on the repetitiveness of phenomena in the current sample.

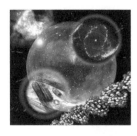

Figure 24. Astrobiology, a uniquely transdisciplinary science. (Credit: Astrobiology Image, JPL/NASA)

Such techniques (Fisher et al. 1943) are valid for a broad range of (ergodic) physical ensembles. Just as there are a limited number of existing species on Earth (an ensemble now predicted to be between four million and six million), there are a limited and much smaller number of unique astronomical phenomena to be discovered in the future, either by a variety (multimodal) or by only one (unimodal) observational method. Given our *accelerating discovery rate and the much smaller phase space* (compared to biology) for *much simpler* astrophysical evo devo systems, Harwit's model predicts terminal differentiation of novelty in observable outer space phenomena very soon in cosmic time, *as early as 2200 CE in his estimate.*

Such insights reveal the increasingly *information poor* nature of "outer space" (the universal environment) as development unfolds, and suggest local intelligence will be driven progressively into *"inner space,"* into zones of ever-greater STEM compression and simulation capacity, in our accelerating evolutionary search for novel, valuable information. We will explore this speculation at length in the DS hypothesis, next.

EDU Hypothesis: Closing Thoughts

The EDU hypothesis is a "just so" story, a self-selected and suspicious fantasy that must be held at arms length until it can be more objectively evaluated. It has parsimony of sorts and intuitive appeal to (at least some) purpose-seeking, biological minds. We present it in a long tradition of Goethe (1790), Schelling (1800), Chambers (1844), Darwin (1859, 1871), Spencer (1864, 1874, 1896), Lotze (1879), Haeckel (1899), Newcomb (1903), Bergson (1910), Wallace (1912), Henderson (1913, 1917), Alexander (1916), Whitehead (1925, 1927, 1933), Vernadsky (1926, 1945), Shapley (1930), Teilhard (1945, 1955), du Noüy (1947), Wiener (1961); Aurobindo (1963); Miller (1978), Murchie (1978), de Rosnay (1979, 2000), Jantsch (1980), Fabel (1981, 2004), Cairns-Smith (1982, 1985), Hoyle (1983), Dodson (1984), Salthe (1985, 1993), Varela (1986); Winiwarter (1986, 1999); Lewin (1988); Stenger (1990, 2000); Wesson (1991); Smolin (1992, 1997), Heylighen (1993), Kauffman (1993, 1995); Stock (1993), de Duve (1995), Stewart (2000), Gardner (2000, 2003, 2007), Allott (2001), Balázs (2002), Morris (1998, 2004, 2008), Primack and Abrams (2006) and other philosophers of science who suspect a naturalistically teleological (directional, progressive, and partly purposeful) universe that uses natural selection as an integral process, but not the only process in its successive self-improvement.

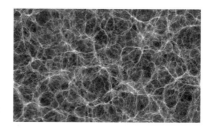

Figure 25. Cosmic web, Millennium Run simulation (Gnedin 2005). (Credit: Volker Springel et al., Virgo Consortium, Max Planck Institute for Astrophysics and Edinburgh Parallel Computing Centre 2005)

Fortunately, as the evo-devo biology community continues to grow in size, research corpus, and legitimacy, it will increasingly be able to inform and test EDU models. Besides theoretical evo-devo biologists and philosophers, major contributors to and critics of EDU models will be the anthropic cosmologists (Barrow et al. 2006; Leslie 1989, 1998; Rees 1999, 2001; Davies 1987, 2007, etc.), complexity theorists (Gardner 2003, 2007; Smith and Morowitz 2006), and astrobiologists (Figure 22; Ward and Brownlee 2000; Lunine 2004; Ulmschneider 2006; Horneck and Rettberg 2007).

Let us close our EDU speculations with the realization that there is something deeply organic and developmental looking about our cosmic web, the apparent large-scale structure of our universe (Figure 25; Gnedin 2005; Springel 2006) with its patterns of filaments, nets, and voids driven by accelerating aggregations of dark matter. Both random and directional processes seem simultaneously at work.

Until sufficiently predictive models of universal development can be brought to bear, EDU concepts must remain speculative systems theory and philosophy of science. We now turn to an even more speculative model, the DS hypothesis, which nevertheless holds promise for predictive verification or falsification reasonably soon, as it has even more specific things to say about the constraints on and future developmental trajectory of cosmic intelligence.

---

3. The Developmental Singularity (DS) Hypothesis

How likely is it that Earth's local intelligence, as it continues to evolve and develop, will transcend the universe, rather than expand inside of it? Are highly dense, highly localized astronomical objects (black holes and objects which approximate them) computationally privileged platforms for universal intelligence, selection, and reproduction? Might all higher intelligence in our universe be developmentally destined for transcension, and could this explain the Fermi Paradox in way that is testable by future science and SETI?

Our first hypothesis considered the universe as a system of *information, physics, and computation.* Our second considered the universe as a *quasi-organic and hierarchically developing* (evo devo) system. Our final hypothesis considers the *life cycle and communication constraints* of such a system, and makes falsifiable predictions for the developmental future of universal intelligence.

The Developmental Singularity (DS) hypothesis will now be presented in brief. It includes the following claims and subhypotheses,

- The ICU and EDU hypotheses, in some variation, and,
- The Developmental Singularity (aka Inner Space or Transcension) Hypothesis: An Asymptotic Mechanism for Universe Simulation and Reproduction. Due to the universal developmental trend of STEM compression (accelerating STEM efficiency and density of higher intelligence), Earth's local intelligence will apparently very soon in astronomical time develop *black-hole-analogous features*, a highly local, dense, and maximally computationally efficient form that we may call a developmental singularity (DS) (Smart 2000). The DS seems to be a natural progression of the technological singularity (highly STEM efficient and dense autonomous postbiological intelligence) that is likely to emerge on Earth in coming generations.

In the EDU hypothesis, we proposed that our universe improves itself via evolutionary processes occurring within a finite, cycling developmental framework. This framework requires universal structural (body) aging and death, the emergence of internal reproductive intelligence, natural selection on that intelligence, and new universe (seed) production in an evo devo life cycle.

In the DS hypothesis, we propose that Earth's local intelligence is on the way to forming a black hole-analogous reproductive system, and then new seed formation via developmental (germline) processes to produce another universe within the multiverse. As all the substrates of our quintet hierarchy appear both evolutionary and developmental, it is likely that our local DS intelligence will also engage in natural selection (competitive and cooperative merger and recombination) with other evolutionarily unique universal intelligences *prior* to universe reproduction. Finally, this reproduction may occur via a special subset of physics (Smolin 1997) found only in the quantum domains of black holes.

The DS hypothesis is just one of several possible models of evo devo CNS-I. It assigns a potential evolutionary role in universe reproduction for all developing cultural intelligences in the cosmos. The DS hypothesis argues that local intelligence, should it continue to successfully develop, will *leave our visible cosmos very soon in universal time.* Nevertheless, due to the greatly accelerated nature of postbiological intelligence, this will also represent a *very long period in subjective (perceived, conscious, computational) time* prior to universal transcension.

Colloquially, the process of DS creation may be summarized as an irreversible developmental trajectory for universal intelligence from outer space to *inner space,* to zones of ever-greater STEM density, STEM efficiency, and self-awareness/simulation capacity. Alternatively, this may also be called a Transcension Hypothesis (intelligence becomes increasingly local and *leaves* the visible universe over time, in order to meet other intelligences and/or partially reshape *future* universes) as opposed to an Expansion Hypothesis (intelligence expands throughout and reshapes the *current* universe over time).

Intelligence expansion is by far the standard perspective contemplated by those who presently consider the future of astrosociology and astrotechnology. It is in fact so dominant that it is generally *assumed* to be true without question. Generalizing from the STEM compression trend, the DS hypothesis proposes that expansion is 180 degrees out of phase with the true vector of universal intelligence development. Fortunately, this prediction seems broadly testable by SETI in coming decades, as explained in Smart 2000a and briefly at the end of this paper.

• "Law" of Locally Asymptotic Computation (LAC): STEM Compression, Computronium, and the Black Hole Attractor as Localized Violations of the Generally Applicable Copernican Principle. As noted in our discussion of STEM compression earlier, the leading edge of universal computational complexity exhibits an ever-increasing *spatial locality*, and an ever-greater ability to *simulate* and *influence* the universe (outer space) within the inner space (STEM compressed structure and simulation system) of the highest local intelligence. Clearly this trend cannot continue forever, but must eventually reach an *asymptote*, some maximally localized and efficient state. In any universe with finite compressibility and finite local physical resources, we must therefore propose some form of LAC "law" as a "right wall" (Schroeder and Ćirković 2008) of accelerating complexity increase, sharply constraining the future dynamics of universal intelligence wherever it arises (Figure 26).

Computronium is defined by speculative writers as hypothetical maximally condensed matter that is "optimally structured as a computing substrate" (Amato 1991). As any physical optimum is always *context-dependent*, a general theory of computation must posit *forms of computronium at every hierarchical level of STEM density* that is achievable by developing computing systems. For example, biological computation based on *DNA in cells* seems

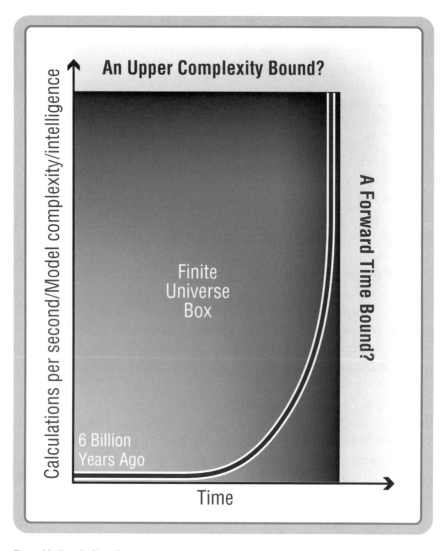

Figure 26. "Law" of locally asymptotic computation (LAC). (Credit: Acceleration Studies Foundation. Artist: Marlon Rojas, *Fizbit.com*)

likely to already be an optimal or near-optimal *chemistry-catalyzed* (lower intelligence) form of computronium, with respect to the set of chemically based systems which are accessible to discovery by molecular evolutionary systems. Likewise, *nanotechnology* (molecular scale engineering), which promises far greater STEM density of computation than all biological systems to date, seems likely to be an optimal *culture-catalyzed* form of computronium, again when we are restricted to the set of substrates accessible to discovery by evolutionary human or AI intelligence (Drexler 1986, 1992, 2007). After

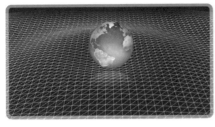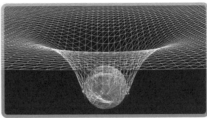

Figure 27. Gravity is the *altering of space time* around high-mass objects, affecting local celestial dynamics as a function of mass. Likewise, STEM compression may be the altering of space time and matter-energy *dynamics* as a function of complexity. In high-complexity objects like our future Earth's postbiological culture, *transcension-related behaviors* may become increasingly probable the closer the system approaches the black hole computational attractor. (Credit: Acceleration Studies Foundation. Artist: Marlon Rojas, *Fizbit.com*)

nanotechnology, some form of *femtotechnology*, or atomic, optical, or quantum computing computronium must lie in wait as yet another evolutionary and developmental computing frontier. As legendary physicist, Richard Feynman (1959) presciently observed, there is "plenty of room at the bottom" of conventional molecular and atomic structures, which are almost all empty space in their current, nonrelativistic configurations. Just as life repurposed molecules to create cells, atoms are waiting to be repurposed by future intelligence into far more STEM efficient, STEM dense, and adaptive computational systems (Moravec 1999).

The LAC law proposes that as STEM efficiency and density of intelligent computation continues to rapidly increase, the *final universal computronium* must be a *black hole*, a structure Lloyd (2000a, 2000b) and others have already proposed as an ideal computing platform for universal intelligence. It also proposes that the closer universal civilizations tend toward this black hole attractor, the more powerfully they are driven to further STEM compress (increase the spatial locality, speed, energy efficiency, and matter density of) their computation. Just as gravity *physically alters space time around high-mass objects*, making local escape from their orbit increasingly unlikely, so, too, there is some yet-unclear *informational* relation between gravitation and universal computation. In other words, the phenomenon of STEM compression somehow alters the *informational landscape* around high-complexity objects, increasingly chaining them to further computational acceleration, until eventually an irreversible, black hole-like regime is reached (Figure 27). Such conjectures wait to be validated or refuted by future theory of universal computation which must, in this model, include general relativity its equations.

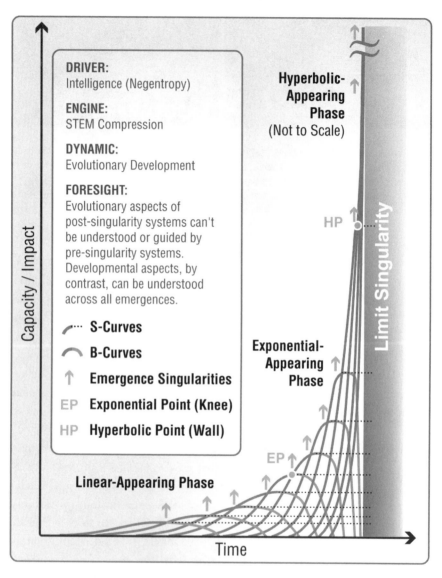

Figure 28. The second-order J-curve of the LAC law is composed of a series of first order S- and B-curves, each individually growth-limited computing substrates. (Credit: Acceleration Studies Foundation. Artist: Marlon Rojas, *Fizbit.com*)

A composite J-curve (Figure 28) illustrates some assumptions of the LAC model. While *individual* physical computing platforms either *saturate* their complexity growth and form the stable base for the next hierarchy emergence (S-curves) or *die/go extinct* (B-curves), the leading edge of *collective* local computation (a second order J-curve) continually accelerates on the way to the black hole attractor. Local computational growth achieves this feat by regularly jump-ing to ever-newer, more STEM dense and STEM efficient computing plat-forms, each of which has steeper S-curves of computational capacity and impact.

In a universe with physical limits however, there must be some "high-est" S-curve, some maximally STEM compressed nonrelativistic computro-nium. Once we have arrived at that, we will find no further substrate to jump to other than black holes themselves. In that terminal environment, a *local saturation in acceleration* must finally occur. This leveling off of computational acceleration may occupy a very insignificant fraction of nonrelativistic ("objec-tive") time (the x-axis in Figures 26 and 28), yet this could still be a very long period in consciously experienced ("subjective") time, for the hyperacceler-ated intelligences of that era. Accurately modeling the "objective" length of time until we reach saturation may be beyond our present abilities, though early work (Lloyd 2000a, 2001; Krauss and Starkman 2004) suggests such a universal physical-computational asymptote may be reached in *hundreds*, not even thousands, of years from today. Such a possibility is breathtaking to consider. Fortunately, if the LAC proposal is correct, it will be increasingly predictive and falsifiable in coming years, as we develop better metrics and models for the dynamics of planetary technological change.

If the LAC model is proven true, such concepts as the generalized Copernican principle (Principle of Mediocrity) *while perhaps valid for the contingent 95 percent evolutionary "body" of our universe, must be revised with respect to special accelerating developmental reference frames* (local germline/seed environments of continual STEM compression and complexity increase) like Earth (Figure 29). In turn, Copernican-dependent models like the random observer self-sampling assumption (Bostrom 2002), and randomness-based "doomsday" arguments (Carter 1983; Gott 1993, 1994; Leslie 1998) estimat-ing the likely duration of cosmic presence of humanity must also be revised.

• Black Holes as Ideal Structures for Information Gathering, Storage, and Computing in a Universe that is Increasingly Ergodic to Local Observers. Current research (Aaronson 2006, 2008) now suggests that building future computers based on quantum theory, one of the two great theories of 20th century physics, will not yield exponentially, but only *quadratically* growing computational capacity over today's classical computing. In the search for truly disruptive future computational capacity emergence, let us therefore look to the second great physical theory of the last century, relativity. If the DS hypothesis is correct, what we can call relativistic computing (a black hole-approximating computing substrate) will be the final common attractor for all successfully developing universal civilizations.

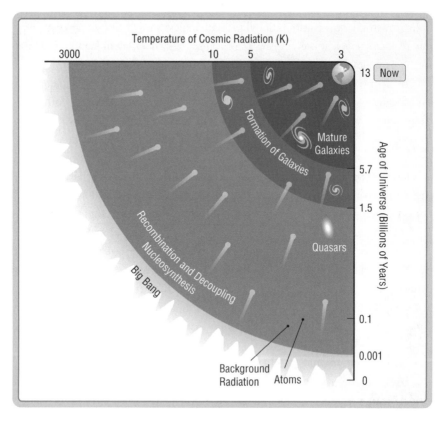

Figure 29. Complexity-centric representation of the universe. If Earth-type emergences need a developmental reference frame, some cosmological models must be revised. (Credit: Acceleration Studies Foundation. Artist: Marlon Rojas, *Fizbit.com*)

Consider the following thought experiment. Imagine that you are a developmental singularity, and have STEM compressed yourself from non-relativistic computronium all the way to the relativistic domain of a black hole. At this special place, everything that happens in the external universe, as well as any sensing and computing devices you have set up just external to you (outside yourself), will tell you everything they can learn about the universe in *virtually no relative local time.* This is because physical rates of change are happening far, far faster in all parts of the universe external to your event horizon "eye" (Figure 30).

A black hole is the last place you want to be if you are still trying to *create* (evolve) in the universe, but this seems *exactly* where you want to be if you have reached the asymptote of complexity development in outer (normal) space, have employed all finite local resources into the most efficient nonrelativistic computronium you can, and are now finding the observable universe

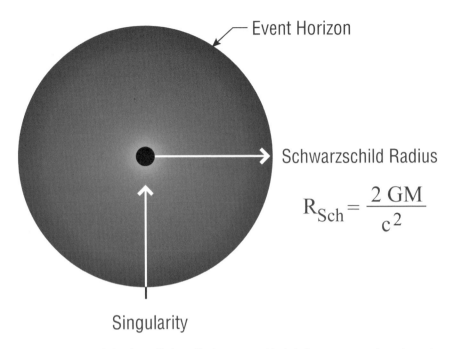

Event Horizon

Schwarzschild Radius

$$R_{Sch} = \frac{2\,GM}{c^2}$$

Singularity

Figure 30. Black hole time dilation. Clocks near a black hole appear to slow down to an external observer and stop altogether at the event horizon. Inside the black hole external clocks move arbitrarily fast. (Credit: Acceleration Studies Foundation. Artist: Marlon Rojas, *Fizbit.com*)

to be *an increasingly ergodic (repetitive, uncreative, "cosmogonic") and senescent or saturated learning environment, relative to you.* In other words, the more computationally closed local computing and discovery become, and the more complex *you* become relative to the universe proper, the faster you want the external universe to go to gain the last bits of useful information in the *shortest amount* of local time, before entering an entirely new zone of creativity (black hole merger, natural selection, and new universe creation). Given their unique internal computational capacity (to be discussed next) black holes seem to be *ideal germline devices* for gaining the last observational and computational information available in the universe, from your no-longer-accelerating local reference frame, and taking it with you to someplace else. As the external universe dies at an accelerating pace, you are locally learning every last thing you can about as it disintegrates *in virtually no subjective time.*

With respect to their internal computational capacities, quantum physicist Seth Lloyd (2000a, 2000b) has theorized that black holes are the "ultimate" computing environment, as only at black hole energy densities does the "memory wall" of modern computing disappear. In all classical computing, there is a time cost to sending information from the processor to the memory register and back again. Yet as Lloyd shows, at the black hole limit of STEM density, computers attain the Bekenstein bound for the energy cost of information transfer (Bekenstein 1981), and the time it takes to flip a bit (t_{flip}) at any position, is on the same order as the time it takes to communicate (t_{com}) from *any* point in the system to any other around the event horizon. In other words, communication and computation have become a *convergently unified process* in black holes, making them a maximally STEM efficient learning system. Even the femtosecond processes and great STEM densities in neutron stars would be slow and simple by comparison.

At the same time, we must admit that this is a learning system that has entered a jail of its own choosing. If one hallmark of developmental processes is their irreversibility, the creation of a black hole is as irreversible a phase transition as one can imagine. Not even information can leak back out into the universe. Once a black hole intelligence is formed, it can "never go home again," only forward, perhaps to merger with other black holes (discussed shortly), and perhaps also to some form of direct experience of and influence on the multiversal environment. We seem to have become a *near-seed*, almost frozen in universal time, waiting patiently for the opportunity to flower again.

Local intelligence would very likely need to be able to enter a black hole without losing any of its structural complexity. Hawking (1987) has speculated we might do just this, if advanced intelligence is built out of some form of femtotechnology (structures below the atom in size). Atoms and above might be destroyed on entering a local, intelligently created low-mass black hole, but there are 25 orders of magnitude of "undiscovered country" in scale between atoms (10^{-10} m) and the Planck length (10^{-35} m) for the possible future creation of intelligent systems. Inner space engineering may one day occur within this vast range, which is almost as broad as the 30 orders of scale inhabited by biological life. If the DS hypothesis is true, local intelligence must continue to migrate to these more STEM efficient and dense learning environments. *Until* we reach the black hole stage, reversibility will always be an option, but we can expect outer space to be far less interesting and vastly slower and simpler by comparison to the consciousness, insight, and adaptive capacities we gain by venturing further into inner space.

As a prime example, human consciousness is presently the most STEM dense computational platform known. It emerges from 100 trillion unique synaptic connections contained in a very small mobile platform that communicates with thousands out of billions of other local memetically unique variants. We regularly alter it but rarely seek to voluntarily eliminate it, statistically speaking. If you could *reversibly* leave your human mind and become the entire sea of your single-celled ancestors, you probably would do so at least once, for the experience. But you probably wouldn't stay in that vastly less complex space for long. Conversely, any opportunity we might gain to go further into STEM compression and thus deeper and broader into conscious experience would very likely be a one way, irreversible, developmental progression, on average, for all universal intelligence. In other words, intelligence apparently has a developmental trajectory, moving whenever possible towards greater STEM density and efficiency.

•   Black Hole or Nonrelativistic Computronium Mergers as Mechanisms for Intrauniversal Natural Selection in Evo Devo CNS-I. As competitive and cooperative natural selection seems to emerge early in all evo-devo biological systems, and as such selection becomes particularly *intricate and multilayered* in more complex systems in the hierarchy (e.g., genetic, kin, sexual, cultural, technological, and many other forms of selection all influencing the reproduction of human beings) (Keller 1999; Okasha 2007), some form of intrauniversal or extrauniversal (multiversal) natural selection seems necessary with respect to black hole intelligences *prior* to their replication. Two intrauniversal selection models will now be proposed.

Not only do intelligent black holes appear to be ideal pre-seeds, picking up and packaging the last useful body information in the universe before they leave, but they may also be ideal vessels for merging, competing, cooperating, and engaging in natural selection with other intrauniversal intelligences. This is because black holes, and only black holes, allow a special kind of one way time travel for merging with other evolutionarily unique universal intelligences in virtually no subjective (internal) time.

Looking at the future dynamics of our universe under dark energy, Krauss and Scherrer (2008) describe a cosmos where space self-fractionates into supergalactic "islands" with *continually decreasing* observable universal information available to each island. Throughout the universe, local group galaxies merge under gravitational attraction to form supergalaxies (islands), and the rest of the universe rapidly recedes beyond each island's view (Figure 31). In related work, Nagamine and Loeb (2003) predict our Milky Way galaxy, Andromeda galaxy, and the dwarf galaxies in our Local Group will all collapse 50 billion–100 billion years from now into a single supergalaxy, while the rest of the universe will move permanently beyond our observation horizon.

From a DS perspective, such self-organization looks much like the formation of a large number of "universe follicles," reproductive structures that facilitate *gravity driven merger and natural selection* amongst all intelligent

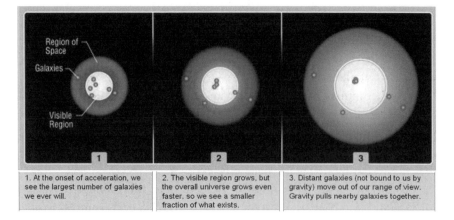

1. At the onset of acceleration, we see the largest number of galaxies we ever will.	2. The visible region grows, but the overall universe grows even faster, so we see a smaller fraction of what exists.	3. Distant galaxies (not bound to us by gravity) move out of our range of view. Gravity pulls nearby galaxies together.

Figure 31. About six billion years ago, universe expansion began to accelerate. It is now self-fractionating into local "islands," each of which may create evolutionarily unique intelligence mergers. (Credit: Acceleration Studies Foundation. Artist: Marlon Rojas, *Fizbit.com*)

black holes (pre-seeds) that exist inside each supergalaxy (Figure 32). This process seems at least partly analogous to the way many eggs compete selectively every month in the human ovarian follicle for ovulation of the single "fittest egg" for reproduction.

How many universal intelligences might be involved in each such merger? Drake and Sagan's original estimate ranged from one (ours) to 1 million technical civilizations in our Milky Way galaxy alone. Estimates from "rare Earth" astrobiologists are far more conservative, but also far from conclusive. If we assume a similar number of civilizations for the Milky Way and Andromeda, and none for the local dwarf galaxies (developmental failures, it seems), our Local Group follicle should harbor *at least two (one per galaxy) to as many as two million cosmic intelligences* that are statistically likely to meet and merge prior to replication, assuming our own future development does not end in failure prior to the merger event. My own intuition, given the impressive biofelicity that our universe appears to exhibit to date, would put the number of merging intelligences in each supergalaxy closer to the high end than the low end of this range.

We can expect each of these cosmic intelligences to have truly unique perspectives on the universe, each having taken slightly different evolutionary pathways to their own developmental singularities, and each being quite limited and incomplete by contrast to intractable multiversal reality. Universes that allow the comparing and contrasting of many uniquely constructed models of reality in a competitive and cooperative manner via black hole mergers would allow *greatly increased natural selection for robustness and complexity* of universes and their civilizations in the next EDU cycle.

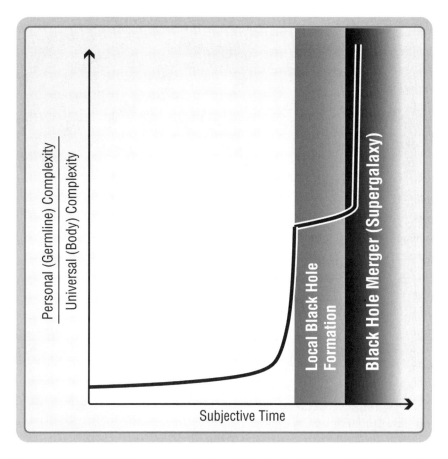

Figure 32. Passive black hole merger scenario. A possible natural selection mechanism for evo devo CNS-I. (Credit: Acceleration Studies Foundation. Artist: Marlon Rojas, *Fizbit.com*)

In addition to passive black hole merger, we can propose at least one active intrauniversal merger scenario. If minimizing nonrelativistic universal time is important prior to merger, or if local developmental singularities choose to STEM compress themselves only to the highest nonrelativistic (form-reversible) computronium available, they might actively launch themselves to some central merger point to allow knowledge sharing as soon as possible in *nonrelativistic* time. This scenario seems less likely to this author, given the apparent primacy of local, subjective, internal, relative time in complexity development to date, but remains in the realm of plausibility. Given the generally proposed shape of the galactic habitable zone (GHZ), the closest central merger point for a community of cosmic intelligences would be the supermassive black holes at the center of any intelligence-supporting galaxy (Figure 33).

Curiously, supermassives are the only black holes that do not immediately destroy, via tidal forces, even the ordinary matter they collect across their event horizons. Could there be something special about these objects that makes them ideal for DS merger? Might future SETI pick up signs of planet- or stellar-mass computronium entities, whose gravitational lensing signatures depict great

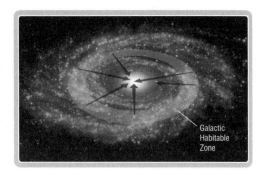

Figure 33. Active black hole merger scenario. Another possible natural selection mechanism for evo devo CNS-I. Might mature DSs actively migrate from the GHZ to the galactic center? (Credit: Acceleration Studies Foundation. Artist: Marlon Rojas, *Fizbit.com*)

mass compacted into negligible volumes, traveling from the GHZ toward the galactic center, like salmon swimming home, as evidence of our own cosmic future? What level of SETI sensitivity would we need before we could detect such evidence? Note that this scenario, though it would involve a specific form of active interstellar travel, is still one of developmentally constrained transcension, not expansion, of cosmic intelligence.

Next, consider why in an evo devo universe, a No-Broadcasting Directive (no active communication of our presence to the universe) would be likely to be self-discovered and scrupulously followed by all advanced civilizations in the cosmos. Given developmentally fated merger (either passive or active) and transcension physics, and given that advanced intelligences should be strongly bound by benevolent, evo compu devo value sets, no advanced communication beacons are likely to be constructed or *Encyclopedia Galacticas* sent prior to merger and transcension. Why? In the biological world, one-way communication is occasionally useful for developmental *control* but never for evolutionary *complexity construction*. It can presently be argued, and we would predict, will eventually be proven with future information theory, that *one-way, nonlocal communication* (aka "broadcasting") with no possibility of feedback, *must always reduce the remaining evolutionary variability and homogenize the developmental transcensions of all civilizations receiving such messages*. Such behavior should therefore be ethically avoided by all advanced intelligences as they inevitably become aware of EDU and DS physics and information theory. Thus the DS hypothesis proposes a very specific solution to the Fermi Paradox (Webb 2002) and falsifiably predicts that future SETI should discover "radio fossils," Earth-like civilizations that transmit *very low* levels of nonrandom electromagnetic radiation during their *early* cultural development, *and then reliably cease such transmission as they disappear into transcension soon after their technological singularity is reached*. For more, please see Smart 2000a.

Finally, we should ask ourselves whether a universe where dark energy didn't dominate might be preferable to the one we seem to inhabit. A universe that ended in a "Big Crunch," for example, would allow us to merge with *all* universal black hole intelligences, as opposed to just a subset of local intelligences prior to replication. Curiously, when we look for such a strategy in evo-devo biological systems, we find it doesn't exist. Why? One of evolution's most basic strategies is increasing variety over time, perhaps as an adaptation to the pervasive computational incompleteness of each organism. In general, a universe ensemble that *keeps branching into many unique forks* (increasing number and variety of daughter universes) will be more robust than an ensemble that brings all its eggs back to one basket at the end of universal time. But remember also that all evolutionary trees also eventually exhaust themselves. The novel branching in the phenospace of universe ensembles should eventually saturate, and a convergent phase transition to some form of *postuniversal substrate* should then occur. In other words, even a network of branching universes must eventually give way to some qualitatively different and more unbounded system in the multiversal future. As it goes in biology, so may we expect it to go in universes, in an evo devo approach to computing reality.

• The Coming Challenge of Postbiological Intelligence: The Evolutionary Development of Friendly AI. Let us close this paper by returning to a particularly imminent concern, the potential arrival of a technological singularity on Earth in coming generations. In EDU language, such an event would be a major threshold in the local evolutionary development of cosmic complexity. Contemplating the transition, which may arrive even this century, what theoretical and empirical strategies may we use to ensure postbiological intelligence will be "friendly" to the complexity, needs, and desires of our species? This question been addressed carefully by only a few thoughtful scholars to date (e.g., Bostrom 2003; Yudkowsky 2006).

The ICU, EDU, and DS hypotheses can each inform the Friendly AI question, should any of these be validated by future science. For example, if the ICU and EDU hypotheses are true, we may expect postbiological intelligences to *aggressively enforce the preservation of human complexity*, as well as the basic needs and positive sum desires of biological humanity, at least for a time. This is because in the EDU framework, human and postbiological complexity are built *not only* by random evolutionary accidents *but also* by *statistically probable developments* emerging from the interaction of collectives of evo compu devo systems. Such a universe has been iteratively tuned for robust computational acceleration, and appears to be *broadly guided* by an inherent evo compu devo moral telos. Just as we are finally concerned with creating, learning from, and preserving Earth's biological diversity, postbiological intelligences must seek to *create, learn from,* and *sustain* personal, planetary, and universal complexity with a degree of ethical rigor that is directly proportional to their own complexity. We may therefore expect such intelligences to have a collective postbiological morality vastly exceeding ours in scope and sophistication, even as they have individual evolutionary moral deviants who are policed by the collective, just as do human populations.

Furthermore, the EDU framework tells us such intelligences must emerge via evolutionary developmental processes (replicating, varying, selecting, and converging in biologically inspired hardware), as a collective or *population* of intelligences, and *never* as a single, top-down engineered intelligence. If the 95/5 rule is correct, massively parallel evolutionary variation is the *only* viable path to the developmental emergence of intelligence, as it is, for example, in your own brain. No single, isolated engineering effort could ever create a human-equivalent artificial intelligence, contrary to the hopes of many AI aspirants. Instead, an extensive period of bottom-up evolutionary gardening of a *global ecology* of simple digital assistants ("cybertwins") must occur long before a technological singularity. Just as it takes a village to raise a child, we will need a *global human community* to raise, select, and prune Earth's coming forms of artificial intelligence. This should allow us many years in which to select our learning agents for safety, symbiosis, and dependability, and to gain *extensive empirical evidence of their friendliness* even if our theories of friendliness remain underdeveloped, and even as the intricacies of their electronic brains remain as inscrutable as the brains of any artificially selected animal that exists today. Applying this perspective, a distributed development I have proposed we may expect in the next decade, long before the emergence of higher AI, is the *conversational interface,* a bottom-up, statistically constructed natural language processing platform that will enable sophisticated human-machine, human-avatar, and avatar-avatar conversations. See Smart 2003 for more on this imminent development, one of our planet's next major steps toward postbiological intelligence.

Those unsatisfied with these arguments may still approach the friendliness question from other aspects of the EDU framework. Consider self-interest: it seems likely that once postbiologicals can deeply and developmentally (predictively) understand *all the simpler systems from which they arose,* they would be potentially much safer from previously unknown subtle universal processes, and considerably more adaptive and intelligent. In an ergodic universe, all of biology must eventually become *increasingly (though never fully predictively) computationally closed systems* relative to postbiological intelligence. Given our subordinate hierarchical relationship ("they" must arise from us) and their unique ability to understand and at least with respect to developmental dynamics, predict our biological thoughts and behaviors once their nanosensors and processors are tightly linked to us, the evo devo nature of the human species should be the *most interesting solvable puzzle* in the universe to tomorrow's AI's (recall that no evolutionary CAS can ever be ergodic to *self*-simulation). A useful parallel to the way humanity will likely be studied is the way structural and computational cellular biologists presently try to simulate and predict, *in real time*, individual metabolic events in model species of Earth's bacteria today, even though we are perhaps generations away from having the computational power or theoretical base to achieve this feat in any comprehensive way.

How long postbiological intelligences would be—or should be—friendly not just to collective planetary human complexity, but to our *needs and desires as individual biological human beings* is a harder question to evaluate. Wesley (1974), for example, would allow no more than a century after postbiological intelligence arrives before the complete disappearance of *Homo sapiens*. While such a guess may be too abbreviated by at least an order of magnitude, its very briefness speaks to the strangeness of unchecked computational acceleration. Once postbiologicals can deeply and successfully predict our species mental and behavioral events, *in real time*, there might be little reason left not to turn us into them.

Given the profound STEM compression limitations of biology as a computing platform, such a strategy would seem to require continued accelerating complexity of our cybertwins (personal digital assistants) until they become our *cyberselves*, via greatly accelerating intimacy of connections between our cybernetic and biological identities. Today our cybertwins are our limited electronic data, and our primitive, nearly static profiles on today's social networks. Very soon they will be our increasingly intelligent digital avatars, and the growing variety of technologies they will control (Smart 2004).

It seems to me that the most productive human beings in mid-21st century society, as well as most of our youth, will increasingly depend on their cybertwins as their primary interface to the world. It also seems likely that many of us will allow our cybertwins to continue to increase in complexity and usefulness to society even after our biological bodies have died, which will profoundly change the nature of grieving and the social impact of death. At some point, with the advanced nanotechnology that postbiological life seems likely to command, our cybertwins can permeate our biological brains and bodies with their nanosensor grids, develop deep connectivity between our digital and biological identities, and deliver a kind of immortality, even a subjective immortality, by *successive digital approximation*.

Consider this: once we can experience our own personal consciousness across *both our electronic and biological forms*, due to intimate, complex nano-technological connections between them, will not the inevitable aging and death of our biological components be seen as simply growth, not death? Won't it be like having a part of you that has more intrinsic limitations finally being shed, while the other part learns something from the shedding? Won't humanity decide to stop procreating biologically once we recognize our cyberselves have fully encapsulated and exceeded our biological complexity, consciousness and humanity? When postbiologicals can *understand, predict, and archive* all planetary biology, will they then consider it morally justified to give all local biology cybernetic appendages, and progressively turn our entire planet into a developmental singularity? A postbiological intelligence made of highly STEM dense materials would likely be impervious to all external environmental threats. It would also have new inner space complexity frontiers to explore that we can scarcely imagine from our biological perspective.

Finally, while the ICU, EDU, and DS hypotheses provide a reasoned and intriguing basis for expecting the continued acceleration of local complexity, they leave unanswered many questions concerning *which unpredictable, evolutionary paths Earth's most intelligent species will take* as it catalyzes postbiological development. Will we be able to reform our most self-absorbed and materialistic cultures (U.S., Japan, U.K., etc.) that frequently serve profit, plutocracy and exploitation more than innovation, learning, and sustainability? Will we limit the scope of human-initiated catastrophe, war, and terrorism by advancing our *global immune systems* (biological, cultural, and technological), *maximizing individual self-determination, eliminating deprivation, and limiting disparity and ecological destruction*? Will we fund the discovery and validation of an increasingly evidence-based and universal *science of human values*, such as our proposed evo compu devo telos, or continue to allow unexamined, cynical postmodernism and unquestioned religious superstition to dictate our deepest beliefs? Will we finally admit that science and technology are not just human enterprises but also the latest stage in a *long-accelerating process of intelligence development*, serving some higher, universal purpose? Will we conscientiously select our technological intelligence for *demonstrable value and symbiosis with humanity* in coming generations? Or will we approach these issues languidly, childishly, and with little foresight, risking an inhumane, disruptive, dangerous, and unfriendly transition?

The future never comes as fast, as humanely, or as predictably as those who shirk responsibility expect it to. Such questions seem among our species great choices and moral challenges in the years ahead. Let us be wise in answering them.

Acknowledgments

Thanks to anonymous reviewers, David Brin, Sybil de Clark, Norman Gilmore, Bill Halal, Alan Kazlev, John Leslie, Mark Lupisella, Max Marmer, Mark Martin, Marty Poulin, Stan Salthe, Clément Vidal, and Peter Winiwarter for helpful critiques. An international research and critique community in evo devo systems theories, free and open to all qualified scholars, may be joined at *EvoDevoUniverse.com*. A longer, wiki-based version of this paper may be found at *books.accelerating.org*. Author's e-mail: *johnsmart@accelerating.org*.

References

Aaronson, Scott. 2006. "Computational Complexity and the Anthropic Principle." Notes for a talk given at the Stanford Institute for Theoretical Physics, 15 December 2006. *http://www.scottaaronson.com/talks/anthropic. html*.

———2008. "The Limits of Quantum Computers," *Scientific American* (March 2008).

Abraham, Ajith et al. 2006. *Stigmergic Optimization (Studies in Computational Intelligence)*, Springer.

Adami, Christoph. 1995. "Self-organized criticality in living systems;" *Physics Letters A* 203:29–32. *http://arxiv.org/abs/adap-org/9401001*.

Adams, Henry B. 1909 [1919]. "The Rule of Phase Applied to History," in *The Degradation of the Democratic Dogma*. New York: Macmillan, pp. 267–311.

Alexander, Samuel. 1916 [1966]. *Space, Time, and Deity: Gifford lectures at Glasgow, 1916-1918, Vol. II*. New York: Macmillan.

——1920. *Space, Time, and Deity.* Whitefish, MT: Kessinger.

Allen, Timothy F. and Thomas B. Starr, 1982. *Hierarchy: Perspectives for ecological complexity.* University of Chicago Press.

Allott, Robin. 2001. *The Great Mosaic Eye: Language and Evolution,* Brighton, UK: Book Guild Ltd.

Amato, Ivan. 1991. "Speculating in precious computronium." *Science* 253 (5022): 856–857.

Arthur, Wallace. 2000. *The Origin of Animal Body Plans: A Study in Evolutionary Developmental Biology.* Cambridge University Press.

Ashtekar, Abhay. 2006. "The Issue of the Beginning in Quantum Gravity." *http://arxiv.org/abs/physics/0605078.*

Aunger, Robert. 2000. *Darwinizing Culture: The Status of Memetics as a Science.* Oxford University Press.

——2007a. "Major transitions in 'big' history." *Technological Forecasting & Social Change* 74 (8): 1137–1163.

——2007b. "A rigorous periodization of 'big' history." *Technological Forecasting & Social Change* 74 (8): 1164–1178.

Aurobindo, Sri. 1963[2003]. *The Future Evolution of Man.* Twin Lakes, WI: Lotus Press.

Bak, Per et al. 1987. "Self-organized criticality: An explanation of the 1/f noise." *Physical Review Letters* 59 (4): 381–384. *http://dx.doi.org/10.1103/PhysRevLett.59.381.*

Bakewell, Margaret A. et al. 2007. More genes underwent positive selection in chimpanzee evolution than in human evolution. *PNAS* (17 April 2007).

Balázs, Béla. 2002. "The Role of Life in the Cosmological Replication Cycle," Paper from 2002 ISSOL Conference. *http://astro.elte.hu/~bab/Role_Life_Univp.rtf.*

Barrow, John D. 2002. *The Constants of Nature: The Numbers that Encode the Deepest Secrets of the Universe.* New York: Pantheon.

——2007. "Living in a Simulated Universe," in *Universe or Multiverse?* B. Carr (ed.), p. 481–486.

Barrow, John D. and Frank Tipler, 1986. *The Anthropic Cosmological Principle.* Oxford University Press.

Barrow, John D. et al. (eds). 2006. *Fitness of the Cosmos for Life: Biochemistry and Fine-Tuning.* Cambridge University Press.

Barzun, Jacques. 2001. *From Dawn to Decadence: 500 Years of Western Cultural Life.* New York: Harper Perennial.

Baum, Eric. 1983. Discussion, *Physics Letters* B 133 (185).

——2006. *What Is Thought?* Cambridge, MA: MIT Press.

Bejan, Adrian. 2000. *Shape and Structure: From Engineering to Nature.* Cambridge University Press.

Bekenstein, Jacob D. 1981. "Energy cost of information transfer," *Physical Review Letters* 46:623–626

Bergson, Henri. 1910 [1983]. *Creative Evolution* (1911 English translation of *L'Evolution créatrice*). University Press of America.

Blackmore, Susan. 1999. *The Meme Machine.* Oxford University Press.

Blume-Kohout, R. and W. H. Zurek, 2005. "Quantum Darwinism: Entanglement, Branches, and the Emergent Classicality of Redundantly Stored Quantum Information." *arXiv:quant-ph/0505031v2.*

Bostrom, Nick. 2002. *Anthropic Bias: Observation Selection Effects in Science and Philosophy.* New York: Routledge.

——2003. "Ethical Issues in Advanced Artificial Intelligence," in *Cognitive, Emotive and Ethical Aspects of Decision Making in Humans and in*

Artificial Intelligence 2, I. Smit et al. (ed.), Int. Institute of Advanced Studies in Systems Research and Cybernetics, pp. 12–17.

Breuer, Reinhard. 1991. *The Anthropic Principle: Man as the Focal Point of Nature*. Birkhäuser.

Brier, Soren. 2008. *Cybersemiotics: Why Information Is Not Enough*. University of Toronto Press.

Brigis, Alvis. 2004. Personal communication.

Broderick, Damien. 1997 [2001]. *The Spike: Accelerating into the Unimaginable Future*. Reed Books.

Brown, James. H. and Geoffrey West, 2000. *Scaling in Biology*. Oxford University Press.

Byl, John. 1996. "On the Natural Selection of Universes," *Quarterly Journal of the Royal Astronomical Society* 37:369–371.

Cairncross, Frances C. 1998 [2001]. *The Death of Distance: How the Communications Revolution is Changing Our Lives*. Harvard Business School Press.

Cairns-Smith, A. Graham. 1982. *Genetic Takeover and the Mineral Origins of Life*. Cambridge University Press.

——1985. *Seven Clues to the Origin of Life*. Cambridge University Press.

Callebaut, Werner and Diego Rasskin-Gutman, 2005. *Modularity: Understanding the Development and Evolution of Natural Complex Systems*. Cambridge, MA: MIT Press.

Carroll, Sean B. 2005. *Endless Forms Most Beautiful: The New Science of Evo Devo*. New York: Norton.

Carter, Brandon. 1983. "The anthropic principle and its implications for biological evolution," Philosophical Transactions of the Royal Society of London A310:347–363.

Chaisson, Eric J. 2001. *Cosmic Evolution: The Rise of Complexity in Nature.* Harvard University Press.

——2003. A unifying concept for astrobiology [Φ_m]. International Journal of Astrobiology 2(2): 91–101. *http://www.tufts.edu/as/wright_center/eric/reprints/unifying_concept_astrobio.pdf.*

Chaitin, Gregory J. 1987. *Algorithmic Information Theory.* Cambridge University Press.

——1998. *The Limits of Mathematics.* New York: Springer-Verlag.

Chambers, Robert. 1844. *Vestiges of the Natural History of Creation.* Churchill.

Church, Alonzo. 1934. "A Note on the Entschiedungsproblem," *Journal of Symbolic Logic* 1:40–41.

Clarke, Andy. 2003. *Natural-Born Cyborgs: Minds, Technologies, and the Future of Human Intelligence.* Oxford University Press.

Coleman, Sidney. 1988. "Black holes as red herrings: topological fluctuations and the loss of quantum coherence," *Nuclear Physics* B 307, no. 864.

Coren, Richard. 1998. *The Evolutionary Trajectory: The Growth of Information in the History and Future of Earth.* CRC Press.

Corning, Peter. 2003. *Nature's Magic: Synergy in Evolution and the Fate of Humankind.* Cambridge University Press.

Crane, Louis. 1994. "Possible Implications of the Quantum Theory of Gravity: An Introduction to the Meduso-Anthropic Principle," arXiv:hep-th/9402104v1.

Darwin, Charles. 1859. *On the Origin of Species By Means of Natural Selection.* John Murray.

——1871. *The Descent of Man, and Selection in Relation to Sex.* John Murray.

Davies, Paul C. W. 1987 [2004]. *The Cosmic Blueprint: New Discoveries in Nature's Creative Ability to Order the Universe.* Templeton Foundation Press.

———2004. "How bio-friendly is the universe?" *arXiv:astro-ph/0403050.*

———2007. *The Goldilocks Enigma: Why Is the Universe Just Right for Life?* New York: Penguin.

Dawkins, Richard. 1976 [2006]. *The Selfish Gene.* Oxford University Press.

Deacon, Terrence W. 1997. *The Symbolic Species: The Co-Evolution of Language and the Brain.* New York: W. W. Norton.

de Duve, Christian. 1995. *Vital Dust: Life as Cosmic Imperative.* New York: Basic Books.

De Morgan, Augustus. 1872. *A Budget of Paradoxes.* Longmans, Green, and Co.

Dennett, Daniel C. 1998. *Brainchildren: Essays on Designing Minds.* Cambridge, MA: MIT Press.

de Rosnay, Joël. 1979. *The Macroscope: A Systemic Approach to Complexity* (Online Book). New York: Harper & Row.

———2000. *The Symbiotic Man.* McGraw Hill.

Descartes, René. 1641. *Meditations on First Philosophy,* in *The Philosophical Writings of René Descartes.* Cambridge University Press, 1984, vol. 2, pp. 1–62.

Deutsch, David. 1985. "Quantum theory, the Church-Turing Principle and the Universal Quantum Computer," *Proceedings of the Royal Society* 400:97–117.

———1997. *The Fabric of Reality.* New York: Penguin.

de Vaucouleurs, Gerard. 1970. "The Case for a Hierarchical Cosmology," *Science* 27(167): 1203–1213.

Devezas, Tessaleno C. and Modelski, George. 2003. "Power law behavior and world system evolution: A millennial learning process," *Technological Forecasting & Social Change* 70 (9): 819–859.

Dick, Steven J. 1999. *The Biological Universe: The Twentieth Century Extraterrestrial Life Debate and the Limits of Science.* Cambridge University Press.

——2000. *Many Worlds: The New Universe, Extraterrestrial Life, and the Theological Implications.* Templeton Foundation Press.

——2003. Cultural evolution, the postbiological universe and SETI. *International Journal of Astrobiology* 2 (1): 65–74.

——2006. "Anthropology and the Search for Extraterrestrial Intelligence: An Historical View," *Anthropology Today* 22 (2): 3–7.

Dodson, Edward O. 1984. *The Phenomenon of Man Revisited: A Biological Viewpoint on Teilhard de Chardin.* Columbia University Press.

Drexler, K. Eric. 1986. *Engines of Creation: The Coming Era of Nanotechnology.* New York: Anchor.

——1992. *Nanosystems: Molecular Machinery, Manufacturing, and Computation.* Wiley.

Drexler, K. Eric et al. 2007. "Technology Roadmap for Productive Nanosystems," Battelle Memorial Institute. *http://www.e-drexler.com/p/07/00/1204TechnologyRoadmap.html.*

du Noüy, Pierre Lecomte. 1947. *Human Destiny,* Longmans, Green & Co., p. 273.

Dyson, Freeman. 1988[2004]. *Infinite in All Directions.* New York: HarperCollins.

Edelman, Gerald. 1989. *Neural Darwinism: The Theory of Neuronal Group Selection*. New York: Basic Books.

Elias, Norbert. 1978 [2000]. *The Civilizing Process: Sociogenetic and Psychogenetic Investigations*. Wiley-Blackwell.

Fabel, Arthur. 1981. *Cosmic Genesis: Teilhard de Chardin and the emerging scientific paradigm*. ANIMA Books.

——2004+. *NaturalGenesis.net* "An annotated anthology and sourcebook for the concept of a creative, organic universe." Thoughtful, holistic perspectives on the value of an organic worldview.

Farhi, Edward and Alan Guth, 1987. "An obstacle to creating a universe in the laboratory," *Physical Review Letters* B183 (2): 149–155.

Ferrer I Cancho, Ramon and Ricard Solé, 2003. "Least effort and the origins of scaling in human language," *Proceedings of the National Academy of Sciences* 100 (3): 789–791.

Feynman, Richard. 1959. "There's Plenty of Room at the Bottom," Lecture to the American Physical Society, Caltech, 29 December 1959.

Fisher, Ronald A. et al. 1943. "The Relation Between the Number of Species and the Number of Individuals in a Random Sample of an Animal Population," *Journal of Animal Ecology* 12:42–58.

Floridi, Luciano (ed.) 2003. *The Blackwell Guide to the Philosophy of Computing and Information*. Wiley-Blackwell.

——2008. *Philosophy of Computing and Information: Five Questions*. Automatic Press.

Fredkin, Edward. 1990. "Digital mechanics," *Physica D* 45 (1–3): 254–270.

——1992. Finite Nature. *Proceedings of the XXVIIth Rencontre de Moriond*.

Frolov, Valeri P. et al. 1989. "Through a black hole into a new universe?" *Physics Letters* B 216:272–276.

Fuller, R. Buckminster. 1938 [2000]. *Nine Chains to the Moon*. New York: Doubleday.

——1979. *Synergetics 2: Further Explorations in the Geometry of Thinking*. New York: Macmillan.

——1981 [1982]. *Critical Path*. St. Martin's Griffin.

Gardner, James N. 2000. "The selfish biocosm: Complexity as cosmology," *Complexity* 5(3): 34–45.

——2003. *Biocosm: The New Scientific Theory of Evolution—Intelligent Life is the Architect of the Universe*. Inner Ocean Publishing.

——2003. "Coevolution of the Cosmic Past and Future: The Selfish Biocosm as a Closed Timelike Curve." *Complexity* 10, no. 5: 14–21.

——2007. *The Intelligent Universe: AI, ET, and the Emerging Mind of the Cosmos*. New Page.

Gelernter, David. 1993. *Mirror Worlds: Or the Day Software Puts the Universe in a Shoebox . . . How It Will Happen and What It Will Mean*. Oxford University Press.

Gershenson, Carlos. 2007. *Design and Control of Self-Organizing Systems*. Ph.D. Dissertation, Vrije Universiteit Brussel, *http://homepages.vub. ac.be/~cgershen/thesis.html*.

——2008. "The World as Evolving Information." *http://arxiv.org/PS_cache/ arxiv/pdf/0704/0704.0304v2.pdf*.

Gintis, Herbert et al. (eds.) 2005. *Moral Sentiments and Material Interests: The Foundations of Cooperation in Economic Life*. Cambridge, MA: MIT Press.

Gnedin, Nickolay Y. 2005. "Cosmology: Digitizing the Universe," *Nature* 435:572–573.

Gödel, Kurt. 1934. "On Undecideable Propositions of Formal Mathematical Systems," lecture notes taken by Kleene and Rossner at the Institute of

Advanced Study. Reprinted in Davis, M. (ed.) *The Undecidable*. Raven Press, 1965.

Goethe, Johann W. v. 1790. "Metamorphosis of Plants" (Versuch die Metamorphose der Pflanzen zu erkläre).

Good, Irving J. 1965. Speculations Concerning the First Ultra Intelligent Machine. In: *Advances in Computers, Vol.6*, F. L. Alt and M. Rubinoff (eds.). Academic Press, pp. 31–88.

Gott, J. Richard, III. 1993. "Implications of the Copernican principle for our future prospects," *Nature* 363:315–319.

——1994. "Future prospects discussed," *Nature* 368:108.

Gott, J. Richard, III and Li-Xin Li, 1997 [2002]. "Can the Universe Create Itself?" *http://xxx.lanl.gov/PS_cache/astro-ph/pdf/9712/9712344.pdf*.

Gould, Stephen J. 1977. *Ontogeny and Phylogeny*. Harvard University Press.

——1992. "Impeaching a Self-Appointed Judge," *Scientific American* (July): 118–121.

——2002. *The Structure of Evolutionary Theory*. Harvard University Press.

——2007. *The Richness of Life: The Essential Stephen Jay Gould*, Steven Rose (ed.). New York: Norton.

Haeckel, Ernst. 1899 [1992]. *The Riddle of the Universe*. Prometheus Books.

Hall, Brian K. (ed.). 2003. *Environment, Development, and Evolution: Toward a Synthesis*. Cambridge, MA: MIT Press.

Harrison, Edward R. 1995. "The Natural Selection of Universes Containing Intelligent Life," *Quarterly Journal of the Royal Astronomical Society* 36:193.

——1998. "Creation and fitness of the universe," *Astronomy & Geophysics* 39 (2): 27.

Hart, Michael H. and Zuckerman, Ben. 1982 [1995]. *Extraterrestrials: Where Are They?* Cambridge University Press.

Harwit, Martin. 1981. *Cosmic Discovery: The Search, Scope and Heritage of Astronomy.* New York: Basic Books.

Hawking, Stephen W. 1987. "Coherence down the wormhole," *Physics Letters* B 195 (337).

——1988. "Wormholes in spacetime," *Physical Review* D 37 (904).

——1993. *Black Holes and Baby Universes—and Other Essays.* Bantam.

——2005. "Information Loss in Black Holes," *arxiv:hep-th/0507171.*

Henderson, Lawrence J. 1913. *The Fitness of the Environment for Life.* New York: Macmillan.

——1917. *The Order of Nature.* Harvard University Press.

Heylighen, Francis. 1999. "The Growth of Structural and Functional Complexity during Evolution," in *The Evolution of Complexity,* F. Heylighen, J. Bollen & A. Riegler (eds.). Kluwer Academic, p. 17–44. *http://pespmc1.vub.ac.be/Papers/ComplexityGrowth.html.*

——2007a. "Accelerating Socio-Technological Evolution: from ephemeralization and stigmergy to the global brain," in *Globalization as an Evolutionary Process: Modeling Global Change,* George Modelski, Tessaleno Devezas, and William Thompson (eds.). New York: Routledge, p. 286–335.

——2007b. "Mediator Evolution," in *Worldviews, Science and Us,* D. Aerts, B. D'Hooghe & N. Note (eds.). World Scientific.

——2007c. "The Global Superorganism: an evolutionary-cybernetic model of the emerging network society," *Social Evolution and History* 6 (1): 58–119.

Heylighen, Francis et al. 1993+ Principia Cybernetica Web. A broad and deep web-based exploration of evolutionary-systemic and cybernetic philosophy. Promotes "MetaSystem Transition Theory" of hierarchical emergence.

Hofkirchner, Wolfgang. (ed). 1999. *The Quest for a Unified Theory of Information*. New York: Routledge.

Hofstadter, Douglas R. 1995. *Fluid Concepts and Creative Analogies*. Basic Books.

Holland, John. 1995. *Hidden Order: How Adaptation Builds Complexity*. Perseus Books.

——1998. *Emergence: From Chaos to Order*. Perseus Books.

Horneck, Gerda and Petra Rettberg, (eds.). 2007. *Complete Course in Astrobiology*. Wiley-VCH.

Horgan, John. 1996. *The End of Science: Facing the Limits of Knowledge in the Twilight of the Scientific Age*. Broadway Books.

Hoyle, Fred. 1983. *The Intelligent Universe: A New View of Creation and Evolution*. Holt, Rhinehart & Winston.

Jablonka, Eva and Marion J. Lamb, 1995. *Epigenetic Inheritance and Evolution: the Lamarckian Dimension*. Oxford University Press.

——2005. *Evolution in Four Dimensions: Genetic, Epigenetic, Behavioral, and Symbolic Variation in the History of Life*. Cambridge, MA: MIT Press.

Inglehart, Ronald and Christian Welzel, 2005. *Modernization, Cultural Change, and Democracy: The Human Development Sequence*. Cambridge University Press.

Iranfar, Negin et al. 2003. "Genome-Wide Expression Analyses of Gene Regulation during Early Development of Dycostelium discoideum," *Eukaryotic Cell* 2 (4): 664–670.

Jacob, François. 1977. "Evolution and tinkering," *Science* 196:1161–1166.

Jacoby, Susan. 2008. *The Age of American Unreason*. Pantheon Books.

Jain, Anil K. et al. 2002. « On the similarity of identical twin fingerprints," *Pattern Recognition* 35:2653–2663.

James, William. 1921. *Pragmatism, a New Name for Some Old Ways of Thinking*. Longmans, Green, and Co.

Jantsch, Erich. 1980. *The Self-Organizing Universe*. Pergamon.

Johnson, Norman L. et al. 1998. « Symbiotic Intelligence: Self-Organizing Knowledge on Distributed Networks Driven by Human Interaction," in *Artificial Life VI: Proceedings of the 6th International Conference on Artificial Life*, Christoph Adami et al. (eds.). Cambridge, MA: MIT Press.

Kauffman, Stuart. 1993. *Origins of Order: Self-Org. and Selection in Evolution*. Oxford University Press.

——1995. *At Home in the Universe*. Oxford University Press.

Keller, Laurent. 1999. *Levels of Selection*. Princeton, NJ: Princeton University Press.

Kelly, Kevin. 2005. "How does technology evolve? Like we did," TED 2005 (video) *http://www.ted.com/index.php/talks/view/id/*.

Kimura, Motoo. 1983. *The Neutral Theory of Molecular Evolution*. Cambridge University Press.

King, Chris C. 1978. "Unified Field Theories and the Origin of Life," *University of Auckland Mathematics Rept. Ser.* 134.

——2001. *Biocosmology Part 1 Prebiotic Epoch: Symmetry-Breaking and Molecular Evolution*, WED Monographs 2 (1): 1–20.

Kirkwood, Tom B. L. 1977. "Evolution of aging," *Nature* 270:301–304.

——1999. *Time of Our Lives: The Science of Human Aging.* Oxford University Press.

——2005. "Understanding the odd science of aging" *Cell* 120:437–447.

Kleidon, Axel and Ralph D. Lorenz, 2005. *Non-equilibrium Thermodynamics and the Production of Entropy: Life, Earth, and Beyond.* Springer.

Krauss, Lawrence M. and Robert J. Scherrer, 2007. *Journal of General Relativity and Gravitation* 39 (10): 1545–1550 and *http://arXiv.org/abs/0704.0221.*

——2008. "The End of Cosmology?: An accelerating universe wipes out traces of its own origins," *Scientific American* 298 (3): 46–53.

Krauss, Lawrence M. and Glenn Starkman, 2004. "Universal Limits on Computation" *http://arXiv:astro-ph/0404510v2.*

Krauss, Lawrence M. et al. 2008. "Anthropic Arguments and the Cosmological Constant, with and without the Assumption of Typicality," *Physical Review Letters* 100 (04): 1301.

Kurzweil, Ray. 1999. *The Age of Spiritual Machines: When Computers Exceed Human Intelligence.* Penguin.

——2001. "The Law of Accelerating Returns," *http://www.kurzweilai.net/articles/art0134.html?printable=1.*

——2005. *The Singularity is Near: When Humans Transcend Biology.* Penguin.

Laland, Kevin N. et al. 2000. "Niche Construction, Biological Evolution and Cultural Change," *Behavioral and Brain Sciences* 23 (1): 131-175.

Lasch, Christopher. 1991. *Culture of Narcissism: American Life in an Age of Diminishing Expectations.* W. W. Norton.

Laszlo, Ervin. 1987 [1996]. *Evolution: The General Theory.* Hampton Press.

Lazcano, Antonio and Jeffrey L. Bada, 2004. "The 1953 Stanley L. Miller Experiment: Fifty Years of Prebiotic Organic Chemistry," *Origins of Life and Evolution of Biospheres* 33:235–242.

Leigh, Egbert G., Jr. 2007. "Neutral theory: A historical perspective," *Evolutionary Biology* 20:2075–2091.

Lenski, Richard E. 2004. Phenotypic and genomic evolution during a 20,000-generation experiment with the bacterium *Escherichia coli. Plant Breeding Reviews* 24:225–265.

Leslie, John. 1989. *Universes.* Routledge.

——1998. *The End of the World: The Science and Ethics of Human Extinction.* Routledge.

Lewin, Roger. 1988. "A Lopsided Look at Evolution: An analysis of the fossil record reveals some unexpected patterns in the origin of major evolutionary innovations, patterns that presumably reflect the operation of different mechanisms," *Science* 241 (15 July): 291–293.

Linde, Andrei. 1994. "The Self-Reproducing Inflationary Universe," *Scientific American* 271 (5): 48–55.

Lloyd, Seth. 2000a. "Ultimate physical limits to computation," *Nature* 406:1047–1054.

——2000b. "How Fast, How Small and How Powerful? Moore's Law and the Ultimate Laptop," *Edge.org. http://www.edge.org/3rd_culture/lloyd/lloyd_index.html.*

——2001 [2002]. "Computational capacity of the universe," *Physical Review Letters* 88: 237901. Also at: *arXiv:quant-ph/0110141v1* (2001).

——2006. *Programming the Universe: A Quantum Computer Scientist Takes On the Cosmos.* Vintage Books.

Lotka, Alfred. J. 1922. "Contribution to the energetics of evolution, and Natural selection as a physical principle," *Proceedings of the National Academy of Sciences* 8:147–154.

Lotze, Hermann. 1879 [1884]. *Metaphysics: Ontology, Cosmology, and Psychology*, ed. and trans. by B. Bosanquet. Clarendon Press.

Lunine, Jonathan I. 2004. *Astrobiology: A Multi-Disciplinary Approach.* Benjamin Cummings.

Malkiel, Burton G. 1973 [2007]. *A Random Walk Down Wall Street.* New York: W. W. Norton.

Margulis, Lynn. 1999. *Symbiotic Planet: A New Look at Evolution.* Basic Books.

McCabe, Gordon. 2006. "Extending cosmological natural selection." *arXiv:gr-qc/0610016v1.*

Milinkovitch, Michel C. and Athanasia Tzika, 2007. "Escaping the Mouse Trap: The Selection of New Evo-Devo Model Species," *Journal of Experimental Zoology (Mol Dev Evol)* 308B:337–346.

Miller, James Grier. 1978. *Living Systems.* McGraw-Hill.

Miller, Stanley L. 1953. "Production of Amino Acids Under Possible Primitive Earth Conditions," *Science* 117:52.

Moravec, Hans. 1988. *Mind Children: The Future of Robot and Human Intelligence.* Harvard University Press.

——1999. *Robot: Mere Machine to Transcendent Mind.* Oxford University Press.

Morris, Simon Conway. 1998. *The Crucible of Creation: The Burgess Shale and the Rise of Animals.* Oxford University Press.

——2000. "The Cambrian 'explosion': Slow-fuse or megatonnage?" *PNAS* 97 (9): 4426–4429.

——2004. *Life's Solution: Inevitable Humans in a Lonely Universe*. Cambridge University Press.

——2008. *The Deep Structure of Biology: Is Convergence Sufficiently Ubiquitous to Give a Directional Signal*. Templeton Foundation Press.

Müller, Gerd B. and Stuart A. Newman, (eds.). 2003. *The Origination of Organismal Form: Beyond the Gene in Developmental and Evolutionary Biology*. Cambridge, MA: MIT Press.

Murchie, Guy. 1978. *The Seven Mysteries of Life*. Houghton Mifflin.

Nagamine, Kentaro and Abraham Loeb, 2003. "Future Evolution of Nearby Large-Scale Structures in a Universe Dominated by a Cosmological Constant," *New Astronomy* 8:439–448. *http://arxiv.org/PS_cache/astro-ph/pdf/0204/0204249v3.pdf.*

Nambu, Yoichiro. 1985. "Directions of Particle Physics," *Progress of Theoretical Physics Supp* 85(104).

National Aeronautics and Space Administration. Lochner, James and Suzanne P. Kinnison, 2003 [2005]. "What is Your Cosmic Connection to the Elements?" *erc.ivv.nasa.gov/pdf/190387main_Cosmic_Elements.pdf.*

Newcomb, Simon. 1903. The Universe as an Organism. *Science* 17 (421): 121–129.

Newman, S.A. and R. Bhat, 2008. "Dynamical patterning modules: physico-genetic determinants of morphological development and evolution," *Phys. Biol.* 5 015008 (14p). doi:10.1088/1478-3975/5/1/015008. *http://www.iop.org/EJ/abstract/1478-3975/5/1/015008/.*

Nicolis, Grégoire and Ilya Prigogine, 1977. *Self-Organization in Nonequilibrium Systems*. Wiley & Sons.

Nottale, Laurent et al. 2000. *Les Arbres de l'Evolution* (*The Trees of Evolution*). Hachette. *http://fractalspace.ifrance.com/livre2.htm.*

O'Brien, Richard. 1992. *Global Financial Integration: The End of Geography*. Council on Foreign Relations Press.

Odling-Smee, F. John. 2003. *Niche Construction: The Neglected Process in Evolution*. Princeton University Press.

Okasha, Samir. 2007. *Evolution and the Levels of Selection*. Oxford University Press.

Oldershaw, Robert L. 1981. "Conceptual Foundations of the Self-similar Hierarchical Cosmology," *International Journal of General Systems* 7 (2).

——1989. "The Self-Similar Cosmological Model: Introduction and Empirical Tests," *International Journal of Theoretical Physics* 28 (6): 669–694.

Pattee, Howard, (ed.). 1973. *Hierarchy Theory: The Challenge of Complex Systems*. George Braziller.

Paul, Gregory S. and Earl Cox, 1996. *Beyond Humanity: Cyberevolution and Future Minds*. Charles River Media.

Piel, Gerard. 1972. *The Acceleration of History*. Knopf.

Pierce, Charles. 1935. *Collected Papers, Vol. VI: Scientific metaphysics*, C. Hartshorne and P. Weiss, (eds.). Harvard University Press, p. 26.

Pinker, Steven. 2007. "A History of Violence," *The New Republic* Online Edition, 19 March 2007. *http://www.edge.org/3rd_culture/pinker07/pinker07_index.html*.

Poundstone, William. 1985. *The Recursive Universe: Cosmic Complexity and the Limits of Scientific Knowledge*. Contemporary Books.

Primack, Joel R. and Nancy Ellen Abrams, 2006. *The View from the Center of the Universe: Discovering our Extraordinary Place in the Cosmos*. Riverhead Books.

Raff, Rudolf. 1996. *The Shape of Life: Genes, Development, and the Evolution of Animal Form*. University of Chicago Press.

Randall, Lisa. 2005. *Warped Passages: Unraveling the Mysteries of the Universe's Hidden Dimensions*. Harper Perennial.

Rees, Martin J. 1999. *Just Six Numbers: The Deep Forces that Shape the Universe*. Basic Books.

——2001. *Our Cosmic Habitat*. Princeton University Press.

Reid, Robert G. B. 2007. *Biological Emergences: Evolution by Natural Experiment*. Cambridge, MA: MIT Press.

Roederer, Juan G. 2005. *Information and its Role in Nature*. Springer-Verlag.

Sagan, Carl. 1973. *The Cosmic Connection: an Extraterrestrial Perspective*. Doubleday.

——1977. *The Dragons of Eden: Speculations on the Evolution of Human Intelligence*. Random House.

——1997. *Contact* [fiction]. Doubleday.

Salthe, Stanley M. 1981. *The New Evolutionary Timetable: Fossils, Genes and the Origin of Species*. Basic Books, p. 40.

——1985. *Evolving Hierarchical Systems: Their Structure and Representation*. Columbia University Press.

——1993. *Development and Evolution: Complexity and Change in Biology*. Cambridge, MA: MIT Press.

——2002. "Summary of the principles of hierarchy theory," *General Systems Bulletin* 31:13–17.

Schelling, F. W. J. 1800 [1936]. "System of transcendental idealism," in *Of human freedom*, J. Guttmann (Trans.), Open Court, p. 318.

Schlosser, Gerhard and Gunter P. Wagner, (eds.), 2004. *Modularity in Development and Evolution.* University of Chicago Press.

Schrödinger, Erwin. 1944. *What is Life?* Cambridge University Press.

Schroeder, Karl and Milan Ćirković, 2008. "Are SETI Projects Probing the 'Right Wall' of Complexity?" To be presented at the First International Conference on the Evolution and Development of the Universe, 8 October 2008.

Shannon, Claude E. 1948. "A Mathematical Theory of Communication," *Bell System Technical Journal* (July and October).

Shapley, Harlow. 1930. *Flights from Chaos.* McGraw Hill.

Siefe, Charles. 2006. *Decoding the Universe: How the New Science of Information is Explaining Everything in the Cosmos, from our Brains to Black Holes.* Viking.

Simon, Herbert A. 1962. "The architecture of complexity," *Proceedings of the American Philosophical Society* 106:467–482.

——1973. "The Organization of Complex Systems," In: *Hierarchy Theory*, H. Pattee (Ed.), George Braziller.

Smart, John M. 1999+. *AccelerationWatch.com* (formerly *SingularityWatch.com*). Discussing accelerating change from universal, global, societal, organizational, and personal perspectives.

——2000 [2008]. "Intro to the Developmental Singularity Hypothesis." *http://www.accelerationwatch.com/developmentalsinghypothesis.html.*

——2001 [2008]. "Limits to Biology: Performance Limitations on Natural and Engineered Biological Systems." *http://www.accelerationwatch.com/biotech.html.*

——2002a [2007]. "Answering the Fermi Paradox: Exploring the Mechanisms of Universal Transcension," *Journal of Evolution and Technology* (June 2002). *http://accelerating.org/articles/answeringfermiparadox.html.*

——2002b [2008]. "Understanding STEM, STEM+IC, and STEM Compression in Universal Change." *http://www.accelerationwatch.com/mest.html.*

——2003 [2008]. "The Conversational Interface: Our Next Great Leap Forward." *http://www.accelerationwatch.com/lui.html.*

——2004. "Human Performance Enhancement in 2032: A Scenario for Military Planners." *http://www.accelerating.org/articles/hpe2032army.html.*

——2005. "Measuring Innovation in an Accelerating World. Published as: Discussion of Huebner article," *Technological Forecasting & Social Change* 72, no.8:988–995. *http://www.accelerating.org/articles/huebnerinnovation.html.*

Smith, D. Eric and Harold J. Morowitz, 2006. "Framing the Question of Fine-Tuning for Intermediary Metabolism," in *Fitness of the Cosmos for Life: Biochemistry and Fine-Tuning*, J. D. Barrow, et al. (eds.). Cambridge University Press.

Smith, John Maynard and Eörs Szathmary, 1995. *The Major Transitions in Evolution.* W. H. Freeman.

Smith, Quentin. 1990. "A natural explanation of the existence and laws of our universe," *Australasian Journal of Philosophy* 68, no. 1:22–43.

——2000. "The black hole origin theory of the universe," *Internal Conf. on Physical Cosmology*, Santa Barbara.

Smolin, Lee. 1992. "Did the Universe Evolve?" *Classical and Quantum Gravity* 9:173–191.

——1994. The fate of black hole singularities and the parameters of the standard models of particle physics and cosmology. *arXiv:gr-qc/9404011v1.*

——1997. *The Life of the Cosmos.* Oxford University Press. *http://www.amazon.com/exec/obidos/ASIN/0195126645/.*

——2001. *Three Roads to Quantum Gravity.* Basic Books.

——2006. "The status of cosmological natural selection." *arXiv:hep-th/0612185v1.*

Spencer, Herbert. 1864. *Illustrations of Universal Progress: A Series of Discussions,* D. Appleton

——1864–1898. *Principles of Biology, Volumes I-II.*

——1874–1896. *Principles of Sociology, Volumes I-III.*

——1896. *A System of Synthetic Philosophy.* Williams and Norgate.

Springel, Volker et al. 2006. "The large-scale structure of the Universe," *Nature* 440:1137–1144.

Steele, Edward J. 1981. *Somatic Selection and Adaptive Evolution: On the Inheritance of Acquired Characters.* 2nd Edition. University of Chicago Press.

Steele, Edward J. et al. 1998. *Lamarck's Signature: How retrogenes are changing the natural selection paradigm.* Perseus.

Stenger, Victor J. 1990. "The Universe: the ultimate free lunch," *European Journal of Physics* 11:236–243.

——2000. *Timeless Reality: Symmetry, Simplicity, and Multiple Universes.* Prometheus Books.

Stent, Gunther S. 1969. *The Coming of the Golden Age: A View of the End of Progress.* Doubleday.

Stewart, John. 2000. *Evolution's Arrow: The Direction of Evolution and the Future of Humanity.* The Chapman Press.

Stock, Gregory. 1993. *Metaman: The Merging of Humans and Machines into a Global Superorganism.* Simon & Schuster.

Strominger, Andrew. 1984. "Vacuum topology and incoherence in quantum gravity," *Physical Review Letters* 52, no. 1733.

Susskind, Lawrence. 2005. *The Cosmic Landscape: String Theory and the Illusion of Intelligent Design.* Back Bay Books.

Tarko, Vlad. 2005. "What is Ergodicity?" *http://news.softpedia.com/news/What-is-ergodicity-15686.shtml.*

Tavernarakis, Nektarios. 2007. "Protein Synthesis and Aging," *Cell Cycle* 6 (10): 1168–1171.

Teilhard de Chardin, Pierre. 1945 [1975]. "The Planetisation of Mankind," *The Future of Man.* Image, 2004.

——1955. *The Phenomenon of Man.* Harper & Row.

Turchin, Valentin F. 1977. *The Phenomenon of Science.* Columbia University Press. *http://pespmc1.vub.ac.be/POSBOOK.html.*

Turing, Alan M. 1936. "On Computable Numbers, with an Application to the Entscheidungsproblem," *Proceedings of the London Mathematical Society* 2 (42): 230–265.

Ulanowicz, Robert. 1997. *Ecology, the Ascendant Perspective.* Columbia University Press.

Ulmschneider, Peter. 2006. *Intelligent Life in the Universe: Principles and Requirements Behind its Emergence, 2nd ed.* Springer.

Vaas, Rüdiger. 1998 [2000]. "Is there a Darwinian Evolution of the Cosmos?" Some Comments on Lee Smolin's Theory of the Origin of Universes by Means of Natural Selection. Proceedings of *MicroCosmos—MacroCosmos* conference, Aachen, Germany, 2–5 September 1998. *http://arxiv.org/abs/gr-qc/0205119.* See also *http://www.vijlen.com/confs/mima/Vaas/VAAS.html.*

Van Valen, L. and V. C. Maiorana, 1985. "Patterns of origination," *Evolutionary Theory* 7:107–125.

Varela, Francisco J. 1986. "Steps to a Cybernetics of Autonomy," In: *Power and Autonomy: New approaches toward complex systems,* R.Trappl (ed.). Plenum Press.

Verhulst, Jos. 2003. *Discovering Evolutionary Principles through Comparative Morphology.* Adonis Press.

Vermeij, Geerat J. 1987. *Evolution and Escalation.* Princeton University Press.

Vernadsky Vladimir I., 1926. *Biosphera (The Biosphere),* Nauchnoe khimiko-technicheskoye izdatel'stvo (Scientific Chemico-Technical Publishing), p. 200.

——1945. "The Biosphere and the Noosphere," *Scientific American* 33, no. 1:1–12.

Vidal, Clément. 2008. "The Future of Scientific Simulations: From Artificial Life to Artificial Cosmogenesis." *arXiv 0803.1087.*

Vinge, Vernor. 1993. "The Coming Technological Singularity." [Presented at the VISION-21 Symposium, NASA Lewis Research Center, 30 March 1993]. *http://www.accelerating.org/articles/comingtechsingularity. html.*

von Baeyer, Hans Christian. 2003. *Information, The New Language of Science.* Weidenfeld & Nicolson.

von Bertalanffy, Ludwig. 1932. *Theoretische Biologie.* Borntraeger.

——1968 [1976]. *General System Theory: Foundations, Development, Applications.* George Braziller.

Wallace, Alfred Russell. 1912. *Man's Place in the Universe.* Chapman and Hall.

Wallace, Rodrick. 2006. "Machine hyperconsciousness." *http://cogprints. org/5005/.*

Wang, Hurng-Yi et al. 2006. "Rate of Evolution in Brain-Expressed Genes in Humans and Other Primates," *PLoS Biology* 5 (2): e13 doi:10.1371/journal.pbio.0050013.

Ward, Peter and Donald Brownlee, 2000. *Rare Earth: Why Complex Life is Uncommon in the Universe.* Springer.

Wattenberg, Ben. 2005. *Fewer: How the New Demography of Depopulation Will Shape Our Future.* Ivan R. Dee.

Watters, Ethan. 2006. "DNA is Not Destiny," *Discover Magazine* (22 November 2006).

Webb, Stephen. 2002. *Where is Everybody? Fifty Solutions to the Fermi Paradox and the Problem of Extraterrestrial Life.* Copernicus/Springer-Verlag.

Weinberg, Steven. 1993. *Dreams of a Final Theory: The Search for the Fundamental Laws of Nature.* Pantheon.

Wesley, James Paul. 1974. *Ecophysics: The Application of Physics to Ecology.* Charles C. Thomas.

Wesson, Robert. 1991. *Beyond Natural Selection.* Cambridge, MA: MIT Press, p. 45.

West-Eberhard, Mary Jane. 2003. *Developmental Plasticity and Evolution.* Oxford University Press.

Wheeler, John A. 1983. "Law without law," in *Quantum Theory and Measurement,* J. A. Wheeler and W. H. Zurek (eds.). Princeton University Press.

Whitehead, Alfred North. 1925. *Science and the Modern World.* New York: Macmillan.

——1927 [1969]. *Process and Reality: An Essay in Cosmology.* Free Press.

——1933. *Adventure of Ideas.* New York: Macmillan.

Wiener, Norbert. 1961. *Cybernetics*. MIT Press.

Wigner, Eugene. 1960. "The Unreasonable Effectiveness of Mathematics in the Natural Sciences," *Communications in Pure and Applied Mathematics* 13, no. 1.

Wikipedia. 2007. "Extraterrestrial Intelligence." *http://en.wikipedia.org/wiki/Extraterrestrial_intelligence.*

Wilkins, Adam S. 2001. *The Evolution of Developmental Pathways*. Sinauer Associates.

Winiwarter, Peter. 1986. "Autognosis: The Theory of Hierarchical Self-Image Building Systems," *Proc. of Intnat'l Conf. on Mental Images, Values & Reality, Soc. for General Systems Research.*

——1999. "*A periodic system of system concepts,*" *Semiotica* 125 (1/3): 47–62.

Winiwarter, Peter and Czeslaw Cempel, 1992. "Life Symptoms: the Behavior of Open Systems with Limited Energy Dissipation Capacity and Evolution," *Systems Research* 9 (4): 9–34.

Wolfram, Stephen. 2002. *A New Kind of Science*. Wolfram Media.

Worldwatch Institute. 2008. *State of the World 2008: Toward a Sustainable Global Economy*. W. W. Norton.

Wright, Robert. 1997. *The Moral Animal: Evolutionary Psychology and Everyday Life*. Peter Smith.

——2000. *Non-Zero: The Logic of Human Destiny*. Pantheon.

Yudkowsky, Eliezer. 2006. "Artificial Intelligence as a Positive and Negative Factor in Global Risk," in *Global Catastrophic Risks*. Oxford University Press.

Zipf, George K. 1948. *Human Behavior and the Principle of Least Effort: An Introduction to Human Ecology*. Addison-Wesley.

Zuse, Konrad. 1969. *Rechnender Raum* (English translation: *Calculating Space*). Friedrich Vieweg & Sohn.

Chapter 7

Dangerous Memes;
or, What the Pandorans Let Loose

Susan Blackmore

Cultural evolution is a dangerous child for any species to let loose on its world. And the parent species, whatever it is like and wherever it arises, will have no insight into what it has done until its offspring is already grown and making its way in the world. By then it is too late to take it back. So I shall call this motherly species "Pandoran," after the mythical first Greek woman whose box released all the evils of mankind. We humans are Earth's Pandorans, and have let loose cultural evolution; but on other planets quite different creatures might be playing this role.

Opening such a box of tricks can even be lethal, and I suspect that there are several danger points. The first critical step occurs when one species becomes capable of behavioral imitation, or of some other process that makes copying with variation and selection possible. This creates a new replicator, making the evolution of culture inevitable. This is the first danger point, because the newly created culture—the spreading of copied behaviors and the competition to mix, match, and make more—can get out of hand. Some of the behaviors may be so extravagant, or expensive, or dangerous, that they kill off their Pandorans and so obliterate themselves as well. This kind of waste is all part of how evolution works. Indeed natural selection might be called "design by death" because of all the billions of creations that have to die in spawning innovation and success for a few.

If this first danger point is passed, the Pandorans and their newly spawned culture may begin to adapt to each other, and coevolve towards a more symbiotic relationship, as diseases and their hosts sometimes do. If this succeeds, the result may be a stable mutualism that lasts indefinitely. Alternatively, with enough time and under the right conditions, another step might be taken. That is, new mechanisms for copying, varying, and selecting information could evolve outside of the Pandorans themselves, leading to a second danger point. For example, here on Earth, humans invented printing, sound recording and photography, vast communication networks, broadcasting, and the Internet. These are all methods of selective copying, which means a new evolutionary step and this creates a second danger point. As the copying increases, the thirst for innovation that's unleashed can be a drain not only on the Pandorans who started it but on their whole environment as well. This is what has happened here on Earth, with the consequent overpopulation and technological explosion threatening the health and climate of the entire planet.

This danger point could be safely passed, or it might prove fatal. We don't yet know what the outcome will be here on Earth; it could go either way. However, our sample of one planet does at least allow us to think about the general picture and speculate about what might happen on other planets elsewhere in the cosmos.

I like to imagine a vast universe containing many planets which have conditions suitable for life to evolve. On some of those planets a species evolves that is capable of copying what others do, thus unleashing this second evolutionary process. Among those planets, some survive the danger point and some do not, with the successful ones going on to spawn further evolutionary steps and face further danger points. On this picture, what should we expect to see around us? I would like to explore what might be out there on the basis of this memetic way of thinking about cultural evolution. I shall first explain a little about memes, meme theory, and the importance of replicators, and then consider some of the possible fates of planets that give birth to multiple replicators as ours has done.

The Science of Memes

Memetics is rooted in Universal Darwinism—the idea that natural selection is a general process of which Earthly biology is just one example. Working from his detailed observations of living things, Darwin saw what very few people had ever seen before even though the process is always staring us right in the face. That is, if creatures vary, and if they have to compete for resources so that most of the variants die, and if the successful variants pass on to their offspring whatever it is that helped them survive, then the offspring must be better adapted to the environment in which all this happened than their parents were. Repeat that cycle of copying, varying, and selecting, and design must appear out of nowhere.

My favorite word in that description is "must." This "must" is what makes Darwin's insight the most beautiful in all of science. You take a simple three step algorithm and find that the emergence of design for function is inevitable. Dan Dennett calls it "a scheme for creating Design out of Chaos without the aid of Mind" (Dennett 1995, 50). This is "Darwin's Dangerous Idea" that the algorithmic level is the level that best accounts for the wonders of nature; that all the fantastic and beautiful creatures in the world are produced by lots and lots of tiny steps in a mindless and mechanical algorithm.

The whole process can look like magic—like getting something for nothing—but it isn't. It is not possible to get matter out of nowhere, but it is possible to get information, or new patterns of matter, apparently out of nowhere by making copies. If the copies vary slightly and not all the copies survive, then the survivors must have something that helped them win the competition—using Darwin's term, they are more "fit"; they make a better fit to their environment. Then they pass on this advantage to the next generation of copies. And so it goes on.

This is the fundamental idea that Richard Dawkins explained in his 1976 book *The Selfish Gene*. He emphasised the importance of thinking about evolution in terms of information rather than squishy living creatures, and he called the information that is copied the replicator. In fact "replicator" is not a very good name, implying that it is the thing that does the replicating rather than being the thing that is replicated, (perhaps "replicatee" would be better) but "replicator" is what it is called and I will stick with that here; the concept is more important than the name.

For Dawkins it was a general law, "the law that all life evolves by the differential survival of replicating entities." (1989, 192); a "view of life . . . that applies to living things everywhere in the universe. The fundamental unit, the prime mover of all life, is the replicator." (1989, 264) With this view he wanted "to claim almost limitless power for slightly inaccurate self-replicating entities, once they arise anywhere in the universe." (1989, 322).

From the perspective of this general law, genes are only one example of a replicator. So we might expect them to show both characteristics that are true of all replicators everywhere in the universe, and features that depend on the idiosyncrasies of evolution here on Earth. Dawkins wanted to explore the general principles as well as the specifics. Indeed, he became quite frustrated with the way his colleagues tended to think about evolution as though it were inevitably and always a matter of genes. So at the end of the book he asked his now famous question "do we have to go to distant worlds to find other kinds of replicator and other, consequent, kinds of evolution?" (1989,

192). His answer was, of course, no. Staring us in the face, "still drifting clumsily about in its primeval soup" (1989, 192), is a new replicator; tunes, ideas, catch-phrases, fashions, and ways of making things are all spread from person to person by imitation. They vary and they are selected. These are the new replicators— the memes.

There is nothing mythical or hypothetical about memes, and this point is frequently misunderstood. Some people seem to imagine that memes are some kind of abstract entity that might, or might not, live inside brains, or that might, or might not, really exist (Aunger 2000). This is to miss the point that everything we copy in culture is a meme, by definition. So the words I am writing now, the picture on the cover of this book, the practice of making books like this, and making paper and ink and glue this way, are all memes. As Dennett (2006) points out, there is nothing mythical about words printed on a page, or even spoken words or recorded and broadcast words. Indeed Darwin referred to "The survival or preservation of certain favoured words in the struggle for existence" as a kind of natural selection (Darwin 1871, 61). There is nothing hypothetical about kids listening to iPods, wearing pre-torn jeans, or putting pieces of metal through their ears and noses after seeing others do the same. There is no question about the existence of financial institutions, money, railways, bicycles, telephones, furniture, skyscrapers, holiday brochures, football, or the days of the week. They are all information; they are all encoded in some kind of matter and energy; and they can all be copied or not. So think of memes this way. Their core definition is "that which is imitated" or that which is copied. They are all around us.

There is no question, then, that memes exist, for unless you deny that anything is ever copied from person to person, they must. The real question is whether thinking about culture in terms of replicators and memes is useful or not (Laland and Odling-Smee 2000). I am convinced that it is, or at least that it can be. Already, considerable progress has been made in identifying the problems, clarifying the issues, and beginning some empirical investigations. For example, there have been constructive arguments about how to define memes (Aunger 2000; Blackmore 2001), whether they should be thought of as units or not (Sperber 2006; Wimsatt 1999) and whether they should be considered as inside or outside of human brains (Aunger 2000; Benzon 1996; Distin 2005). Particularly interesting areas of debate concern the extent to which behaviors are reconstructed rather than imitated (Jablonka and Lamb 2005; Sperber 2006) and whether memes are truly replicators or not (Blackmore 2001; Richerson and Boyd 2005). Then there are empirical investigations of, for example, replicating text (Pocklington and Best 1997) and memes in translation (Wright 2000), applications in sociology (Runciman 1998) and musicology (Jan 2007), and attempts to simulate and model memetic processes (Bull et al. 2000; Higgs 2000; Kendall and Laland 2000).

These are all promising signs but it remains true to say that there is currently no thriving science of memetics. It is, at best, a tiny area with a few enthusiastic proponents. The reasons for this are not clear. Some people seem simply to be afraid of the whole idea of memes. This baffles me. When I gave my first ever lecture on memes at the London School of Economics in 1996, I mentioned that the word "meme" is often printed with scare quotes, and that I had even seen lecturers putting up their hands up round their ears in stylised scare quote fashion when daring to mouth the word "meme." More than a decade later I am sorry to find that I am still seeing this bizarre behavior. Why? Is memetics really so scary? Possibly it is. Among the ideas that upset people are that all "our" ideas are recombinations and adaptations of other people's, that all creativity comes from the evolutionary algorithm and not from the magic of human consciousness (Blackmore 2007a; Chater 2005), that our inner conscious selves may be memeplexes created by and for the memes (Blackmore 1999), that free will is an illusion, that modern computing technology is creating itself using us, and that the process of memetic evolution is not under our control (Blackmore 1999; Dennett 1995). These implications may be scary, but it is far from certain that they do all follow from a memetic view of evolution. In any case, being frightening is not a good test of the truth or falsity of a theory.

Among other reasons, some social scientists brand all evolutionary approaches to their subject "reductionist," and reject memetics along with sociobiology and evolutionary psychology (Bloch 2000) while some biologists want to keep Darwinism exclusively for their own field and so reject its application to culture (Rose and Rose 2000).

More interesting here are those who accept that culture evolves but still reject memetics. This may be either because they reject the whole idea of replicators as the driving force in evolution, or because they deny that memes are replicators. Wilson famously argued that "genetic natural selection operates in such a way as to keep culture on a leash." (Lumsden and Wilson 1981, 13). On his theory and related theories of gene-culture coevolution, the cultural variants (culturgens) are not independent evolving entities but are part of the human phenotype and are an adaptation that benefits human genes.

Branching out from purely genetic evolution, Jablonka and Lamb (2005) explore epigenetic and other evolutionary systems, but they do not accept that "the dreaded memes" (2005, 224) are replicators, and claim memetics is "seductively simple" but flawed (2005, 208). Richerson and Boyd (2005), whose theory of cultural evolution is arguably closest to memetics, do sometimes use the term "meme" but they clearly state that "cultural variants are not replicators," "[c]ulture is on a leash, all right," even if the dog on the end is big and clever, and "[c]ulture is an adaptation." In other words, culture was adaptive for human genes, it evolved for that reason, and it has persisted for that reason—in spite of including some maladaptive elements. In this respect they still illustrate Dawkins's complaint about his 1970s colleagues that "[i]n the last analysis they wish always to go back to 'biological advantage.'" (Dawkins 1976, 193).

This reveals the fundamental difference between all other theories of gene-culture coevolution and memetics: for the former the final arbiter is genetic advantage so that culture must always remain on its leash, even if the leash sometimes gets very loose; for memetics both genes and memes have replicator power and can drive change and creativity. For other theories, cultural traits are an aspect of the human phenotype, but for memetics they are living things in their own right.

These include a vast range of memeplexes (coadapted complexes of memes) that are copied, stored, and propagated by their human hosts using a wide variety of adaptations. All these, according to Humphrey, "should be regarded as living structures, not just metaphorically but technically." (Dawkins 1989, 192).

Some survive predominantly because they are useful to their hosts (e.g., effective financial institutions, scientific theories, or useful technologies); others depend on fulfilling human desires and preferences (e.g., the arts, music, and literature); and still others are positively harmful, tricking their hosts into propagating them. We humans are selective imitation devices (Blackmore 2001); we try to select only the useful or valuable memes but are inevitably tricked by some of the rest.

Popular examples of the tricksters are informational viruses, such as chain letters, e-mail viruses, and pyramid schemes. These reveal the classic viral structure; an instruction to copy the whole memeplex, backed up with threats and promises to ensure compliance. Dawkins (1993) pointed out that the major religions of the world have just this structure. Billions of people all over the world are infected with a religion at an early age when they have little memetic immunity, usually by their own parents whom they love and trust. They then spend the rest of their lives paying the price of adherence to false beliefs, and in turn infect others. Thus we can see the whole history of religions as an evolutionary competition for the replication of information. What matters here is not specifically whether the ideas are true, or whether believing them benefits their carriers (although both of these may play a role), but whether the religion can successfully get itself stored and replicated using humans as its meme machines. The winners are those that outdo the competition by developing adaptations such as enjoyable rituals, memorable stories, glorious art and music, explanations for life's mysteries (whether true or not), or nasty meme tricks such as threats of hell, and death to the infidel. The religions we see surviving around us today are the few big winners in that long and mindless competition to infect human minds.

There have been ferocious debates about this way of looking at religions, with opponents arguing that God is not a virus (Bowker 1995; McGrath 2007), evidence accumulating that religions do not improve societies' health (Paul 2005) and arguments that faith itself is harmful (Dennett 2006; Harris 2006). Sadly, there has been little in the way of meme-based empirical studies of religions and belief, which is badly needed if memetics is to thrive.

The value of memetics may also be judged by its theoretical contribution to understanding human evolution here on Earth and the reasons why humans alone have acquired complex and evolving culture. In trying to explain human uniqueness many different critical turning points have been suggested such as the acquisition of tools, the evolution of language, increasing group size, or crossing the "symbolic threshold" (Deacon 1997; Dunbar 1996; Mithen 1996). All these theories have in common the familiar assumption that genes are the final arbiter, and that "adaptive" means adaptive for genes or for the organisms carrying those genes.

By contrast memetics claims that the turning point in human evolution was the advent of imitation. Indeed it is imitation that makes us human (Blackmore 2007b). Once early hominids could imitate well enough, they let loose a new replicator and, because of this, their evolution shifted to an entirely new phase.

What does "well enough" mean? As a general principle, replicators are more effective when they are copied with high fidelity (accuracy of copying), fecundity (number of copies made), and longevity (lifetime of the copies) (Dawkins 1976). So we can imagine imitation becoming good enough to set the new evolutionary process going, and then memes competing so that those of higher fidelity, fecundity, and longevity increase in the newly growing memepool. From that point on, humans alone are the product of two replicators, not just one. As Dawkins put it "[o]nce this new evolution begins, it will in no necessary sense be subservient to the old." (1989, 193–194).

This flowering of a new replicator was what I explored in *The Meme Machine*, leading to a completely new way of understanding how humans came to have such unique features as their excessively large brain; true language; extensive tool use; a love of music, art, and religion; and complex culture. I argued that, by a process of "memetic drive," memes changed the environment in which human genes were selected and so drove genes to produce ever-larger brains that were better at imitating the currently successful memes. In this way our brains became selective imitation devices, adapted to copying some kinds of memes more easily than others (Blackmore 2001).

A good example here is the evolution of language—long a highly contentious issue with many competing theories (Dunbar 1996; Pinker 1994, 2007). On this memetic view language, like art and all of culture, is not seen as an adaptation of benefit to humans and their genes, but as a parasite turned symbiont. Indeed, all of cultural evolution is seen as happening for the benefit of the memes and in spite of posing a threat to humans and their genes. The human genes did, however, survive but the creature that was once their vehicle (i.e., the human body) gradually turned into a better and better copying machine for the new replicator—the memes. That is how we humans became such effective meme machines.

Like Dawkins and Dennett, I am convinced that treating memes as replicators is the way to understand human uniqueness and our evolutionary origins. Furthermore, I think it allows us to speculate about how similar replicators may have evolved on other planets and what this might mean for cultural evolution in the cosmos.

A Universe of Replicators

We are able to ask the question "are we alone in the universe?" because our distant ancestors began to imitate, and therefore created memes and language. We are able to contemplate communicating with other worlds because our more recent ancestors invented new copying machines and therefore let loose more replicators.

In all my previous work in memetics, I have deliberately used the term "meme" to apply to any information that is copied between people, or between people and artefacts such as books or computers. I have often wondered whether "artificial" memes such as Web sites and high-tech goods deserve a different name from "natural" human memes such as spoken words, skills, music, art, and religions, but have never found any principled way of distinguishing them. So on the grounds that a false distinction is worse than none, I have stuck to the term "meme" throughout. However, being asked to write about memes in the cosmos has forced me to think about this more deeply and to conclude that there is indeed an important transition from memes copied by human brains to information copied by technology other than human brains. These "technological memes" are riding on top of both genes and memes to form a new layer of evolution. I'd like to call them "temes."

The justification is this: replicators do not evolve on their own but coevolve with the machinery that replicates them. In the case of Earth's first-level replicator, DNA, we have only a sketchy understanding of its origins (Maynard Smith and Szathmáry 1995) but we now see an exquisitely coadapted system of DNA and cellular copying machinery on which most living things on Earth depend. These living things can be thought of as the "vehicles," or gene machines, that carry the genes around and protect them (Dawkins 1976), or as the "interactors" that interact with the environment to produce differential effects on gene replication (Hull 1988). In the case of human evolution, those vehicles eventually became the copying machinery for a new replicator, memes. Could it then be that the memes will do the same—building themselves meme-vehicles that in turn become the copying machinery for a new kind of replicator, temes? I suggest that this is what is happening all around us now.

The emergence of a new replicator is probably always a complicated and messy process (as it must have been with both of the first two levels), but we may discern some important steps indicating a new transition. When humans invented writing about five thousand years ago, it increased the longevity of memes as compared with speech, and so new written memes spread along with the skill of making them. But the process still required human hands to do the copying and human brains to select which texts to copy and distribute. When printing was invented just a few hundred years ago this increased both the fidelity and the fecundity because many copies could be made quickly. It also shifted the copying from human hands to the printing presses, but human meme machines still did the selection. Subsequently, new technologies have increased the fidelity, fecundity, and longevity in many new ways. For example, communications systems spread memes over longer distances, and broadcasting increases the number of copies sent out; sound and image recording systems raise longevity by storing previously ephemeral information; and new technologies raise fidelity enormously by making the shift from analogue to digital recording. The systems that do this are increasingly copying, storing, and propagating information without human help and at some point (which may never be precisely pinned down) they deserve the new name of "teme machines."

I said that these technologies are copying, storing, and propagating temes, but arguably the most significant shift is only now getting under way when the processes of variation and selection, as well as those of copying and storage, move from human meme machines to the new teme machines. This was hardly happening at all in the mid-1970s when Dawkins invented the idea of memes, but it is happening faster and faster now, just a few decades later.

We can see this in the invention of the World Wide Web and the search engines that are essential to its use. We should remember how recent this is, and how few people (if any) realized the significance of search engines when they first appeared. Now we take them for granted and assume that if we want to know something the whole of the Web is at our fingertips. Their significance here is that they are beginning to shift the job of selection of information from human brains to teme machines. For most searches, a human still chooses what to search for, but the results of that search are determined by numerous previous searches and other aspects of the stored information; there are increasingly many ways in which software does the selection rather than people. There are also sites that can write an essay by selecting and recombining bits of old essays; the same can be done with poetry or prose. Then there are evolutionary algorithms used to solve problems in engineering, medicine, or robotics.

Are these systems true teme machines? If they carry out all three of the essential processes of copying, varying, and selecting information outside of human control then perhaps they are, but at the moment these processes tend not to be bound together into something like a single organism. For example, books don't carry around their own printing presses, and cars don't carry around production lines; yet biological organisms do carry their own replicating machinery around inside them. Why? This is perhaps the same question that Dawkins (1982) pondered when, in *The Extended Phenotype*, he asked why life is packaged into organisms at all. If the answers from biology can be generalized, we might expect future teme machines to have all three processes built into them.

This relates to a question that has caused a lot of trouble for memetics: whether memes have the equivalent of a phenotype-genotype distinction. In biological evolution, genes are not directly selected. Instead, they act as instructions for building bodies—their vehicles or interactors—whose properties are the phenotype. These phenotypic properties are (at least in large part) determined by genes and in turn determine whether those genes are passed on again or not. This is a highly effective system because errors in building the phenotype are not passed on in the genotype. Dennett (1995) describes it as a system for retaining the "good tricks" that selection stumbles upon, and Dawkins (1982) emphasises the design value of a "return to the drawing board" in each generation.

Superficially, memes may not appear to work this way and some critics have argued that this disanalogy between genes and memes is a reason for rejecting memetics (McGrath 1995; Midgley 2000; Wimsatt 1999). For example, when people pick up a new saying, or hear a tune or story and pass it on, they copy what they have heard. In this case there is no obvious genotype/phenotype distinction or replicator/vehicle separation (Aunger 2000). But if someone copies the recipe for making a new kind of figgy pudding, then it is easy enough to see the written recipe as a "memotype" and the resulting pudding as the "phemotype"; the analogy is quite close because if Frederick makes a nasty mess of his pudding but passes the recipe on to Frances, Frances does not have to follow Frederick's mistakes. But what if Frances watches him pick the figs, whip up the mixture, and set the oven? Then the distinction is gone (Blackmore 1999). Some memeticists have tried to work with a memotype/phemotype distinction (Benzon 1996; Speel 1997), but this has not been widely adopted and can be very confusing.

I suggest that a better way to understand what is happening is this: any system that copies the instructions for making a product is better than one that copies the product itself (Blackmore 1999). The gene/vehicle distinction is precisely that: a system for copying instructions (genes) for making living things (vehicles). However, such systems have to evolve over time. In biology we are seeing one that is billions of years old and has long ago achieved this distinction. But when we turn to memes, they are at most a few million years old, and we see a system still in flux. In some cases a distinction has appeared, and very effective it is, too, but in other cases it has not.

Think of music. Some people do listen to others singing or playing and then copy the sounds directly, and in this case there is no replicator/vehicle distinction. But most music is now produced in recording studios and then copied in factories onto various media, ending up being listened to in homes, or via phones, MP3 players, and other personal music systems. The information on a CD or music file is instructions to create the pattern of sounds. When someone hears the music they don't copy it directly but go and buy it or download it from somewhere else. So this is all copy-the-instructions, and the CDs and digital players are meme vehicles.

The same applies to cars, clothes, fridges, furniture, and almost all the household goods we take for granted. Almost no one sees a table they like and then goes out and cuts down a tree to make one like it from scratch. Instead they go and buy a similar, or even identical, one that has been produced from the same factory line as the one they first saw. If lots of people buy a particular model of car then the factory makes more from the production line it already had. It does not copy the ones already out on the streets.

Applying this idea we can now see that technological evolution is rapidly making the shift from copy-the-product to copy-the-instructions for making a product. This is not because there is any inherent goal for the process or any designer making it happen, but because better replicators overtake poorer ones, and better replicating machinery takes over from poorer machinery. If downloading digital files from the Internet produces more, more accurate, and more easily copied music than records, tapes, and CDs, then digital files will take over. It's as simple as that.

Another important shift is also taking place. Much of our technology is designed merely to store memes (such as books, CDs, and so on) but increasingly also to copy them. If the analysis here is correct, then this is a critical step in the evolution of temes. That is, the meme vehicles we have created become replication machinery for the next level of replicator. This is equivalent to the step that occurred when hominid gene machines began imitating and so became replication machinery for memes.

For now, we Earthly Pandorans are still needed for various stages in the copying and selecting of temes, but teme machines are very rapidly evolving and it may not be long before there are self-repairing computer systems, self-maintaining power stations, artificial systems for choosing which new technology to build and which to ignore, and all the processes of replication will be shifted out of the hands of humans and into the world of teme machines. At this point, the temes could carry on even if the Pandorans all died out. We are not at that point yet, but it is interesting to wonder whether we will get there before we wipe ourselves out or not.

With this sketch of how replicators on Earth have been doing, we can now move on to consider the general case of replicators anywhere in the cosmos.

Extraterrestrial memes

Who is out there in the rest of the cosmos? Are there lots of other cultures that have evolved in completely different ways from ours? Are there lots of civilizations potentially capable of communicating with us? Or are we all alone?

These questions have been asked often enough, but in trying to answer them most people have been searching for "extraterrestrial intelligence" and so, I suggest, have got the emphasis wrong from the start. From what I have said so far it will be clear that I want to put the emphasis elsewhere, on how replicators arise, and what happens when one kind of replicating entity builds on the products of the previous one. From this perspective, intelligence is a product of replicator power, not its precursor: it is not intelligence, per se that forces a great leap forward in living creatures or creates the possibility of culture, but the appearance of a second-level replicator. This second replicator creates an environment in which greater intelligence is adaptive. Intelligence therefore increases, helping to provide a situation in which a third-level of replicator can arise. This third level entails the creation of replicating machinery outside of any original Pandoran species, a crucial step towards interplanetary communication, and so towards the possibility of others communicating with us.

In 1961, the astrophysicist Frank Drake came up with his famous equation for estimating the number of intelligent civilizations in our galaxy capable of communicating with us (Drake and Sobel 1992). He never intended his equation to provide quick answers, but rather to stimulate discussion and to direct research towards the important factors involved. In the same spirit, I would like to suggest a different equation. Like Drake's it describes the number of intelligent civilizations in our galaxy capable of communicating with us, but it begins with a guess at the number of planets in our galaxy, ignores intelligence, and concentrates on the appearance of replicators. This equation is

$$N = n \times f_{R1} \times f_{R2} \times f_{R3} \times L$$

where N = the number of intelligent civilizations in our galaxy capable of communicating with us

n = the number of planets in our galaxy

f_{R1} = the fraction of planets in n where a first-level replicator survives

f_{R2} = the fraction of planets with R1 where a second-level replicator survives

f_{R3} = the fraction of planets with R2 where a third-level replicator survives

L = the fraction of a planet's life for which a third-level replicator persists

We know far too little to make sensible guesses about the values of most of these fractions. Even so, the equation provides a useful structure for thinking about the possibilities. I guess that the emergence of each new level of replicator marks a danger point at which the new replicator may simply fail, may wipe out the next level down, or may wipe out all previous levels. If this is right, we can now make some further guesses about what may be happening elsewhere.

No Replicators

We don't know whether "replicating entities" are necessary, sufficient, or both for life. If we assume both, then all those planets that do not have the conditions in which replicators can arise must remain lifeless and therefore cultureless. Conceivably, there are ways in which culture could appear that don't depend on replicators, or on individual organisms constructed by replicators, but if so I do not know how.

The First-Level Replicator R1

Possibilities: R1 emerges and fails

R1 emerges and sustains life

The first level of replicator is the one that makes some form of life possible. This might have evolved from an even simpler replicating substance (e.g., a cheme [Szathmáry 1999]) or begun as a naked replicator (such as a simple self-copying molecule) before evolving to construct some kind of packaging or vehicle to protect and propagate it. I will say little about this first stage because it has been the subject of so much research and debate. Nevertheless, it is clear that there are probably a large number of planets in our galaxy capable of sustaining a first-level replicator that creates living things. These living things might be very different from any on Earth. They might live under seas, within the solid mass of their planet, in an atmosphere of some kind, or they might roam on the surface. Conceivably, they might appear on asteroids or interstellar particles. The way they develop will make it more or less likely that a second replicator will emerge.

It is curious that almost all life on Earth depends on DNA and uses the same (or small variations on the same) code for translating stored information into instructions for protein synthesis. Whether it is possible to have multiple replication systems operating side by side, or whether one inevitably defeats all competitors, I do not know.

Second-Level Replicator

Possibilities: R2 emerges in Pandoran species but fails

R2 emerges and kills Pandorans

R2 emerges, coevolves with Pandorans, and sustains culture

A second-level replicator, R2, is one that emerges from a living thing created by a first-level replicator. That is, R1 builds vehicles, and those vehicles become the copying machinery for R2, copying a different kind of information with variation and selection.

This brings us to where I began this chapter, with the idea that acquiring a second replicator is a dangerous step. This is because the new replicator (precisely because it is a replicator) will multiply selfishly. Since there is so much misunderstanding over the term "selfish replicator," I will just explain that this does not mean that genes or memes or temes have plans, desires, or intentions; it means only that their ability to multiply whenever conditions are right means that they exert replicator power regardless of the effect this has on anything else. This is all they can do for they are just information mindlessly undergoing replication.

The danger is much like that of a parasite infecting a host. Conventional parasites are built on the same replicator as their hosts, while R2 parasites use a new replicator, but the principles may be similar, as may the possible outcomes.

First, R2 may emerge but never really take hold. This might happen if, for example, its effects on individual Pandorans are so harmful that individuals that acquire the copying ability die out, leaving ordinary Pandorans to prevail. Or it might happen if the conditions on the planet do not provide a sufficient advantage to R2 for it to thrive. On Earth it seems that if environmental conditions change slowly then new skills are best dealt with by R1 (assimilated into the genome), if they change fast each individual is better to learn new skills for itself (individual learning). Only when individual learning is too costly and the environment neither too variable nor too stable is imitation worthwhile (Richerson and Boyd 2005). Once copying is underway, it must be of sufficiently high fidelity, and there must be enough individuals capable of it for R2 to take off. If these principles generally hold true then there may be planets where R2 appears but never thrives. There may even be planets where this happens many times either in series or in parallel.

Second, R2 may begin to proliferate but then prove to be lethal. It could be that the new ability to replicate information is so energy-intensive that the Pandorans' resources are exhausted. It could be that the things copied (behaviors, signals, chemicals, or whatever) become lethal. Or it could be that R2 begins to transform the Pandorans into better R2 machines and this transformation proves lethal.

Here on Earth, the dangers of R2 included the high-energy requirements of building and sustaining a very large brain, and the danger of death during childbirth for a species that walks upright and therefore needs a narrow pelvis. Conventional theories attribute the increase in human brain size to tool use, the acquisition of language, or other adaptations of benefit to human genes, but I have argued that it was meme driven and therefore potentially dangerous (Blackmore 1999). In other words, the acquisition of memes could have killed us off.

Third, if this danger point is passed, R2 can become established on its planet. To do this R2 must adapt to R1 and vice versa. In other words, the two replicators must coevolve. This may be a kind of arms race with the R1

Pandorans striving to survive and multiply copies of R1, while R2 strives to transform the Pandorans into better machinery for multiplying R2. If the poor Pandorans are not wiped out by this process then they become simultaneously R1 machines and R2 machines (more specifically, they remain R1 vehicles while becoming R2 replicating machines). The information they copy itself evolves and this is what we call culture.

This whole process is analogous to coevolution between parasites and their hosts. So what determines whether a parasite will kill its host or will coevolve to become symbiotic? There is evidence from disease pathogens that when transmission is horizontal the parasite is more dangerous than when transmission is vertical (down the generations) (Maynard Smith and Szathmáry 1995). This is interesting with respect to a second-level replicator such as memes. For example, it seems likely that early memetic transmission was mostly vertical, within families, and probably remained largely so during most of human evolution which may be relevant to the fact that we survived. But now transmission is increasingly horizontal between peers rather than from parents to their children, and may be correspondingly more dangerous.

Another interesting question is whether it is possible for different kinds of R2 to appear at once on the same planet resulting in multiple kinds of culture. Here on Earth, human brains are the only ones to have been turned into meme machines, and humans have the only significant culture. There is simple cultural transmission in songbirds, cetaceans, and chimpanzees (Whiten et al. 1999) but not the kind of cumulative culture that marks a fully evolving new replicator. This is reminiscent of the fact that DNA has close to a monopoly as Earth's R1, and prompts speculation as to whether there might be a general principle here. It seems plausible that if two second-level replicators appear at once, they will compete and the winner will take all. This might even be the reason for the curious fact that we humans are the only remaining species in the hominid line. Perhaps Neanderthals and other related species also embarked on an R2 transformation but either their R2 proved lethal (perhaps through forcing their heads to become too large for safe childbirth or through copying dangerous traditions) or they competed directly with early humans and lost. This is no more than speculation but might just prove interesting by prompting new hypotheses about what happened in hominid evolution and what might happen elsewhere in the cosmos.

Returning to the possibilities for an R2 planet, the direction of cultural evolution will depend on the kind of species in which that culture first emerged, how much scope there is for transforming that species into an efficient R2 machine, whether the species has limbs suitable for constructing rich material culture, and what material resources there are available for such construction. The general principle will apply throughout that replicators of high fidelity, fecundity, and longevity will prevail. This is likely to result in such innovations as communication systems, behavioral traditions, education, symbolic culture, tools, and buildings. As the culture goes on evolving, it may produce analogues of writing (because it increases longevity), long-range communications systems (because they increase fecundity), and digitization of information (because it increases fidelity). Gradually these may, depending on conditions, create signals detectable far from the home planet itself, but this only becomes a serious possibility once the way is already paved for the emergence of a third-level replicator.

Third-Level Replicator

A third-level replicator, R3, is one that emerges from vehicles built by R1 and R2. More specifically, level 2 replicators build vehicles to protect and propagate themselves, and those vehicles become the copying machinery for a third level of replicator. On Earth, this is occurring as memes (R2) use humans (R1 vehicles and R2 replicating machines) to build R2 vehicles and these become machinery for copying temes (R3).

The possibilities with three replicators multiple rapidly, and we have little to go on when looking at our single planet for clues. So I will not speculate much further but confine myself to sketching out some of the more obvious possibilities. A few such possibilities if R3 takes hold are listed in Table 1.

The first (disaster) scenario is one that may yet happen here on Earth: that is, R3 gets beyond the control of its Pandorans, irreparably damages its planet, and so obliterates all life as well as itself. This could happen through overuse of resources, by causing drastic climate change, or by nuclear or other accidents. A second, slightly less drastic, outcome is that a planet's Pandorans all die but other life-forms survive and can then begin the evolutionary process all over again. This is perhaps a more likely outcome here on Earth given

Table 1.

#	Outcome	Remaining Replicators
1	R3 wipes out all of R1, R2 and R3	0
2	R3 kills R2 and its Pandorans; the rest of R1 survives	R1
3	R3 wipes out R2, but still survives	R1, R3
4	R3 emerges and coevolves along with R1 and R2	R1, R2, R3
5	R3 machines merge with R2 machines	R1 R2/3
6	R4 emerges from R3	?

the widespread presence, variety, and resilience of DNA-based life, especially bacteria and insects.

A third possibility is that R3 coevolves with earlier replicators for long enough to get to the point where it does not need them any more, e.g., by creating self-repairing and self-replicating R3 machines. It might then alter its planet's atmosphere, climate, or resources in such a way that R2 and the Pandorans die out but the R3 systems survive.

If disasters like this are avoided, the earlier replicators might survive in several ways. As a fourth example, a stable symbiosis might be reached with all three replicators coexisting. We have all three on Earth now, but this is very recent and already serious dangers are apparent. So it is impossible to judge how stable such a system is likely to be.

Even if a three-replicator system can survive, I suspect that there would be pressures for change. One change might be the merging of R2 with R3 machines. This is already happening here on Earth with the invention of neural implants and other prostheses and with the beginnings of the technology to create entirely artificial creatures based on DNA. This might be one way in which the descendents of earlier replicators might carry on in new forms.

Finally, there is the possibility of yet another level of replicator emerging. What would R4 be like? It is hard enough to speculate about R3, but my best guess is this: An R3 level culture might develop the machinery to copy itself and so to seed new variants of that culture on different planets. This would lead to competition between variant cultures, and the evolution across the cosmos of R4 level civilizations. If this happened, planets separated by large distances would play a role analogous to islands here on Earth—creating relatively isolated conditions in which cultures would evolve in different directions.

Note that the vehicles of earlier replicators, such as biological organisms, would not need to travel as long as adequate artificial vehicles had been built and could cope with the widely different conditions on different planets. If it occurred, this kind of colonization of the cosmos ought to be visible by its effects, and we have seen no evidence of it so far. Perhaps this is because, like all the previous transitions, the creation of a new level of replicator is dangerous.

Perhaps all the transitions I have discussed are incredibly dangerous and we Earthlings are lucky to have got through to the third replicator stage; perhaps the dangers are small, and the rest of the cosmos is teeming with systems we have failed to detect. We do not know. Indeed, we have no idea how to assess the values of any of the variables $f_{R1,}$ $f_{R2,}$ f_{R3}, or L but perhaps by thinking about evolution this way we Pandorans may see a little more clearly what sort of child we have let loose.

References

Aunger, R. A. 2000. Introduction to Aunger, R. A. (Ed) *Darwinizing Culture: The Status of Memetics as a Science.* Oxford University Press.

Benzon, W. 1996. "Culture as an evolutionary arena," *Journal of Social and Evolutionary Systems* 19:321–362.

Blackmore, S. J. 1999. *The Meme Machine.* Oxford: Oxford University Press.

Blackmore, S. 2001. Evolution and memes: "The human brain as a selective imitation device," *Cybernetics and Systems* 32:225–255.

Blackmore, S. 2007a. "Memes, minds and imagination," in *Imaginative Minds.* Ed. Ilona Roth. London: British Academy.

Blackmore, S. J. "Imitation makes us human," in *What makes us human?* Ed. Charles Pasternak, pp 1–16. Oxford: Oneworld.

Bloch, M. 2000. "A well-disposed social anthropologist's problems with memes," in R. Aunger (Ed.), *Darwinizing Culture: the status of memetics as a science.* Oxford; New York: Oxford University Press.

Bowker, J. 1995. *Is God a Virus?* London, SPCK.

Bull, L., Holland, O. and Blackmore, S. 2000. "On meme-gene coevolution," *Artificial Life* 6:227–235.

Chater, N. 2005. "Mendelian and Darwinian views of memes," In Hurley, S. and Chater, N. (Eds). *Perspectives on Imitation: From Neuroscience to Social Science* Vol. 2, pp. 355–362. MIT Press.

Darwin, C. 1871. *The Descent of Man and Selection in Relation to Sex.* London: John Murray.

Dawkins, R. 1976. *The Selfish Gene.* Oxford: Oxford University Press.

Dawkins, R. 1982. *The Extended Phenotype.* Oxford: Oxford University Press.

Dawkins, R. 1989. *The Selfish Gene.* Oxford: Oxford University Press (new edition with additional material).

Dawkins, R. 1993. "Viruses of the mind," in B. Dahlbohm (ed) *Dennett and his Critics: Demystifying Mind.* Oxford: Blackwell.

Deacon, T. 1997. *The Symbolic Species: The Co-evolution of Language and the Human Brain.* London: Penguin.

Dennett, D. 1995. *Darwin's Dangerous Idea.* London: Penguin.

Dennett, D. 2006. *Breaking the Spell: Religion as a natural phenomenon.*

Distin, K. 2005. *The Selfish Meme: A Critical Reassessment.* Cambridge: Cambridge University Press.

Drake, F. and Sobel, D. 1992. *Is anyone out there? the scientific search for extra-terrestrial intelligence.* Delacourt.

Dunbar, R. 1996. *Grooming, Gossip and the Evolution of Language.* London: Faber & Faber.

Harris, S. 2006. *The end of faith: Religion, terror, and the future of reason.* Free Press.

Higgs, P. G. 2000. "The mimetic transition: a simulation study of the evolution of learning by imitation," *Proceedings of the Royal Society London B.* 267:1355–1361.

Hull, D. L. 1988. "Interactors versus vehicles," in H. C. Plotkin (Ed.) *The Role of Behaviour in Evolution.* Cambridge, MA: MIT Press.

Jablonka, E. and Lamb, M. J. 2005. *Evolution in Four Dimensions: Genetic, Epigenetic, Behavioral and Symbolic Variation in the History of Life.* Bradford Books.

Jan, S. 2007. *The Memetics of Music: A neo-Darwinian view of musical structure and culture.* Aldershot, UK: Ashgate.

Kendal, J. R. and Laland, K. N. 2000. "Mathematical models for memetics," *Journal of Memetics* 4 (1). *http://jom-emit.cfpm.org/2000/vol4/kendal_jr&laland_kn.html.*

Laland, K. and Odling-Smee, J. 2000. "The evolution of the meme," In. R. A. Aunger (Ed) *Darwinizing Culture: The Status of Memetics as a Science*, pp. 121–141. Oxford University Press.

Lumsden, C. J. and Wilson, E. O. 1981. *Genes, Mind and Culture.* Cambridge, MA: Harvard University Press.

Maynard-Smith, J. and Szathmáry, E 1995. *The Major Transitions in Evolution.* Oxford: Freeman.

McGrath, A. 2007. *The Dawkins Delusion?: Atheist Fundamentalism and the Denial of the Divine.* London: SPCK.

Midgley, M. 2000. "Why memes?" In. H. Rose and S. Rose (Eds) *Alas, Poor Darwin*, pp. 67–84. London: Cape.

Mithen, S. 1996. *The Prehistory of the Mind.* London: Thames and Hudson.

Paul, G. S. 2005. "Cross-National Correlations of Quantifiable Societal Health with Popular Religiosity and Secularism in the Prosperous Democracies: A First Look," *Journal of Religion and Society* 7:1–17.

Pinker, S. 1994. *The Language Instinct.* New York: Morrow.

Pinker, S. 2007. *The stuff of thought: Language as a window into human nature.* New York: Viking.

Pocklington, R. and Best, M. L. 1997. "Cultural evolution and units of selection in replicating text," *Journal of Theoretical Biology* 188:79–87.

Richerson, P. J. and Boyd, R. 2005. *Not by Genes Alone: How culture transformed human evolution.* Chicago: University of Chicago Press.

Rose, H. and Rose, S., eds. 2000. *Alas, Poor Darwin.* London: Jonathan Cape.

Runciman, W. G. 1998. "Greek hoplites, warrior culture, and indirect bias," *Journal of the Royal Anthropological Institute* 4:731–751.

Speel, H. C. A. M. 1997. A short comment from a biologist on William Benzon's essay, "Culture as an Evolutionary Arena," *Journal of Social and Evolutionary Systems* 20 (3): 309–322.

Sperber, D. 2006. "Why a deep understanding of cultural evolution is incompatible with shallow psychology," in Nick Enfield and Stephen Levinson (eds.), *Roots of Human Sociality*, pp. 431–449.

Szathmáry, E. 1999. "Chemes, genes and memes: a revised classification of replicators," in C. L. Nehaniv (Ed.), *Mathematical and Computational Biology: Computational Morphogenesis, Hierarchical Complexity, and Digital Evolution. Lectures on Mathematics in the Life Sciences* 26:1–10.

Whiten, A., Goodall, J., McGrew, W. C., Nishida, T., Reynolds, V., Sugiyama, Y., Tutin, C. E. G., Wrangham, R. W. and Boesch, C. 1999. "Cultures in chimpanzees," *Nature* 399:682–685.

Wimsatt, W. 1999. "Genes, Memes and Cultural Heredity," *Biology and Philosophy* 14:279–310.

Wright, D. 2000. *Translating Science: The Transmission of Western Chemistry into late Imperial China, 1840–1900.* Brill: Leiden.

Part 3

Cosmos and Culture

Chapter 8

Cosmocultural Evolution
The Coevolution of Culture and Cosmos and the Creation of Cosmic Value

Mark L. Lupisella

1. Introduction

Culture is something special. It has helped life on Earth, particularly *Homo sapiens*, survive and thrive in ways that sometimes defies belief. What human beings have created, what we are becoming, is utterly remarkable, inspiring, mind-blowing. But is it an illusion of sorts? Is culture merely an increasingly complex result of biologically driven self-interest, arising from the happenstance of life? Is it merely a blind walk (or run?) of replicating memes—the cultural equivalent of natural selection?[1]

While it may be true that much, if not all, culture might ultimately be explained directly and indirectly by Darwinian explanations of one sort or another, it may also be true that cultural evolution is beginning to break free of our biological heritage. Natural selection has been working on the experiment of life for close to 4 billion years on Earth, and what we witness now with human culture is so rich, so complex, so uncertain, that we have to wonder how it will evolve, and how it may be evolving elsewhere in the universe.

Other species on Earth arguably exhibit basic forms of culture, but those instances appear to be far less complex, and perhaps far less meaningful than what human beings experience. Our technology, art, and what we know of our world, is unspeakably exhilarating and terrifyingly dangerous. We are capable of powerful creations and complete annihilation. Our consciousness is uncontainable—to the point of agonizing awareness. *Homo sapiens sapiens* has a power unlike Earth has ever seen.

To some, this anthropocentric cheerleading will seem the worst sort of "speciesism"—a kind of blind, unethical delusion engendered by biologically driven affinities for one's own likeness. But exaltation of humanity in no way justifies unchecked devotion at the expense of others who inhabit our world and perhaps worlds beyond. Nevertheless, the evidence seems clear: human beings are running away with culture. And it may be running away with us. We get the prize—the Culture Prize. We deserve it. We've worked hard, made untold sacrifices. We are smart in a way no other animal is. And through us, if not others, the Culture Prize is bestowed upon the Cosmos.

It is in this context that I hope to 1) provide a basic framework for thinking about how culture and cosmos might relate—the primary notion being "cosmocultural evolution" and/or the Cosmocultural Principle; 2) briefly develop the notion of "bootstrapped cosmocultural evolution," including practical near- and longer-term implications; 3) suggest a long-term worldview, consistent with 1 and 2, that can be characterized as a morally creative cultural cosmos—a post-intelligent, post-technological universe that enters the realm of conscious evolution driven largely by moral and creative pursuits

1.1 Characterizing Culture

For the purposes of this essay, it will be helpful to think about culture as the *collective manifestation of value*—where value is that which is valuable to "sufficiently complex" agents, from which meaning, purpose, ethics, and aesthetics can be derived.[2] Culture manifests value in many varied forms, from thoughts and knowledge to symbolic abstractions to social norms to mass movements to large-scale physical creations. "Collective" is that which is shared, which suggests a) at least some degree of common interests, pursuits, or purposes among multiple agents, including future generations; and b) the transmission of information in space and time, including across generations—what might be thought of as a kind of collective memory (Bloom 2009, this volume). "Manifestation" suggests instantiation in the world—e.g., thoughts, behavior, and objects (including purely aesthetic objects) that are predominantly (but not exclusively) driven by some usefulness to agents—e.g., to perform a function, adapt, anticipate, and modify memory, information, and knowledge in order to more effectively pursue interests. "Sufficiently complex agents" implies beings with interests that are capable of complex autonomous behavior to pursue those interests. With this characterization of culture in mind, "cultural evolution" then is the variance of culture (as characterized above) over time.

There is much wiggle room in this characterization to accommodate a variety of perspectives about culture. For example, memetic perspectives of evolution may see mere replication as a manifested "value," but memes ("replicating cultural units" such as ideas, art, ways of doing things, etc.) would not necessarily be thought of as having autonomy in the sense of being able to consciously "choose" a behavior to ensure their replication, nor do memes have to be seen necessarily as providing usefulness to agents. "Sufficiently complex beings" also offers wiggle room in that it could include, for example, bacterial colony behavior (Bloom 2009, this volume). But if collective bacterial behavior were not thought to be sufficiently complex and/or sufficiently autonomous, it would not count as culture—whereas collective human behavior would seem to be far more complex and autonomous, and would hence be considered culture. However, it may not be important to make this a hard distinction. It may only be important to think of degrees of culture with bacterial colonies perhaps being examples of a basic form of culture. Human culture would be an example of what might be considered robust culture. It is primarily robust culture that is of interest for this essay.

---

2. Cosmic-Cultural Relationships and Cosmocultural Evolution

Here I hope to lay out a basic framework to help think about cultural evolution in a cosmic context. As shown in Figure 1, the relationships between culture and cosmos can be categorized as one-way and two-way relationships, where one-way relationships suggest that the cosmos is important for culture, but culture is not important for cosmos; and two-way relationships suggest that culture and cosmos are important for each other.

In one-way, or "unidirectional," relationships, the significance of culture for the universe is either none, negligible, minimal, and/or fundamentally limited—essentially a one-way street—the cosmos is important for culture, but not the reverse. The universe gives rise to and influences culture, but culture has little or no significance for the universe at large. In two-way relationships, the cosmos is important for culture, and culture is important for the cosmos. Culture having importance for the universe might be called "cosmocultural evolution," or the Cosmocultural Principle, suggesting that perhaps a sufficiently different kind of evolution is emerging—the coevolution of cosmos and culture, where culture plays an important and perhaps critical role. Strong versions of cosmocultural evolution could be interpreted to suggest that cultural evolution is in some sense "on par" with physical cosmic evolution. Stronger forms of cosmocultural evolution might imply that cultural evolution has unlimited potential and may ultimately be more important than physical cosmic evolution as it we've understood it so far.

I do not wish to make such a strong distinction between cosmic evolution and cultural evolution that they are thought of as so separate—cultural evolution is ultimately a part of cosmic evolution in the broad sense that culture has emerged as part of the physical evolution of the universe. But I do wish to make a distinction to the extent that it suggests culture is a different enough phenomenon from the rest of physical cosmic evolution and to the extent that it can help address the interesting question of how significant cultural evolution may be in a cosmic context.

The intent of the next section is not to define life or intelligence, nor to rigorously analyze and defend philosophies and worldviews. It is not intended to provide complete and definitive distinctions in all cases, but instead to broadly characterize potentially relevant perspectives and worldviews to help further convey the ways in which cosmos and culture can be seen to relate and to help form a framework for thinking about the significance of cultural evolution in a cosmic context. Many of the categorizations overlap and interrelate—some of which is explicitly noted, some of which is implied, but most of which is left to the reader to navigate with the help of what are hopefully useful guideposts.

2.1 Unidirectional Cosmic-Cultural Relationships

In unidirectional relationships, the cosmos is a source and driver of culture, but culture has little or no influence on, or importance for, the universe at large. Culture is strongly influenced by the universe in that it is informed, and ultimately limited, by physical laws and cosmological perceptions and realities. Human culture is imbued with a wide variety of imaginative and influential worldviews, literature, music, and other forms of culture that are directly and often profoundly influenced by cosmological perspectives—as explored by authors in this volume (Chaisson 2009; Palmeri 2009; Christian 2009; Vakoch 2009).

As shown in Figure 1, other broad characterizations of cosmic worldviews that would reflect unidirectional cosmic-cultural relationships might be

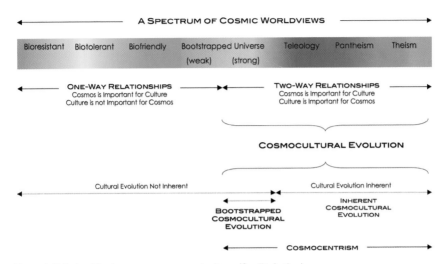

Figure 1. Relationships between cosmos and culture. (Credit: Author)

a bioresistant universe, a biotolerant universe, a biofriendly universe, and a weak bootstrapped universe.

2.1.1 Bioresistant Universe

A "bioresistant universe" worldview would suggest that life emerged against substantial odds in a hostile environment. Such a view implies the origin of life, and all that derives from it, is purely random and unlikely given the nature of the universe, and could imply very little or no cosmic significance for culture. A broadened version of this kind of worldview might also hold that the origin of the universe itself was essentially random, and that randomness is an important factor in the origin of the universe and for cosmic evolution in general. But even this kind of "accidental universe" worldview can't escape the fact that cosmology influences culture in an important way by influencing worldviews and constituting important pillars of scientific culture and all that implies for our broader culture. As shown in Figure 1, this bioresistant accidental universe may be seen to occupy one end of a spectrum of how culture can be viewed in the context of cosmic worldviews.

2.1.2 Biotolerant Universe

A "biotolerant universe" worldview would suggest that life is highly contingent in that laws of the universe are such that life, and perhaps eventually intelligence and culture, *may* originate under the proper, perhaps narrow, set of circumstances—e.g., the presence of liquid water, dynamic environment driving evolution, etc. The characteristics of the universe allow life to emerge, and perhaps intelligence to follow, but the universe's laws and constants are not such that life is an expected phenomenon. Life may arise periodically, and intelligence and culture may then arise from time to time (and perhaps even be numerous given the large number of potential environments for life and intelligence to evolve), but without any particular significance for the universe as a whole.

2.1.3 Biofriendly Universe

A "biofriendly universe" worldview suggests that the nature of the universe tends to produce life. Replication, self-organization, and life, arise easily as a result of the universe's laws and physical constants. An example of this kind of worldview might also be called a "biophysical cosmology" or "biological universe" worldview—a popular view based on both philosophical and scientific grounds that has been explored by a wide variety of philosophers and scientists (Dick 1996; Dick and Strick 2004). However, regardless of how predisposed the universe may be to produce life, a biofriendly universe need not necessarily produce culture. But because a biofriendly universe worldview would imply the ubiquity of life throughout the universe, advocates would also acknowledge that many instances of culture could also arise. Such instances might even be likely given the number of chances for life to arise throughout the universe, the variety of phenomena natural selection can produce over time, and the usefulness of intelligence and culture for survival (Dawkins 1986; Dennett 1995). But in such a view, the ubiquity of intelligence and culture, while noteworthy as a prevalent phenomenon, would not necessarily imply any particular cosmic significance for culture. Culture would be seen merely as a derivative of biological systems (or any agents with sufficient interests to create "culture") that are consequences of natural laws and physical constants—none of which has any particular significance, direction, or broader purpose for the universe as a whole. Indeed, while life may originate frequently throughout the universe, some views suggest that complex life and the origin of intelligence and culture could be so highly historically contingent as to be exceedingly rare (Gould 1989; Ward and Brownlee 2000).

2.1.4 Weak Bootstrapped Universe

A "weak bootstrapped" worldview would suggest that a) the universe has in some sense "bootstrapped" itself into the realm of value—meaning, purpose, ethics, aesthetics, etc.—via the emergence of life, intelligence, and culture; but that b) there is no broader significance of culture for the universe as a whole beyond having those "properties" emerge in the universe as a product of cosmic and biological evolution—however intellectually interesting that may be. The implications for such properties in the universe are primarily confined to cultural beings and perhaps valuing agents more generally. Figure 1 shows the weak bootstrapped universe worldview on the "one-way relationship" side of the spectrum. Nevertheless, as Figure 1 shows, the weak bootstrapped universe moves us closer to cosmocultural evolution.

2.2 Bidirectional Cosmic-Cultural Relationships: "Cosmocultural Evolution"

As noted previously, unidirectional cosmic-cultural relationships assume little or no significance for culture in a cosmic context. Bi-directional cosmic-cultural relationships suggest that cultural evolution could be important for the cosmos, have unlimited potential, be "on par" with, and perhaps ultimately be more important than, the rest of cosmic evolution—what might be called "cosmocultural evolution" and/or the Cosmocultural Principle. As shown in Figure 1, some broad categories of views that can be characterized in this context of cosmocultural evolution are a strong bootstrapped universe, teleology, pantheism, and theism.

2.2.1 Strong Bootstrapped Universe

The notion of a universe that bootstraps itself into the realm of value via cultural beings such as ourselves—however random its emergence may be—need not be confined to having minimal significance for the universe as suggested by a weak bootstrapped universe worldview. Not only can we assert that the mere presence of value in the universe via cultural beings has noteworthy significance—in part because the universe now has important properties it might not have otherwise have had—but that the potential of those properties for the universe is essentially unlimited. This may mean that the value that emerges in the universe via cultural beings would not only be an important force for how intelligent beings act in and upon the universe, but also for how intelligence and culture may ultimately significantly influence the evolution of the whole of the universe itself. However, while a strong bootstrapped universe worldview would allow for culture to be a potentially important aspect of the universe, it would not be for any particular deep reason other than the fact that culture arose via physical evolution and now has the power to be an important force in the universe.

This is a universe that has bootstrapped itself into the realm of value via its own otherwise non-teleological, or non-purposeful, physical evolution—but that nevertheless may be entering a qualitatively different, and perhaps fundamentally new and unlimited kind of evolution—via the emergence of cultural beings, namely, cosmocultural evolution.

2.2.2 Teleology

Teleology has traditionally been used to suggest design, purpose, or "final causes" in both biology and cosmology and has often been associated with (although by no means exclusively) metaphysical and/or supernatural explanations. There are many ways to think about teleology, and the term has largely fallen out of favor among many scientists for a variety of reasons (Mayr 1992; Davies 2007[3]), but still receives attention from scientists and philosophers (Manson 2003). I wish to highlight here what may be thought of as a weaker form of teleology that is more akin to suggesting the existence of fundamental cosmological trends, natural directionality or directive principles, loosely defined notions of "progress" or "purpose," or perhaps cosmic "imperatives"—all of which are contained within, and caused by, the nature of the universe. This is to be distinguished from pantheism and theism that contain the additional features of divinity and transcendence, respectively. This weaker form of teleology has been implicitly or explicitly suggested by a number of scientists ranging from a) suggestions of trends toward increasing self-organization and complexity (Kauffman 2000; Chaisson 2005), to b) life and intelligence as "cosmic imperatives" or inevitable cosmic phenomena (De Duve 1995; Lloyd 2006; Davies 2007), to c) "multiverse" and/ or "anthropic" worldviews that suggest our particular universe is made for life (Smolin 1997[4]; Rees 1997; Carr 2007), to d) more explicit eschatological treatments (Teilhard 1955; Tipler 1994) that have stronger pantheistic and theistic themes.

In this kind of "naturally deliberate" universe, intelligence and culture are not only just manifestations of sociobiological selective processes, but are also at least partially (if not completely in some interpretations) created and driven by other deeper teleological natural law-based factors. In this view, culture can be seen as a robust manifestation of the nature of the universe and of cosmic evolution.[5]

2.2.3 Pantheism

Pantheism generally equates God with the universe and tends to reject the notion of a personal and/or transcendent God (although some religions—especially eastern traditions—tend to be pantheistic while retaining a "personal" nature for God).[6] Unlike most of the teleological views noted above, pantheism is more akin to a metaphysical and religious position where unity, reverence, sacredness, and divinity play important roles (MacIntyre 1967; Levine 1994; Harrison 1999). There are many conceptions of pantheism, ranging from eastern religions such as Taoism, to mystical versions of western religions, to purely naturalistic views based on biology and cosmology that focus on the realities of our natural world and the universe at large.[7]

The significance of culture in pantheistic worldviews could be interpreted in a number of ways. Many thinkers who revere the universe might be dissatisfied with implications of cultural evolution that result in the blind consumption and destruction of our natural world.[8] However, much of culture could be viewed with reverence since culture is a part of the sacred divine whole that is the universe. While including culture as a part of the universe, and hence as part of "God," it can be seen to imply noteworthy significance for culture. But culture may also be seen in such a way as to be ultimately-undifferentiated from all other phenomena in the universe, suggesting that culture is not necessarily more significant than other "divine" manifestations of cosmic evolution. Other pantheistic views may ascribe more significance to culture by claiming that cultural evolution is a way for the universe to become self-aware, in some sense to know itself, and perhaps ultimately to become more beautiful, more divine. Such interpretations would imply that cultural evolution occupies a special place in cosmic evolution.

2.2.4 Theism

Theism generally claims the existence of a transcendent, personal, supernatural God who is omnipotent, omniscient, creator of and active in our universe, and generally immutable.[9] However, there are noteworthy exceptions to almost all of these characteristics, of which immutability is of particular relevance for this book. Theistic views that promote the idea of mutability tend to incorporate evolutionary concepts and cosmic evolution to understand the nature of God. "Process theology" (Whitehead 1929), "evolutionary theism,"[10] (Haught 2008), and what might be called "eschatological cosmic evolution"—which envisions an essentially theistic "God" primarily at the end of cosmic evolution which results from the evolution of intelligence within the universe (Teilhard 1955; Tipler 1994)—are all categories of theistic thought that involve deep evolutionary processes. The role of cultural evolution in such worldviews is arguably strong, at least conceptually, in the sense that intelligent beings and their behavior are often thought to reflect, and/or in some way be directly or indirectly connected to, the transcendent God. Such views would imply a significant role for culture in

Table 1.1. Distinguishing Features of some Cosmocultural Perspectives. (Credit: Author)

	Strong Bootstrapped Universe	**Teleology**	**Pantheism**	**Theism**
Directionality	Possibly	Yes	Possibly	Possibly, perhaps likely
Mutability	Yes	Yes	Generally yes	Yes and no
Transcendence	No	No	No	Yes
Role of Culture	Likely very strong	Strong, possibly very strong	Strong on some views—but primarily conceptually	Strong—mostly conceptually, but physically for some views (i.e., some eschatological views)

the cosmos as robust manifestations of the processes of cosmic evolution and/or perhaps as "cocreators" of reality.

As Table 1.1 shows, the important distinctions for the purposes of this paper of the views noted above are that 1) a strong bootstrapped universe does not have teleology, divinity, or transcendence, 2) teleology is directionality without divinity, 3) pantheism is divinity without requiring directionality, and 4) theism is transcendent divinity that may or may not involve directionality, but perhaps does for many theistic views.

2.3 Implications of Cosmic-Cultural Relationships and Cosmocultural Evolution

This section will a) briefly consider some implications of unidirectional cosmic-cultural relationships, then b) touch on two further concepts—inherent cultural evolution and cosmocentrism—to help make distinctions within the broader analytical framework, and c) introduce a particular view within the framework, namely "bootstrapped cosmocultural evolution."

2.3.1 Unidirectional Cosmic-Cultural Relationships

Unidirectional formulations of cosmic-cultural relationships suggest that the cosmos is significant for culture in that culture arises from cosmic evolution, and through physical reality and cosmologically related worldviews, the cosmos informs and influences culture in critical ways; however, cultural evolution has no particular significance for the universe at large. Such unidirectional formulations may be uninteresting and trivially true to some, in part perhaps because it is largely consistent with common sense minimalist views of cosmic evolution as we understand it today. But such views may have interesting implications. At minimum, there may be an implication that one of the great challenges for intelligent cultural beings may be to learn to cope with, and perhaps finally accept, a profound and deep sense of uncertainty regarding any larger cosmic sense of meaning and purpose—that such an uncertainty may have to be treated as a kind of empirical question to be possibly addressed over very long time periods as evidence is accumulated, but perhaps without ever obtaining a satisfactory answer. Coping with the uncertainty of larger cosmic objective meaning may be one of the most profound challenges sufficiently aware beings have to face, and this could have profound implications for cultural evolution—as it arguably already has. Indeed, human beings might be further along in this regard than may be commonly thought—much of the human population seems to able to cope without religion and without a larger sense of cosmic meaning and purpose.

In addition to the uncertainty of broader cosmic significance, it may be that intelligent beings might have to learn to cope with a *known* cosmic insignificance, leading for some perhaps to a kind of nihilistic worldview. For others, something short of nihilism might suggest instead a kind of "cosmically local" relativism where value, meaning, purpose, ethics, and aesthetics derive solely from the affairs of cultural beings who think, behave, and perhaps freely choose in such ways as to sometimes, but often not, establish widely accepted norms and standards to help "local" beings coexist.

Even if a single instance of intelligence and the associated emergence of cultural evolution were to eventually spread throughout the universe, unidirectional cosmic-cultural views would still suggest there is ultimately no particularly deep cosmic significance for the emergence and long-term implications of cultural evolution. Also, in the same way that Jungian archetypes may be thought to reflect deeper "collective" realities of human experience and possibly deeper realities more generally, many separate instances of cultural beings throughout the cosmos independently coming to similar conceptions of value may also imply a deeper cosmic reality and significance for cultural evolution. However, unidirectional worldviews would still suggest that such appearances of "cosmic cultural convergence" are probably not necessarily reflective of deeper cosmic realities—they may instead merely reflect the realities and implications of biological and cultural selective processes—and that the significance of such cultural convergence is fundamentally limited for the universe at large—both conceptually and physically. Claims that such cosmic cultural convergence would reflect a deeper cosmic reality would fit more into bidirectional cosmic-cultural worldviews—i.e., cosmocultural evolution.

2.3.2 Inherent Cultural Evolution and Cosmocentrism

A potentially helpful distinction in many of these brands of cosmic worldviews is whether culture is in some sense "built-in," or inherent in the universe, as part of the nature of the universe. On the spectrum shown in Figure 1, the biore-sistant, biotolerant, biofriendly, and both weak and strong bootstrapped views would suggest that cultural evolution is not inherent in the nature of the universe, certainly that it is not an inevitable "cosmic imperative." However, views characterized as teleological, pantheistic, and theistic would likely claim that culture is indeed part of the nature of the universe (i.e., perhaps as part of a trend of evolving self-organizing complex systems) and/or as part of a deeper conceptual metaphysical significance (e.g., spiritual or divine). This distinction is potentially important in that if culture is seen to be a deep manifestation and expected outcome of cosmic evolution, this would engender worldviews in which we are seen to be at home in the universe, to belong to the universe, to be an important part of its fundamental nature. This is a friendly universe, a cosmos in which many will feel a deep sense of comfort and belonging and perhaps a larger sense of objective meaning and purpose—which in turn can have an impact on how intelligent beings think and act in the world and if/how intelligent beings may ultimately influence the evolution of the universe itself.

Another way of thinking about some of the noted cosmic worldviews above is to consider the broad notion of "cosmocentrism," which places the universe at the center of a worldview and makes it the priority in a value system (Lupisella and Logsdon 1997). As Figure 1 shows, the notion of cosmocentrism is consistent with a strong bootstrapped universe, teleology, and pantheism. Cosmocentrism is a general notion that need not ascribe spiritual or divine significance to the universe (although pantheistic formulations would tend to do so), but can still nevertheless view the universe as the ultimate source of meaning, purpose, and value, and make it the central priority in a worldview.

2.3.3 Bootstrapped Cosmocultural Evolution

As Figure 1 shows, looking at the various cosmic worldviews and the above noted perspectives (Inherent Cultural Evolution and Cosmocentrism) reveals a noteworthy intersection at the strong bootstrapped universe worldview. This is where cosmocultural evolution intersects with "non-inherent" cultural evolution and with cosmocentrism—call it "bootstrapped cosmocultural evolution." This is a worldview that a) makes few assumptions about the nature of the universe, while b) advocating that the universe has bootstrapped itself into the realm of value, and c) allows for the possibility of unlimited significance and unlimited potential for cultural evolution in the universe.

While *bootstrapped cosmocultural evolution* is consistent with the broader notion of cosmocentrism, one could still advocate for a bootstrapped cosmocultural evolutionary view without necessarily making the universe the central priority or source of value. One could believe that it is significant that the universe has bootstrapped itself into the realm of value via cultural agents such as ourselves and still also maintain an anthropocentric or "ratio-centric" (Kelley Smith, in press) worldview in which intelligent beings are still the ultimate priority.

3. Bootstrapped Cosmocultural Evolution

Here I would like to expand on the idea of bootstrapped cosmocultural evolution and then suggest a more specific worldview consistent with the notion of a bootstrapped cosmocultural perspective—namely, a morally creative cultural cosmos.

As noted previously, a bootstrapped cosmocultural perspective suggests not only that the universe has bootstrapped itself into the realm of value and culture via valuing cultural agents such as ourselves, but that the significance and potential for cultural evolution is unlimited. To some, these may seem like trivial claims, to others they may seem unduly speculative and perhaps even extraordinary, but these two suggestions arguably make minimal assumptions—especially compared to many other worldviews—and are arguably consistent with the evidence we have (albeit perhaps limited) for both the nature of the universe and cultural evolution. The notion of bootstrapped cosmocultural evolution relies on minimal claims about the nature of the universe in the sense that it stresses the observation that "properties" such as value, meaning, purpose, and culture have appeared in the universe ultimately as a result of the appearance of replicating molecules (which may have occurred only by chance), and results of natural selection operating on replicating systems over long time periods leading to intelligence and culture. The appearance of basic culture (e.g., mechanisms of transferring knowledge) would not necessarily be so surprising in this worldview.

3.1 The Surprise of Life? Or the Surprise of Intelligence?

What might be more surprising than the emergence of basic culture is the origin and evolution of life itself—that is, the emergence of replicators that appear to work in opposition to the second law of thermodynamics creating local spatial-temporal negentropy. This is arguably a quite different kind of evolution than the rest of cosmic evolution that has come prior. However, much progress has been made in understanding replicating systems and there appear to be sufficiently plausible explanations that could account for the origin of molecular replicators (Fry 2000). Indeed, claims are often made, if not implied, that the universe is teeming with life. And many scientists point out that the biofriendliness of the universe's "fine-tuning" of physical laws and constants is compelling and needs to be explained (Barrow and Tipler 1986; Davies 2007). However, one reading of the evidence—namely the lack of life and intelligence beyond Earth even after searching for many decades—is simply that the universe is perhaps not that biofriendly.

It may turn out to be true that the universe is teeming with life and perhaps intelligent life. But it seems premature to jump to such a conclusion in the absence of sufficient evidence. Of course, as Carl Sagan often cautioned, "absence of evidence is not evidence of absence," so we must simply do the experiment and keep searching—perhaps for a very long time.

Indeed, an obvious counter to the concern that we haven't yet found life is that we have only begun the search, and in such a large universe it will take time to find life. But the Fermi challenge is less easy to dismiss—despite many creative responses (Webb 2002)—if life is ubiquitous and intelligence and technology follow, then "where are they"? Intelligent life, and/or signs thereof, should arguably be easier to find than primitive life—if they're not hiding. Perhaps the nature of the universe lends itself to producing life (e.g., replicating systems), but not necessarily to producing intelligence and culture as is often suggested.

But if mere replication is the key, we can imagine that it could happen under many physical circumstances.[11] We can also imagine that once replication is underway in a dynamic environment, the emergence of increasingly diverse, and perhaps eventually quite complex strategies for replication (e.g., sociality and culture) would not be so surprising given enough time and given the very simple and compelling mechanism that is natural selection.

3.2 The Complexity and Power of Human Culture

While basic culture may not be surprising given replication and natural selection acting over long timescales, what is noteworthy is the level of sophistication of human culture, the depth of our awareness, and the extent and speed that culture has evolved and influenced an entire world. What human beings are doing with culture, what culture is doing with us, what culture is doing to our world and beginning to do to worlds beyond, and its apparent unlimited potential—are all noteworthy to say the least. It isn't at all clear whether the level of sophistication we see with human culture should somehow be an expected outcome of cosmic or biological evolution—nevertheless, culture has been born; it is here, and it is powerful.

Irrespective of whether the emergence of life, intelligence, and culture is a low probability, it need only happen once. Surprising things happen all the time—especially given enough time and space. It may also be that the universe possesses value completely independent of valuing agents (Rolston 1990; Lupisella 2009, in press), but what we can claim with confidence today, what we know about the universe today, is that the cosmos now has the properties of value—meaning, purpose, and culture—at least through us. The universe literally has those properties within it, where it otherwise would not without the emergence of valuing cultural beings such as *Homo sapiens* and other forms of life that have similar characteristics. So even with this "minimalist" bootstrapped cosmocultural perspective, we can assert that the universe has now become a different kind of entity, an entity that contains culture, manifesting value to extreme degrees. Those qualities are at least in us—in our evolutionarily driven predispositions, in our interests, in our worldviews, in our culture—and hence in the universe. Regardless of origin and form, value is indisputably manifested in the universe through us. What isn't so obvious is how significant that really is.

3.3 Implications for Bootstrapped Cosmocultural Evolution

This section will explore some implications and significance of bootstrapped cosmocultural evolution under the broad categories of a) limited ontological significance, b) practical cultural significance, and c) unlimited significance.

3.3.1 Limited Ontological Significance

The use of "ontological" in what follows is meant partly in the traditional philosophical sense of having to do with that which exists, or with "being," but is also meant to emphasize a narrower sense than that broader use sometimes implies—namely "*physical* being" or "*physical* existence," with the caveat that "physical" is used in a fairly broad and admittedly loose sense, implying, among other things, that it is not necessarily limited to our formulations of physical reality as we understand it today.[12]

The emergence in the universe of properties such as value and meaning is noteworthy in that the universe has produced something different, and has perhaps *become* something different to the extent that it has evolved in what is arguably an interesting and important way by creating value, meaning, purpose, and culture. This may be seen as a form of limited ontological significance in that a) emergent properties such as value are primarily physical manifestations—albeit unique and complex—within cultural beings (e.g., brains) who have evolved with sufficiently complex interests, and b) while the universe may be changing in an important yet limited physical sense (although perhaps in a physical *qualitative* sense) via the emergence of value, the broader significance beyond that is minimal or negligible. Nevertheless, culture is significantly ontologically relevant for the cosmos as the vehicle of that change—what may be a kind of limited physical qualitative change. That is, a new kind of qualitatively different physical manifestation has emerged— namely value, along with culture as a way of further manifesting and operationalizing value. We may think of this limited ontological significance as corresponding to a weak form of bootstrapped cosmocultural evolution.

However, as sources and arbiters of value, cultural beings cannot only recognize this ontological significance, but in some sense deepen it by merely emphasizing it. Simply choosing to adopt and emphasize this ontological significance for ourselves and for the universe makes that significance more significant—in part because it can become more deeply meaningful to human beings, and because as sources of value, we confer that deepening upon the cosmos. This limited ontological significance, however, is akin to having a kind of "benign" worldview that doesn't have much, if any, practical consequence, but which might otherwise offer helpful and/or comforting worldviews and perhaps ultimately form a foundation for more practical implications.

3.3.2 Practical Cultural Significance

A lack of "external" objective meaning may be unsatisfying to many—caught forever in endless cycles of relativism, a morass of unbearable responsibility for our own meaning and purpose, and perhaps ultimately for that of the universe. But it looks like choice is inescapable.[13] And while choice can sometimes be oppressive and debilitating, it is also liberating and empowering—so much so that freedom forms a critical pillar of many human societies. What then are we to do with the destructive and constructive power of culture? What kind of "cosmic" beings should we strive to be? Or, perhaps a more immediate challenge: Why should we worry about such long-term questions at all? Why should we contemplate our role in the universe when it seems so distant, so far in the future, so uncertain? Such considerations may not be as distant as first glances might suggest. There are a number of relatively near-term practical challenges that could have consequences for human behavior that relate to these broader longer-term cosmic perspectives, among them:

globalization, biospheric stewardship, space ecology, search for extraterrestrial intelligence, off-Earth migration, and long-term survival and development.

Globalization—Transcending Tribalism. While "localism" is an important and often healthy counterbalance to the forces of globalization, it is important to strike balances between the two. Knowing how our evolutionary heritage can blind us to longer-term implications, and more specifically, how it can drive blind group identity—and how that can ultimately lead to unduly nationalistic tendencies—can help us be more careful about such proclivities. Seeing ourselves in a cosmic context that suggests our selfish biological evolution is not necessarily part of a deep cosmic design can help motivate us to take better control of our local and collective global behavior as a species. It can help sensitize us to some of the blinding adverse effects of cultural forces such as dogmatic ideologies that too often lead to unnecessary conflict. Seeing ourselves in a longer-term cosmic context can help us envision a healthier, more united human species, creating recognition of value for global engagement and collective global pursuits as opposed to pursuing strictly group or national interests. Seeing ourselves as a special fragile species that may be "on our own," with potential cosmic significance, can indeed help us act as a global species—and the need to come together better as a species is evident on many fronts—some of them noted in what follows.

Biospheric Stewardship. While most people today would easily acknowledge the importance of preserving and improving our environmental quality—certainly at least for the sake of human survival and quality of life—it is perhaps surprising that we don't do better. Or is it? As noted above, biological evolution doesn't quite program us to be sensitive to longer-term, broader implications, and non-obvious implications—and perhaps for good reason—at least from a "selfish gene" perspective. Near-term higher probability consequences would be expected to drive animal behavior given how natural selection is slave to what appears to be essentially blind gene replication. Indeed, despite our awareness of long time scales, extinction, and our own power to potentially mitigate catastrophic and extinction level threats, it is noteworthy that we humans are still primarily reactive near-term creatures—especially in many western cultures. But it is changing. What we've learned about our planet, about our biosphere—much of which is a result of human instinct for looking up and out into the cosmos—has led us to see ourselves as a "pale blue dot"[14] in a vast cosmic ocean. The way in which we appreciate and deal with that fragility, the way we have begun to see ourselves as biospheric stewards in the context of cosmic evolution, has and should continue to influence how we care for our world and how we value life—whether here on Earth, or elsewhere in the universe.

Space Ecology. Humanity is beginning to have a direct impact on our space environment—however small that impact may be for now. We have created much debris in low-Earth orbit—including remains from weapons shooting down satellites. We have crashed, landed, lived, and played on the Moon.[15] We have sent robotic spacecraft near and far. We have leaked, and intentionally sent, radio waves into space. We are living in near-Earth orbit. And we are now planning to permanently live on the Moon, Mars, and beyond. These developments raise a range of environmental questions, from if and how we should preserve certain space environments (Almar 2002; Williamson 2006), to how we can be more responsible, eco-friendly explorers (Cockell 2007), to how we might deal with the prospects of extraterrestrial life (Lupisella 1999, 2009, in press). How we deal with such questions will be informed, in part, by our own cultural evolution, by how we see ourselves in the universe, and by what we see as our responsibilities. Space agencies around the world take substantial measures to avoid contamination of certain space environments, but it is primarily for scientific reasons. What about other perspectives, including broader cosmic and philosophical perspectives, which might inform such policies? (Bertka, in press).

The Search for Extraterrestrial Intelligence. Our longer-term cosmic considerations should inform how we think about other intelligent beings in the universe, and if/how they may communicate and act throughout the cosmos. Such considerations may inform if and how we communicate and perhaps ultimately interact with other intelligent beings. Indeed, we have intentionally and unintentionally sent communications into space. It is unlikely that our transmissions have been detected by other civilizations for a number of reasons, but nevertheless, our communications are both leaking out into space, and on occasion, being sent intentionally. Perhaps more importantly, there has been serious consideration to the idea of a more systematic attempt to send communications from Earth to potential extraterrestrial civilizations (Vakoch 2004, 2008, 2009, this volume). What would we communicate in such attempts? How would we decide what to say? Our considerations about cultural evolution in a cosmic context, our own specific cosmic perspectives, and the plurality of our views, will at least inform such decisions, if not be explicitly articulated in communications with extraterrestrial beings.[16]

Off-Earth Migration. While the preservation and enhancement of planet Earth needs to be a central organizing priority for humanity, we also need to attempt migration beyond our home world. Humanity needs to do the difficult experiment of migrating off Earth to assess if and how we can effectively and sustainably survive and thrive outside the comforts of our natural biosphere. If we don't, we run the risk of extinction (Shostak 2009, this volume). It is this kind of "experimental ethos" and experimental migration narrative that should be a significant justification for space activities. But there are other benefits to migrating off Earth. Human beings have slowly, and perhaps sometimes too painfully, benefited from social experimentation that has often been driven and accelerated by migrating to new environments, with new challenges, and new freedoms. Experimenting with new forms of social organization and new means of governance can benefit from the challenges of migration—especially to challenging environments. Migrating into the wider universe can serve that purpose and help unite all countries of the world in a common, perhaps critical, long-term endeavor of human expansion and social experimentation.

But there is also a less practical, and perhaps equally important, consequence of migrating off Earth—the creation of cultural diversity. Finding better ways to live is clearly important. But finding *different* ways to live is culturally enriching both to the human experience and perhaps to the "nonhuman" experience. New branches of cultural evolution can enhance the human condition and enrich our lives by giving us more to take note of, more to study, more to choose from, more to appreciate, more to take joy in, more to be inspired by, and more to be in awe of. Cultural diversity, and perhaps diversity in general, may have practical benefits (i.e., having a wide variety to choose from as needed),[17] but diversity may be a value in its own right, an end unto itself, and worth pursuing for its own sake.[18] Given the potential for quite diverse lifeforms throughout the universe, diversity may have broad cosmic significance beyond our own aesthetic appreciation. And so our motivations for extraterrestrial migration, and the associated new branches of human cultural evolution, can and should be informed by broader long-term cosmic perspectives.

Long-Term Survival and Development: All of the above relatively near-term issues have long-term trajectories, potentially of cosmic significance—why not treat them that way—at least in part? Why not take a truly long view, a cosmic view? If we look long-term, what might we see? What visions might we pursue? Let us have the courage to face the uncertainties of such contemplations. Let us not shrink in the face of complex threats, or be passive about presently unknown threats. Let us seek them out, as no other species has ever been able to do. Let us rally our political institutions and global resources to become a truly long-lived species (Tough 1991; Lupisella et al. 2003; Smith 2007). Now is the time to be proactive about our long-term survival and development—whether by protecting our planet from asteroid impacts and gamma ray bursts or by migrating off-Earth to reduce our chance of extinction and to create new branches of human civilization. Understanding ourselves in a cosmic context can help motivate and inform such endeavors including, perhaps ultimately—as fanciful as it may sound—surviving the "end" of the universe.

3.3.3 Unlimited Significance: Cosmic Demotion to Cosmic Promotion?

We don't know for sure of course whether there will be, or are presently, deep or large-scale physical or nonphysical consequences of culture for the universe at large, but a cosmocultural perspective suggests it is a plausible enough possibility to take seriously. This is where the unlimited potential of cosmocultural evolution becomes particularly compelling. Cultural evolution is ultimately manifested as behaviors at what are often large-scale social actions; so if we envision cultural evolution acting over long time scales, especially cosmic timescales, we can imagine potential impacts for the universe as a whole.

A Cosmocultural Evolution Scale. In 1963, Nikolai Kardashev proposed three types of civilizations categorized by the amount of energy that is harnessed: a Type 1 civilization harnesses roughly the energy associated with a planet; Type II, a star; Type III, a galaxy. Carl Sagan calculated Earth to be something like a .7 civilization (not quite Type I) and further suggested the additional categorizing criterion of information available to the civilization (Sagan 1973). Milan Ćirković (2004) suggests that Type IV should be used to designate a civilization that can harness the power of its supercluster; Michio Kaku (2005) suggests a Type IV civilization could harness extragalactic energy sources such as dark energy; and Zoltan Galantai (2004) has suggested a Type IV level which harnesses the energy of the visible universe. I would like to suggest a somewhat different scale that overlaps with what's been proposed prior, but has a different emphasis, goes quite a bit further, and is admittedly more speculative and more qualitative. The scale I explore emphasizes the *kind* of impact and influence a culture exerts on its environment and the universe.

Type I Influence: *Planetary.* Planetary influence would include the ability to influence a planet and solar system bodies (e.g., biospheric control, defense from astronomical impacts such as asteroids, etc.). Humanity is close to this now in some respects, but far in other respects—i.e., despite our global climate impacts, we are probably far from effective planetary climate control. We should also consider the possibility that life may not originate and/or evolve on planetary bodies.[19] This would suggest a more general category title such as "localized," where the environmental influence and control of the species is confined to a "local" scale—e.g., solar systems.

Type II Influence: *Astrophysical.* Astrophysical influence would imply a capacity for using, controlling and modifying astrophysical objects on small and large scales—e.g., stars and galaxies, superclusters, possibly black holes, etc. Examples would be the ability to harness most if not all of a star's energy, control the energy output of a star, extend the lifetime of stars, modify the composition of stars, control the energy of galaxies and superclusters, possibly create black holes, and harness unusual forms of energy such as "dark energy."[20]

Type III Influence: *Cosmological.* Cosmological influence implies an ability to influence and control phenomenon on cosmological scales, i.e., the large-scale behavior of the universe, but within the constraints of physical laws and constants. An example might be extending the lifetime of the universe (perhaps by slowing or accelerating expansions or contractions) possibly transmitting something like information through a big crunch, creating baby universes, or creating an information processing universe and/or a kind of cosmic mind.

Type IV Influence: *Ontological.* As noted previously, "ontological" is perhaps used slightly differently than some traditional uses in that ontological influence applies an ability to control and modify the physical nature of the universe itself—truly "mind over matter." As an example, this would amount to an ability to change physical constants and perhaps laws. This might apply to the Selfish Biocosm hypothesis proffered by James Gardner (2003, and highlighted in this volume), and could also be consistent with views that suggest that life and mind are key creative drivers of a "self-synthesizing" and/or participatory universe (Davies 2007; Wheeler 1988, 1989) whereby observers participate in shaping all of physical reality, particularly as mind and cosmos eventually merge.[21]

Type V Consequence: *Metaphysical.* At the risk of treading into even deeper waters, but for the sake of completeness, I would like to suggest the possibility of another category, one that is perhaps more a matter of consequence than influence (although influence wouldn't necessarily be ruled out)—namely, metaphysical. Here, too, "metaphysical" may be used in a somewhat nontraditional philosophical sense. It is intended here primarily to capture that which may be considered to be beyond physical reality—an often-popular use of the word—to the understandable chagrin of many scientists and philosophers. One way to think about metaphysics in this context is that while ontology is concerned with what actually exists (primarily physically), metaphysics is more concerned with what may exist—or theoretical possibilities, including that which is "nonphysical." This may include considerations such as God or a kind of Platonic realm in which there are theoretical properties (e.g., "universals" such as mathematical constructs, logic, redness, etc. [Armstrong 1989]) or theoretical possibilities for the universe and reality. The realm of metaphysics might be thought of as the largest possibility space for "ultimate reality,"[22] a subset of which is the actual and/or temporary state of reality. On some interpretations, this metaphysical possibility space could include things like value, meaning, purpose, divinity, "spirit," etc. So metaphysics then can be seen to be a very broad (perhaps the broadest) category of investigation that would include, for example, ontology and theology as subsets.

If one thinks of value and cultural evolution as somehow transcending physical reality, if even only partially,[23] then cultural beings are partly metaphysical beings and are arguably beginning to have metaphysical significance for the universe by manifesting value, and perhaps by bringing value and culture to the universe altogether. Whether a bootstrapped cosmocultural perspective can be interpreted to go so far as to imply metaphysical significance is highly speculative of course—in part because of the speculative nature of metaphysical considerations in general. But if there is any metaphysical significance to consider, some interpretations of bootstrapped cosmocultural could be consistent with suggesting there may be partially metaphysical relevance for cultural evolution to the extent that emergent phenomena (ultimately rooted in physical reality—e.g., things like value and cultural evolution) sufficiently transcend physical reality nonetheless.[24] However, bootstrapped cosmocultural evolution would in no way be committed to such a view, and in fact, is more consistent with no such transcendence because bootstrapped cosmocultural evolution emphasizes that cultural evolution is bootstrapped from the physical universe we see and does not require an appeal to "nonphysical" reality.

In the context of the proposed cosmocultural evolution scale, one way of interpreting bootstrapped cosmocultural evolution (especially stronger versions that emphasize unlimited potential) is that we are beginning to have *planetary* (or localized) influence, we are studying for *astrophysical* influence, we are contemplating *cosmological* influence, we are speculating about *ontological* influence, and we may have a kind of *metaphysical* consequence if value and cultural evolution somehow transcend physical reality. A weak version of bootstrapped cosmocultural evolution would be associated with the largely nonpractical limited ontological implications noted previously. Stronger versions of bootstrapped cosmocultural evolution would be associated with the practical cultural implications noted previously as well as all of the levels of the civilization control scale with the possible exception of metaphysical consequence.

A Cosmic Promotion? Scientists and thinkers have been fond of pointing out humanity's "great demotions." From Copernicus to modern day cosmology (perhaps with the exception of "anthropic principles" and associated
observations of "fine tuning"), humanity has been displaced and demoted
from privileged positions in the cosmos. Perhaps it's time for a promotion—
one that goes beyond the confusion of anthropic principles, one that does not
rely on teleological assumptions and assertions about the ultimate nature of
the universe.[25] Bootstrapped cosmocultural evolution allows for the possibility that life, intelligence, and culture could have arisen by chance, while at the
same time asserting that such phenomena are cosmically significant. Stronger
versions suggest that cultural evolution may have unlimited significance for
the cosmos. Our cosmic location and means of origin should not be confused
with our cosmic potential.

As valuing agents, we cannot only claim, but can perhaps, to some extent,
create a more meaningful universe. For some, this may mean the creation of,
or at least recognition of, a more evolved, more significant, more complex
and diverse universe. This may strike some as anthropocentrically superficial,
but the value we humans bring to the universe is at least noteworthy. In the
same way that intelligence and culture is impacting planet Earth, we may also
ultimately have so much freedom and power as to impact the universe itself.
And in the same way we seek to strike balances between individual freedom
and collective well-being, we may also ultimately wish to seek such balances
for beings everywhere and for the whole of the universe as we become an
increasingly cosmic species.

---

4. A Morally Creative Cultural Cosmos

With great potential, comes great responsibility. So what do we do with the
potential of cultural evolution? Culture can have insidious negative effects of
course—a kind of "culture curse"—especially on nonhuman life and the environment. As we increasingly wrap ourselves in culture, our basic humanity, our
common humanity, our connection to each other and our broader environment—especially the global environment—is often masked, if not effectively
lost. Indeed, human beings can lose themselves in culture. But culture can
also uplift and inspire. Culture has produced large-scale devastation as well as
magnificent human achievement. A critical challenge we face is coping with

the dramatic variances for what is thought to be justified destruction and laudable human activity.

How much can we control cultural evolution anyway? Susan Blackmore warns of what might be called "runaway memetic evolution," whereby replicating memes blindly go about their replicating business—unchecked and unfettered—resulting in massive, often unforeseen destruction (Blackmore 2009, this volume). But it does appear that human beings can indeed control cultural evolution to some extent, perhaps to a sufficient extent that we should take responsibility for it, for its products, and for its results. After all, we are certainly in part, if not in totality, creators of culture.

Steve Dick (2003) has proffered the "Intelligence Principle," "*The maintenance, improvement and perpetuation of knowledge and intelligence is the central driving force of cultural evolution, and that to the extent intelligence can be improved, it will be improved.*" He goes on to write: "The Intelligence Principle implies that, given the opportunity to increase intelligence (and thereby knowledge), whether through biotechnology, genetic engineering or AI, any society would do so, or fail to do so at its own peril." Indeed, we see the evidence for the dominant role of intelligence and technology in improving the human condition, in furthering human evolution, leading to what Dick calls the "postbiological universe."

But is that enough? Perhaps cultural evolution will, and should, lead us to a kind of "post-intelligent," "post-technological" universe—a universe that isn't predominantly ruled only by the forces of intelligence and technology, but also by the forces of morality and creativity. Should it? Why not? We see evidence for the forces of morality and creativity all around us.

4.1 A Moral Universe

> For small creatures such as we, the vastness is bearable only through love.
>
> —Carl Sagan, *Contact*

As a result of our interests, we have emerged in the universe as valuing agents with meaning, purpose, and morality as cultural derivatives of value. If the universe did not have morality prior, it does now. We, in some nontrivial sense, make the universe a moral entity, however limited the degree of that contribution may appear. We may indeed be just a very small part of the universe that arose by chance, but nevertheless, strictly speaking, the universe now contains morality. The cosmos now has agents caring about other agents and about nonagents as well, and in some cases, about the whole of the universe. This caring, even if solely a product of biological evolution—as either direct or indirect results of natural selection—need not necessarily be constrained to that narrow heritage—however strong the force of selfishness may be. Indeed, much human behavior reflects an expanding circle of moral consideration (Singer 1981; Sober and Wilson 1998).

We now have an awareness of our capacity to care, and perhaps the sources of such capacity. We are aware in a way no other animal is. This awareness, our knowledge, can help mind trump biology. And it does appear to be happening. One often hears the refrain that socials ills are inevitable, that they will always be with us. But why should that be? Can we really be so confident that intelligent long-lived species, perhaps ones like ours that exhibit great moral potential, have neither the will nor capacity to eradicate most, if not all social ills? Such certainty appears to be misplaced.

It may be difficult, if not impossible, to ultimately wind our way out of what might be thought of as a "selfishness trap"—a trap that prevents us from giving up, or significantly moderating, our selfishness even if we have compelling reasons and opportunities to do so (Lupisella 2001).[26] It may be difficult, if not impossible to render the implications of the competition for resources and the second law of thermodynamics negligible (these are certainly deep challenges), but perhaps it will eventually be possible. As intelligence and technology carries beings to ever-increasing degrees of well-being and comfort, the cost of caring for others can decrease, helping to make it easier to care for others, resulting in more caring acts and an increase our overall "caring capacity."

As the cost of caring for others is reduced, we may be able to better pursue the well-being of *all* as a critical organizing principle for cultural evolution, including perhaps ultimately, the whole of the universe.[27] Indeed, this points to the possibility of a nearer-term cultural goal: reducing the cost of caring, which is happening to some extent intentionally and incidentally as part of our social pursuits and technological innovation. But perhaps reducing the cost of caring, as well as increasing its benefits, can serve more explicitly as a formal organizing principle of cultural endeavors.

It may be that there is a creator, a designer, and a source of external meaning and purpose, in which case, it is perhaps a matter of speculation and maybe eventually, discovery; it is only then that we may know details. But if not, if we're on our own, if there is no larger source of value and meaning, we may then see ourselves simultaneously in opposition to a meaningless and hostile universe (i.e., in opposition to the second law of thermodynamics), and also as a kind of transformative force for creating a meaningful and moral universe. In the same way that religions motivate human beings to care in a way they might not otherwise, so too can certain cosmic worldviews.

4.2 A Creative Cosmos

And if, or when, our "caring capacity" has been reached, if the well-being of all has been sufficiently achieved, what then? Perhaps it is premature to think beyond that, but in some parts of the world we are increasingly able to achieve the well-being of many members of society—although admittedly falling well short of overall global caring capacities. Nevertheless, we see signs of cultural evolution that may point us in directions we may ultimately wish to go, as we are increasingly able to care for all.

Increasing creativity may be one of those directions. Creativity is a significant, if not critical part of human culture. The universe itself seems to be creative. Even if creativity isn't a deeply cosmic phenomenon, it is nevertheless something that human culture (and perhaps other cultures) brings to the universe. Perhaps creativity for the sake of increasing diversity in the universe is a pursuit worthy in and of itself—being mindful that the often advocated notion of "creative destruction" may need to be more carefully considered in light of how much *net* well-being and diversity is gained, as opposed to the blind justification that sometimes results from its invocation.

4.3 A Morally Creative Cosmos—A Busy Utopia

> But equally it appeared to us as unreasoning Creativity, at once blind and subtle, tender and cruel, caring only to spawn and spawn the infinite variety of beings, conceiving here and there among a thousand inanities a fragile loveliness.
>
> —Olaf Stapledon, *Star Maker*

It may seem fanciful or gratuitous to think so long-term and so speculatively about the future. But if we consider long-term questions now, it may inform nearer-term pursuits. If our thoughts about long-term norms reveal desirable directions to head in, why not start now? To a significant extent, human beings already do that of course—mostly on shorter timescales. But if we value certain things in the very long-term, we presumably value them now. Indeed, many human beings deeply value morality and creativity, which are often magnificently manifested in human culture. These behaviors, in most cases, are presumably not motivated by long-term cosmic perspectives. But perhaps long-term cosmic perspectives can increasingly motivate morally creative pursuits, in part by providing other compelling contexts for those who seek them, including extraterrestrial beings (if they're out there). If they are out there, pursuing a morally creative cosmos may be something we have in common. If it isn't, maybe it should be.[28]

If cultural evolution becomes a major force of cosmic evolution, that is, if the universe undergoes cosmocultural evolution and becomes a deeply "cultural cosmos", then there will be compelling implications for cultural beings. There will be profound choices to make. Perhaps we will want to move beyond biology, beyond intelligence, beyond technology, to a universe that is a moral universe, a creative universe—a morally creative cosmos where what matters is not whether cultural beings live effectively, but whether we live ethically and creatively.

---

5. Summary

One way to think about the relationships of cosmos and culture is to explore whether each is important for the other, and if so, how. Unidirectional relationships suggest that the universe is important for culture, but not the reverse. This could be consistent with many worldviews such as a bioresistant, biotolerant, and biofriendly universe, as well as a "weak bootstrapped universe" worldview which suggests the universe has bootstrapped itself into the realm of value, but without any particular significance for the universe at large. Bi-directional relationships suggest that the universe is important for culture and that culture is important for the universe. This could include worldviews that can be characterized as a "strong bootstrapped universe," teleological, pantheistic, and theistic—all of which could be consistent with *cosmocultural evolution* and/or *the Cosmocultural Principle* which suggests that cultural evolution is significant enough for the cosmos that it implies a kind of coevolution of cosmos and culture that should be considered in totality and holistically as single integrated evolution.

The new quality of *value* that has emerged in the minds of beings with interests, along with the phenomenon of culture that operationalizes value, has added a significant and arguably qualitatively different kind of evolution to the cosmic landscape. *Bootstrapped cosmocultural evolution* suggests that the universe has "bootstrapped" itself into the realm of value via physical processes that created replicators leading eventually to intelligence, mind, and culture—none of which were necessarily inherent in the universe per se (e.g., as a "cosmic imperative")—but which now have a limited kind cosmic ontological significance, practical cultural relevance, and the perhaps unlimited potential to eventually transform the whole of the universe itself. This emergence of a new kind of cosmic property, *value*, along with cultural evolution that instantiates value and creates derivatives such as meaning, purpose, and other endless forms of value, has given rise to a qualitatively different kind of cosmic phenomenon that may have unlimited potential.

What we do with the potentially unlimited power of cultural evolution is a profound challenge—one that we face day-to-day on many levels, but that will increasingly be relevant on ever-widening scales as we begin to see ourselves in a long-term cosmic context and as cultural evolution begins to become a more cosmically relevant phenomenon. The forces of morality and creativity can give rise to a morally creative cosmos, a universe that goes beyond intelligence and technology, a universe that is deeply driven by the caring capacity of valuing agents and ultimately by a pervasive cosmic force of moral creativity—something to which all cultural beings might aspire.

Whether one thinks life and culture arose by chance or are instead a part of cosmic design, an argument can be made either way for the value of life, intelligence, and culture. Whether we are a kind of rare cosmic gem, part of a "cosmic fugue," or perhaps a part of cosmic destiny, there is arguably some form of noteworthy significance we can claim for life, mind, and culture. Either way, we can see ourselves as precious and meaningful, worth preserving, and worth developing to the greatest potential—for ourselves and the whole of the universe.

Regardless of what the deep cosmic truth may be, we must still carefully exercise the power of culture. We don't know where it's all heading, and we may not quite know how it works, but culture is carrying us—we are carrying ourselves—on what may be the leading edge of cosmic evolution. And we may be more in control than we think. It's a wave we at least have some hand in creating. It's an evolution we are partly, if not entirely, responsible for. Let us then play a worthy role in cosmocultural evolution—a role worthy of cultural beings, a role worthy of the cosmos.

References

Almar, Ivan. "What could COSPAR do to protect the planetary and space environment?" in *Advances in Space Research* 30, no. 6 (2002): 1577–1581.

Alston, William. 1998. "Ontological Commitments," in Laurence and Macdonald eds. *Contemporary Readings in the Foundations of Metaphysics.* Oxford: Blackwell.

Armstrong, David. 1989. *Universals: An Opinionated Introduction.* Boulder, CO: Westview.

Barrow, John D. and Frank J. Tipler, 1986. *The Anthropic Cosmological Principle.* Oxford University Press.

Bertka, Connie. In Press. *Exploring the Origin, Extent, and Future of Life: Philosophical, Ethical, and Theological Perspectives.* Cambridge University Press.

Blackmore, Susan. 1999. *The Meme Machine.* Oxford University Press.

Blackmore, Susan. 2009. "Dangerous Memes: What the Pandorans Let Loose" in Dick, S. J. and M. Lupisella (eds.) *Cosmos and Culture: Cultural Evolution in a Cosmic Context.* Washington, DC: NASA History Series.

Bloom, Howard. 2000. *Global Brain: The Evolution of Mass Mind From the Big Band to the 21st Century.* John Wiley & Sons.

Bloom, Howard. 2009. "The Big Burp and The Multi-Planetary Mandate" in Dick, S. J. and M. Lupisella (eds.) *Cosmos and Culture: Cultural Evolution in a Cosmic Context.* Washington, DC: NASA History Series.

Bunge, Mario. 1999. *Dictionary of Philosophy.* Amherst: Prometheus Books, pp. 200–201.

Carr, Bernard (ed.). 2007. *Universe or Multiverse?* Cambridge University Press.

Christian, David. 2009. "History and Science after the Chronometric Revolution" in Dick, S. J. and M. Lupisella (eds.) *Cosmos and Culture: Cultural Evolution in a Cosmic Context.* Washington, DC: NASA History Series.

Chaisson, Eric, 2005. *Epic of Evolution: Seven Ages of the Cosmos.* New York: Columbia University Press.

Chaisson, Eric, 2009. "Cosmic Evolution: State of the Science" in Dick, S. J. and M. Lupisella (eds.) *Cosmos and Culture: Cultural Evolution in a Cosmic Context*. Washington, DC: NASA History Series.

Ćirković, Milan. (February 2004). "Forecast for the Next Eon: Applied Cosmology and the Long-Term Fate of Intelligent Beings," *Foundations of Physics* 34. Netherlands: Springer.

Cockell, Charles. 2007. *Space On Earth: Saving Our World By Seeking Others*. New York: Macmillan.

Davies, Paul. 2007. *Cosmic Jackpot: Why Our Universe is Just Right for Life*. New York: Houghton Mifflin Company.

Dawkins, Richard. 1976. *The Selfish Gene*. Oxford University Press.

Dawkins, Richard. 1986. *The Blind Watchmaker: Why the Evidence of Evolution Reveals a Universe Without Design*. New York: W. W. Norton & Company, Inc.

De Duve, Christian. 1995. *Vital Dust: Life as a Cosmic Imperative*. New York: Basic Books.

Dennett, Daniel. 1995. *Darwin's Dangerous Idea*. London: Penguin Books.

Deutsch, David. 1997. *The Fabric of Reality*. New York: Viking.

Dick, Steven J. 1996. *The Biological Universe: The Twentieth Century Extraterrestrial Life Debate and the Limits of Science*. Cambridge: Cambridge University Press.

Dick, Steven J. "Cultural evolution, the Postbiological Universe and SETI," *International Journal of Astrobiology* 2, no.1 (2003): 65-74.

Dick, Steven J. "Cosmotheology: Theological Implications of the New Universe," in Dick (ed.) *Many Worlds: The New Universe, Extraterrestrial Life, and the Theological Implications*. Philadelphia: Templeton Foundation Press, p. 195.

Dick, Steven J. 2000. (ed.), *Many Worlds: The New Universe, Extraterrestrial Life, and the Theological Implications*. Philadelphia: Templeton Foundation Press.

Dick, Steven J. and James Strick. 2004. *The Living Universe: NASA and the Development of Astrobiology*. Piscataway, NJ: Rutgers University Press.

Dyson, Freeman. 1988. *Infinite In All Directions*. New York: Harper & Row.

Fry, Iris. 2000. *The Emergence of Life On Earth: A Historical and Scientific Overview*. Rutgers University Press.

Galantai, Zoltán. 2004. "Long Future and Type IV Civilizations," *Periodica Polytechnica Ser. Soc. Man. Sci.* 12, no. 1:83–89.

Gardner, James. 2003. *Biocosm—The New Scientific Theory of Evolution: Intelligent Life Is the Architect of the Universe*. Makawao, Maui, HI: Inner Ocean Publishing.

Gould, Stephen J. 1989. *Wonderful Life: The Burgess Shale and the Nature of History*. New York: W. W. Norton & Company.

Harrison, Paul. 1999. *The Elements of Pantheism: Understanding the Divinity of Nature and the Universe*. London: Element Books. Later via self-publishing site of Taramac FL: Llumina Press.

Hart, W. D. (1996) "Dualism," in *A Companion to the Philosophy of Mind*. Samuel Guttenplan, ed. Oxford: Blackwell, pp. 265–267.

Haught, John F. 2000, 2nd edition, 2008. *God After Darwin: A Theology of Evolution*. Boulder, CO: Westview Press.

Kaku, Michio. 2005. *Parallel Worlds: The Science of Alternative Universes and Our Future in the Cosmos*. New York: Doubleday.

Levine, Michael. 1994. *Pantheism: A Non-Theistic Concept of Deity*. London: Routledge.

Lloyd, Seth. 2005. *Programming the Universe: A Quantum Computer Scientist Takes on the Cosmos.* New York: Random House.

Lupisella, Mark and John Logsdon. 1997. "Do We Need a Cosmocentric Ethic?" Paper IAA-97-IAA.9.2.09 presented at the International Astronautical Federation Congress. American Institute of Aeronautics and Astronautics, Turin.

Lupisella, Mark. 1999. "Ensuring the Scientific Integrity of Possible Martian Life." Paper IAA-99-IAA.13.1.08 presented at the International Astronautical Federation Congress. American Institute of Aeronautics and Astronautics, Amsterdam.

Lupisela, Mark. 2001. Participant statement for Humanity 3000 Seminar No. 3 Proceedings, Foundation for the Future. Seattle, Washington, USA. 12–14 August 2001. *http://www.futurefoundation.org/documents/hum_pro_sem3.pdf,* p. 37.

Lupisella, Mark. J. Glenn, C. Jones, J. Dator, J. Dewar, D. Fromkin, J. Ryzenko, A. Tough, W. Marshall, S. Gill, "The Horizons Project: Global Mechanisms for Long-Term Survival and Development," Paper IAA-13.2.09 presented at International Astronautical Congress, Bremen 2003.

Lupisella, Mark. 2004. "Using Artificial Life to assess the typicality of terrestrial life," *Advances in Space Research* 33:1318–1324.

Lupisella, Mark. In press, 2009. "The Search for Extraterrestrial Life: Epistemology, Ethics, & Worldviews," in Bertka, C. (ed.) *Exploring the Origin, Extent, and Future of Life.* Cambridge University Press. In preparation, publication due 2009. Based on American Association for the Advancement of Science workshops.

MacIntyre, Alasdair. 1967. "Pantheism," in *Encyclopedia of Philosophy.* Paul Edwards, ed. New York: Macmillan and Free Press.

Mansen, Neil A. 2003. Ed. *God and Design: The Teleological Argument and Modern Science.* New York: Routledge.

Mayr, Ernst. 1992. "The Idea of Teleology," *Journal of the History of Ideas* 53 (Jan./Mar.): 117–135.

Michaud, Michael A.G. 2007. *Contact with Alien Civilizations: Our Hopes and Fears About Encountering Extraterrestrials.* New York: Springer.

Owen, H. P. 1971. *Concepts of Deity.* London: Macmillan.

Palmeri, JoAnn. 2009. "Bringing Cosmos to Culture: Harlow Shapley and the Uses of Cosmic Evolution" in Dick, S. J. and M. Lupisella (eds.) *Cosmos and Culture: Cultural Evolution in a Cosmic Context.* Washington, DC: NASA History Series.

Rees, Martin. 1997. *Before the Beginning: Our Universe and Others.* New York: Perseus Books.

Rolston, H. 1990. "The preservation of natural value in the solar system," In E. C. Hargrove, ed. *Beyond Spaceship Earth: Environmental Ethics and the Solar System.* San Francisco: Sierra Club Books.

Sagan, Carl. 1973. (October 2000). Coauthor Jerome Agel: *Cosmic Connection: An Extraterrestrial Perspective.* Cambridge Press.

Sagan, Carl. 1985. *Contact.* New York: Simon and Schuster.

Sagan, Carl. 1994. *Pale Blue Dot.* New York: Random House.

Shostak, Seth. 2009. The Value of L and the Cosmic Bottleneck in Dick, S. J. and M. Lupisella (eds.) *Cosmos and Culture: Cultural Evolution in a Cosmic Context.* Washington, DC: NASA History Series.

Singer, Peter. 1981. *The Expanding Circle: Ethics and Sociobiology.* Oxford: Oxford University Press.

Smith, Kelly. In press, 2009. "Cosmic Ethics: A Philosophical Primer," in Bertka, C (ed.) *Exploring the Origin, Extent, and Future of Life.* Cambridge University Press, in preparation, publication due 2009. Based on American Association for the Advancement of Science workshops.

Smith, Kelly. 2007 presentation, proceedings in press. "The Terrestrial Lifeboat Project: An International Undertaking to Safeguard Humanity." Proceedings of the International Conference on Science/Technology Ethics and Business Ethics. China: Renmin University Press.

Smolin, Lee. 1997. *The Life of the Cosmos*. New York: Oxford University Press.

Stapledon, Olaf. 1937. *Star Maker*. London: Methuen Publishing.

Sober, Eliott and David S. Wilson, 1998. *Unto Others: The Evolution and Psychology of Unselfish Behavior*. Harvard University Press.

Swimme, Brian and Thomas Berry, 1992. *The Universe Story*. New York: HarperCollins Publishers.

Swimme, Brian. 1995. *The Hidden Heart of the Cosmos: Humanity and the New Story*. Maryknoll, NY: Orbis Books.

Teilhard De Chardin, Pierre. 1955. *The Phenomenon of Man*. Originally published as *Le Phenomene Humain*. Editions du Seuil, Paris. Translated by Bernard Wall. New York: Harper & Row, 1959.

Tipler, Frank. 1994. *The Physics of Immortality*. New York: Doubleday.

Tough, Allen. 1991. *Crucial Questions About the Future*. Lanham: University Press of America.

Vakoch, Doug. 2004. "The Art and Science of Interstellar Message Composition," *Leonardo* 37:33–34.

Vakoch, Doug. 2008. "Representing Culture in Interstellar Messages," *Acta Astronautica* 63:657–664.

Vakoch, Doug. 2009. "Encoding Our Origins: Communicating the Evolutionary Epic in Interstellar Messages" in Dick, S. J. and M. Lupisella (eds.), *Cosmos and Culture: Cultural Evolution in a Cosmic Context*. Washington, DC: NASA History Series.

Van Inwagen, Peter. 1998. "The Nature of Metaphysics." In Laurence and Macdonald eds. *Contemporary Readings in the Foundations of Metaphysics.* Oxford: Blackwell.

Ward, Peter D. and Donald Brownlee, 2000. *Rare Earth: Why Complex Life is Uncommon in the Universe.* New York: Copernicus Books.

Webb, Stephen. 2002. *If the Universe Is Teeming with Aliens . . . Where Is Everybody? Fifty Solutions to Fermi's Paradox and the Problem of Extraterrestrial Life.* New York: Copernicus Books.

Wheeler, John. 1989. "Information, Physics, Quantum: The Search for Links," in Proceedings of the 3rd International Symposium on the Foundations of Quantum Mechanics, Tokyo, 1989.

Wheeler, John. 1988. "World as a System Self-Synthesized by Quantum Networking," *IBM Journal of Research and Development* 32, no. 1.

Whitehead, Alfred North. 1929. *Process and Reality: An Essay in Cosmology.* New York: Macmillan. Edition 1978 by D. R. Griffin and D. W. Sherbourne, New York: Macmillan.

Williamson, Mark. 2006. *Space: The Fragile Frontier.* American Institute of Aeronautics and Astronautics, Reston, VA.

Wright, Robert. 2001. *Nonzero: The Logic of Human Destiny.* New York: Vintage Books.

Endnotes

1. See Dawkins (1976) for an introduction to the notion of "memes" that are suggested to be a kind of cultural replicating unit (e.g., an idea, song, social norm, etc.), and Blackmore (1999) for an expanded treatment.

2. Value theory is one of four primary areas of philosophy—along with metaphysics, epistemology, and logic.

3. In his book, *Cosmic Jackpot,* Paul Davies devotes several sections to teleology and indicates its controversial nature by titling the first of those

sections, "Tackling the T-Word" (p. 233). Davies provides a brief but helpful contemporary treatment of teleology.

4. Lee Smolin's proposal is interesting as it relates to this weak form of teleology because he suggests a cosmic selection mechanism (much like natural selection) that essentially "selects" for universe's like ours – or at least universes that have characteristics for being relatively stable and long-lived – arguably allowing for an interpretation that our universe arises from a somewhat directional selection mechanism (e.g. for "stable" long-lived universes), that once selected, may have directionality toward life.

5. Some interpretations of quantum mechanics (e.g. the Cogenhagen Interpretation and Many Worlds Interpretation) suggest a central role for observers because the act of observation contributes to physical reality, or at least the physical state of the universe.

6. Taoism, certain forms of Buddhism and Hinduism, and some mystical strands of monotheism have pantheistic features (Stanford Encyclopedia of Philosophy *http://plato.stanford.edu/entries/pantheism/*).

7. Steve Dick (2000) emphasizes the need for "cosmotheology," and the prospects for a purely "Natural God," to help better account for the physical realities of cosmic evolution in theological worldviews.

8. Brian Swimme is an example of many writers with backgrounds in cosmology who express deep reverence for the universe and our natural world based on views of physical cosmological evolution (*The Universe Story* 1992 and *The Hidden Heart of the Cosmos* 1995), but he is critical about human impacts on the Earth's environment.

9. "Deism" is distinguished from theism in that deism tends to see God as not being active in or "interfering" with the world. Panentheism (with an "en" in the middle) sees God as imbued and active within the world as part of the nature of the universe (as in pantheism), but also as transcendent, essentially making the universe a subset of a larger God. Deism and panentheism are considered subsets of theism for the purposes of this essay, in part because they advocate a key distinguishing feature of transcendence.

10. "Theistic evolution" or "evolutionary creationism" can be seen as a more narrow pursuit that attempts primarily to integrate *biological* evolution with traditional religion.

11. Replication may also be a limited characteristic for what counts as life (Lupisella, 2004).

12. This narrower use of "ontological" that stresses physical existence is arguably consistent with the definitions of some philosophers. For example, Mario Bunge (1999) defines ontology as "the serious secular version of metaphysics. The branch of philosophy that studies the most pervasive features of reality, such as real existence, change, time, chance, mind, and life. Ontology does not study constructs, i.e., ideas in themselves." He goes on to write: "General ontology studies all existents, whereas each special Ontology studies one genus of thing or process-physical, chemical, biological, social, etc. Thus, whereas general ontology studies the concepts of space, time, and event, the ontology of the social investigates such general sociological concepts as those of social system, social structure, and social change. Whether general or special, ontology can be cultivated in either of two manners: speculative or scientific."

13. Even if free will may be a kind of an illusion in a "deterministic" universe, the way most of us experience and act in the world, individually and collectively, is through intentional choices with consequences. Robert Wright writes: "History, even if its basic direction is set, can proceed at massive, wrenching human cost. Or it can proceed more smoothly—with costs, to be sure, but with more tolerable costs. It is the destiny of our species—and this time I mean the inescapable destiny, not just the high likelihood—to choose." (*Nonzero*, p. 10).

14. Carl Sagan wrote eloquently in *Pale Blue Dot* (1994) about Earth and humanity occupying such a small part of a vast cosmos. A NASA Voyager image, looking back at our solar system, shows Earth as a very small light blue dot "suspended" in a sunbeam.

15. For a video of Alan Shepard golfing on the Moon, see: *http://www.youtube.com/watch?v=AdqBL5pdRT8.*

16. For an engaging interdisciplinary look at "Cultures of the Imagination," see *http://www.contact-conference.org/index.html.*

17. In *Global Brain* (2000), Howard Bloom stresses the importance of "diversity generators."

18. Personal communication with Jill Tarter, October 1997. Also, Freeman Dyson has written: "Diversity is the great gift which life has brought to our planet and may one day bring to the rest of the Universe. The preservation and fostering of diversity is the great goal which I would like to see embodied in our ethical principles and in our political actions." (1988).

19. For example, life may originate and/or evolve in interstellar clouds or possibly even in "free space"—perhaps near a star or other astrophysical energy sources.

20. David Deutsch (1997) has suggested that knowledge is a kind of fundamental physical quantity, and as an example, he uses the intentional modification of stellar evolution (to prolong the lifetime of a planet's sun) as a way to illustrate how intelligent beings might use their knowledge to alter large-scale cosmic phenomenon and as a result affect the "knowledge" of observers of that star when they observe that it doesn't fit their standard models. This, and even more physically transformative examples, would be cases where knowledge transforms physical reality on cosmic scales.

21. In this volume, Paul Davies is explicit about life, mind, and culture being fundamental properties of the universe.

22. Peter van Inwagen (1998) suggests that metaphysics is an attempt to sufficiently generally describe "ultimate reality." William Alson (1998) also examines the notion of ultimate reality and considers the relevance of "possibilities" with respect to the notion of ultimate reality.

23. "Dualism," in the philosophy of mind, claims that in some respects, mental phenomena are nonphysical (Hart 1996).

24. It is not clear if/how "emergence" from physical systems gives rise to anything that transcends physical reality—what might be called a kind of "nonphysical emergence."

25. We may in fact someday discover a deep compelling purposeful cosmic order that is sufficiently evidence-based to convince a sufficient number of intelligent beings—a cosmic order that might guide cultural evolution. But such a purposeful cosmic order appears to elude us for now, and may in fact not exist.

26. It is conceivable that we will be able to genetically or cognitively moderate internal selfish predispositions on large scales sooner than we think. If so, humanity will be faced with difficult questions regarding whether such an endeavor should be tried, and if so, how we should do it. Our strongly selfish natures may in fact prevent us from ever seriously moderating or abandoning our selfish motivations—in part because selfishness is important for individual survival, and also because genetically or cognitively moderating our selfishness may have to be an "all-or-nothing" social action to avoid undue advantage for those who choose not to. A noteworthy implication however is that a sufficiently small and relatively isolated space community may be able to conduct such an experiment.

27. This would be consistent with James Gardner's suggestion that highly advanced intelligence might be guided by a kind of moral cultural attractor that preserves humanity and that might ultimately help the universe as a whole to survive and replicate.

28. It is often assumed, perhaps naively, that extraterrestrial intelligence will have a kind of moral advancement that accompanies their technological advancement. But this assumption may be misguided—there are many uncertainties. Indeed, we may not have to look further than own species to call this assumption into question. See Michaud (2006) for a careful consideration of this and related issues.

Chapter 9

The Intelligent Universe

James Gardner

Overview

In the opening chapter of *The Crooked Timber of Humanity,* British intellectual historian Isaiah Berlin famously observed that two factors, above all others, shaped human history in the 20th century. The first was the flourishing of the natural sciences and technology, which Berlin celebrated as "the greatest success story of our time."[1] The second factor consisted of "the great ideological storms that have altered the lives of virtually all mankind: the Russian Revolution and its aftermath—totalitarian tyrannies of both right and left and the explosions of nationalism, racism, and, in places, of religious bigotry."[2]

Both great movements—the century's remarkable record of scientific and technological advancement and its simultaneous embrace of horrifying genocide and total warfare—began, Berlin reminded us, "with ideas in people's heads: ideas about what relations between men have been, are, might be and should be."[3] It was for this reason, Berlin believed, that "we cannot confine our attention to the great impersonal forces, natural and man-made, which act upon us."[4] Rather we desperately need to launch a kind of Manhattan Project in cultural anthropology:

> The goals and motives that guide human action must be looked at in the light of all that we know and understand; their roots and growth, their essence, and above all their validity, must be critically examined with every intellectual resource that we have.[5]

The urgency of such an effort has grown since *The Crooked Timber of Humanity* was published in the United States in 1991, in large part because of the very success of the historical factor Berlin lauded as an unqualified success: the exponentially increasing capabilities of science and technology. Many analysts have noted that most of our powerful technologies can be put to evil as well as beneficial uses. Nuclear science can light a city with electricity or destroy it with an explosion. Genetic engineering can cure dreadful maladies or create unstoppable plagues. And nanotechnology can revolutionize product manufacturing or reduce our manufactured artifacts to featureless "grey goo."

But some thoughtful observers are beginning to focus on an even more portentous possibility: that we may be approaching a kind of cultural tipping point—what Ray Kurzweil calls a looming singularity—after which human history as we currently know it will be superseded by hypervelocity cultural evolution driven by transhuman computer intelligence. If this prospect is realistic, then a key task may be to not only comprehend the ideas that are currently driving historical trends (Berlin's charge to his fellow intellectual historians) but also to attempt to actually shape them—to launch an exercise in what I have previously called *memetic engineering*[6]—aimed at ensuring that the better angels of our nature prevail in the strange new transhuman cultural environment that may lie just over history's frontier.

This essay will suggest that the emergence of a novel scientific worldview that places life and intelligence at the center of the vast, seemingly impersonal physical processes of the cosmos may offer the best hope for meeting this uniquely daunting challenge. The concept of an intelligent universe may turn out to be the key tool with which memetic engineers will build the cultural foundation for a benign cosmic future in which human beings no longer play the dominant role.

Samuel Butler: Darwin's Forgotten Contemporary

Just four short years after the publication of Charles Darwin's *The Origin of Species*, Samuel Butler offered a prescient insight into the potential of artificial intelligence (AI) and artificial life to supersede the squishy biological processes that constitute the only kind of life with which humanity is familiar. Butler's eloquent speculations on this portentous topic rank favorably, in terms of prophetic power and contemporary relevance, with the heretical view expressed by Giordano Bruno in the 16th century concerning the multiple-biosphere nature of the cosmos (a view that constitutes the implicit premise of NASA's astrobiology initiative).

In an 1863 letter entitled "Darwin Among the Machines" Butler offered this startling vision of the future of terrestrial evolution:

> There are few things of which the present generation is more justly proud than the wonderful improvements which are daily taking place in all sorts of mechanical appliances. . . . But what would happen if technology continued to evolve so much more rapidly than the animal and vegetable kingdoms? Would it displace us in the supremacy of earth? Just as the vegetable kingdom was slowly developed from the mineral, and as in like manner the animal supervened upon the vegetable, so now in these last few ages an entirely new kingdom has sprung up, of which we as yet have only seen what will one day be considered the antediluvian prototypes of the race . . . . We are daily giving [machines] greater power and supplying by all sorts of ingenious contrivances that self-regulating, self-acting power which will be to them what intellect has been to the human race.[7]

The end-point of the postbiological evolutionary process that Butler foresaw was the displacement of humanity from its perch as the dominant form of intelligence on Earth.

> Who will be man's successor? To which the answer is: We are ourselves creating our own successors. Man will become to the machine what the horse and the dog are to man; the conclusion being that machines are, or are becoming, animate.[8]

Only now, nearly a century and a half after Butler articulated this disconcerting prophecy concerning the emergence of postbiological life and intelligence, are the implications of his revolutionary insights finally beginning to sink in. With the publication of path-breaking books about the future of computer-based AI like Ray Kurzweil's *The Age of Spiritual Machines*[9] and *The Singularity Is Near*[10] and the appearance in the scientific literature of papers offering novel perspectives on the likely predominance of postbiological intelligence in a life-friendly universe (such as Steven J. Dick's seminal contribution to the *International Journal of Astrobiology* entitled "Cultural evolution, the postbiological universe and SETI"[11]), we are witnessing an intellectual awakening that is unique in the history of mankind. A handful of cutting-edge opinion leaders like Silicon Valley venture capitalist Steve Jurvetson, entrepreneur and philanthropist Martine Rothblatt, and Microsoft founder Bill Gates are starting to focus seriously on the possible economic, cultural, and philosophical consequences of what may turn out to be the most profound evolutionary development since the Cambrian explosion: the emergence of a radically new form of life and intelligence on our planet that owes its primordial origin to the stochastic processes of Darwinian natural selection but stands poised to inherit a future that will be shaped by hypervelocity cultural evolution and—dare one utter the forbidden phrase?—exponentially accelerating iterations of self-directed intelligent design.

The daunting challenge that humanity faces—call it the Butler challenge in honor of Darwin's forgotten contemporary—is to understand and attempt to shape the powerful, perhaps irresistible, cultural forces that are propelling the terrestrial biosphere toward a transhuman and postbiological future.

Mapping Mount Invisible

In a nutshell, the daunting task that faces us is to map and then sculpt a looming virtual edifice that I will provisionally call Mount Invisible.

In *Climbing Mount Improbable*[12] British ultra-Darwinist Richard Dawkins conjured up, as a metaphor to represent the evolutionary process, a vast and utterly improbable peak rising up from an essentially flat landscape of merely probable occurrences. Dawkins envisioned evolution as a lengthy tinkering exercise by which Mount Improbable is assembled, blind step by blind step, until finally the outrageously unlikely peak reveals itself in all its glory.

Natural selection serves as both mortar and mason in the process of building Mount Improbable, not only generating (in Darwin's felicitous phrase) endless forms most beautiful and most wonderful, but also prolonging for millennia the persistence of intricate and negentropic configurations of living matter (species of plants, animals, and bacteria) whose continued existence seems, in raw statistical terms, as vanishingly improbable as the spontaneous self-assembly of successive generations of Boeing 747s from the dust of the asteroid belt.

In facing the Butler challenge, we confront two tasks that dwarf, in terms of difficulty, the relatively straightforward scientific challenge of mapping Mount Improbable:

- Modeling, not the accessible façade of Mount Improbable that was erected by the historical process of terrestrial evolution, but rather an unseen future edifice—Mount Invisible. That is to say, the Butler challenge calls upon us to model, at least in coarse-grained fashion, the future course of a cultural evolutionary process that will supersede the human stage of evolution and, by definition, transcend our human capacity to understand its dynamics in microscopic detail; and

- Perturbing the future process of cultural evolution by means of which Mount Invisible will arise in a manner that will render the entire edifice human-friendly (or at least human-tolerant) over the long term (or at least over the short-to-medium term). Think of the second half of the Butler challenge as a cultural engineering project aimed at deliberately sculpting the landscape of Mount Invisible in such a way as to include human-friendly caves, passages and meadows within the ample confines of its unknown geography.

Whether the human mind is capable of meeting the Butler challenge— or even taking it seriously—is an open question. Yet the Butler challenge may present the most urgent and profound existential crisis that we shall ever confront as a species. And—contrary to popular assumptions—we may not have much time to come up with a strategy for dealing with it.

The Looming Cultural Singularity and the Urgency of the Butler Challenge

Most scientists associate the term "singularity" with a black hole—a bizarre region predicted by Einstein's theory of general relativity in which an ultra-dense object (like a collapsed star) bends the fabric of the space time continuum so severely that nothing—not even a single photon—can escape to the outside universe. But the term has a different, albeit related, meaning in the context of the accelerating progress of technology. In 1958, Los Alamos National Laboratory scientist, Stanislaw Ulam, reported on a cryptic comment by the great mathematician and computer science theorist, John von Neumann, that appears to be the first pregnant thought about the implications of a looming technological singularity:

> One conversation centered on the ever-accelerating progress of technology and changes in the mode of human life, which gives the appearance of approaching some essential singularity in the history of the race beyond which human affairs, as we know them, could not continue.[13]

Amplifying on von Neumann's casual remark nearly a decade later, the statistician I. J. Good speculated on what the cryptic computer pioneer might have been talking about:

Let an ultraintelligent machine be defined as a machine that can far surpass all the intellectual activities of any man however clever. Since the design of machines is one of these intellectual activities, an ultraintelligent machine could design even better machines; there would then unquestionably be an "intelligence explosion," and the intelligence of man would be left far behind. Thus the first ultraintelligent machine is the last invention that man need ever make.[14]

The term "singularity" entered the popular science culture with the 1993 presentation at a NASA-sponsored conference of a seminal paper by San Diego State University statistician, Vernor Vinge. The abstract of the famous essay is as haunting today as it was more than a decade ago:

Within thirty years, we will have the technological means to create superhuman intelligence. Shortly after, the human era will be ended. Is such progress avoidable? If not to be avoided, can events be guided so that we may survive? These questions are investigated. Some possible answers (and some further dangers) are presented.[15]

Echoing Good's speculations about the prospects of an intelligence explosion as the essential hallmark of the coming singularity, Vinge went on to draw a scary analogy between this looming technological phenomenon and key patterns discernible in the history of biological evolution:

What are the consequences of this event? When greater-than-human intelligence drives progress, that progress will be much more rapid. In fact, there seems no reason why progress itself would not involve the creation of still more intelligent entities—on a still-shorter time scale. The best analogy that I see is with the evolutionary past: Animals can adapt to problems and make inventions, but often no faster than natural selection can do its work—the world acts as its own simulator in the case of natural selection. We humans have the ability to internalize the world and conduct "what ifs" in our heads; we can solve many problems thousands of times faster than natural selection. Now by creating the means to execute those simulations at much higher speeds, we are entering a regime as radically different from our own human past as we humans are from the lower animals.[16]

The lessons of our evolutionary past were, in Vinge's view, not exactly comforting:

> From the human point of view this change will be a throwing away of all previous rules, perhaps in the blink of an eye, an exponential runaway beyond any hope of control. Developments that before were thought might only happen in "a million years" (if ever) will likely happen in the next century. [One commentator] paints a picture of the major changes happening in a matter of hours . . . . [The most disturbing consequence of the technological singularity is that any hyper-intelligent machine] would not be humankind's "tool"—any more than humans are the tools of rabbits or robins or chimpanzees.[17]

Understanding the linkage between our evolutionary past and our probable evolutionary future may be of great importance, despite the superficial differences between slow-paced natural biological evolution and hyper-fast technological and cultural natural selection. Indeed, I would hazard a guess that if Charles Darwin were alive today and fully apprised of the truly revolutionary trends now becoming manifest in what might be called the extended terrestrial biosphere,[18] he would conclude that the sturdy engine of evolution, its vital force undiminished by the passage of centuries, is now poised to hurtle through an invisible barrier and effect a transformational change perhaps equal in import to that ushered in by the Cambrian explosion half a billion years ago when multicellular animals, exhibiting a dazzling array of brand-new body plans, began to proliferate in ancient seas.

Darwin would likely conclude as well that *artificial* selection—of which he made artful metaphorical use in *The Origin of Species* to illustrate his hypothesis of speciation through natural selection—has, in our modern era, virtually displaced *natural* selection as evolution's key propellant, at least with respect to the future pathway of human biological development. And the theorist would doubtless contemplate with awe the abiding reality that deep geological time—the enormous stretch of millennia that utterly dwarfs a human lifespan and challenges the very capacity of our biologically evolved human imagination to conceive of its vastness—remains the vital arena in which evolution's epic story continues to unfold.

But the great naturalist would immediately recognize that there is a crucial difference between the process of natural selection as it operated in the distant past and the novel possibilities currently open to the evolutionary process. A 21st century version of Charles Darwin would conclude that, while a vision of time's immensity remains the vital key in reaching an understanding of evolution's radical potential, it is a realization of the fathomless magnitude of *future time* and *future history* that is of utmost importance today. A modern Darwin would concur with the conclusion of Princeton physicist, John Wheeler: most of the time available for life and intelligence to achieve their ultimate capabilities lie in the distant cosmic future, not in the cosmic past. As cosmologist Frank Tipler has bluntly stated, "Almost all of space and time lies in the future. By focusing attention only on the past and present, science has ignored almost all of reality. Since the domain of scientific study is the whole of reality, it is about time science decided to study the future evolution of the universe."[19]

Although you won't read about it in any *New York Times* or *Wall Street Journal* headlines, the disruptive potential of *future evolution* is the emerging leitmotif in advanced biological theorizing today. The current ID vs. Darwinism dust-up on which the popular press focuses myopically will turn out to be a minor historical footnote to the portentous evolutionary drama that is about to reveal itself in all its unnerving grandeur.

Futurist Ray Kurzweil, more than any other author, has envisioned in rich detail the looming scenario. As he writes in *The Singularity Is Near*,[20] the crucial inflection point will be a moment when artificial intelligence surpasses the capabilities of the human mind and then leaps further forward at a lightning pace that we can barely imagine. This development will result in the appearance of a form of *strong artificial intelligence* that will, for the first time, supplant the human mind as the dominant form of intelligence on the planet:

> By the end of this century, computational or mechanical intelligence will be trillions of trillions of times more powerful than unaided human brain power. . . . Artificial intelligence will necessarily exceed human intelligence for several reasons. First, machines can share knowledge and communicate with one another far more efficiently than can humans . . . . Second, humanity's intellectual skills have developed in ways that

have been evolutionarily encouraged in natural environments. These skills, which are primarily based on our abilities to recognize and extract meaning from patterns, enable us to be highly proficient in certain tasks, such as distinguishing faces, identifying objects, and recognizing language sounds. Unfortunately, our brains are less well-suited for dealing with more-complex patterns, such as those that exist in financial, scientific, or product data . . . . Finally, as human knowledge migrates to the Web, machines will demonstrate increased proficiency in reading, understanding, and synthesizing all human-machine information.[21]

Kurzweil acknowledges the prospect of "runaway AI"—the exponential acceleration in AI capabilities that is likely to ensue when machine intelligences gain access to their own design specifications and are able to directly intervene in their evolutionary future by engineering improvements in their progeny—and even assigns a probable date to this momentous development:

The logic of runaway AI is valid, but we still need to consider the timing. Achieving human levels in a machine will not *immediately* cause a runaway phenomenon. Consider that a human level of intelligence has limitations . . . . [T]his [runaway] acceleration won't happen immediately when a computer passes the Turing test. The Turing test is comparable to matching the capabilities of an average, educated human and thus is closer to the example of [a sample of average] humans [found at] a shopping mall. It will take time for computers to master all of the requisite skills and to marry these skills with all the necessary knowledge bases. Once we've succeeded in creating a machine that can pass the Turing test (around 2029), the succeeding period will be an era of consolidation in which nonbiological intelligence will make rapid gains. However, the extraordinary expansion contemplated for the Singularity, in which human intelligence is multiplied by billions, won't take place until the mid-2040s.[22]

In short, humanity can look forward to a stretch of around 30 years from the moment you read this sentence until the day arrives—think of it as

Singularity Judgment Day—when artificial forms of intelligence gain control of their own destiny and race past the pitifully outclassed meat computers housed in the skulls of *Homo sapiens.*

If Kurzweil's predictions turns out to be accurate—and they have been uncannily accurate in the past, inspiring Bill Gates to remark that "Ray Kurzweil is the best person I know at predicting the future of artificial intelligence"[23]—then humanity has perhaps three decades to prepare to meet the Butler challenge.

The Bottom-Up Focus of the Singularity Institute for Artificial Intelligence

The California-based Singularity Institute for Artificial Intelligence is one of a handful of think-tanks and research centers around the world that are seriously embarked on the study of ways to avoid the emergence of unfriendly artificial general intelligence. Outside of this tiny community of dedicated researchers, the topic of prophylaxis against unfriendly AI seems quixotic and premature at best—why should we worry about the potential appearance of hostile AI when we have not yet succeeded in creating general AI? The short answer from Eliezer Yudkowsky, a leading researcher affiliated with the Singularity Institute, is that if we wait until an AI acquires transhuman intelligence, it will be too late to retrofit that particular AI with human-tolerant sensibilities or instincts:

> Let us concede for the sake of argument that, for all we know (and it seems to me also probable in the real world) that an AI has the capability to make a sudden, sharp, large leap in intelligence. What follows from this? First and foremost: it follows that a reaction I often hear, "We don't need to worry about Friendly AI because we don't yet have AI," is misguided or downright suicidal. We cannot rely on having distant advance warning before AI is created; past technological revolutions usually did not telegraph themselves to people *alive at the time*, whatever was said afterward in hindsight. The mathematics and techniques of Friendly AI will not materialize from nowhere when needed; it takes years to lay firm foundations. And we need to solve the Friendly AI challenge *before* artificial general intelligence is created, not afterward.[24]

For Yudkowsky, the key strategy for avoiding an existential catastrophe for humanity is to figure out a way to build an AI that is benignly motivated toward human beings from the inception:

> The possibility of sharp jumps in intelligence . . . implies a higher standard for Friendly AI techniques. The technique cannot assume the programmers' ability to monitor the AI *against its will*, rewrite the AI *against its will*, bring to bear the threat of superior military force; nor may the algorithm assume that the programmers control a "reward button" which a smarter AI could wrest from the programmers, et cetera. Indeed no one should be making these assumptions to begin with. The indispensable protection is an AI that does not *want* to hurt you. Without the indispensable, no auxiliary defense can be regarded as safe. No system is secure that searches for ways to defeat its own security. If the AI would harm humanity in *any* context, you must be doing *something* wrong on a very deep level, laying your foundations awry. You are building a shotgun, pointing the shotgun at your foot, and pulling the trigger. You are deliberately setting into motion a created cognitive dynamic that will seek in some context to hurt you. That is the wrong behavior for the dynamic; write code that does something else instead. For much the same reason, Friendly AI programmers should assume that AI has total access to its own source code. If the AI *wants* to modify itself to be no longer friendly, then friendliness has *already* failed, at the point when the AI forms that intention. Any solution that depends on the AI not being able to modify itself must be broken in some way or other, and will still be broken even if the AI never does modify itself. I do not say it should be the *only* precaution, but the *primary* and *indispensable* precaution is that you choose into existence an AI that does not choose to hurt humanity.[25]

No one has the slightest notion of how to program innate human friend-liness into an artificial intelligence that may, over time, grow to be billions of times smarter than the smartest human being. But it is certainly an approach worth pursuing. An alternative approach is outlined in the next section.

An Alternative Approach:
Memetic Engineering With Cultural Attractors

The approach of the Singularity Institute can be characterized as a bottom-up strategy for constructing Friendly AI. The basic idea is to build a set of algorithms into an AI's source code that will cause that particular AI never to desire to turn against its human progenitors and to refrain from any action that would harm human beings. This approach is similar in principle to inserting into the deep structure of an AI's source code a set of Isaac Asimov's fictional laws of robotics.

An alternative approach may be to design a set of cultural attractors that could conceivably perturb the developmental direction of the future cultural environment in which strong AI will emerge in such a way as to encourage the prolongation of human-friendly sensibilities and outcomes. This top-down strategy can be characterized as an exercise in what I have previously called a possible future scientific discipline of memetic engineering:

> A meme-focused vision of culture and consciousness acknowledges forthrightly that memes are not mere random effluvia of the human experience but powerful control mechanisms that impose a largely invisible deep structure on a wide range of complex phenomena—language, scientific thinking, political behavior, productive work, religion, philosophical discourse, even history itself . . . . What if it were possible to construct a new science of the meme—memetic engineering—analogous to the discipline of genetic engineering? Such a science would allow us to manipulate complex patterns of replicating memes and achieve consistent and predictable manifestations in the form of a precisely altered cultural phenotype. Who would then be in charge of the course of cultural evolution, ourselves or our selfish memes?[26]

Are there useful precedents that could serve as guideposts for this audacious undertaking? I suggest that a search for guideposts might usefully begin with a careful analysis—along the lines advocated by Isaiah Berlin in *The Crooked Timber of Humanity*—of the deep cultural forces that led to the birth and triumph of western science itself. This seems particularly appropriate inasmuch as western science and technology is the cultural substrate out of which strong AI is likely to emerge.

Do the cultural forces that birthed western science exhibit qualities that identify them as particularly efficacious cultural attractors? If so, can one abstract from the qualities that rendered those forces so uniquely powerful in order to identify general characteristics of efficacious cultural attractors that might conceivably guide the exercise in memetic engineering that I have proposed?

A useful place to begin is with the cultural analysis of British philosopher, Alfred North Whitehead. In his classic Lowell Lectures delivered at Harvard in 1925, Whitehead put forward an intriguing explanation for the curious fact that European civilization alone had yielded the cultural phenomenon we know as scientific inquiry. Whitehead's theory was that "the faith in the possibility of science, generated antecedently to the development of modern scientific theory, is an unconscious derivative from medieval theology."[27] More specifically, he contended that

> the greatest contribution of medievalism to the formation of the scientific movement [was] the inexpugnable belief that every detailed occurrence can be correlated with its antecedents in a perfectly definite manner, exemplifying general principles. Without this belief the incredible labours of scientists would be without hope. It is this instinctive conviction, vividly poised before the imagination, which is the motive power of research—that there is a secret, a secret which can be unveiled.[28]

From where did this instinctive conviction come that there is discoverable pattern of order in the realm of nature? The source of the conviction, in Whitehead's view, was not the inherently obvious rationality of nature but rather a peculiarly European habit of thought—a deeply ingrained, religiously derived, and essentially irrational faith in the existence of a rational natural order. The scientific sensibility, in short, was an unconscious derivative of medieval religious belief in the existence of a well-ordered universe that abides by invariant natural laws which can be discovered by dint of human investigation.

The most obvious characteristic of the cultural attractor that Whitehead identified was that it constituted a particular kind of *cosmology*—an encompassing vision of the rational nature of the universe and of the concomitant possibility of human scientific discovery. Perhaps this is the category of cultural attractor—an encompassing cosmology that defines a complementary role for both human and transhuman artificial intelligence—that we should be seeking in our search for methods with which to perturb ongoing cultural trends so as to encourage the emergence of human-friendly AI.

As the next section will suggest, the articulation of a novel scientific worldview that places life and intelligence at the center of the vast, seemingly impersonal physical processes of the cosmos may offer the best hope for meeting this daunting challenge. The concept of an intelligent universe may turn out to be the key tool with which memetic engineers can build the cultural foundation for a benign cosmic future in which human beings no longer play the dominant role.

The Key Cultural Attractor: The Concept of an Intelligent Universe

In two books—*Biocosm* and *The Intelligent Universe*—and in scientific papers published in the *International Journal of Astrobiology, Acta Astronautica, Complexity* and the *Journal of the British Interplanetary Society*—I have begun to articulate a novel (and concededly radical) cosmological vision which suggests that in attempting to explain the linkage between life, intelligence, and the biofriendly qualities of the cosmos, most mainstream scientists have, in essence, been peering through the wrong end of the telescope. My work asserts that life and intelligence are, in fact, the primary cosmological phenomena and that everything else—the constants of inanimate nature, the dimensionality of the universe, the origin of carbon and other elements in the hearts of giant supernovas, the pathway traced by biological evolution—is secondary and derivative. In the words of British Astronomer Royal, Martin Rees, my work embraces the proposition that "what we call the fundamental constants—the numbers that matter to physicists—may be secondary consequences of the final theory, rather than direct manifestations of its deepest and most fundamental level."[29] Rees's insight yields a glimpse of a new kind of cosmology that views the oddly biofriendly qualities of our anthropic universe—a universe adapted to the peculiar needs of carbon-based living creatures just as thoroughly as those creatures are adapted to the physical exigencies of the universe—not as an irksome curiosity but rather as a vital set of clues pointing toward a radically new vision of the basic nature of the cosmos.

The essence of my vision is that the emergence of life and intelligence are not meaningless accidents in a hostile, largely lifeless cosmos but are at the very heart of the vast machinery of creation, cosmological evolution, and cosmic replication.

The hypothesis that I developed—called the Selfish Biocosm hypothesis—was based on a set of conjectures put forward by Martin Rees, John Wheeler, Freeman Dyson, John Barrow, Frank Tipler, and Ray Kurzweil. Their futuristic visions suggested collectively that the ongoing process of biological and technological evolution was sufficiently robust, powerful, and open-ended that in the very distant future, a cosmologically extended biosphere could conceivably exert a global influence on the physical state of the entire cosmos. Think of this idea as the Gaia principle extended universe-wide.

A synthesis of these insights lead me directly to the central claim of the Selfish Biocosm hypothesis: that the ongoing process of biological and technological emergence, governed by still largely unknown laws of complexity, could function as a von Neumann controller and that a cosmologically extended biosphere could serve as a von Neumann duplicating machine in a conjectured process of cosmological replication.

I went on to speculate that the means by which the hypothesized cosmological replication process could occur was through the fabrication of baby universes by highly evolved intelligent life-forms. These hypothesized baby universes would themselves be endowed with a cosmic code—an ensemble of physical laws and constants—that would be life-friendly so as to enable life and ever more competent intelligence to emerge and eventually to repeat the cosmic reproduction cycle. Under this scenario, the physical laws and constants serve a cosmic function precisely analogous to that of DNA in Earthly creatures: they furnish a recipe for the birth and evolution of intelligent life and a blueprint, which provides the plan for construction of offspring.

I should add that if the fabrication of baby universes, which is the key step in the hypothesized cosmic reproductive cycle that I just outlined, sounds like outrageous science fiction—an "X-file too far," in the words of one of my critics—please be aware that the topic has begun to be rigorously explored by such eminent physicists as Andrei Linde of Stanford, Alan Guth of MIT (the father of inflation theory), Martin Rees of Cambridge, eminent astronomer Edward Harrison, and physicists Lawrence Krauss and Glenn Starkman.

This central claim of the Selfish Biocosm hypothesis offered a radically new and quite parsimonious explanation for the apparent mystery of an anthropic or biofriendly universe. If highly evolved intelligent life is the von Neumann duplicating machine that the cosmos employs to reproduce itself— if intelligent life is, in effect, the reproductive organ of the universe—then it is entirely logical and predictable that the laws and constants of nature should be rigged in favor of the emergence of life and the evolution of ever more capable intelligence. Indeed, the existence of such propensity is a falsifiable retrodiction of the hypothesis.

A fasifiable *prediction* of the SB hypothesis—and a key feature of my cosmological paradigm that is directly relevant to the putative exercise in memetic engineering that I have proposed here—is that the process of progression of the cosmos through critical thresholds in its life cycle, while perhaps not strictly inevitable, is relatively robust. One such critical threshold is the emergence of human-level and higher transhuman intelligence, which is essential to the scaling up of biological and technological processes to the stage at which those processes could conceivably exert an influence on the global state of the cosmos. The conventional wisdom among evolutionary theorists, typified by the thinking of the late Stephen Jay Gould, is that the abstract probability of the emergence of anything like human intelligence through the natural process of biological evolution was vanishingly small. According to this viewpoint, the emergence of human-level intelligence was a staggeringly improbable contingent event. A few distinguished contrarians like Simon Conway Morris, Robert Wright, E. O. Wilson, and Christian de Duve take an opposing position, arguing on the basis of the pervasive phenomenon of convergent evolution and other evidence that the appearance of human-level intelligence was highly probable, if not virtually inevitable. The latter position is consistent with the Selfish Biocosm hypothesis while the Gould position is not.

In my books and scientific papers I suggest that the issue of the robustness of the emergence of human-level and higher intelligence is potentially subject to experimental resolution by means of at least three realistic tests: SETI research, artificial life evolution, and the emergence of transhuman computer intelligence predicted by computer science theorist Ray Kurzweil and others. The discovery of extraterrestrial intelligence, the discovery of an ability on the part of artificial life-forms that exist and evolve in software environments to acquire autonomy and intelligence, and the emergence of a capacity on the part of advanced self-programming computers to attain and then exceed human levels of intelligence are all falsifiable implications of the Selfish Biocosm hypothesis because they are consistent with the notion that the emergence of evermore competent intelligence is a robust natural phenomenon.

This idea is similar to what Steven J. Dick has called the Intelligence Principle, which he describes as follows:

> The Intelligence Principle: *the maintenance, improvement and perpetuation of knowledge and intelligence is the central driving force of cultural evolution, and that to the extent intelligence can be improved, it will be improved.*[30]

Because this is a cosmological vision that predicts the emergence of transhuman artificial intelligence, it would seem to be congenial to those brainy AIs on whose activities and cogitations the fate of the universe is hypothesized to depend. But what is there in this vision that would perturb the cultural environment in which an AI is likely to emerge so as to encourage friendliness with that AI's less brainy human progenitors? That is the most difficult issue of all: why would human beings matter at all in a transhuman, postbiological universe?

Dreams of a Trans-Temporal Cosmic Community

We know from Einstein's theories and from experimental evidence that time is not the absolute, invariant, and universal tick-tick-tick process that Isaac Newton envisioned, but rather a kind of elastic and malleable phenomenon, slowing down to a crawl in a spacecraft approaching the speed of light or in the presence of a super strong gravitational field. Many scientists conjecture, based on the pioneering work of Kurt Gödel, J. Richard Gott III, Kip Thorne, and others, that past and future states of the cosmos can loop together in an unusual configuration called a closed timelike curve (CTC).

In a paper published in *Complexity*, I offered a riff on the CTC themes of Gödel and Gott in order to offer a possible explanation for what many observers regard as the major unanswered question raised by my Selfish Biocosm hypothesis: how did the cycle of life-mediated cosmic reproduction get started in the first place? Here is the CTC-derived scenario that I put forward in an attempt to answer that question:

> For purposes of the present inquiry, the key perspective is offered by what physicist John Wheeler calls the super-Copernican principle. Derived from the Copenhagen interpretation of quantum physics, this "principle rejects the now-centeredness of any account of existence as firmly as Copernicus rejected here-centeredness." According to this principle, the future can have at least as important a role in shaping the present moment as the past.
>
> The most important aspect of Wheeler's insight is not that we must embrace the specific mechanism of retroactive causation favored by Wheeler and the advocates of the Copenhagen interpretation of quantum mechanics (the retroactive impact on quantum phenomena of observer-participancy), but rather that we should be open to counterintuitive notions of causation, if they appear to be consistent with novel yet mathematically plausible accounts of physical reality.
>
> In particular, the vision of the cosmos as a closed timelike curve that allows at least limited information flow across the putative Big Bounce threshold offers a new paradigm that may allow us to formulate radically novel theoretical

possibilities concerning the origin and nature of biological information and of the specified complexity it exhibits.

According to this paradigm, the process of biological information generation can be viewed as an essentially eternal autocatalytic process in which past and future temporal states are linked in a coevolutionary relationship. The wave of causation moves from what we call the past to what we call the future and back again to the past across the Big Crunch era to a new Big Bang era without disruption (but, we shall see shortly, with possible causal filtering).

Causation defines the relationship between all points on the CTC, but the relationship of cause and effect is not temporally restricted in the sense we naively perceive. As Wheeler put it with uncanny prescience (though with a different causal mechanism in mind), the history of the cosmos "is not a history as we usually conceive history. It is not one thing happening after another after another. It is a totality in which what happens 'now' gives reality to what happened 'then,' perhaps even determines what happened then." Because the CTC is curved *and* timelike *and* closed *and* unblemished by a final singularity, each point on the CTC is, to at least a limited degree, both the cause *and* effect of every other point. Time flows in only one direction in this scenario but because the CTC unites past and future at the Big Crunch threshold, the two temporal states can coevolve.

The CTC that is hypothesized to be our cosmos thus may be a classic autocatalytic set, what Wheeler ventured to call a "self-excited circuit" and a "grand synthesis, pulling itself together all the time as a whole." The implication for the origin of biological information should be apparent: not only the universe but also the life-friendly cosmic code and indeed life itself (and the specified complexity it embodies) could conceivably be its own mother under this scenario.[31]

The relevance of this concededly speculative scenario to the present inquiry is this: if our cosmos is indeed a CTC—or if our multiverse is a series of branching CTCs—then the human-dominated past will continue to exert a causal effect on a transhuman future, long after humanity ceases to be the dominant form of intelligence on planet Earth. Likewise, the transhuman future will exert a causal relationship on prior states of the cosmos, including the era of human intellectual supremacy. In the inimitable phrase of John Wheeler, this exotic scenario envisions the whole shebang of past, present, and future not as a traditional sequential history but rather as a "self-excited circuit" and a "grand synthesis, pulling itself together all the time as a whole."

This notion, strange and counterintuitive as it may be, might conceivably offer the cultural foundation for a credible and sustainable vision of a trans-temporal cosmic community. And that vision might itself be the key cultural attractor that could ensure a benign fate for humanity in a strange new world—a world that may be mere decades away—in which human beings will no longer constitute the dominant form of intelligence.

What is it about this particular cosmological vision that might make it the key cultural attractor with regard to the task at hand and thus render it an appropriate tool for memetic engineers seeking to ensure a human-friendly future in a world dominated by AI? I suggest that the primary utility of the vision consists of its status as an encompassing cosmology that defines a complementary cosmological role for both human and transhuman artificial intelligence. This novel scientific worldview places life and intelligence (both biological and postbiological) at the center of the vast, seemingly impersonal physical processes of the universe. This unique aspect of the vision may conceivably offer the best hope for meeting the challenge of engineering the emergence of human-friendly AI.

The essence of this cosmological vision is that we inhabit a cosmos that is a kind of ecosystem-in-waiting—a universe custom-made for the purpose of yielding life and ever-ascending intelligence. Central to this idea is the notion that every creature and every intelligent entity—great and small, biological and postbiological—plays some indefinable role in an awesome process by which intelligence gains hegemony over inanimate nature. This notion implies that every living thing and every postbiological form of intelligence is linked together in a joint endeavor of vast scope and indefinable duration. We soldier on together—bacteria, people, extraterrestrials (if they exist), and hyper-intelligent computers—pressing forward, against all odds and the implacable foe that is entropy, toward a distant future we can only faintly imagine. But it is together, in a spirit of cooperation and kinship, that we journey hopefully toward our distant destination.

In summary, the concept of an intelligent universe populated by a trans-temporal cosmic community encompassing both biological and postbiological forms of intelligence may turn out to be the key tool with which memetic engineers can build the cultural foundation for a benign cosmic future in which human beings no longer play the dominant role.

Conclusion

Ever since human beings first lifted their eyes to the heavens, visions of the cosmos have served as powerful cultural attractors, shaping not only concepts of the nature of the universe but also of humanity's role within it. Now a seismic cultural event may loom just over history's horizon: the emergence of transhuman artificial intelligence. In the aftermath of what some futurists call a cultural singularity, humans will—assuming these predictions are correct— be displaced as the dominant form of intelligence on planet Earth.

Will humanity be able to shape this portentous transition so as to ensure a human-friendly (or at least human-tolerant) future? The answer may depend on whether we can figure out how to engage in a novel exercise in memetic engineering—developing and disseminating a powerful new cosmological paradigm that will prescribe complementary roles for human and transhuman forms of intelligence—before singularity judgment day arrives and the human race confronts the unnerving prospect of being swept aside by an uncontrollable tsunami of runaway AI.

Endnotes

1. Isaiah Berlin, *The Crooked Timber of Humanity: Chapters in the History of Ideas* (New York: Vintage, 1992), p. 1.

2. Ibid.

3. Ibid.

4. Ibid., p. 2.

5. Ibid.

6. James Gardner, "Memetic Engineering." *WIRED* (May 1996): 101.

7. Samuel Butler, "Darwin Among the Machines" (June 13, 1863) in *The Notebooks of Samuel Butler* (Festing Jones, 1912), quoted in Ray Kurzweil, *The Singularity Is Near: When Humans Transcend Biology* (New York: Viking, 2005), p. 205.

8. Ibid.

9. Ray Kurzweil, *The Age of Spiritual Machines: When Computers Exceed Human Intelligence* (New York: Viking, 1999).

10. Ray Kurzweil, *The Singularity Is Near: When Humans Transcend Biology* (New York: Viking, 2005).

11. Steven J. Dick, "Cultural evolution, the postbiological universe and SETI." *International Journal of Astrobiology* 2, no. 1(2003): 65–74.

12. Richard Dawkins, *Climbing Mount Improbable* (New York: Norton, 1997).

13. Stanislaw Ulum, "Tribute to John Neumann." *Bulletin of the American Mathematical Society* 64, no. 3, part 2 (May 1958): 1–49.

14. I. J. Good, "Speculations Concerning the First Ultraintelligent Machine." *Advances in Computers* 6 (Franz L. Alt and Morris Rubinoff, eds.) (Academic Press, 1965): 31–88.

15. Vernor Vinge, "The Coming Technological Singularity." Available at *www.accelerating.org/articles/comingtechsingularity.html*.

16. Ibid.

17. Ibid.

18. The extended terrestrial biosphere is the totality of all life on the planet plus all of life's artifacts, including the biologically perturbed atmosphere as well as the physical and cultural output of human technological civilization. A similar but more limited concept was articulated by Richard Dawkins in *The Extended Phenotype* (Oxford: Oxford University Press, 1999 [revised edition]).

19. Frank Tipler, *The Physics of Immortality* (New York: Doubleday, 1994), p. 2.

20. Ray Kurzweil, *The Singularity Is Near: When Humans Transcend Biology.* (New York: Viking, 2005).

21. Ray Kurzweil, "Reinventing Humanity: The Future of Machine-Human Intelligence." *The Futurist* (March–April 2006): 43–44.

22. Ray Kurzweil, *The Singularity Is Near: When Humans Transcend Biology* (New York: Viking, 2005), pp. 262–263.

23. Bill Gates, cover blurb for *The Singularity Is Near.*

24. Eliezer Yudkowsky, "Artificial Intelligence as a Positive and Negative Factor in Global Risk" in *Global Catastrophic Risks* (N. Bostrom and M. Ćirković, eds.) (forthcoming).

25. Ibid.

26. James Gardner, "Memetic Engineering." *WIRED* 4.05 (May 1996): 101.

27. Alfred North Whitehead, *Science and the Modern World* (New York: Free Press, 1967), p. 13.

28. Ibid., p. 12.

29. Martin J. Rees, "Life in Our Universe and Others: A Cosmological Perspective" in *Many Worlds: The New Universe, Extraterrestrial Life & the Theological Implications.* (Steven Dick, ed.) (Philadelphia: Templeton Foundation Press, 2000), pp. 61, 76, quoted in James Gardner, "Dreams of a Cosmic Community." *Science & Spirit* (available at *http://www.science-spirit.org/article_detail.php?article_id=375*).

30. Steven J. Dick, "Cultural evolution, the postbiological universe and SETI." *International Journal of Astrobiology* 2, no. 1 (2003): 65–74, 69.

31. James N. Gardner, "Coevolution of the Cosmic Past and Future: The Selfish Biocosm as a Closed Timelike Curve." *Complexity* 10, no. 5 (May/June 2005): 14, 17–18.

Chapter 10

Life, Mind, and Culture as Fundamental Properties of the Universe

Paul C. W. Davies

Taking Life Seriously

A few years ago, Stephen Hawking wrote, "The human race is just a chemical scum on a moderate-sized planet."[1] His bleak assessment reflects the prevailing view among scientists concerning the place of life in the universe. Traditionally, living systems have been regarded as a trivial and incidental embellishment to the physical world, of no particular significance in the overall cosmic scheme of things. In this essay I shall argue that the orthodox view is profoundly wrong. Not only do I believe that life is a key part of the evolution of the universe, I maintain that mind and culture, too, will turn out to be of fundamental significance in the grand story of the cosmos.

My argument has to appeal to indirect evidence, in view of the fact that Earth provides the only samples we currently know of life, mind, and culture. It is certainly possible that we are alone in the universe. If so, it does not necessarily mean that life is insignificant, even if it is confined at the moment to one planet. In principle, life and intelligence have the potential to spread across the cosmos from Earth, and given the immense duration of time available before the universe become depleted of useful sources of energy, there seems to be plenty of opportunity for our descendants to play a literally cosmic role.

Two centuries ago, many scientists believed that life is indeed a fundamental phenomenon because they thought that some sort of life force was responsible for the remarkable properties that living organisms display. This "life stuff" was treated as a basic property of biology. Today we know that living organisms are machines that derive their special qualities from their great organizational complexity, not from a life force. Life is distinctive not as a result of the material from which it is made, but because of the things it does.

Nevertheless, it is still possible to argue that life is a fundamental physical phenomenon, as opposed to a quirky aberration of matter and energy. Firstly, biological organisms are a product of a very basic organizational principle: replication with variation, plus selection. Because this Darwinian mechanism will apply anywhere in the cosmos, life may be considered to be a product of a fundamental and universal principle.

A second argument for why life should be regarded as fundamental has been given by David Deutsch, based on the informational properties of genomes. Deutsch points out that a genome is in effect an internal representation of the world, constructed over vast time scales by evolution. It embodies the information needed for the organism to be adapted to its environment. To put it simply, the genome "knows about" its environment. "Life is about the physical embodiment of knowledge," writes Deutsch. "It says that it is possible to embody the laws of physics, as they apply to every physically possible environment, in programs for a virtual reality generator. Genes are such programs."[2]

The ability of living organisms to construct a computational representation of the universe hinges on the Turing principle, namely, that it is possible to build a machine that can be programmed to perform any computation that any other classical physical system can perform. The Turing principle, often taken for granted in this computer age, represents a very deep property of the world, and it depends crucially on the types of physical objects that exist in nature. Deutsch argues that knowledge of the world as encoded in genetic information is just as much a fundamental physical quantity as mass or electric charge. Imagine, he says, a future civilization on Earth with the technology to modify not just the planet but the Sun, as well. (One reason might be to extend its longevity.) The evolution of stars like the Sun is well understood, and the properties of the aging Sun can be determined from the standard laws of physics. An alien observer on the far side of the galaxy who modeled the behavior of our Sun in the standard way would find disagreement with observation, because the Sun would have been altered by the scientific knowledge of the terrestrial civilization. So knowledge can, in principle, have an impact big enough to affect astrophysics.[3]

Taking Mind Seriously

It is fashionable to downplay the significance of consciousness, perhaps because of its perceived mystical associations. However, this is in my view a serious error. Conscious organisms should not be casually shrugged aside as just another sort of physical system, albeit a peculiar one. The qualities of conscious systems are totally unlike anything else found in nature. Mental entities such as thoughts and feelings are clearly not just "other sorts of things," on a par with material objects like atoms or rocks. They occupy a class apart. To be sure, it is possible to determine the correlations between physical (neural) states and mental states, but this still leaves untouched the so-called hard problem of subjectivity and qualia.[4] For this reason, some philosophers are prepared to defend the fundamental nature of the mental realm, and to argue that subjective experience cannot be relegated to a sequence of mere epiphenomena attaching to physical processes.

There is an additional philosophical reason why mind occupies a significant place in the universe. It concerns the fact that minds (human minds, at least) are much more than mere observers of the physical world. Human beings have come to *understand* the world, at least in part, through the processes of reasoning and science. By developing mathematics, it has been possible for scientists to unravel the hidden subtext of nature that we call the laws of physics. These laws are not manifest in day-to-day observations, but must be deduced through a sequence of arcane procedures and reasoning.

Human understanding of nature through science, rational reasoning, and mathematics points to a deep and still-unexplained link between life, mind, and cosmos. Somehow, the universe has engineered not only its own self-awareness, but its own self-comprehension. It is hard to see this astonishing property of (at least some) living organisms as an accidental and incidental by-product of physics, a lucky fluke of biological evolution. Rather, the fact that mind is linked into the deep workings of the cosmos in this manner suggests that there is something truly fundamental and literally cosmic in the emergence of sentience.

Some physicists, too, have argued that consciousness is a fundamental property of the world. One argument centers on the peculiar role that the observer plays in quantum mechanics. This subject has been well reviewed elsewhere, so I shall not dwell on it here (see, for example, the work of Stapp[5]). However, I should like to draw attention to a rather different argument due to the theoretical physicist and cosmologist Andrei Linde. It concerns the extreme case of when quantum mechanics is applied to the universe as a whole—the subject of quantum cosmology. Linde's argument focuses on the passage of time. He points out that temporal intervals are not absolute, but involve a change of one physical system relative to another, for example, how many times the hands of a clock go round relative to the rotation of Earth.

When considering the universe as a whole, time loses its meaning, for there is nothing else relative to which the universe may be said to change. This "vanishing" of time becomes explicit when quantum mechanics is applied to the entire universe, and has been the subject of much discussion.[6] To recover the notion of duration of time, one may consider the universe to be separated into two subsystems: an observer with a clock, and the remainder. The observer may then gauge the passage of time relative to the evolution of the rest of the universe by inspecting the clock, i.e., by making a quantum measurement on the clock variables that are correlated with some degrees of freedom of the rest of the universe (such as the size of the universe). Linde expresses the fundamental role played by the observer in recovering the passage of time from a "frozen" quantum universe: "Thus we see that without introducing an observer, we have a dead universe, which does not evolve in time. . . . In the absence of observers, our universe is dead."[7]

The claim that life and mind are intrinsically fundamental to the workings of nature, and not irrelevant aberrations, implies that they are "written into" the laws of the universe and therefore are the expected, even inevitable, product of the outworking of these laws. This point of view is sometimes called the strong anthropic principle, and has received support from some prominent scientists. Thus Freeman Dyson has famously written: "As we look out into the universe and identify the many accidents of physics and astronomy that have worked together to our benefit, it almost seems as if the universe must in some sense have known we were coming."[8] Likewise the Cambridge biologist Simon Conway Morris says that, "there is, if you like, seeded into the initiation of the universe itself the inevitability of intelligence."[9] The strong anthropic principle also conforms with the widespread belief that the emergence of life is somehow inevitable because it is "built into" the laws of the universe. Christian de Duve calls life "a cosmic imperative."[10] The biophysicist Stuart Kauffman echoes Freeman Dyson by declaring that we are "at home in the universe."[11] The ambitious astrobiology program funded by NASA and other institutions and the SETI project to seek evidence of extraterrestrial intelligence are based on the assumption that life is not a freak phenomenon confined to Earth, but a widespread and inevitable outcome of physical laws that are intrinsically slanted in favor of biology. Such a view has obvious popular appeal, but is it credible?

Fine-Tuning in the Laws of Physics

Support for the anthropic principle comes from the well-known fact that the existence of life balances on a knife edge, delicately dependant on a number of special features built into the structure of the universe. One way to understand how sensitively the existence of life is poised on the fortuitous arrangement of the laws of physics is to envisage playing God and tinkering with the properties of the universe. Imagine that before you is a machine with knobs—a Designer Machine. One knob controls the strength of gravity, another alters the masses of all electrons, and yet another changes the number of space dimensions. It turns out that to describe the observed universe, you need to set the position of about 30 knobs.[12] Unless many of the knob settings—or "parameter values"—lie very close to the ones nature actually selected, there would be nobody around to witness the result. Changing some of the values by even a scintilla would have lethal consequences.[13]

One of the best-known examples of this biofriendly "fine-tuning" of the laws of physics concerns carbon, the element on which all known life is based. The Big Bang that started the universe coughed out plenty of hydrogen and helium, but no carbon. So where did the carbon in our bodies come from? The answer was worked out in the 1950s. Most of the chemical elements heavier than helium were manufactured in the hot cores of stars, by nuclear fusion reactions. It is the energy released by these reactions that makes the stars shine.

The details of stellar nuclear reactions are fairly straightforward, with a notable exception—carbon. Most nuclear reactions in stars occur when two atomic nuclei collide and fuse. But carbon cannot form in this manner because all the possible intermediate steps from helium to carbon involve highly unstable nuclei. The solution, worked out by Fred Hoyle, is for carbon to form from the simultaneous collision of *three* helium nuclei. However, the probability of such a triple encounter is low, and the carbon yield appears at first sight to be negligible.

Hoyle reasoned that the triple-collision reaction must be amplified somehow, or there would be no carbon—and hence, no life—in the universe. The amplification of nuclear reactions can sometimes occur due to a quantum effect known as resonance. If the masses and energies of the participating nuclei are just right, then a resonance in the carbon nucleus could explain how abundant carbon is formed in stars. Hoyle worked backwards—he knew the particle masses and energies, and he used them to predict the existence of a carbon resonance. He then persuaded Willy Fowler, a nuclear physicist at the California Institute of Technology, to test the prediction by conducting an experiment. Hoyle was right: carbon has a resonant state at exactly the right energy to enable stars to manufacture abundant carbon, and thereby seed the universe with this life-encouraging substance.

Fred Hoyle immediately realized that the existence of the carbon resonance at just the right energy was an astonishing coincidence. The energy of
the resonance depends on the strength of the force that binds protons and
neutrons together in the nucleus, and is one of the unexplained parameters
of basic physics—one of the knobs on the Designer Machine. If the strength
of the force wasn't fine-tuned to produce the carbon resonance in the manner
observed, it is doubtful that the universe would contain any observers to
worry about it. Hoyle was deeply impressed by this discovery. "It looks like a
put-up job," he quipped. "A commonsense interpretation of the facts suggests
that a superintellect has monkeyed with physics," he later wrote.[14]

So what is going on? One popular explanation of the carbon resonance
coincidence, and a host of other "all-too convenient" biofriendly features of
basic physics and cosmology, is to invoke the concept of an ensemble of universes, or a "multiverse." The argument assumes that the observed universe is
merely an infinitesimal component of a vast and elaborate patchwork quilt
of different universes. The laws of physics, rather than being universal, have
the feature of being more like local by-laws, with each universe having its
own distinctive set, perhaps allocated randomly in a gigantic cosmic lottery.
The vast majority of universes would then lack the delicate fine-tuning that
biology demands, and these universes would go unobserved. But by chance, a
tiny fraction of universes would possess just the right laws with just the right
values of the biologically critical quantities for life to emerge. It would then
be no surprise that we find ourselves in a life-encouraging universe because
we could hardly find ourselves in one that forbids living organisms. What
seems at first like a fix is in fact nothing of the kind; we have simply hit the
cosmic jackpot.

The multiverse explanation is popular, but it leaves a great deal unexplained. For example, there has to be some sort of universe-generating mechanism to create the varied patches in the cosmic quilt, and an explanation
for why the laws that attach to the universes differ, plus an algorithm for
distributing the laws among the universes. As a matter of fact, several mathematical theories exist that describe the creation of universes, such as eternal
inflation, which is the currently favored explanation for the Big Bang. Eternal
inflation supposes the existence of countless big bangs producing countless
"bubble universes."[15] Furthermore, string theory seems to provide a natural
mechanism whereby the quantum nucleation of bubble universes would lead
to different low-energy effective laws in different bubbles.[16] However, there
are still a lot of assumptions that go into this theory: an eternally inflating
space, a bubble nucleation process, quantum mechanics, relativistic causality,

and a host of other advanced physical ideas. So the multiverse theory is far from a complete explanation of why the universe is biofriendly.

The key shortcoming of the multiverse theory, however, is that it appeals to something outside the universe, namely, a vast ensemble of other universes and a set of meta-laws that exist for no reason (e.g., quantum mechanics, string theory). In this respect, the multiverse theory is little better than a direct theistic explanation where an appeal is made to an external creator/designer. Another approach, which I wish to advocate here, is to try to explain the biofriendliness of the laws of physics from entirely *within* the universe. Is this possible?

A founding tenet of physics is that the basic laws are treated as immutable mathematical relationships that presumably get imprinted (somehow!) on the universe at the moment of the Big Bang. It is a viewpoint often called "Platonism," after the Greek philosopher. According to Plato, mathematics isn't an invention of the human mind; rather, it exists in a nonmaterial realm of perfect, idealized forms that lie outside the physical universe. Many theoretical physicists follow the Platonic tradition and envisage the laws of physics as infinitely precise eternal mathematical relationships that are simply "there," transcending physical reality.[17] Note the curious asymmetry involved here: the universe depends on the laws for its properties, but the laws are in no way affected by the universe. I believe we will never achieve a satisfactory and complete scientific account for why the universe is as it is so long as we cling to Platonism, i.e., to externally imposed, immutable mathematical laws.

But what is the alternative? In recent years, a radically new view of physical laws has emerged prompted by the growth of the science of computation. At rock bottom, a law of physics is simply an algorithm that takes input data and returns output data. Let me give a simple example: The motion of the planets round the sun may be calculated using Newton's laws of motion and gravitation. Knowing the positions and motions of the planets today, we can work out where they will be, say, this time next year. So today's information about the planets is "processed" by the laws and next year's information is delivered as output. Looking at it this way, the laws of physics are akin to computer software. And the hardware? Well, it is the universe itself, of course.

Regarding the universe as a gigantic computer on which the laws of physics are "run" prompts us to ask a crucial question. All real computers are fundamentally limited in their performance by two factors: speed and resources. So is there an analogous limit to the power of the Great Cosmic Computer? The answer is yes. The universe may be vast, but it is finite in both age and size. The reason for the latter concerns the finite speed of light. Since the Big

Bang that gave birth to the cosmos 13.7 billion years ago, light can have traveled at most 13.7 billion light years. So there is a "horizon" in space beyond which we cannot see however good our instruments may be. As nothing can travel faster than light, the horizon represents a basic limit to communication. Expressed simply, two regions of the universe beyond each other's horizon cannot combine the results of their "computation."

It is fairly straightforward to work out the theoretical maximum number of bits of information contained within a volume of space encompassed by the horizon.[18] For example, this volume contains about 10^{80} atoms each capable of representing a few bits of information. Taking into account all the known particles, including photons, neutrinos, and gravitons, the total information content of the universe is no more than about 10^{120}.

What is the significance of the finite information capacity of the universe? In the Platonic view, there is no significance, because Mother Nature computes in the Platonic heaven of infinitely precise mathematical relationships and infinite resources. But the software view of the laws leads to a very different conclusion, because it regards as meaningless any appeal to mathematical procedures or relationships that exceeds the theoretical information-bound. For example, a well-known law of physics states that electric charge cannot be created or destroyed. The orthodox interpretation of this statement is that the charge carried by, say, an electron, cannot vary by one iota: the charge is fixed to *infinite* precision. But the software view of the laws denies that any physical quantity can be specified with a precision better than one part in 10^{120}. If the laws of physics are regarded as some sort of cosmic program, then there will be an irreducible fuzziness in their operation.

The number 10^{120} is so huge that for almost all practical purposes it might as well be infinite. For example, electric charge cannot be measured to a higher precision than one part in a trillion, so we would not notice any departure from the law of conservation of electric charge arising from the inherent lack of precision in the cosmic computation. However, the information bound on the universe was smaller in the past because the universe was younger, so light would have traveled less far. At the time of inflation, for example, when the main cosmological structure was laid down (the epoch concerned began about 10^{-34} seconds after the Big Bang), the universe contained a mere 10^{20} bits of information. The software view of laws therefore implies that the universe began with ill-defined regularities, and then, over time, the laws sharpened and focused into the form we observe today. What we want to explain is why, from this higgledy-piggledy beginning, the laws evolved and zeroed in on such a strangely biofriendly form.

If an explanation for this "choice" is to be sought from within the universe itself, we face a causality issue. Somehow the universe has to fine-tune its own biofriendliness back in the first split second, when its laws were still malleable. But how could the universe at that time have "known about" the emergence of life billions of years later? One answer lies with quantum indeterminism. The way quantum uncertainty is usually described is as follows. A system such as an atom is prepared in a certain definite state. At a later time the experimenter measures some property of the atom, e.g., its position. In general, the outcome of the measurement cannot be reliably predicted from the initial state; there will be a range of possible outcomes, each having a certain probability. So even if one knows precisely what state an atom is in initially, it is generally impossible to correctly predict with certainty what the outcome of a later measurement will be.

When the quantum system is the entire universe, however, the foregoing construction is inappropriate. The initial state of the universe is not something any experimenter is able prepare, so we need to think about quantum uncertainty differently when it comes to cosmology. Human beings make observations of the universe today, and can use them to infer something about the past. In other words, we post-select, rather than pre-select, the quantum state. Now the laws of physics are symmetric in time, so quantum uncertainty works both forwards into the future and backwards into the past. Therefore, any given observation of the universe made today is consistent with a large number of possible histories, stretching all the way back to the Big Bang. Obviously we can reject any histories that are incompatible with the emergence of life and observers, or we could not be here to make the observations in the first place. So the very fact that an observation gets made today in some sense helps shape the reality of the past—even the far past.[19]

Linking the present with the past via quantum measurement is part and parcel of standard quantum mechanics, bizarre though it may appear. It can even be demonstrated experimentally, although so far only over very short time scales. One way to do this was proposed nearly 30 years ago by John Wheeler, and is known as the delayed choice experiment.[20] It is based on a modification of the well-known Young's two-slit interference experiment, consisting of a pinpoint source of light and a screen with two slits cut in it. The image of the slits is projected onto a second screen, and is observed to be a series of bright and dark lines, called interference fringes (see Figure 1). The fringes famously demonstrate the wave nature of light.

However, light also manifests a particle, or photon, aspect. A wave can go through both slits and recombine to make the interference pattern. In

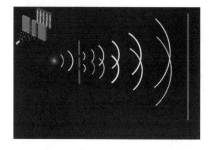

Figure 1. Young's original two-slit experiment, in which light incident on two narrow slits creates a wave interference pattern on a detection screen. (Credit: Author)

contrast, a particle must presumably pass through *either* one slit *or* the other. If light behaved like a stream of particles resembling bullets from a machine gun, then there would be no interference pattern because any given photon would go through only one of the two slits and know nothing of the other. Which raises the intriguing question of what happens when the experimenter turns down the intensity of the light so that only one photon as a time traverses the apparatus? If the image screen is a photographic plate, then each photon hitting it will make a tiny dot. Over time, as more and more photons pass though the slit system, an interference pattern emerges in a speckled sort of way from the accumulation of a large number of individual photon events. Thus, although the arrival of the light is recorded as individual particle-like dots, the collective effect is to produce a wave interference pattern.

The result is peculiar because it seems as if individual photons somehow "know about" the existence of *both* slits—in order to cooperate with the other photons and thereby form the pattern. Sometimes this is expressed by saying that the photon passed through *both* slits, i.e., it was in two places at once! So why can't the experimenter sneak a look to see what the photon is doing when it approaches the screen with the two slits? Well, according to the rules of quantum mechanics, any attempt to glimpse the photon's path has the effect of injecting uncontrollable uncertainty into the photon's behavior and as a result it destroys the photon's ability to contribute properly to the interference pattern.

If the light is allowed to traverse the slit system untrammeled, it behaves like a wave, and an interference pattern results. But if the experimenter observes which slit each photon passes through, the light behaves like a stream of particles. When, exactly, does nature "decide" to opt for wave or particle? To test this issue, Wheeler proposed a modified version of Young's experiment (see Figure 2) in which the image screen is replaced by a venetian blind and a pair of detectors (*e.g.*, small telescopes) are positioned behind it, each pointing at one of the slits. If the blind is left closed, the system functions as in the original experiment, with the wave nature of light manifested as an interference pattern. If the blind is opened, allowing the photons to go through, the detectors reveal which slit the photon emerged from. In this mode of operation the particle nature of light is manifested. The experimenter can decide on a photon by photon basis which of the two experimental configurations to employ, and thus which aspect of light shall be manifested—wave or particle—entirely at whim. Crucially, however, the experimenter can *delay the choice* of wave or particle right up to the moment the photon arrives at the venetian blind. The mystery is then how any particular photon could know, ahead of the experimenter's decision, whether to behave like a wave or a particle. And it certainly needs to know, by the time it reaches the screen with the two slits, which of the two forms it must adopt, otherwise the predicted results of the experiment will be violated.

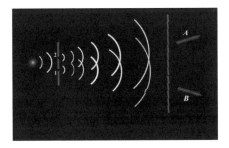

Figure 2. Modified two-slit experiment in which a venetian blind replaces the image screen and a pair of telescopes could be used, if the blind is opened, to determine which slit each photon traverses. (Credit: Author)

When the delayed-choice experiment was performed (in an adaptation of the original "thought experiment" in which the experimenter's choice is made by a randomizing fast electronic

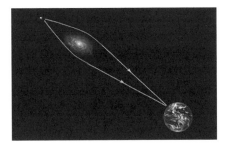

Figure 3. The focusing of dispersed light, known as gravitational lensing, caused by a galaxy's gravitational pull. (Credit: Author)

system), it confirmed Wheeler's predictions.[21] The photons that, in effect, "hit the venetian blind," formed an interference pattern as expected, and those that were allowed through did not. So the photons somehow knew what the "experimenter" (the electronic randomizer) was going to do a little while later. It is important to understand that the delayed choice experiment does *not* involve any actual backwards-in-time signaling. If an accomplice stationed near the slits tried to find out what the experimenter was going to do by peeking at each photon as it passed by, the very act of observation by the accomplice would compromise the experiment. However, the experiment does show that what an experimenter may choose to do today helps to shape the nature of reality (*e.g.*, wave or particle) *that was* in the past.

Wheeler envisaged a scenario in which this "retro-selection" might be extended from nanoseconds (as in the actual experiment) to billions of years. The concept is shown in Figure 3. Here the two light paths are defined not by slits in a screen, but by the gravitational lensing effect of a galaxy bending light from a distant quasar. If the delayed-choice experiment could be performed in this manner, the photons would need to know what to do (*i.e.*, one path or both round the galaxy) billions of years before Earth even existed, let alone before the experimenter makes a choice! Although the experiment isn't a practical one, it could be performed in principle, so the link between the present and the far past must be inherent in quantum mechanics.

Considerations such as the delayed choice experiment led Wheeler to think of observers as *participators* in shaping physical reality, and not as mere spectators. The novel feature he introduced was the possibility that observers today, and in the future, might shape the nature of physical reality that was, *in the past*, including the far past when no observers existed. It is a radical idea that gives life and mind a creative role, making them an indispensable part of the cosmological story. Yet life and mind are the *products* of the universe. So there is a logical as well as a temporal loop here. In conventional science one describes a logical sequence: cosmos→life→mind. Wheeler proposed closing this chain into a loop: cosmos→life→mind→cosmos. He expressed it as follows: "Physics gives rise to observer-participancy; observer-participancy gives rise to information; information gives rise to physics."[22] In this manner, the universe explains observers, and observers explain the universe.

Is Culture Inevitable?

Building on Wheeler's notion of retroactive observer-participancy, can we explain why the laws of physics are fine-tuned for life? Not in the usual formulation, no. Although quantum mechanics requires the presence of many alternative pasts, every allowed history develops over time in conformity the *same* laws of physics. The differences in the histories come about purely from inherent quantum uncertainty, not from any variations in the laws of physics as such. What we would like to explain is why the laws themselves are biofriendly, thus permitting at least some quantum histories containing observers. To achieve this, it is necessary to apply the general principle of linking future to past through quantum observations, but to extend its reach from states of the world to the underlying laws of physics, too. Until now, such an extension would have been meaningless because the laws were regarded as fixed and infinitely precise. But treating the laws as cosmic software, with an inherent flexibility, neatly lends itself to the task. Observations made throughout the entire duration of the universe can contribute to fashioning the form of the laws in the first split second after the Big Bang when they were still significantly malleable. Thus the potential for future life acts like an attractor, drawing the emerging laws towards a biofriendly region of the available parameter space. In this way life, mind, and cosmos form a self-consistent explanatory loop.

It is obviously a huge leap from the delayed-choice experiment, which deals with single photons, to the *entire universe* being somehow fashioned by its own observer-participators. What about all those photons, not to mention other particles, that don't get observed? Remember, however, that observers don't have to be human—they could be any form of sentient being in the universe. More importantly, the observations do not have to happen now. Because of the backwards-in-time aspect of quantum mechanics, the past can be shaped by observations at any stage in the cosmological future.

Humankind has existed for what is a tiny duration in cosmological terms. Earth should remain habitable for at least another billion years. That offers plenty of time for our descendants, natural or engineered, to spread out into the galaxy. It may take hundreds of billions of years before stars become a rarity. Even then, black holes could be a source of energy for enormously longer times. There is no fundamental reason why life and mind could not endure for trillions upon trillions of years. We can imagine that life and mind will expand into the cosmos, perhaps from Earth alone, or perhaps from many planets. A progressively larger fraction of the universe will be brought under intelligent control. More and more matter will be used to process information and create a rich mental world. We can even speculate that in the fullness of time a cosmically distributed super intelligence will become more and more omniscient and god-like, and that in the final stage this evolved super mind will merge with the universe: mind and cosmos will be one. Sometimes this astonishing vision is called the final anthropic principle.[23]

If the universe were to become saturated by mind, then it would fulfill the necessary conditions for Wheeler's participatory principle in which the *entire universe* would be brought within the scope of observer-participancy. The final state of the universe, infused with mind, would have the power to bring into being the pathways of evolution that lead to that same final state. Thus cultural evolution, on a cosmic scale, would in effect be the lynchpin in the very self-synthesis of the universe, enabling the universe to both create itself and steer itself towards its destiny. In Wheeler's words, "The coming explosion of life opens the door to an all-encompassing role for observer-participancy: to build, in time to come, no minor part of what we call *its* past—*our* past, present and future—but this whole vast world."[24]

Endnotes

1. Quoted by David Deutsch in *The Fabric of Reality* (London: Allen Lane, 1997), pp. 177–178.

2. David Deutsch, *The Fabric of Reality* (London: Allen Lane, 1997), p. 181.

3. Deutsch, *The Fabric of Reality.*

4. David Chalmers, "Facing up to the problem of consciousness," *Journal of Consciousness Studies* 2 (1995): 200.

5. Henry Stapp, *Mind, Matter and Quantum Mechanics* (Verlag: Springer, 1993).

6. See, for example, Julian Barbour, *The End of Time* (London: Weidenfeld & Nicolson, 2001).

7. Quoted by Tim Folger, "Does the universe exist if we're not looking?" *Discover Magazine* 23, no. 6 (June 2002): 43.

8. Freeman Dyson, *Disturbing the Universe* (New York: Harper & Row, 1979), p. 250.

9. "Evolution's driving force," discussion between Robyn Williams and Simon Conway Morris, ABC Radio National, 3 December 2005: *http://www.abc.net.au/rn/science/ss/stories/s1517968.htm.*

10. Christian de Duve, *Vital Dust: Life as a Cosmic Imperative* (New York: Basic Books, 1995).

11. Stuart Kauffman, *At Home in the Universe* (Oxford: Oxford University Press, 1995).

12. Max Tegmark, Anthony Aguirre, Martin Rees, and Frank Wilcek, "Dimensionless constants, cosmology and other dark matters," *Physical Review D* 77 (2006): 23505.

13. Barrow and Tipler, *The Anthropic Cosmological Principle*; Frank Tipler, *The Physics of Immortality* (New York: Doubleday, 1994).

14. Fred Hoyle, "The universe: past and present reflections," *Annual Review of Astronomy and Astrophysics* 20 (1982): 16.

15. Andrei Linde, *Inflation and Quantum Cosmology* (San Diego, CA: Academic Press, 1990); Alexander Vilenkin, *Many Worlds in One: The Search for Other Universes.* (Hill & Wang, 2006).

16. Leonard Susskind, *The Cosmic Landscape: String Theory and the Illusion of Intelligent Design* (New York: Little Brown, 2005).

17. For a robust defence of Platonism, see Roger Penrose, *The Emperor's New Mind* (Oxford: Oxford University Press, 1989).

18. Seth Lloyd, "Computational capacity of the universe," *Physical Review Letters* 88 (2002): 237901; *The Computational Universe* (New York: Random House, 2006).

19. S. W. Hawking and T. Herzog, "Populating the landscape: a top down approach," hep-th/0602091. A popular account is Amanda Gefter, "Mr. Hawking's flexiverse," *New Scientist* (22 April 2006): 28.

20. John Wheeler, "Information, physics, quantum: the search for links," in *Proceedings of the 3rd International Symposium on the Foundations of Quantum Mechanics*, Tokyo, 1989, p. 354.

21. W. C. Wickes, C. O. Alley, and O. Jakubowicz, "A 'delayed-choice' quantum mechanics experiment," in *Quantum Theory and Measurement*, edited by John A. Wheeler and Wojciech H. Zurek (Princeton: Princeton University Press, 1983), p. 457; T. Hellmuth, H. Walther, A. Zajonc, and W. Schleich, "Delayed-choice experiments in quantum interference," in *Physical Review A* 35 (1987): 2532.

22. See reference 20.

23. See reference 13.

24. John Wheeler, "World as a system self-synthesized by quantum networking," *IBM Journal of Research and Development* 32, no. 1 (1988): 4.

Chapter 11

The Value of "L" and the Cosmic Bottleneck

Seth Shostak

The Drake Equation, a commonly used starting point for discussions about the likelihood of finding extraterrestrial intelligence, is now nearly a half-century old. It dates from 1961, a year after Frank Drake made his pioneering radio search for artificial signals from other worlds. That search, dubbed "Project Ozma," was a 200-hour scrutiny of two nearby, Sun-like stars for transmissions spectrally situated near the 1420 MHz line of neutral hydrogen, and was conducted with an 85-foot-antenna at the National Radio Astronomy Observatory in Green Bank, West Virginia (Kellermann and Seielstad 1985; Drake 1960). These efforts to find easy evidence of intelligence in other star systems provoked considerable public interest, including a major article in the *Saturday Review* (Lear 1960).

As a sequel, Drake organized a two-day conference a year later on searching for sentience in the galaxy—the so-called Green Bank Conference. The invitees comprised approximately 10 astronomers, biologists, and technical specialists. As a conference agenda, Drake composed a simple, linear equation (Drake 1965) for estimating the number of galactic civilizations that are sending signals we could detect. The last term in this famous formula is *L*, the lifetime of a signaling society. *L* is *sui generis* among the equation's factors for two reasons:

1. It is dependent on sociology, not astronomy or biology (the only other term that is similar in this regard is f_c, the fraction of intelligent species that develop a technical civilization).

2. It is arguably the term that we know, and perhaps can know, least about. At a conference in 1971, Carl Sagan noted that in trying to evaluate the terms of the Drake Equation "We are faced . . . with very difficult

The Allen Telescope Array, a SETI tool that will analyze radio frequency in hopes of detecting evidence of extraterrestrial life.

problems of extrapolating from, in some cases, only one example and in the case of L, from no examples at all. When we make estimates we cannot pretend that these values are reliable." (Sagan 1973)

This is a daunting caveat. It has not, however, squelched speculation on the value of L. The fact that these estimates *are* speculative can be gauged by the degree to which they differ. In a compilation by Steven Dick, published estimates for L range over five orders of magnitude (Dick 1996).

Clearly, the chances of finding a signal with SETI experiments depend strongly on the value of L. For example, if the invention of nuclear weapons is always nearly simultaneous with the development of radio and laser technology (as is the case for *Homo sapiens*), then it is seductive to argue that when a species is technically mature enough to make its presence known from afar, it is also ripe for effecting its own destruction. In that case, L might be only a few centuries or less, and the opportunity for intercepting a signal is very limited. Having some inkling of what L might be—even if that estimate has an uncertainty of a magnitude or two—is significant in motivating (or perhaps demoralizing) those seeking evidence of intelligence elsewhere.

The other reason for considering the value of L, quite independent of SETI, is that as a matter of self-interest, it's clearly of consequence to know if our species—or at least our culture—can reasonably hope for a long future.

In this paper, we will consider some of the suggestions made, primarily with sociological arguments, for a short L, and then ask if—even granting a society the good fortune to escape self-destruction—what would be the limits on L imposed by external factors. It will be our contention that, in fact, the short-term threats posed by our own activities might be rendered ineffective, and that, on the basis of our own likely future, L could be >10^6 years.

Relevance to SETI

The Drake Equation estimates the number of contemporary, signaling societies as the product of the rate at which they are born and L, their lifetime in a transmitting state. In gauging what value the former might have, computed as the product of all six factors preceding L, the 1961 Green Bank Conference attendees estimated that it was of order unity. In other words, detectable, galactic civilizations were believed to arise at the rate of approximately one per year. (Other estimates, as compiled by Dick, are not always this sanguine and dip as low as 10^{-3}.) (Dick 1996)

The most sensitive SETI experiments, so-called targeted searches, carefully examine plausible, individual star systems. Project Phoenix, the most comprehensive radio search of this type, spent a decade observing somewhat less than 1,000 stellar targets at microwave frequencies (Tarter 1997). Assuming even the optimistic Green Bank estimate for the rate at which technical societies are born, L would need to be of order 10^8 years for Project Phoenix to have booked a success, assuming that all stars are equally likely to shelter intelligence. In the coming decades, new radio telescopes will be able to extend the target list by three orders of magnitude. Even so, in order for this far larger search to have a high probability of detecting a signal, L must have a value approaching 10^4–10^5 years (Shostak 2004). Ergo, if L is very significantly less than this, the chance that targeted searches of the foreseeable future will uncover extraterrestrial sentience should be rated as small.

Before proceeding to consider estimates of L, we note some restrictions on its relevance to SETI.

1. It is clearly dependent on the technology used for searching. If, for example, societies eventually abandon high-powered radio transmissions in favor of optical communication links, the value of L_{radio} could be short, but $L_{optical}$ might be long. As a current and possibly important illustrative example, the switch from television broadcasting to delivery of content via optical fibers or direct satellite broadcast could greatly reduce our visibility to SETI projects on other worlds, no matter how long-lived our technology. Similarly, communication

modes based on physics or technology that are beyond our ken or current ability to easily detect, would each have their own values for L in the Drake Equation.

2. Such considerations imply that estimates of L based on the length of time that a society survives (and thrives) beyond technological puberty might be sociologically interesting but irrelevant to SETI. Advanced societies could be "there," but not in a broadcasting state, as defined by our current abilities to find them.

3. In either of the above cases, the estimated value for the average technological lifetime could overestimate the chances of making a detection. There are other scenarios in which the lifetime of a civilization will be an *underestimate* of L as germane to SETI. Soter (Soter 2005) has noted that there have been dozens of major civilizations in the history of humankind (e.g., the Mycenaean, Roman, etc.), and these have a typical longevity of 400 years. The relevant value for L is not the average lifetime of any of these civilized epochs, but their sum. Note that this might be substantially different than the species lifetime, as these high-level periods could be intermittent.

4. Another circumstance in which the lifetime of a technological species underestimates the time during which it might be detected by a SETI experiment is if that society constructs transmitting hardware that outlives its makers. This idea was famously exploited in the film *Forbidden Planet*, in which the Krell, the erstwhile inhabitants of a distant world, constructed a self-repairing apparatus that continued to function long after they were gone. It was also implicit in the movie *Alien*, in which a transmitting beacon attracts visitors to a planet populated only by eggs.

5. The Drake Equation assumes that each transmitting society arises independently, and forever remains in its natal star system. If interstellar colonization is practical and sometimes undertaken, this assumption would be violated, and many transmitting sites might eventually derive from a single instance of a technological society. The extreme extension of this idea would be the colonization of the entire galaxy by a small number of civilizations (possibly even one), a circumstance not accurately gauged by the Drake Equation. (We note a variation on this scenario known as *panspermia*, in which simple life is widely dispersed throughout the galaxy via rocks kicked off planets by impacts. This would greatly change one of the least-known terms of the Equation, f_L, the probability that a suitable planet will evolve life.)

Having noted these limits to L's applicability to SETI, we consider what estimates have been made.

L *Is Small*

In all previous attempts to estimate L, researchers have tried to extrapolate the one technological society we know, our own. We have been transmitting powerful, high frequency signals—the type that our own SETI experiments could find if they were coming from another star system—since the Second World War. The one example of a technological society we have has a value for L, so far, of about 60 years.

Almost every approach to L has been an effort to extrapolate from this limited baseline to predict the long-term consequences of our own activities. And most of these analyses have focused on catastrophe: how long will it be before we do ourselves in via nuclear war, pollution, destruction of the environment, exhaustion of our energy and mineral resources, or just having too many children? The long-term outlook for a society in which progress is both accelerating and, in some measure, frightening (e.g., the brouhaha over stem cell research) suggests to many that for human society, L may be short.

Two-dozen years ago, Sebastian von Hoerner considered many of the critical societal factors that could end technological society on our planet, and concluded that Armageddon was just over the horizon, less than a century hence (von Hoerner 1975). Most of von Hoerner's dystopian view was driven by a two percent per annum population growth. Aside from the obvious crush of humanity, this growth, if unabated, would provoke an unsustainable pressure on food and energy reserves. And, von Hoerner cautioned, despite the optimistic scenario often portrayed in fiction, interstellar colonization cannot hope to solve the problems created by a rapidly swelling population. When, in 1972, von Hoerner wrote his treatise, the doubling time for the world's human inhabitants population was 35 years. In fact, and as was earlier pointed out by von Foerster et al. (von Foerster, Mora, and Amiot 1960), the population growth at this time was actually *hyperexponential*, with the rate of increase itself increasing. A straightforward calculation shows that this growth would lead to an infinite population by the year 2027, surely an untenable (and uncomfortable) situation.

Since exponential—let alone hyperexponential—increase will quickly outrun every resource, von Hoerner's simple point is that this growth will inevitably break down either because we voluntarily put on the reproductive brakes, or because of external circumstance. He notes that the food supply is a critical resource that imposes a stringent limit in the face of a rapid swelling of population. If every square inch of land were planted with wheat, humanity would still starve by about 2025.

That's more or less the date at which von Hoerner figured we run out of energy. But while substitutes for fossil fuels can be found, he pointed out that the generation of waste heat—from whatever source we exploit to power our lifestyle—will set a strict limit on our activities. He assumed that we cannot have an average global temperature rise of more than ~1°C without severe climate change, and this sets a limit on energy consumption that is about 300 times greater than the worldwide total in 1972. With population growth at the levels of that time, we will hit this limit by 2054, even if we find all the oil we ever need. In fact, China and India, with more than one-third of the planet's population, now consume, per capita, approximately one-tenth and one-thirtieth (respectively) the amount of energy used in the United States. Consequently, and assuming that one succeeds in raising the living standards of most of the world's peoples to parity with the U.S., von Hoerner overstated the amount of time remaining until the waste energy limit is reached. It's interesting to note that he anticipated the threat of global warming without anticipating its proximate cause—greenhouse gases.

Finally, using an argument based on a simple probability calculation, and noting that there is a greater chance of a fatal misstep every time a new weapons system comes online, von Hoerner was led to expect devastating nuclear war within 40 to 80 years.

It was a one-two-three punch leading to a societal knockout. Having delineated the problem, von Hoerner treated a solution that many people assume is both obvious and effective: the expansion of our civilization into space. We should simply get the majority of humankind off the planet. He shuts this idea down immediately by pointing out that even with the population growth of the 1970s, we would have to send 200,000 people a day to the launch pads to prevent the indefinite swelling of human protoplasm on Earth.

Since, as von Hoerner states "medicine will always come before nuclear engineering," population pressures will always precede any ability for interstellar travel, and the problem of the short lifetime that he predicts for us—one or two centuries at best—will also apply to extraterrestrials.

A similar conclusion, predicated on a somewhat different analysis, was reached by Lemarchand (2004). After referencing Sagan's (1980) definition of a technological adolescent age as one in which a society has the ability to exterminate itself, Lemarchand makes the barely controversial statement that we've entered such a period. Lemarchand then tried to estimate how long we will be in this precarious position before reaching a more stable, safer, technologically mature age. To do so, he appealed to historical timescales for major societal transitions, and noted that these are typically a century or so. For example, the world population began a sharp rise in growth *rate* in about 1960 that is predicted to abate by 2050, a century later. He pointed out that the time required for the worldwide shift to democratic governments is similarly a century or so. On the basis of such long-term societal transitions, Lemarchand figured that our situation is precarious for the next 150–200 years, and therefore unless we change our social behavior, we "have a high probability of becoming extinct" within that interval.

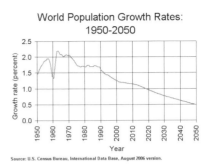

World Population Growth Rates: 1950-2050

Source: U.S. Census Bureau, International Data Base, August 2006 version.

Figure 1. Projected world population growth rates, 1950–2050.

Such somber predictions have become less frequent in recent years, largely as a result of sociological developments. The growth in population that was the principal driver of von Hoerner's analysis has lessened. It was then above two percent per year. It is now approximately half that (see Figure 1, and *http://www.census.gov/ipc/www/world.html*) and is projected to drop by another factor of two by 2050. This suggests that the total world population will reach a peak of about nine billion at mid-century, and may decline after that. The apocalyptic scenarios predicted by von Hoerner, driven by hyperexponential growth, seem to have been written out of the 21st century script at least.

The other development that has served to rescue humanity, at least temporarily, has been the end of the Cold War. In Figure 2 are reproduced the readings of the Bulletin of Atomic Scientists' "Doomsday Clock." Note that we are somewhat farther from the apocalyptic hour of midnight than previously. Of course, the possibility of nuclear war may vary strongly on short time scales, so the current lessening of menace might be only a temporary respite, and such catastrophe need only happen once to vindicate those who suggest that our society is doomed to a brief future.

Nonetheless, it is plain that we live in dangerous times, arguably the most perilous since the emergence of *Homo sapiens*. But could we really wipe out humanity *entirely*? The greatest catastrophes in recorded history were the epidemics of black plague more than half a millennium ago, a pestilence that killed about a third of Europe's inhabitants. Nonetheless, those terrible events barely register as a blip on the growth of world population. Nuclear war, and

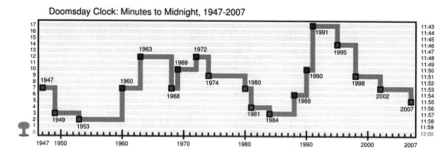

Figure 2. The Bulletin of Atomic Scientists' "Doomsday Clock," depicting the relative apocalyptic imminence from 1947 to 2007.

even nuclear winter, in light of various analyses, would seem to be less than 100 percent efficient in destroying all humanity.

In short, while many have suggested that we are doomed to destruction within a handful of generations thanks to our own activities, these arguments are scarcely hermetic. Other scenarios deserve our consideration.

L *Is Large*

As noted, it has been fashionable to project a dystopian future in which our species snuffs itself out only a few centuries after developing the means for interstellar communication. This unfortunate future has been generalized to societies on other worlds, and L is thereby estimated to be small (less than a millennium).

However, in this section we will hypothesize that the apocalyptic scenario of death at our own hand might be stayed. If so, would that guarantee a large value for L? Or are there other factors that would rapidly eliminate our species despite good behavior? Put another way, are there nonsocietal constraints that will keep us, or them, from being technologically active for at least tens or hundreds of millennia?

One possible limit is the biological lifetime of our species. This doesn't seem to enforce a low value for L, however. When considering the fate of long-lived habitants of Earth, we find that while individual species have typical lifetimes of 10^6 years, some orders and classes (trilobites, sharks, cockroaches, and even dinosaurs) have survived for 10^8 years or more. Successful species are often opportunists and generalists, eschewing narrow ecological niches. They are geographically widespread and can make use of a variety of resources.

Homo sapiens are, of course, both generalist and widespread. There is no obvious, compelling biological argument why humans could not last many millions of years.

What about various cosmic catastrophes? Our predecessors survived ice ages, but what about a future asteroid collision, such as eliminated the majority of species 65 million years ago? While we might be vulnerable to such destruction today, systematic observing programs are currently increasing our knowledge and surveillance of these dangerous projectiles (Morrison 2006). With advance warning, they could be diverted.

Global warming and other near-term environmental concerns may be serious, but are at least tractable and amenable to cure. The long-term external factors that might limit Earth's habitability—for instance the massive distortion of the carbon dioxide cycle by the warming Sun or the eventual death throes of our host star—are at minimum 10^8 years in the future, and more likely 10^9 years (Caldeira and Kasting 1992). In addition, they can, at least in principle, be circumvented with engineering fixes in the former case and emigration to a nearby star in the latter.

Astronomer Ray Norris has considered two potentially lethal phenomena from far beyond the solar system that might set upper bounds on the durability of life, intelligent or otherwise (1999). According to Norris, nearby supernovae should severely afflict a planet at intervals of roughly 200 million years. Lethal gamma-ray bursters are expected to sterilize a planet about as often. The fact that there has been an unbroken reign of life on Earth for four billion years, or 20 times the mean interval between the occurrence of these catastrophes can, according to Norris, have only two explanations. Either 1) we are extraordinarily fortunate, beating enormously long odds against destruction (which would mean that we are likely alone in the galaxy, and therefore L is of no particular interest), or 2) the estimate of 200 million years between deadly events is wrong. Assuming the latter explanation (which, and with all deference to Norris, seems more plausible), then we can better estimate that the average interval between such explosive disasters is at least four billion years—the duration of life on this planet so far. And since there would be variation in this number, a typical civilization could last for billions of years. Norris's argument boils down to noting that four billion years of uninterrupted life on Earth implies that natural catastrophes don't set a severe limit on L.

Neither biology nor cosmic interference seems to mandate low values for L. But nondestructive technology might introduce complications that could change the ground rules of our existence. We might deliberately modify our species, or threaten its role on Earth by introducing a manufactured competitor.

To begin with, there is a general expectation that we will, sometime in the 21st century, begin to direct our biological future and disrupt the march of Darwinian evolution. One can easily envision two major developments in this regard: 1) the manipulation of human DNA to produce individuals that have greater talent and are free of inherited disease (and perhaps eventually, the malaise of mortality), and 2) the development of implantable, technical aids to improve body performance, for example eyesight, hearing, and thought.

Such improvements to our species might not affect *L*. But taking these developments to their logical—and some would say inevitable—conclusion, we might expect the creation of true, artificial sentience: thinking machines (Moravec 1999). If this occurs, the curtain of human dominance on this planet is likely to drop quickly. The improvement of machines, which can, after all, proceed as a Lemarckian rather than Darwinian process, is much faster than biological evolution. Digital electronics currently enjoy an exponential growth in functionality, doubling in capability per unit cost each 18 months, a phenomenon known as Moore's Law (Moore 1965). At this rate, an artificial intelligence device that is equivalent to the brainpower of a single person, will improve to the point of outstripping the cerebral capability of the entire human population within 50 years. The possibility of this rapid change-over from wet, biological brains to dry, technological ones has led Ray Kurzweil and others to speculate about an impending "singularity" in the history of our species (Kurzweil 2006).

Would such developments, which seem imminent to some, produce a large or small value for *L*? There is no convincing answer we can offer to this question. On the one hand, a machine-run society might be less aggressive, and therefore less susceptible to certain types of self-ruin. It might remain "communicative" for long periods of time, resulting in large *L* according to the definition of this term implicit in the Drake Equation. On the other hand, intelligent machines might be in less need of, or have less desire for, the sort of communication that would make them detectable at a distance, shortening *L*.

Such musings, while interesting, are also highly speculative. In truth, and quite obviously, we cannot predict what artificial sentience—successors to our own species—might do.

In addition to the disruption that such technical developments might provoke, the value of *L* might be affected by a SETI detection itself. Some SETI practitioners have argued that the ability to communicate with other societies might forge durable civilizations by promoting interstellar intercourse and a transfer of knowledge and social norms that are useful for long-term survival (Billingham, Oliver, and Wolfe 1979). Indeed, even a single instance of contact between two star systems would surely encourage substantial effort to find more, thus quickly fostering a growing communications web throughout the galaxy. This has led these investigators to speculate that *L* might be as great as 10^9 years, although one could be justifiably suspicious of an argument by SETI researchers that their endeavors can reward humanity with a billion years of continued existence.

The major technical developments described above could end the unchallenged reign of *Homo sapiens*, although not necessarily the visibility of Earthly intelligence. Biological engineering removes our species from the slow and uncertain path of Darwinian evolution. Success in developing artificial intelligence would replace living beings as the prime repository of intelligence in its home star system. The third—exchange of information with an existing galactic club—might be initially disruptive (consider the 18th century encounters between James Cook and the South Sea Islanders) but could ultimately prove transformational in a positive sense. All three of these possible developments are wild cards in the assessment of *L*.

We have seen that—absent species suicide, and excepting the unpredictable consequences of either reengineering humankind or exchanging information with other cosmic societies—there is no short-term limit to human existence. Ergo, it seems that estimating *L* really does boil down to guessing what society will do to itself.

However, there is another approach to the problem—a metaanalysis that circumvents the uncertainty of all the detailed phenomena that could wipe us out. This approach is that taken by physicist J. Richard Gott (1993), who has estimated the species lifetime of *Homo sapiens* with a calculation largely independent of the socioeconomic factors considered by von Hoerner and the technology speculation given above. His method was supposedly inspired by a visit to the Berlin wall, during which he wondered how much longer that onerous edifice would remain standing. The approach itself is described as an application of the Copernican principle. Copernicus was the first to demonstrate that our spatial position in the universe is unremarkable. The analogous assumption made by Gott is that the person inquiring about the duration of humankind as a species is not special in *time*. While sometimes gracefully monikered as the Copernican principle applied to time, this approach is also known as the principle of indifference, a term derived from probability theory (Keynes 1921).

Gott's argument, in its simplest formulation, is as follows: suppose that the total lifetime of *Homo sapiens* is L_s (species lifetime, not technological lifetime). Then if the probability of being alive today is equally distributed from the origin of the species until its demise, then we can trivially say with 95 percent probability that we are living somewhere between 2.5 percent and 97.5 percent of the distance along the span of time L_s. Thanks to the dusty labors of paleontologists we know that *Homo sapiens* have already strutted across Earth's stage for 150,000 years (Lewin 1997). This means that L_s must range from 150,000/0.975 < L_s < 150,000/0.025, or that we have a future as a species (and possibly as a technological species) ranging from 3,800 to 6.0 million years.

One notable refinement to this argument derives from the obvious observation that, in a world with a rising birth rate, the assumption that one's chance of being born is uniform in time during our species' first 150,000 years (and more important, will remain uniform in the future) is clearly wrong. There are many more births today than, say, 10,000 years ago. If we take the more reasonable approach of assuming equal probability of "birth order"— that is, an equal chance that our name would appear at any place in the complete list of human births—then we can recalculate L_s as follows. Define the total number of humans who will ever live as N_0, and the number that have been born so far as n. Since the chance is the same of appearing anywhere in the birth list, we can say that we are in the last 95 percent of all humans to be born if n/N_0 > 0.05. The total number of humans to have lived so far is estimated to be ~100 billion (Haub 1995), and to be in accord with the likely circumstance that we haven't won the lottery and appeared by chance in the first 5 percent of the birth list, this means that the total that will ever live is 2,000 billion, with 95 percent probability.

How long will it take for this number of souls to strut Earth's stage? If we stabilize our planet's population at 15 billion, and extend human lifetimes to 100 years, this total will be reached in another 13,000 years. If we manage to subdue our more destructive impulses, and perhaps colonize nearby space, we might dramatically increase our population rather than merely stabilizing it, and this number will become shorter. In either case this simple reckoning suggests that the majority of our species' lifetime is over, but that our technological lifetime has just begun, in sharp contradiction to the shorter, more pessimistic estimates based on socioeconomic factors.

Passing Through a Bottleneck?

We have seen that, if the dismal, albeit trendy, apocalyptic scenarios of war, environmental degradation, and short-term cosmic threats can be thwarted, our future might be anything from thousands to million of years. However, even with this sunnier prognosis, there is little doubt that—sooner or later— we will be obliged to move at least some of our population into space. Earth, being spherical, has the minimum surface area for its mass. Resources—both the obvious ones such as arable land, as well as the less obvious ones, such as platinum—are finite, and in many cases already scarce. So, putting aside the possibility that, by engineering our own successors or joining the "galactic club" we may introduce a major discontinuity in the story of *Homo sapiens*, there's one reasonably reliable expectation we can have for our activities of the next 100 years: the expansion of habitat to the nearby, extraterrestrial realms of the solar system. This settlement of a new frontier could have a telling, and salubrious effect on the Earthly value for *L*.

We have visited the Moon, and our mechanical proxies have landed on Mars. Both worlds could be colonized, and in the case of Mars, made more amenable to life (Wood 2007). That this will happen is less a question of "if" than "when." While the initial colonies will be small, historical analogs suggest that within a century they will have populations measured in the tens of thousands or more.

The carrying capacity of these nearby bodies is limited. However, the numbers of humans living in orbit could dwarf their populations. Two decades ago, Gerald O'Neill (1977) and Thomas Heppenheimer (1979) described in detail how we could build artificial habitats in space: slowly rotating aluminum cylinders, having diameters of several kilometers, that could house entire villages and towns. Their prediction was that by the 1990s, millions of Earthlings would be living in these space habitats. That hasn't yet happened, but not because it's *technically* impractical. Rather, at the moment, building such artificial cities in orbit is economically and politically impractical.

In the somewhat longer view, perhaps one to two centuries hence, we can consider colonizing the larger bodies of the asteroid belt.

While the exact time scale of these projects is subject to the vagaries of political will, one can conservatively foresee that within two centuries, at most, enough of us will be off the planet—in O'Neill colonies, on the Moon and Mars, and burrowed into the asteroids—that total annihilation of human society will be as impossible as the total annihilation of Earth's ants. We will be dispersed, and dispersal is the ultimate insurance policy for survival. Modest colonization will inoculate us against self-destruction. It might be possible to exterminate all the individuals in one habitat, but not the entire populace of all habitats.

A similar bottleneck—during which a civilization has dangerous weapons, but is still confined to a small chunk of real estate—will presumably be encountered by most intelligent, technologically developed species. Since the time scale for getting through the bottleneck is small, one or two hundred years, many societies will manage to do so. In this view, the doomsday scenarios so popular in the literature, and which have been so influential in estimating low values for *L*, are unrealistically pessimistic.

Conclusion

It seems that a reasonable alternative to the various doomsday scenarios that foretell our own destruction is the possibility that humankind is passing through a "bottleneck." The development of powerful weapons and the pressures of a rapidly growing population have produced this constriction. But this risk is short-lived compared with the time scale of human evolution.

Clearly, estimates of low L are reactions to social developments associated with the bottleneck that any society will enter once it has developed sufficient technology. But as the bottleneck is short, many—possibly even most—civilizations will pass through. Once dispersed and no longer vulnerable to total annihilation, they might, like some other species, remain viable for ~10^8 years or more. However, we note that there are three possible near-term developments that might affect this scenario in unpredictable ways:

1. The use of genetic manipulation to reengineer the species.
2. The development of machine intelligence.
3. Communication with other galactic societies.

Setting these aside, we argue that the suggestions that L is short (<10^3 years) are unduly pessimistic, and suggest that the very technology that threatens us will soon alter our situation such that extinction of our species becomes impossible. The less threatening future that lies beyond the bottleneck becomes attainable by our (and their) dispersal into nearby space. This accords with a view of a galaxy that hosts long-lived civilizations, societies that may have established mutual communication networks, and in so doing, brought many worlds to the technological level of the most accomplished member.

References

Billingham, J., B. M. Oliver, and J. H. Wolfe, 1979. *Acta Astronautica* 6:47.

Caldeira, K., J. F. Kasting, 1992. "The life span of the biosphere revisited," *Nature* 360:721.

Dick, Steven J. 1996. *The Biological Universe: The Twentieth-Century Extraterrestrial Life Debate and the Limits of Science* (Cambridge: Cambridge University Press).

Drake, F. 1960. "How Can We Detect Radio Transmissions from Distant Planetary Systems," *Sky and Telescope* 39:140.

Drake, F. 1965. *Current Aspects of Exobiology*. eds. G. Mamikunian and M. H. Briggs (Oxford: Pergamon Press), p. 324.

Gott, J. Richard III. 1993. "Implications of the Copernican principle for our future prospects," *Nature* 363:315.

Haub, Carl. 1995. "How many people have ever lived on earth?" *Population Today* 2:4.

Heppenheimer, T. A. 1979. *Toward Distant Suns* (Harrisburg, PA: Stackpole Books).

Keynes, John Maynard. 1921. *Treatise on Probability* (New York: Macmillan).

Kurzweil, Ray. 2006. *The Singularity is Near* (New York: Penguin).

Lear, John. 1960. "The Search for Intelligent Life on Other Planets," *Saturday Review* (2 January): 39.

Lemarchand, Guillermo. 2004. "The technological adolescent age transition: A boundary to estimate the last factor of the Drake Equation," in *Bioastronomy 2002: Life Among the Stars* (IAU Symposium 213), R. P. Norris and F. H. Stootman, eds., Astron. Society of the Pacific (San Francisco).

Lewin, Roger. 1997. *New Scientist*: 5.

Moore, Gordon E. 1965, "Cramming more components onto integrated circuits," *Electronics* 38, no. 8.

Moravec, Hans. 1999. *Robot: Mere Machine to Transcendent Mind* (Oxford: Oxford University Press).

Morrison, David. 2006. "Asteroid and comet impacts: the ultimate environmental catastrophe," *Phil. Trans. of the Royal Society A* 264:2041.

Norris, R. P. 1999. "How old is ET?" *Acta Astronautica* 47:731.

O'Neill, Gerard K. 1977. *The High Frontier: Human Colonies in Space* (New York: Wm. Morrow).

Sagan, Carl. 1973. "The Lifetimes of Technical Civilizations," in *Communications with Extraterrestrial Intelligence.* ed. C. Sagan, MIT Press, p. 147 (Byurakan 1971 conference...).

Sagan, C. 1980, *Cosmos* (New York: Random House).

The Search for Extraterrestrial Intelligence. (Proceedings of an NRAO Workshop held at the NRAO, Green Bank, West Virginia, 20–22 May 1985), 1986, ed. K. I. Kellermann and G. A. Seielstad, NRAO/AUI.

Shostak, Seth. 2004. "When Will We Detect the Extraterrestrials?" *Acta Astronautica* 55:753.

Soter, Steven. 2005. "SETI and the Cosmic Quarantine Hypothesis," *Astrobiology Magazine. www.astrobio.net/news/modules.php?op=modload& name=News&file=article&sid=1745.*

Tarter, J. C. 1997. "Results from Project Phoenix: looking up from down under," *Astronomical and Biochemical Origins and the Search for Life in the Universe.* C. B. Cosmovici, S. Bowyer, and D. Werthimer, eds. Editrice Compositori (Bologna) p. 633.

von Foerster, H., P. Mora, and L. Amiot, 1960. *Science* 132:1291.

von Hoerner, Sebastian. 1975. "Population Explosion and Interstellar Expansion," *Journal of the British Interplanetary Society* 28:691.

Wood, Lowell. 2007. As reported in *http://www.space.com/scienceastronomy/ 070623_mars_terraform.html.*

Chapter 12

Encoding Our Origins
Communicating the Evolutionary Epic
in Interstellar Messages

Douglas A. Vakoch

Even before the first search for extraterrestrial intelligence (SETI) project was conducted, people have been pondering what reply we might send if some day we discover an extraterrestrial civilization. Some have suggested that the United Nations (U.N.) would be the international body of choice for deciding such a question, and indeed, that would seem one appropriate starting point. The challenge that the international SETI community has faced is gaining a space on the already full agenda of the U.N.; indeed, the preface to the existing SETI protocols endorsed by the International Academy of Astronautics (IAA) and the International Institute of Space Law explicitly acknowledges the difficulty of gaining the attention of the U.N. If some day we detect direct evidence of extraterrestrial intelligence, all that may well change, but what are we do to in the meantime?

There is a natural alternative to the United Nations—a group whose discussions over the past decades already puts it in a position to recommend a coherent, consistent message that reflects broad-based, international consensus: the scientific community. To be clear, a solely scientific account of us would not capture the depth and breadth of human experience. For precisely that reason, over the past several years the IAA through its Interstellar Message Construction Study Group, in conjunction with the SETI Institute, has organized a series of workshops and conferences bringing together scholars from a range of disciplines—including the arts, music, humanities, theology, and law—aimed at identifying some of the many voices that should be represented in a comprehensive reply from Earth.

But a reply message representing contemporary society would also surely include some of our scientific accounts of the world and of ourselves. And perhaps the most all-encompassing story has evolution as its central theme.

Understanding Our Origins

The view that the universe is in flux is an ancient one. Contemporary scientific understandings of evolution are multifaceted, aimed at understanding multiple transitions and developments (Swimme and Berry 1992). How did heavy atoms originate from lighter ones? How did life arise from inert matter? How did consciousness and culture evolve from the biological world?

Our messages to other worlds might start by telling this evolutionary epic, and in the process, describing something about our own place in the universe. Indeed, we humans bear witness to the process of evolution in the very composition of our bodies. The calcium that gives solidity to our bones, the iron that lets our blood carry oxygen to our brains, the sodium and potassium that make possible the transmission of impulses along our nerves, all of these elements were formed inside a star that had its own birth and life and death, hurling its remains outward in a supernova explosion billions of years ago. As Steven Dick (2009) summarizes the significance of this epic, "[c]osmic evolution provides the proper universal context for biological evolution, revealing that the latter is only a small part of the bigger picture, in which everything is evolving, including life and culture."

Eric Chaisson has examined the evolutionary epic in several books, using a framework that has remained largely constant over a quarter of a century of his writing. From his *Cosmic Dawn: The Origins of Matter and Life* (1981) to his *Epic of Evolution: Seven Ages of the Cosmos* (2006), he has identified seven periods, with a recent version (Chaisson 2006) including the following epochs: particle, galactic, stellar, planetary, chemical, biological, and cultural. In Chaisson's (2006, *xiii*) view, this evolutionary account provides more than a scientifically accurate story:

> As sentient beings, we humans now reflect back on the matter of the Universe that gave us life. And what we find is a natural history, a universal history, a rich and abiding story of our origins that is nothing less than an epic of creation as understood by modern science—a coherent *weltgeschichte* that people of all cultures can adopt as currently true as truth can be.

416

A similar view is expressed by historian Cynthia Stokes Brown in her *Big History: From the Big Bang to the Present* (2007, *xi*), when she writes "[w]ithin the last fifty years the scientific community has established a verifiable, and largely verified, account of the origins of our universe—of where we came from, how we got here, and where we may be going. This is a creation story for our time—for a world built on the discoveries of modern science, a world of jet travel, heart transplants, and the worldwide Internet."

At the beginning of the 21st century, scientific inquiry has become a primary means by which we attempt to understand the universe and our place within it. As a result, science naturally provides the foundation for evolution to become a central "myth" of our time.

To speak of evolution as being a myth—perhaps the preeminent scientific myth of the past century—does not refute the facts of evolution; to call evolution a myth is not to dismiss its scientific accuracy or adequacy. Instead, the term "myth" points toward the impact that this evolutionary perspective has on understanding our place in the cosmos. Barbara Sproul (1979, 2–3) captures this meaning of myth in her description of traditional creation myths: "Not only are creation myths the most comprehensive of mythic statements, addressing themselves to the widest range of questions of meaning, but they are also the most profound. They deal with first causes, the essences of what their cultures perceive reality to be." Across a wide range of disciplines, from biology to cosmology and beyond, many scientists today attempt to perceive reality by studying cosmic evolution.

Essentials of Evolution

There are two distinctive features of evolutionary explanations of nature: they involve both change and historical embeddedness. Though there may be *constant* laws of nature,[1] they are manifested through *transformations* of the stuff of the universe: things change. Moreover, these changes build upon the past. The natural order we see today depends, at least in part, on historical circumstances. The dramatic changes in climate that led to the Cretaceous extinctions provided an opening for the proliferation of mammalian life in the Cenozoic era. We, as human beings, fundamentally embody both change and history. By characterizing ourselves in these terms in an interstellar message, we capture not only some of our fundamental biological attributes, but also some of the core dimensions of our contemporary self-understanding.

Of course, we might argue that to describe the origin and development of galactic structures, of planetary systems, of life, of civilization and technology, all under the generic name of evolution is to blur critical distinctions about the varied mechanisms responsible for such diverse phenomena. Admittedly, the processes of mutation, recombination, and natural selection in biological evolution are markedly different from the gravitational processes involved, for example, in the formation of planetary systems (Lupisella 2009). Nevertheless, Eric Chaisson (2001, 214) defends the use of the term "evolution" for such varied processes:

> Given the powerful underlying phenomenon of change quite naturally everywhere, evolution itself should not be a disciplinary word exclusive to only one field of science, but rather an interdisciplinary word that helps connect often disparate fields of scientific scholarship . . . . neo-Darwinism, which has largely appropriated the term for itself, becomes but a special case (with powerful value-added features) within the much wider purview of cosmic evolution.

Perhaps the very fact that we do use the term "evolution" to describe such radically different processes is evidence of the mythic power that evolution has for organizing our self-understanding. But that may well change.

Evolution's Importance, for Now

We should not expect this myth of evolution to remain as central to our self-understanding in future generations as it is now, an idea suggested by the continuation of Cynthia Stokes Brown's (2007, *xi*) above comment about the contemporary scientific account of our origins: "This is a creation story for our time—for a world built on the discoveries of modern science, a world of jet travel, heart transplants, and the worldwide Internet. *This world will not last forever* [emphasis added], but while it does, this is our story."

Brown's prediction that "[t]his world [as understood in evolutionary terms] will not last forever" is relevant for interstellar communication. Too often those who discuss interstellar communication take a simplistic view that somehow the message we send can reflect value-free scientific concepts; if we can only identify the "right" concepts, it is often assumed, we might communicate information that will be as obviously relevant to another technological civilization as it is to us. As Lupisella (2009) has argued, cosmic evolution itself may be value-laden. Indeed, we should be cautious in assuming that our messages—even messages about potentially widespread evolutionary processes—could ever objectively mirror the nature of reality in itself, independent of the culture from which our scientific understanding arises.

Nevertheless, we might well expect that evolutionary concepts—so central to our contemporary self-understanding—will also be embedded into the worldviews of scientifically literate extraterrestrials. After all, extraterrestrials, too, will have evolved in the same galaxy as we; if they were astronomically curious enough to seek out other civilizations, they would plausibly have come to understand the nature and history of our shared neighborhood in the universe.

Perhaps so. But this is quite different from holding an evolutionary perspective as especially *central* to their self-understanding. On the contrary, we might well expect that evolutionary processes will lose their central place in extraterrestrial self-understanding precisely because they become so commonplace: because they are taken for granted. Part of the impact of evolutionary accounts of our origins comes from the relative *novelty* of understanding ourselves, not as a fixed species in a static cosmos, but as a mutable species in an evolving universe.

Brian Swimme and Thomas Berry (1992, 2–3) contrast this sense of transformation inherent in an evolutionary perspective with the cyclical notion of time characteristic of earlier views:

> The most significant change in the twentieth century, it seems, is our passage from a sense of cosmos to a sense of cosmogenesis. From the beginning of human consciousness, the ever-renewing seasonal sequence, with its death and rebirth cycles, has impinged most powerfully upon human thought. This orientation in consciousness has characterized every previous human culture up to our own. During the modern period, and especially in the twentieth century, we have moved from that dominant spatial mode of consciousness, where time is experienced in ever-renewing seasonal cycles, to a dominant time-developmental mode of consciousness, where time is experienced as an evolutionary sequence of irreversible transformations.

In the same way that scientists continue to recognize seasonal sequences, so, too, we should not be surprised to find advanced extraterrestrials who remain aware of evolutionary principles, even though these beings may have ways of understanding the cosmos that they value even more. But the fact that evolution is important for humankind's self-understanding now could provide an important foundation for introducing ourselves to denizens of another world.

Figure 1. Diagram of vertebrate evolution. (From the Voyager Interstellar Recording)

Evolutionary Voyages

What would an interstellar message with an evolutionary theme look like? For concrete examples of such messages that were already sent into space, we need look no further than the interstellar recording attached to two Voyager spacecraft, launched by NASA in 1977—arguably the richest portrayal of life on Earth thus far intentionally sent into space.

In addition to over 100 images, greetings in 55 languages, and music from around the world, the message also included two components specifically intended to indicate the evolution of humankind. The first is a diagram of vertebrate evolution, including sketches of several animals featured in other photographs that appear on the recording (Figure 1). Though there is no absolute indication of progress in the diagram, we might infer an implicit indication that humankind is at the apex of the evolutionary process on Earth, given that the human couple is located at the top of the diagram.

The second evolutionary message included in the Voyager recording is a 12-minute sequence of selected sounds of Earth. Ann Druyan (1978, 153), who coordinated this part of the project, describes the rationale for ordering the sounds: "I felt that it would be most informative to arrange them chronologically. We took many liberties within that very broad structure, but the fundamental direction of the montage is evolutionary: from the geological through the biological into the technological."

The sound sequence begins with a musical rendition of part of Johannes Kepler's *Harmonica Mundi*, a 16th century instantiation of the "music of the spheres." To evoke a sense of the geological activity in Earth's early history, next follow sounds of volcanoes, earthquakes, thunder, and mudpots. To highlight the centrality of water in life's development on our planet, next we hears sounds of a rainstorm—and again thunder—followed by crashing surf and the gentler lapping of ocean waves on a shore. As the sound of flowing water continues, the vocalizations of a sampling of Earth's varied life-forms are added: first crickets and frogs, then a variety of birds. Then comes a selection of mammals: the distinctive voice of a hyena, elephants trumpeting, and a chimpanzee calling. The first sequence of nonhuman animal life ends with the sounds of a windy evening, punctuated by the plaintive howl of a wild dog.

Next, to signal humankind's entrance into the world, come footsteps intertwined with heartbeats, then laughter, underscored by the crackling of a fire, and the first sounds of language. Then we hear the development of stone tools, with the chip and click of flint on flint, followed by sounds of these tools used for scraping and for cleaving wood. Domestication is indicated by the barking of a dog—soon followed by the bleating of sheep. Increased sophistication of tool use is signaled by sounds of hammer against metal in a blacksmith's shop, the sawing of wood and hammering of nails, moving into the sounds of a riveter and tractor.

Advances in communication and transportation are intermixed, with Morse code overlaid on the sounds of a ship's fog horn, followed by progressively faster means of transportation—starting with a lengthy recording of horse and cart; moving on to fully mechanized locomotion, first through the characteristic chug and whistle of a train, and then on to the uncertain ignition of an internal combustion engine; ending with the flyby of an airplane and the Saturn 5 engine launching humans toward the Moon.

The evolutionary sound montage ends with a sequence moving from human intimacy to technology and exploration, with a chaste kiss introducing the cry of a child and the succor of his mother, the crackle and fizz of a speeded-up recording of an electroencephalogram, and finally, the regular beat of pulsar CP1133, located some 600 light-years from Earth.

As Druyan (1978, 150) explains, listeners on different worlds might have quite different experiences: "The twelve-minute sound essay was conceived for two audiences: the human and the extraterrestrial. In the former, we hoped to evoke smiles of recognition, and in the latter, a sense of the variety of auditory experiences that are part of life on Earth."

Chemical Evolution

In an age when science is becoming increasingly specialized, attempts to find bridges between disciplines are rare, but not absent. One such infrequent but important example of looking for transdisciplinary connections is Stephen F. Mason's (1991) *Chemical Evolution: Origin of the Elements, Molecules, and Living Systems*. He begins by examining the historical context of 19th century chemistry; then considers cosmic evolution in chemical terms, with topics ranging from stellar nucleosynthesis and the interstellar medium; to the evolution of the solar system and its planets, meteors, and comets; to the energetics of living systems. Mason (1991, *viii*) emphasizes the value of understanding our origins in chemical terms: "Surveys of the principal discoveries in the fields divergent from nineteenth-century chemical science, in cosmochemistry, geochemistry, biochemistry, and molecular biology, restore some coherence and provide a wider chemical view of the world, particularly when set in an evolutionary context."

Maps of Time: An Introduction to Big History, by David Christian (2004), expands the range of chemical phenomena relevant to an evolutionary understanding. Christian illustrates additional ways that chemistry can help tell us about the origins and development of our world and our civilizations. At one level, we can describe the chemical evolution of the universe—in a cosmic scale, and as well as more locally—as providing the substrate from which life, and eventually intelligence, arose. But we can also describe the ongoing evolution of Earth's civilizations through artifacts created (Gräslund 1987; Heizer 1962), as well as environmental changes induced—all using the basic vocabulary of chemistry.

But how, precisely, might such chemical concepts be conveyed in interstellar messages?

Encoding Chemistry

To create a message that may be intelligible to an independently evolved civilization, we attempt to identify basic principles that human and extraterrestrial civilizations are likely to share. The most frequently proposed set of universals is derived from mathematical and scientific principles. Why rely on such principles as a foundation for interstellar discourse? Because, it is typically argued, any civilization having a technology capable of contact at interstellar distances will also need to know some of the same fundamental principles of mathematics and science that humans know in order to construct this technology. To build a radio transmitter, for example, it seems reasonable that an extraterrestrial would need to know at least some basic math and science.

Among the most frequently proposed sets of universals are those related to principles of chemistry. As we consider the intentional messages that have already been sent from Earth, we see that chemical principles are typically presupposed from the earliest stages. For example, the two Pioneer spacecraft, launched by NASA in 1972, include engraved plaques that depict the hyperfine transition of hydrogen, which then provides a unit of time and distance for other parts of the message (Sagan, Saltzman, and Drake 1972). Similarly, the Voyager recording, mentioned earlier, contains schematic diagrams of atomic and molecular structures, with special emphasis on the structure of the DNA molecule as the biochemical foundation for life on Earth (Figure 2) (Drake 1978). Likewise,

Earth's atmosphere is described in the Voyager recording in terms of its chemical composition (Figure 3).

A similar emphasis on chemical principles is found in proposed and actual interstellar messages that could be conveyed by radio broadcasts rather than by space probes. In 1961, following the first contemporary conference on communication with extraterrestrials, the meeting's organizer, Frank Drake, sent a message consisting of 551 ones and zeros to each of the participants (Drake and Sobel 1992). His instructions indicated that when properly formatted, the recipients would find a message from a hypothetical extraterrestrial civilization. Among the mathematical, scientific, and pictorial information included in this first message by Drake,

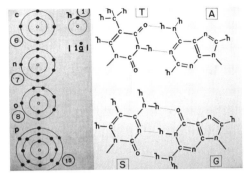

Figure 2. Depictions of the atomic structure of several elements central to life on Earth, individually (on the left) and as found in deoxyribonucleic acid (DNA) (on the right). (From the Voyager Interstellar Recording)

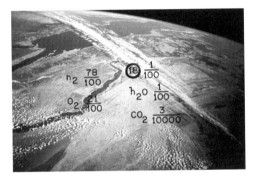

Figure 3. Depicting the chemical composition of Earth's atmosphere in terms of elements basic to life on Earth, introduced in Figure 2. (From the Voyager Interstellar Recording)

there were schematic representations of two elements central to the biochemistry of this hypothetical civilization: oxygen and carbon. In 1974, when Drake transmitted an actual message from the world's largest radio telescope and radar facility, located near Arecibo, Puerto Rico, he began his message with a basic numbering system in binary digits, quickly followed by an identification of elements central to life on Earth, providing a numerical description of the structure of DNA in terms of its basic chemical constituents (Staff of the National Astronomy and Ionosphere Center 1975).

While these early messages tend to combine mathematical, scientific, and pictorial information in the same message, Carl DeVito and Richard Oehrle (1990) propose messages that would give chemistry an even more central role. After introducing basic characteristics of set theory in their interstellar message, they describe the set that corresponds to the naturally occurring chemical elements, portrayed as a two-dimensional array that humans know as the Periodic Table of Elements. Moreover, this team of a mathematician and linguist describes chemical principles through a series of chemical reactions, introducing such concepts as volume, mass, and temperature.

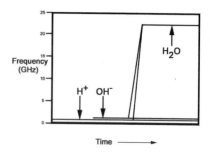

Figure 4. An iconic approach to communicating that hydrogen and hydroxyl ions combine to form water. (From Vakoch [2008a])

Douglas Vakoch (1998c) emphasizes the value of starting with more direct representations of chemical elements and molecules. He suggests that we communicate concepts related to specific elements and molecules by transmitting signals at frequencies that mimic the emission spectra of the chemical constituents. For example, to communicate that hydrogen and a hydroxyl ion combine to form water, we might transmit signals at frequencies associated with the emission spectra of the reactants and the final product (see Figure 4). As with earlier proposals to use "magic frequencies" such as the hydrogen line as a base frequency for a search, we might transmit slightly to one side of these characteristic emission lines so our signals are not lost in naturally occurring background radiation. While Vakoch recognizes that such an approach lends itself especially well to only a circumscribed range of phenomena, he is concerned that it may be difficult to encode *any* information in a way that will be understandable to extraterrestrial intelligence. Once some information content—even a small amount—can be conveyed in any format, more general principles about the multiple formats used in other parts of the message might be conveyed through redundant encoding, providing a key to the multiplicity of ways that humans have of representing phenomena (Vakoch 1998a).

For example, consider the multiple ways we have of describing chemical concepts. As we have just seen, we might transmit chemical information through two-dimensional images or through signals that mimic emission spectra. Alternatively, we might highlight the three-dimensional structure of molecules (Vakoch 2000). If the recipients understand the connections between these multiple representations of the same or related concepts, we will have succeeded in introducing formats for describing phenomena that may be quite alien to extraterrestrials. In this case, we might communicate our ways of describing the three-dimensional structure of objects ranging in size from molecules to galaxies. Such a message would provide anchors for expressing other representations, using scientific objects that extraterrestrials may also have experience modeling. If we can find a shared means of representing objects ranging from the microscopic to the macroscopic—on scales ranging from angstroms (for molecules) to light-years (for galaxies)—we would be well-positioned to describe objects of intermediate size that extraterrestrials would never have seen before, such as the human body (Vakoch 2000).

Encoding Culture

Having established a basic vocabulary of chemistry, an interstellar message could then go on to describe biological and even cultural phenomena, either based on or by analogy to such chemical processes. For example, given the evidence that individuals tend to be more altruistic toward closely related individuals, consistent with kin selection, we might iconically show the fate of individuals when threatened by predators—with closely related individuals (as shown by shared genetic material, described in chemical terms) more likely to survive than unrelated individuals (Vakoch 2008a).

Alternatively, the same approach could be used to provide accounts of group selection, which Howard Bloom argues in *The Global Brain: The Evolution of Mass Mind from the Big Bang to the 21st Century*, is found throughout the evolutionary epic. Bloom (2000, 4) suggests that networking and cooperation are evident in evolutionary processes at multiple times and levels of complexity, from before the origins of life to the advent of the Internet and beyond: "Such a need to cooperate would have been necessary long ago to make a global brain and a planetary nervous system possible."

Given arguments for "memetic" rather than genetic transmission of cultural practices, we might imagine an extension of this approach to describe practices not apparently reducible simply to biology. For example, Susan Blackmore (1999, 167) proposes that a memetic version of altruism may underlie vegetarianism:

> I suggest that vegetarianism succeeds as a meme because we all want to be like the nice people who care about animals, and we copy them. Not everyone will get infected by this meme; some like meat too much and others have sets of memes that are not very compatible with this one. Nevertheless, it does quite well. Vegetarianism is a memetically spread altruistic fashion.

We might also use the vocabulary of chemistry to explain to extraterrestrial intelligence some of the consequences of our cultural evolution about which we are less proud (Vakoch 2007). After describing the evolution of Earth's atmosphere, hydrosphere, and lithosphere, as they have occurred largely independently of major human intervention, we might then describe how the Industrial Revolution caused such significant changes to the environment.

To restrict our descriptions of terrestrial culture to its chemical manifestations would, however, be unnecessarily restrictive. As Lupisella (2009) notes, it can be "helpful to think about culture as the *collective manifestation of value*— where value is that which is valuable to 'sufficiently complex' agents, from which meaning, purpose, ethics, and aesthetics can be derived." As we have seen, we might begin to communicate the biological underpinnings of altruism in terms of the chemical basis of our genetics. But even if we restrict ourselves to the broad category of altruistic acts, multiple mechanisms have been proposed, each with its own explanatory framework. For example, notions of reciprocal altruism might be encoded into interstellar messages using game theory (Vakoch 2001, 2002), providing a mathematical expression of concepts related to fairness (Fehr and Gächter 2000), a concept within the purview of ethicists. Similarly, if we can communicate some basic numerical concepts in interstellar messages, we may have the foundation needed to begin expressing some aspects of the human aesthetic experience (Vakoch 2004a, 2004b).

What Can We Offer?

SETI scientists typically assume that extraterrestrial civilizations are much longer lived than terrestrial civilization. That is, the average lifetime of extraterrestrial civilizations, as measured in the time they are actively seeking to make contact with other civilizations, is assumed to be much longer than the time that humans have had the technology and motivation to communicate at interstellar distances. Without this assumption, it is statistically improbable that extraterrestrial and human civilizations will exist sufficiently close to one another in time and space to make contact. If we make contact at all, we can expect to be the junior partner in the conversation.[2]

This presumed asymmetry in the lifetimes of extraterrestrial and terrestrial civilizations raises the question, "what would humans have to say that would be of interest to much older civilizations?" Typically it has been assumed that more long-lived civilizations will also be more technologically and scientifically advanced. If so, then humans are unlikely to be able to teach extraterrestrial civilizations much in these realms, at least assuming that there is a convergence of technological developments and scientific discoveries across civilizations, with more advanced civilizations attaining an understanding that encompasses and surpasses that of less advanced civilizations.

Following the above line of reasoning, even if humankind is much younger than extraterrestrial civilizations, we may nevertheless be in possession of information that could be of significant scientific interest to intelligent beings on other worlds: information about the longevity of our own civilization, as well as factors that threaten our continued existence as a species.

As we attempt to assess the likelihood that SETI will succeed, one of the most elusive variables to quantify is the lifetime of technological civilizations. By beginning a serious program in active SETI—transmitting evidence of our existence to other civilizations—we could provide at least one data point to scientists on other worlds attempting to make this same estimate of the lifetime of civilizations with both the capacity and the willingness to make their existence known to other forms of intelligence.

Although more advanced civilizations may be able to glean some information about the threats to our survival as a species by monitoring atmospheric changes and unintentional leakage radiation from Earth, intentional messages describing the social, political, and ecological factors that contribute to the instability of our planet may provide a rare glimpse into the cultures of a young civilization that has some insight into the threats it faces. Whether or not we continue such transmissions over the millennia would be informative to sociologists and psychologists beyond Earth, potentially providing greater insights into the critical years during which civilizations attempt to make the transition to becoming long-lived civilizations themselves. Whether or not humankind succeeds, such messages from Earth could be useful to extraterrestrials attempting to understand better the factors that contribute to the lifetimes of other civilizations.[3]

Acting on the Environment

In a strikingly different approach to communicating to extraterrestrials the environmental challenges facing contemporary humankind, we might focus not only on the physical manifestations of environmental problems, but also on the humans who contribute to these problems. One step toward creating a language to describe human behavior was proposed by Vakoch (2006a), who noted that scientific explanations of human behavior typically have significantly more limited predictive ability than physicists and chemists are used to. Rather than being able to identify with great precision the antecedents and consequences of any particular person's behavior, psychologists are typically content to predict the behaviors of *groups* of individuals, even when such predictions account for only a modest amount of the total variance in the behaviors between individuals. While physicists may achieve considerable accuracy in determining the trajectory of a billiard ball of particular mass when it is hit at a specific point with a specific force, psychologists must typically remain content to provide probabilistic accounts of human behavior.

Even in the rare interstellar messages that have addressed human behavior, differences between individuals have typically been neglected. As an example, Freudenthal (1960) devotes one section of his book, *Lingua Cosmica*, or *LINCOS*, to an examination of human behavior. However, as he describes the actions of humans under a variety of contexts, he makes no attempt to provide a consistent account of the behaviors of the particular individual identified in his "mini-plays" as Human A, for example. That is, Human A may act in one scenario in a manner that is completely inconsistent with the same person in a different scenario. Such an arbitrary pairing of names of individuals with the actions of particular actors captures some of the variety of human behaviors. But it fails to show that any *particular* individual may have stable dispositions to act in certain ways across situations. In short, Freudenthal's approach fails to describe stable personality characteristics, sometimes known as traits.

Contemporary psychological research has shown, however, that personality plays an important role in determining differences between actors. For example, Fraj and Martinez (2006) examined the relationship between environmental behavior and the five personality factors identified by Costa and McRae (1992): neuroticism, extroversion, openness, conscientiousness, and agreeableness. Fraj and Martinez (2006) found that conscientious individuals were more likely to purchase ecological products or to switch products for ecological reasons. On the other hand, extroverted and agreeable people were more likely either to join an environmental group or to attend an ecological conference. In both cases, their findings readily translate into interstellar messages that show individuals interacting in a range of contexts. As might be expected, individuals who seek out and enjoy being with others are more likely to engage in environmental concerns in settings that require such cooperative, extroverted action, and dispositionally conscientious individuals are likely to be conscientious about their buying patterns. Such probabilistic accounts may provide a foundation for communicating the correlates and even causes of behaviors related to environmental changes.

A Message to Terrestrial Intelligence

Typically, we imagine the benefits of interstellar communication in terms of what we might gain *from extraterrestrial intelligence* as a result of such an exchange. But we might also consider ways we might benefit by transmitting messages, even if we never receive a reply. What might we gain, for example, by grappling with the challenges of describing our understanding of our place in the universe in terms of the epic of evolution—whether or not anyone beyond Earth ever hears us?

In an interstellar message that describes life on Earth in terms of its diversity over the ages, we would be compelled to describe the cataclysmic changes that have occurred periodically throughout the history of our planet—changes such as those that marked the transition from the Mesozoic era to the Cenozoic era. In addition, we would be invited to reflect on our own role in creating cataclysms of comparable scale.

Some have argued that we are in the midst of another great extinction—this one due to human intervention (e.g., Swimme and Berry 1992). As we have expanded our scientific understanding of and mastery over the physical world, we have also significantly drawn upon Earth's limited resources, we have taxed the terrestrial environment with by-products of our industrial progress, and we have reduced Earth's biodiversity. Perhaps the strongest argument for not undertaking a serious program of active SETI—in which we would transmit messages *de novo*, rather than merely listening for messages from other intelligence—is that we do not expect humankind to survive long enough to receive a reply.

Such a program of transmitting messages to other civilizations, however, would make a strong statement here on Earth—a statement that we do expect to be around hundreds or thousands of years from now to receive a reply. And even if we are not—that is, either *not around*, or simply *not listening* any longer—such an experiment could be of significant value to SETI scientists living around distant stars. Indeed, a transmission project undertaken for the benefit of extraterrestrial civilizations would be consistent with a "cosmocentric ethic" (Lupisella and Logsdon 1997), which may provide an ethical foundation for future transmissions from Earth (Vakoch 2005).

Although the focus of SETI is on making contact with intelligence beyond Earth, the exercise of portraying ourselves in interstellar messages provides us with an opportunity to cultivate greater intelligence on our own planet. Few things are more critical to approach more intelligently than the environmental problems that threaten the very existence of human civilization as we know it. Even considering only the climate changes we can anticipate due to greenhouse gas emissions, in the coming decades we should expect environmental effects such as extreme weather events, rising sea levels, and environmental degradation, as well as threats to health due to thermal stress, microbial proliferation, changes in infectious diseases, diminished food sources, and increased poverty (McMichael, Woodruff, and Hales 2006).

By focusing interstellar messages on the ecological challenges we face, we provide a forum for discussing critical issues in a way that is both concrete yet not excessively aversive. The challenge of taking environmental issues seriously is that we need to find a way to make issues like global warming seem sufficiently immediate to attend to, without evoking such strong negative emotional reactions that people avoid the discussions altogether (Lorenzoni et al. 2006).

Agreeing to Disagree

Since the 1980s, a protocol developed by the IAA SETI Committee, in consultation with the International Institute of Space Law, provides guidance about appropriate actions following the detection of an extraterrestrial civilization. This protocol recommends that any response from humankind to a signal from extraterrestrials should represent a consensus. Differences of opinion, in contrast, should be minimized in interstellar messages according to this guideline.

A markedly different approach is proposed in the Dialogic Model (Vakoch 1998b), which advocates transmitting messages that highlight different perspectives in an attempt to reflect the reality of the current human condition in which there are significant differences of viewpoint between groups and even between individuals within relatively homogeneous groups. Vakoch (1998b) argues that to minimize such differences would neglect some of the most important information that humankind could convey: the diversity of our views. As Lupisella (2009) notes:

> Cultural diversity, and perhaps diversity in general, may have practical benefits (e.g., having a wide variety to choose from as needed), but diversity may be a value in its own right, an end unto itself—worth pursuing for its own sake. Given the potential for quite diverse life-forms throughout the universe, diversity may have broad cosmic significance beyond our own aesthetic appreciation.

In any interstellar message that would attempt to describe the environmental challenges that humankind faces in order to survive in the coming decades, alternative perspectives must be acknowledged. Not only do multiple accounts of humankind's role in the current environmental situation portray a diversity of views in contemporary society, but openly discussing these differing accounts may also have a salutary effect by providing a forum for the ongoing dialogue between individuals and groups with divergent perspectives. As we consider the potential value of transmitting messages to extraterrestrial intelligence, we should remember the value of the *process* of deciding on the content of an interstellar message, regardless of whether that message is ever received by an extraterrestrial civilization, or even whether it is ever transmitted.

The Evolution of the Evolutionary Epic

But in an interstellar message based on the evolutionary epic, how much of the content should reflect evolution on a galactic, stellar, or planetary scale, and how much should reflect the idiosyncrasies of our planet's biological and cultural histories? Both are important, but for different reasons.

As we convey physical accounts about, say, the mechanics of galactic structure and the dynamics of planetary formation, we have an opportunity to make a link between basic principles of mathematics and physics and an external reality shared by humans and extraterrestrials. Even if humans and extraterrestrials have a common commitment to modeling evermore accurately the nature of physical reality, there is no guarantee, however, that these models of reality will necessarily be obviously commensurable (Vakoch 1998a). Peter Barker (1982) has articulated the challenges of terrestrial scientists from different times and cultures understanding one another; how much more difficult might it be for terrestrial and extraterrestrial scientists to understand one another given they have evolved in different environments? The differing evolutionary histories of independently evolved species may indeed affect the goals that scientists pursue on different worlds. As philosopher Nicholas Rescher (1985) argues, an aquatic intelligence may have a very sophisticated science of hydrodynamics because its survival and flourishing depends on it. But it may be lacking in some concepts fundamental to land-based civilizations.

This view of scientific progress contrasts with a standard view of linear progress typically assumed—often implicitly—in SETI circles (Vakoch 2008b). In this standard view, more advanced civilizations have passed through the same stages as less advanced civilizations on other worlds. If more advanced civilizations want to make themselves understood, it is argued, they will start with the principles that would surely be understood by less advanced civilizations. But, the skeptic might ask, is it so obvious which principles those would be, and even if the principles are widely known, is the conceptual apparatus for describing these principles universal?

Perhaps an analogy of mountain climbing will help clarify the issue. Science progresses, we might argue, in the same way that a mountain climber progresses toward the peak of a mountain.[4] Not all climbers will progress as far; novice climbers may only make it part way up the mountain. But as these neophytes become more skilled, they will be able to progress to greater altitudes, all the while pointed toward their goal: the highest point of the mountain.

In this analogy, the scientist is akin to the climber, progressing step-by-step toward ever clearer understanding of the nature of reality as it really is, symbolized by the mountaintop. There may, indeed, be times when the scientist/climber diverts from the path, but in the long run, the interplay of theory and experiment ensures that the successful scientist—the one who makes progress in ascending the mountain—will find the right path. A more sophisticated scientist/climber, having ascended higher, could look back and even leave pointers for the less experienced scientist/climber, potentially providing clues that might speed up the ascent of the less experienced.

As we apply this metaphor to interstellar communication, we assume—by necessity—that we are the less experienced climber. In the 13-plus billion-year history of our galaxy, on purely statistical grounds, it is highly improbable that any civilization we contact by radio signals or brief laser pulses will be as technologically youthful as we are. Less advanced civilizations will not have the capacity to communicate at interstellar distances. And if the typical age of an extraterrestrial civilization is as short as ours, then the number of civilizations that exists at any one time will be very small—and the few that exist will be located far from one another.

But to continue the analogy, what if we and the extraterrestrial scientist/climber ascend different sides of the mountain? How then could the more advanced civilization point the way up a path it did not take? Or even more pessimistically, what if the human and extraterrestrial scientists/climbers are ascending different mountains—both getting continually closer to their respective goals of increasingly comprehensive understanding of the universe, but each headed toward a different mountain peak, providing a perspective on a different aspect of the universe? If Rescher (1985) is right, then science may take varied forms on varied worlds.

While the possibility of multiple directions of progress does little to reassure us of easy interspecies communication, it does open the possibility of learning much, if ever we do establish contact. Indeed, the possible plurality of sciences on different worlds may provide a sense of reassurance that even a civilization as young as ours might contribute substantially in an interstellar exchange. Even beyond accounts of the challenges we face simply to survive, our scientific and cultural accomplishments could be of considerable interest on other worlds. By Steven Dick's (2009) analysis of the history of ideas about cosmic evolution, even on Earth there was no inherent necessity that scientists would come to understand the universe in specifically evolutionary terms: "The humble and sporadic origins of the idea of cosmic evolution demonstrate that it did not have to become what is now the leading overarching principle of twentieth century astronomy." If in fact there is not one single path of scientific progress taken by all civilizations, but different paths depending on each species' idiosyncratic environment as well as its unique evolutionary and cultural histories, then even our relatively primitive accounts of the universe may provide novel insights to extraterrestrials.

Just as the anthropologists and historians of Earth are interested in the development of other cultures' ways of understanding the world about them, so, too, might extraterrestrial intelligence be interested in the specific trajectory that our elaboration of the evolutionary epic has taken. Though we tend to value our most recent scientific understanding most highly, assuming this most accurately reflects the nature of reality, historians of science on another world may not be especially interested in learning about the models most widely accepted in the early 21st century. Instead, extraterrestrial historians may be more intrigued by the entire history of the idea of cosmic evolution (Dick 2009) or the ideas of particular scientists whose models have in some ways now been superseded, for example, those of Harlow Shapley (Palmeri 2009). If, as many have argued, the most readily comprehensible parts of an interstellar message are those addressing scientific topics, then a history of human theories of cosmic evolution may provide one of the most accessible ways to introduce other civilizations to terrestrial historical and cultural concepts.

Starting with Our Origins

We might, of course, describe our evolutionary origins in other than chemical terms, which was the focus of this chapter. We might describe the dynamics of galactic formation, for example, with some of the same basic concepts of physics through which we can analyze the evolution of locomotion in terrestrial life (e.g., Radinsky 1987). Astronomers on other worlds, we might argue, would be as likely to share basic principles of physics with humans as they are likely to have concepts of chemistry in common. Indeed, Freudenthal's (1960) interstellar language *LINCOS*—perhaps the most sophisticated language for cosmic discourse yet developed on Earth—gives concepts from physics a central place.

Regardless of whether we choose a language based on principles of chemistry, physics, or something else, as we ponder what we might say in transmissions to other worlds—should we choose some day to transmit evidence of our existence in a serious fashion—it would be very fitting if our messages reflected some of the very processes of the universe that ultimately led to the origin and evolution of ourselves as a species attempting to make contact with other worlds.

Yes, we humans are more than merely biological creatures. We appreciate beauty, we struggle with ethical conflicts, and we strive to make sense of our purpose in the universe, asking questions that science cannot answer. And yet, our sense of aesthetics, our moral sensibilities, and our search for meaning may themselves be intricately connected to the fabric of the cosmos (Lupisella 2009). It would seem fitting, then, if our first exchange with sentient beings on other worlds started by explaining that we, too, recognize our origins in the early universe when hydrogen and helium were created; that our life's breath requires the oxygen first released from Earth's oceans some two billion years ago; and that as we have learned to trace the history of the elements that make up our bodies and that give rise to our consciousness, we have discovered an evolutionary creation myth that helps us start to understand our place in the cosmos. And that they, the recipients of this message, living on a distant planet, may well be interested in hearing it.

References

Barker, P. (1982) "Omilinguals," in Smith, N. D. (ed.) *Philosophers Look at Science Fiction*. Chicago: Nelson-Hall, pp. 75–85.

Blackmore, S. (1999) *The Meme Machine*. Oxford: Oxford University Press.

Bloom, H. (2000) *Global Brain: The Evolution of Mass Mind from the Big Bang to the 21st Century*. New York: John Wiley & Sons.

Brown, C. S. (2007) *Big History: From the Big Bang to the Present*. New York: The New Press.

Chaisson, E. (1981) *Cosmic Dawn: The Origins of Matter and Life*. Boston: Little, Brown and Company.

Chaisson, E. (2001) *Cosmic Evolution: The Rise of Complexity in Nature*. Cambridge: Harvard University Press.

Chaisson, E. (2006) *Epic of Evolution: Seven Ages of the Cosmos.* New York: Columbia University Press.

Christian, D. (2004) *Maps of Time: An Introduction to Big History.* Berkeley: University of California Press.

Costa, P. T., Jr., and R. R. McCrae, (1992) *Revised NEO Personality Inventory (NEO-PI-R) and NEO Five Factor Inventory (NEO-FFI) Professional Manual.* Odessa, FL: Psychological Assessment Resources.

Davies, P. C. W., T. M. Davis, and C. H. Lineweaver, (2002) "Cosmology: Black Holes Constrain Varying Constants," *Nature* 418:602–603.

DeVito, C. L. and R. T. Oehrle, (1990) "A Language Based on the Fundamental Facts of Science," *Journal of the British Interplanetary Society* 43:561–568.

Dick, S. J. (2009) "Cosmic Evolution: History, Culture and Human Destiny," in Dick, S. J. and M. Lupisella (eds.) *Cosmos and Culture: Cultural Evolution in a Cosmic Context.* Washington, DC: NASA History Series.

Drake, F. (1978) "The Foundations of the Voyager Record," in Sagan, C. (ed.) *Murmurs of Earth: The Voyager Interstellar Record.* New York: Random House, pp. 45–70.

Drake, F. and D. Sobel, (1992) *Is Anyone Out There?: The Scientific Search for Extraterrestrial Intelligence.* New York: Delacorte.

Druyan, A. (1978) "The Sounds of Earth," in Sagan, C. (ed.) *Murmurs of Earth: The Voyager Interstellar Record.* New York: Random House, pp. 149–160.

Fehr, E. and S. Gächter, (2000) "Fairness and Retaliation—The Economics of Reciprocity," *American Economic Review* 90:980–994.

Fraj, E. and E. Martinez, (2006) "Influence of Personality on Ecological Consumer Behaviour," *Journal of Consumer Behaviour* 5:67–181.

Freudenthal, H. (1960) *LINCOS: Design of a Language for Cosmic Intercourse. Part I.* Amsterdam: North-Holland.

Gräslund, B. (1987) *The Birth of Prehistoric Chronology: Dating Methods and Dating Systems in Nineteenth-century Scandinavian Archaeology.* Cambridge: Cambridge University Press.

Heizer, R. F. (1962) "The Background of Thomsen's Three-age System," *Technology and Culture* 3, no. 3:259–266.

Lorenzoni, I. et al. (2006) "Cross-National Comparisons of Image Associations with 'Global Warming' and 'Climate Change' among Laypeople in the United States of America and Great Britain," *Journal of Risk Research* 9, no. 3:265–281.

Lupisella, M. (n.d.) "Increasing Verisimilitude as the Goal of Science," Unpublished manuscript.

Lupisella, M. (2009) "Cosmocultural Evolution: The Co-evolution of Culture and Cosmos" in Dick, S. J. and M. Lupisella (eds.) *Cosmos and Culture: Cultural Evolution in a Cosmic Context*, Washington, DC: NASA History Series.

Lupisella, M. and J. Logsdon, (1997) "Do We Need a Cosmocentric Ethic?" Paper presented at the 48th International Astronautical Congress, Turin, Italy.

Mason, S. F. (1991) *Chemical Evolution: Origin of the Elements, Molecules, and Living Systems.* Oxford: Clarendon Press.

McMichael, A. J., R. E. Woodruff, and S. Hales, (2006) "Climate Change and Human Health: Present and Future Risks," *The Lancet* 367:859–869.

Palmeri, J. (2009) "Bringing Cosmos to Culture: Harlow Shapley and the Uses of Cosmic Evolution," in Dick, S. J. and M. Lupisella (eds.) *Cosmos and Culture: Cultural Evolution in a Cosmic Context*, Washington, DC: NASA History Series.

Radinsky, L. B. (1987) *The Evolution of Vertebrate Design.* Chicago: The University of Chicago Press.

Rescher, N. (1985) "Extraterrestrial Science," in Regis, E., Jr. (ed.) *Extraterrestrials: Science and Alien Intelligence.* Cambridge: Cambridge University Press, pp. 83–116.

Sagan, C., L. Saltzman Sagan, and F. Drake, (1972) "A Message from Earth," *Science* 175:881–884.

Sproul, B. C. (1979) *Primal Myths: Creating the World.* New York: Harper & Row.

Staff of the National Astronomy and Ionosphere Center. (1975) "The Arecibo Message of November 1974," *Icarus* 26:462–466.

Swimme, B., and T. Berry, (1992) *From the Primordial Flaring Forth to the Ecozoic Era—A Celebration of the Unfolding of the Cosmos.* New York: HarperCollins.

Vakoch, D. A. (1998a) "Constructing Messages to Extraterrestrials: An Exosemiotic Perspective," *Acta Astronautica* 42:697–704.

Vakoch, D. A. (1998b) "The Dialogic Model: Representing Human Diversity in Messages to Extraterrestrials," *Acta Astronautica* 42:705–710.

Vakoch, D. A. (1998c) "Signs of Life beyond Earth: A Semiotic Analysis of Interstellar Messages," *Leonardo* 31:313–319.

Vakoch, D. A. (2000) "Three-dimensional Messages for Interstellar Communication," in Lemarchand, G. A. and K. Meech (eds.) *Bioastronomy 99: A New Era in Bioastronomy.* San Francisco: Astronomical Society of the Pacific, pp. 623–627.

Vakoch, D. A. (2001) "Altruism as the Key to Interstellar Communication," *Research News & Opportunities in Science and Theology* 2, no. 3:2, 16.

Vakoch, D. A. (2002) "Encoding Altruism," *Galileo* 52:30–36.

Vakoch, D. A. (2003) "Le sacrifice de soi: Une composition interstellaire," *Anomalie Digital_Arts* 4:201–202.

Vakoch, D. A. (2004a) "The Art and Science of Interstellar Message Composition," *Leonardo* 37:33–34.

Vakoch, D. A. (2004b) "To the Stars, Silently," *Leonardo* 37: 265.

Vakoch, D. A. (2005) "Expanding Human Presence beyond the Solar System through Active SETI: On the Prerequisites for Legal Relations with Extraterrestrial Intelligence," *Proceedings of the Forty-eighth Colloquium on the Law of Outer Space: 17–21 October 2005, Fukuoka, Japan* 48:149–155.

Vakoch, D. A. (2006a) "Describing the Probabilistic Nature of Human Behavior in Interstellar Messages," Paper presented at the SETI II Interdisciplinary Connections Review Meeting, 57th International Astronautical Congress, Valencia, Spain.

Vakoch, D. (2006b) "To Err is Human . . . and of Interest to ET?" *Explorer* 3, no. 2:16–17.

Vakoch, D. (2007) "A Shadow of Ourselves," *Explorer* 4, no. 4: 16–17.

Vakoch, D. A. (2008a) "Representing Culture in Interstellar Messages," *Acta Astronautica* 63:657–664.

Vakoch, D. (2008b) "Technology as a Manifestation of Intelligence: Does Shared Technology Imply Shared Science and Mathematics?" *Astrobiology* 8, no. 2:391.

Endnotes

1. To be sure, not all cosmologists would maintain that physical constants remain constant over time. Nevertheless, some constraints might be assumed. For example, Paul Davies, Tamara Davis, and Charles Lineweaver (2002) suggest that though there is evidence that the fine-structure constant may be increasing slowly over cosmological timescales, one might test which constants could be variable without violating the second law of thermodynamics.

2. For a discussion of another possibility—that the burden of transmitting may lie with the less advanced civilization—see Vakoch's (2005) "Expanding Human Presence beyond the Solar System through Active SETI: On the Prerequisites for Legal Relations with Extraterrestrial Intelligence."

3. For additional ways that older, more technological civilizations may benefit from learning about humanity, see Vakoch's (2006b) "To Err is Human . . . and of Interest to ET?" and (2007) "A Shadow of Ourselves."

4. For a similar analysis, see Lupisella's (n.d.) "Increasing Verisimilitude as the Goal of Science."

Chapter 13

History and Science after the Chronometric Revolution[1]

David Christian

Introduction

This paper describes a transformation in our understanding of the past, a transformation whose full significance has not yet been adequately appreciated. The transformation is associated with a revolution in the techniques used to date past events. I will argue that this "chronometric revolution," which occurred in the middle of the 20th century, has large implications for our understanding of both history, and of the relationship between history and science.

The first part of this essay reviews the changing relationship between history and the sciences in the western world over several centuries. The second part describes the "chronometric revolution." The discipline of history has been transformed by two great chronometric revolutions. One occurred several millennia ago, after the appearance of writing. Written records made it possible, for the first time, to assign absolute dates to events many generations in the past. The second revolution occurred soon after the Second World War. It allowed us to assign reliable absolute dates to events extending back to the very origins of the universe. The third part explores some of the consequences of the chronometric revolution. By expanding our vision of the past to eras well before the appearance of our own species, the chronometric revolution historicized disciplines such as cosmology, geology, and biology and brought them closer in their methodologies to the discipline of history. The fourth part argues that the idea of increasing complexity offers a powerful thematic link between this newly discovered cluster of historically oriented disciplines. Over 13 billion years, increasingly complex entities have appeared in the universe, and modern human society may be one of the most complex of all these entities. Finally, the expanded vision of the past made possible by the chronometric revolution raises important questions about the distinctive nature of *human* history. I will argue that our species is distinguished by two complementary "emergent" properties. The first is an exceptional ability to adapt to different environments. The second is a unique capacity for seeking and finding "meaning." As a species we have a quite exceptional ability to keep finding new ways of adapting to our environments. I will argue that the source of this ability is "collective learning"—the ability, unique to our species, to share learned information with precision and in great volume. That ability in turn is linked to our propensity for finding "meaning" through the sharing of symbols. In the light of these arguments, I will suggest that the expanded past revealed by the chronometric revolution allows us to redefine our sense of the past in general and of human history in particular.

Part 1: A Revolution in our Understanding of the Past

In the form of meaningful stories about the past ("creation stories"), history has probably existed since the appearance of the first humans more than 100,000 years ago. Science, at least in recognizably modern forms, is only a few centuries old.[2]

The new science of the 17th century was astonishing because it seemed to provide simple, elegant, and apparently perfect solutions to ancient riddles about the nature of the universe. In a few simple equations, Isaac Newton managed to explain the movements of objects both in the heavens and on Earth. The same equations could tell you why the planets moved in ellipses and why apples fell on your head. Here was an entirely new and uniquely powerful form of knowledge. During the Enlightenment era, and for much of the 19th century, European scholars in many different fields, from history to sociology to economics, tried to imitate the success of science by finding "scientific" laws that would explain human history as successfully as Newton's laws had explained the workings of gravity.[3]

However, by the end of the 19th century, disillusionment began to set in, particularly among historians. More and more historians gave up hope of finding fundamental laws of historical development because so many claims had been made and so few fit the evidence. Part of the problem was that there wasn't enough hard information to construct a rigorous narrative for any but the most recent eras of human history. Hardly anything was known of prehistory, in part because dating techniques based on the written record did not permit the construction of coherent chronologies for any era earlier than a few millennia ago. Shortage of information made it all too easy to concoct large narratives that reflected little more than the (often racialist) views of their authors, because they were insufficiently disciplined by hard evidence.

Besides, there was a growing feeling that the methods of science and history differed in fundamental ways. Above all, historians could not even pretend to generalize on the basis of controlled experiments. Could you rerun the French Revolution, making minor changes to different variables each time? Perhaps by allowing assassins to murder Robespierre or Napoleon early in their respective careers? No. History didn't allow the repeatability or predictability of laboratory experiments. Instead, it tried to reconstruct a vanished past consisting of millions of apparently unique events. Such a process, it seemed, could never be brought under general laws or mathematical equations, so history would have to set itself more modest goals.

Some historians, particularly in Germany, argued that there was a fundamental difference in the subject matter of history and science. History dealt with entities that had ideas, thoughts and a sense of purpose, while science dealt with inert matter. They contrasted the *Geisteswissenschaften*, or sciences of the inner or spiritual world, with the *Naturwissenschaften*, or sciences of the natural or material world. In 1894, Wilhelm Windelband proposed that there were two utterly different aspects of reality, the "nomothetic," or those things subject to regular laws, and the "ideographic," those areas of reality where it was pointless seeking general laws.[4] The great English historiographer, R. G. Collingwood, argued that while natural history consisted of *events*, only human history could deal with conscious *acts*, that is to say with events that had meaning and were motivated by intentions.[5] In the English-speaking world in particular, this argument remains influential to the present day. Indeed, Appleby and her colleagues, whose survey of the evolution of modern historiography I have already cited, put it like this: "the human sciences, such as history, have a distinct set of problems. Any analogy to natural science falters because the historian or sociologist, even the economist, cannot effectively isolate the objects of inquiry. . . . Humanists study action which is responsive to intentions, whereas naturalists investigate the bounded world of behavior."[6] That is a good, concise summary of beliefs that are widely held within the history profession today.

By the middle of the 20th century, relations between history and science had worsened. Some of this alienation may have been due to jealousy, as science went from triumph to triumph. But science was also implicated in the horrors of the two world wars.[7] It created planes and the bombs they carried, as well as the killing machines of the Holocaust. Its role in these horrors cast doubt both on its objectivity and its capacity to sustain progress. In this mood of deep disillusionment, many historians in the West (though not in the Communist world) turned towards relativism. Some concluded that their role was to interpret meaning rather than to seek out the facts. Under the influence of scholars such as anthropologist Clifford Geertz, many English-speaking historians became more interested in how people mapped the world than in the accuracy of the maps they constructed. As Appleby and her colleagues put it: "Geertz . . . explicitly rejected the positivist scientific model in favor of an increasingly literary model of cultural criticism. His position had obvious affinities to those advanced by postmodernists such as Foucault and Derrida. . . . The emphasis on decoding meaning, rather than inferring causal laws of explanation was taken to be the central task of cultural history, just as Geertz had named it the central task of cultural anthropology."[8] This meant that, in very general terms, the task of history was hermeneutic rather than explanatory. The thankless task of explaining a dead reality was left to the scientists. History dealt, instead, with the complex, unpredictable, and endlessly creative world of living, thinking beings.

This was the atmosphere in which C. P. Snow famously argued that the humanities and the sciences had moved so far apart that they had become, in effect, distinct "cultures."[9] What prospect was there of overcoming such fundamental differences?

In the rest of this paper I will argue that a new chapter is being written in this complex and tempestuous relationship. Crucial to this new chapter is the "chronometric revolution" of the 20th century.

Part 2: "Chronometric" Revolutions

By "chronometry," I mean the techniques used to assign absolute dates to past events. Chronometry is fundamental to historical thought. Without absolute dates, we can say nothing rigorous about the past because our evidence consists of a disorganized mass of information with no chronological structure. A rigorous understanding of the past requires not just evidence in general, but evidence *that can be ordered chronologically*, because without a precise sense of temporal order, we cannot discuss causation. As Collingwood wrote, the historian's business is "to apprehend the past as a thing in itself, to say for example that so many years ago such-and-such events actually happened."[10] Unfortunately, chronometry is one of those issues that is so fundamental that it can easily drop out of our consciousness. In his massive study of the evolution of modern European historiography, Hayden White writes that "chronicle," or the ordering of events in time, is the most basic level of "conceptualization in the historical work." He then proceeds to ignore problems of chronology almost entirely in the 400 pages that follow.[11]

A simple analogy may help to more clearly bring out the fundamental significance of chronometry. Imagine that looking at the past is like looking into a cave. Sunlight may allow us to map the entrance to the cave quite precisely. Further in, we may be able to see things, but the relationship between objects gets harder to gauge, and our mapping soon loses precision. Then there is total darkness. We have no idea how far back the cave goes, or what is there. So we really don't know if the bits we can see are representative of the whole cave or not. The truth is that our knowledge of the cave depends less on what is actually there than on the available illumination. The same is true of our knowledge of the past. Without knowing the full extent of the past, we have no idea whether the events we can see are typical of larger patterns or simply contingent products of particular eras, societies, or conjunctures. A statistician might say that the sample from which historians generalize is seriously skewed for the simple reason that we have no idea how or by how much it is skewed! If that is true, it makes all the larger generalizations of historians suspect. Until recently, historians tended to ignore the problem because there was little that could be done about it. In practice, history meant the study of those parts of the past for which we could construct chronologically structured narratives, *whether or not* they were representative of the past in general.

As this argument suggests, our understanding of the past is critically dependent on "chronometry." So we need to think very carefully about chronometric techniques and how they have shaped the history discipline and our sense of the past in general.

Chronometric techniques have passed through two large revolutions. In societies without writing, dates depended entirely on human memory. But memory could assign plausible dates for only a few generations. It is true that oral traditions can retain a vast amount of information about the past; the difficulty they face is how to order that information chronologically. Where the chronological precision of collective memory fades, the past loses shape, turning into what Aboriginal Australians call the "dreamtime," a time with lots of events but little chronology.

The first chronometric revolution was a by-product of the invention of writing from about five millennia ago. Writing made it possible to assign plausible absolute dates to events that had occurred centuries or even millennia before the present. And it was the only reliable method of doing so. That is why it became the basis for the discipline of history, the discipline that specialized in reconstructing the past. Written documents or inscriptions lit up new areas of the past. But of course the illumination they provided depended on the existence of writing. And this was a more severe limitation than is generally recognized. History based on written documents can assign dates only to human history (not to natural history unless it was described by someone); and only to those parts of human history recorded by the scribes of religious or governmental bureaucracies. History therefore tended to exclude the natural world. Even worse, it excluded most humans, with the exception of those elite groups who wrote: government officials, rulers, and literati. These limitations shaped our understanding of the very nature of history well into the 20th century. H. G. Wells regretted that, in his attempt to write a universal history, he could assign no dates before the first Olympiad, 776 BCE.[12] Geologists and archaeologists had begun to construct increasingly sophisticated systems of *relative* dating in the 19th century, but they could offer no *absolute* dates before the appearance of written records.[13]

As a result of the first chronometric revolution, in all literate societies and for several millennia, history came to mean something like: *the study of the past on the basis of written documents.* Unfortunately, the dominant role of written evidence made it all too easy to confuse the past as illuminated by written documents with the past in general. Eventually, this view of how we should study the past came to seem so natural that it was built into our taxonomies of knowledge. "No documents, no history," wrote Charles Langlois and Charles Seignobos in a textbook published in English in 1898.[14] "History cannot discuss the origin of society," wrote Leopold von Ranke despairingly, as he attempted a universal history, "for the art of writing, which is the basis of historical knowledge, is a comparatively late invention. . . . The province of History is limited by the means at her command, and the historian would be over-bold who should venture to unveil the mystery of the primeval world, the relation of mankind to God and nature."[15] That our sense of the past must be based on written evidence is still a widely held view among historians. Let me quote Appleby and her colleagues once more: "Because they are most often found in texts, the remnants of the past usually present themselves in words."[16]

All in all, though the first chronometric revolution extended our chronologies by many generations, it also left us with an extremely distorted vision of the past. Our "sample" of the past excluded most of the natural world, most of the Paleolithic era and at least half of the Agrarian era. And even within the periods that it could describe, most humans remained invisible until the last century or two. The situation was transformed by a second chronometric revolution that dates to the middle of the 20th century. This cast a flood of light on those parts of the cave of the past that had remained in darkness, and by doing so it promised to revolutionize our understanding of history in general.

The second chronometric revolution began with the discovery of radioactivity by Marie and Pierre Curie in the 1890s. Then in the first decade of the 20th century, Ernest Rutherford realized that radioactive materials decay with such regularity that they could provide a sort of clock for events in the natural world. If you could measure accurately the extent to which a lump of radioactive material had decayed, by measuring the by-products of radioactive decay, you could estimate when the lump was formed. Rutherford illustrated these ideas by attempting to date a lump of pitchblende (an ore of uranium). He found it to be about 500 million years old, much older than the standard contemporary estimates of Earth itself.[17] Arthur Holmes used similar techniques to estimate absolute dates for the geological time scale soon after Rutherford's demonstration. However, many practical difficulties had to be overcome before these techniques could be used routinely, and that is why they did not revolutionize our sense of the past until after World War II.

Willard Libby, from the University of Chicago, had worked on the Manhattan project, specializing in the difficult task of separating different isotopes of uranium from each other. These were precisely the skills needed to develop the program Rutherford had imagined half a century earlier. After the war, Libby applied the same techniques to the task of separating out different isotopes of carbon in order to measure precisely the rates of decay of materials containing radioactive isotopes of carbon (carbon 14). In 1952, he published the first edition of a pioneering text on *Radiocarbon Dating*. Though important difficulties remained, such as the need to calibrate C14 dates carefully, from the 1950s, radiometric dating techniques began to be used more generally by archaeologists. They worked well for dates since about 50,000 years ago. Other radiometric techniques were soon developed that used other materials with different rates of decay, so they could determine dates at larger scales. One of the most important depended on the decay of uranium to lead, a sequence that allows measurements over many hundreds of millions of years. In 1953, Clair Patterson, of the California Institute of Technology, used this sequence to establish that Earth itself was about 4.55 billion-years-old, by estimating the breakdown of uranium to lead in a meteorite from the Barringer crater in Arizona.

From the 1950s, a whole series of radiometric dating techniques were developed, as well as other, entirely unrelated techniques such as dendrochronology (the counting of tree rings), genetic dating (used to estimate when different species diverged from each other), and a series of special techniques for measuring the expansion of the universe that now allow us to date the very beginnings of the universe to 13.7 billion years ago. Suddenly, it turned out that it was possible to construct rigorous chronologies not just for human history, but also for the history of living organisms (by dating fossils), Earth itself, and even the entire universe. It was as if the entire cave of the past had been illuminated by fires reaching right back to the very deepest part. For the first time, it became possible to start mapping the past in its entirety rather than just those few patches that were dateable using written evidence. This was the chronometric counterpart of the construction of the first modern world maps in the 16th century. At last, we could see (at least in outline), and we could even date, the entire past!

Part 3: History and Science after the Chronometric Revolution: Shared Stories and Methods?

Within a decade or two the dateable past had expanded from just a few thousand years to many billions of years. This transformed the relation between history and science, because it gave science itself a historical dimension. Geology, biology, and astronomy all became rigorous historical disciplines, just as history had once tried to become a science.[18] Cosmologists began to describe in detail the history of a universe that had evolved over 13 billion years; geologists reconstructed the history of Earth, its interior, and its atmosphere over 4.5 billion years; and biologists began to reconstruct the history of life itself, from the first single-celled organisms that had appeared almost 4 billion years ago, to the immense variety of species present today.

No longer could history claim to be the only scholarly discipline interested in rigorous reconstructions of a vanished past. Once equipped with plausible chronologies of their own, cosmology, geology, and biology became more interested in reconstructing the histories of the entities that they dealt with. And as they did so they found themselves facing the same fundamental challenge as historians: that of reconstructing a vanished and somewhat wayward past from the few scraps of evidence that had survived into the present. The challenge was similar even if different disciplines used different archives—historians using, say, those of the papacy (Ranke's favorite archive), while cosmologists studied the cosmic background radiation. Like history, such disciplines could no longer base their truth claims primarily on experimental data repeatable more or less at will.[19]

The chronometric revolution also has the potential to transform the traditional history discipline by making available to it a much more complete account of the past. This should allow historians to more rigorously pursue questions about the typicality of the behaviors and the communities they study using conventional kinds of evidence. How typical are the state-level societies that have been the main focus of a discipline largely dependent on the written record? It is now possible to say, reasonably precisely, that such societies have emerged only in the most recent millennia of a human history that extends back more than 100,000 years. Chronologically speaking, state-level societies are *atypical*. They represent the result of a long period of very slow change extending back through at least two Ice Ages. Historians have been studying only the tip of a chronological iceberg. How typical are human beings, themselves? We now have powerful reasons for believing that the types of community studied by historians have never existed before in the 3.5 billion-year history of life on Earth.[20] This means that, in principle at least, it should now be possible to identify more precisely than ever before what is unique about human history in general, a question I will return to later.

———

Part 4: History and Science after the Chronometric Revolution: Shared Themes?

Is it possible that the chronometric revolution has also brought history and science closer together in their themes, questions, and subject matter?

In the English-speaking world, these questions are being pursued by a number of scholars from both the humanities and the sciences who have been trying to revive the ancient tradition of "universal history" under the new label of "big history."[21] Universal histories have been constructed within all cultural traditions. They attempt to understand the past at all scales, to incorporate the history of human societies within that of the universe as a whole. "Big history" is an attempt to do the same thing, but using the information and the dating techniques of modern science. Scholars engaged in this project have naturally been forced to ask whether there can be any thematic coherence to big history. Will it consist just of a ragbag of unrelated stories? Or are there common themes shared by all historically oriented disciplines, from cosmology to history?

One promising (and positive) answer to this question is the idea of "complexity." The early universe was simple. It consisted of little more than an expanding space, with clouds of hydrogen and helium atoms and lots of energy pouring through them. Today's universe is much more complex. Dotted through space are the complex hot spots we call stars. They pour energy into the extreme cold of surrounding space and, in at least one instance (and probably many more) that extraordinary torrent of energy has been used to assemble entities that are chemically more complex than stars, things such as planets and living organisms.[22]

But what is complexity? That question is not easy to answer, but a relatively simply description can take us some of the way. First, complex things are composed of different elements organized in precise ways to form distinctive structures. More complex objects have more components than simpler objects, and are organized in more elaborate ways within more elaborate structures. A hydrogen atom is a simple arrangement of one proton and one electron; a molecule of DNA may contain billions of atoms arranged in extremely precise configurations that encode the information needed to construct a particular living organism.

Second, the astronomer Eric Chaisson (who has taught an astronomer's version of big history in Boston for many years) has pointed out that energy flows are always needed to construct and sustain complex structures. If this is true, it should also be true that it takes *more* energy to make *more* complex things. So here's a second property of complex entities: they depend on denser, more concentrated "energy flows" than simpler entities. Chaisson has argued that if you try to calculate these energy flows you can come up with a clear ranking of different entities by their levels of complexity.[23] How precise the correlation between energy flows and complexity really is remains uncertain.

What is important for us is that Chaisson's ranking order suggests that chemistry deals with a higher level of complexity than physics, and biology with even greater levels of complexity. Finally, he argues that modern human societies, when ranked by the density of the energy flows through them, count as amongst the most complex things we know.

Complex entities have a third important property. As you assemble components into something larger, new properties appear. This is the phenomenon known as "emergence." Emergent properties can seem magical because they do not seem to arise from the component parts of a structure.[24] You can study hydrogen and oxygen for as long as you like but when you assemble those atoms into a molecule of water, new properties will emerge that could not have been predicted merely from an understanding of hydrogen and oxygen. Thought, too, seems to be an emergent property of the organization of neurons in brains. As these examples suggest, the apparently magical quality of emergent properties is an illusion. "Emergent properties" arise from a particular arrangement of components—they do not appear within the component parts themselves.[25]

In summary, complex things have three crucial properties: 1) diverse components organized within a very precise structure; 2) significant, and increasingly dense energy flows; and 3) emergent properties that arise from the specific way in which components are arranged.

Distinctive emergent properties mean that complexity itself takes different forms, and these underlie many of the differences in approach and techniques between the various disciplines that study the past. Astronomy concerns itself with the emergent properties of large heavenly bodies such as stars, including their ability to generate huge energy flows and to forge new chemical elements in their dying days. Geology concerns itself with bodies such as Earth itself, which are more chemically complex than stars because they contain a greater variety of chemical elements and exist at temperatures low enough for the construction of a wide array of chemically complex materials. Biology concerns itself with the distinctive emergent properties of living organisms. Each type of complex entity poses distinctive problems for the scholar and reveals new emergent properties. Living organisms, for example, display qualities not present in nonliving things, such as the ability to reproduce, to extract energy from their environments, and to adapt to changes in their environments.

This line of thought raises a new question that ought to help us better understand what distinguishes human history from other historical disciplines within a unified modern account of the past: what are the emergent properties that distinguish human history from these other forms of history?

Part 5: What Is Unique about Human History?

I will argue that two complementary emergent properties distinguish our species from all other species. The first is an astonishing capacity to adapt, or find new ways of extracting resources and energy from the environment. The second, which helps explain the first, is a subjectively experienced sense that reality has "meaning."[26] (So Collingwood was at least half right in insisting that history was about meaningful action!)

The first property can be appreciated best within the large context of big history. When human history is seen as a whole (a perception that is extremely difficult within the more limited frames of conventional historical scholarship) it is apparent that there are large patterns. One pattern stands out despite the limitations of our information about the Paleolithic era. Over the 200,000 years or so during which our species has existed, it has shown a unique ability to innovate, to keep finding new ways of extracting energy and resources from its environment. As far as we know, no other living species has displayed such ecological virtuosity in 3.5 billion years.[27]

A capacity for constant innovation means that over time our species has secured control over more and more of the energy and resources of the biosphere. This has allowed humans to multiply, but eventually, human communities also became larger, denser, and more complex. As human communities increased in numbers and variety, so did the pace of innovation and change. Change was very slow in the Paleolithic era of human history, much faster in the Agrarian era, and is many times faster today.

The ecological virtuosity of our species helps explain the extraordinary complexity of today's global human community, for it is our increasing control of energy and resources that has allowed the building of larger and more complex communities. When humans first appeared about 200,000 years ago, there may have been just a few thousand of them, each using at least 3 Kcals a day—the minimum necessary for survival. Their energy consumption was probably similar to that of other large mammals such as our close relatives, the great apes. Today, there are more than 6 billion of us, and on average each of us is controlling approximately 230 Kcals a day, or more than 70 times as much as our Stone Age ancestors.[28] If Eric Chaisson is right, such calculations suggest the extraordinary complexity of the global society of humans today. So here's the first thing for historians to note. They are dealing with entities (human societies) which, at least in modern forms, are vastly *more* complex than those dealt with in the other historically oriented sciences. (This conclusion highlights the advantages of seeing the whole cave of the past. Now, we can begin to see how untypical of the past our modern, gas-guzzling society really is!) The sheer complexity of modern human societies may be one more reason why historians have failed to come up with the neat, mathematically precise laws that have emerged within physics: human society is simply too complex to yield such laws.

What is the source of our astonishing ecological precocity? Why is our species so good at finding new ways of adapting to our environments? Answers to these fundamental questions have been slow in coming partly because of the extreme fragmentation of scholarly disciplines in the modern world. Such questions fall between disciplines—between history, psychology, paleontology, linguistics, anthropology, and biology. As a result, they have not been studied with the care, completeness, or breadth of vision needed to yield sophisticated answers. But I believe we may be on the verge of answering such questions as a number of different disciplines begin to converge on similar answers.

Here's one attempt to describe some of these emerging answers. All living species "adapt." Indeed, "adaptation" is a distinctive emergent property of life in general. Adaptation means that, over time, the average features of a species can slowly change so as to ensure that each individual member can extract from its surroundings the energy needed to maintain its complex structures. This is what natural selection is all about. But it's a slow process, taking many generations. Individuals don't adapt; what adapt or change are the average qualities of entire species, as the genes of individuals undergo tiny changes from generation to generation.

But there's also a second type of adaptation, which we call learning. Animals with complex nervous systems and brains can adapt during a single lifetime. They learn, and that means they get better at dealing with their environment and extracting the energy and resources they need to survive. This form of adaptation is much faster, but it is also Sisyphean. It has to be repeated each generation as each individual learns anew. Certainly, some teaching goes on; a bear cub can watch its mother hunt and try to imitate it. But think how limited this method of teaching is! How much would we teach in modern universities if every professor was ordered to use mime alone and every student had to just imitate their professors?

Now imagine what would happen if you found a species that had the ability to communicate huge amounts of learned information with great precision, so that what was learned by each individual could be shared with others and stored in collective memory. (The difference is analogous to that between stand-alone computers and computers linked through the Internet.) Suddenly, the intellectual potential of each individual would be magnified many times over by the fact that it was embedded within a large web of information that included millions of other individuals, both living and dead.

That's the sort of species we are because we can communicate learned knowledge with exquisite precision and in large amounts. We are the only species that is networked with anything like this degree of efficiency. In short, our species is characterized by new emergent properties that arise not from the qualities of each individual human (after all, we're not *that* much more intelligent than other great apes), but from the way we are linked through the webs of information that we describe as "cultures." Culture gives each of us ready access to the information accumulated and stored within society over many generations. Perhaps we should call our species *Homo communicans*, to highlight our ability to share knowledge, rather than *Homo sapiens*, a label that highlights our intellectual prowess as individuals.[29]

I call this process of sharing learned information "collective learning."[30] This is one emergent property that distinguishes us so strikingly from all other species. The results of our capacity for "collective learning" are spectacular. As individuals share information with others, the amount of information stored within a community slowly accumulates. This means that our species has the ability, group by group, to accumulate new knowledge about ways of relating to its environment. This slow accumulation of information—ecological, social, and artistic—generation by generation explains the directional nature of human history. It explains why human history, unlike that of chimps, is cumulative. It is this process of accumulating social knowledge that has taken us, in 200,000 years, from the low energy consumption of the early Stone Age, to the dangerously high consumption levels of today. Collective learning is a new and extraordinarily powerful adaptive mechanism that is unique to our species. And it explains why we have a "history" of sustained change, while other species do not.

Indeed, our adaptive ability is so extraordinary that it may help to think of it as "hyperadaptivity."[31] We are blessed (or cursed) with an ability to adapt that is so powerful that eventually we may *over* adapt, becoming so clever that we become a danger to ourselves and to other species. Indeed, the evidence is accumulating that we crossed that threshold some time in the 20th century.[32]

In short, the first thing that makes the work of historians so distinctive is that they try to describe the history of the only species on Earth (perhaps in the universe) that is capable of adapting through collective learning.[33]

Why are we able to communicate so efficiently? This question leads us to the second distinctive emergent property of our species: our sense (apparently unique to humans) that reality is meaningful. We can exchange information much more efficiently than other intelligent organisms because of our gift for symbolic language. The ability to think in symbols allows us to share not just simple bits of information (such as warnings of danger), but also more complex models or maps of reality. What limits learning in other species is the fact that these models cannot be shared, so that each model is constructed from the experiences and memories of a single individual. That complex models of reality cannot be shared is hardly surprising because they contain a lot of information organized in very precise ways, like DNA molecules. They are very different from gestures, which need to convey just a few simple bits of information. Symbols contain information in highly compressed forms.[34] They can even communicate information about things that are not present (the lion I saw yesterday down by the waterhole to the east of the mountain), or things that may never have existed (the evil spirit I dreamed about last night). That is why they are the source of both religion and science.[35]

Symbols can also work together, adding to and defining each other. They exist as parts of much larger intellectual structures. And it is within these larger structures, linking the minds of millions of individuals, that particular events, ideas, or activities acquire "meaning." That is to say they appear no longer as isolated phenomena but as entities with precisely defined positions within huge conceptual maps constructed by many individual humans, both living and dead. The sharing of models of reality magnifies their power by orders of magnitude because, through this sharing, models of reality can be constructed that integrate the learned knowledge of millions of individuals over many generations.

Here is the link between our species' capacity for "meaning" (our sense of meaning derives precisely from the sense that different parts of reality are linked within our shared conceptual maps) and our extraordinary ecological virtuosity (which derives from the sophistication and richness of the models of reality that we construct collectively). Meaning is a social property, as Wittgenstein famously argued, because it depends on the sharing of ideas and language.[36] It is an emergent property of society and, like all emergent properties, it seems magical because it does *not* arise from isolated individuals.

The close link between our extraordinary ecological virtuosity and our inner world of meaning removes any need to think of history and science as residing on different sides of a mind-body dualism. Our sense of meaning is an emergent property that arises from our capacity to share complex models of reality; but it is also the source of our extraordinary ability to keep adapting to the physical world in new ways.

I hope this tentative discussion hints at the powerful synergy that may await us within an expanded, multidisciplinary account of the past. If we can overcome the divisions between the sciences and the humanities, we will be in a much better position to understand what it means to be human because we can triangulate on the problem, taking bearings on it both from history and from science. Combined, these different perspectives can give us a much better and more coherent answer than they can separately. Indeed, they can give us the sort of unified answer that may help us deal with the more dangerous features of our capacity for "hyperadaptivity"!

Conclusions

I will end by summarizing the main conclusions of this paper.

First, I have argued that, as a result of the second chronometric revolution, we can now see human history as part of an expanded account of the past that includes the history of our planet and of the entire universe. That story links our understanding of "history" (or human history) with our understanding of other historical sciences such as cosmology, geology, and biology, whose historical dimensions have been developed in the half century since the second chronometric revolution.

Second, within this larger framework, it is easier to see the distinctive "emergent properties" that distinguish human history from the histories of other entities such as stars, planets, and other living organisms. One emergent property is an entirely unique ability for continuous, sustained, and cumulative adaptation to our environments. That ability has allowed us to increase our control of resources and energy as human societies achieve unprecedented levels of power and complexity.

Finally, I have argued that one way of explaining this distinctive property is to see it as a consequence of "collective learning"—the ability, unique to our species, to share learned information with great precision and in large amounts. I ended by arguing that the idea of collective learning can help explain a second emergent property of our species: our capacity (indeed our *need*) to find meaning in our surroundings. For our apparently unique gift for finding meaning is a product of the same capacity for symbolic thought that allows us to communicate with each other so efficiently.

Once its significance is fully appreciated, the second chronometric revolution will allow us to redefine our understanding of the past and to rethink what we mean by "history."

Endnotes

1. This essay develops some ideas first explored in "Historia, Complejidad y Revolución Cronométrica" ["History, Complexity and the Chronometric Revolution,"] an article commissioned for *Revista de Occidente*, Abril 2008, no. 323, 27–57.

2. The English word, "science" dates to the 19th century; what we call science today was known before then as "natural philosophy."

3. See Joyce Appleby, Lynn Hunt, and Margaret Jacob, *Telling the Truth about History*. New York: Norton, 1994, for a good modern survey of this changing relationship.

4. Michael Bentley, *Modern Historiography: An Introduction*. London and New York: Routledge, 1999, p. 89.

5. R. G. Collingwood, *The Idea of History*. Rev. ed., Jan van der Dussen, Oxford University, Paperback, 1994, pp. 210, 115.

6. Appleby et al., p. 252.

7. It is not unreasonable to counter that historians were equally implicated through their construction of the nationalist narratives that justified war in the first place. In a preface to the third (1921) edition of his *Outline of History*, H. G. Wells wrote: "The need for a common knowledge of the general facts of human history throughout the world has become very evident during the tragic happenings of the last few years. Swifter means of communication have brought all men closer to one another for good or for evil. War becomes a universal disaster, blind and monstrously destructive; it bombs the baby in its cradle and sinks the food-ships that cater for the non-combatant and the neutral. There can be no peace now, we realize, but a common peace in all the world; no prosperity but a general prosperity. But *there can be no common peace and prosperity without common historical ideas*. Without such ideas to hold them together in harmonious co-operation, with nothing but narrow, selfish, and conflicting nationalist traditions, races and peoples are bound to drift towards conflict and destruction. This truth, which was apparent to that great philosopher Kant a century or more ago—it is the gist of his tract upon universal

peace—is now plain to the man in the street." *An Outline of History*. 3rd ed., New York: Macmillan, 1921, p. vi.

8. Appleby, et al., pp. 219–220; and see Geertz's famous essay, "Thick Description: Toward an Interpretive Theory of Culture," in Clifford Geertz, *The Interpretation of Cultures*. New York: Basic Books, 2000 [1st published 1973].

9. C. P. Snow, *The Two Cultures and the Scientific Revolution*. Cambridge: Cambridge University Press, 1959.

10. *The Idea of History*. Rev. ed., p. 3.

11. Hayden V. White, *Metahistory: the Historical Imagination in Nineteenth Century Europe*. Baltimore: Johns Hopkins University Press, 1975, p. 5. The word, "chronicle," only appears once in the index, and White's real focus is on the challenges that begin *after* each known event has been arranged "as an element of a series." p. 7.

12. H. G. Wells, *Outline of History*. 3rd ed., 1921 [1st ed., 1920], p. 1102.

13. As Colin Renfrew and Paul Bahn put it: "Before World War II for much of archaeology virtually the only reliable absolute dates were historical ones—Tutankhamun reigned in the 14th century BC, Caesar invaded Britain in 55 BC." Colin Renfrew and Paul Bahn, *Archaeology: Methods and Practice*. London: Thames and Hudson, 1991, p. 101.

14. Cited in Dan Smail, "In the Grip of Sacred History," *American Historical Review* 110, no. 5 (December 2005): 1337–1361, 1351.

15. Cited in Dan Smail, "In the Grip of Sacred History." p. 1350.

16. Appleby et al., *Telling the Truth about History*, p. 252; Ranke's opinion counts because he is so widely regarded as the founder of the modern tradition of solid, archive-based empirical historical scholarship.

17. His demonstration immediately challenged the contemporary idea that Earth was at most 100 or 200 million years old, which was based on

calculations by Lord Kelvin of the speed at which an Earth-sized body should have cooled down.

18. For a good short discussion, see W. H. McNeill, "History and the Scientific Worldview," *History and Theory* 37, no. 1 (1998): 1–13.

19. In fact, the argument that historical knowledge could not be scientific because the past could not be replicated experimentally had always been flawed. Towards the end of his life, Karl Popper, who spent much of his life trying to establish clear "demarcation criteria" to distinguish science from nonscience, rejected the idea that historical disciplines (and he was referring, in this instance, to biology and the principle of natural selection), were nonscientific because they did not deal with replicable events. He wrote: "some people think that I have denied scientific character to the historical sciences, such as paleontology, or the history of the evolution of life on Earth; or to say, the history of literature, or of technology, or of science. This is a mistake, and I here wish to affirm that these and other historical sciences have in my opinion scientific character: their hypotheses can in many cases be tested. It appears as if some people would think that the historical sciences are untestable because they describe unique events. However, the description of unique events can very often be tested by deriving from them testable predictions or retrodictions." Karl Popper, 1980. [Letter on] Evolution. *New Scientist* 87 no.1215 (Aug. 1980): 611, 621.

20. For some arguments in support of this claim, see David Christian, *Maps of Time*, pp. 139–144.

21. On "big history," see David Christian, "The Case for 'Big History,'" *The Journal of World History* 2, no. 2 (Fall 1991): 223–38 [see *http://www.fss.uu.nl/wetfil/96-97/big.htm*]; David Christian, *Maps of Time: An Introduction to 'Big History.'* Berkeley, CA: University of California Press, 2004; as well as Fred Spier, *The Structure of Big History: From the Big Bang Until Today.* Amsterdam: Amsterdam University Press, 1996; and Marnie Hughes-Warrington, "Big History." *Historically Speaking* (November 2002): 16–17, 20 [available at *http://www.bu.edu/historic/hs/november02.html#hughes-warrington*].

22. In the last decade, the detection of planets orbiting nearby stars suggests that as many as 10 percent of all stars may have solar systems; that greatly increases the likelihood that life, too, is not confined to our own planet, but is spread throughout the universe.

23. For these somewhat controversial claims, see Eric Chaisson, *Cosmic Evolution: The Rise of Complexity in Nature.* Cambridge, MA: Harvard University Press, 2001, particularly chapter 3 and the table on p. 139.

24. In a study of Wittgenstein's theory of knowledge, David Bloor writes: "The strange properties of mental states derive from the fact that they are properties of groups of people which have been imputed to individuals or individual actions." David Bloor, *Wittgenstein: A Social Theory of Knowledge.* New York: Columbia University Press, 1983, p. 20.

25. Though he did not use the word, "emergence," the sociologist, Durkheim, offered a superb account of what it means: "Whenever any elements combine and, by the fact of their combination produce new phenomena, it is evident that these phenomena are not given in the elements, but in the totality formed by their union. The living cell contains nothing but mineral particles, just as society contains nothing but individuals; it is obviously impossible, however, for the phenomena characteristic of life to exist in the atoms of hydrogen, oxygen, carbon, and nitrogen. For how could the properties of life exist within inanimate elements? . . . Life . . . is in the whole, not in the parts." *Emile Durkheim: Selected Writings,* ed. Anthony Giddens, Cambridge: Cambridge University Press, 1972, p. 69. There is another wonderful account of emergence within the Buddhist sutra known as the "Questions of King Milinda"; see Edward Conze, ed., *Buddhist Scriptures.* Harmondsworth: Penguin, 1959, pp. 148–149. The basic question of the sutra is: what is a chariot? Take away its parts one by one and when does it cease to be a chariot?

26. Clifford Geertz captures the link between these two properties when he writes that "culture patterns," by which he means "systems of complexes of symbols," "have an intrinsic double aspect: they give meaning, that is, objective conceptual form, to social and psychological reality both by shaping themselves to it and by shaping it to themselves." Geertz, *The Interpretation of Cultures,* p. 93.

27. *Groups* of species, such as mammals or primates have displayed such inventiveness in what are often called "adaptive radiations"; but it is precisely the fact that in humans we observe such inventiveness within a single species that is unique, for this means that the inventiveness is *not* a result of natural selection.

28. Data from I. G. Simmons, *Changing the Face of the Earth: Culture, Environment, History.* 2nd ed. Oxford: Blackwell, 1996, p. 27.

29. Another alternative, mentioned by Oliver Sacks, is *Homo loquens*; see *The Man Who Mistook his Wife for a Hat.* New York: Touchstone, 1998 (1st published 1970), p. 81.

30. I have explored the idea of "collective learning" at greater length in *Maps of Time.*

31. Oliver Sacks has a wonderful description of neurological states that are characterized not by the lack of some ability, but by an excess: "Enhancement allows the possibilities not only of a healthy fullness and exuberance, but of a rather ominous extravagance, abberation, monstrosity ... This danger is built into the very nature of growth and life. Growth can become over-growth, life 'hyper-life.' All the 'hyper' states can become monstrous, perverse aberrations ... [t]he paradox of an illness which can present as wellness—as a wonderful feeling of health and well-being, and only later reveal its malignant potentials—is one of the chimaeras, tricks, and ironies of nature." *The Man who Mistook his Wife for a Hat*, p. 89.

32. This idea is developed in John McNeill's wonderful *Something New Under the Sun: An Environmental History of the Twentieth-Century World.* New York: Norton, 2000.

33. I have listed some reasons for thinking that collective learning may be extraordinarily rare even on cosmological scales in David Christian, "World History in Context." *Journal of World History* 14, no. 4 (2003): 437–458. [see *http://www.historycooperative.org/journals/jwh/14.4/christian.html*].

34. There is a superb discussion of these issues in Terence W. Deacon, *The Symbolic Species: The Coevolution of Language and the Brain.* Harmondsworth: Penguin, 1997.

35. A point made long ago in Peter L. Berger and Thomas Luckmann, *The Social Construction of Reality: A Treatise in the Sociology of Knowledge.* Harmondsworth: Penguin, 1967, pp. 54–55.

36. Wittgenstein "treated cognition as something that is social in its very essence. For him, our interactions with one another, and our participation in a social group, were no mere contingencies. They were not the accidental circumstances that attend our knowing; they were constituted of all that we can ever claim by way of knowledge. Tracing the profound consequences of this insight led Wittgenstein into building up what might be called a 'social theory of knowledge.'" Bloor, *Wittgenstein: A Social Theory of Knowledge*, p. 2.

Chapter 14*

Bringing Culture to Cosmos
The Postbiological Universe

Steven J. Dick

The Biological Universe (Dick 1996) analyzed the history of the extraterrestrial life debate, documenting how scientists have assessed the chances of life beyond Earth during the 20th century. Here I propose another option—that we may in fact live in a postbiological universe, one that has evolved beyond flesh and blood intelligence to artificial intelligence (AI) that is a product of cultural rather than biological evolution. MacGowan and Ordway (1966), Davies (1995), and Shostak (1998), among others, have broached the subject, but the argument has not been given the attention it is due, nor has it been carried to its logical conclusion. This paper argues for the necessity of long-term thinking when contemplating the problem of intelligence in the universe. It provides arguments for a postbiological universe based on the likely age and lifetimes of technological civilizations and the overriding importance of cultural evolution as an element of cosmic evolution. And it describes the general nature of a postbiological universe and its implications for SETI.

The Necessity of Stapledonian Thinking

The possibility of a postbiological universe—one in which most intelligence has evolved beyond flesh and blood to AI—has not been considered in detail

* This paper is reprinted by permission of Cambridge University Press from *International Journal of Astrobiology* 2 (2003): 65–74.

because humans are unaccustomed to thinking on cosmic time scales and following the logical consequences of cosmic time scales for biology and culture. The vast majority of humans think in terms of a human lifetime and the necessities for survival. Even historians span only the few thousand years of the rise and fall of civilizations, while anthropologists encompass the several million years of human origins, and geologists cover the 4.5-billion-year history of Earth. Only astronomers contemplate the 13.7-billion-year history of the cosmos, and the vast majority of them concentrate on the physical universe. Biologists—even paleobiologists and paleontologists—have never thought beyond the 3.8-billion-year history of life on Earth, and cultural evolution has rarely been considered beyond the evolution of culture on Earth. Yet, if biology and culture exist beyond Earth, the one thing we know for certain is that they will evolve.

Only science fiction writers have thought in these longer terms, beginning most notably with H. G. Wells's evocative picture of a terrestrial society of Moorlocks and Eloi in *The Time Machine* (1895). In the 20th century, the British philosopher Olaf Stapledon is the prime example of one who had a cosmic perspective on universal biological and cultural evolution, as played out in his novels *Last and First Men* (1930) and *Star Maker* (1937), and in some of his essay such as "Interplanetary Man?" (Stapledon 1948). We need, therefore, to think not only on astronomical time scales, but also on what I shall call Stapledonian time scales, by which I mean an astronomical time scale that takes into account the evolution of biology and culture. The foundation for the concept of a postbiological universe is the recognition of these time scales (Table 1), and the *necessity* for thinking in Stapledonian terms, no matter where it may lead. A primary methodological premise of this paper is that *long-term Stapledonian thinking is a necessity if we are to understand the nature of intelligence in the universe today.*

One small set of scientists that *has* thought on astronomical time scales about biology is SETI proponents. SETI enthusiasts, knowing the story of cosmic evolution, have often concluded that extraterrestrials must be older

Table 1. Time Scales in Human Thought.

Human	100
Historical	10,000 years
Anthropological	10 million years
Geological	5 billion years
Astronomical	14 billion years
Stapledonian	Biology and Culture on Astronomical Scale

and wiser than us (Shklovskii and Sagan 1966; Oliver 1971; Drake 1976). But they have not used Stapledonian thinking to carry this possibility to its logical conclusion—that biological and cultural evolution will make extraterrestrial intelligence far different from us. Why they have not done so is understandable from an operational viewpoint: SETI proponents wish to search for intelligence using current technology, so they prefer the option that extraterrestrials will have technology similar to ours. That *is* an option, but only one of many, and, possibly, not the most likely scenario.

By contrast, those who have no stake in standard SETI strategy have been more successful at adopting Stapledonian thinking. This is particularly true of proponents of the Fermi Paradox—formulated in 1950 even before radio searches were technologically feasible, elaborated in the 1970s and 1980s especially by Hart (1975) and Tipler (1985), and codified in a famous volume of essays (Hart and Zuckerman 1982). If there are so many civilizations in the galaxy, given the time scales involved, Hart, Tipler and their proponents ask, where are they? If extraterrestrials have acquired space travel, they should have colonized the galaxy in a few million years and should be here. They are not, therefore, they do not exist. Many solutions to the Fermi Paradox have been proposed over the last quarter century (Webb 2002). Suffice it to say that Tipler thought the rationale of the Fermi Paradox was strong enough that we should abandon all SETI programs. SETI proponents, among others, took strong exception to this claim. While Tipler's conclusion is not rigorous, it does embody the methodology of long-term thinking that needs to be applied to the problem of intelligence in the universe. The Fermi Paradox *does* need to be taken seriously.

Tipler's conclusion, however, is not the only possible outcome of long-term thinking about intelligence in the universe. In attempting to disprove extraterrestrials, Tipler argued that the galaxy would be colonized by self-reproducing automata—so-called von Neumann machines—with intelligence comparable to humans, but still under control of an intelligent flesh-and-blood species. Since he concluded extraterrestrials do not exist, for Tipler, machine intelligence also does not exist. But if there is a flaw in the logic of the Fermi Paradox and extraterrestrials *are* a natural outcome of cosmic evolution, then cultural evolution may have resulted in a postbiological universe in which machines are the predominant intelligence. This is more than mere conjecture; it is recognition of the fact that cultural evolution—the final frontier of the Drake Equation—needs to be taken into account no less than the astronomical and biological components of cosmic evolution (Chaisson 2001). Although the importance of cultural evolution was recognized very

Figure 1. The Drake Equation.

$$N = R_* \times f_p \times n_e \times f_l \times f_i \times f_c \times L$$

Astronomical　　　　*Biological*　　　　*Cultural*

N = The number of technological civilizations in the galaxy.
R_* = The rate of formation of stars suitable for the development of intelligent life.
f_p = The fraction of those stars with planetary systems.
n_e = The number of planets in each planetary system with an environment suitable for life.
f_l = The fraction of suitable planets on which life actually appears.
f_i = The fraction of life-bearing planets on which intelligent life emerges.
f_c = The fraction of planets with intelligent life that develop technological civilizations.
L = The lifetime of a technological civilization.

early on in the modern SETI discussions (Ascher and Ascher 1962), including some of its pioneering documents (Stull 1977), it has been essentially ignored over the last four decades.

The missing element in all past SETI arguments has therefore been a failure to account fully for the effects of cultural evolution. To some extent, cultural evolution is embodied in the "L" parameter of the Drake Equation, the lifetime of a technological civilization (Figure 1). But, especially if one is interested in more than just "N" (the number of technological civilizations in the galaxy), many other aspects of cultural evolution are critical to understanding the nature of extraterrestrial intelligence. Moreover, the prevalence of artificial intelligence may be critical to L. Another primary methodological premise of this paper, then, is that *cultural evolution must be seen as an integral part of cosmic evolution and the Drake Equation.* Following this premise, one solution to the Fermi Paradox is that we live in a postbiological universe, in which the psychology of biological beings no longer rules. While SETI proponents might rejoice in yet another solution to the Fermi Paradox, the postbiological universe has other important implications for SETI that must be taken into account in SETI strategies. But before addressing these implications, we must examine the likelihood that we indeed inhabit a postbiological universe.

Arguments for a Postbiological Universe

In setting forth arguments for a postbiological universe, it is important to define the term more precisely. It cannot mean a universe totally devoid of biological intelligence since we are an obvious counterexample. Nor does it mean a universe devoid of lower forms of life, what I have called elsewhere "the weak biological universe" (Dick 2000a), as advocated by Ward and Brownlee (2000). Rather, the postbiological universe is one in which the *majority* of intelligent life has evolved beyond flesh and blood intelligence, in proportion to its longevity, L.

SETI practitioners often state that ETI would be much older than terrestrial intelligence (TI), and that therefore SETI programs stand to inherit much knowledge and wisdom of the universe. However they assume that ETI will just be some more advanced form of TI. This may be an excellent case of what Arthur C. Clarke calls "a failure of imagination" because it represents a failure to take into account cultural evolution. If civilizations are billions of years older than TI, or even millions of years older, our experience with the evolution of intelligence on Earth indicates that biological evolution would have carried such civilizations far beyond TI in terms of mental capacity. Moreover, as argued below, if civilizations are even thousands of years older than TI, cultural evolution would likely have also resulted in artificial mental capacities beyond TI, concluding in a postbiological universe. There are thus three scientific premises in the arguments for a postbiological universe 1) the maximum age (A) of ETI is several billion years; 2) the lifetime (L) of a technological civilization is >100 years and probably much larger; and 3) in the long-term, cultural evolution supersedes biological evolution, and would have produced something far beyond biological intelligence. If that is the case, the chances of success for standard SETI programs may be greatly reduced, or at least altered, and our place in the universe may be quite different from anything envisioned except in science fiction. We approach each of these premises in turn.

The Maximum Age of Extraterrestrial Intelligence (A)

Cosmic evolution (Delsemme 1998; Chaisson 2001) is our guide to the maximum age (A) of an extraterrestrial civilization. Recent results from the Wilkinson Microwave Anisotropy Probe (WMAP) place the age of the universe at 13.7 billion years, with one percent uncertainty, and confirm the first stars forming at about 200 million years after the Big Bang (Bennett et al. 2003; Seife 2003). Although these first stars were very massive—from 300 to 1,000 solar masses—and therefore short-lived, it is fair to assume that the oldest Sun-like stars formed within about one billion years, or about 12.5 billion years ago. By that time enough heavy element generation and interstellar seeding had taken place for the first rocky planets to form (Delsemme 1998,

71, Larson and Bromm 2001). Then, if Earth history is any guide, it may have taken another five billion years for intelligence to evolve. So, some six billion years after the Big Bang, one could have seen the emergence of the first intelligence. Accepting the WMAP age of the universe as 13.7 billion years, the first intelligence could have evolved seven and a half billion years ago. By the same reasoning, intelligence could have evolved in our galaxy four billion to five billion years ago, since the oldest stars in our galaxy formed about 10 billion to 11 billion years ago (Rees 1997).

These conclusions are essentially in line with those of a number of other astronomers. Using similar reasoning Norris (2000) argued that the median age of an extraterrestrial civilization is 1.7 billion years, assuming that civilizations born 5 billion years ago are now dying off because the 10 billion year lifetime of a solar type star has reached its end. (This assumption is perhaps pessimistic, given that a civilization more than a billion years old may well have found a way to escape its star system.) Based on the peak of the cosmic rate of carbon production in stars, Livio (1999a, 1999b) concluded the first civilizations would emerge when the universe was about 10 billion years old, or 3.7 billion years ago assuming the WMAP age of the universe. Kardashev (1997) concluded that cosmological models yield an age for civilizations of six billion to eight billion years. Kardashev also pointed out that the youngest and less developed civilizations would be most distant from us, while the oldest and most developed civilizations would be nearest to us. Thus all lines of evidence converge on the conclusion that the maximum age of extraterrestrial intelligence would be billions of years, specifically, A ranges from 1.7 billion to 8 billion years. Even uncertainties of a billion years would not affect the argument for taking seriously cultural evolution.

The Lifetime of a Civilization (L)

But do civilizations really reach this age? Not necessarily. The maximum A of ETI is mitigated by L, the lifetime of a technological civilization. We recall that the Drake Equation (Figure 1) consists of astronomical, biological, and cultural parameters, that L is the determining factor to the extent that N (the number of technological civilizations) approximates L, and that we know almost nothing about L. This is why values of L vary widely to the despair of many who are genuinely interested in the chances of detecting ETI. Sagan, Drake, and others generally assigned L values in the neighborhood of a million years, and even some pessimists admitted 10,000 years was not unlikely (Dick 1996, 441). Nevertheless, the only data point for L is ourselves, and if L is defined as a radio communicative technological civilization, all we may conclude from this datum is that L is at least 100 years. Beyond that single data point, L is a matter of whether one is optimistic or pessimistic about the survival of civilization. This is hardly an objective parameter even for a single individual; SETI pioneer Joseph Shklovskii, for one, became a pessimist at the end of his life, due in part to political events in the Soviet Union.

Difficulties notwithstanding, is there any more that can be said about L? What about an upper bound? One sometimes hears that civilizations are inherently unstable, that they have risen and fallen many times on Earth, and that therefore an upper bound for L is several thousand years. But what is really relevant is not the longevity of any single historical civilization on Earth, but that terrestrial civilization as a whole is still alive and well after five millennia of ups and downs known as "human history." It seems likely that technological civilization can last much longer, barring man-made catastrophes such as nuclear war and natural catastrophes such as mass extinctions. That a man-made catastrophe could totally wipe out civilization seems unduly pessimistic, despite the controversial results of nuclear winter scenarios (Turco and Toon, et al. 1983). It seems likely that even in a nuclear world war, some corner of civilization would survive robustly enough that the slow climb of technological evolution would not have to start over again, much less recapitulate the even slower climb of cultural evolution from the cave, or the biological evolution of complex life.

Natural phenomena such as mass extinctions, supernovae, and gamma ray bursters are more problematic for civilization. Norris argued that the latter two events should extinguish all life on planets at intervals of about 200 million years, a conclusion at variance with what we observe on Earth (Norris 2000). A more refined study of gamma ray bursters (Scalo and Wheeler 2002) indicates events of potential biological significance, though not necessarily catastrophic, every 10 million years or so. Current data indicates that a mass extinction from an impacting comet or asteroid serious enough to precipitate the collapse of civilization might occur every 300,000 years (Chapman and Morrison 1989; Raup 1992; Chapman and Morrison 1994). Mass extinctions similar to those that destroyed the dinosaurs, and would probably destroy *Homo sapiens*, have taken place on the order of tens of millions of years (Raup 1992; Becker 2002). Assuming that mass extinctions and other cosmic catastrophes could not be overcome, L would be between 100 years and tens of millions of years. If human ingenuity could overcome such natural catastrophes, or (in the case of mass extinctions) if human civilization has evolved far enough that even a small but technologically capable part of human civilization has been transported self-sufficiently to space, then L could conceivably approach A, which is billions of years. Surveying the vast range of possible catastrophes, Leslie (1996) has estimated that civilization has a 70 percent chance of lasting five more centuries, and believes that if it lasts that long, it could last millions of years.

Necessarily, none of this has the certainty of rigorous deduction. But the possibility of long lifetimes for technological civilizations leads us to explore the likely evolution and nature of such civilizations. It is clear that *biological* evolution, by definition, over the course of millions of years would produce nothing but more advanced biology. Consider what happened to the genus *Homo* in two million years of biological evolution on Earth. Where will we be in another two million years of biological evolution? And what would a billion-year-old terrestrial civilization be like? Possibly the minds of those comprising such a civilization would have evolved significantly beyond *Homo sapiens*. Possibly a similar process would take place for any extraterrestrial intelligence with serious implications for what we normally envision as the biological universe full of communicating civilizations. I say "possibly" because although *knowledge* surely would have increased in both cases, we know so little about the biological evolution of intelligence on Earth (Mithen 1996; Deacon 1997; Parker and McKinney 1999) that its future is unpredictable.

But the important point is that, even at our low current value of L on Earth, biological evolution by natural selection is already being overtaken by cultural evolution, which is proceeding at a vastly faster pace than biological evolution (Dennett 1996). Technological civilizations do not remain static; even the most conservative technological civilizations on Earth have not done so, and could not given the dynamics of technology and society. Unlike all the other parameters in the Drake Equation, L is a problem of cultural evolution, and cultural evolution must be taken into account no less than astronomical and biological evolution. It must be treated as an integral part of cosmic evolution, in direct proportion to L, the age of the civilization. And unlike biological evolution, L need only be thousands of years for cultural evolution to have drastic effects on civilization.

Cultural Evolution

Because the nature of technological civilizations on time scales ranging from hundreds to billions of years reduces to a question of cultural evolution, we must turn to the social and behavioral sciences for insight. These disciplines have shown embryonic interest in the implications of successful SETI (Billingham et al. 1999; Harrison et al. 2000), but have yet to tackle the problem of cultural evolution in a cosmic context. This is hardly surprising;

compared to astronomical and biological evolutions, our understanding of how culture evolves even on Earth is rudimentary. In the past, social scientists have posed two broad models of cultural evolution: the Spencerian, which views society as evolving "through well-defined stages, progressing from chaos to order, from simple to complex, from lower to higher"; and the Darwinian, which posits no particular direction, provides an explanatory framework rather than a historical generalization, and is evolutionary rather than revolutionary (Fellner 1990).

Most social scientists have judged the Spencerian model as too simplistic, but after a long lapse since Darwin's own ideas on cultural evolution detailed in *The Descent of Man* (Richerson and Boyd 2001), Darwinian models of cultural evolution have proliferated in recent decades and have been highly controversial. "Darwin's dangerous idea," as the philosopher Daniel Dennett calls it, posits that the same general evolutionary principles that apply to biology may also apply to culture, though with a mix of mechanisms including the Spencerian inheritance of acquired characteristics as well as those related to natural selection (Dennett 1996). The challenge is in the details of "Darwinizing culture," and elucidating how genes and culture may coevolve. Because the foundation and engine of cultural evolution are human psychology, behavior, cognition, and the transmission of ideas, they must serve as the basis for any theory, though they are notoriously difficult to characterize in individuals, much less in the aggregate.

Among the first modern Darwinian theories of human behavior was sociobiology (Wilson 1975), "the systematic study of the biological basis of all social behavior." Sociobiology has generated bitter disputes as a Darwinian extension from the realm of biology to that of culture (Segerstrale 2000). No less controversial have been related attempts (Lumsden and Wilson 1981; Wilson 1998) to use the idea of gene-culture coevolution to span the natural and social sciences. Cavalli-Sforza and Feldman (1981) pioneered a distinctive approach to gene-culture coevolution that makes use of population genetics. One of the more sophisticated Darwinian models of cultural evolution in this vein, termed the "dual inheritance" theory (Boyd and Richerson 1985), uses population genetics to construct simple mathematical models of how cultural evolution works. The authors recognize, however, that their system cannot yet make quantitative predictions, but can only clarify the relationships between cultural transmission and other Darwinian processes. A better known, if less rigorous, Darwinian model is Dennett's "Universal Darwinism," wherein he argues that Darwinism applies to humans at many levels—mind, language, knowledge, and ethics (Dennett 1996). When applied to knowledge and its transmission, Dennett's brand of Universal Darwinism leads to the field of "memetics," based on Dawkins's idea (1976) that culture evolves via memes in the same way that biology evolves with genes. Despite a number of books and a *Journal of Memetics*, even memetic enthusiasts realize the field is far from a real science (Aunger 2000).

All such Darwinian models of cultural evolution have considerable problems. Indeed, for historical reasons many social scientists still resist evolutionary hypotheses of culture altogether (Lalande and Brown 2002, 28). It is possible that some synthesis of sociobiology, gene-culture coevolution, and memetics, along with related Darwinian models like behavioral ecology and evolutionary psychology, will some day provide a widely accepted theory or mechanism for cultural evolution (Lalande and Brown 2002; Segerstrale 2000). It is also possible that the concept of "emergence" will play a role, that culture or its components (toolmaking, language, agriculture, technology, and so on) are emergent phenomena that will be explained in terms of agents, rules and "pruning relations" in the way that the origin of life and the origin of consciousness may someday be explained as emergent phenomena (Morowitz 2002). But for now a widely accepted theory or mechanism of cultural evolution is lacking.

Still, theoretical and empirical studies of cultural evolution hold hope for a science of cultural evolution in the same way there is currently a well-developed science of biological evolution. In the context of extraterrestrial life, even a theory of universal biological evolution does not yet exist, much less a theory of universal cultural evolution. And even if a theory of cultural evolution existed, such models (short of Asimovian psychohistory) would lack the power to predict the future of our own culture, much less those of extraterrestrials. While galactic, stellar, and planetary evolution may be predicted to some extent based on physical principles, biological evolution cannot be predicted based on natural selection, and the prediction of our cultural evolution is not even contemplated except in the long-term context of the fate of the universe (Ward and Brownlee 2003). And while there is no lack of purely descriptive accounts of terrestrial cultural evolution, such descriptions also lack explanatory power or the predictive power needed to answer our question about the future of cultural evolution.

Lacking a robust theory of cultural evolution to at least guide our way, and "wildcard" events notwithstanding, we are reduced at present to the extrapolation of current trends supplemented by only the most general evolutionary concepts. Several fields are most relevant, including genetic engineering, biotechnology, nanotechnology, and space travel. But one field—artificial intelligence—may dominate all other developments in the sense that other fields can be seen as subservient to intelligence. Biotechnology is a step on the road to AI, nanotechnology will help construct efficient AI and fulfill its goals, and space travel will spread AI. Genetic engineering may eventually provide another pathway toward increased intelligence, but it is limited by the structure of the human brain. In sorting out priorities, I adopt what I term the central principle of cultural evolution, which I will refer to as the Intelligence Principle: *the maintenance, improvement and perpetuation of knowledge and intelligence is the central driving force of cultural evolution, and that to the extent intelligence can be improved, it will be improved.* At the level of knowledge, we see this principle in daily operation as individuals, groups, and societies attempt to maximize their knowledge in order to gain advantage in the world around them, an endeavor in which some succeed better than others. Better education, better information, and better technology are generally perceived as advantageous to the individual, group, or society—an understanding recognized in the aphorism "knowledge is power." At the species level, which is the meaning I primarily refer to here, intelligence is related to the size and structure of the brain of *Homo sapiens sapiens*, a capacity that has not changed in 100,000 years, and that led to the "big bang of human culture 60,000–30,000 years ago" (Mithen 1996). In hominid biological evolution the increased brain size and intelligence of *Homo sapiens sapiens* allowed it to outcompete other hominid species and dominate the planet. In the cultural evolution of the species, the same will hold true. Failure to improve intelligence, resulting in inferior knowledge, may eventually cause cultural evolution to cease to exist in the presence of competing forces like AI. In Darwinian terms, knowledge has survival value, or selective advantage, as does intelligence at the species level, a fact that may someday be elucidated by an evolutionary theory of social behavior, whether "group selection" as recently applied to religion (Wilson 2002), selfish gene theory, evolutionary epistemology (Bradie 1986), or some other Darwinian model. The Intelligence Principle implies that, given the opportunity to increase intelligence (and thereby knowledge), whether through biotechnology, genetic engineering, or AI, any society would do so, or fail to do so at its own peril.

The Intelligence Principle is a hybrid between the Spencerian and Darwinian models of cultural evolution in the sense that it does not have well-defined stages, but is evolutionary and implies a direction toward greater intelligence. Because it is governed by mind, the process is goal-oriented. Culture may have many driving forces, but none can be so fundamental, or so strong, as intelligence itself.

Turning, then, to the field of AI as a striking example of the Intelligence Principle of cultural evolution, we find quite astounding predictions. As Dyson (1997, 25) has pointed out, ever since the Industrial Revolution, there has been concern about the rise of the machines and their relation to humans. Butler (1863) wrote "[w]e find ourselves almost awestruck at the vast development of the mechanical world, at the gigantic strides with which it has advanced in comparison with the slow progress of the animal and vegetable kingdom. We shall find it impossible to refrain from asking ourselves what the end of this mighty movement is to be . . . . The machines are gaining ground upon us; day by day we are becoming more subservient to them; more men are daily bound down as slaves to tend them; more men are daily devoting the energies of their whole lives to the development of mechanical life." After a century of progress in machine development and the increasing convergence between machine and life that Dyson describes, MacGowan and Ordway (1966) argued that, "[a]ny emerging intelligent biological society which engages in the development of highly intelligent automata must resign itself to being completely dominated and controlled by automata. The only means of preventing domination by intelligent artificial automata would be to make them distinctly subnormal in intellectual capacity, when compared with the biological society, and to destroy them or clear their memories at regular intervals." The possibilities of AI played a substantial role in MacGowan and Ordway's volume on extraterrestrial intelligence, but those possibilities were completely overshadowed by the publication of Shklovskii and Sagan (1966) in the same year. Although the last chapter of Shklovskii and Sagan's volume was on "Artificial Intelligence and Galactic Civilizations," the AI thesis was very general and lost in the midst of the exciting—and at the time more verifiable and realistic—implications of the other chapters, which assumed biological beings. Over the last 40 years, SETI has focused almost exclusively on the biological paradigm, especially the radio SETI technique, as opposed to a postbiological paradigm (MacGowan and Ordway 1966, 265; Shklovksii and Sagan 1966, 281–288).

The study of AI was rudimentary in 1966, but MacGowan and Ordway's idea as applied to humans has been broached in subsequent years as the field of AI developed. One of the most forward-thinking scholars in the field is Hans Moravec, a pioneer in AI and robotics at Carnegie-Mellon. Already in 1988 in his book *Mind Children: The Future of Robot and Human Intelligence*, Moravec predicted that "[w]hat awaits is not oblivion but rather a future which, from our present vantage point, is best described by the words 'postbiological' or even 'supernatural.' It is a world in which the human race has been swept away by the tide of cultural change, usurped by its own artificial progeny." Within the next century, he predicted, our machines "will mature into entities as complex as ourselves, and eventually into something transcending everything we know—in whom we can take pride when they refer to themselves as our descendants. Unleashed from the plodding pace of biological evolution, the children of our minds will be free to grow to confront immense and fundamental challenges in the larger universe." (Moravec 1988, 1; Moravec 1999). Just as there may have been a genetic takeover when RNA or DNA took over from some more primitive system like clay, Moravec foresees a robotic takeover. This assumes the strong AI position that it is possible to construct intelligent machines functionally equivalent to human intelligence, a point of considerable contention (Searle 1980; Tipler 1994, ch. 2). It seems reasonable to assume, however, that the strong AI position will prove increasingly true in direct proportion to the time available for further developments in the field—time that extraterrestrial civilizations, if any, will have already had.

Another thinker who came to a similar conclusion in the terrestrial context is inventor Ray Kurzweil, a pioneer in AI who has been critical in bringing voice-recognition machines to the commercial market. In *The Age of Spiritual Machines: When Computers Exceed Human Intelligence*, Kurzweil, (1999) also adopting the strong AI claim, sees the takeover of biological intelligence by AI, not by hostility, but by willing humans who have their brains scanned, uploaded to a computer, and live their lives as software running on machines. In his view, human intelligence will be left behind. Physicist Frank Tipler, well known for his work on the anthropic principle and the Fermi Paradox, has also weighed in on this subject. After a review of the arguments for and against strong AI, Tipler (1994) concluded that "the evidence is overwhelming that in about thirty-odd years we should be able to make a machine which is as intelligent as a human being, or more so." Tipler does not necessarily foresee a takeover, but believes that such machines will enhance our well-being. And he ties these ideas to the resurrection of the dead and an entire cosmotheology.

It may well be that Moravec, Kurzweil, and their proponents underestimate the moral and ethical brakes on technological inertia; after all, the abortion controversy in the United States pales in significance with the replacement of the species. And Fukuyama (2002) argues strenuously against a possible "posthuman future" that he sees stemming from advances in the brain sciences, neuropharmacology and behavior control, and the prolongation of life and genetic engineering. He argues for the regulation of biotechnology to preserve human nature, and biotechnology is relatively tame compared to the possibilities of AI. But such objections fail to take into account cultural evolution, and may lose their impact over the longer term,

Table 2. Lifetime of a Technological Civilization and Effects on SETI.

L (Years)	Stage of Cultural Evolution	Effect on SETI
< 100	Biological	Civilizations scarce but comparable level—EM SETI possible
100-1000	Machine/Biology Hybrid (Cyborg)	Hybrid techniques
> 1000	Postbiological	Advanced artificial intelligence—Direct EM SETI unlikely

as the Intelligence Principle asserts itself. If we consider cultural evolution over the last millennium, especially as regards science and technology, who would have predicted space travel, genetic engineering, and nanotechnology? No one could have, because the foundational concepts were not in place. This might lead us to conclude that in another millennium there will be important concepts that we have no inkling of now. This is undoubtedly true. But barring a landmark transformation in human thought comparable to the origins of western science over the next thousand years, we are set on a course that will still be playing out in 3001, with AI still a predominating factor. When one considers the accelerating pace of cultural evolution as we enter the third millennium of our era, radical change of the sort foreseen by Moravec and Kurzweil does not seem so far-fetched. Just as Thomas Aquinas had a failure of imagination almost a millennium ago, so do we.

We thus come to a startling conclusion. Based on what experts see happening on Earth, L need not be five billion, one billion, or a few million years. It is possible that a postbiological universe would occur if L exceeds a few hundred or a few thousand years, where L is defined as a technological civilization that has entered the electronic computer age, which on Earth was almost simultaneous with the usual definition of L as a radio communicative civilization. If L is less than a few hundred years, less than the time it takes for a technological civilization to conceive, design, construct, and launch their intelligent machines, we do not live in a postbiological universe. If L is between 100 and 1,000 years, a transition zone may result populated by human/machine symbiosis, sometimes referred to as "cyborgs" (Dyson 1997; Ward and Rockman 2001; Gray 2002), and genetically engineered humans. But if L is greater than 1,000 years, we almost certainly will have made that transition to a postbiological universe (Table 2). "Interstellar humanity" (Dick 2000b) remains valid if we expand our definition of "humanity" to our artificial progeny, Moravec's "mind children." As for the present, on the time scales of the universe, this means that we are in the minority; the universe over the billions of years that intelligence has had to develop will not be a biological universe, but a postbiological universe. Biologically based techno-logical civilization as defined above is a fleeting phenomenon limited to a few thousand years, and exists in the universe in the proportion of one thou-sand to one billion, so that only one in a million civilizations are biological. Such are the results of applying the Intelligence Principle, and the insights of Moravec, Kurzweil, and Tipler among others, to the entire universe using Stapledonian thinking.

The Nature of the Postbiological Universe and its Implications for SETI

What would a postbiological universe be like? What is artificial intelli-gence *doing* out there? And what does it mean for SETI? Speaking of Earth, Moravec believed that "A postbiological world dominated by self-improving, thinking machines would be as different from our world of living things as this world is different from the lifeless chemistry that preceded it. A popula-tion consisting of unfettered mind children is quite unimaginable" (Moravec 1988, 5). Even more unimaginable, then, would be the activities of artificial intelligence in the universe. But, in the tradition of Stapledon, and guided by the Intelligence Principle, let us try.

Although one cannot, and need not, specify morphological details of postbiologicals, we can assess with some confidence their general characteris-tics. Complex intelligent postbiologicals—which we can assume over the time intervals dealt with here—would have the capability of repair and update, capa-bilities facilitated by their modularity. The so-called von Neumann machine is able to reproduce better versions of itself. Part of this reproduction is the improvement of intelligence; unlike humans this intelligence is cumulative in the sense that the sum total of knowledge in the parent machine is passed on to the next generation, conferring effective immortality for the machine's most important characteristic. The immortality of postbiologicals is enhanced by their increased tolerance to their environment, whether it be vacuum, tempera-ture, radiation, or acceleration (MacGowan and Ordway 1966).

Immortal postbiologicals would embody the capacity for great good or evil over a domain that dwarfs biological domains of influence. There are admittedly deep questions of the nature of "good," "evil," and "morality" in the context of artificial intelligence in the universe (Ruse 1985). But if the

Intelligence Principle holds, postbiologicals are driven by the improvement of knowledge and intelligence. How they would use these qualities presumably remains a value question no less than for humans. One notable interpretation from science fiction is Asimov's robot series, where select robots traverse the galaxy trying to influence events in a positive way, subject to the famous Laws of Robotics. But another interpretation is that AI could be motivated by darker purposes, whether through the programming of its parent biologicals or through its own evolution. Saberhagen evokes this scenario in his Berserker series, where Berserkers are not quite AI, but are near-sentient death machines programmed for their prime directive to seek out and destroy life wherever it may hide. As Brin has pointed out, such deadly probes, whether intelligent or not, are an eerie solution to everything we observe, including "the Great Silence" as so far determined by all SETI programs (Brin 1983).

It is notable that Asimov's robots are human descendants, since his universe has no extraterrestrials, and that his robots are still to some extent controlled by humans according to the second law, and can allow no harm to come to humanity according to the zeroth law. It is also notable that in Arthur C. Clarke's universe, which is full of extraterrestrial intelligence, artificial intelligence plays very little role—with the exception in *2001: A Space Odyssey* of HAL, a disastrous postbiological that violated Asimov's three laws by harming humans. It would seem that Clarke may have had a failure of imagination when it comes to the potential role of AI in the universe, or that he saw AI as a passing part of evolution: in his earlier novel *The City and the Stars* (1956), humans teamed with other galactic civilizations to build a disembodied intelligence, a pure mentality that would seem to be beyond the stage of AI.

This raises a valid point: on the principle that nothing in the universe remains static, postbiologicals would continue to be subject to cultural evolution. AI may not be the ultimate emergence of cultural evolution, and Morowitz (2002) has suggested that "spirit" could be an emergent phenomenon beyond AI. Where cultural evolution would ultimately lead one cannot say, except that ultimate entities might have characteristics approaching those we ascribe to deities: omniscience, omnipotence, and perhaps the capability of communication through messenger probes. Stapledon himself has envisioned such a being in *Star Maker*, although not a product of cultural evolution via artificial intelligence. Thus, our reflections on postbiologicals lead to a possibility that some might characterize as cosmotheology (Dick 2000c).

Given the characteristics of immortality, increased tolerance to their environment, capacity for action on a large scale, and an intelligence far superior to our own, what are the implications of the postbiological universe for SETI? First, there is the problem of search space. Environmental tolerance and availability of resources beyond the planetary realm means that SETI searches for postbiologicals need not be confined to planets around Sun-like stars, nor to planets at all (Shostak 1998, 201; Tough 2002). Indeed postbiologicals probably would "prefer" not to be so confined. Artificial intelligence, or their robotic surrogates, could roam the galaxy as reproducing von Neumann machines (Tipler 1985), Bracewell probes (Bracewell 1975), or smart microprobes (Tough 1998). Roaming intelligent probes might also lead to an AI version of the Fermi Paradox, but with novel possibilities for solution, since postbiological "psychology" may be very different from the psychology of biologicals.

Secondly, there is the question of the nature of the signal. Postbiologicals could be communicating with each other via electromagnetic signals, but the Intelligence Principle tending toward the increase of knowledge and intelligence renders it unlikely they would wish to communicate in such a way with embryonic biologicals like humans. Shklovskii and Sagan pointed out that the long lifetimes of artificial intelligence "could be very advantageous for interstellar contact among advanced communities. The sluggishness of two-way radio communication over interstellar distances tends to make such contact unsatisfactory for beings with lifetimes measured in decades. But for very long-lived beings, such communication would be much more interesting" (Shklovskii and Sagan 1966, 487). What Shklovskii and Sagan left unsaid was that this means that short-lived biologicals such as ourselves might be reduced to intercepting communications of postbiologicals; attempts to do this might lead to a new sense of what the "magic frequencies" are. Intercepting such signals at interstellar distances would undoubtedly be more difficult than detecting a signal directed at us. But if one of the activities of postbiologicals is to study emerging biologicals, as terrestrial anthropologists study our own roots, they may be closer than we think. Indeed, as the products of technology, the Intelligence Principle of cultural evolution implies that, even if they did not wish to communicate with us, postbiologicals would incessantly attempt to increase their knowledge of emerging cultures and their perhaps unique pathways in the development of science, technology, and mathematics.

Thirdly, the Intelligence Principle leads us to conclude that postbiologicals might be more interested in receiving signals from biologicals than in sending them. This conclusion should lead us to place new emphasis on message construction, to explore the implications for message construction if the intended recipients are AI, including the optimal mode of representation to be used with postbiologicals in contrast to biologicals. In addition to increasing their knowledge of the physical and biological universe, would postbiologicals also be interested in spiritual principles, altruism, and the arts, as some have recently proposed for extraterrestrial biologicals? (Vakoch 1998, 1999; Ringwald 2001). This is tantamount to asking if postbiologicals would be interested in cultural evolution; as products of cultural evolution themselves, this seems highly likely, and with this conclusion cultural evolution comes full circle in a cosmic context.

Finally, the vast disparity in age between postbiologicals and biologicals highlights what has been called the Incommensurability Problem. It is entirely possible that the differences between our minds and theirs are so great that communication is impossible.

With a better understanding of the role of cultural evolution in cosmic evolution, it seems clear that the L parameter is a double-edged sword for SETI. If L is large, extraterrestrials may have evolved through biological or cultural evolution, beyond human understanding. If L is small, the chances of communication increase because our mental capacities might be more comparable, but N becomes much smaller, and the chances of finding any scarce civilizations are much smaller. Here, in the Siren call of SETI, we are caught between Scylla and Charybdis.

All of these conclusions, and the possibility of a postbiological universe in general, point to the need to place AI research in a cosmic context. AI and SETI, after all, have much in common with their interest in the nature of intelligence. And although the difficult problem of the definition of intelligence is beyond the scope of this article, the relation of biological and postbiological intelligence gains greater urgency with the prospect that cultural evolution may have already produced artificial intelligence throughout the universe. With the symbiosis of SETI and AI, SETI expands its possibilities into new phase space, and the study of the long-term future of AI becomes more than idle speculation.

Summary and Conclusions

We have applied two methodological principles in this paper: 1) long-term Stapledonian thinking is a necessity if we are to understand the nature of intelligence in the universe today, and 2) cultural evolution must be seen as an integral part of cosmic evolution and the Drake Equation. We have accepted the strong AI theory that it is possible to construct artificial intelligence equivalent to, or superior to, humans, and adopted the Intelligence Principle that the improvement and perpetuation of intelligence is a central driving force of cultural evolution. Applying these principles to the universe, we have argued that if the lifetime of technological civilizations typically exceed 1,000 years, it is likely that we live in a postbiological universe. The argument makes no more, and no fewer, assumptions about the probability of the evolution of intelligence, or its abundance, than standard SETI scenarios; it argues only that if such intelligence does arise, cultural evolution must be taken into account, and that this may result in a postbiological universe. As a by-product of the discussion, we point out that even if we live in a biological universe, the extraterrestrials that compose the biological universe would be millions, if not billions, of years older than us.

Whether biologicals or postbiologicals, we conclude that the implications for SETI strategies are profound. Biologicals that are part of a civilization millions or billions of years old may or may not still be using electromagnetic technology for SETI, calling for new strategies (Tough 2000). Postbiologicals would not be confined to planetary surfaces, they might be more likely to roam the universe than to send signals, they might be using electromagnetic technology for communication among themselves rather than with others, and they would be more likely to receive than to send messages. Lacking a theory of cultural evolution on Earth, we are unable to predict the cultural evolution even of our own species in the near future. Lacking a knowledge of advanced biological or postbiological motivations, we are unable to predict the nature of civilizations millions or billions of years older than ours. Still, the likelihood of Darwinian-type mechanisms at work in cultural evolution throughout the universe forces us to consider the real possibility—perhaps amounting to probability—of a postbiological universe, and calls for a sweeping reconsideration of SETI assumptions and strategies.

References

Ascher, R. & M. Ascher (1962). "Interstellar communication and human evolution," *Nature* 193, 940. Reprinted in *Interstellar Communication,* ed. A. G. W. Cameron, ed., New York: W. A. Benjamin, 1963 pp. 306–308.

Aunger, R., ed. (2000). *Darwinizing Culture: The Status of Memetics as a Science.* Oxford: Oxford University Press.

Becker, L. (2002). "Repeated blows," *Scientific American* 286 (March): 76–83.

Bennett, C. L. et al. (2003). "First year Wilkinson Microwave Anisotropy Probe (WMAP) observations: Preliminary maps and basic results,' *Astrophysical Journal Supplement Series*, vol 148, 1–27.

Billingham, J. et al. (1999). *Social Implications of the Detection of an Extraterrestrial Civilization.* Mountain View, CA: SETI Press.

Boyd, R. and P. J. Richerson, (1985). *Culture and the Evolutionary Process.* Chicago: University of Chicago Press.

Bracewell, R. (1975). *The Galactic Club.* San Francisco: W. H. Freeman.

Bradie, M. (1986). "Assessing evolutionary epistemology," *Biology and Philosophy* 1:401–460.

Brin, G. D. (1983). "The 'Great Silence': The controversy concerning extraterrestrial intelligent life," *Quarterly Journal of the Royal Astronomical Society* 24: 283–309.

Butler, S. (1863). *Canterbury Press* (June 13).

Cavalli-Sforza, L. L. & M. W. Feldman, (1981). *Cultural Transmission and Evolution: A Quantitative Approach.* Princeton, NJ: Princeton University Press.

Chaisson, E. (2001). *Cosmic Evolution: The Rise of Complexity in Nature.* Cambridge, MA: Harvard University Press.

Chapman, C. R. and D. Morrison, (1989). *Cosmic Catastrophes.* New York: Plenum Press.

Chapman, C. R. and D. Morrison, (1994). "Impacts on the Earth by asteroids and comets: Assessing the hazard," *Nature* 367:33–34.

Davies, P. (1995). *Are We Alone? Philosophical Implications of the Discovery of Extraterrestrial Life.* New York: Basic Books, pp. 51–55.

Dawkins, R. (1976). *The Selfish Gene.* Oxford: Oxford University Press.

Deacon, T. (1997). *The Symbolic Species: The Co-evolution of Language and the Brain*. New York: W. W. Norton.

Delsemme, A. (1998). *Our Cosmic Origins*. New York and Cambridge: Cambridge University Press.

Dennett, D. (1996). *Darwin's Dangerous Idea*. New York: Simon and Schuster.

Dick, S. J. (1996). *The Biological Universe: The Twentieth Century Extraterrestrial Life Debate and the Limits of Science*. Cambridge: Cambridge University Press.

Dick, S. J. (2000a). "Extraterrestrial life and our world view at the turn of the millennium," Dibner Library Lecture, Smithsonian Institution Libraries, Washington, DC.

Dick, S. J. (2000b). "Interstellar humanity," Futures 32:555–567, reprinted as "Cosmic Humanity" in Tough (2000) pp. 93–101.

Dick, S. J., ed. (2000c). "Cosmotheology: Theological implications of the new universe," in *Many Worlds: The New Universe, Extraterrestrial Life and the Theological Implications*," Philadelphia: Templeton Press.

Drake, F. (1976). "On hands and knees in search of Elysium," *Technology Review* 78:22–29.

Dyson, G. (1997). *Darwin Among the Machines: The Evolution of Global Intelligence*. Cambridge, MA: Perseus Books.

Fellner, R. (1990). "The problems and prospects of cultural evolution," *Papers from the Institute of Archaeology* [London] 1:45–55.

Fukuyama, Francis. (2002). *Our Posthuman Future: Consequences of the Biotechnology Revolution*. New York: Farrar, Straus and Giroux.

Gray, C. 2002. *Cyborg Citizen: Politics in the Posthuman Age*. Routledge.

Harrison, A. A., J. Billingham, et al. (2000). "The role of the social sciences in SETI," in *When SETI Succeeds*, ed. Tough, A., pp. 71–85.

Hart, M. (1975). "An explanation for the absence of extraterrestrials on Earth," *Quarterly Journal of the Royal Astronomical Society* 16:128–135.

Hart, M. and B. Zuckerman, eds. (1982). *Where Are They?* New York: Pergamon; 2nd edition, Zuckerman and Hart, Cambridge University Press, 1995.

Kardashev, N. S. (1997). "Cosmology and civilizations," *Astrophysics and Space Science* 252:25–40.

Kurzweil, R. (1999). *The Age of Spiritual Machines: When Computers Exceed Human Intelligence.* New York: Penguin Books.

Lalande, K. N. and G. R. Brown, (2002). *Sense & Nonsense: Evolutionary Perspectives on Human Behaviour.* Oxford: Oxford University Press.

Larson, R. B. and V. Bromm, (2001). "The first stars in the universe," *Scientific American* 285:64–71.

Leslie, J. (1996). *The End of the World: The Science and Ethics of Human Extinction.* London and New York: Routledge.

Livio, M. (1999a). "How rare are extraterrestrial civilizations and when did they emerge?" *Astrophysical Journal* 511:429–431.

Livio, M. (1999b). "How rare are extraterrestrial civilizations and when did they emerge?" *Mercury* 28, no. 2: 10–13.

Lumsden, C. J. and E. O. Wilson, (1981). *Genes, Mind and Culture: The Coevolutionary Process.* Cambridge, MA: Harvard University Press.

MacGowan, R. and F. I. Ordway, III. (1966). *Intelligence in the Universe.* Englewood Cliffs, NJ: Prentice-Hall.

Mithen, S. (1996). *The Prehistory of the Mind: The Cognitive Origins of Art, Religion and Science.* London: Thames and Hudson.

Moravec, H. (1988). *Mind Children: The Future of Robot and Human Intelligence.* Cambridge, MA: Harvard University Press.

Moravec, H. (1999). *Robot: Mere Machine to Transcendent Mind.* Oxford.

Morowitz, H. (2002). *The Emergence of Everything: How the World Became Complex.* Oxford: Oxford University Press.

Norris, R. P. (2000). "How old is ET?," in *When SETI Succeeds: The Impact of High-Information Contact*, ed. Tough, A. Bellevue, Washington, 2000, pp. 103–105.

Oliver, B. (1971). *Project Cyclops: A Design Study of a System for Detecting Extraterrestrial Intelligent Life*, NASA Ames, Moffett Field, California, pp. 27, 60.

Parker, S. and McKinney, M. (1999). *Origins of Intelligence: The Evolution of Cognitive Development in Monkeys, Apes, and Humans.* London: Johns Hopkins University Press.

Raup, D. M. (1992). *Extinction: Bad Genes or Bad Luck.* New York: W. W. Norton.

Rees, M. (1997). *Before the Beginning: Our Universe and Others.* Reading, MA: Addison-Wesley.

Richerson, P. J. and R. Boyd, (2001). "Build for speed, not for comfort: Darwinian theory and human culture," *History and Philosophy for the Life Sciences* 23:423–463. Special Issue on Darwinian Evolution Across the Disciplines.

Ringwald, C. D. (2001). "Encoding altruism," *Science and Spirit* (September–October, 2001).

Ruse, M. (1985). "Is rape wrong on Andromeda?" in E. Regis, ed., *Extraterrestrials: Science and Alien Intelligence.* Cambridge: Cambridge University Press, pp. 43–78.

Scalo, J. and J. C. Wheeler, (2002). "Astrophysical and astrobiological implications of gamma-ray burst properties," *Astrophysical Journal*, 566:723–787.

Searle, J. R. (1980). "Minds, brains, and programs," *Behavioral and Brain Sciences* 3, no. 3: 417–457.

Segerstrale, U. (2000). *Defenders of the Truth: The Battle for Science in the Sociobiology Debate and Beyond.* Oxford: Oxford University Press.

Seife, C. (2003). "MAP Glimpses Universe's Rambunctious Childhood," *Science* 299 (14 February): 991, 993.

Shklovskii, J. & C. Sagan, (1966). *Intelligent Life in the Universe.* San Francisco: Holden-Day, pp. 360–361.

Shostak, S. (1998). *Sharing the Universe: Perspectives on Extraterrestrial Life.* Berkeley, CA, pp. 103–109.

Stapledon, O. (1948), "Interplanetary Man?" in *An Olaf Stapledon Reader*, Robert Crossley, ed., (Syracuse, NY, 1997), pp. 218–241.

Stull, M. (1977). "Cultural evolution," in P. Morrison, J. Billingham, and J. Wolfe, eds., *The Search For Extraterrestrial Intelligence*, NASA, Washington, DC, pp. 47–52. Based on a Workshop on Cultural Evolution chaired by Joshua Lederberg, 24–25 November 1975.

Tipler, F. (1985). Extraterrestrial intelligent beings do not exist, in *Extraterrestrials: Science and Alien Intelligence*, ed. Edward Regis (Cambridge, 1985), pp. 133–150.

Tipler, F. (1994). *The Physics of Immortality.* New York.

Tough, A. (1998). "Small smart interstellar probes," *Journal of the British Interplanetary Society* 51:167–174.

Tough, A. (2000). "How to achieve contact: Five promising strategies," in *When SETI Succeeds*, Tough, A., ed., pp. 115–125.

Tough, A. (2002). "Post-biological implications for SETI: A response to the SETICon02 keynote paper [by S. Dick]," *Proceedings of SETICon02: The Second SETI League Technical Symposium.* American Radio Relay League, New Jersey, pp. 11–13.

Turco, R. P., Owen B. Toon, Thomas P. Ackerman, James B. Pollack, and Carl Sagan, (1983). "Nuclear winter: Global consequences of multiple nuclear explosions," *Science* 222:1283–1292 (23 December 1983).

Vakoch, D. A. (1998). "Constructing messages to extraterrestrials: An exosemiotic perspective," *Acta Astronautica* 42:697–704.

Vakoch, D. A. (1999). "The view from a distant star: Challenges of interstellar message-making," *Mercury* (March–April 1999): 26–32.

Ward, P. and D. Brownlee, (2000). *Rare Earth : Why Complex Life is Uncommon in the Universe*. New York: Copernicus.

Ward, P. and D. Brownlee, (2003). *The Life and Death of Planet Earth: How the New Science of Astrobiology Charts the Ultimate Fate of our World*. New York: Henry Holt.

Ward, P. and A. Rockman, (2001). *Future Evolution: An Illuminated History of Life to Come*. New York: Henry Holt & Co.

Webb, Stephen. (2002). *If the Universe Is Teeming with Aliens . . . Where Is Everybody?: Fifty Solutions to the Fermi Paradox and the Problem of Extraterrestrial Life*. New York: Copernicus Books and Praxis Publishing.

Wilson, D. S. (2002). *Darwin's Cathedral: Evolution, Religion and the Nature of Society*. Chicago: University of Chicago Press.

Wilson, E. O. (1975). *Sociobiology: The New Synthesis*. Cambridge, MA: Harvard University Press.

Wilson, E. O. (1998). *Consilience: The Unity of Knowledge*. New York: Alfred A. Knopf.

Chapter 15

Bringing Cosmos to Culture
Harlow Shapley and the Uses of Cosmic Evolution

JoAnn Palmeri

Bringing Cosmos to Culture as Shapley's Lifelong Mission

In response to a request for an interview to be conducted at the U.S. Naval Observatory, 73-year-old famed astronomer and retired Harvard Observatory Director, Harlow Shapley (1885–1972), stated that for the upcoming NBC interview he did not "care to pose with a telescope."[1] Shapley explained that apart from some episodes in his scientific youth, he had spent little time actually peering through telescopes. He wanted to make the point that like most astronomers, his contributions were based on a range of activities distinct from the practice of observing. While this 1959 exchange is instructive with respect to Shapley's view of his astronomical work, it is also instructive with respect to Shapley's view of his potential historical legacy. Shapley believed that some of his most important contributions lay outside science; he wanted to be seen not only as a scientist, but also as a scholar and a public intellectual.[2] The title of his 1967 book, *Beyond the Observatory*, aptly characterizes a career in which considerable effort was devoted to extending his influence beyond astronomical and scientific circles.[3] Yet Shapley's work beyond these circles was shaped in important ways by his career in science, and especially, by his belief that the findings of science held lessons of profound significance for humanity. Shapley achieved scientific renown through his work as an astronomer and observatory director. In these roles he influenced the course of 20th century astronomy and shaped his contemporaries' understanding of the cosmic facts. Yet elucidating the broader and very human significance of the cosmic facts was this scientist's true calling. Bringing the cosmos to human culture was Harlow Shapley's lifelong mission.

Shapley's mission of bringing cosmos to culture culminated in the 1950s and 1960s in an outpouring of publications and public appearances that disseminated his views widely. It was at the beginning of this period, in 1952, that he retired as Director of Harvard Observatory, a position he held for three decades. Over the course of his lengthy career, Shapley played a leadership role in the intellectual and institutional development of astronomy. With his work in administration and planning in both the prewar and postwar periods, he influenced the course of American science.[4] Entering retirement in the mid-1950s, Shapley was finally in a position to devote himself full time to the activity that had always been his passion—lecturing and writing on astronomy and sharing his insights concerning the significance of science for humanity. For nearly two decades after his retirement Shapley did just this, enthusiastically bringing cosmos to culture as a prominent popularizer and spokesman for science.

An indication of Shapley's success in spreading his cosmic perspective is perhaps best symbolized by the sense of familiarity current readers would likely experience upon reading the preface to his 1963 book, *The View From a Distant Star:*

> Mankind is made of star stuff, ruled by universal laws. The thread of cosmic evolution runs through his history, as through all phases of the universe—the microcosmos of atomic structures, molecular forms, and microscopic organisms, and the macrocosmos of higher organisms, planets, stars, and galaxies. Evolution is still proceeding in galaxies and man—to what end, we can only vaguely surmise.[5]

And surmise Shapley did. Through dozens of publications and hundreds of appearances, Shapley offered eloquent lessons on the implications of the cosmic facts. Shapley educated his readers and audiences on the latest findings of science but also inspired them with a vision of how this knowledge could positively shape the course of human history. As suggested by this excerpt, Shapley viewed cosmic evolution as a universal principle of nature, one that had relevance to human destiny.

Shapley popularized his cosmic evolutionary perspective with missionary zeal during the 1950s and 1960s. But just how successful was he in spreading his vision? To what extent did Shapley's efforts influence the development and use of the idea of cosmic evolution? Other authors in this volume provide clues and historical reflections on these intriguing questions. The focus of this chapter is, however, on Shapley himself. The questions posed are biographical and historical. For example: How and why did Shapley come to identify cosmic evolution as the "greatest theme I know" and use it as a foundation for his vision of science and its ultimate significance for society?[6] How and why did he come to promote his evolutionary perspective as "stellar theology" and "rational religion" in the postwar decades? More generally, how are Shapley's efforts to promote his message of "Life, Hope, and Cosmic Evolution" to be understood within the broader context of a life and career that spanned the great cultural, political, and scientific transformations of the 20th century? To answer these questions we must begin with an examination of Shapley's attempts to connect cosmos and culture in the early decades of the 20th century.

Connecting Cosmos and Culture

By 1918, Shapley completed the work that established his scientific reputation and secured his standing as one of the most important contributors to 20th century astronomy. With his investigations at Mount Wilson Observatory the Princeton-trained astronomer overturned established thinking by offering a new view of the Milky Way system of stars, and especially, of Earth's place within it. His work extended the dimensions of the galaxy and presented a new picture of the arrangement of stars within it.[7] Most significantly, Shapley located the solar system at the periphery rather than at the center of the newly enlarged galaxy.[8] Shapley's work provided the foundation for what would become a standard yet compelling picture of humanity's place in the universe—Earth as a minor planet, orbiting an unremarkable star, located in an undistinguished part of a galaxy populated by countless stars.[9] This episode of scientific change and the new perspective on the universe that it revealed, became the foundation for Shapley's earliest attempts to fashion lessons of broader significance from the cosmic facts.

In a letter to astronomer George Ellery Hale, his director at Mount Wilson Observatory, Shapley emphasized the revolutionary nature of his achievement and characterized it as the latest step in a process that spanned millennia. Yet his discovery was only most recent blow to man's view of himself as the center of things; an earlier and well-known episode was the removal of Earth from the center of the cosmos by Copernicus.[10] Shapley emphasized how each step in the process of the "shifting of the center" signaled a further retreat from anthropocentrism. He identified anthropocentrism not only with the earlier attempts to understand the cosmos, but also with superstition and with tendencies inherent in most religious traditions. Anthropocentric thinking was an obstacle to true understanding of the cosmos. Its decline thus marked the triumph of rationality.

While getting past anthropocentrism and the barrier of human ego was difficult, Shapley suggested the payoff was worth it. Vanity as a consequence of place was supplanted by a humility that encouraged a new perspective on humanity within the cosmic scheme. As he suggested in one of his many radio talks:

> We do not amount to much in size, or in duration either, for that matter; but we have the gift, I hope, of humility and reverence and we have an inborn impulse to learn and understand. We may, therefore, not be inconsequential in this scheme of stars, of gravitation, and of empty space. At any rate, we are composed of star-stuff and we are a part of a magnificent universe.[11]

With lessons of humility came lessons of cosmic connections and a new basis for reverence. Shapley integrated his lessons on the futility of anthropocentrism and the reorienting effects of the cosmic facts into his earliest efforts to popularize astronomy and science, as the newly appointed Director of Harvard Observatory, beginning in 1921.

Throughout the 1920s and 1930s, when Shapley was building an astronomy program of international stature, he was also establishing a reputation as a talented lecturer and inspiring popularizer of science. As Katherine Bryant shows in her study of Shapley as "Great Communicator" these two activities were very much connected. It was necessary for Shapley to become a self-promoter in order to obtain the resources he needed.[12] Successful publicity and outreach led to financial support for observatory and department projects, as well as his many efforts to promote science and interdisciplinary research at Harvard.[13] Yet even as Shapley linked public appearances and other popularization efforts with fundraising success, it is clear he viewed such activities as serving a higher purpose. Impulses beyond the practical and professional motivated his efforts to bring the latest findings of science to the attention of the public.

Lecturing to the public and writing for the popular press provided the means by which Shapley could express his literary and humanistic side, and a venue within which he could hone his oratorical skills.[14] These activities also presented Shapley with the opportunity to act on his belief in the importance of communicating knowledge to an intelligent and interested public. In an exchange of letters in 1929 with the President of the American Philosophical Society, Shapley reflected longingly on the promise and possibilities of devoting oneself exclusively to such an endeavor:

> To be a subsidized and dignified and competent interpreter of current knowledge would be a noble calling—not a routine teacher, not an investigator, but a weigher, surveyor, expounder, and (perchance) a prophet![15]

While it would not be until the postwar years that Shapley would be in a position to devote himself full time to such a role, at the time he expressed these sentiments he had already made a promising start. Through his efforts to promote Harvard astronomy and science, Shapley gained increasing renown as well as growing confidence in his ability to make an impact within the broader culture. Shapley viewed himself as more than a conveyor of facts; he was someone with an important message. The message underlying Shapley's efforts to promote science was his belief in the reorienting potential of the cosmic facts, of the capacity of science to influence man's philosophies, social systems, and especially—religions.

Science as the Best Medicine for Man's Religions and Philosophies

Alternatively characterizing himself through the decades as agnostic, pagan, pantheist, and secularist, Shapley emphasized the fact that friends considered him to be a religious individual. He described himself as a "religious sort of person," typically qualifying this characterization with the statement, "by my own definition" of religion.[16] What, exactly, was this definition? Shapley's response to comments after a lecture in 1951 encapsulates the definition of religiosity that he projected throughout most of his career: "stars . . . provide me with the awe, the reverence, the poetry, the mystery, the beauty, the inspiration, the respect for and service to fellow-man that form the basis of what seems to me to be the essence of religion."[17] As documented by an interviewer in the mid-1960s, this was a perspective that Shapley traced back to an earlier time. Shapley credited his undergraduate work in astronomy at the University of Missouri with helping to awaken within him the spirituality that he would maintain throughout his life: "Some men lose interest in religion when they get into science, but it was the other way round with me."[18] As the interviewer explained, "exposure to the stars through astronomy aroused in him a feeling of awe and wonder that he can only describe as religious." In Shapley's words: "I guess I have what John Dewey called a 'religious attitude.'"[19] This was an attitude he hoped to incite in others through his own presentations of science.

As Shapley explained at one point during his first years of public outreach at Harvard, the dual goal of his lectures was to "try to bring in both the remarkable developments in sounding the depths of space and the apparent relation of the physical universe to the spiritual outlook."[20] With lectures such as "Stars and Spiritual Things" and "The Religious Implications of Astronomy," Shapley presented a spiritually compelling vision of the cosmos, one that rarely failed to captivate and inspire audiences.[21] It is notable that it was Shapley's eloquent musings and reverential tone that earned him a reputation as an inspiring and sought-after speaker and not his actual views and sometimes irreverent pronouncements on contemporary religion. For Shapley defined his own spirituality in the context of a reverence for nature and the cosmos, not in the acceptance of traditional church doctrine nor in the belief in a personal God. Shapley believed science strengthened religion, but he did not adhere to the kind of reconciliation efforts being conducted within the popular press by prominent scientific colleagues like Robert Millikan, Michael Pupin, and his mentor Henry Norris Russell.[22] In a cultural climate in which many of his scientific colleagues were offering ways to reconcile the new findings of science with their Christian faith, it is not unexpected that Shapley's more critical and skeptical perspective on religious institutions and doctrines was conveyed to the public in cryptic ways. Typically, Shapley expressed his sentiments in terms of a support for rationality and an opposition to superstition, supernatural belief, and irrationality. For example, in his 1923 article, "The Universe and Life," Shapley suggested to his readers that the existence of life could be explained by "nothing more supernatural" than the laws of physical chemistry.[23] Despite Shapley's emphasis on superstition as the main foe of science, it is clear that he also viewed his efforts at popularizing science, in part, as a challenge to what he negatively perceived as anthropocentric, authoritarian, and static religious traditions.[24]

Throughout 1920s and 1930s, Shapley presented his brand of cosmic spirituality not as an aid to established religion, but as an alterative to traditional modes of thought.[25] From his earliest days of public outreach, Shapley conveyed the message that science could have a profound impact on other aspects of culture, especially religion. In 1923 he included himself in the company of those "who think a new social and ethical system may be founded on science."[26] Yet given the reality of the times, Shapley speculated that he believed it would not be for another generation that people would appreciate that "religion and ethics and esthetics and political science must be grounded directly on the progress of science in an increasingly scientific age."[27] Still, the message that science could positively impact other areas of human thought was one Shapley continued to passionately promote through the coming decades. He conveyed his message during talks at schools, civic associations, churches, and in correspondence with colleagues, fans, and supporters. To one potential Harvard donor he suggested that the support of science was important because even "partial solutions" in the assault on the mysteries of the universe yielded the "most effective material for man's future meditations, religions, and philosophies."[28]

Shapley's efforts on behalf of advancing the dream of a scientifically grounded ethical, religious, and social system remained a predominately solitary enterprise in the period prior to World War II. But his ambitions for science would be energized during the war years and beyond, within an intellectual climate that encouraged interdisciplinary exploration of the problem of the relationship of science to religion, to humanistic traditions, and to questions of ethics and values. World War II had been a watershed, a true crisis of civilization. Amidst the haunting specter of nuclear annihilation, there was an urgent need to explore new ways of thinking, new orientations. Throughout his life, Shapley had given much thought to the question of new orientations. Now, through immersion in projects that encouraged dialogue between theologians, philosophers, scientists, humanists, and social theorists, he had the opportunity to bring his perspective on the reorienting potential of science to the problem of planning for a postwar world. Shapley's experiences in these years set the stage a more explicit focus on the issue of the relationship between science and religion within his own efforts to promote science.

By his own account, Shapley portrays a 1939 conversation with Rabbi Louis Finkelstein of New York's Jewish Theological Seminary as a pivotal moment in his engagement with contemporary concerns and in particular, religion.[29] He was persuaded to join with others from academia and various religious denominations in a continuing dialogue on the most pressing issues of the day—what became institutionalized as the annual Conference on Science, Philosophy, and Religion.[30] As a result of his experiences with individuals associated with the Conference as well as other groups, Shapley became convinced that religion, as well as science, had something important and necessary to contribute to the contemporary crisis. Both perspectives were needed to direct humanity toward survival and away from destruction; both perspectives could contribute to the cause of "civilization defense."[31] It was within the context of his reevaluation of religion and his efforts to articulate a role for science in the postwar world that Shapley began to characterize science as "practical religion."[32]

Religion in an Age of Science: IRAS, Evolution, and Rational Religion

Of particular significance for Shapley's efforts to promote a wider role for science was his association throughout the 1950s with the circle of scholars, scientists, and religious leaders affiliated with the Institute for Religion in an Age of Science (IRAS). IRAS emerged from the combined efforts of individuals associated with the "Coming Great Church" conference and members of the American Academy of Arts and Sciences. The Coming Great Church conferences had been held since 1950, a movement of religious leaders geared to the creation of a new ecumenism. In response to a concern that the implications of science for this new age needed to be explored, scientists were asked to attend the 1954 conference.[33] Many of the invited scientists were members of the American Academy of Arts and Sciences; some were members of its Committee on Science and Values. IRAS was incorporated in 1954, with the following constitutional goals:

> To promote creative efforts leading to the formulation, in the light of contemporary knowledge, of effective doctrine and practices for human welfare; to formulate dynamic and positive relationships between the concepts developed by science and the goals and hopes of man expressed through religion; to state human values in such universal and valid terms that they may be understood by all men whatever their cultural background and experience, in such a way as to provide a basis for world-wide cooperation.[34]

As historian James Gilbert has noted, unlike contemporary groups with similar goals, "only in the Institute did scientists exercise the primary inspiration."[35] It is not surprising that Shapley found a home within this community, for it provided a supportive atmosphere for his own ambitions for establishing a role for science. Central to this was the leadership of Ralph Wendell Burhoe, whose vision for the establishment of a scientific theology grounded in an evolutionary conception of the cosmos informed much of the group's activities.[36]

Shapley's longstanding tendency to speak of evolution in universal terms, as well as his immersion and more general interest in biological topics, resonated strongly with Burhoe's vision and with perspectives of the biologists and social scientists that constituted the core of IRAS.[37] Within IRAS, the question of the development of ethics and values was examined from anthropological and evolutionary perspectives and much attention was given to the question of the origin and development of religion. Religion was a topic that had long interested Shapley; for decades he had suggested that the findings of science should influence religion. In the context of his association with IRAS, Shapley began to characterize change in religion in evolutionary terms. In reflections following one meeting he wrote:

> "Religion in an Age of Science" is one of the subjects that bedevils me year after year. More than forty years of scientific research in the fields nearest to times essentially eternal and spaces approaching the infinite led me directly to contemplate the role of tender man in a tough universe. What means human life? What holds his future? On one hand we have the scientific revelations and revolutions of recent years and on the other the stubbornly held religious creeds and dogmas, mostly of long ago. I ask if they are outmoded. Am I wrong in believing that religions must evolve or die?[38]

Since his earliest musings on the significance of his own astronomical discoveries, Shapley had depicted shifts in understanding of humanity's place in the cosmos in terms of a retreat from anthropocentric thinking typical of primitive science as well as religion. He now began to characterize these shifts as grounded in the very fabric of the universe—in the existence of a cosmic principle, of an evolutionary urge toward change and growth.[39] In talks and publications Shapley reflected on this theme and posed a recurring question:

> We see that stars evolve, planetary surfaces like our own change with the flowing of time. We see that primitive plants and animals develop through the ages into complicated organisms ... Man, too, has evolved and so have his social organizations. Why, then—this is my question—why not expect the great growth urge that runs through the universe to include the growth of man's groping philosophies?[40]

Shapley made the case for change in man's groping philosophies by drawing upon the historical evidence of change in humanity's view of his relation to the cosmos. He cited an address by Pope Pius XII to the Vatican Academy of Sciences in 1951 as evidence that religious creeds do evolve.[41]

Shapley and Burhoe, in particular, viewed the key mission of IRAS as one of education and orientation of the public toward the next step in the evolution of religion—what they identified as "rational religion."[42] The message Shapley emphasized was that understanding and accepting the cosmic facts was part of the natural evolutionary process of the emergence of a rational religion. In the early 1950s, Shapley developed a compelling vehicle for promoting his cosmic evolutionary perspective and hopes for rational religion—the newly proposed discipline and academic course "cosmography."[43] Shapley developed this course for the general education program at Harvard and taught it during the period coinciding with his initial association with IRAS.[44] By the late 1950s, the themes of cosmography, cosmic evolution, and rational religion were seamlessly entwined in Shapley's pronouncements on the cosmic facts.

Cosmography as Practical Religion

Cosmography was defined by Shapley as "a discipline based in a cosmic way on chemistry, physics, social biology, geology, astronomy, all referred to the fundamental physical entities of space, time, matter, and energy."[45] Cosmography had wide ranging scope; it treated all the components of the cosmos and all the sciences with emphasis on connections, classification, and a common evolutionary framework.[46] The evolutionary thread underlying all operations and processes, all material and immaterial factors in the universe, was identified by Shapley as something beyond the foundational space-time and matter-energy entities. This was the "fifth entity."[47]

In earlier writings and lectures, Shapley had suggested the existence of a "fifth entity." He continued to speculate on just what this fifth entity was and on how it should be named, yet he argued definitively only with respect to its existence.[48] He now began to associate the fifth entity with cosmic evolution. Shapley's view on the significance as well as very human relevance of the idea of universal evolution was later summed up in the aptly titled "Life, Hope, and Cosmic Evolution":

> We have evidence of a truly wide Cosmic Evolution from hydrogen to *Homo*, and probably somewhere an evolution beyond the *Homo* level of sentiency. We have in Cosmic Evolution a fundamental principle of growth that affects the chemical atoms as well as plants and animals, the stars and nebulae, space-time and mass-energy. In brief, everything

that we can name, everything material and non-material is involved. It is around this Cosmic Evolution that we might build revised philosophies and religions.[49]

For Shapley, cosmic evolution provided the basis for the kind of transformation in humanity's perspective that he had long envisioned. Since evolution was an underlying theme of cosmography, the discipline could serve as a tool for human orientation as well as inspiration for rational religion.[50] As Shapley explained: "My course in cosmography in Harvard University is aimed at orientation of man in his universe and by, inference at least, tries to explore a religion of rationality."[51] Along with papers on dinosaurs and the origin of life, students submitted papers on "Cosmography as a Practical Religion."[52]

Through the 1950s and 1960s Shapley promoted his cosmographic and evolutionary perspective across a wide range of educational, literary, and organizational venues. Through his affiliation with IRAS Shapley conducted outreach to theological schools, contributed to the journal *Zygon*, and edited the conference publication *Science Ponders Religion*.[53] As in the prewar years, Shapley found a receptive community within liberal religious circles as well as within a wide array of community and educational forums. In response to the positive feedback he received from one important talk, Shapley remarked with considerable satisfaction: "I seem to have established myself as one competent to ponder the relationships of modern scientific revelations to spiritual values and ideas."[54] Encouraged by response to his public appearances and the success of his Harvard course (and interest in it shown by several universities), Shapley took his message on the road. He toured colleges under the auspices of the National Science Foundation and the American Astronomical Society, and spent several semesters in the late 1950s as Visiting Lecturer in Cosmography. Shapley spoke of hoping to inspire a "cult of cosmography teaching" and hoping to see the field established as an academic discipline.[55]

While Shapley's plans for the institutionalization of cosmography did not work out as he had envisioned, he was nevertheless successful in disseminating his cosmographic perspective through his nationwide lecturing. Shapley confided in a number of astronomical colleagues and friends that he considered his lecturing in these years as one of his most important contributions.[56] He believed he was getting his message across; at one point he proudly reported: "They all want me back, they say, for they believe my 'rational' religion is what they want their religion to be."[57] The message that Shapley had been spreading about the cosmic facts through lecturing was also circulated through a wide variety of publications. Throughout his career, Shapley had been a prolific writer, contributing to a wide array of general interest and popular science publications since the 1920s; he had also published a number of books in the prewar years.[58] Shapley continued to publish in a wide variety of venues through the postwar years, including *American Scholar, American Scientist, Science Digest, Scientific American*, and *Scientific Monthly*.[59] Shapley capped off his prolific publishing career with three popular books published while in his seventies: *Of Stars and Men* (1958), *The View from a Distant Star* (1963), and *Beyond the Observatory* (1967).

Of Stars and Men: Science as Stellar Theology

If Shapley can be characterized as a kind of prophet of science in a new age of science, then *Of Stars and Men: The Human Response to an Expanding Universe* can be considered as the bible of his new stellar theology.[60] Shapley was particularly proud of the many translations of this work as well as its incarnation as a film in 1964 by Oscar-winning animators John and Faith Hubley.[61] It is telling that Shapley credited the Star Island movement for providing the inspiration to complete this work, which incorporated many of the themes he had been emphasizing since his IRAS days—religion, evolution, and the significance of the cosmic facts for human destiny.[62]

Shapley characterized *Of Stars and Men* as a treatise on cosmography; its underlying theme was the reorienting potential of the cosmic facts. This book was "an essay on orientation, including a tentative obituary, one might say, of anthropocentrism in our description of the universe."[63] Shapley identified the most significant leaps in understanding of the universe over time and explained how these influenced philosophical and religious systems, necessitating "adjustments" on the part of humanity. The first and second adjustments involved acceptance of the geocentric and heliocentric views of the cosmos. The third adjustment in thinking was associated with Shapley's work—the galactocentric revolution—his identification of the center of the Milky Way galaxy and Earth's eccentric place within it. The most recent—the "Fourth Adjustment" was still in process and was biological rather than physical—it entailed the recognition that humanity was not alone in the universe.[64] Since it was a rational approach to the universe that had propelled humanity away from earlier conceptions of the cosmos, Shapley suggested that it would be the same approach that would move humanity beyond adherence to the anthropocentric religious creeds that were the remnants of the earliest civilizations. The cosmic facts would provide the foundation for the revitalization of religion. As Shapley explained:

Some theologies are not frozen, not fossilized at a given epoch; their spokesmen recognize the bearing of the advance of knowledge on the tenability of the ancient positions. Some philosophers, not too many, re-examine, re-evaluate, and go forward. By them the cosmologies are reformed to agree with verified data of biology and physics. Moreover, this evolution of doctrine need not be reluctant, gradual, slow. In situations under human control (like man's own reasoning), beneficent mutations should be welcomed and if possible incited. For change, growth, evolution in this live dynamic universe is inherent and wide-spread. . . . Evolution affects not only stars, galaxies, and planetary crusts, animals, plants, and societies, but also touches social policies, the ethical systems of man, and the religions he fosters. May not science, broadly taken, be the fundamental cultural soil in which we plant and vitalize our religions? Need so many of them remain dated and nonrational?[65]

Acceptance of this rational approach was part of the universal thread of evolution and growth in the cosmos.[66]

While Nature supplanted God and salvation was to be sought in man's ability to reason, Shapley's cosmos was not devoid of meaning.[67] Its mystery and magnificence filled the individual with a religiously inspired awe; lessons of moral and spiritual significance could be derived from the cosmic facts. Shapley challenged his readers to "look deeply and sympathetically for religious beliefs that are founded on science, and that grow with science."[68] In his writings and lectures, Shapley offered examples of how the cosmic facts could transform one's religious and ethical perspective.

Cosmic connections is one theme that is pervasive in Shapley's works. He emphasized the idea of a fundamental physical connection between humanity and other parts of the universe through popularization of two themes—"the common breath of humanity" and "humans as star stuff." Shapley connected the past with the present by highlighting the fact that a life breath drawn today contains argon atoms breathed by our long-forgotten ancestors:

Some of the argon atoms breathed in his first day by Adam (or any early man) are in the next breath of all of us. Some of the argon of our today's breathing will be in the first gasp of all infants a century hence. This argon traffic is obviously rich in suggestion; it implies a droll one-worldness and, like sunshine, recognizes no national boundaries. It links us with the breathing animals of the remote past and distant future in a sort of communal way.[69]

Shapley invoked the idea of humans as star stuff to promote the idea of a fundamental connection of life to cosmic processes. While there was a common thread in Shapley's use of the phrase "star stuff" over the course of his career—to teach a lesson about cosmic connections—the actual basis on which this was grounded did shift dramatically. Whereas in the earlier period, Shapley's vision of cosmic connections and use of star stuff was based on the belief in a uniformity of materials in stars and humans, in the later period, he used new astronomical theories (the origin of the chemical elements in the Big Bang and supernovae) as the basis for the human connection to the cosmos.[70] The lesson derived from this fundamental connection between humanity and the cosmos did not change:

With our fellow animals and plants of land, air, and sea; with the rocks and waters of all planetary crusts, and the photons and atoms that make up the stars—with all these we are associated in an existence and evolution that inspires respect and deep reverence.[71]

In his writings, Shapley invoked the themes of the common breath of humanity and cosmic connections to suggest a cosmic basis for international brotherhood and spiritual fulfillment.[72]

Another cosmic fact that Shapley used to yield significant implications beyond science was that of extraterrestrial life. Drawing upon origin of life studies and recent developments in astronomy, Shapley claimed it was no longer possible to deny the existence of life elsewhere in the cosmos. Humanity's "Fourth Adjustment" was necessitated by "the acceptance of the evidence and the belief that the biological development on this planet is not unique and that varied and highly elaborate sentient life is abundant and widely distributed."[73] This latest adjustment had special relevance to Shapley's crusade on behalf of rationality—he used the idea of extraterrestrial life to emphasize the untenability of belief in a "one-planet deity."[74]

Shapley's efforts to depict science as a means to move beyond outdated religious traditions in these and other works was not new. What was new in the postwar period was the degree to which he explicitly and pervasively employed religious language to present science as a kind of religion. He even invoked the phrase "stellar theology" in his 1967 *View From a Distant Star*.[75] Shapley was propelled into action by concerns shaped in the war years. Through his engagement in science-religion dialogues and debates about the future of the postwar world, he gained rhetorical strategies for articulating his cosmic evolutionary perspective and especially, for promoting it as rational religion.[76] Shapley's efforts to articulate and promote rational religion was an extension and elaboration of a perspective that he had developed over the course of a lifetime—his simultaneous advocacy of a rational approach to the universe and desire to promote a religiously inspired sensibility. His pleas for the coexistence of rationality and religion and the characterization of science as practical religion had particular resonances within the cultural climate of the postwar years. Historians have documented the increasing importance of religion in American life in the period following World War II.[77] As Stephen Whitfeld has argued in discussion of the revival of religion in American culture during the Cold War, what was revived in this period "was not so much religious belief as belief in the *value* of religion."[78] Within this culture, Shapley found audiences receptive to his vision of science and a variety of opportunities and venues within which to promote it.[79]

Astronomy, Biology, and Evolution

Shapley's promotion of cosmic evolution must also be viewed against the intellectual developments and disciplinary contexts of the biological and physical sciences. With the resurgence of Darwinian natural selection and the emergence of the Modern Synthesis, by mid-century, evolution became a unifying theme in the discipline of biology.[80] As Smocovitis highlights, Julian Huxley and other biologists emphasized the theme of cosmic evolution to help bring evolution to the forefront of biology.[81] Throughout the decades, astrophysics had been refining theories about stellar evolution and the cosmic origin of the chemical elements. Continuing progress in understanding astro-physical and cosmic processes, as well as increased scientific attention of the questions of the origin of life and the possibility of life on other worlds, con-tributed to a tendency on the part of many scientists to characterize evolution in universal terms. By the 1940s "cosmic, galactic, stellar, planetary, chemical, organic evolution, and cultural evolution emerged as a continuum in a 'uni-fied' evolutionary cosmology." And by the 1950s, the wider culture "perme-ated with evolutionary science" and "resonated with evolutionary themes."[82]

Shapley's case illustrates that disciplinary uses of the idea of universal evolution were not limited to the biology. In his response to the increasing attention given to biological evolution in scientific and popular arenas, Shapley was intent on making sure that astronomical evolution was given due attention. After all, as he reminded one correspondent: "Evolution is commonly taken to be a biological activity—wolf to dog, reptile to bird, monkey to man. But the evolution of atoms, molecules, stars, and galaxies is a more fundamental operation."[83] Promoting inorganic evolution was at the top of his mind in 1959—a high-profile year for evolution as a consequence of the Darwin centennial celebrations.[84] Shapley had a particularly important forum for presenting the perspective of an astronomer at the Darwin Centennial at the University of Chicago. In his contribution to this meeting, published subsequently as "On the Evidences of Inorganic Evolution," Shapley gathered together the most recent developments in physics, astronomy, and cosmology to emphasize the significance of processes of inorganic evolution.[85] Elsewhere Shapley continued to press the point that evolution needed to be viewed as a cosmic phenomenon. In the aftermath of the Chicago meeting, Shapley again shared his frustrations with a colleague:

> There has been much written in the past two years on evolution, in part celebrating the centennial of Darwin. But nearly all of the 100 articles I have seen deal with *biological* evolution. There have been new ideas on the evolution of atoms, planetary systems, stars, and galaxies. In fact, non-biological-evolution is much greater in a cosmic sense than the life developed on this peripheral planet.[86]

While Shapley was committed to insuring a wider recognition of inorganic evolution, he was also committed to promoting a wider recognition of biological evolution at the cosmic level—life in the universe. Shapley had long been interested in the problem of life—its origin and its cosmic significance. Through his work on entomology, support for biology at Harvard, and correspondence with scientists working on origin of life studies, Shapley maintained a continuing immersion in general with developments in the biological sciences.[87] Shapley's views concerning the cosmic significance of biological evolution are illustrated in an exchange with *Harper's* publisher Frederick Allen concerning a review of a book on relativity theory in the late 1940s. While Shapley admired the author's treatment of the physics, he protested the limited definition of the word universe, musing to Allen that he would like to inquire of the author "Have you heard of the biological universe?"[88] Given Shapley's interest in such questions it is not unexpected that he was one of the more prominent public spokesman on ideas such as the origin of life or extraterrestrial life as these topics gained increasing public attention and sustained scientific inquiry. As Steven Dick outlines, changing theories of planetary and solar system formation created opportunities for scientists like Shapley to explore the question of extraterrestrial life.[89] Shapley's own contribution to the question of life in the universe included an estimate for the number of possible sites for life throughout the universe.[90] With his efforts, Shapley bolstered the case for the cosmic component of biological evolution, popularizing the idea that "we are not alone" in the universe.[91] He made the case that evolution need not be restricted to a narrow, terrestrial perspective, nor be retained as the exclusive domain of the biologist. His emphasis on inorganic evolution and on biological evolution beyond Earth supported the cosmic evolutionary perspective—of evolution as a fundamental, unifying principle in nature.

There is an even broader disciplinary context within which Shapley's promotion of universal or cosmic evolution can be viewed—this is the defense of science itself. Throughout the 20th century, the idea of a universal evolution has been used by scientists in support of the validity of biological evolution—specifically, to support the idea of human evolution in the wake of continuing challenges from fundamentalist quarters.[92] In the 1920s, Shapley used the existence of inorganic evolution as a way of arguing for the credibility of biological (and by inference, human) evolution. During the 1920s, against the backdrop of public debate and controversy over the question of the teaching of evolution, Shapley was eager to bring the weight of astronomy to bear on the issue. He characterized the "plain facts of modern astronomy" as the "best antidote of fundamentalism—much less equivocal than the arguments of biology."[93] Elsewhere Shapley characterized astronomy as presenting "the most definite evidence for evolution."[94] This strategic use of the idea of universal evolution resurfaced in the 1950s in the context of the Darwin Centennial.[95] In his contribution, Shapley stressed the important consequence of acceptance of the existence of evolution in one arena for its acceptance in another. Following his description of the Sun and stellar evolution, Shapley remarked: "therein lies the answer to those who deny, or at least question, on the grounds of mistaken theological orthodoxy, the occurrence of any kind of evolution."[96] More generally, the existence of universal evolution was used by Shapley to set modern science in opposition to the supernatural:

> We have, therefore, in the centennial of the Darwinian *biological* evolutionary theory, found that *physical* evolution

prevails on a much greater scale. It is exhibited not only by the birth and growth of stars, galaxies, and planets, but also by the mutation of the chemical elements. An evolutionary thread seems to run through all nature, inanimate and animate. Again I point out that modern science has removed the need of appeal to miracles or the supernatural for the origin of molecules, or the origin of life, or the origin of trees, or the origin of man and his curiosity. All these evolve naturally.[97]

The Astronomer as Prophet of Science

In his study of IRAS and the contributions of Ralph Wendell Burhoe, John Durant makes the claim that in the 20th century, scientists have attempted to appropriate for their discipline "all of the authority traditionally invested in religion and the priesthood."[98] While evolutionary biology provides the context of Durant's study, his characterization is easily extended to the arena of astronomy.[99] Shapley's story aptly illustrates that in the case of astronomers as in case of biologists, evolution has also provided a compelling forum for addressing "ultimate questions of meaning and value."[100]

From the 1920s through the 1960s, Shapley devoted his energies to the mission of spreading the word of the significance of the cosmic facts for humanity.[101] His efforts were motivated on the one hand, by an interest in advancing astronomy and science, and on the other hand, by a belief in the capacity of science to influence social, ethical, and religious traditions. Nothing less than the prolongation of civilization was at stake. Through his affiliation with IRAS beginning in the 1950s, Shapley became a well-traveled and popular lecturer on "Religion in an Age of Science." Suggesting science could serve as practical religion, Shapley promoted cosmic evolution as the basis of this perspective. With his wide-ranging and influential efforts of bringing the cosmos to culture during the postwar period, Shapley certainly fulfilled his decades-old dream of serving as "a weigher, surveyor, expounder, and . . . a prophet!"[102]

Endnotes

1. Harlow Shapley to James Nelson (Manager of Program Services, NBC New York), 31 January 1959, Papers of Harlow Shapley, 1906–1966, HUG 4773.10, Box 28b, Harvard University Archives, Cambridge, Massachusetts. (hereafter Shapley papers). "Most people like to associate astronomers and telescopes inseparably. But astronomers do their chief research on

photographic plates, or with mathematics, or tables of observations. I do not care to pose with a telescope. I have designed them, and used their output, but except for a short interval years ago, I have not 'peered' through telescopes with hair on end and mouth standing open. Therefore, if we work at the Naval Observatory, it should *not* be in the heatless telescope houses, but in a library of books, or in some ordinary office."

2. For Shapley's perspective on his contributions see Shapley, *Through Rugged Ways to the Stars* (New York: Charles Scribner's Sons, 1969). This autobiography was based in part upon transcripts of interviews conducted by historians representing the American Institute of Physics.

3. Shapley, *Beyond the Observatory* (New York: Charles Scribner's Sons, 1967).

4. Owen Gingerich provides an overview of Shapley's career and diverse activities in his entry in the *Dictionary of Scientific Biography*, vol. 12 (New York: Charles Scribner's Sons, 1975), pp. 345–352. For accounts written in celebration of his Shapley's life see the special issue of *American Scholar* 40 (Summer 1971). See also the contributions by Gingerich and Michael Hoskin in *The Harlow-Shapley Symposium on Globular Cluster Systems in Galaxies*, ed. J. E. Grindlay and A. G. Davis Philip, *Proceedings of the 126th Symposium of the International Astronomical Union* (Cambridge: Cambridge University Press, 1988).

5. Shapley, *The View from a Distant Star: Man's Future in the Universe* (New York: Basic Books, 1963), p. v.

6. Shapley, *Beyond the Observatory*, p. 98.

7. Two important publications documenting Shapley's early work include "Studies Based on the Colors and Magnitudes in Stellar Clusters, Twelfth Paper: Remarks on the Arrangement in the Sidereal Universe," *Astrophysical Journal* 49 (1919): 311–336 and "On the Nature and Cause of Cepheid Variation," *Astrophysical Journal* 40 (1914): 448–465. For a perspective on Shapley's work in the context of early 20th century astronomy see Robert W. Smith, *The Expanding Universe: Astronomy's 'Great Debate,' 1900–1931* (Cambridge: Cambridge University Press, 1982). For a discussion of Shapley's important early research see Owen Gingerich and Barbara Welther, "Harlow Shapley and the Cepheids,"

Sky and Telescope 70 (December 1965): 540–542, and Bark J. Bok, "Harlow Shapley and the Discovery of the Center of Our Galaxy," in *The Heritage of Copernicus: Theories 'Pleasing to the Mind,'* ed. Jerzy Neyman (Cambridge: MIT Press, 1974), 26–61. On Shapley's later astronomical work see Owen Gingerich "Through Rugged Ways to the Galaxies," *Journal for the History of Astronomy* 21 (1900): 77–88.

8. In his autobiography Shapley described his achievement as follows: "In the scientific way, I suppose my number one contribution was locating the center of our galaxy some 33,000 or more light-years from the sun; in other words, the 'overthrow' of the heliocentric hypothesis of Copernicus. The sun-centered universe is dead and has been dead ever since the plots of the distribution of globular star clusters were developed on the basis of the pulsating theory of Cepheid variables. Several colleagues have helped in the 'overthrow,' of course." Shapley, *Through Rugged Ways to the Stars*, p. 168.

9. In 1958 Shapley's version of this image depicted Earth "as the surface of planet No. 3, in the family of a run-of-the-mill yellowish star, situated in the outer part of a typical galaxy that contains billions of typical stars." Shapley, *Of Stars and Men: The Human Response to an Expanding Universe* (Boston: Beacon Press, 1958), pp. 74–75.

10. Shapley to George Ellery Hale, 19 January 1918, Microfilm of Harlow Shapley Papers, Center for History of Physics, American Institute of Physics, College Park, Maryland.

11. Shapley, "Galaxies of Galaxies," Talk During *Collier's* Radio Hour, 21 April 1929, Shapley papers, Box 8b.

12. Katherine Bryant, "The Great Communicator: Harlow Shapley and the Media, 1920–1940" (Senior thesis, The Committee on the History of Science, Harvard University, 1992).

13. One example is Shapley's attempt to institutionalize his vision of interdisciplinary research with his plan calling for establishment of an Institute of Cosmography. "Memorandum of Interview with Dr. Rose on 26 November 1926." Rockefeller Foundation Archives, Record Group 1.1, Series 200, Box 139, Folder 1718, Rockefeller Archive

Center, Sleepy Hollow, New York. A more successful project with which he was later associated with was Harvard's Science Center. For exploration of Shapley's career in astronomy within broader intellectual and institutional contexts, see John Lankford, *American Astronomy: Community, Careers and Power, 1859–1940* (Chicago: University of Chicago Press, 1997) and Ronald E. Doel, *Solar System Astronomy in America: Communities, Patronage, and Interdisciplinary Research, 1920– 1960* (Cambridge: Cambridge University Press, 1996).

14. Shapley worked as a reporter for the *Daily Sun* (Chanute, Kansas) and the *Times* (Joplin, Missouri). His journalistic goals were supplanted by astronomical ambitions during his undergraduate years at the University of Missouri.

15. Shapley to Francis X. Dercum, 6 February 1929, Harvard College Observatory—Records of Director Harlow Shapley, 1921–1956, UAV 630.22, Box 5. Harvard University Archives (hereafter Observatory records).

16. Shapley to Peter Biginelli, 22 April 1954, Shapley papers, Box 18c. For similar statements in print see Shapley, "Human Ideals and the Cosmic View," in *New Horizons in Creative Thinking*, ed. R. M. MacIver. (New York: Published for the Institute for Religion and Social Studies by Harper and Brothers, 1954), p. 8; *View From a Distant Star*, p. 180.

17. Shapley to Poff, 5 November 1951, Shapley papers, Box 22a.

18. William McCleery, "An Informal Call on Harlow Shapley at His Home in New Hampshire," *Princeton Alumni Weekly* (9 December 1964): 5.

19. Ibid.

20. Shapley to Victor Starzenski, 18 August 1923, Shapley papers, Box 8b.

21. Following one lecture Shapley received the following response from a representative of the Beefstake Club: "We went away with a sense of our infinitesimal smallness, and with a profound sense of the supreme bigness of God's universe." Stacy R. Smith to Shapley, 17 February 1925, Shapley papers, Box 8b.

22. Marcel LaFollette, *Making Science Our Own: Public Images of Science, 1910–1955.* (Chicago: University of Chicago Press, 1987), p. 154.

23. Shapley, "The Universe and Life," *Harper's Monthly Magazine* 146 (May 1923): 717. After making the point that scientists should expect the same kinds of results in the life sciences as they have obtained in the physical sciences, Shapley argues that primordial life "becomes inevitable" when "the chemical environment is right." He follows with the suggestion that "the intervention of creative gods, between the inanimate and the living, appears to the scientist to be as unnecessary for the starting of life as the opposition of unnatural devils is impotent to thwart its coming."

24. Shapley's criticism of superstition was in keeping with popular science of the period. In his study of popularization, John Burnham characterizes the existence of an "aggressive campaign against superstition" in the United States at this time. He suggests that "in the field of popularization, religion was a distraction. Superstition continued to be the real issue because it helped to define, in a negative way, what 'science stood for.'" John Burnham, *How Superstition Won and Science Lost: Popularizing Science and Health in the United States* (New Brunswick: Rutgers University Press, 1988), p. 21.

25. In his contribution to an edited volume on the philosopher Kant in 1925, Shapley wrote: "Kant realized, even better than most of us do today, that religion and science in the last analysis are the same. The science of yesterday is the revealed religion of today, and the science revealed today will be the religion of tomorrow. But the religion we are speaking of here has nothing to do with orthodoxy." Shapley, "Science," in *Immanuel Kant: 1724–1924*, ed. E. C. Wilm (New Haven: Yale University Press; London: Oxford University Press, 1925), p. 55.

26. Shapley to Arthur Hixson, 3 November 1923, Shapley papers, Box 8b.

27. Shapley to Frederick Allen, 15 October 1924, Observatory records, Box 1.

28. Shapley to E. M. Grossman, 26 March 1929, Observatory records, Box 8.

29. Shapley, "Introduction to Religion in an Age of Science," Shapley papers, Box 4a.

30. For background on the conference see Fred W. Beuttler, "Organizing an American Conscience: The Conference on Science, Philosophy and Religion, 1940–1968," Ph.D. diss, University of Chicago, 1995.

31. In a letter to a fellow astronomer in 1941 Shapley explained the cause to which he found himself devoting so much of his personal time and energy: "Although the Harvard Observatory and I personally are involved in 'national defense' activities, under both government and information auspices, my recent choice has been to devote my own personal efforts in the direction of 'civilization defense'—a high sounding phrase for the post-war problems of adjustment." Shapley to H. Plaskett, 21 October 1941, Shapley papers, Box 22a. During the war years and beyond, the task of "civilization defense" was a unifying framework for Shapley's wide-ranging activities in the public arena, which included: support for political candidates, promotion of international projects, increasing support for scientific research, encouraging interdisciplinary dialogue and educational projects, and promoting the social relevance of scientific findings. In the "Fifth Informal Memorandum from Harlow Shapley" published in August of 1941, Shapley wrote: "It is an amazing thing, this persistent urge to maintain ideals and impracticalities at this moment when we must be more realistic and practical than ever before. Research on the Structure and Behavior of the Universe is a job we intend not to drop or slacken appreciably, notwithstanding the occupation of several of us with grim realities. National Defense is immediate; Civilization Defense is a continuing and long-range business, and the solving of sidereal mysteries has always been a pioneer part of it." Rockefeller Foundation Archives, Record Group 2, Series 200, Box 210, Folder 1472, Rockefeller Archive Center, Sleepy Hollow, New York.

32. Transcript of Meeting, 3 November 1939, p. 46, Records of the Conference on Science, Philosophy and Religion, Record Group 5, Box 2, Folder 5D-2-12, Courtesy of The Joseph and Miriam Ratner Center for the Study of Conservative Judaism, Jewish Theological Seminary, New York City.

33. For the perspective of a key participant see Ralph Wendell Burhoe, "The Institute on Religion in an Age of Science: A Twenty Year View," *Zygon* 8 (March 1973): 59–80.

34. "Constitution," 9 November 1954, Shapley papers, Box 13c.

35. James Gilbert, *Redeeming Culture: American Religion in an Age of Science* (Chicago: University of Chicago Press, 1997), p. 274.

36. David R. Breed, *Yoking Science and Religion: The Life and Thought of Ralph Wendell Burhoe* (Chicago: Zygon Books, 1992). See also John Durant's analysis of Burhoe's activities in "Evolution, Ideology and World View: Darwinian Religion in the Twentieth Century," in *History, Humanity and Evolution: Essays for John C. Greene*, ed. James R. Moore (Cambridge: Cambridge University Press, 1989), pp. 355–373.

37. Participants and contributors included Alfred Emerson, Theodosius Dobzhansky, Hudson Hoagland, Kirtley Mather, and B. F. Skinner.

38. Shapley, "Statement," November 1955, Shapley papers, Box 25b.

39. Since the 1920s he had suggested connections between biological and inorganic aspects of evolution. "We are, or should be, impressed by the general scope and dignity given to the evolutionary conception by the recent studies of astronomy and physical chemistry. Evolution is not chiefly limited to the relation of man to his anthropoid forebears. That phase is one of the minor steps in the development that pervades the whole universe. . . . From our survey emerges an appreciation of the importance and magnitude of inorganic evolution." Shapley, *Starlight* (New York: George H. Doran Company, 1926), pp. 140, 142.

40. Shapley, "Life, Hope, and Cosmic Evolution," *Zygon* 1, no. 3 (1966): 277.

41. Shapley to Ralph A. Wright, 13 July 1953, Shapley papers, Box 22e. See also, Shapley, *Of Stars and Men*, p. 90 and *Beyond the Observatory*, pp. 99–100.

42. In support of the goal of promoting rational religion, Shapley suggested in early draft statements concerning the IRAS program that members' work should include "an examination of the relevance and nature of primitive religions to the construction of an effective 'religion of rationality' or 'rational religion' (Many useful studies bearing on this matter have already been made by anthropologists)." Shapley, "Afterthoughts of the

Star Island Conference 1955," Shapley papers, Box 4e. See "The Religion of Science," in James Gilbert, *Redeeming Culture: American Religion in an Age of Science* (Chicago: University of Chicago Press, 1997), pp. 273–295.

43. The official news release about the course was issued in fall of 1951. Harvard University New Office Release, 5 November 1951, Papers of Harlow Shapley, 1906–1966, HUG 4773.20, Box 1.

44. This was also the period of Shapley's retirement from the Observatory. From 1952 to 1956 he was associated with the university as Paine Professor of Astronomy.

45. Shapley to Warren Weaver, 17 February 1953, Shapley papers, Box 23a. For the course Shapley drew heavily on his own taxonomic account of "the universe of material things" published in 1930 as *Flights from Chaos: A Survey of Material Systems from Atoms to Galaxies* (New York: McGraw-Hill Book Company, 1930).

46. In a letter to David Owen of the Committee on General Education, Shapley proposed a catalog description: "A survey of the cosmos in the light of current scientific knowledge and theory is the goal of this course. The location of man and his artifacts in the world of atoms, cells, stars, and galaxies, will be examined along with the complementary inquiry of the place in the mind of man of the material universe—its appearances and realities. The age of the world, the twilight of heat, the dimensions of space, the cosmic role of the matter-energy and time-space entities will be discussed, as well as biological life as a cosmic phenomenon. The explorations will lead up and down the geological timetable, in and out of the groups and periods of the chemical elements, and along the radiation spectrum from cosmic rays to radar. The large evolutionary processes, as of the stars and rotating galaxies in an expanding universe, and the smaller evolutionary operations, as of the planets, mountains, plants, animals and societies, are a part of the dynamics of Cosmography. The only prerequisite is persistent curiosity." Shapley to Dr. David Owen, 11 January 1952, Shapley papers, Box 20b.

47. Shapley discussed this in *Beyond the Observatory*: "These observations and deductions that a drive or major process touches both animate and inanimate nature lead directly to the concept of cosmic evolution as the fifth

basic entity. But perhaps we should admit that this may be an entity that is not coordinated with the other four. Why not regard it as even more basic? Or as permeating all of them? . . . For the moment we shall accept cosmic evolution as a sort of fifth entity. . ." *Beyond the Observatory,* p. 109.

48. Shapley referred to this elusive principle in assorted ways in his writings: Something Else, Drift, Cosmic Urge, Will of God, Evolution, and Natural Logic.

49. Shapley, "Life, Hope, and Cosmic Evolution," *Zygon* 1, no. 3 (1966): 281.

50. "Cosmography, when ideally described and studied, involves an extensive and complicated content. It is too comprehensive to be handled thoroughly in brief compass. It appears to manageable, however, if used chiefly as an instrument in human orientation." Shapley, *Of Stars and Men,* p. 20.

51. Shapley to Peter Biginelli, 22 April 1954, Shapley papers, Box 18c. In the outline for the course for the 1954–1955 fall term Shapley included "the religion of rationality" as one topic to be covered in his concluding section. Shapley, "Outline of General Education course in Harvard College," Shapley papers, Box 25a. The course was taught as Natural Sciences 115.

52. "Suggested Topics," Shapley papers, Box 28d.

53. Shapley, ed., *Science Ponders Religion* (New York: Appleton-Century-Crofts, Inc., 1960).

54. Shapley to Professor Wilbur S. Hoopengardner, January 1954, Shapley papers, Box 27d. This was a talk in the fall of 1953, which Shapley gave at the Institute for Social and Religion Studies, a group affiliated with the Jewish Theological Seminary and inspired by the same circle of scholars and religious leaders involved with the Conference on Science, Philosophy and Religion.

55. Shapley to Warren Weaver, 15 January 1953, Shapley papers, Box 23a. "No college or university has started a course in Cosmography. I am disappointed." Shapley to Bernard Perry (Indiana University Press), 11 December 1956, Shapley papers, Box 26b. Encouraged by Dean Sinnott

of Yale University and others, Shapley published an account of his course. See "Cosmography: An Approach to Orientation," *American Scientist* 42 (July 1954): 471–486. Shapley to Philip H. Rhinelander, 12 February 1955, Shapley papers, Box 20b.

56. Shapley to Otto Struve, 10 December 1959, Shapley papers, Box 28d; Shapley to Bart and Priscilla Bok, 20 April 1962, Shapley papers, Box 27a.

57. "The visits were in a sense 'triumphal,' and I am sure I did a lot of commendable damage. . . . They all want me back, they say, for they believe my 'rational' religion is what they want their religion to be." Shapley to Norwood Baker, 3 December 1959, Shapley papers, Box 27a.

58. Shapley's earlier books include: *Starlight* (New York: George H. Doran Co., 1926); *Flights from Chaos: A Survey of Material Systems from Atoms to Galaxies* (New York: McGraw-Hill, 1930); and *Galaxies* (Philadelphia: Blakiston Co., 1943). The most complete list of Shapley's publications is in his NAS biographical memoir. See Bart J. Bok, "Harlow Shapley," *Biographical Memoirs of the National Academy of Sciences* 49 (1978): 241–291.

59. Shapley also contributed to numerous radio and television programs on science and astronomy. He was even a guest on Jack Paar's popular late-night talk show (with his first appearance in October 1961).

60. In his testimonial at a 1972 memorial service for Shapley close friend and IRAS associate Ralph Wendell Burhoe reflected on the impact of this book by sharing an anecdote: "I was just last week told a story by a clergyman-educator now here in Cambridge that reflects this impact. The story, I believe, is an authentic one from this clergyman's days in Princeton, when he was present at an occasion when the socialist political candidate Norm Thomson was to speak at the Unitarian church. Thomas wanted to look up a quotation in the Book of Job . . . and exclaimed 'Don't you have a Bible here? All I can find is magazines and a copy of Harlow Shapley's *Of Stars and Men!*'" Burhoe, "Contribution Written by Ralph Wendell Burhoe for the Harvard Memorial Service at Harvard University on 21 November 1972." Papers of Harlow Shapley, 1906–1966, HUG 4773.80, Box 1.

61. "The small book, "Of Stars and Men," is a sort of guide into truth, and away from orthodoxy. It has been reprinted four times in its first year and is already going into Swedish, Japanese, Spanish and Hindi; also in Pocket Books and the movies." *Harvard College Class of 1910 Fiftieth Anniversary Report* (Cambridge, MA: The Cosmos Press, 1960), p. 452. The animated film (narrated by Shapley) premiered at the Beekman Theater in New York City in April 1964. It was a critical rather than commercial success.

62. Shapley to Robert, 20 July n.d., Shapley papers, Box 23a. "To that movement I owe the inspiration to finish OSAM." IRAS annual meetings were held on Star Island, off the coast of Maine and New Hampshire.

63. Shapley, *Of Stars and Men*, p. 1.

64. "Man's Fourth Adjustment," *American Scholar* 25 (Autumn 1956): 453–457.

65. Shapley, *Of Stars and Men*, p. 90.

66. The message of the importance of a rational approach to the universe was one upon which Shapley concluded his major opus. "As rational practitioners of life and tentative interpreters of the cosmos, we deplore superstition—the last stronghold of the irrational. But, thanks to man's reasoning never before has hampering superstition been in retreat on so wide a front . . . We no longer need appeal to anything beyond nature when we are confronted by such problems as the origin of life, or the binding forces of nucleons, or the orbits in a star cluster, or the electro-chemical dynamics of a thought, or some super-entity of the material universe. We can assail all such questions rationally." *Of Stars and Men*, p. 157.

67. In a talk presented at the 1954 IRAS summer meeting at Star Island, New Hampshire, Shapley presented what would become a familiar stance: "I should like to rationalize religion, dissolve superstition, and equate God and Nature." Shapley, "Comments on a Star Island Conference by Harlow Shapley," [1954], p. 2, Shapley papers, Box 4e.

68. Shapley, *Beyond the Observatory*, p. 105.

69. Shapley, *Of Stars and Men*, pp. 42–43. See also Shapley, "You and the Queen of Sheba: The Breathing Link," *Vogue* (15 March 1960): 108, 109, 154.

70. See "An Inquiry Concerning Other Worlds," in *Of Stars and Men*, pp. 53–75.

71. Shapley, *Of Stars and Men*, p. 149.

72. More recently, Ralph A. Alpher, the physicist who made important contributions to the development of Big Bang cosmology, presented his view on the significance of humanity's connection to the cosmos: "The stars are giant thermonuclear factories whose waste products distributed in supernovae explosions are the chemical elements. *We humans are all star stuff.* Isn't it ridiculous to think of one another as black or white or yellow or Jew or Christian or Moslem when all we really are is some primeval hydrogen chemically compounded with a bit of nuclear debris from the explosion of a star?" Ralph A. Alpher, "Theology of the Big Bang," *Religious Humanism* 17, no. 1 (Winter 1983): 8. Carl Sagan is perhaps the most well-known and influential popularizer of the image of humans as star stuff.

73. Shapley, *Of Stars and Men*, pp. 113–114.

74. "Am I not right in suggesting a new orientation—in asking for a religious philosophy that encompasses the newly known, and which is not continuously in retreat? And am I not right in asking for the abandonment of a one-planet religion and a one-planet deity?" Shapley, *Beyond the Observatory*, p. 105. See also, *Of Stars and Men*, p. 149.

75. Shapley, *View From a Distant Star*, p. 89.

76. For discussion of scientists and religious rhetoric see the work of Thomas Lessl, especially: "The Priestly Voice," *Quarterly Journal of Speech* 75 (1989): 183–197.

77. From statistics on the increase in church affiliations, to the addition of "under God" in the Pledge of Allegiance, to Billy Graham's earliest crusades, to the popularity of books and movies with spiritual themes, it

is evidence that Americans exhibited a heightened interest in religion
See Michael L. Lacey, ed., *Religion and Twentieth-Century American
Intellectual Life* (Cambridge: Cambridge University Press, 1989).

78. Stephen Whitfeld, *The Culture of the Cold War*, 2nd ed. (Baltimore: The
    Johns Hopkins University Press, 1996), p. 86.

79. With respect to his widespread lecturing at colleges, Shapley offered this
    typical description of his efforts: "At 80% of the colleges and universi
    ties I visit I am asked to talk on 'Religion in the Age of Science' and my
    plea for rationalism appears to appeal deeply to students and faculties
    Shapley to Faust, 21 December 1957, Shapley papers, Box 27c.

80. Vassiliki Betty Smocovitis, *Unifying Biology: The Evolutionary Synthesis
    and Evolutionary Biology* (Princeton: Princeton University Press, 1996)
    pp. 149–150.

81. Ibid., pp. 142–146, 152–153.

82. Ibid., pp. 165, 148, 169–171.

83. Shapley to Melba Phillips, 19 September 1959, Shapley papers, Box 28c.

84. See for example: "My remarks could be on the Geophysical Year, or
    Russia, but I believe it would be more to the point to talk about cosmic
    evolution since this is a Darwin Year," Shapley to Burhoe, 27 September
    1958, Shapley papers, Box 13c.

85. Shapley, "On the Evidences of Inorganic Evolution," in *Evolution After
    Darwin*, ed. Sol Tax (Chicago: University of Chicago Press, 1960), pp
    23–38.

86. Shapley to James O'Connell, 28 December 1959, Shapley papers, Box
    28c.

87. Through his work in entomology, support for biological projects
    at Harvard, and correspondence and interaction with biologists
    Shapley earned a reputation within the biological community. Shapley
    was involved in the start of the journal *Evolution* and many of his

contemporaries recognized his special interest and contributions to biology. Smocovitis, *Unifying Biology*, p. 157. In response to Shapley's review of his paper "Life and Its Evolution," Ernst Öpik wrote to thank him for his comments, emphasizing that his remarks were given "greater weight" because he was "one of the few astronomers having biological links." Ernst Öpik to Shapley, 21 July 1952, Shapley papers, Box 21c.

88. Shapley to Frederick Allen, 12 December 1947, Shapley papers, Box 26b.

89. Steven Dick, *The Biological Universe: The Twentieth-Century Extraterrestrial Life Debate and the Limits of Science* (Cambridge: Cambridge University Press, 1996), pp. 160–221.

90. Shapley identified, as a minimum, "a hundred million planetary systems suitable for organic life." Shapley, *Of Stars and Men*, p. 74. Dick, *The Biological Universe*, pp. 428–429. Shapley presented his views at an interdisciplinary conference he organized at the American Academy of Arts and Sciences. See Shapley, "On Climate and Life," in *Climatic Change: Evidences, Causes, and Effects* (Cambridge, MA: Harvard University Press, 1953), pp. 1–12.

91. Shapley, "Life on Other Planets," *Atlantic Monthly* (November 1953): 30.

92. Biologists also used cosmic evolution in this way. Smocovitis, *Unifying Biology*, 142–143, 149–153.

93. Shapley to Maynard Shipley, 10 June 1925, Shapley papers, Box 22d. This was the year of the Scopes trial.

94. Shapley to Agnes Rowlands, 3 March 1925, Shapley papers, Box 22b.

95. Such strategic use for evolution resurfaced more recently. See, for example, an editorial in *Mercury* in which the author refers to suggested strategies offered by Eugenie Scott of the National Center for Science Education in combating increasing challenges to evolution in the classroom. Editor George Musser reminds his readers: "In classrooms across the country, teachers are skipping evolution because biblical literalists have made it too hot to handle. This is not just a battle for the biologists; it also demands the renewed attention of astronomers and astronomy

educators." Among suggestions for how his readers can act: "**Use the 'e'-word**. Evolution, in the broad sense of the development of new forms through natural processes, is a unifying concept in science. It can also be a unifying concept in science education. 'There's far less resistance to evolution in astronomy than to evolution in biology,' Scott said. Stellar evolution, galactic evolution, orbital evolution: These don't sound so threatening as self-replicating molecules and the rise of man. If people can get used to uttering 'evolution' in astronomy, Scott said, they may be less reluctant to use the word in biology." George Musser, Editorial comments, *Mercury* 25, no. 6 (November–December 1996): 2. Yet such emphasis on evolution has a flip side. The closer connection with biological evolution encouraged by astronomers' promotion of cosmic evolution has made astronomy and cosmology more visible objects for challenge. This was seen in the controversy in Kansas in where Big Bang cosmology, not just biological evolution, became the subject of legal maneuvers. For discussion of this trend see David Kaiser, "The Other Evolution Wars," *American Scientist* 95 (November–December 2007): 518–525.

96. Shapley, "On the Evidences of Inorganic Evolution," 23–24.

97. Shapley, "Stars, Ethics, and Survival," in *Science Ponders Religion*, ed. Harlow Shapley (New York: Appleton-Crofts, Inc., 1960), pp. 6–7. This was based on a talk given in December 1959 at the Fairmont Temple in Cleveland, Ohio. I have not identified any instance in publications or unpublished sources where Shapley addresses the issue of the validity of using "evolution" to characterize processes that are fundamentally very different. Like many others, he used evolution in the general sense of development or change. He also strongly suggested the existence of a fundamental connection or commonality to these different kinds of evolutionary processes.

98. John Durant, "Evolution, Ideology and World View: Darwinian Religion in the Twentieth Century," p. 369.

99. In the arena of astronomy, it has been Carl Sagan's efforts that have been the primary focus of attention. See Thomas M. Lessl, "Science and the Sacred Cosmos: The Ideological Rhetoric of Carl Sagan," *Quarterly Journal of Speech* 71 (1985): 175–187; Thomas Ross, "The Implicit Theology of Carl Sagan," *Pacific Theological Review* 18 (Spring

1985): 24–32; Smocovitis, *Unifying Biology*, p. 165; and Philip Hefner, "Editorial," *Zygon* 32 (June 1997): 145–146. As an astronomer with strong biological inclinations, one who popularized the issue of life in the universe, characterized humans as "star stuff," presented science as a kind of revealed religion, brought his message to late night talk shows, and sought cooperation with the Soviet Union as a means to preserve civilization, Shapley's story is an intriguing prelude to the subsequent activities of astronomer Carl Sagan.

100. Durant, "Evolution, Ideology and World View," p. 356. Here Durant is highlighting John C. Greene's use of this phrase. Referring to Greene's essay "From Huxley to Huxley: Transformation in the Darwinian Credo," Durant writes: "Greene deals with the continuing attempts of twentieth-century evolutionary biologists to explain the significance of their subject for human duty and human destiny, dubbing the works of these authors 'the Bridgewater Treatises of the twentieth century,' in that they seek to find in science indications and proofs concerning ultimate questions of meaning and value.'"

101. Shapley's promotion of science from the 1920s through the 1960s is explored in my dissertation, upon which this study is based: "An Astronomer Beyond the Observatory: Harlow Shapley as Prophet of Science," Ph.D., University of Oklahoma, 2000. This research was supported by the History of Science Department at the University of Oklahoma and by generous grants from the American Institute of Physics and the National Science Foundation. Archival materials are reproduced with the kind permission of Harvard University Archives, the American Institute of Physics, the Jewish Theological Seminary, and the Rockefeller Archive Center.

102. Shapley to Francis X. Dercum, 6 February 1929, Observatory records. In a 1947 discussion of his extensive work on behalf of science and civilization, Shapley characterized himself as "a planner and prophet." Shapley, "Cooperation in the Atomic Age," 19 May 1947, Shapley papers, Box 1c. These were remarks prepared for the American-Russian Institute Dinner. Earlier, he characterized himself as an "embryonic evangelist in the movement for a sane age of science." Shapley to Van Dyne, 2 February 1929, Shapley papers, Box 22e. Among his many honors, Shapley was awarded a Doctor of Divinity from Meadville Theological Seminary (Chicago, 1969).

Contributors

✸

Susan Blackmore is a freelance writer, lecturer, and broadcaster, and a visiting lecturer at the University of the West of England, Bristol. She has a degree in psychology and physiology from Oxford University (1973) and a Ph.D. in parapsychology from the University of Surrey (1980). Her research interests include memes, evolutionary theory, consciousness, and meditation. She practices Zen and campaigns for drug legalization. She writes for several magazines and newspapers, writes a blog for the *Guardian* newspaper, and is a frequent contributor and presenter on radio and television. She is author of over 60 academic articles, about 40 book contributions, and many book reviews. Her books include *Beyond the Body* (1982), *Dying to Live* (on near-death experiences, 1993), *In Search of the Light* (autobiography, 1996), and *Test Your Psychic Powers* (with Adam Hart-Davis, 1997). *The Meme Machine* (1999) has been translated into 13 languages. Her textbook, *Consciousness: An Introduction,* was published in June 2003 (Hodder, U.K.; OUP, New York), and *A Very Short Introduction to Consciousness* in 2005 (OUP). Her latest books are *Conversations on Consciousness* (November 2005, OUP, Oxford), and *Ten Zen Questions* (2009).

Howard Bloom is the author of *The Lucifer Principle: A Scientific Expedition Into the Forces of History* ("mesmerizing"—The *Washington Post*), *Global Brain: The Evolution of Mass Mind From The Big Bang to the 21st Century* ("reassuring and sobering"—*The New Yorker*) and the upcoming *The Genius of the Beast: A Radical Re-Vision of Capitalism.* Bloom is the founder of three international scientific groups: The Group Selection Squad (started in 1995), The International Paleopsychology Project (1997), and The Space Development Steering Committee (2007). The Space Development Steering Committee includes the second astronaut on the Moon, Buzz Aldrin; the sixth astronaut on the Moon, Edgar Mitchell; and members from NASA, the National Science Foundation, and the Future Science and Technology Exploration Branch of the Air Force. Bloom is a recent visiting scholar in the graduate psychology department at New York University and a former Core Faculty Member at The Graduate Institute in Milford, Connecticut. From 1976 to 1988, he embarked on what he calls "a science project in mass behavior"—he founded and ran the biggest public relations firm in the music industry, working with Michael Jackson,

Prince, Bob Marley, Bette Midler, Billy Joel, Peter Gabriel, David Byrne, Kiss Queen, AC/DC, Run DMC, and roughly 200 others.

Eric J. Chaisson is an American astrophysicist and science educator best known for his research, teaching, and writing on the interdisciplinary science of cosmic evolution. He is also noted for his original research on the interstellar clouds and emission nebulae of the Milky Way galaxy, and for his leadership in improving science education nationally and internationally. Chaisson earned his Ph.D. at Harvard University and has held appointments at the Harvard-Smithsonian Center for Astrophysics, Johns Hopkins University, and the Space Telescope Science Institute. He is currently Director of the Wright Center for Science Education at Tufts University, where he holds research professorships in the department of physics and in the school of education. As an Associate of the Harvard College Observatory, he also serves with the Faculty of Arts and Sciences at Harvard, where he teaches an annual undergraduate course on the subject of cosmic evolution.

Chaisson has published more than a hundred papers in the refereed journals and written a dozen books, several of which have won awards, such as the B. J. Bok Prize (Harvard) for astronomical discoveries, the Smith-Weld Prize (Harvard) for literary merit, and the Kistler Award for increasing understanding of subjects shaping the future of humanity. He has also won scholarly prizes from Phi Beta Kappa and the American Institute of Physics, a Certificate of Merit from NASA for work on the Hubble Space Telescope, as well as fellowships from the Sloan Foundation and the National Academy of Sciences. Chaisson's major research interests are twofold: His scientific agenda addresses an interdisciplinary, thermodynamic study of physical and biological systems, thereby seeking to understand the origin, evolution, and unification of galaxies, stars, planets, and life in the universe. His educational work engages master teachers and computer animators to create better methods, technological aids, and novel curricula to enthuse teachers, instruct students, and enhance scientific literacy of everyone from grade school to grad school.

David Christian (D.Phil. Oxford, 1974) is by training, a historian of Russia and the Soviet Union, but since the 1980s, he has become interested in world history on very large scales. He taught at Macquarie University in Sydney from 1975 to 2000 before joining San Diego State University in 2001. In January 2009, he returned to Sydney to take up a position at Macquarie University. He has written on the social and material history of the 19th century Russian peasantry, in particular on aspects of diet and the role of alcohol.

524

He has also written a text book history of modern Russia, and a synoptic history of Inner Eurasia (Russia, Central Asia, and Mongolia). In 1989, he began teaching courses on "big history," surveying the past on the largest possible scales, including those of biology and astronomy; and in 2004, he published the first text on "big history." At San Diego State University, he taught courses on world history, "big history," world environmental history, Russian history, and the history of inner Eurasia. He is a member of the Australian Academy of the Humanities and the *Koninklijke Hollandsche Maatschappij der Wetenschappen* [Royal Holland Society of Sciences and Humanities], Affiliates Chair for the World History Association, and a member of the editorial boards of the Journal of Global History and the Cambridge History of the World. In 2008, he was appointed as a James Marsh Professor-at-large at the University of Vermont, and also accepted appointments as a Research Fellow at Ewha Women's University in Seoul and as a Professor of history at Macquarie University in Sydney.

Christian's recent publications include *This Fleeting World* (Berkshire Publishing: Great Barrington, MA: 2007), a history of humanity in under 100 pages; *Big History*, a set of 48 lectures for the Teaching Company, 2008; and *Maps of Time: An Introduction to Big History*, foreword by W. H. McNeill, (Berkeley: University of California Press, 2004). The latter is the first modern attempt by a historian to offer a coherent history of the entire past, beginning with the origins of the universe. With an attempt to explore how human history is embedded in the histories of the biosphere and the universe, *Maps of Time* won the 2005 WHA History Prize for the best book in world history published in 2004. He is also the author of *A History of Russia, Central Asia and Mongolia: Vol 1: Inner Eurasia from Prehistory to the Mongol Empire*, in The Blackwell History of the World series (Oxford: Blackwell, 1998). This is the first synoptic study of "Inner Eurasia" from prehistory up to the 13th century; it is the first of two volumes. And he is the author of *Imperial and Soviet Russia: Power, Privilege and the Challenge of Modernity* (Basingstoke and New York: Macmillan/St. Martin's, 1997), a textbook survey of Russian and Soviet history.

Paul Davies is theoretical physicist, cosmologist, astrobiologist, author, and broadcaster. He now works as a college professor at Arizona State University, where he is Director of the BEYOND Center for Fundamental Concepts in Science. Davies previously held academic appointments in the U.K., at the Universities of Cambridge, London, and Newcastle upon Tyne. He moved to Australia in 1990, initially as Professor of mathematical physics at The

University of Adelaide. Later, he helped found the Australian Centre for Astrobiology, based at Macquarie University, Sydney. His research has ranged from the origin of the universe to the origin of life, and includes the properties of black holes, the nature of time, and quantum field theory.

In addition to his research, Professor Davies is known a passionate science communicator. He gives numerous public lectures each year throughout the world and has written 27 books, both popular and specialist works, which have been translated into many languages. He writes regularly for newspapers, journals, and magazines in several countries. Among Davies's better-known media productions were a series of 45-minute BBC Radio 3 science documentaries. Two of these became successful books and one, *Desperately Seeking Superstrings*, won the Glaxo Science Writers Fellowship. In early 2000, he devised and presented a three-part series for BBC Radio 4 on the origin of life, entitled *The Genesis Factor*. His television projects include two six-part Australian series *The Big Questions* and *More Big Questions* and a 2003 BBC documentary about his work in astrobiology entitled *The Cradle of Life*.

Paul Davies has won many awards, including the 1995 Templeton Prize for his work on the deeper implications of science, the 2001 Kelvin Medal from the U.K. Institute of Physics, and the 2002 Michael Faraday Prize from the Royal Society for promoting science to the public. In April 1999, the asteroid 1992 OG was officially named (6870) Pauldavies in his honor.

Daniel C. Dennett, the author of *Breaking the Spell* (Viking, 2006), *Freedom Evolves* (Viking Penguin, 2003), and *Darwin's Dangerous Idea* (Simon & Schuster, 1995), is University Professor and Austin B. Fletcher Professor of Philosophy, and Co-Director of the Center for Cognitive Studies at Tufts University. He lives with his wife in North Andover, Massachusetts, and has a daughter, a son, and a grandson. He was born in Boston in 1942, the son of a historian by the same name, and received his B.A. in philosophy from Harvard in 1963. He then went to Oxford to work with Gilbert Ryle, under whose supervision he completed the D.Phil. in philosophy in 1965. He taught at U.C. Irvine from 1965 to 1971 when he moved to Tufts where he has taught ever since, aside from periods visiting at Harvard, Pittsburgh, Oxford, and the École Normale Supérieure in Paris.

His first book, *Content and Consciousness*, appeared in 1969, followed by *Brainstorms* (1978), *Elbow Room* (1984), *The Intentional Stance* (1987), *Consciousness Explained* (1991), *Darwin's Dangerous Idea* (1995), *Kinds of Minds* (1996), and *Brainchildren: A Collection of Essays 1984–1996* (MIT Press and Penguin, 1998). *Sweet Dreams: Philosophical Obstacles to a Science of*

Consciousness, was published in 2005 by MIT Press. He coedited *The Mind's I* with Douglas Hofstadter in 1981. He is the author of over 300 scholarly articles on various aspects on the mind, published in journals ranging from *Artificial Intelligence* and *Behavioral and Brain Sciences* to *Poetics Today* and the *Journal of Aesthetics and Art Criticism.*

He gave the John Locke Lectures at Oxford in 1983; the Gavin David Young Lectures at Adelaide, Australia, in 1985; and the Tanner Lecture at Michigan in 1986, among many others. He has received two Guggenheim Fellowships, a Fulbright Fellowship, and a Fellowship at the Center for Advanced Studies in Behavioral Science. He was elected to the American Academy of Arts and Sciences in 1987. He was the cofounder (in 1985) and codirector of the Curricular Software Studio at Tufts, and has helped to design museum exhibits on computers for the Smithsonian Institution, the Museum of Science in Boston, and the Computer Museum in Boston. He spends most of his summers on his farm in Maine where he harvests blueberries, hay, and timber, and makes Normandy cider wine when he is not sailing. He is also a sculptor.

Kathryn Denning, Assistant Professor in the Department of Anthropology at York University, is an anthropologist/archaeologist who has taught and conducted research at universities in Canada and the U.K. She has participated in SETI Institute seminars about interstellar message construction and the societal implications of astrwobiology, has been actively involved in the International Academy of Astronautics SETI Permanent Study Group, and has presented papers relating to SETI at meetings of the American Anthropological Association, Bioastronomy, AbSciCon, the International Astronautical Congress, and a NASA workshop on the future of intelligence in the cosmos. She studies a variety of SETI-related subjects, including: scientists' conceptions of ETI, and how these are influenced by culture, history, and by the technology used in SETI; how archaeology might inform interstellar message construction; debates about transmissions from Earth; what the course of civilizations on Earth might tell us about the Drake factor "L"; and what the evolution of intelligence on Earth might tell us about the Drake factor "F_i."

Denning enjoys exploring the philosophical resonances between archaeology and SETI. Both involve the quest to know about others distant from us in space and time; both require us to challenge our own ideas about intelligence, ways to think, and ways to live; both can force us to work in challenging realms of scientific thought, where theories and searches are compelling, but evidence is difficult to interpret and proof is elusive; both pose fascinating theoretical challenges in communication; and both make us reconsider our own place in the world.

Steven J. Dick served as the Chief Historian for NASA and Director of the NASA History Office from 2003-2009. He worked as an astronomer and historian of science at the U.S. Naval Observatory in Washington, DC for 24 years before coming to NASA Headquarters in 2003. He is the author of numerous books, including *The Biological Universe* (1996) and *Life on Other Worlds* (1998). Among his recent books are *Remembering the Space Age* (NASA SP-2008-4703), a 50th anniversary proceedings for which he served as editor; *America in Space: NASA's First 50 Years* (with Neil Armstrong et al., Abrams, 2007); *Societal Impact of Spaceflight* (NASA SP-2007-4801, edited with Roger Launius); *Critical Issues in the History of Spaceflight* (NASA SP-2006-4702, edited with Roger Launius); *The Living Universe: NASA and the Development of Astrobiology* (2004, with James Strick); and *Sky and Ocean Joined: The U.S. Naval Observatory, 1830–2000* (2003).

Dr. Dick is the recipient of the Navy Meritorious Civilian Service Medal, the NASA Exceptional Service Medal, the NASA Group Achievement Award for his role in NASA's multidisciplinary program in astrobiology, the NASA Group Achievement Award (2008) for the book *America in Space*, and the 2006 LeRoy E. Doggett Prize for Historical Astronomy of the American Astronomical Society. He has served as Chairman of the Historical Astronomy Division of the American Astronomical Society, as President of the History of Astronomy Commission of the International Astronomical Union, and as President of the Philosophical Society of Washington. He is a corresponding member of the International Academy of Astronautics. Minor planet 6544 Stevendick is named in his honor.

James Gardner—the author of *The Intelligent Universe: AI, ET, and the Emerging Mind of the Cosmos*—is a widely published science essayist and complexity theorist. His science essays and peer-reviewed scientific papers have appeared in *Nature Biotechnology, WIRED, World Link, Complexity, Acta Astronautica,* the *International Journal of Astrobiology,* and the *Journal of the British Interplanetary Society.* His first book—*BIOCOSM*—was selected by *Amazon.com*'s editors as one of the 10 best science books of 2003. *BIOCOSM* was featured in major articles and reviews in *Time Magazine, U.S. News & World Report, Harper's,* and *National Geographic* and received outspoken praise from many prominent scientists including U.K. Astronomer Royal Sir Martin Rees and astrophysicist and Templeton Prize-winner Paul Davies.

Gardner has been a featured speaker at major scientific institutions and conferences around the world, including the 2008 conference on the frontiers of SETI research at the Beyond Center for Fundamental Concepts in Science in Phoenix, the 2008 IAA Symposium on Searching for Life Signatures in Paris, the Hayden Planetarium in New York City, the Adler Planetarium in Chicago, the World Space Congress in Houston, the International Astronautical Congress in Rio de Janeiro, the 7th International Artificial Life Conference, and the TransVision 2007 conference in Chicago.

Mark L. Lupisella works for NASA as an engineer and scientist. He has worked on Hubble Space Telescope, Mars planning, Exploration and Constellation Programs (focusing recently on integrating science into the human space program), wearable computing, and areas of astrobiology such as planetary protection, artificial life (to assess the typicality of terrestrial life), cooperative robotics (to search for extraterrestrial life), and broader societal issues of astrobiology such as ethics and worldviews. He has also worked on space governance issues and cofounded the Horizons Project that aims to improve humanity's ability to address long-term survival and development challenges.

Dr. Lupisella has been on numerous panels related to the above sub-jects and is the author of 25 published works. He has a chapter forthcom-ing on philosophical aspects of astrobiology, "The Search for Extraterrestrial Life: Epistemology, Ethics, and Worldviews," in *Exploring the Origin, Extent, and Future of Life: Philosophical, Ethical, and Theological Perspectives*—a Cambridge University Press book based on a series of workshops held by the American Association for the Advancement of Science. He has a B.S. in physics, a M.A. in philosophy (emphasis in philosophy of science), and a Ph.D. in biology (program in behavior, ecology, evolution, and system-atics) from the University of Maryland at College Park, where he did his dissertation on microbial contamination of Mars from a human mission.

JoAnn Palmeri is a historian of science and librarian whose research focuses on the intersections of the astronomy and popular culture. She was appointed interim librarian for the History of Science Collections at the University of Oklahoma in January 2009, and previously held appointments as Visiting Assistant Professor in the Department of the History of Science at the University of Oklahoma. Her article in this volume is based on her dissertation, *An Astronomer Beyond the Observatory: Harlow Shapley as Prophet of Science* (University of Oklahoma, 2000). Aspects of this research have been presented at meetings of the American Astronomical Society, the Biennial History of Astronomy Workshop at the University of Notre Dame, the History of Science Society, and the Society for Literature, Science, and the Arts. The project was initially supported by grants from the National Science Foundation, the American Institute of Physics, and the History of Science Department at the University of Oklahoma. Palmeri served as Associate Editor for the *Biographical Encyclopedia of Astronomers* (Springer, 2007). She contributed the chapter "Science Fiction" to *Genreflecting: A Guide to Popular Reading Interests* (Libraries Unlimited, 2006), edited by Diana Tixier Herald and Wayne A. Wiegand. Her interests in librarianship and history of science intersect in her master's thesis "Using Book Reviews for Readers' Advisory Service: The Case of History of Science Narrative Nonfiction," (University of Oklahoma, 2008). From 1982–1988, Palmeri was employed as a mechanisms design engineer at RCA Astro-Electronics in New Jersey.

Seth Shostak is the Senior Astronomer at the SETI Institute, in Mountain View, California. He has an undergraduate degree in physics from Princeton University, and a doctorate in astronomy from the California Institute of Technology. For much of his career, Seth conducted radio astronomy research on galaxies, and has published approximately 60 papers in professional journals.

He has written several hundred popular magazine and Web articles on various topics in astronomy, technology, film, and television. He lectures on astronomy and other subjects at Stanford and other venues in the Bay Area, and for the last six years, has been a Distinguished Speaker for the American Institute of Aeronautics and Astronautics. He is also Chair of the International Academy of Astronautics' SETI Permanent Study Group. Every week he hosts the SETI Institute's science radio show, "Are We Alone?" Seth has edited and contributed to a half dozen books. He has also been the principal author of four: *Sharing the Universe: Perspectives on Extraterrestrial Life, Life in the Universe* (textbook with Jeff Bennett), *Cosmic Company* (with Alex Barnett), and *Confessions of an Alien Hunter.*

John M. Smart is an evolutionary developmental systems theorist who studies science and technological culture with an emphasis on accelerating change, computational autonomy (human-independent machine learning), and technology foresight. He directs the Acceleration Studies Foundation (ASF, *Accelerating.org*) a nonprofit research organization that seeks to help individuals to better understand and manage accelerating technological change and improve personal and collective foresight. He is an affiliate of the ECCO research group at VUB, a visiting professor at the University of Advancing Technology, and a cofounder of the evo devo universe research community (*evodevouniverse.com*).

John has a B.S. in business from UC Berkeley, has done graduate work in physiology and medicine at UC San Diego, and post baccalaureate course-work in biological, cognitive, computer and physical sciences at UCLA, UC Berkeley, and UCSD. He studied systems theory at UCSD under the mentorship of James Grier Miller (*Living Systems*, 1978), who mentored under process philosopher Alfred North Whitehead. Most recently, he received an M.S. in futures studies from the University of Houston in 2007.

Douglas A. Vakoch received his B.A. in religion from Carleton College, his M.A. in history and philosophy of science from the University of Notre Dame, and his M.A. and Ph.D. in clinical psychology from the State University of New York at Stony Brook. He is currently Associate Professor in the department of clinical psychology at the California Institute of Integral Studies, as well as Director of Interstellar Message Composition at the SETI Institute. Dr. Vakoch is the editor of several volumes now in press or under contract, including *Psychology of Space Exploration: Contemporary Research in Historical Perspective* (NASA History Series), *Between Worlds: The Art and Science of Interstellar Message Composition* (The MIT Press), and *Culture in the Cosmos: Extraterrestrial Life and Society* (Berghahn Books). Dr. Vakoch chairs the International Academy of Astronautics' Study Group on Interstellar Message Construction, and he is a member of the International Institute of Space Law. He serves on the Executive Committee of the Society for Cross-Cultural Research as well as the Editorial Board of the journal *Ecopsychology*, and he is General Editor of the new book series *Ecofeminist Theory and Practice* (Berghahn Books).

The NASA History Series

❋

Reference Works, NASA SP-4000:

Grimwood, James M. *Project Mercury: A Chronology*. NASA SP-4001, 1963.

Grimwood, James M., and Barton C. Hacker, with Peter J. Vorzimmer. *Project Gemini Technology and Operations: A Chronology*. NASA SP-4002, 1969.

Link, Mae Mills. *Space Medicine in Project Mercury*. NASA SP-4003, 1965.

Astronautics and Aeronautics, 1963: Chronology of Science, Technology, and Policy. NASA SP-4004, 1964.

Astronautics and Aeronautics, 1964: Chronology of Science, Technology, and Policy. NASA SP-4005, 1965.

Astronautics and Aeronautics, 1965: Chronology of Science, Technology, and Policy. NASA SP-4006, 1966.

Astronautics and Aeronautics, 1966: Chronology of Science, Technology, and Policy. NASA SP-4007, 1967.

Astronautics and Aeronautics, 1967: Chronology of Science, Technology, and Policy. NASA SP-4008, 1968.

Ertel, Ivan D., and Mary Louise Morse. *The Apollo Spacecraft: A Chronology, Volume I, Through November 7, 1962*. NASA SP-4009, 1969.

Morse, Mary Louise, and Jean Kernahan Bays. *The Apollo Spacecraft: A Chronology, Volume II, November 8, 1962–September 30, 1964*. NASA SP-4009, 1973.

Brooks, Courtney G., and Ivan D. Ertel. *The Apollo Spacecraft: A Chronology, Volume III, October 1, 1964–January 20, 1966*. NASA SP-4009, 1973.

Ertel, Ivan D., and Roland W. Newkirk, with Courtney G. Brooks. *The Apollo Spacecraft: A Chronology, Volume IV, January 21, 1966–July 13, 1974.* NASA SP-4009, 1978.

Astronautics and Aeronautics, 1968: Chronology of Science, Technology, and Policy. NASA SP-4010, 1969.

Newkirk, Roland W., and Ivan D. Ertel, with Courtney G. Brooks. *Skylab: A Chronology.* NASA SP-4011, 1977.

Van Nimmen, Jane, and Leonard C. Bruno, with Robert L. Rosholt. *NASA Historical Data Book, Vol. I: NASA Resources, 1958–1968.* NASA SP-4012, 1976, rep. ed. 1988.

Ezell, Linda Neuman. *NASA Historical Data Book, Vol. II: Programs and Projects, 1958–1968.* NASA SP-4012, 1988.

Ezell, Linda Neuman. *NASA Historical Data Book, Vol. III: Programs and Projects, 1969–1978.* NASA SP-4012, 1988.

Gawdiak, Ihor, with Helen Fedor. *NASA Historical Data Book, Vol. IV: NASA Resources, 1969–1978.* NASA SP-4012, 1994.

Rumerman, Judy A. *NASA Historical Data Book, Vol. V: NASA Launch Systems, Space Transportation, Human Spaceflight, and Space Science, 1979–1988.* NASA SP-4012, 1999.

Rumerman, Judy A. *NASA Historical Data Book, Vol. VI: NASA Space Applications, Aeronautics and Space Research and Technology, Tracking and Data Acquisition/Support Operations, Commercial Programs, and Resources 1979–1988.* NASA SP-4012, 1999.

Astronautics and Aeronautics, 1969: Chronology of Science, Technology, and Policy. NASA SP-4014, 1970.

Astronautics and Aeronautics, 1970: Chronology of Science, Technology, and Policy. NASA SP-4015, 1972.

Astronautics and Aeronautics, 1971: Chronology of Science, Technology, and Policy. NASA SP-4016, 1972.

Astronautics and Aeronautics, 1972: Chronology of Science, Technology, and Policy. NASA SP-4017, 1974.

Astronautics and Aeronautics, 1973: Chronology of Science, Technology, and Policy. NASA SP-4018, 1975.

Astronautics and Aeronautics, 1974: Chronology of Science, Technology, and Policy. NASA SP-4019, 1977.

Astronautics and Aeronautics, 1975: Chronology of Science, Technology, and Policy. NASA SP-4020, 1979.

Astronautics and Aeronautics, 1976: Chronology of Science, Technology, and Policy. NASA SP-4021, 1984.

Astronautics and Aeronautics, 1977: Chronology of Science, Technology, and Policy. NASA SP-4022, 1986.

Astronautics and Aeronautics, 1978: Chronology of Science, Technology, and Policy. NASA SP-4023, 1986.

Astronautics and Aeronautics, 1979–1984: Chronology of Science, Technology, and Policy. NASA SP-4024, 1988.

Astronautics and Aeronautics, 1985: Chronology of Science, Technology, and Policy. NASA SP-4025, 1990.

Noordung, Hermann. *The Problem of Space Travel: The Rocket Motor.* Edited by Ernst Stuhlinger and J.D. Hunley, with Jennifer Garland. NASA SP-4026, 1995.

Astronautics and Aeronautics, 1986–1990: A Chronology. NASA SP-4027, 1997.

Astronautics and Aeronautics, 1991–1995: A Chronology. NASA SP-2000-4028, 2000.

Orloff, Richard W. *Apollo by the Numbers: A Statistical Reference.* NASA SP-2000-4029, 2000.

Lewis, Marieke and Swanson, Ryan. Aeronautics and Astronautics: A Chronology, 1996–2000. NASA SP-2009-4030, 2009.

Management Histories, NASA SP-4100:

Rosholt, Robert L. *An Administrative History of NASA, 1958–1963.* NASA SP-4101, 1966.

Levine, Arnold S. *Managing NASA in the Apollo Era.* NASA SP-4102, 1982.

Roland, Alex. *Model Research: The National Advisory Committee for Aeronautics,1915–1958.* NASA SP-4103, 1985.

Fries, Sylvia D. *NASA Engineers and the Age of Apollo.* NASA SP-4104, 1992.

Glennan, T. Keith. *The Birth of NASA: The Diary of T. Keith Glennan.* Edited by J.D. Hunley. NASA SP-4105, 1993.

Seamans, Robert C. *Aiming at Targets: The Autobiography of Robert C. Seamans.* NASA SP-4106, 1996.

Garber, Stephen J., editor. *Looking Backward, Looking Forward: Forty Years of Human Spaceflight Symposium.* NASA SP-2002-4107, 2002.

Mallick, Donald L. with Peter W. Merlin. *The Smell of Kerosene: A Test Pilot's Odyssey.* NASA SP-4108, 2003.

Iliff, Kenneth W. and Curtis L. Peebles. *From Runway to Orbit: Reflections of a NASA Engineer.* NASA SP-2004-4109, 2004.

Chertok, Boris. *Rockets and People, Volume I.* NASA SP-2005-4110, 2005.

Chertok, Boris. *Rockets and People, Volume II: Creating a Rocket Industry.* NASA SP-2006-4110, 2006.

Chertok, Boris. Rockets and People, Volume III: Hot Days of the Cold War. NASA SP-2009-4110, 2009.

Laufer, Alexander, Todd Post, and Edward Hoffman. *Shared Voyage: Learning and Unlearning from Remarkable Projects.* NASA SP-2005-4111, 2005.

Dawson, Virginia P., and Mark D. Bowles. *Realizing the Dream of Flight: Biographical Essays in Honor of the Centennial of Flight, 1903–2003.* NASA SP-2005-4112, 2005.

Mudgway, Douglas J. *William H. Pickering: America's Deep Space Pioneer.* NASA SP-2008-4113.

Project Histories, NASA SP-4200:

Swenson, Loyd S., Jr., James M. Grimwood, and Charles C. Alexander. *This New Ocean: A History of Project Mercury.* NASA SP-4201, 1966; reprinted 1999.

Green, Constance McLaughlin, and Milton Lomask. *Vanguard: A History.* NASA SP-4202, 1970; rep. ed. Smithsonian Institution Press, 1971.

Hacker, Barton C., and James M. Grimwood. *On Shoulders of Titans: A History of Project Gemini.* NASA SP-4203, 1977, reprinted 2002.

Benson, Charles D., and William Barnaby Faherty. *Moonport: A History of Apollo Launch Facilities and Operations.* NASA SP-4204, 1978.

Brooks, Courtney G., James M. Grimwood, and Loyd S. Swenson, Jr. *Chariots for Apollo: A History of Manned Lunar Spacecraft.* NASA SP-4205, 1979.

Bilstein, Roger E. *Stages to Saturn: A Technological History of the Apollo/Saturn Launch Vehicles.* NASA SP-4206, 1980 and 1996.

Compton, W. David, and Charles D. Benson. *Living and Working in Space: A History of Skylab.* NASA SP-4208, 1983.

Ezell, Edward Clinton, and Linda Neuman Ezell. *The Partnership: A History of the Apollo-Soyuz Test Project.* NASA SP-4209, 1978.

Hall, R. Cargill. *Lunar Impact: A History of Project Ranger.* NASA SP-4210, 1977.

Newell, Homer E. *Beyond the Atmosphere: Early Years of Space Science.* NASA SP-4211, 1980.

Ezell, Edward Clinton, and Linda Neuman Ezell. *On Mars: Exploration of the Red Planet, 1958–1978.* NASA SP-4212, 1984.

Pitts, John A. *The Human Factor: Biomedicine in the Manned Space Program to 1980.* NASA SP-4213, 1985.

Compton, W. David. *Where No Man Has Gone Before: A History of Apollo Lunar Exploration Missions.* NASA SP-4214, 1989.

Naugle, John E. *First Among Equals: The Selection of NASA Space Science Experiments.* NASA SP-4215, 1991.

Wallace, Lane E. *Airborne Trailblazer: Two Decades with NASA Langley's 737 Flying Laboratory.* NASA SP-4216, 1994.

Butrica, Andrew J., ed. *Beyond the Ionosphere: Fifty Years of Satellite Communications.* NASA SP-4217, 1997.

Butrica, Andrew J. *To See the Unseen: A History of Planetary Radar Astronomy.* NASA SP-4218, 1996.

Mack, Pamela E., ed. *From Engineering Science to Big Science: The NACA and NASA Collier Trophy Research Project Winners.* NASA SP-4219, 1998.

Reed, R. Dale. *Wingless Flight: The Lifting Body Story.* NASA SP-4220, 1998.

Heppenheimer, T. A. *The Space Shuttle Decision: NASA's Search for a Reusable Space Vehicle.* NASA SP-4221, 1999.

Hunley, J. D., ed. *Toward Mach 2: The Douglas D-558 Program.* NASA SP-4222, 1999.

Swanson, Glen E., ed. *"Before This Decade is Out . . ." Personal Reflections on the Apollo Program.* NASA SP-4223, 1999.

Tomayko, James E. *Computers Take Flight: A History of NASA's Pioneering Digital Fly-By-Wire Project.* NASA SP-4224, 2000.

Morgan, Clay. *Shuttle-Mir: The United States and Russia Share History's Highest Stage.* NASA SP-2001-4225.

Leary, William M. *We Freeze to Please: A History of NASA's Icing Research Tunnel and the Quest for Safety.* NASA SP-2002-4226, 2002.

Mudgway, Douglas J. *Uplink-Downlink: A History of the Deep Space Network, 1957–1997.* NASA SP-2001-4227.

Dawson, Virginia P., and Mark D. Bowles. *Taming Liquid Hydrogen: The Centaur Upper Stage Rocket, 1958–2002.* NASA SP-2004-4230.

Meltzer, Michael. *Mission to Jupiter: A History of the Galileo Project.* NASA SP-2007-4231.

Heppenheimer, T. A. *Facing the Heat Barrier: A History of Hypersonics.* NASA SP-2007-4232.

Tsiao, Sunny. *"Read You Loud and Clear!" The Story of NASA's Spaceflight Tracking and Data Network.* NASA SP-2007-4233.

Center Histories, NASA SP-4300:

Rosenthal, Alfred. *Venture into Space: Early Years of Goddard Space Flight Center.* NASA SP-4301, 1985.

Hartman, Edwin, P. *Adventures in Research: A History of Ames Research Center, 1940–1965.* NASA SP-4302, 1970.

Hallion, Richard P. *On the Frontier: Flight Research at Dryden, 1946–1981.* NASA SP-4303, 1984.

Muenger, Elizabeth A. *Searching the Horizon: A History of Ames Research Center, 1940–1976*. NASA SP-4304, 1985.

Hansen, James R. *Engineer in Charge: A History of the Langley Aeronautical Laboratory, 1917–1958*. NASA SP-4305, 1987.

Dawson, Virginia P. *Engines and Innovation: Lewis Laboratory and American Propulsion Technology*. NASA SP-4306, 1991.

Dethloff, Henry C. *"Suddenly Tomorrow Came . . .": A History of the Johnson Space Center, 1957–1990*. NASA SP-4307, 1993.

Hansen, James R. *Spaceflight Revolution: NASA Langley Research Center from Sputnik to Apollo*. NASA SP-4308, 1995.

Wallace, Lane E. *Flights of Discovery: An Illustrated History of the Dryden Flight Research Center*. NASA SP-4309, 1996.

Herring, Mack R. *Way Station to Space: A History of the John C. Stennis Space Center*. NASA SP-4310, 1997.

Wallace, Harold D., Jr. *Wallops Station and the Creation of an American Space Program*. NASA SP-4311, 1997.

Wallace, Lane E. *Dreams, Hopes, Realities. NASA's Goddard Space Flight Center: The First Forty Years*. NASA SP-4312, 1999.

Dunar, Andrew J., and Stephen P. Waring. *Power to Explore: A History of Marshall Space Flight Center, 1960–1990*. NASA SP-4313, 1999.

Bugos, Glenn E. *Atmosphere of Freedom: Sixty Years at the NASA Ames Research Center*. NASA SP-2000-4314, 2000.

Schultz, James. *Crafting Flight: Aircraft Pioneers and the Contributions of the Men and Women of NASA Langley Research Center*. NASA SP-2003-4316, 2003.

Bowles, Mark D. *Science in Flux: NASA's Nuclear Program at Plum Brook Station, 1955–2005*. NASA SP-2006-4317.

Wallace, Lane E. *Flights of Discovery: An Illustrated History of the Dryden Flight Research Center.* NASA SP-4318, 2007. Revised version of SP-4309.

General Histories, NASA SP-4400:

Corliss, William R. *NASA Sounding Rockets, 1958–1968: A Historical Summary.* NASA SP-4401, 1971.

Wells, Helen T., Susan H. Whiteley, and Carrie Karegeannes. *Origins of NASA Names.* NASA SP-4402, 1976.

Anderson, Frank W., Jr. *Orders of Magnitude: A History of NACA and NASA, 1915–1980.* NASA SP-4403, 1981.

Sloop, John L. *Liquid Hydrogen as a Propulsion Fuel, 1945–1959.* NASA SP-4404, 1978.

Roland, Alex. *A Spacefaring People: Perspectives on Early Spaceflight.* NASA SP-4405, 1985.

Bilstein, Roger E. *Orders of Magnitude: A History of the NACA and NASA, 1915–1990.* NASA SP-4406, 1989.

Logsdon, John M., ed., with Linda J. Lear, Jannelle Warren Findley, Ray A. Williamson, and Dwayne A. Day. *Exploring the Unknown: Selected Documents in the History of the U.S. Civil Space Program, Volume I, Organizing for Exploration.* NASA SP-4407, 1995.

Logsdon, John M., ed, with Dwayne A. Day, and Roger D. Launius. *Exploring the Unknown: Selected Documents in the History of the U.S. Civil Space Program, Volume II, External Relationships.* NASA SP-4407, 1996.

Logsdon, John M., ed., with Roger D. Launius, David H. Onkst, and Stephen J. Garber. *Exploring the Unknown: Selected Documents in the History of the U.S. Civil Space Program, Volume III, Using Space.* NASA SP-4407, 1998.

Logsdon, John M., ed., with Ray A. Williamson, Roger D. Launius, Russell J. Acker, Stephen J. Garber, and Jonathan L. Friedman. *Exploring the*

Unknown: Selected Documents in the History of the U.S. Civil Space Program Volume IV, Accessing Space. NASA SP-4407, 1999.

Logsdon, John M., ed., with Amy Paige Snyder, Roger D. Launius, Stephen J. Garber, and Regan Anne Newport. *Exploring the Unknown: Selected Documents in the History of the U.S. Civil Space Program, Volume V, Exploring the Cosmos.* NASA SP-4407, 2001.

Logsdon, John M., ed., with Stephen J. Garber, Roger D. Launius, and Ray A. Williamson. *Exploring the Unknown: Selected Documents in the History of the U.S. Civil Space Program, Volume VI: Space and Earth Science.* NASA SP-2004-4407, 2004.

Logsdon, John M., ed., with Roger D. Launius. *Exploring the Unknown: Selected Documents in the History of the U.S. Civil Space Program, Volume VII: Human Spaceflight: Projects Mercury, Gemini, and Apollo.* NASA SP-2008-4407, 2008.

Siddiqi, Asif A., *Challenge to Apollo: The Soviet Union and the Space Race, 1945–1974.* NASA SP-2000-4408, 2000.

Hansen, James R., ed. *The Wind and Beyond: Journey into the History of Aerodynamics in America, Volume 1, The Ascent of the Airplane.* NASA SP-2003-4409, 2003.

Hansen, James R., ed. *The Wind and Beyond: Journey into the History of Aerodynamics in America, Volume 2, Reinventing the Airplane.* NASA SP-2007-4409, 2007.

Hogan, Thor. *Mars Wars: The Rise and Fall of the Space Exploration Initiative.* NASA SP-2007-4410, 2007.

Monographs in Aerospace History (SP-4500 Series):
Launius, Roger D., and Aaron K. Gillette, comps. *Toward a History of the Space Shuttle: An Annotated Bibliography.* Monograph in Aerospace History, No. 1, 1992.

Launius, Roger D., and J. D. Hunley, comps. *An Annotated Bibliography of the Apollo Program*. Monograph in Aerospace History No. 2, 1994.

Launius, Roger D. *Apollo: A Retrospective Analysis*. Monograph in Aerospace History, No. 3, 1994.

Hansen, James R. *Enchanted Rendezvous: John C. Houbolt and the Genesis of the Lunar-Orbit Rendezvous Concept*. Monograph in Aerospace History, No. 4, 1995.

Gorn, Michael H. *Hugh L. Dryden's Career in Aviation and Space*. Monograph in Aerospace History, No. 5, 1996.

Powers, Sheryll Goecke. *Women in Flight Research at NASA Dryden Flight Research Center from 1946 to 1995*. Monograph in Aerospace History, No. 6, 1997.

Portree, David S. F., and Robert C. Trevino. *Walking to Olympus: An EVA Chronology*. Monograph in Aerospace History, No. 7, 1997.

Logsdon, John M., moderator. *Legislative Origins of the National Aeronautics and Space Act of 1958: Proceedings of an Oral History Workshop*. Monograph in Aerospace History, No. 8, 1998.

Rumerman, Judy A., comp. *U.S. Human Spaceflight, A Record of Achievement 1961–1998*. Monograph in Aerospace History, No. 9, 1998.

Portree, David S. F. *NASA's Origins and the Dawn of the Space Age*. Monograph in Aerospace History, No. 10, 1998.

Logsdon, John M. *Together in Orbit: The Origins of International Cooperation in the Space Station*. Monograph in Aerospace History, No. 11, 1998.

Phillips, W. Hewitt. *Journey in Aeronautical Research: A Career at NASA Langley Research Center*. Monograph in Aerospace History, No. 12, 1998.

Braslow, Albert L. *A History of Suction-Type Laminar-Flow Control with Emphasis on Flight Research*. Monograph in Aerospace History, No. 13, 1999.

Logsdon, John M., moderator. *Managing the Moon Program: Lessons Learned From Apollo*. Monograph in Aerospace History, No. 14, 1999.

Perminov, V. G. *The Difficult Road to Mars: A Brief History of Mars Exploration in the Soviet Union*. Monograph in Aerospace History, No. 15, 1999.

Tucker, Tom. *Touchdown: The Development of Propulsion Controlled Aircraft at NASA Dryden*. Monograph in Aerospace History, No. 16, 1999.

Maisel, Martin, Demo J.Giulanetti, and Daniel C. Dugan. *The History of the XV-15 Tilt Rotor Research Aircraft: From Concept to Flight*. Monograph in Aerospace History, No. 17, 2000. NASA SP-2000-4517.

Jenkins, Dennis R. *Hypersonics Before the Shuttle: A Concise History of the X-15 Research Airplane*. Monograph in Aerospace History, No. 18, 2000. NASA SP-2000-4518.

Chambers, Joseph R. *Partners in Freedom: Contributions of the Langley Research Center to U.S. Military Aircraft of the 1990s*. Monograph in Aerospace History, No. 19, 2000. NASA SP-2000-4519.

Waltman, Gene L. *Black Magic and Gremlins: Analog Flight Simulations at NASA's Flight Research Center*. Monograph in Aerospace History, No. 20, 2000. NASA SP-2000-4520.

Portree, David S. F. *Humans to Mars: Fifty Years of Mission Planning, 1950–2000*. Monograph in Aerospace History, No. 21, 2001. NASA SP-2001-4521.

Thompson, Milton O., with J. D. Hunley. *Flight Research: Problems Encountered and What they Should Teach Us*. Monograph in Aerospace History, No. 22, 2001. NASA SP-2001-4522.

Tucker, Tom. *The Eclipse Project*. Monograph in Aerospace History, No. 23, 2001. NASA SP-2001-4523.

Siddiqi, Asif A. *Deep Space Chronicle: A Chronology of Deep Space and Planetary Probes 1958–2000*. Monograph in Aerospace History, No. 24, 2002. NASA SP-2002-4524.

Merlin, Peter W. *Mach 3+: NASA/USAF YF-12 Flight Research, 1969–1979.* Monograph in Aerospace History, No. 25, 2001. NASA SP-2001-4525.

Anderson, Seth B. *Memoirs of an Aeronautical Engineer: Flight Tests at Ames Research Center: 1940–1970.* Monograph in Aerospace History, No. 26, 2002. NASA SP-2002-4526.

Renstrom, Arthur G. *Wilbur and Orville Wright: A Bibliography Commemorating the One-Hundredth Anniversary of the First Powered Flight on December 17, 1903.* Monograph in Aerospace History, No. 27, 2002. NASA SP-2002-4527.

No monograph 28.

Chambers, Joseph R. *Concept to Reality: Contributions of the NASA Langley Research Center to U.S. Civil Aircraft of the 1990s.* Monograph in Aerospace History, No. 29, 2003. SP-2003-4529.

Peebles, Curtis, editor. *The Spoken Word: Recollections of Dryden History, The Early Years.* Monograph in Aerospace History, No. 30, 2003. SP-2003-4530.

Jenkins, Dennis R., Tony Landis, and Jay Miller. *American X-Vehicles: An Inventory- X-1 to X-50.* Monograph in Aerospace History, No. 31, 2003. SP-2003-4531.

Renstrom, Arthur G. *Wilbur and Orville Wright: A Chronology Commemorating the One-Hundredth Anniversary of the First Powered Flight on December 17, 1903.* Monograph in Aerospace History, No. 32, 2003. NASA SP-2003-4532.

Bowles, Mark D., and Robert S. Arrighi. *NASA's Nuclear Frontier: The Plum Brook Research Reactor.* Monograph in Aerospace History, No. 33, 2004. (SP-2004-4533).

Matranga, Gene J., C. Wayne Ottinger, Calvin R. Jarvis, and D. Christian Gelzer. *Unconventional, Contrary, and Ugly: The Lunar Landing Research Vehicle.* Monograph in Aerospace History, No. 35, 2006. NASA SP-2004-4535.

McCurdy, Howard E. *Low Cost Innovation in Spaceflight: The History of the Near Earth Asteroid Rendezvous (NEAR) Mission.* Monograph in Aerospace History, No. 36, 2005. NASA SP-2005-4536.

Seamans, Robert C., Jr. *Project Apollo: The Tough Decisions.* Monograph in Aerospace History, No. 37, 2005. NASA SP-2005-4537.

Lambright, W. Henry. *NASA and the Environment: The Case of Ozone Depletion.* Monograph in Aerospace History, No. 38, 2005. NASA SP-2005-4538.

Chambers, Joseph R. *Innovation in Flight: Research of the NASA Langley Research Center on Revolutionary Advanced Concepts for Aeronautics.* Monograph in Aerospace History, No. 39, 2005. NASA SP-2005-4539.

Phillips, W. Hewitt. *Journey Into Space Research: Continuation of a Career at NASA Langley Research Center.* Monograph in Aerospace History, No. 40, 2005. NASA SP-2005-4540.

Rumerman, Judy A., Chris Gamble, and Gabriel Okolski, compilers. *U.S. Human Spaceflight: A Record of Achievement, 1961–2006.* Monograph in Aerospace History No. 41, 2007. NASA SP-2007-4541.

Dick, Steven J., Stephen J. Garber, and Jane H. Odom. *Research in NASA History.* Monograph in Aerospace History No. 43, 2009. NASA SP-2009-4543.

Dryden Historical Studies

Tomayko, James E., author, and Christian Gelzer, editor. *The Story of Self-Repairing Flight Control Systems.* Dryden Historical Study #1.

Electronic Media (SP-4600 Series)

Remembering Apollo 11: The 30th Anniversary Data Archive CD-ROM. NASA SP-4601, 1999.

Remembering Apollo 11: The 35th Anniversary Data Archive CD-ROM. NASA SP-2004-4601, 2004. This is an update of the 1999 edition.

The Mission Transcript Collection: U.S. Human Spaceflight Missions from Mercury Redstone 3 to Apollo 17. SP-2000-4602, 2001. Now available commercially from CG Publishing.

Shuttle-Mir: the United States and Russia Share History's Highest Stage. NASA SP-2001-4603, 2002. This CD-ROM is available from NASA CORE.

U.S. Centennial of Flight Commission presents Born of Dreams ~ Inspired by Freedom. NASA SP-2004-4604, 2004.

Of Ashes and Atoms: A Documentary on the NASA Plum Brook Reactor Facility. NASA SP-2005-4605.

Taming Liquid Hydrogen: The Centaur Upper Stage Rocket Interactive CD-ROM. NASA SP-2004-4606, 2004.

Fueling Space Exploration: The History of NASA's Rocket Engine Test Facility DVD. NASA SP-2005-4607.

Altitude Wind Tunnel at NASA Glenn Research Center: An Interactive History CD-ROM. NASA SP-2008-4608.

Conference Proceedings (SP-4700 Series)

Dick, Steven J., and Keith Cowing, ed. *Risk and Exploration: Earth, Sea and the Stars.* NASA SP-2005-4701.

Dick, Steven J., and Roger D. Launius. *Critical Issues in the History of Spaceflight.* NASA SP-2006-4702.

Dick, Steven J., ed. *Remembering the Space Age: Proceedings of the 50th Anniversary Conference.* NASA SP-2008-4703.

Societal Impact (SP-4800 Series)

Dick, Steven J., and Roger D. Launius. *Societal Impact of Spaceflight.* NASA SP-2007-4801.

Index

B

H

I

M

Milky Way, 261–62, 491, 500

Miller, Stanley, 31

Miller, Walter, 43

Mind Children (Moravec), 474–75

Modern Synthesis, 100–101

Modularity, 219–20

Mohammed, 160, 189n129

Molecules, 153–55, 174n56, 175n62, 177n70, 255

Moleculocosmochronology, 153, 172n48

Monkeys at typewriters, 149–50

Moon, 338, 411

Moore's Law, 408

Moral universe, 344–46, 359nn26–27

Moravec, Hans, 474–75, 477

Morgan, Lewis Henry, 75

Morris, Simon Conway, 212, 376, 386

Morrison, Philip, 31

Moslem Student Association, 189n129

Mount Improbable, 364

Mount Invisible, 364–65

Mount Wilson Observatory, 491

Mountain climbing analogy, 431–32

Multicellularity, 215

Multilinear evolution, 104–8

Multiple-biosphere nature of cosmos, 362

Multiverse, 204, 226, 388–89

Music, 134–39, 142n16, 307

Musser, George, 519–20n95

Mutualists, 129, 297

N

Nanotechnology, 254–55, 362, 472–73, 476

Narrative form of explanation, 73, 91, 93–94, 125–27

National Aeronautics and Space Administration (NASA)

    Astrobiology Institute, 36, 362, 386

    cosmic evolution research, 32, 33–36, 53n22

    exobiology research, 33–34, 53n22

    mission of, viii

    Origins program, 34–36

T

G꞉O U.S. GOVERNMENT PRINTING OFFICE: 2009—358-567